Jawaharlal Nehru

By Frank Moraes

REPORT ON MAO'S CHINA

JAWAHARLAL NEHRU: A Biography

Jawaharlal Nehru

∽ A BIOGRAPHY ∽

by

FRANK MORAES

THE MACMILLAN COMPANY · NEW YORK

1958

© THE MACMILLAN COMPANY 1956

Published simultaneously in Canada

Fifth Printing, 1958

Printed in the United States of America

Frontispiece reproduced by courtesy of
the Press Information Bureau, Government of India.

The Author

Oxford-educated, barrister-at-law of Lin-
coln's Inn, and editor of *The Times of India,*
Frank Moraes has closely observed Nehru's
career for many years.

In 1952 Mr. Moraes was one of a group
of Indians invited to China by Mao Tse-tung
on a five-week tour of the country. *Report
on Mao's China* is Mr. Moraes' candid account of what the delegation saw and heard
during this visit.

Library of Congress catalog card number: 56-11656

For
My Son Dom

Best of Friends
and
Liveliest of Critics

PREFACE

This book presents Jawaharlal Nehru against the background of the Indian nationalist movement, and is thus primarily a political biography. It also projects Nehru through Indian eyes, and in doing so attempts to explain and elucidate the more controversial aspects of his personality and politics.

Although I have discussed various facets of the Prime Minister's career with a great many people, the conclusions I have reached and the interpretations I have placed on his actions are necessarily my own. The manuscript was read by several friends, to all of whom I am indebted for their comment and criticism. I am particularly grateful to D. G. Tendulkar, author of *Mahatma*, a source book of invaluable help; to Donald Thomas, V. B. Kulkarni, Mahendra Desai, and Shaun Mandy. My thanks are also due to B. Krishnaswamy, who cheerfully and patiently typed the entire manuscript, helping me with many valued suggestions. For details on Harrow and various anecdotes relating to the Prime Minister's stay there, I am indebted to Raja Maharaj Singh, former Governor of Bombay and himself an Old Harrovian.

FRANK MORAES

CONTENTS

Jawaharlal Nehru

Scale of Miles

0   500

CHINA

AFGHANISTAN

KASHMIR
AND
JAMMU
(IN DISPUTE)

PUNJAB

P.E.P.S.U.

HIMACHAL
PRADESH

BILASPUR

Lhasa

PAKISTAN

RAJASTHAN

New
Delhi
DELHI
(FED. DIST.)

AJMER

UTTAR PRADESH

N E P A L

BHUTAN
SIKKIM

A S S A M

VINDHYA
PRADESH

CUTCH

MADHYA
BHARAT

BHOPAL

BIHAR

W. BENGAL

PAK

MANIPUR

TRIPURA

SAURASHTRA

BOMBAY

I N D I A

MADHYA PRADESH

ORISSA

Calcutta

BURMA

Bombay

HYDERABAD

Goa

A N D H R A

Bay of

Bengal

*Arabian
Sea*

MYSORE

Madras

COORG

MADRAS

ANDAMAN &
NICOBAR IS.

TRAVANCORE-
COCHIN

CEYLON

© *The New York Times*

INDIA AFTER INDEPENDENCE

1

"A TRYST WITH DESTINY"

I⊤ was the night of August 14, 1947.

As drums rolled and conches blew the midnight hour, India moved from foreign rule to freedom.

In the cities lights glittered from house fronts and public buildings, playing on the streets and squares where the multihued holiday crowds mingled in gay, fantastic patchwork quilts of colour and light.

There were light and movement in the villages too. On hills and mounds and by the gaunt trees of the countryside, bonfires gleamed.

That night in Delhi crowds milled around the approaches to Parliament House, where, within the circular pile of red and white sandstone, the people's constituent assembly met to witness the last act in the transfer of political power.

The scene within the chamber was colourful but subdued. For the most part the members were dressed in sober homespun white, but here and there a bright turban flashed its colours like a peacock at a poultry show. In the public galleries the women's saris looked like so many rainbows, their colours enhanced by the sheen of satin and the shimmer of silk.

Slowly the hands of the clock moved towards midnight, and a hush descended on the house.

From the front row of seats facing the President a slight slim man, dressed in a pale cream *achkhan*[1] and wearing an immaculately white *khadi*[2] cap, rose to his feet. In the glare of the flash bulbs

---

[1] A long coat buttoned up to the neck.
[2] Handwoven cloth from handspun yarn.

which suddenly illumined the chamber, his face looked tense. There were shadows under his eyes. The chiselled profile had a hint of fatigue. He seemed wan and weary. Even the red rose flaunting a challenge from his buttonhole drooped slightly.

As he spoke his face was transformed. The tired lines vanished. The voice, at first low and metallic, grew in volume, was suddenly buoyant and vibrant. Jawaharlal Nehru was speaking.

"Long years ago we made a tryst with destiny, and now the time comes when we shall redeem our pledge, not wholly or in full measure, but very substantially." The opening sentence struck an authentic chord, for India was about to enter the agony of partition. But India was also to be free.

"At the stroke of the midnight hour," continued Nehru, "when the world sleeps, India will awake to life and freedom. A moment comes, which comes but rarely in history, when we step out from the old to the new, when an age ends, and when the soul of a nation, long suppressed, finds utterance. It is fitting that/at this solemn moment we take a pledge of dedication to the service of India and her people and to the still larger cause of humanity."

He paused.

"That future," he warned, and his voice was solemn and strangely sad, "is not one of ease or resting but of incessant striving so that we might fulfil the pledges we have so often taken and the one we shall take today. The service of India means the service of the millions who suffer. It means the ending of poverty and ignorance and disease and inequality of opportunity."

There came a reference to the Mahatma as Nehru quoted one of his master's many memorable phrases: "The ambition of the greatest man of our generation has been to wipe every tear from every eye. That may be beyond us, but so long as there are tears and suffering, so long our work will not be over."

He ended with an invocation. "To the people of India whose representatives we are," he declared, "we make appeal to join us with faith and confidence on this great adventure. This is no time for petty or destructive criticism, no time for ill-will or blaming others. We have to build the noble mansion of free India where all her children may dwell."

It was a speech worthy of the occasion, the greatest which Jawaharlal Nehru, no natural orator, had so far made. More than a charter of freedom, it was a testament of faith.

*   *   *

For Nehru freedom meant much more than the end of an old road. It meant the beginning of a new. Behind him that night stretched the long story of the past, with its milestones of toil, tragedy and triumph. But clearly, also, rose a vista of the future. Freedom was not the end, only the means to an end.

Both India and he had made a long and arduous trek to that goal. When freedom came Nehru was fifty-eight. The formative years were long past, and ahead lay new problems and crises.

Of those fifty-eight years some twenty-seven had been spent in political toil and struggle. Over ten years had been spent in jail. Nehru went to prison for the first time in December, 1921. He emerged from his last and longest term of jail—1,041 days—on June 15, 1945, a little over two years before he became the first Prime Minister of independent India. In between he had been in and out of prison seven times.

Yet not until he was thirty-one did he come into contact with the Indian peasants. Ironically enough, the British Government was responsible for precipitating the contact. Under the mistaken notion that he might attempt to have dealings with some Afghan envoys who were in India to negotiate a peace agreement following the brief Afghan War of 1919, Nehru was served with an externment order from the hill station of Mussoorie, where he was on a holiday with his mother and wife. Having then no other immediate preoccupations, he accompanied some two hundred peasants from his home town of Allahabad into the countryside.

Until then, he writes in his autobiography, his outlook was "entirely bourgeois." "I was thrown, almost without any will of my own, into contact with the peasantry." Sooner or later that association was inevitable. But the manner of its establishment is interesting. The year 1920 marks a decisive turning point in Nehru's political life. Until his incursion into the villages he had never realised what the peasantry was and what it meant to India. "Ever since then," he writes, "my mental picture of India always contains this naked hungry mass."

Of the thirty-one years before that, the first fifteen were spent as the only son—for eleven years as the only child—in a patrician and wealthy household. Nehru's introspective nature, the moodiness which occasionally seizes him, and his strong sense of separateness, as of a being apart, derive from his lonely boyhood. Prison intensified it.

The family were Kashmiri Brahmins whose ancestors had migrated in the early eighteenth century from the mountain vale of Srinagar to the plains of Hindustan. Nehru's father, Motilal, an assertive, self-willed man, was a highly successful lawyer. The son lived very much under the imperious shadow of his father. His mother doted on him.

Aside from his father, the only other significant personal influence in his life was Gandhi. In time the trio represented by the two Nehrus and Gandhi became known irreverently as the Father, Son and Holy Ghost.

Nehru met the Mahatma for the first time during Christmas week, 1916, at the annual meeting of the Indian National Congress in Lucknow. Four years had elapsed since his return from England after a stay of over seven years in school and college. Jawaharlal was then twenty-seven. Gandhi was twenty years his senior.

Neither seems to have made an immediate impression upon the other. Gandhi's autobiography, entitled *The Story of My Experiments with Truth*, which was dictated in prison between 1922 and 1924 and published in 1925, contains not a single reference to Jawaharlal, but mentions his father, Motilal. In his autobiography Nehru, describing his first meeting with Gandhi, writes: "All of us admired him for his heroic fight in South Africa, but he seemed very distant and different and unpolitical to many of us young men."

We can picture the meeting between the two. Nehru wore European clothes, and his manner, slightly stilted and self-conscious, was a hangover from Harrow and Cambridge. His shyness gave him an air of disdain. He was untried and assertive. Of those years he himself recalls, "I was a bit of a prig, with little to commend me."

To Gandhi, clad in a coarse cotton *dhoti* [3] and long coat and wearing his native *Kathiawadi*,[4] or turban—he was to adopt his famous loincloth only in 1921—Nehru must have seemed equally distant and different. Perhaps, being a good judge of men, he noted the purpose

---

[3] A piece of cloth worn as a lower garment by many Hindus.
[4] From the district of Kathiawad in western India.

behind the petulance of the young man's mouth. The patrician stared from the proud dark eyes, but there was sensitivity in them.

Much of what the Mahatma preached seemed to Nehru medieval and revivalist. Gandhi, he confesses, was a very difficult person to understand. "Sometimes his language was almost incomprehensible to an average modern." But instinctively Nehru sensed in the older man a leader who, although gentle in mien, was moved by a hard resolve and purpose. He spoke in a new idiom and wielded a new weapon. He insisted on action. A wrong, he said, should provoke not only protest but resistance, and such resistance must be non-violent.

At this early stage in their association, however, it was the elder Nehru who was nearer to Gandhi.

No two men could have been more dissimilar than Gandhi and Nehru's father, Motilal. Yet not only did they work together as political colleagues, but both men, separately and together, left their imprint on Jawaharlal. In his autobiography Nehru suggests that Motilal was attracted to Gandhi as a man. That was so. But it is more likely that the primary urge which drew the father into the Gandhian orbit was the fact that his son had stepped inside it.

Motilal was neither meek nor mild, but a natural autocrat. He was a man of strong likes and dislikes, dogmatic, proud, combative, with a tremendous zest for life and good living. In his heyday he burned the candle at both ends and a bit in the middle. Nature had been prodigal of her gifts to him. He was a magnificently handsome man with a fine presence and, when the mood moved him, great courtliness and charm. There was something Roman in his carriage and in the proud tilt of his head.

Motilal's temper was fierce and inflammable, but his laughter swept like a gale through his house. Where he sat was the head of the table. He loved company, and almost every evening friends congregated at his house, the wine flowing as freely as the talk. As a child Jawaharlal once saw his father drinking a glass of claret. Horrified by its red colour, he ran to his mother and told her that his father was drinking blood.

Gandhi had nothing of the sybarite in him. The days when he had donned Western dress, essayed to play a violin and laboured painfully at ballroom dancing were far behind. He talked a new language in terms of a new common denominator—the ordinary Indian whom he saw as the lowly peasant in the village and the worker in the city slum. In dress and language Gandhi looked extraordinarily like a peasant. He had the peasant's patience, his kindliness, his good humour, his teasing sense of fun, most of all his earthy shrewdness. His voice purred its way into an unwilling listener's heart. He had a quality of unyielding earnestness which attracted the Nehrus, both father and son.

Motilal had no use for saints. In a foreword to a booklet entitled *Thought Currents*, which contained selections from Gandhi's writings, he wrote: "I have heard of saints and supermen, but have never had the pleasure of meeting them, and must confess to a feeling of scepticism about their real existence. I believe in men and things manly." The inference is that he regarded and respected Gandhi not as a saint but as a man.

Motilal had been contemptuous of politicians. He felt that those who took to politics were failures in life. He admired Englishmen and their ways, and very early in life adopted Westernized habits. A country, he thought, got the politicians it deserved, and India's political tribe impressed him not at all—until Gandhi came, and Jawaharlal fell under his spell.

The one quality in Gandhi which impressed Motilal as it did his son was his insistence on action. Until the Mahatma came, India abounded in politicians who with a few notable exceptions talked and talked and did nothing. This was especially so of the Congress, where nationalism was confined to armchair politicians who revelled in marathon speeches and in the passing of resolutions. Somnolence went with sonority.

If the man in Motilal was attracted by Gandhi's creed of action, the lawyer was momentarily repelled by the idea of a challenge to established authority. By training and temperament the elder Nehru was a constitutionalist, and his mind could not readily attune itself to defiance of the law. He was upset when Gandhi invited his followers to court imprisonment by breaking "unjust laws," and he asked angrily what sort of pressure the Mahatma thought this would bring on the Government.

Foremost in his mind was the thought of his impetuous son. The proud old aristocrat resented fiercely the idea of Jawaharlal going to jail. Such a thing had never happened in his family. He tried to find out what jail life would be like—by surreptitiously sleeping on the floor of his own bedroom. In the end, like Jawaharlal, Motilal rationalised the Mahatma's ideas to fit into the framework of his own traditional tenets.

Even before Gandhi came, Motilal had been moving away from the orthodox political moderates with whom he was earlier associated. The detention in June, 1917, of Dr. Annie Besant, the theosophist leader who had identified herself with the Indian nationalist movement, led him to join the Home Rule League which she had founded some nine months before her arrest. There is an engaging comment on Dr. Besant's detention in the diary of Mr. Edwin Montagu, then British Secretary of State for India: "I particularly like the Shiva [5] who cut his wife into fifty-two pieces only to discover that he had fifty-two wives. This is really what happened to the Government of India when it interned Mrs. Besant."

Nevertheless, it is doubtful if the elder Nehru would have thrown himself into the Congress movement had it not been for the repression following Satyagraha Day [6] in April, 1919. An orgy of rioting and firing culminated in the massacre of Jallianwallah Bagh when General Dyer wantonly fired on a crowd of unarmed Indians, using on his own admission 1,605 rounds, until his ammunition was almost exhausted. According to an official estimate 379 persons were killed and at least 1,200 wounded. This outrage and other horrors perpetrated after it, including the infamous Crawling Order which required all Indians to crawl on their bellies through a lane in Amritsar where an Englishwoman had previously been attacked by a mob, touched Motilal's pride to the quick. Even then he justified his course of action to his own mind by arguing that under British rule there was no constitution in India and no real rule of law. Therefore resistance to it was justified.

Nehru describes the kinship between his father and Gandhi as a meeting between introvert and extrovert. Motilal was an exuberant extrovert. Gandhi, though intrinsically an introvert, differed from

[5] A Hindu deity, lord of destruction and creation.

[6] This was staged on Gandhi's direction as a protest against the Rowlatt Bills which provided for arrest and trial without due process of law. It called for the suspension of all activities and the closure of business houses and stores on that day. *Satyagraha*, meaning literally "force of truth," came to signify non-violent resistance.

most introverts by being as mindful of the welfare of others as of his own.

Both men had much of the autocrat in their make-up. "Behind all his courteous interest," Nehru writes of Gandhi, "one has the impression that one is addressing a closed door." This is not surprising. Men who argue from first principles as Gandhi did invariably tend to be dogmatic, because their surrender of first principles would be moral cowardice and betrayal. Motilal, although intolerant of opposition, was often open to persuasion.

Between father and son flowed a curious ambivalence of thought. Much in his son's thinking dismayed and daunted the father. Despite Motilal's attempts to keep in step politically with Jawaharlal, he was burdened by his background. For him the plunge into Gandhian politics meant a sharp break with his past life, professional and personal. It meant a shedding of expensive tastes and a reduction in his standard of living. At sixty a man rarely changes his habits or opinions.

Only when his reason backed by the trained mind of a lawyer had weighed everything did he join Gandhi in his campaign, writes Jawaharlal. There he is wrong. Without the filial urge of Jawaharlal it is doubtful if Motilal would have followed the Mahatma. His was a surrender not so much to the Mahatma as to his son. Like Jawaharlal, he combined intensity of thought with intensity of feeling. The borderland between the two is dim. And in groping between the one and the other it is as easy to deceive oneself as unconsciously to mislead others. Motilal would probably have liked his son to believe that conviction, and not emotion, had influenced his decision. He was too fond a father not to know how his son would like him to behave.

Nehru had none of Motilal's constitutional scruples about defying the established order. With Gandhi he saw India in the dumb misery of a peasant's eyes. Freedom was meaningless without a change in the social and economic order. But Nehru's concepts of change differed vastly from those of the Mahatma.

Gandhi, he felt, was vague in the definition of objectives, political and economic. Although his thinking was basic, even elemental, the Mahatma's approach to problems was pragmatic, dealing with each issue as it arose and unwilling to peep into the future. Politically Gandhi hesitated for a long time before committing India to complete independence, and even after the Congress party had adopted independence as its goal he was reluctant to give the objective a clear character and content. Economically, he appeared to be even more vague. The Mahatma's views on machinery and modern civilisation irked Nehru. He resented his frequent stress on the religious and spiritual aspect of the civil-disobedience movement. What had religion to do with politics? In Gandhi's thinking private wealth constituted a trust. Nehru regarded this view as economic heresy. He quotes Tom Paine's remark on Edmund Burke, "He pities the plumage but forgets the dying bird." Nehru absolves Gandhi of forgetting the dying bird. "But why," he asks peevishly, "so much insistence on the plumage?"

Gandhi's praise of poverty and suffering also seemed to him a dangerous form of idealisation and an incitement to the more selfish and greedy to perpetuate the old order of things. Although the ascetic life might suit individuals, Jawaharlal could see no especial virtue in it as a social ideal. Interpreted in mass terms it was mass masochism.

Even on non-violence, which was the sheet anchor of the Mahatma's political faith, Nehru differed with his master. He admired the moral and ethical elements in non-violence but he could not give absolute allegiance to it as a political creed. It could never be a religion, only a policy and a method judged ultimately by results. If Nehru accepted non-violence as a political weapon it was not because he regarded it as a dogma, but merely as the right policy for India in the conditions which prevailed.

In their attitude to economic, political and social problems, even temperamentally, a gulf separated the two men. Yet both bridged the chasm in a common cause. The reasons which led Nehru to follow the Mahatma, in themselves compelling but confused, give a clue to the paradox of his character. There were moments when he wondered whether the signposts pointed in the right direction. Sometimes he was weary and dispirited. But always, inevitably, the Mahatma drew him like a magnet.

What impressed Jawaharlal most of all was the fact that Gandhi in wiping out the stain of servitude was wiping out the stain of fear. Nehru has always admired courage. The rebel in Gandhi attracted him. Courage, the Mahatma had said, is the one sure foundation of character. Without courage there is no morality, no religion, no love.

Cowardice is a contagious crime. It was what the prophets had preached before him: "Fear and be slain. Believe and live."

Gandhi had also a genius for communicating this quality to others. He showed India how to shed fear. He gave to the Indian people, particularly the masses, a new sense of pride and backbone. He taught them to walk erect. His instinct enabled him to see unerringly into the hearts and minds of his people.

Characteristically Nehru rationalised those of the Mahatma's ideas which he could not accept. It is interesting to see how his mind persuades his conscience of many things. Thus, though he could not give an absolute allegiance to the doctrine of non-violence, he accepted it as the right policy for Indian conditions. It was also a worthy weapon. "A worthy end," Nehru argues, "should have worthy means leading up to it. That seemed not only a good ethical doctrine but sound practical politics, for the means that are not good often defeat the end in view and raise new problems and difficulties."

For the sake of the larger loyalties Nehru is prepared to keep some of his most cherished beliefs in the background. But, characteristically again, he does not abandon them. Few legends are less justified than the legend of Nehru as a man of vacillation and instability. If Nehru knows anything he knows his mind.

Over many years he has thought, read and observed deeply, and on most matters he has reached definite conclusions. Indeed, his activities, writings and speeches, long before he assumed the Prime Ministership, reveal inexorably the shape of things to come.

Although Nehru sometimes subordinated his own ideas to those of Gandhi, his influence on the tempo and direction of the nationalist movement was considerable and decisive. His was the spur which prodded the Congress party into adopting complete independence as its political objective. In the light of this it might seem ironical that his was also the decisive voice which after freedom kept India in the Commonwealth—but as a republic. Nehru, unlike Gandhi, who preferred to move step by step, has always been eager to define ultimate objectives, whether political, economic or social. In 1931, at the Karachi session of the Congress, he sponsored a resolution on economic policy which advocated for the first time the nationalisation of key industries and services. Earlier, in 1927 in Madras, he had associated himself with a Republican conference which was still-born because it met on that occasion for the first and last time. In the summer of 1929 the All-India Congress Committee, assembling in Bombay, considered a recommendation, at the instance of the United Provinces [7] Provincial Congress Committee, for the adoption of an economic programme on socialist lines. The preamble to this programme which outlined the socialist ideal was accepted by the Central Committee, but consideration of the detailed programme was deferred. The Congress thus committed itself to the principle of socialism, although Nehru confesses ruefully that "most members probably did not realise what they were doing."

Nehru did much more than rationalise Gandhi and Gandhism to India's educated youth. He provided the perfect complement to the Mahatma even if his approach to most problems differed radically from his leader's. Gandhi was more concerned with means than with ends, more interested in specific problems than in distant objectives. His means were often ends, so therefore a method, non-violence, became a mission. The Mahatma's approach to most problems was intuitive rather than intellectual. He was moved more by his conscience than by his mind. This thing is right, said Gandhi; therefore it is rational. Nehru, on the other hand, says: This thing is rational; therefore it must be right.

If Gandhi made India aware of herself, Nehru made Indians aware of others. In March, 1926, he revisited Europe after an absence of over thirteen years, and stayed abroad for a year and nine months, returning to India in December, 1927. This visit influenced his political thinking profoundly, and in turn was to influence the trend of Congress thought. Nehru came back from Europe with the uneasy feeling that nationalism was not enough. For the first time the conviction grew upon him that if India's struggle for freedom had to have a global significance it must be related to the many vital movements occurring outside the country. It must be part of the broad stream of world progress.

He set about enlarging his countrymen's political vision. Unless India, he argued, was trained and prepared to see its struggle in the wider context of world events, its own progress would be lopsided and its outlook insular. Here he provided a corrective to the subjectivism which the Gandhian philosophy encouraged. Alongside a

[7] The United Provinces now known as Uttar Pradesh is Nehru's home state.

hitherto introvert nationalism he helped India to develop an objective outlook and to be conscious of the neighbours around her and of the problems of more distant lands and peoples. He helped make India extrovert.

During the same European tour Nehru came decisively under the impact of socialism, and in turn sought to shape Congress policies to this end. Although the greater part of his stay abroad was spent in Switzerland because of his wife's health, he also travelled in France, England and Germany. As a representative of the Indian National Congress he attended the Congress of Oppressed National-ities at Brussels in February, 1927. The Brussels Congress founded the League Against Imperialism. Later, in November, accompanied by his father, wife and younger sister Krishna,[8] Nehru visited Moscow for the tenth anniversary celebrations of the Soviet. They were in Moscow for about four days. It was Nehru's first visit to the Soviet capital.

In his autobiography he confesses that he did not then know much "about the fine points of Communism." He owed it no doctrinal adherence, and his acquaintance with it at the time was limited to its broad features. But, like many thoughtful Indians, he was impressed by Soviet Russia's will to progress and the social and industrial trans-formation she had wrought in the comparatively short space of a dec-ade. On the other hand he disliked intensely some of Communism's manifestations—its ruthless suppression of opposition, its unnecessary violence and its spirit of wholesale regimentation. He thought many Communists vulgar and needlessly aggressive.

Nehru recalls how, although not lacking in goodwill to the Com-munists, he found himself at the committee meetings of the League Against Imperialism more often on the side of the Anglo-American members "on petty matters of argument." He discovered a similarity between their outlook and his, "in regard to method at least," and both combined in objecting to the Communists' declamatory and long-winded resolutions which often resembled manifestoes.

To Nehru's mind the gravitational pull of Marxism is its scientific approach. Its theory and philosophy excited him. "History came to have a new meaning for me." But stimulated though he was by Marx's scientific approach, Nehru was not prepared to swear by everything

[8] Now Mrs. Raja Hutheesing.

taught by Marx and Lenin. His own mind, exposed to the free air of democratic thought and learning, was allergic to rigid ideologies. It was impossible in any case to reconcile Gandhism and its stress on the individual with Marxism and its stress on the State. Planning there must be, but in India it could only be planning for democracy and freedom. This is what Nehru seeks to achieve. His El Dorado is a State ensuring economic security and liberty. Therein it differs from the Communist ideal which guarantees only economic security.

Clearly Nehru, even in the Mahatma's lifetime, had a more decisive influence on his country's political thought than he is normally credited with. To a large extent Gandhi chose the means, but it was Nehru primarily who defined the ends. Time and again he deplored the lack of cohesive thought behind Congress actions.

By December, 1927, when he returned from his European trip, his own mind was made up on most problems. From then onward he tried to train and prepare his countrymen to march along the route he planned.

In the twenty years from 1927 to 1947 when independence came, Nehru preached a doctrine which was unpopular in many orthodox Congress quarters. He insisted that nationalism was not enough, that India, even though politically subservient, must see her struggle in the larger context of world developments and upheavals. The results were seen in the Congress denunciation of Hitler and Nazism and of Japan's aggression in Manchuria. Italy's invasion of Abyssinia provoked many protest meetings and demonstrations throughout the country. In 1936 Nehru, while in Europe, declined a pressing invitation to call on Mussolini, at a time when some Western statesmen were inclined to see many shining virtues in the Duce. Republican Spain evoked wide sympathy in India. The betrayal of Czechoslovakia was received with dismay.

Many of his own colleagues scoffed at Nehru's seeming obsession with other countries while his own country lay in bondage. Events have proved that Nehru's was the longer and wiser view. Inside India an atmosphere of international awareness grew along with the urge for freedom. When India became independent her leaders and people were prepared for action and for cooperation on an international plane.

Nehru's influence on his country's political and economic thinking has therefore been considerable. On many important issues it has been decisive. In a sense he created a climate for the implementation of his own ideas, for his thinking was always ahead of that of his Indian contemporaries, and independence found him in the unique position of being able to put through his ideas. His habit of trying to see things steadily and to see them whole yielded good dividends.

Nehru saw more clearly than Gandhi did that the middle-class intellectual was the most revolutionary force in India. By defining India in terms of peasants and workers, Gandhi simultaneously broadened the base of the Congress party and of the nationalist struggle. Nehru agreed with this basic approach. But his distinctive contribution to the nationalist movement is that by reducing Gandhism to an intellectual equation and interpreting it in radical terms, he drew to its active support the country's revolutionary middle-class intellectuals. Without Gandhi, India would have achieved freedom eventually, but along a different road. It is doubtful if without Nehru, Gandhi would have attracted the educated middle class who formed the backbone of Britain's tenuous administrative structure in India. The collapse of their loyalty to the Raj ultimately meant the collapse of the Raj itself.

As long as Gandhi lived, Nehru had to temporise in order to achieve his ends. This has misled many into thinking that Jawaharlal had no mind of his own and that he could be easily converted or persuaded. The truth is that, like Fabius, he tries to conquer by delay. He has a streak of femininity, of which his father was innocent, which occasionally finds vent in petulance. But, like his father, he has also a core of ruthlessness which over the past seven years has become increasingly evident and assertive. Today he is an audacious and calculating leader.

About Nehru there is a sense of history and hustle. He seems always to be burdened by the thought of having too much to do in too little time. Since the night of August 14, 1947, that feeling has grown. He spoke then of India's having a tryst with destiny. But he too, standing on the threshold of India's independence, had a date with destiny.

2

BOYHOOD

In the heart of the Himalayas lies the lovely land of Kashmir. "Learning, lofty houses, saffron, icy water and grapes: things that even in heaven are difficult to find are common there." So wrote the chronicler of *Rajatarangini*,[1] a Sanskrit record of the early and fabulous days of Kashmir.

In the late sixteenth century, in 1588, Akbar, the great Mogul Emperor of India, incorporated Kashmir in his domain. Earlier Hindu and Buddhist monarchs had ruled the land until about 1294 when it passed into Muslim hands. Of the Mogul rulers, the wayward, unregenerate but sensitive Jehangir, Akbar's favourite son and successor, was drawn strongly towards this mountain land. Jehangir loved nature, and Kashmir's birds and flowers, its green valleys and streams with their majestic background of mountains and glaciers enchanted him. "Wherever the eye reaches," he wrote in his autobiography, "there are verdure and running water. The red rose, the violet and the narcissus grow of themselves; in the fields there are all kinds of flowers and all sorts of sweet scented herbs, more than can be calculated."

Nehru's ancestors came from this land of enchantment. They were, as are the vast majority of Kashmiri Hindus, Brahmins enjoying the honorific of Pandit, which means Man of Learning. The original family name was not Nehru but Kaul.

Around 1716, some nine years after the death of the Emperor Aurangzeb, who was Jehangir's grandson, a Sanskrit and Persian scholar, Raj Kaul, migrated to the imperial capital of Delhi, probably

[1] It means River of Kings.

at the instance of the then Emperor Farrukhsiar who during a visit to Kashmir had been attracted by his scholarship. Raj Kaul was granted a *jagir* (piece of land) with a house by a canal. The Persian term for canal is *nahar,* and it was from the accident of living alongside a *nahar* that the name of *Nehru* is derived. For a long time the family was known as Kaul-Nehru. Later the Kaul was dropped.

Although scholars, Jawaharlal's ancestors were mostly in government employment. His great-grandfather, Pandit Lakshmi Narayan Nehru, was a lawyer, and in this capacity was attached to the East India Company at the phantom court of the dying Mogul Empire. His grandfather, Pandit Ganga Dhar Nehru, was *kotwal,* or police officer-in-charge, of the city of Delhi. This was some time before the Indian Mutiny of 1857.[2] Fair-skinned like most Kashmiris, Ganga Dhar is depicted in an old painting as a red-bearded man with reflective blue eyes. He died in 1861 at the age of thirty-four.

Around 1858 the Nehru family joined the fugitive caravan fleeing Delhi in the turmoil following the Mutiny, and migrated to the neighbouring town of Agra, which contains the famous Taj Mahal. There on May 6, 1861, Nehru's father, Motilal, who was Ganga Dhar's youngest son, was born. He was a posthumous child, Ganga Dhar having died three months earlier. By an interesting coincidence he was born on the same day, month and year as the poet Rabindranath Tagore. Commenting on the coincidence many years later Nehru remarked that apart from Gandhi and Motilal, Rabindranath Tagore had "a very considerable influence over me." The major influences, he admitted, were those of his father and Gandhiji. "I came into contact with Tagore rather in the later years when I had been conditioned more or less by my father and Gandhiji," Nehru explained. Nevertheless, Rabindranath had a very considerable influence over me."

Motilal had two brothers, both very much older than he, Bansi Dhar and Nandlal. On their father's death the infant Motilal became their responsibility. Not long after, the eldest brother, Bansi Dhar, took employment with the British Government and as a member of the judicial department was transferred to various places. The care and

---

[2] This rebellion against the British was put down with a heavy hand, and in 1858 the government of India was transferred from the East India Company to the British Crown.

education of Motilal thus devolved on his second brother Nandlal, to whom he was deeply attached.

Nandlal was for a while the Diwan or Prime Minister of a princely estate called Khetri in Rajputana. After this he practised as a lawyer in Agra, and when the High Court was transferred from there to Allahabad he moved to the latter place. Since then Allahabad [3] has been the home of the Nehrus.

Young Motilal was a lively, high-spirited lad not greatly addicted to formal learning but naturally intelligent. As a boy his education was confined to Persian and Arabic, but he studied English later. He went through school and college in Kanpur and Allahabad, although he never graduated. This lapse came about in a curious if typical way. Motilal took his first examination but thought he had fared badly. Thereupon he decided to skip the rest and, playing truant, spent his time looking around the Taj. Actually, he had done quite well in his first paper.

At the Muir Central College in Allahabad, Motilal came under the influence of British professors who liked his youthful independence and initiative. Jawaharlal recalls how even in his later years his father would reminisce affectionately about the English principal of his college—one of whose letters he had carefully preserved. From this time date Motilal's Westernized habits and dress and his geniune liking and admiration for Englishmen.

Faced with the choice of a career Motilal decided to emulate his favourite brother and become a lawyer. He appeared for the High Court Vakil's [4] examination and topped the list, winning a gold medal. The law at that time was one of the few professions open to Indian talent.

After three years of apprenticeship in the district court at Kanpur, Motilal moved to the loftier realms of the High Court at Allahabad and settled to legal practice at that centre. About this time Nandlal died. To Motilal, who had grown up under Nandlal's affectionate care, his brother's sudden death was a heavy blow. He had loved him greatly. Aside from their mother, a woman of imperious personality and tremendous will, much of whose strong-mindedness Motilal inherited, there was hardly any other personal influence in his life.

[3] It is in the State of Uttar Pradesh, known formerly as the United Provinces.
[4] Vakil means lawyer.

The burden of supporting his brother's family now fell on Motilal. He plunged into work. As a lawyer he was more effective in the role of advocate than in that of jurist, being impatient of the smaller niceties of the law but quick to grasp the broad essentials of a case. His mind was keen and resourceful. He was by temperament combative. He loved nothing better than a fight, and his assertive advocacy aided by the vigour of his personality cut a quick swath to success.

Politics had then very little appeal for him, and in the India of those days political aspirations were limited to the removal of minor grievances and to pleas for larger representation in the administrative services and local government. Motilal was twenty-four when in 1885 the Indian National Congress in which he and his son were later to play a dominating part met for its first session in Bombay. The Congress owed its inception to a Scotsman, Alan Octavian Hume, who was a former member of the Indian Civil Service. At this session Hume called for "three times three cheers for Her Majesty the Queen Empress," and the delegates responded enthusiastically. Exactly forty-four years later, in 1929, the Congress party met at Lahore under the presidentship of Jawaharlal Nehru to proclaim complete independence as India's political goal.

According to the custom then prevailing in India, marriage was contracted at an early age. Motilal was married twice. He was around twenty when he married a Kashmiri girl of a family settled in Lahore, but she died shortly after the birth of a son who in turn did not survive his mother for long. Motilal's second wife, Swaruprani, was only a little over fifteen when she entered the Nehru household as a bride. Her husband was seven years her senior.

Like her husband, Swaruprani was the last child of her family, also Kashmiri Brahmins, settled in Lahore, and of a younger stock than the Nehrus. The family name was Thussu. She was tiny, being hardly five feet tall, smalled-boned, dainty and exquisite, like a porcelain figurine. Her son writes of her "amazingly small and beautiful hands and feet."

Notwithstanding her doll-like delicacy, Swaruprani was a person of considerable fortitude and character. In the coming years she was to have more than a woman's fair share of tribulation. Married to a man even then well set on the road to fame and fortune, she lacked nothing of the material adjuncts to comfort, ease and happiness. For thirty years Swaruprani knew the splendour and luxury of an affluent home until along with her husband she voluntarily shed the past and all that went with it to follow the Mahatma.

The Nehru household, when she entered it, was a typical Hindu joint family comprising Motilal, Nandlal's sons and a considerable cohort of cousins, children of his father's sisters, all living under one roof and presided over by the strong-willed matriarch who was Motilal's mother. It was no easy thing for a young bride of near sixteen to adjust herself to this environment, the more so since she was not mistress of the household. Motilal lavished on her the love and care of a devoted husband, but it is doubtful whether, until she reigned in her own household, which she did a few years later, Swaruprani felt any different from a bird in a golden cage.

Motilal, already a successful lawyer but still to reach the fabulous heights he achieved later, was then living in a house standing in a lane in one of Allahabad's more congested localities. The entrance to the lane was said to be haunted. Here, on November 14, 1889, Jawaharlal was born, and here he lived for three years.

In 1889 a twenty-year-old Indian, Mohandas Karamchand Gandhi, who was studying in London to be a barrister, called on Cardinal Manning to congratulate him on his attitude to the London dockers' strike. In that year Bernard Shaw published his *Fabian Essays*, and Gustave Eiffel confounded his critics by completing the Eiffel Tower in Paris. Japan was granted a constitution, and the Suez Canal was neutralised. A would-be dictator, General Georges Boulanger, fled from France. In India the Congress party's fourth annual session in Bombay was presided over by an Englishman, Sir William Wedderburn. Another Englishman, Charles Bradlaugh, the atheist Member of Parliament, addressed it.

Jawaharlal's boyhood was lonely. Although the household was full of children, they were considerably older than he. Portraits of those days show him as a boy with wistful eyes, and dressed in a variety of costumes from embroidered pantaloons and coat with jewelled slippers, to a sailor's rig and a Scots kilt. A fervent admirer of the British character, Motilal was determined that his son should be brought up in Western ways.

Until the age of sixteen when he went to Harrow, Jawaharlal never attended school. He was educated at home by a series of English governesses and private tutors, but of these only one, a part Irish theosophist of the name of Ferdinand T. Brooks, made any impression on the boy.

Brooks had been recommended to Motilal as Jawaharlal's tutor by Dr. Annie Besant. His father was Irish, his mother was Belgian and he was born on board a steamer bound for South America. As a young man Brooks was attracted to Indian philosophy, learned Sanskrit and translated the Bhagavad-Gita, a celebrated religious poem contained in the *Mahabharata*, which is the great epic poem of the Hindus. He was an ardent theosophist, of a deeply devotional nature, with a strongly religious pietist streak in him which in the eyes of his young charge must have contrasted strangely with Motilal's robust secularism.

Brooks was about twenty-six when he came as tutor to Jawaharlal, then a boy of eleven. He was to die later in tragic circumstances. Fanatically wedded to the truth as he saw it, Brooks parted company with Dr. Besant when that lady proclaimed Krishnamurthy as the coming Messiah. He was earning a precarious livelihood when his body was found in a river, drowned in circumstances which left the cause of his death a mystery. The influence of this strongly introvert character on Jawaharlal, albeit temporary, was also considerable.

Brooks developed in Jawaharlal two interests which have endured —a taste for reading and a curiosity in science and its mysteries. Apart from his religious bent, he appears to have been a man of much sensitivity, imagination and understanding. Between them, tutor and pupil rigged up a little laboratory, and there Jawaharlal felt for the first time the quick stir of wonder which still seizes him when confronted with scientists and scientific matters. Here he learned his early lessons in elementary physics and chemistry.

Brooks was with him for nearly three years, and in this period he encouraged his pupil's liking for English literature. Jawaharlal's reading, though wide, was haphazard and discursive. He read many of the novels of Scott, Dickens and Thackeray. He was attracted by Lewis Carroll and by Kipling's *Jungle Books* and *Kim*. Fridtjof Nansen's account of his Arctic adventures, *Farthest North*, excited his imagination and he followed breathlessly the exploits of Anthony Hope's hero in *The Prisoner of Zenda*. He came to know of Mark Twain and H. G. Wells and Conan Doyle's stories of Sherlock Holmes. He thought Jerome K. Jerome's *Three Men in a Boat* "the last word in humour."

Two other books seem to have specially impressed his youthful imagination, and he mentions them in his autobiography. They were Du Maurier's *Trilby* and *Peter Ibbetson*. Jawaharlal gives no reason for his especial choice, but it is possible that the boy discovered there the first faint glimmerings of a philosophy of life which the man was later to embrace. "And this I know," says a character in *Peter Ibbetson*, "the longer and more strenuously and complete one lives one's life on earth, the better for all. It is the foundation of everything."

Brooks also developed in his young charge a love for English poetry, and though his other preoccupations leave Jawaharlal little time today to indulge this taste his love for the arresting phrase and evocative thought persists. The strong streak of melancholy in his character was probably also enhanced by this association.

At the height of the partition killings in 1947, an acquaintance relates how he quoted to Nehru a line from the noted Hindi poet Maithili Sharan Gupta: "The history of man is the history of the devil." Jawaharlal, bowed with care and grief, heaved a sigh and repeated the line slowly.

A similar incident is related of a dinner party. There was a programme on the sitar [5] after dinner, and the host, knowing that his guest had had a very tiring day, suggested that he should retire.

"Oh, no," protested Nehru. "I haven't heard the sitar for a very long time."

Thereupon a fellow guest broke in, as is often the custom in parts of the country, with an Urdu quotation from northern India's most celebrated troubadour Ghalib: " 'It was love, Ghalib, that brought me to this pass. Or else I too would have been of some use.' "

Nehru, nodding melancholy assent, gently repeated, " 'It was love, Ghalib . . .' "

As a boy he was fascinated by Gustave Doré's illustrations to *Don Quixote*, but his visual judgment even today is less sure than his aural. His ear is more certain than his eye, and music and song have a stronger appeal to him than the sweeping brush and broad canvas of an artist. But he can be moved, even intoxicated, by the beauty of sky and stars, by the majesty of mountains and the breathless won-

[5] An Indian musical instrument.

der of nature stirring at dawn to new life. Brooks opened to him a window on a new world.

The only Indian tutor Jawaharlal had was a venerable pandit who was engaged to teach him Hindi and Sanskrit. An old friend of the family recalls seeing a beautifully printed edition of the *Samaveda*, the third of the four holy books of Hinduism, among the boy's Sanskrit texts. Nehru confesses that "after many years' effort" his knowledge of Sanskrit was about as small as his subsequent knowledge of Latin at Harrow. His Hindi is fluent but it is less proficient than his English. He probably thinks in English. During his last term of imprisonment in Ahmednagar fort, Nehru shared a cell with Maulana Abul Kalam Azad, the noted Muslim divine who is now India's Education Minister. Azad has related how Nehru talked in English in his sleep. "He not only talks in English," wrote Azad. "He dreams in English."

As Motilal prospered, the family's standard of living improved. When Jawaharlal was three the father decided to move from his house in the haunted lane of the old city to a newer part of Allahabad where he rented a bungalow in an area occupied mainly by Europeans. Jawaharlal lived here until he was ten, when Motilal moved to a residence he had bought for himself known as Anand Bhawan (Abode of Happiness).

Anand Bhawan, a large rambling house ringed with verandahs, stood in spacious grounds and had an indoor swimming pool, the first of its kind in Allahabad. Here Jawaharlal learned to swim. He recalls how on first moving to his new home he watched the labourers at work on the structures and embellishments which his father had ordered. Boy-like, he was entranced by the digging and building operations.

Anand Bhawan, donated later by Motilal to the nation and rechristened Swaraj Bhawan (Abode of Freedom), stands on a reputedly sacred spot where according to some traditions the deity Rama [6] met his half-brother Bharata, on Rama's return from his fourteen years' exile. Nearby is the Bharadwaj Ashram where legend has it that the sage Valmiki, author of the *Ramayana*, once stayed. The

---

[6] His life forms the subject of the *Ramayana*, one of the two famous epics of India. The other epic, *Mahabharata*, contains about 220,000 lines and is probably the longest poem in the world.

city of Allahabad, the ancient Prayaga, is also on hallowed ground, for here the heavenly river Ganga meets the Jumna and the fabled subterranean stream Saraswati. At the meeting place of these three rivers known as Triveni, or "the triple braid," pilgrims foregather from all parts of India, once annually for the Magh Mela and once in every twelve years for the great Kumbh Mela, a mammoth religious festival fair which goes back to the Vedic times.[7]

In these early formative years Jawaharlal spent his time mainly between his English tutors and his mother. His cousins were much older than he, and though he often listened to their grown-up talk the gulf of years prevented any affinity or companionship between them. One can imagine the little boy listening wide-eyed and not always comprehendingly to the conversation of his youthful elders. Some of it seeped into his sensitive, highly imaginative mind and stayed there.

Much of this talk was concerned with the overbearing, often in-sulting behaviour of Europeans and Eurasians towards Indians. Jawa-harlal heard of railway compartments being reserved for Europeans which no Indian, however crowded the train, might enter. He heard of benches and chairs being similarly labelled in public parks. Some-times one or the other of his cousins was involved in an encounter. Jawaharlal relates how these accounts created in him a feeling of strong resentment against the alien rulers of his country. At the same time he does not recall cherishing any hostile sentiments towards individual Englishmen. His own governesses and tutors were English and his father's house was wide open to English friends. "In my heart," he confesses, "I rather admired the English."

Of his father he saw little, and much of it from a distance. Off and on Motilal took time to play with his son, putting him through his paces in cricket and tennis. Sometimes father and son regaled them-selves flying a kite. Occasionally of an evening as Motilal sat talking and drinking with his friends, the boy would peep from behind a curtain, trying to take in the flow of conversation and laughter. He was tremendously impressed by his father, by his robust talk, his great echoing laugh, his vitality, strength and magnetism. He thought him clever and full of courage. Now and again the eavesdropper was noticed, and on these occasions his father would pull him into the

[7] Between 1500 and 1000 B.C.

room and seat him on his knee. Jawaharlal confesses that these occasions somewhat awed him.

"I grew up," Nehru was to recall many years later, "in a rather composite environment."

If he admired his father he was also more than slightly afraid of him. Motilal had charm and a sense of humour, but his temper was something awful to behold. "Even in after years," writes Jawaharlal, "I do not think I ever came across anything to match it in its own line." The *patria potestas* was very much in evidence in Motilal's attitude to his household. By nature overbearing, he was inclined to be somewhat feudal in his treatment of servants. When moved to wrath by a domestic's ineptitude he thought nothing of rising from the table and then and there thrashing the unfortunate man with his own hands. A youthful Indian friend of the family, fresh from Cambridge, recounts one such incident at the breakfast table at Anand Bhawan. He describes the episode as "odd and inexcusable." On Jawaharlal his father's attitude to his servants undoubtedly made an impression. The boy's fear was mixed with resentment, and something at least of his instinctive sympathy for the helpless underdog is traceable to these early years.

On one occasion Jawaharlal himself felt the weight of his father's wrath. He was about six years old when, wandering into his father's study one day, he noticed two fountain pens on his table. Two, he argued, were not necessary for one man at the same time. He helped himself to one. When the loss was discovered he was too terrified of his father's wrath to confess. But the missing pen was traced to him, and his father beat him severely. "Almost blind with pain and mortification at my disgrace, I rushed to my mother, and for several days various creams and ointments were applied to my aching and quivering little body."

It was on his mother that Jawaharlal leaned in those early years. She doted on him, and the boy, aware of her excessive, indiscriminating love, tried, as he confesses, to dominate her a little. She was his confidante, and to her he told some of his dreams, disappointments and yearnings. Loneliness gave an edge to his imagination. He used to dream of astral bodies, and imagined himself flying vast distances high up in the air without any appliance, alone and dominant. This escapist fantasy was to haunt him in later years. "This dream," he writes, "has indeed been a frequent one throughout my life; and sometimes it has been vivid and realistic and the countryside seemed to lie underneath me in a vast panorama."

From his mother and aunt, the widow of Nandlal, Jawaharlal heard, as Indian children of his age do, the old, old tales of Indian mythology and folklore. His mother told him of the adventures of the great Rama [8] which form the theme of the oldest of Sanskrit epic poems, Valmiki's *Ramayana*. From her too he learned the story of the *Mahabharata* detailing, among other things, the war between the Kauravas and the Pandavas for a kingdom, the ruins of whose capital, known as the "elephant city," are faintly discernible on an old bed of the Ganga about sixty miles northeast of Delhi.

Another of the boy's early confidants was Munshi Mubarak Ali, a patriarchal-looking Muslim who served as a sort of major-domo to the household. Often the companionless lad sought the old man's company and, snuggling up to him, listened to tales from the *Arabian Nights* and to stories of the Indian rebellion of 1857. Mubarak Ali's family had been ruined by the Mutiny, during which some British soldiers had hanged his father before his mother's eyes. Sorrow, as it sometimes does, had made Mubarak gentle and understanding, and the boy, looking at the lined face, the white locks and beard of his old friend, thought him the epitome of human wisdom. "The memory of him," Jawaharlal wrote many years later, "remains with me as a dear and precious possession."

Some at least of the brooding melancholy which is part of Nehru's nature might be traced to this solitary boyhood. With no companions of his own age at home, he sought instinctively the company of his mother and of sympathetic elders such as his aunt and Mubarak Ali. He was left very much to himself, and this isolation sharpened his thought and imagination. The sense of living a life apart, alone and sure, is reflected in his dream of flying high up in an empyrean void. But always there was the earth below.

Although Jawaharlal saw little of his father, and feared him, his admiration and affection for him remained as strong as ever. On his side Motilal, though never as demonstrative as the mother, loved his son intensely. His work absorbed him, and Jawaharlal's education was a matter which he felt could be left safely to the hands of com-

[8] The seventh incarnation of the god Vishnu.

petent tutors. The mother was never in the best of health. Since her son's birth she had suffered from a number of intermittent ailments, and her health was indifferent. Life with an ailing mother and later with an ailing wife was to influence Nehru profoundly. He learned to value good health. Fitness became a fetish with him.

Motilal's masculine assertiveness appealed to the feminine streak in his son. The father's attitude to women, particularly to his own womenfolk, was one of amused toleration. He dismissed family squabbles as the creation of women's folly. He was not particularly religious, and was inclined to treat religion half humorously as a woman's affair.

"My father was not exactly a religious man," Nehru once remarked. "But he respected the Hindu religion since he had been brought up in it."

Jawaharlal's own ideas on religion were hazy, and his tutor, Brooks, a determined theosophist, had therefore little difficulty in influencing his pupil his way. He instilled in him an interest in theosophy by introducing him to the works of Madame Blavatsky and by exposing him to discussions on the more esoteric aspects of this creed. Jawaharlal, then thirteen, was fascinated. He decided to join the Theosophical Society.

Motilal had been a member of the Society when Madame Blavatsky was in India, and was initiated into it by her. Founded by this formidable personage in 1875 in New York, the Society had been transferred to Madras in India in 1882. With the advent of Dr. Annie Besant, friend of Bradlaugh and Bernard Shaw, theosophy began to have an appeal for the urban Indian intellectual who was attracted and intrigued by its references to the Hindu and Buddhist scriptures. Mrs. Besant, perhaps the greatest natural orator of her day, was in wide vogue, and, hearing some of her speeches in Allahabad, Jawaharlal was thrilled. He asked his father's permission to join the Society, and was hurt when Motilal laughingly assented, displaying more amusement than interest in the affair. Motilal himself had ceased his association with theosophy within a short time of joining the Society.

Mrs. Besant presided at Jawaharlal's ceremony of initiation. Not long after, the thirteen-year-old boy attended the Theosophical Convention at Banaras where he saw the bearded Colonel Henry Olcott. His interest in theosophy, like that of his father, was short-lived. It did not long survive Brooks's departure from the household, but while this spiritual fever seized him he went about, as he recalled later, in an aura of pallid piety. Significantly his interest in theosophy palled not because he saw anything wrong in its tenets but because many of the persons associated with the movement seemed to him to live in an impractical, unreal world and priggishly regarded themselves as the elect.

Two years earlier, when Jawaharlal was eleven, a daughter was born to his parents. His father at the time was away in England, and the boy, sitting anxiously in the verandah of his house, learned of the new arrival from the doctor. That somewhat cross-grained individual amused himself by remarking that the advent of a sister need not disturb the brother unduly. Had it been a son he would have had a share in his father's patrimony. Jawaharlal was not amused. But he was exhilarated by the thought of having a baby sister. She was named Sarup (the Beautiful One) and grew up to be the celebrated Mrs. Vijayalakshmi [9] Pandit.

Motilal, with his wide circle of English friends, had always been impressed by the products of British public schools. He decided to send his son to one, and was fortunate to find a vacancy at Harrow. Jawaharlal was then sixteen, slightly above the normal age for entering a British public school.

A year before an event had occurred which absorbed the attention of India's educated middle class and was to affect Asian nationalism deeply. This was the Russo-Japanese War of 1904–1905. In one of his letters [10] to his daughter Indira, Nehru writes: "Early in the twentieth century an event occurred which had a great effect on the mind of Asia. This was the defeat of Tsarist Russia by Japan. . . . I remember well how excited I used to get when news came of the Japanese victories. I was about your age then." In a later letter [11] to his daughter he describes the Japanese triumph as "a great pick-me-up for Asia."

[9] Kashmiri brides are given a new name on their marriage. Vijaya means victory, and Lakshmi is the goddess of fortune.

[10] Dated November 22, 1932. This is one of a series of letters which Nehru wrote to his daughter while in different prisons between October, 1930, and August, 1933. His periodic absences in prison gave him little opportunity to supervise his daughter's education, and the letters were designed to tell her something of world history. See *Glimpses of World History* by Jawaharlal Nehru (London, Lindsay Drummond, 1939).

[11] Dated December 7, 1932.

About the only war which Jawaharlal had followed before this was the Boer War between 1899 and 1902 in which his sympathies were with the Boers, possibly a reflection of his latent antipathy to British rule in India. For the first time he read newspapers avidly in an effort to follow the news. The Russo-Japanese conflict excited his interest more keenly, for Japan symbolised an Asian country in conflict with a European power. He bought a number of books on Japan and delighted in the exotic prose of that literary exquisite, Lafcadio Hearn. The war stimulated his imagination. He dreamt of himself, sword in hand, fighting like one of Lafcadio Hearn's knightly heroes for the freedom of his country.

In May, 1905, Jawaharlal sailed for England with his father, mother and his four-year-old sister Sarup. On the train between Dover and London he opened a newspaper and read of Admiral Togo's decisive victory over the Russian fleet at Tsushima. "I was in high good humour," he notes.

It was in this mood that he entered upon his life in England.

3

HARROW AND CAMBRIDGE

In 1905 England was in the gaudy heyday of the Edwardian era. In December of that year a Liberal administration headed by Sir Henry Campbell-Bannerman took office. Germany was already launched on its armament race with Britain, and World War I was nine years away. About this time the suffragettes began their militant campaign for votes for women. There was a new toy, the motor car; and, travelling at twenty miles an hour, the world of fashion talked of "these fast, forward and frantic days. . . . The rush through the air is positively exhilarating."

Society took its tone from the gruff, gay and avuncular Edward VII. For the so-called higher orders it was a decade of spacious and opulent living in a world dominated by the glitter of great hostesses and celebrated beauties. The boa and ruffle were conspicuous features of feminine fashion. Crinolines and bustles had died in the boudoirs of Victorian England, and feminine contours were settling down to the "straight-fronted corset." Feminine shapes were full-blown in the style of Dana Gibson's drawings.

Masculine fashions were also changing. The sleek shining "topper," soon to be followed by the soft hat and "bowler," had replaced the Victorian "stovepipe." "Boaters" or straw hats were in vogue. The privileged drove to long-drawn sumptuous dinners in one-horse broughams, and London's streets were plied by a variety of vehicles, including steam buses, hansoms and four-wheel cabs. It was an age of leisure and plenty, a little vulgar in its ostentation, where the "higher" and "lower" orders pursued contentedly their separate ways.

Jawaharlal joined Harrow in the Christmas term of 1905 and left at the end of the summer term in 1907. He was sixteen at the time, three years older than most entrants to an English public school. Harrow school, about ten miles from London, is an ancient foundation established in 1572 in the reign of Elizabeth I by John Lyon, a yeoman of the neighbourhood. It was restricted originally to scholars of the parish of Harrow, but about 1660 it began to receive "foreigners," that is, boys from other parishes who paid for their education. In time the connotation of the term "foreigners" was liberalised and extended.

There were four or five Indian boys at Harrow when Jawaharlal entered it. The son of an Indian prince, the Gaekwar of Baroda, was one of them. He was an ardent cricketer much senior to Jawaharlal, and left soon after his arrival. The present Maharaja of Kapurthala, then heir-apparent to his father, was another, and Jawaharlal relates how this prince, when teased and tormented by his British companions, would expatiate on what he would do with them if ever they set foot in Kapurthala. The most notable of his British contemporaries was to win fame in World War II. Today he is Field-Marshal Lord Alexander of Tunis. Sir Walter Monckton, friend of the Duke of Windsor, and destined to be guide and philosopher to kings and princes, was also at Harrow at this time. Both Alexander and Monckton were senior to Nehru, and neither has any vivid recollection of his Indian contemporary.

Left alone among strangers, Jawaharlal was at first lonely and homesick. Harrow, on the model of English public schools,[1] is divided into a number of residential "houses," and it was in the largest of these, the Headmaster's, that Nehru was placed. The Headmaster, the Reverend Joseph Wood, D.D., was an amiable, popular man and a good scholar. Unlike his predecessor, the Reverend J. E. C. Welldon, who at one time was Bishop of Calcutta, Wood was no heavy-handed disciplinarian. Nehru's "house," although nominally under the Headmaster, was in the immediate charge of a Housemaster, the Reverend Edgar Stogdon, himself an old Harrovian and later Vicar of Harrow. Like Wood, Stogdon was a genial, kindly personality well liked by the boys.

The battle of Waterloo might have been won on the playing fields of Eton, but Harrow has also produced its quota of distinguished

[1] An English public school is the equivalent of an American private school.

soldiers and statesmen. These include among British Prime Ministers the names of Peel, Palmerston, Baldwin and Winston Churchill. By an irony which his father would have greatly relished, another Old Harrovian was also destined to be a Prime Minister—the first Prime Minister of independent India.

There are few records of Jawaharlal at Harrow. On his own admission, although he adjusted himself in time to his new surroundings, he was "never an exact fit." This was not from want of trying. At Harrow, as at most English public schools, cricket and football are compulsory for all the boys except the medically exempted. Jawaharlal did not shirk games, and he did his quota of work. He was keen on the Harrow School Corps which he joined, and a photograph shows him in uniform, very slim and erect, his boyish face a little tense beneath a shako. His Housemaster, who was commanding officer of the corps, speaks of Jawaharlal's "quite good capabilities as a soldier."

Stogdon also relates that when a shield for shooting was won by Harrow from among a number of competitors, the carriage conveying the winning team was relieved of its horses and dragged up Harrow hill by a number of schoolboys. Among them were Nehru and the future Lord Alexander.

Some thirty-five years after Nehru had left school, Stogdon wrote the following assessment of his young charge: "I was then Housemaster to the Headmaster, Dr. Wood, and Nehru was in the house—a very nice boy, quiet and very refined. He was not demonstrative but one felt there was great strength of character. I should doubt if he told many boys what his opinions were, or the masters with whom he had a good name, as he worked well and seldom (almost never) gave trouble."

It is a shrewd and perceptive judgment. Already the reserved, somewhat secretive strain in Nehru's make-up was apparent, as was also his latent strength of character. Part of this reserve derived from the mental gap between him and his companions who, like English boys of their age and class, were interested chiefly in games. In a letter to his father Jawaharlal complains how dull most of his English colleagues were. Yet he was no prig. It was only that his interests were wider than theirs; he read more books and newspapers than they did, and in general knowledge he was ahead of them. When his form master asked his pupils to name the members of the new Liberal government in Britain the Indian boy, to the master's great surprise, was the only one able to give him any information on the subject. He named nearly all the members of Campbell-Bannerman's Ministry.

Jawaharlal's zest for science which Brooks had nursed and nurtured remained. Aviation was at that time in its infancy, and its progress excited him. In 1905 the Wright brothers, Wilbur and Orville, made forty-five flights in the longest of which they remained in the air for half an hour and travelled 24½ miles. In the following year Alberto Santos-Dumont flew a distance of 250 yards in twenty-one seconds in a machine of his own construction. Jawaharlal followed these pioneer efforts with close interest. Speed, with its aerial concomitants of separateness and dominion, had always fascinated him and is reflected in his favourite dream. He wrote to his father predicting that he might soon be able to pay him a week-end visit to India by air.

Harrow reflected the leisured world outside with its predilections and prejudices. There were a few Jews in the school, including some in Jawaharlal's House, and the boy detected an undercurrent of anti-Semitic feeling. Although he had no opinions on the matter, he confesses he was influenced by the atmosphere sufficiently "to think that it was the proper thing to have this feeling." His regard for the artificial proprieties which were part and parcel of his environment momentarily overcame his innate sense of social justice. He was growing fast, but the social conscience of later years had still to develop.

Although immature in some ways Jawaharlal soon had a feeling of having outgrown his stay in Harrow. He came to like the place, but the sense of intellectual restraint and confinement irked him somewhat. Perhaps also the grey skies of England depressed the Indian boy alive to the colour, movement and vibrant light of his own homeland. Harrow, although standing in spacious grounds with buildings dating from the seventeenth to the nineteenth century, had an intellectually cloistered air. So at least it seemed to the youthful Nehru.

He longed for the wider world of the university. A book which intensified this feeling was one of G. M. Trevelyan's three volumes on Garibaldi and his struggle for Italian freedom, which Jawaharlal won as a prize for good work in school. So absorbed was he by its story that he obtained the other two volumes and studied the Garibaldi epic carefully. In his mind, already politically conscious as far as his own country was concerned, he equated Italy with India. Why, he asked, should India not wage a similar struggle? The culture of the Mediterranean, of Italy and Greece, had long attracted Britain's upper classes. Was not Byron a Harrovian?

It is interesting to see how this parallel between India and Italy burned itself in his mind and stayed in his memory. Many years later, in his autobiography,[2] Nehru was to return to the theme. Writing of Italy's political divisions, and comparing them with India's, he remarks that despite diversity the unity persists. He sees Banaras in the image of Rome. Even when Italy lay politically prostrate, its cultural life coursed through the veins of Europe. So, he mused, has India's through Asia's.

His Asian consciousness aroused by the Russo-Japanese War, Jawaharlal eagerly followed political events at home which in turn has been influenced by developments in and outside India. Asia's educated classes felt that Europe was losing its predominant world position, for the Boer War, although concluded in Britain's favour, had not shown the British military machine to advantage; the Turks had routed the Greeks, and from the Near East came news of the massacres of Christians. Fearful of the encroachments of Tsarist Russia, the British administration in India had inflated the might of the Russians, and when Japan scored a series of resounding victories over that country their reverberations were heard throughout Asia.

Inside India these external developments generated a feeling of vague unrest accompanied by acts of violence in various parts of the country. Two months before Campbell-Bannerman's Liberal government assumed office in Britain, a new Viceroy, Lord Minto, who was previously Governor-General of Canada, arrived in India. Lord Morley was Secretary of State for India, and between them the Viceroy and Secretary of State set to work out a cautious advance in representative government for the country. There was no question of giving India or Indians a parliamentary system or democratic control.

Jawaharlal followed these events closely, scanning the English newspapers for news from India. The accounts they contained were meagre and scrappy, but informative enough to reveal that a new political upsurge was under way at home. It was the first since the great revolt

[2] Published in April, 1936.

of 1857. Apart from terrorism another weapon was being deployed—the boycott of British goods which was accompanied by a drive to support *swadeshi,* or homemade products. "All this," wrote Jawaharlal, "stirred me tremendously but there was not a soul in Harrow to whom I could talk about it." Sometimes during the holidays he would meet other Indian students and friends, and they would discuss events at home excitedly and with no little emotion.

India was pulsating with life. From 1904, when the idea of partitioning Bengal [3] was mooted, nationalism took a more assertive form. Already the moderate tactics of the Indian National Congress had found a formidable opponent in Bal Gangadhar Tilak, who in 1907 made an unsuccessful attempt to capture that body. Tilak, an orthodox Brahmin, was an aggressive nationalist. He came from Maharashtra in western India, which with Bengal and the Punjab was the cradle of the new political renaissance. A vigorous speaker, Tilak was also trenchant with his pen, and the columns of the Marathi newspaper *Kesari,*[4] which he founded, were widely read for their direct and pungent prose. He was active on the political scene long before Gandhi, and suffered his first term of imprisonment in 1897[5] for an article which allegedly incited to sedition.

The anti-partition movement in Bengal stirred Tilak to renewed effort. He was no believer in quiescent philosophies, and he preached the gospel of incessant agitation, direct and indirect, to be reinforced if necessary by violence. He mobilised religion in the cause of politics and resuscitated the annual festival of Ganesh, god of wisdom and remover of obstacles, whom the people of Maharashtra hold high among the deities of the Hindu pantheon. Bengal flattered him by imitation, reviving the tantric ritual[6] and the cult of Kali, a goddess renowned as the militant consort of the god Shiva, protector and annihilator, "the three-eyed, the blue-throated, the tranquil." In Bengal the movement was led by a florid orator, Bepin Chandra Pal,

[3] Bengal was partitioned in 1905, the eastern area being separated with its own capital at Dacca. The partition, which was fiercely opposed, was reversed in 1911 when Eastern Bengal was again brought under Calcutta. In 1947 the partition of India again saw the partition of Bengal more or less on the lines of the 1905 division.

[4] It means Lion.

[5] He was sentenced to eighteen months' rigorous imprisonment.

[6] A ritual which gives prominence to the female energy of the deity Vishnu, or Shiva, their active nature being personified in the persons of their Saktis or wives.

and by a young Cambridge-educated Indian, Aurobindo Ghose, who later was to retire from politics and set up as a sage in his ashram at Pondicherry.

Like many of Tilak's followers, the opponents of the Bengal partition were not squeamish about the use of violence. In 1908, shortly after Nehru left Harrow, a bomb factory was discovered at Maniktollah in Bengal following the accidental killing of two English women at Musaffarpur by a bomb meant for the local British magistrate. There followed the Maniktollah conspiracy trial, which aroused country-wide interest and excitement. For his comments on this case, Tilak was sentenced to six years' imprisonment.

Aside from Bengal and Tilak's stamping ground, Maharashtra, there was unrest in the Punjab. Although the grievances here were more agrarian than political, they manifested themselves in political demonstrations and riots. These were spearheaded by two local leaders, Lala Lajpat Rai, known popularly as "the Lion of the Punjab," and Sardar Ajit Singh, both of whom were deported by the British Government.

To Jawaharlal, following these events with emotional interest and fervour, the world of Harrow suddenly seemed very small. Yet he wept when he left Harrow. Even if he was not altogether attuned to its atmosphere, Jawaharlal was infected by its traditions and fellowships, and the impact here was again emotional. "I know," writes his Housemaster, the Reverend Edgar Stogdon, "that he very specially liked the Harrow school songs." He did. To this day the library at Anand Bhawan contains an enormous dog-eared book of his Harrow school songs. Among Nehru's favourites are the fag song "Jerry, You Duffer and Dunce," and "When Grandpapa's Grandpapa Was in the Lower Lower First," which he sometimes sings lustily with his nieces, nephews and grandchildren. In 1952, while in London for the Commonwealth conference, Nehru attended the Old Harrovian dinner and took an impish delight in singing the school song "Forty Years On" in the company of another Old Harrovian, also a Prime Minister, Winston Churchill. Ten years had passed since Churchill's war-time government in Britain had sent Nehru to jail for his last and longest term of imprisonment.

What thoughts, one wonders, assailed the two Prime Ministers as together they sang the slightly doleful refrain?

"Forty years on, growing older and older,
Shorter in wind as in memory long,
Feeble of foot and rheumatic of shoulder,
What will it help us that once we were strong?"

In October, 1907, Nehru went to Trinity College, Cambridge. He was then approaching eighteen, a slim handsome dark-haired youth with sensitive eyes, speaking English in the consciously clipped accents of a British public school boy.

Cambridge then excelled in the teaching of natural sciences, economics, and philosophy. At the Cavendish Laboratory was the celebrated physicist Sir J. J. Thomson, absorbed in his epoch-making research into the conduction of electricity through gases, the determination of the charge and mass of the electron and the analysis of positive rays. Nehru, with his attachment to science, chose the Natural Science Tripos, his subjects being chemistry, geology and botany. But his interests were broader, and his mind, naturally inquisitive, roved over a wide horizon. Politics and economics attracted him and he had always been drawn towards history and literature. He read widely, if desultorily.

The three years which Nehru spent at Cambridge coincided with an interesting intellectual ferment in Europe as the world moved through a fading twilight into the darkness of a global war. Bergson was in eruptive mood, and nearer home H. G. Wells and Bernard Shaw were challenging old social and economic values. Shaw's *Major Barbara* appeared in 1905, in the same year as Wells's *A Modern Utopia*, and at Cambridge Shavian wit and wisdom were culled eagerly from the celebrated prefaces. In these effervescent years Einstein propounded his special relativity theory. In 1908 Thomas Hardy completed his *Dynasts*, and about this time a Spaniard by the name of Pablo Picasso founded cubism. Freud had published the first of his psychopathological treatises shortly before the turn of the old century. At the end of the first decade of the new century his study entitled *Psychoanalysis* was released.

Sex and morality figure large in the discussions of undergraduates fumbling their way to new experiences. Nehru discussed sex with his companions from a theoretical and therefore consciously lofty viewpoint. They bandied the names of Block and Krafft-Ebing, of Havelock Ellis and Otto Weininger. The tone of their talk was superior.

Few of them had had any sexual experience, certainly not Nehru, who confesses that his approach to sex was "rather timid," and then and for many years after he left Cambridge, theoretical. He had no religious inhibitions on the subject, and sex in his mind was not associated with sin, but his natural shyness and diffidence prevented him from embarking on experience.

Two authors who at this period moulded much of his political and economic thinking were Lowes Dickinson and Meredith Townsend. Townsend's *Asia and Europe* particularly impressed him and influenced the pattern of his political thought. Already his Asian consciousness was seeking an intellectual basis and foundation. His interest in poetry remained, and was quickened by certain events. Swinburne died in the spring of 1909 to be followed by George Meredith a few weeks later. Among Nehru's favourite poetry is the lyric verse of Swinburne, and he is still fond of reciting the nostalgic opening lines of Swinburne's "Rondel":

> These many years since we began to be
> What have the gods done with us? What with me?
> What with my love? They have shown me fates and fears,
> Harsh springs, and fountains bitterer than the sea,
> Grief a fixed star, and joy a vane that veers
> These many years.

Auden, Masefield, Walter de la Mare, Spender, Eliot and Yeats are among the poets whose books adorn the shelves of his library at Anand Bhawan.

It would be misleading to imagine that Nehru read and thought deeply on the intellectual developments of his day. His interest in them, he admits, was superficial, and although his mind was stirred by some of their manifestations he was not sufficiently absorbed or stimulated to burrow deep below the surface. The winds of artistic and intellectual creativeness blew around him, and, inhaling them, he savoured some of their passing fragrance. Having come to Cambridge by way of Harrow, he lived in an atmosphere and against a background vastly different from those of most of his Indian contemporaries. Something of the dilettantism of Oscar Wilde and Walter Pater infected the university life of his time. Most other Indian students, inured to more earnest ways of life, were immune to this pervasive influence. But the aesthetic with its appeal to the senses and the imagination drew Jawaharlal like a magnet. His father, always generous, made him a handsome allowance which Nehru, in what he was later to dub this "cyrenaic" period of his life, often exceeded. He lived a soft, easy existence immersed in work and games and amusements. The only thing which occasionally clouded his mind was the political struggle in India which he continued to follow.

Among his Indian contemporaries were some who were to be associated with him in the nationalist movement. One of them was J. M. Sen Gupta, who was senior to him, and who left Cambridge soon after Nehru went up. Sen Gupta was to be prominent in Bengal politics. The others included Syed Mahmud of Bihar, now a minister in Nehru's cabinet, Tassaduk Ahmad Khan Sherwani from his own province, and Saif-ud-Din Kitchlew, who with the advent of freedom was to leave the Congress, flirt with the Communists and become India's first recipient of the Stalin Peace Prize.[7]

Another Indian acquaintance in London who was later to become a valued friend and colleague was Sri Prakasa, now Governor of Madras. Prakasa went up to Cambridge a year after Nehru left the university and first encountered him in December, 1911, in the house of a mutual Indian friend in London. He recalls how Nehru, dressed in immaculate Western clothes, entered the drawing room and, standing before the fire, held forth on a variety of topics at some length. Evidently he knew his host and hostess well, for after a while, remarking that he was hungry, he asked for some food. The food was produced, and at a comparatively late hour, when the buses and "tubes" had stopped and taxis were hard to come by, Nehru with Prakasa stepped out into the night. Prakasa lived close by, but Jawaharlal's residence was a considerable distance away.

"How are you getting home?" Prakasa asked.

"Don't worry about me," said Nehru shortly. "I can look after myself." And he vanished into the night.

It was the sort of reply, says Prakasa, which he would give today—"for nothing in him has changed."

There was, of course, another side to Nehru's nature. If he was inclined to be reserved, even curt with acquaintances, he could be gaily ebullient and demonstrative in the company of close friends.

[7] He was awarded this in 1952.

One of these, Dr. Khan Sahib,[8] brother of the famous Frontier Gandhi, Abdul Ghaffar Khan, was then a student at St. Thomas's Hospital, London. "Hardly a day went by when I was in London, when we did not meet," Nehru wrote many years later. Other friends recall how in an exuberance of high spirits Nehru sometimes clambered on to the shoulders of Dr. Khan Sahib while the latter, holding the tails of his professional frock coat, waltzed around the room.

This combination of friendly ebullience and conscious reserve, of introspectiveness and high spirits survives to this day. Nehru gambols with his grandchildren like a schoolboy, sometimes stopping his car on the drive to get on to one of their tricycles and pedal merrily in the garden of the Prime Minister's residence. With close friends and relatives he can be solicitous, even tender. But he has his moments of glacial reserve. Then the blinds of his mind are drawn and the windows shuttered.

Nehru did not keep aloof from the other Indian students in Cambridge or London, but it is possible that he spoke an idiom which most of them did not easily understand or appreciate. His shyness and sensitivity gave him an air of hauteur. His direct, often abrupt speech was not calculated to win friends and influence people. He left no impress on the life of the university or indeed on the hundred-odd Indian students studying at Cambridge in his time. Few of them in later years had any recollection of even meeting him. At Cambridge the Indian students had a society of their own known as the Majlis which Nehru frequented. It met weekly when a debate was held, very often on a political theme concerning India. Jawaharlal's shyness and reserve prevented him from speaking often, and his incursions into public speech were few and far between. The Majlis manner and style of debate were modelled on the University Union, and this irritated Nehru, who was concerned equally with content. He felt that less attention was paid to matter than to form. A similar diffidence deterred him from taking part in the discussions of his college debating society known as "The Magpie and Stump." Here there was a rule that a member not speaking for a whole term must pay a fine. Nehru often paid the fine.

To Cambridge came many Indian visitors, including a few political notabilities. Among them was the Bengal leader Bepin Chandra Pal,

[8] Now a minister in the Pakistan cabinet.

a man given to torrid and tumultuous oratory. Like Gladstone addressing Queen Victoria, he was wont to talk to an audience, even of one, as if it were a public gathering. Pal addressed about a dozen Indian students in a small sitting room. His oratory rumbled and thundered over their heads. "The volume of noise was so terrific," says Jawaharlal, "that I could hardly follow what he was saying."

He was more impressed by the Punjab leader Lala Lajpat Rai, who spoke in a less extravagant manner than Pal. He also heard Gopal Krishna Gokhale, a politician of high calibre and perspicacity, who as a moderate was stoutly opposed to Tilak's volatile extremism. Gokhale, a cautious, far-sighted politician, was unfortunately to die early. He died in February, 1915, at the age of forty-nine.

In India the year 1907 had seen a renaissance of nationalism. At the annual session of the Congress party at Surat that year, Tilak sought to challenge the dominance of the Moderates but failed. He withdrew from the Congress, rejoining it only in 1916. Nehru's father, Motilal, was present at Surat when the Congress session broke up in disorder. Disapproving of the extremists, he yet admired Tilak as a man of deeds, however misguided some of his activities might seem. Tilak's imprisonment in 1908 immobilised him for six years, but India continued to simmer in the three areas of Bengal, Maharashtra and the Punjab. In Bengal the cult of violence was openly preached in the columns of *Yugantar*,[9] edited by Bhupendranath Dutt, brother of the famed Swami Vivekananda. Dutt was sentenced to a long term of imprisonment. Alongside him was another arresting and unusual figure, Aurobindo Ghose, whose literary gifts were embellished with political acumen and a capacity for philosophical thought. Aurobindo preached his ideas in the columns of the powerful *Bande Mataram*.[10] Between 1906 and 1910 he was prosecuted on three occasions and was imprisoned for about a year in 1908. In 1910 the British Government launched the third prosecution against him, but Aurobindo had already taken refuge in the then French settlement of Pondicherry, where he renounced politics to take up the life of a recluse and sage. He died in 1950 in the famous ashram he had founded there.

Jawaharlal was twenty when in 1910 he left Cambridge, having secured a second-class honours degree in the Natural Science Tripos.

[9] New Age.
[10] Hail Motherland.

Thus his academic record at school and college was average and undistinguished. His choice of science at the university influenced his habit of mind and gave him a measure of intellectual poise, for in the opening years of the twentieth century science was positive and assured. He lacked, however, the one-track mind of the specialist. His interests were diffuse, and consequently there grew in him a precision of thought accompanied by a loose, even untidy, mode of speech. This tendency to look around rather than into a subject persists.

At Cambridge his nationalism, which was stirred as a boy by the Russo-Japanese War, found an emotional vent in the happenings in India. But quite clearly his political convictions, such as they were, had as yet no firm foundations and the later axiom of non-cooperation with British rule had then no place in his thinking. In consultation with his father Jawaharlal toyed for a while with the idea of joining the Indian Civil Service, but this proposition was soon abandoned in favour of the paternal profession. It was decided that he should become a lawyer, two considerations influencing this choice. Jawaharlal was twenty, and the minimum age limit in the competitive examination for the Indian Civil Service was twenty-two. He would thus have had to wait another three years in England—for if successful an extra year of apprenticeship was entailed—and already his family chafed at his absence from home. Moreover, as an Indian Civil Servant he was likely to be posted to various distant places far removed from Allahabad, and this was no agreeable prospect for a fond father and a doting mother.

From Cambridge, accordingly, Jawaharlal went to London where he stayed for the next two years, "eating" his dinners [11] at the Inner Temple, and passing his examinations—as he remarks—"with neither glory nor ignominy." He was vaguely restive, and at one period found an outlet in a bout of gay parties with some old Harrow friends. At that time he had something of his father's taste for good living. While in London he liked to frequent fashionable restaurants and sample his wine with the care and air of a connoisseur. He enjoyed downing magnums of champagne in company. He acquired a taste but never a habit for wine. Partly this period of physical ebullience was a reaction to the mental restiveness which left him uncertain and

---

[11] The ritual of eating a certain number of dinners every term is obligatory for the Bar examinations in London.

dissatisfied. But even at its most exuberant peak this period was a passing phase.

There was much to attract him elsewhere. Nehru traces the beginnings of his interest in socialism to his Cambridge days when the Fabianism of Shaw and the Webbs attracted him, but he confesses that his interest was academic. He was also drawn by the intellectual liveliness of Bertrand Russell and John Maynard Keynes many of whose lectures he attended although his own university curriculum was scientific, not economic. This interest he maintained in London. The Fabians were active in London, and to the man who later was to propound the principle of peaceful co-existence, the theory of the inevitability of gradualness had its appeal. He was interested in, but by no means overwhelmed by, socialist ideas. In the summer of 1910 Jawaharlal visited Ireland, where the beginnings of the Sinn Fein movement intrigued him. To many Indians in those days Ireland was as infectious and inspiring an ideal as the Italy of Garibaldi and Mazzini. In England the suffragette movement was then at its height, and Jawaharlal's interest was provoked by this spectacle of militant femininity.

In the summer of 1912 he completed his examinations and was called to the Bar. During his stay of over seven years in England he had been home twice, spending his time there with his family at Allahabad and at the hill station of Mussoorie. While at Cambridge he had acquired a second sister, Krishna, who was born in November, 1907. Earlier another son had been born to his parents but had died in infancy.

The years had wrought many changes in Jawaharlal. Away from home he had exchanged his lonely boyhood for an independent but still largely isolated existence. If this had sharpened his sense of independence it had also given an edge to his introspectiveness. He had as yet no settled moorings, social, political or intellectual. He lived in a hazy half-world, at home neither in East nor West, in India nor England. Most of what he knew of India's storied past, of her folklore, legend and song he had learned as a boy from his mother and aunt and the adult friends of his childhood such as Munshi Mubarak Ali. On this had been superimposed the pattern of a Western education, first at home and then abroad at Harrow, Cambridge and London. "I have become," he wrote many years later, "a queer mixture of the

East and West, out of place everywhere, at home nowhere." And he noted the feeling of spiritual loneliness which it created "not only in public activities but in life itself."

Nehru is, as he himself once described T. S. Eliot, "a torn being," not mentally but emotionally and psychologically. This gives him a sort of Janus look and accounts for the contradictions in his personality. Here is a revealing episode of later days.

"If you come to my place," said an Indian university professor at Allahabad, "I can arrange for you to meet a few groups of keen students trying to think."

Nehru paced the corridor in which they stood.

"Ah, yes," he said, stopping suddenly before the professor and grasping his arm. "But what about the groups inside me?"

From this rootlessness stemmed the restiveness, particularly of his early years as an exile back in India. "I am a stranger and alien in the West; I cannot be of it," he lamented. "But in my own country also, sometimes, I have an exile's feelings."

He had gone to England in a mood of adventure and discovery. But he returned to his homeland—to discover India. It is not without significance that many years later a book of his was to bear the title *Discovery of India.*

4

THE GATHERING STORM

OVER India in 1912 hung a haze of political lassitude and torpor. Tilak was in prison, and since his withdrawal from the Congress after the stormy Surat session of 1907 the Moderates, willing to cooperate with the British Government in working the Morley-Minto reforms, were in the ascendant. The Morley-Minto reforms of 1909 established an Imperial legislature at the centre with an official majority and permitted one Indian to enter that British holy of holies, the Viceroy's executive council. In the provinces the local legislatures known as provincial councils contained a majority of Indian members, but they had no authority to displace the British governors' executive councils, which were impervious to any legislative verdict. The reforms also introduced the principle of separate representation for Hindus and Muslims, thereby hardening political cleavages and rivalries between the two communities—a system that some forty years later was to find its logical culmination in Pakistan.

Even Bengal where the anti-partition movement had stirred political feeling for the first time among the lower middle classes and, to some extent, the masses, was quiescent, the British Government having undone the partition in 1911, thereby restoring Bengal's unity and peace. Six years earlier, the formation of the Muslim League, which the authorities actively encouraged, had created a counterpoise to the Congress which was predominantly Hindu, and the acceptance of the principle of separate communal representation for Hindus and Muslims, adopted in the Morley-Minto reforms, weakened the possibilities of a united Hindu-Muslim front against the Raj. The British administration held sway on the Roman principle of divide and rule.

Politics were thus confined to the Moderates, who were busy jostling for office. In December, 1912, shortly after his return from England, Nehru attended a Congress session for the first time at Bankipore in Bihar. Himself clad in a lounge suit, he was disconcerted to see that a great many of his fellow delegates had donned morning coats and well pressed trousers for the occasion. It appeared to him to be more of a social gathering than a political assembly. "Very much an English-knowing upper-class affair" was his verdict.

Uneasy and uncertain in this artificially arid atmosphere, Nehru felt that the political world of India was unreal. From England he had thought of it in terms of tumult and triumph, of suspense, sacrifice, effort and excitement. Here was something altogether different, not only drab but pedestrian. The spectacle of over-dressed politicians gabbling in a void would have been faintly comic were its implications not so disturbing. In Nehru this unexpected situation induced the old feeling of frustration.

Life in the law courts, once the freshness of novelty had worn off, proved equally listless. The lawyer's profession calls for some exacting qualities—a mind capable of finding intellectual excitement in the intricacies of a mortgage or entail, a temperament willing "to die for an idea or do battle over an egg," an imperviousness to judicial jaundice, vast industry, persistence, precision and patience. Accomplishment is something different from creativeness, as the artist in Nehru soon realised. He was no Buzfuz prepared to talk automatically to his brief, and the prospect of a favourable verdict, while satisfying, was not sufficiently stimulating. He wanted to do things, not merely to achieve them. He lacked the lawyer's temperament, and his was not the mind to harness itself to the rote and routine of the law. Its taste soured. Intangibles, save the stimulus of ideas which intrigue him, have rarely interested Nehru, and he thought the intangibles of the law enervating to a degree.

Unlike his father, Nehru did not find the company of fellow lawyers particularly congenial or bracing. He felt that their talk outside the jargon of the law was flat, dull and insipid. Their intellectual horizon appeared to be curiously limited, and the boundaries of their interests seemed plotted, marked and defined with all the precision and exactitude of a legal conveyance. They conformed to a pattern, and the pattern palled. Nehru has never troubled to conceal his intellectual arrogance. He was nearly twenty-four, and both politically and professionally he felt at a dead end. As always, he chafed at inaction. Life at home was not uncongenial, and in his father he rejoiced in a stimulating if often contentious companion. They did not always see eye to eye on politics, Motilal's views being more moderate than his son's. A few years before, while in London, shortly after coming down from Cambridge, Jawaharlal, piqued by one of his father's studiously moderate utterances on political affairs, had written to him, sarcastically suggesting that no doubt the British Government was delighted with his views. Motilal was infuriated by this distant display of filial impertinence. He worked himself into one of his tremendous rages and talked of summoning his son home. Happily, more temperate counsels prevailed.

Repelled by the ineffectualness of the Congress, Nehru was at first attracted by a moderate organisation. This was the Servants of India Society which Gopal Krishna Gokhale had founded in 1905 in Poona, modelling it on the famous Society of Jesus and exacting from its members pledges of poverty, good works and obedience. Nehru had heard Gokhale speaking at Cambridge. Although he did not agree with his moderate views, being more inclined to Tilak's aggressive tactics, he was even then impressed by Gokhale's integrity and his sense of dedicated service. Since Tilak's withdrawal from the Congress in 1907, Gokhale's influence in that organisation had grown perceptibly. Nehru saw him again at the Bankipore Congress session in December, 1912, and his respect for the moderate leader was reinforced by Gokhale's earnestness and serious approach to politics and public affairs. Here at least was a man, who, however moderate, was doing something. The spirit of service and sacrifice which animated the Society drew Jawaharlal's admiration, but neither then nor later did he entertain any thought of joining it. Perhaps he remembered his early juvenile plunge into theosophy. The aura of good works and pallid piety was not for him.

It was about this time that the name of Gandhi came into Nehru's ken. In November, 1913, Gandhi, heading a band of some 2,500 Indian indentured labourers, marched from Natal into the Transvaal as a protest against the failure of the South African Government to honour its undertaking to repeal an annual tax on the labourers. India heard again of the novel weapon of satyagraha, which means literally holding on to truth but which came to signify non-violent resistance. Gandhi had first employed this method in South Africa as far back as 1907, but in 1913 it achieved a resounding triumph. Nehru, impressed and intrigued by the possibilities of the new technique, was thrilled by the thought "that a community of poor down-trodden ignorant workers and a group of petty merchants, far from their home country, should take up this brave attitude." Action had always stimulated and inspired him.

The Balkan Wars, a prelude to World War I, also had their repercussions in India. In 1911 Italy's unprovoked attack on Turkey and its occupation of Tripoli, Cyrenaica and the Dodecanese Islands stirred feeling in India, where Turkey was regarded as an Oriental power. Resentment was especially sharp among the Indian Muslims who looked upon the Sultan of Turkey as the Khalif or head of Islam. The Balkan Wars of 1912–1913 when Greece, Serbia, Montenegro and Bulgaria ranged themselves against the Turks intensified this feeling, and a medical team known as the Red Crescent Mission was despatched to aid the Turkish wounded. A member of this group, Dr. M. A. Ansari, whom Jawaharlal had met in London in 1905, was to be associated closely with the nationalist movement.

When the First World War broke out in August, 1914, sympathy in India was divided. Among the politically conscious elements there was little real enthusiasm for the Allied cause, and Turkey's entry on the side of Germany dulled it further. The Princes rallied to the British, and among the upper middle classes there was some show of vocal support. While few entertained any illusions about the Kaiser's Germany, educated Indians by and large took a vicarious pleasure in seeing their British rulers humbled. Nehru confesses that he viewed the war with mixed feelings. If his sympathy was with any country it was with France, whose culture he greatly admired. As during the Russo-Japanese War, Jawaharlal and his father followed the course of hostilities in the daily newspapers and discussed it keenly.

For the most part the war seemed far away, and not until the debacle of Mesopotamia, for which the British authorities in India had taken a special responsibility, was its impact felt in the country. Then, if anything, opinion hardened. There were stories of "press-gang" methods being brought into play, particularly in the Punjab, where forced recruiting was resorted to in order to procure men for the army and labour corps. In all, over a million Indians volunteered or were impressed into war service. Censorship of news combined with the Defence of India Act which provided for summary arrest and imprisonment gave currency to alarmist rumours and some unrest.

In this hothouse atmosphere nationalist feeling slowly came to life again. Tilak was released on June 17, 1914, after six years of imprisonment. "I feel like Rip Van Winkle," he declared. While in prison he had worked on a commentary on the Gita, where Krishna, the most popular of Hindu deities, expounds to his kinsman Arjuna his philosophical doctrines. Tilak characteristically interpreted these as a gospel of action, thereby giving a political twist to a religious theme and making an allegory of a dialogue. The book was published in mid-1915 and sold furiously. Earlier, an attempt to bring Congress moderates and extremists together in the persons of Tilak and Gokhale had proved abortive. On February 19, 1915, Gokhale died, and with his passing the influence of the moderates was weakened. "This side of life," he murmured as he lay dying, "has been good to me. It is time I should go and see the other."

Gandhi, after a three-month stay in England on his way back from South Africa, arrived in Bombay on January 9, 1915. Except for a year's residence in India between 1901 and 1902 and an earlier shorter stay in 1896, he had not visited his homeland since he sailed for South Africa in April, 1893. On the advice of Gokhale he decided to abstain from active politics for a year, and utilised the period to tour the country. India was marking time.

Not until 1916 was this truce from politics broken. With the exception of Bengal and the Punjab, where sporadic acts of violence were fiercely repressed, India as a whole was politically quiescent. Indeed, there was no such thing as active non-cooperation with the war effort. At this period Jawaharlal himself saw nothing incongruous in applying to join the newly formed Indian Defence Force, but political developments caught up with this decision and made it inoperative. While he was in London, Gandhi on behalf of a number of Indians had pledged unconditional support to the authorities, and his wife, Kasturba, like Jawaharlal's mother, was busily engaged in knitting and sewing garments and other comforts for the troops. On June 3, 1915, the King's birthday honours announced the award to

Gandhi of a British decoration, the Kaisar-i-Hind medal, "for services to the British empire." The days of non-cooperation were still five years away.

Nehru remained an uneasy spectator of these events. At this period he was a patriot pure and simple, his nationalism submerging even the vague socialism of his university days. He was still shy, still reserved, proud and very sensitive. Public speaking terrified him, and not until three years after his return from England, in 1915, could he be persuaded to mount a platform and speak. When he did, attacking a new Act which muzzled the press, he was more than slightly embarrassed when a lawyer friend of his father embraced him and kissed him publicly on the dais. Nehru read in that effusive act a significant meaning, for politics in those days was confined largely to speaking, and here, hey presto, was a new recruit.

Because it saw two major schisms healed, albeit temporarily, the year 1916 is a landmark in the political story of modern India. The war had never been popular, particularly with the Muslims, who resented the idea of fighting Turkey. "It is a sore point," declared Maulana Mazharul Haq, the President of the Muslim League in 1915, "that the Government of our Khalif should be at war with the government of our King-Emperor." In 1915 the Muslim League and the Congress held their annual sessions in Bombay at the same time. The Young Turks movement led by Enver Pasha had earlier attracted the attention of Indian Muslims, and the idea of Indian nationalism based on Hindu-Muslim unity was being vigorously canvassed, among others, by Maulana Abul Kalam Azad, India's Education Minister today, and the two Ali brothers, Mohamed and Shaukat, now both dead. Azad, born in Mecca in 1888, wielded a robust pen, and his paper Al Hilal was widely read by the Urdu-speaking world. The Ali brothers and Azad were interned early in the war.

These developments brought about a radical change in the Muslim outlook which found expression at the Lucknow session of the Congress in December, 1916. At this session the Congress and the Muslim League finalised an agreement known as the Lucknow Pact. The Pact had been initiated earlier in the year at Allahabad at a meeting of the All-India Congress Committee which was held at the residence of Jawaharlal's father, Motilal. While the Congress conceded the principle of separate electorates for Muslims, the League surrendered the

Muslims' privileges of voting in both the general and separate electorates. Motilal had long felt that political progress was difficult without Hindu-Muslim unity. For him the Pact was an encouraging
portent of the shape of things to come.

To Jawaharlal also this *rapprochement* between the two major
communities was welcome. He had always reacted strongly to the
notion of religious influences in politics. Even Tilak's aggressive
nationalism, while attracting him, had simultaneously repelled him
because of its deep religious motivations. Nehru felt that such manifestations were reactionary.

Tilak, a militant nationalist, was until 1916, at least, also a militant
Hindu. In December, 1915, the simultaneous sessions of the Congress
and the Muslim League in Bombay signified the beginning of the
Hindu-Muslim entente. Some ten months later the entente was
strengthened when Mohamed Ali Jinnah, destined to be the founder
of Pakistan but at that time an ardent nationalist, presided over a
Congress conference at Ahmedabad. Jinnah was the President-elect
of the Muslim League for the December session of that year. Tilak
attended the Ahmedabad conference, thereby signifying the healing
of another breach—that between Congress moderates and extremists
dating back to 1907. At this conference the Maharashtrian leader also
endorsed the plan for constitutional reforms agreed to between the
Congress and the League. This plan, while incorporating the Hindu-
Muslim agreement on separate representation for Muslims, demanded
elected majorities in the provincial and central legislatures, along with
a status for India commensurate with that "of an equal partner in the
Empire with the self-governing Dominions."

It was at the Lucknow Congress that Nehru met Gandhi for the
first time. Gandhi's work in South Africa had stirred the imagination
and admiration of his countrymen, but he was still a largely unknown
political entity inside his homeland. At the Bombay Congress session
the year before, he had failed to be elected to a committee and had to
be nominated by the President. The story is told that while at Lucknow he entered a room occupied by some important delegates who
had assembled for a meeting, and was unrecognised by the majority of
them. His slight emaciated figure clad in a coarse *dhoti* and long coat
with a Kathiawadi turban piled high on his head must in any case
have seemed incongruous among those well clad, well shod person-

ages. Neither on Nehru nor on the session as a whole did Gandhi make any strong impact. It was Tilak who dominated the Lucknow meeting.

Being a clever tactician with a flair for organisation, Tilak chose his time and ground shrewdly. In April, 1916, he formed the first Home Rule League in India which Mrs. Annie Besant, the Theosophist leader who by now was immersed in Indian politics, emulated. Her organisation, known as the All-India Home Rule League—to distinguish it from Tilak's—was founded in Madras in September of the same year and, like Tilak's, drew many adherents. "The price of India's loyalty," she declared, "is India's freedom."

Jawaharlal joined both leagues but worked especially for Mrs. Besant's. Along with Tilak this indomitable sixty-nine-year-old Irish woman, who had been elected President of the Theosophical Society in 1907, galvanised Indian politics into renewed life. It was she who had recommended Ferdinand Brooks as a tutor for Jawaharlal, and the magic of her oratory had impressed Nehru even as a boy and lingered with him as a man. Neither of the leagues, however, percolated to the masses. They attracted only the intelligentsia drawn almost entirely from the middle classes.

"Mrs. Besant," Nehru remarked long after, "had a very powerful influence on me in my childhood, and even later when I entered political life her influence continued."

It did not, however, overwhelm Gandhi's later influence which in fact submerged it.

Mrs. Besant was not the only woman whose oratory moved Nehru. He found the lyric eloquence of Sarojini Naidu, poetess and politician and the first Indian woman to be President of the Congress, equally evocative. Plainly, his patriotism had strong emotional roots.

Few events during the war excited India more than the developments in Ireland. As a student Jawaharlal, while on a visit to Ireland, had watched with interest the first faint beginnings of Sinn Fein which Arthur Griffith had founded in 1900. Now the Easter rebellion of 1916 stirred his heart and mind. He was moved by Roger Casement's speech from the dock, and marvelled at the invincible spirit which animated it. Of course, the Easter rebellion was another of those faithful failures.

"But," asked Nehru, "was that not true courage which mocked at almost certain failure and proclaimed to the world that no physical might could crush the invincible spirit of a nation?"

Inside India events pointed to the same invincible pattern, though less dramatically. Gandhi was launching his first indigenous experiments in satyagraha. Early in 1917 the cause of the oppressed labourers in the indigo plantations at Champaran in north Bihar drew Gandhi to the foothills of the Himalayas. Here he found himself faced by the implacable opposition of the British planters supported by the British Raj. He was served with a notice to quit Champaran, but refused to do so until his inquiry into the labourers' grievances was completed, and thereupon he received a summons to appear in court. Gandhi complied, and the firm, dignified tone of his speech as the accused so disconcerted the Government that the higher authorities immediately ordered the case against him to be withdrawn. Moreover, he was allowed to continue his inquiries, and the Government, shamed into action, itself appointed an official committee of investigation with which Gandhi was associated. Its report led to the Champaran Agrarian Act which largely redressed the indigo labourers' grievances. As Gandhi later described it, it was "the first direct object lesson in civil disobedience." In July, 1918, Gandhi staged a second triumph in the Khedda district of Gujerat in western India. Here the peasants waged a four months' non-violent struggle before their pleas for redress were substantially granted.

Neither of these two episodes had the sharp dramatic appeal of Ireland's sombre struggle. But the employment of a weapon unusual in political warfare had produced results in India more successful than those obtained by the violent tactics of the Sinn Fein in Ireland. Many in India paused to think.

Meanwhile, the mounting tempo of events in the country found an echo in the Nehru household, where the high-spirited and impetuous son was posed against the calm, ruthless logic of a fond father. Aware of his son's impulsive nature, Motilal was haunted by the fear that Jawaharlal would embark on terrorist ways. He knew that this path led inevitably to prison or the gallows. Inside his own mind the elder Nehru was fighting a battle between the tug of his son's ardent nationalism and his own moderate, more sober inclinations. By temperament and training he recoiled from extreme ways. As a lawyer he was wont to argue coolly, almost cold-bloodedly, from premises to a conclusion. The heart of the father finally triumphed over the mind of the lawyer; but, as his son was to do later, Motilal rationalised what his reason could not easily accept.

The turning point came with Mrs. Besant's internment in June, 1917. Far from discouraging the cry for Home Rule, this action intensified the popular demand and induced many Moderates to identify themselves with the movement. Among them was Motilal, who had always cherished a high regard and respect for Mrs. Besant. He joined the Home Rule League and some time later became its President at Allahabad. A nationalist wave swept the country.

The war had been going badly for the Allies and disaster overtook the Mesopotamian campaign owing largely to the collapse of the medical and commissariat arrangements for which the British authorities in India had assumed the responsibility. Mr. Austen Chamberlain,[1] then Secretary of State for India, resigned and was succeeded by Mr. Edwin Montagu, who lost no time in announcing the British Government's intention to institute another series of constitutional reforms. As part of this policy of conciliation, Mrs. Besant was released in September.

Political agitation now assumed a constructive form concentrating on extracting the maximum concessions from the Government. In October the All-India Congress Committee and the Council of the Muslim League held a joint meeting at Allahabad, and later in the year a deputation representative of both these organisations waited on the Viceroy, Lord Chelmsford, and Mr. Montagu, who had come out to India to see things for himself. Broadly, the Congress-League plea was for self-government with parliamentary power of the purse and control of the executive. "In any crisis or struggle," said Tilak, "a contented self-governing India is the greatest and surest asset of the empire." Neither the Congress nor the League saw anything anomalous in the concept of a British Empire which included a self-governing India.

The actual reforms conceded by the Montagu-Chelmsford proposals published in July, 1918,[2] fell far short of these demands, for although the two new central legislatures, the Assembly and the

[1] Later Sir Austen Chamberlain of Locarno fame.
[2] These were embodied in the Government of India Act passed in December, 1919.

Council of States, had elected majorities, each contained a strong official bloc, and the Viceroy had the over-riding power of negativing such legislation as he thought undesirable. In the provinces legislative councils, elected on a wider franchise, were set up, and a system of checks and balances known as dyarchy was introduced in the provincial executive whereby certain "reserved" subjects such as finance and law and order were the sole responsibility of the Governor and his councillors, while certain other innocuous portfolios described as "transferred" subjects were entrusted to ministers who were responsible to the legislature.

Both the Congress and the Muslim League joined in denouncing the reforms as inadequate. Gandhi, although inclined at first to support the scheme, dubbed it later "a whited sepulchre." Since 1916, when Tilak had returned to the Congress a year after Gokhale's death, the Moderates had steadily lost ground. In August, 1918, there came a definite parting of the ways when certain leading Moderates absented themselves from a special Congress meeting summoned in Bombay to discuss the reforms. The dissidents, who accepted the Montagu-Chelmsford proposals and agreed to work them, organised themselves as a separate group which later emerged as the National Liberal Federation.

Meanwhile, resentment at the war against Turkey had alienated the Muslims who were apprehensive about the future of the Khalif and of the *Jazirat-ul-Arab* (the islands of Arabia), which included the holy cities of Mecca and Medina. The Hindu-Muslim entente remained firm through this ferment and unrest.

In 1917 the Government of India, disquieted by the murmur of mounting political trouble, had appointed a committee presided over by Mr. Justice Rowlatt to investigate the question of sedition and the course of criminal conspiracies. By a clumsy juxtaposition its report was released shortly after the appearance of the Montagu-Chelmsford proposals, and Indian opinion was quick to contrast its clear-cut penal recommendations with the vague and tentative suggestions incorporated in the reform plan. The Rowlatt Committee's proposals that judges should try political cases without juries in certain notified areas and that provincial governments should be armed with powers of internment were speedily incorporated in two bills, one of these being a temporary measure intended to deal with the situation arising from the expiry of the Defence of India Act. The other was of a permanent nature; and among various penalties, the mere possession of a seditious document, "with intention to publish or circulate it," was summarily punishable with imprisonment.

Here was a major *casus belli*, and the battle was joined with vigour. The text of the Rowlatt Bills appeared in February, 1919, some three months after the end of the war. Although the war saw a business boom in which Indian capital partly shared, it generated a rising spiral of prices and in time a slump causing widespread unemployment among the white-collar workers. Thus economics conspired with politics to render the general situation uneasy.

The Rowlatt Bills, condemned as the Black Bills, brought Gandhi to the centre of the political stage. They also marked another advance in Motilal's progress away from the Moderates to aggressive nationalism; but father and son were by no means yet politically in step, and Jawaharlal still strained at the leash.

Motilal's initial reactions to the Montagu-Chelmsford reforms were not unlike Gandhi's first thoughts. The reforms might prove the springboard to better things. Jawaharlal did not share his father's cautious optimism but, like Gandhi later, was inclined to see in them "a whited sepulchre." The Rowlatt Bills, however, offended the lawyer in Motilal and seemed to transgress all notions of constitutional propriety. They were "lawless laws."

"What can we do?" Congress members asked.

"Do?" said Gandhi. "Once the bills become law we offer satyagraha."

But before launching on this extreme step, Gandhi appealed to the Viceroy to withdraw the obnoxious measures. Lord Chelmsford refused. At this period Gandhi was seriously ill, but he set about organising the Satyagraha Sabha,[3] whose members were pledged to disobey the Rowlatt Act if it was applied to them, and to court jail openly and deliberately.

The reactions of Motilal and Jawaharlal to this novel move were strikingly different. To the younger Nehru here "at last was a way out of the tangle, a method of action which was straight and open and possibly effective." Motilal was by no means as enthusiastic, being in fact totally opposed to this thirst for jail-going which must

[3] Sabha means Body or Organisation.

inevitably involve his son. He peremptorily asked Gandhi to come to Allahabad. What passed between the elder Nehru and Gandhi can be guessed, but the outcome was that Gandhi counselled Jawaharlal to do nothing precipitate.

Characteristically Gandhi appealed both to the filial love of the son and his loyalty to the political gospel as the Mahatma preached it.

"Don't push your father too much," he counselled Jawaharlal. "Don't cause him pain."

In effect he was advising Nehru to "go slow."

For the time being, at least, Motilal had his way. But not for long.

Faced with the Viceroy's insistence on putting the Rowlatt Bills on the statute book,[4] Gandhi called upon the country to observe a hartal or day of mourning to be signalised by the general stoppage of all business. March 30th was initially fixed upon as Satyagraha Day, but the date was later switched to April 6th. It was the first time India's people were called upon to stage a national demonstration on a country-wide scale, and it is a tribute to Gandhi's insight into the mind of the people that he sensed how strongly its symbolical significance would strike them.

Jawaharlal worked hard to make the day a success in his own province. But the response not only of the United Provinces but of the whole country exceeded the calculations either of the Congress or of the Government. India rose in a vast surge of life not only in cities and towns but in distant villages; and as the ripples gathered into waves and the waves moved in a relentless tide towards the shore the Canutes of Delhi took fright. The age-old fear of alien rulers—fear of the unknown—seized them.

By a strange mischance the wire announcing the postponement of Satyagraha Day from March 30th to April 6th did not reach the Delhi Congress organisers in time, and in Delhi, accordingly, the day was observed on March 30th. Delhi's reaction was a foretaste of things to come. On the famed Chandni Chowk, or Street of Silver, in the oldest quarter of this ancient city, Hindus and Muslims fraternised, joining in common protest against the high-handedness of their rulers. Every business house was closed, and in the Jumma Masjid, where once the Emperor Aurangzeb had prayed with his Muslim brethren, a Hindu leader, Swami Shraddhanand, clad in his saffron

---

[4] By a strange irony the Act was not applied in a single instance.

sanyasi's robes, addressed a vast Muslim gathering. Such a spectacle was unprecedented. The local British authorities, unnerved by this unusual demonstration of solidarity, decided to break up the meetings and processions by force. Accordingly, the military and police were summoned, and firing was resorted to, resulting in some casualties.

On the official Satyagraha Day, April 6th, firing by the military and police on unarmed demonstrators occurred in various cities and towns. In the Punjab—particularly at Amritsar and Lahore—the crowds retaliated and there were arson, rioting and attacks on Europeans. Gandhi was arrested on April 8th on his way from Bombay to Delhi; and although he was brought back to Bombay and released almost immediately on April 10th the news of his arrest touched off further disorders in Bombay and Ahmedabad.

On April 15th martial law was declared in the Punjab, and a curtain descended on the reign of terror inaugurated by the authorities which culminated in the massacre at Jallianwalla Bagh under the order of General Dyer.[5] Various humiliations, degrading in their refinements, were heaped upon the Punjab's hapless people, and these only came to an end when martial law was lifted on June 9th. When the full horror of the Punjab atrocities was revealed, opinion throughout India was moved to a pitch of flaming indignation, Indo-British relations deteriorated to a point never reached since the 1857 rebellion, and Whitehall was compelled to appoint a committee of inquiry, comprising four British and four Indian members, presided over by Lord Hunter. The committee submitted two reports, dividing along racial lines, but both reports severely criticised General Dyer, who was later retired from the army. None the less, the fact that his action was applauded by certain sections in England—he was actually presented with a gold sword allegedly emanating from "the ladies of England"—did nothing to lessen racial resentment.

On Motilal these happenings had a decisive effect. Henceforth his political lot was to be cast with Gandhi and Jawaharlal; and although subsequently he had occasion to disagree with both on certain

[5] According to the official estimates, 379 Indians were killed, including 87 villagers, and at least 1,200 were wounded. Dyer, on his own admission, had his troops fire 1,605 rounds on the crowd, which had assembled for a meeting, "until my ammunition was almost exhausted."

trends and policies, he remained, until his death on February 6, 1931, an unyielding and militant nationalist. Yet it seems certain that but for the accident of having an only son imbued with such high patriotic ardour, the elder Nehru would have pursued more moderate and sedate politics. Although by temperament combative, his mind could not easily equate itself with a mass outlook. By later identifying Jawaharlal with the masses, he was able to sympathise with the common cause, idealising it in the person of his son, and thereby resolving the argument in his own mind.

Gandhi's capacity to be all things to all men found a vivid illustration in his impact on Motilal.

Gandhi, as Jawaharlal has often testified, was the person who kept everybody together. "He had a part of everybody's faith in him and also his own self-discipline."

Himself of an imperious nature, Motilal respected the firm unyielding approach of the Mahatma, but at the same time he noted that there was no personal aggressiveness in the man. Here was an individual novel and distinctive whose words and actions carried the stamp of greatness. He was not only great but effective. He seemed capable of "delivering the goods."

If the Punjab happenings brought father and son politically nearer, they also brought Jawaharlal for the first time into close political contact with Gandhi. With the lifting of martial law, the Congress embarked on aid and inquiry, the relief work being entrusted to Swami Shraddhananda and another leader, Pandit Madan Mohan Malaviya, who had been actively associated with the foundation of the Hindu University at Banaras. The inquiry was mainly under the direction of Motilal and the Bengal leader Deshbandhu [6] Das, who was later to work closely with Jawaharlal and his father. Gandhi, who was permitted to enter the Punjab in the second half of October, took considerable interest in these proceedings.

The younger Nehru, deputed to assist Das, was greatly attracted toward him. Das, an affluent lawyer from Calcutta, though temperamentally emotional, was a political realist with a high degree of practical common sense and legal acumen—qualities which were later to make Motilal regard him as a valued counsellor and friend. With

[6] Deshbandhu was a popular title conferred on Das. It means "friend of the country."

Das, Jawaharlal often visited the so-called Jallianwalla Bagh,[7] in reality, as one British observer described it, "resembling a very large sunken swimming bath with perpendicular sides," an area of ground surrounded, with the exception of one low wall, by tall tenements. It was on a mass of unarmed people huddled in this pit that Dyer had felt compelled to exhaust his ammunition. Jawaharlal heard the gory details of many grim incidents and also visited the lane where Indians had been required to crawl on all fours as reprisal for an attack on an Englishwoman.

In his autobiography he describes how, travelling towards the end of the year 1919 by the night train from Amritsar to Delhi, he was kept awake by a rubicund-faced British general describing to his British companion in loud declamatory tones how he had dealt with a crowd at Amritsar. It was Dyer exulting over Jallianwalla. The general descended at Delhi station the next morning clad, writes Nehru, "in pyjamas with bright pink stripes and a dressing gown."

Gandhi took keen interest in the inquiry of the Congress, and Jawaharlal saw a great deal of him. He was puzzled by much of what Gandhi said which was vastly different from his own approach to things, and some of his proposals to the committee seemed novel. But Gandhi had a habit of arguing his point gently but with firmness and unusual earnestness. He generally got his way, and Nehru noticed that generally he also proved right. There grew in him, as yet not fully captivated or convinced by the Mahatma, a lingering, reluctant respect for his political insight.

It was also the first occasion when Motilal had the opportunity of working in close association with the Mahatma and of watching his mental processes and actions. Like Jawaharlal he was often mystified by the manifestations of the Mahatma's mind but like his son he could not help noting that the results were generally effective.

Jawaharlal already saw Gandhi on a more elevated plane. He sensed in him a new revolutionary force in action. Gandhi, he reflected, was always thinking of the mass mind of India. He was of and for the people.

Gandhi had almost imperceptibly seized the political initiative, and at the Amritsar Congress in December, 1919, over which Motilal presided, he, and not Tilak, who was also present, was the centre of

[7] Bagh means "garden."

all eyes. For the first time the slogan *Mahatma Gandhi ki jai* [8] came to be heard. It was Tilak's last conference, for he was to die in August of the next year. Jawaharlal detected a new spirit in this Congress induced partly by the absence of the Moderates who, despite Motilal's invitation to join the Amritsar deliberations, preferred to hold a separate conference of their own at Calcutta under their new label of Liberals. Their eyes were directed to the reforms which were proclaimed on December 24th. But at Amritsar a new spirit, broad-based on the masses, was stirring.

Amritsar saw the return of the Ali brothers, released from jail, and both these stalwart Muslim leaders immediately joined the Congress. Muslim fears on the future of the Khilafat were partly justified by the Treaty of Sèvres which curtailed the temporal powers of the Khalif. Gandhi made the Khilafat cause his own, and by doing so bound the Muslims closer to the Congress.

Jawaharlal accompanied the Mahatma to more than one meeting with the Khilafat leaders, and grew to appreciate, even if he did not always understand, his novel methods of work. Gandhi, he found, could speak gently while speaking dictatorially. He could be "clear-cut and hard as a diamond." He was incisive, purposeful, and knew his mind. During this period Gandhi was propagating his two ideas of non-violence and non-cooperation which together made satyagraha. He canvassed these ideas both with the Congress and the Khilafat leaders, the term "non-cooperation" actually occurring to him at a joint meeting of these leaders at Delhi in November, 1919.

Nehru did not completely share Gandhi's enthusiasm for the Khilafat cause, which was more religious than political in its motivations. Although primarily concerned with the temporal power of the Khalif this Muslim movement, like some of its Hindu counterparts, was not unallied with certain elements of conservativism and bigotry. In Gandhi's view, however, there was nothing obscurantist in a movement which affected the mass of Muslims and represented a genuine grievance calling for redress. It was also, he felt, an effective banner for Hindu-Muslim unity.

On May 28, 1920, the Khilafat committee, meeting in Bombay, adopted Gandhi's non-cooperation programme. Earlier in March the publication of the Congress report on the Punjab atrocities had

[8] Hail to Gandhi.

provoked deep feeling throughout the country, and in memory of the Amritsar happenings it was decided that thereafter the week from April 6th to April 13th should be observed as a National Week. With the calculated nonchalance of which he was sometimes capable, Gandhi, in an appeal for service and sacrifice, called upon the people to "treat hanging as an ordinary affair of life."

On May 30th the All-India Congress Committee, assembling at Banaras, decided to refer Gandhi's non-cooperation programme to a special session of the Congress to be summoned in Calcutta in September. On June 9th the Khilafat committee met at Allahabad and reiterated its support, and on July 28th, despite the fact that the Congress had so far not officially considered or accepted the proposal, Gandhi set August 1st as the date for inaugurating non-cooperation.

On that day Tilak died in Bombay. From his deathbed he said: "Unless swaraj is achieved, India will not prosper. It is vital for our existence." By a coincidence Jawaharlal, who had been touring the province of Sind with Gandhi, arrived with him in Bombay that morning. Both of them joined the mammoth funeral procession which ended at the seaside by the sands of Chowpatty where Tilak's remains were cremated on a pyre of sandalwood.

"My strongest bulwark is gone," wrote Gandhi. Obviously the Mahatma realised that he was the country's leader for so far only Tilak had challenged his political primacy.

5

DISCOVERY OF INDIA

In a letter to John Gunther written about 1938, two years after his wife's death, Nehru says: "I suppose my father and Gandhiji have been the chief personal influences in my life. But outside influences do not carry me away. There is a tendency to resist being influenced. Still influences do work slowly and subconsciously. My wife influenced me considerably in many ways, though unobtrusively."

They were married in Delhi in March, 1916, on Vasanta Panchami, a day which heralds the coming of spring, and is dedicated to the goddess Saraswati, patroness of the arts and sciences, of speech and learning. Nehru's bride, Kamala, was about seventeen at the time. She came of a Kashmiri family of the name of Kaul [1] who had settled in Delhi. Tall and slim, with natural poise and a virginal freshness of look which was never completely to desert her even through the stresses and strains of the subsequent years, Kamala had much of her husband's character and temperament.

Like Jawaharlal, she was sensitive and proud, impulsive in her judgements, wilful, high-spirited, quick in her likes and dislikes. Towards strangers or persons she disliked she could be reserved to the point of seeming frigid. But she was warm-hearted, even gay, in the company of friends and intimates. Unlike Jawaharlal, Kamala had had no formal education and was unsophisticated, though by no means artless. She had very definite opinions, and liked to express them. A certain child-like strain in her character enhanced her lack of sophistication and made her at times embarrassingly direct in her speech. It was not a love marriage but an arranged match, one report

[1] This was an adopted name, the original family name being Atal.

having it that Kamala's youthful beauty had so attracted the attention of Jawaharlal's mother at a party that she resolved on making her her son's wife.

In 1916 the floodtide of nationalist politics had yet to overwhelm the Nehru household. For another four years, at least, Motilal was to preserve his lavish way of life, living in a palatial home surrounded by a retinue of servants, cars, dogs and carriages and all the gilded paraphernalia which wealth can buy. The house was full of Persian rugs, silver, Dresden china and Venetian glass. In the stables were horses, and ponies for the children. And a cavalcade of guests moved ceaselessly in and out of Anand Bhawan. Motilal's hospitality was royal.

The marriage of Nehru coincided with a period of political flux which was reflected in the doubts and urges of his own mind. Not until 1921, when he went to prison for the first time, were these mental conflicts and contradictions partially resolved. Certain doubts persisted, but the basic problem of active resistance to alien rule was settled.

Those five years were lonely years for Kamala. Nehru's habit of dramatising events which move him and of projecting them on a three-dimensional plane of his own devising often leads him to forget his immediate environment. His mind, once aroused, soars on its own wings much as in his favourite dream his body, unaided, soars through the air. In that period, with the unthinking thoughtlessness of youth, he took Anand Bhawan with all it contained, including his bride, very much for granted. In later years he was to regret this deeply, and the survival of a guilt complex is clear in the written references to his wife. "She gave me strength," he wrote after her death in February, 1936, "but she must have suffered and felt a little neglected. An unkindness to her would almost have been better than this semi-forgetful casual attitude."

Both being quick-tempered and self-willed, they quarrelled easily in those early years. With their differing backgrounds, educational and social, they found it difficult to adjust themselves to each other, and Kamala's lack of sophistication must often have seemed to the impatient Jawaharlal an inability to follow and grasp not only the nuances of Indian politics but even their more direct manifestations. Only later did he visualise her in the one role she cherished—that of political comrade and companion. Unhappily her subsequent illness could only have intensified this desire and given an edge to her sense of frustration. In this respect her husband compares her to Chitra in Rabindranath Tagore's play of that name: "I am Chitra. No goddess to be worshipped, nor yet the object of common pity to be brushed aside like a moth with indifference. If you deign to keep me by your side in the path of danger and daring, if you allow me to share the great duties, then you will know my true self." But Jawaharlal was to sense this urge of hers only in the early months of 1930.

Twenty-one months after their marriage, in November, 1917, their daughter and only child, Priyadarshini Indira,[2] was born. Jawaharlal's mother had been in indifferent health since the birth of her first-born, and by a tragic coincidence his wife was to suffer a similar fate. A series of illnesses made her an invalid for the greater part of her married life, and the onset of tuberculosis hastened her end. The conjunction of an ailing mother and wife has made Nehru acutely conscious of the value of physical fitness and well-being. It also explains his keen solicitude for the sick and ailing. "In a sick room," writes his sister Krishna, "Jawahar is an ideal nurse. His gentleness and understanding are infinite under the most trying circumstances, and his patience is unlimited."

When in the latter half of 1920 Motilal decided to cast his political lot with the Mahatma, partly in an effort to keep a vigilant eye on his son, the character of the Nehru household changed. As a first step Motilal gave up his enormous practice at the bar, and the sharp slump in income compelled a drastic revision in his high scale of living. Overnight he sold his horses and carriages, reduced his vast retinue of servants, and curtailed expenditure in every direction. From satins and silks the women of the household took to *khadi* [3] saris and coarse linen.

The person on whom this sudden metamorphosis made the least impact was Jawaharlal, for, though reared in affluent circumstances all his life, he was never a slave to them and could shed them easily. His resilience of mind and body explains not only his physical adaptability but his bouts of prodigious industry. He can be impervious to

[2] Now Mrs. Pheroze Gandhi, and her father's hostess at Prime Minister's Residence, New Delhi.
[3] Rough hand-spun, hand-woven cloth.

environment but rarely to ideas, and Gandhism had intoxicated him with the potency of a new elixir. Although himself an individualist, he is at home more with the masses than with the classes.

"You are so aloof," complained a Congress colleague, "I bet you haven't a single real friend."

Jawaharlal's mind seemed far away. Then, very slowly and deliberately, he said, "I like to open my heart before the crowd."

He discovered this quite by accident, and the accident was to change his outlook fundamentally on many things. In May, 1920, his mother and wife being both unwell, he decided to take them for a holiday to the hill station of Mussoorie. His father, who had then not yet relinquished his practice, was busy on an important case. At the hotel where the Nehrus stayed were members of the Afghan delegation who had come to India to negotiate a peace treaty with the British following King Amanullah's brief war of 1919. Jawaharlal, having no interest in them, never met them. But for some obscure and complicated reason the British authorities feared that he might, and asked him for an undertaking that he would have no dealings with them.

Jawaharlal thought the request preposterous, and refused.

Thereupon he was served with an externment order requiring him to leave the district within twenty-four hours, which he did. Subsequently, on his father's intervention, the order was rescinded, and a fortnight later Jawaharlal returned with Motilal to Mussoorie. Almost the first spectacle which greeted him at the hotel was his baby daughter, Indira, in the arms of one of the members of the Afghan delegation. They had read of the episode in the papers, and, interested by it, had started sending Jawaharlal's mother a basket of fruits and flowers every day.

In the intervening fortnight at Allahabad, Jawaharlal, left to his own resources, heard of a peasant march on Allahabad and decided to visit their encampment on the banks of the Yamuna. There were about two hundred peasants gathered there under the leadership of a man named Baba Ramachandra. They begged Nehru to help free them from the exactions of the oppressive taluqdars (landlords) who apart from levying heavy imposts were subjecting them to all manner of indignities. They pleaded with him to come to their village and see conditions for himself.

Nehru, at first unwilling to go, was finally persuaded by their appeals. With a few companions he accompanied the peasants back to their village and stayed among them for three days. "That visit was a revelation to me," he wrote. He had never stayed in a village before, and the dumb misery of the starving peasants clad in rags, hungry and emaciated, was a new and overwhelming experience. They told him stories of the oppression and humiliations heaped on them, of the cruelty of the landlords' agents, the rapacity of the moneylenders, the kicks and beatings they were subjected to, their ejectment from their land and miserable hovels.

Here was a world completely new to Nehru. He was appalled and moved to indignation by their tales. What touched him was their simple faith in him and his colleagues to work a miracle and better their lot. As they spoke, their pinched tired faces glowed with excitement and their eyes glistened with hope.

Nehru wrote:

Looking at them and their misery and overflowing gratitude, I was filled with shame and sorrow, shame at my own easy-going and comfortable life and our petty politics of the city which ignored this vast multitude of semi-naked sons and daughters of India, sorrow at the degradation and overwhelming poverty of India. A new picture of India seemed to rise before me, naked, starving, crushed and utterly miserable. And their faith in us, casual visitors from the distant city, embarrassed me and filled me with a new responsibility that frightened me.

From henceforth Nehru was to see India largely in terms of the oppressed peasantry. The memory of the simple faith of these simple people, the forgotten men and women of India, haunted him. He returned to the countryside again and again, paying brief visits to the villages in his own province, talking to the peasants, listening to their grievances and trying to instil in them a determination to improve their own lot. In the process he found he had overcome his shyness on the platform. He discovered he could talk to the peasants with no trace of self-consciousness, and, speaking directly, tell them what was in his heart and mind.

Some of the districts through which he moved in his peasant pilgrimage had once formed part of the ancient kingdom of Ayodhya where Rama, scion of the solar race and hero of the *Ramayana*, had legendarily ruled. Nehru discovered that the illiterate peasants by some mnemonic process could recite verses from the *Ramayana,* and their lives were coloured by the legends of Rama and his wife Sita. The cry of "Sita-Ram," echoing from village to village, brought hundreds of peasants to a meeting or for some other community purpose much as the roll of drums in the African jungles carries a message. Nehru was fascinated. He was in the process of discovering India.

His frequent visits to the villages helped to develop the peasants' courage and give their resistance to oppression some backbone. He taught them to organise themselves and work in unison, to shed the fear which so often gripped them and left them grovelling before the majesty of a landlord's wrath.

About this time Gandhi was preaching his creed of sacrifice in the columns of his weekly journal *Young India.* On June 16, 1920, he wrote: "No country has ever risen without being purified through the fire of suffering. The mother suffers so that her child may live. The condition of wheat-growing is that the seed grain should perish. Life comes out of death. Will India rise out of her slavery without fulfilling this eternal law of purification through suffering?"

The message of the Mahatma, Nehru discovered in his rural journeyings, had spread to the villages, which were astir with the new *mantra*⁴ of non-violent non-cooperation. There was spring in the peasants' step, and the light of a new hope was in their eyes. Although few, if any, of them, understood the political implications of *swaraj* (self-government), they were quick to appreciate that only by their own efforts and organised strength could political freedom for the country mean economic betterment for themselves. Looking at them Nehru realised the basic logic of the Gandhian approach.

"He is taking the masses with him," he reflected, "not merely converting the elect."

The curse of litigation, to which the peasants were particularly addicted, had made them the prey of the moneylenders. Nehru, together with other of his Congress colleagues, tried to induce the peasants to settle their disputes out of court through the agency of their own *panchayats* or village councils. The response was impressive and litigation diminished in volume, the peasants gaining confidence and strength in the process. Congress's creed of non-violence also restrained them in great measure from violent ways.

⁴ A sacred formula or invocation.

In his journeyings through the villages Nehru was always accompanied by police officials who were detailed to watch his movements.
Not all of them were accustomed either to villages or to striding over
rough country in the heat of the noonday sun. Jawaharlal took an
almost malicious delight in out-walking them, and he relates with
glee the tale of an official, "a somewhat effeminate youth from Lucknow," who dogged his footsteps clad in patent-leather pumps and,
unable to maintain the pace, dropped by the wayside.

Imbued with confidence in the new method of collective action,
the peasants on at least one occasion successfully deployed it against
the local authorities. In the autumn of 1920 many hundreds of them
collected in the court compound and around the jail of a district
where a few peasant leaders were being held for some petty offence,
and the spectacle so unnerved the authorities, new to this type of
demonstration, that after a formal trial the arrested peasants were discharged and released.

The peasants saw in this a chain of cause and effect, and they tried
it again. But this time the authorities were in no mood to relent, and
the police opened fire on the demonstrators, killing a few of them.
Nehru, who had been away in Calcutta during the first incident, was
in the neighbourhood during the second. He hurried to the trouble
spot, which was by a riverbank, but was stopped by the military at a
bridge. As he waited there he heard the sound of firing, and not long
after he was surrounded by some two thousand frightened and be-
wildered peasants. Nehru addressed them, trying to take the edge off
their fear and excitement, and in this he was successful. The peasants, hearing him, dispersed quietly to their homes.

But the spirit of unrest was abroad in rural India, and with it came
a reign of official repression. Other incidents of police firing on peasants occurred through the closing months of 1920, and at the opening
of the new year an episode took place in which Nehru was again involved. A group of ignorant and credulous peasants, told by the
servants of one landowner that Mahatma Gandhi wished them to
loot the property of a rival landowner, went about it with a will, in
the process raising cries of *Mahatma Gandhi ki jai*.

Hearing about this, Nehru was furious. He summoned a meeting of
the local peasants, some six thousand of whom assembled to hear
him, and berated them, calling on them to hang their heads in shame

for the disgrace they had brought on their movement. He demanded that the guilty persons should publicly confess to their sins by raising their hands. In the presence of numerous police officials, about two dozen hands went up.

Nehru, once the heat of anger had died in him, knew what this meant. So did the peasants. The freedom of those who had confessed was not worth a day's purchase, and their arrests would signalise many hundreds more. Speaking to the peasants privately, Nehru was touched by the artless minds of these simple folk who more often than not took their neighbours on trust and believed implicitly in what they were told. But now it was too late. Over a thousand arrests were made in the district, and several received vindictively long sentences. "In later years when I went to prison," Nehru wrote, "I came across some of them, boys and young men, spending their youth in prison."

But the peasants' sufferings and sacrifices were not in vain, for the British authorities, concerned by this evidence of rural unrest, hastened the introduction of tenancy legislation to improve the peasants' lot. In the widely affected district of Oudh the *kisan* (peasant) was given a hereditary tenancy, although in practice this was not always possible to maintain. Slowly economic and political ideas were percolating to the masses.

In the course of this new experience Nehru lighted on a discovery. He realised that the masses acted on him like a tonic, that while he poured into them his energy and mental ferment they gave him in return renewed strength and sustenance, sinew, fibre and muscle. Between him and these starving down-trodden people a communion of thought and action was established based on mutual regard and respect. It explains Nehru's extraordinary hold on the Indian masses, different in character from the Mahatma's, but almost equally pervasive.

No Indian leader, including Nehru, has understood the Indian masses so acutely and instinctively as the Mahatma did. Nehru, unlike Gandhi, has not equated himself with the masses in dress, habits and mode of living. He sees no virtue in ascetism for ascetism's sake, and he abhors the notion of idealising poverty. "I hate poverty," he has declaimed more than once.

Yet, like Gandhi, his heart is in the villages, not in the towns. He writes of beginning "to understand a little the psychology of the crowd, the difference between the city masses and the peasantry, and I felt at home in the dust and discomfort, the pushing and jostling of large gatherings, though their want of discipline often irritated me." He had not, like Gandhi, come down to the level of the masses. He kept, as he describes, his "separate mental perch"; but, like Gandhi, Nehru is imbued with a passion for social justice and for decency in human relationships. Like Gandhi, he hides behind the outer crust of the politician a core of genuine humanity.

One quality bound Gandhi and Nehru irresistibly to the common people. Both, though in differing degrees, represented the idea of renunciation, the symbol of men who had spurned wealth which attracts but does not bind. In the minds of the peasantry there stirred the immemorial respect of the Indian for those who renounce the world's goods in order to benefit their fellow men.

Nehru himself in analysing this phenomenon is unusually humble. "I am vain enough in many ways," he confesses, "but there could be no question of vanity with these crowds of simple folk. There was no posing about them, no vulgarity, as in the case of many of us, of the middle classes who consider ourselves their betters. They were dull certainly, uninteresting individually, but in the mass they produced a feeling of overwhelming pity and a sense of ever-impending tragedy."

That sense of urgency continues to haunt Nehru, and makes some see in him a radical not over-concerned with democratic means. The magnitude of India's problems, social, economic and political, would overawe and chasten the most egotistic of leaders. If Nehru is seized by a sense of history and hustle, it is as much because of the problems confronting him as because of the paradox he represents. Doomed to pass his life living amongst crowds, he is one of the loneliest of men. Yet the masses stimulate him, and he resolves the paradox by seeing the crowd not as an impersonal unit but as a conglomeration of living and sentient individuals.

Nehru has many qualities of leadership but lacks one supreme gift— the ability to decentralise work by entrusting some of it to others. He likes to do all the work himself. His secretiveness and mistrust of others make him a bad judge of men and, while not isolating him from the masses, lead him to surround himself with a cohort of inferior lieutenants. When faced with a problem he is fond of urging that the disease should be cured, and not the symptoms. But he would like to combine in himself the roles of diagnostician, physician, surgeon and nurse.

It is this tendency for concentration, this habit of method rather than mind, which leads some to see in Nehru as India's Prime Minister a strong dictatorial strain. The concentration of multiple duties in one hand invariably leads to the concentration of power, to the growth of a Caesar legend which in turn retards the building up of democratic traditions in a country inured by long years of foreign rule to look up to authority, to be governed rather than to govern. But in Nehru the impulse to be the primary driving force derives more from a sense of urgency than from any calculated desire to be dictatorial. Democratic processes, he realises, are somewhat slower than in an autocratic regime. "But," he warns, "any vital change in a nation takes time to consolidate. You cannot impose it." But presumably an individual can determine and influence its tempo.

There is no aridity in his sense of intellectual aristocracy, though he can be tart-tongued when moved to irritation. An English friend of India who is also a Quaker, Horace Alexander, recounts two typical incidents.

Nehru, on a visit to Birmingham, was staying with Alexander, when the well known British noveliest Naomi Mitchison came in. On being introduced to Nehru she promptly squatted on the floor.

"Why this curious behaviour?" inquired Jawaharlal, slightly nettled.

"It seemed appropriate," was Miss Mitchison's reply.

Nehru was not amused.

On the other hand he can be extraordinarily charming, particularly in the company of individuals like Churchmen with whom he has no strong affinities. Alexander writes of a Dutch cleric, "now one of the best known leaders of Church life in Europe," who was entirely captivated by Nehru.

"There," he told Alexander, "is just the type of man who can capture the imagination, the devotion, the idealism of youth today, a selfless champion of the oppressed."

Nehru, oddly enough, produced a different though equally agreeable reaction on a former Archbishop of Canterbury, the late Dr.

Lang, who figured prominently in the abdication of the Duke of Windsor.

"Dear! Dear!" said His Grace after meeting him. "Such a pleasant and charming man. Who would imagine that he could shake up a continent?"

In the twilight of the twenties Nehru had no idea that he would live to shake up a continent. Gandhi's call to his countrymen to leave the cities and go into the villages had drawn many hundreds of others besides Jawaharlal into the countryside. They, like Nehru, were beginning to discover India. But on none was the impact so direct and forceful or the internal urge to action so explosive.

Motilal, watching his son closely, was sensitive to these changes. He had earlier prevented him from taking precipitate action when Gandhi's formation of the Satyagraha Sabha threatened a spate of prison-going. But now events culminating with Jallianwalla Bagh had stolen a march on him, and the horror of the Punjab happenings had stirred both his patriotism and pride. He had parted company with the Moderates, and his Presidency of the Amritsar Congress in December, 1919, sealed and symbolised the break.

Yet even now he found it hard to reconcile himself to the idea of his son's going to prison, and for himself also the plunge into Gandhian politics meant a sharp severance with his past. Tilak's death, on August 1, 1920, had coincided with the inauguration of the non-cooperation campaign. On that day Gandhi, in a letter to the Viceroy, Lord Chelmsford, surrendered his British decorations and titles, including the Kaisar-i-Hind gold medal and the Zulu war medal.

The special Congress session to consider Gandhi's non-cooperation programme was scheduled to be held in the first week of September, 1920. On August 11th Gandhi published in *Young India* his famous article expounding and explaining his doctrine of non-violence:

I do believe that where there is only a choice between cowardice and violence I would advise violence. . . . I would rather have India resort to arms in order to defend her honour than that she should in a cowardly manner become or remain a helpless witness to her own dishonour. But I believe that non-violence is infinitely superior to violence, forgiveness is more manly than punishment. Forgiveness adorns a soldier. But abstinence is forgiveness only when there is the power to punish; it is meaningless when it pretends to proceed from a helpless creature. A mouse hardly forgives a cat when it allows itself to be torn to pieces by her. . . . Strength

does not come from physical capacity. It comes from an indomitable will.
. . . Non-violence is the law of our species as violence is the law of the
brute. The spirit lies dormant in the brute, and he knows no law but that
of physical might. The dignity of man requires obedience to a higher law,
to the strength of the spirit. . . . Non-violence in its dynamic condition
means conscious suffering. It does not mean submission to the will of the
evil-doer but it means the putting of one's whole soul against the will of
the tyrant. Working under this law of our being, it is possible for a single
individual to defy the whole might of an unjust empire to save his honour,
his religion, his soul and lay the foundation for that empire's fall or re-
generation.

Twenty-seven years were to pass before India achieved its freedom.
In that article Gandhi sounded the bugle note to whose call millions
of his countrymen were to respond during these fateful years.

As August waned and September drew near, Gandhi toured the
country preaching his message of non-violent revolt. On August 10,
1920, the Allies imposed the Treaty of Sèvres on Turkey, curtailing
the temporal power of the Khalif, a move which angered the Indian
Muslims who under the leadership of the spectacular Ali brothers,
Mohamed and Shaukat, had already made common cause with
Gandhi. On his tours the Mahatma was accompanied by the Ali
brothers, and unity between Hindus and Muslims was acclaimed in
the popular cry *Hindu-Musalman ki jai.*[5] The twin objectives of the
non-cooperation programme were freedom for India and the righting
of the Khilafat [6] wrongs.

Lala Lajpat Rai, who had returned recently after long years of exile
in America, presided over the Calcutta session. Some eleven years
previously, when Lord Minto was Viceroy, he had been deported from
India for leading an agitation in the Punjab which had earned him the
title of Lion of the Punjab. Although hitherto identified with aggressive nationalism, he was opposed to the non-cooperation programme, which he thought unreal and impracticable.

He was supported in this by a considerable phalanx of the Old
Guard, including Bengal's Deshbandhu Das, Mrs. Annie Besant and
Mohamed Ali Jinnah, who after the next session of Congress at
Nagpur in December was to sever his association with this body. Das

[5] Hail to Hindu-Muslim unity.
[6] Kaliph was the religious title of the Sultan of Turkey in his capacity of Head
of Islam. Khilafat means the suzerainty of the Kaliph.

was especially opposed to the boycott of the new legislatures established by the Montagu-Chelmsford reforms.

Motilal, who had spent many anxious days considering the matter, finally decided to follow the Mahatma. The decision meant a complete break with his past life, personal and political. But it enabled him to keep in step with his son. In consonance with the principle of non-cooperation, he was obliged to abandon his fabulously lucrative practice at the bar, boycott foreign goods, withdraw from association with his many British friends and remove his younger daughter Krishna from the British school she was attending. It was arranged for tutors to teach her at home.

"I was bowled over by Gandhi straight away," Nehru confesses. "But with Father it was different. He could not leap as I did. The process was long-drawn, even painful. Father was not the man to bend his will to anyone else's. But once he was convinced and had made up his mind he never changed."

The new spirit infecting the country was reflected at the Calcutta session which for the first time saw a preponderance of khadi-clad members drawn largely from the lower middle classes and inclined more to the use of Hindi or their own indigenous language than English. A new earnestness and enthusiasm were visible. The base of the Congress was broadened. The Gandhian era in the politics of Congress had begun.

So the country moved slowly but massively towards non-cooperation. Calcutta adopted Gandhi's programme, but the final imprimatur was given only at the annual session at Nagpur in December. "If there is sufficient response to my scheme," Gandhi promised at Calcutta, "you can gain *swaraj* in the course of a year."

Between the sessions at Calcutta and Nagpur, Gandhi embarked on another extensive tour of the country. He found not only the masses but a fair proportion of the classes responsive to his message and appeal. The boycott of the elections to the new legislatures, which were held in November, was especially successful and more than any other single factor swung Congress's Old Guard behind the Mahatma. Almost two-thirds of the voters abstained. Reporting his experiences of the elections at a township near Allahabad, the well known British journalist, the late Sir Valentine Chirol of *The Times*, London, wrote: "There was nothing to show that this was the red-letter day in the history of modern India which was to initiate her people into the great art of self-government. . . . From eight in the morning till past twelve not a single voter had presented himself in the course of the whole day."

On December 26th the Congress met at Nagpur under the Presidency of a South Indian leader, Mr. Vijayaraghavachari. In the opening stages Deshbandhu Das, supported by Mohamed Ali Jinnah, opposed the non-cooperation programme on various counts, particularly on the demand for the boycott of the law courts. But the overwhelming majority sided with Gandhi, and with a few minor amendments the original Nagpur resolution was presented to the public assembly and passed, Deshbandhu Das actually sponsoring the resolution.

"Many of us who worked for the Congress programme," wrote Nehru, "lived in a kind of intoxication during the year 1921. We were full of excitement and optimism and buoyant enthusiasm. We sensed the happiness of a person crusading for a cause." The old uncertainties and fears had vanished. Hope stirred in the air again. With Wordsworth, Nehru might have felt:

> Bliss was it in that dawn to be alive,
> But to be young was very heaven.

He was thirty-one, and the wonder and excitement of a new experiment which might end in actual achievement seized his questing mind.

Lord Reading succeeded Lord Chelmsford as Viceroy in April, 1921. He came armed with a big reputation, for he had served successfully as ambassador to the United States and as Lord Chief Justice in Britain. Bland and suave, with an agreeable presence and an ingratiating manner, he was a man with a nimble and resourceful wit but lacked the prime quality of a great administrator. Reading was incapable of decision.

In mid-May, at the new Viceroy's invitation, Gandhi met Reading at Simla; but their talks, though cordial and frank, were inconclusive. They had six talks covering collectively nearly thirteen hours and ranging from the Treaty of Sèvres to the meaning of *swaraj*. In a letter to his son (the present Lord Reading), the Viceroy wrote: "Our conversations were of the frankest; he [Gandhi] was supremely courteous, with manners of distinction. . . . He held in every way to his word in the various discussions we had."

But Indo-British relations were deteriorating, and there was talk of an impending show-down on both sides. As the morale of the Indian people grew under the stimulus of a new idea and ideal, the nerve of the British authorities, "puzzled and perplexed," as Lord Reading confessed later in the year, began to give way. Like children, they were afraid to walk in the dark—the dark unknown—and, like children, they conjured up all manner of sinister images which imperilled them. The old fear—fear of the unknown—gripped them. Repression got under way.

Through the greater part of this decisive year of 1921 Nehru worked in the rural areas, scouring the villages of the United Provinces, until he had gone through most of them carrying with him, like the boy in "Excelsior," a banner with a strange device—non-cooperation. Once again, sharing the peasants' sufferings and sorrows, he mused and wondered over their patience and toil. They laboured ungrudgingly, like their own oxen fastened uncomplainingly to the plough. They symbolised India for they were India—meek, mild, patient, persistent, with the agony of unrequited effort in their eyes.

Nehru moved closer to them. And in the poem of the American poet, Edwin Markham, entitled "The Man with the Hoe," he saw mirrored the tragedy and betrayal of his own people. He was to quote that poem often:

> Bowed by the weight of centuries he leans
> Upon his hoe and gazes on the ground,
> The emptiness of ages in his face,
> And on his back the burden of the world.
>
> . . . .
>
> Thru this dread shape the suffering ages look;
> Time's tragedy is in that aching stoop;
> Thru this dread shape humanity betrayed,
> Plundered, profaned and disinherited,
> Cries protest to the Judges of the world,
> A protest that is also prophecy.

India, endowed with a prophet, was rising in protest.

6

IN PRISON

THROUGHOUT 1921 the land was in ferment. With other leaders of Congress Gandhi toured the country preaching his message of non-violence. The secret of *swaraj*, he insisted, lay in constructive work. Through the charkha, or spinning wheel, said Gandhi, India could spin her way to freedom, and he set about propagating the cult of the charkha which in Indian eyes soon became the emblem of patriotism and to the British authorities a symbol of sedition. Gandhi also urged Hindu-Muslim unity, and called upon Hinduism to purify itself by shedding the curse of untouchability. "I regard untouchability as the greatest blot on Hinduism," he declared.

Nehru worked largely in the villages, and his constant journeyings through the rural areas gave him a keener insight into the mass mind and an understanding of mass psychology. He felt completely at home in a crowd, particularly a crowd of peasants. He could talk to them easily, without the self-consciousness which oppressed him in an urban drawing room or on a city platform. He found their trust and enthusiasm infectious, and in turn he tried to instil in them the message and meaning of *swaraj*. Freedom would not descend like manna from the heavens. It would come only through the disciplined will of a people, and non-violent non-cooperation was a hard school of discipline.

More and more he found himself drawn towards the Mahatma. Nehru sensed a fire beneath Gandhi's icy calm and, although not attracted by the metaphysics of the Bhagavad-Gita, he liked to read the verses, recited daily at the Mahatma's ashram, which lay down what a man should be like—"He who does the task dictated by duty, caring nothing for fruit of the action. He is a Yogi." He admired and envied Gandhi's mental poise so strangely allied with a passion for action and a sense of ruthless resolve.

There were things about the Mahatma which he did not understand, some with which he did not agree. There was, Nehru felt, a revivalist streak in Gandhi's political teachings, giving them at times an evangelical fervour bordering on the religious. Why make so much of Hinduism and Islam? Why encourage, albeit unconsciously, the Moulvis [1] and Swamis [2] to flavour politics with piety and prayers? Gandhi's frequent references to Rama Raj (Rule of Rama) as a golden age to which India should return nonplussed Nehru. Yet many years after Gandhi's death, Nehru in a characteristic mood of rationalisation was to interpret the Mahatma's Rama Raj as "a kind of Welfare State." To the younger man at that time progress lay in the future. Let the dead past bury its dead.

But these were fads and peculiarities; and, often discussing Gandhi among themselves, Nehru and his colleagues would console themselves with the half humorous resolve that when *swaraj* came his idiosyncrasies would not be encouraged. For the present they must be tolerated. Yet Nehru confesses that "I came nearer to a religious frame of mind in 1921 than at any other time since my boyhood. Even so I did not come very near." The moral and ethical aspects of nonviolent non-cooperation attracted Nehru, who was also impressed by Gandhi's insistence that worthy ends should have worthy means. Gandhi had a curious, almost uncanny knack of seeing into the minds and hearts of the Indian people and of reaching out to them. His methods might be novel, his ideas a trifle mildewed. But there was a basic strength and resolve in the man which he could communicate to others.

"There were no rough edges or sharp corners about him," Nehru noted, "no trace of vulgarity or commonness in which unhappily our middle classes excel. Having found an inner peace he radiated it to others and marched through life's tortuous ways with firm and undaunted step." Gandhi was in almost all ways the antithesis of Nehru's father, Motilal. Yet both men—physically and temperamen-

[1] Muslim divines.
[2] Hindu religious preachers.

tally poles apart—shared a natural kingliness. Gandhi had the majesty of the meek. There was about Motilal an air of leonine dignity. Caught between these two strongly contrasting personalities, Nehru was influenced by both, by his father's rational approach to all problems and by Gandhi's habit of at once drawing strength from the people and communicating it to them.

As the tempo of the non-cooperation movement mounted, the British authorities embarked on a policy of small-scale repression. Restraint orders were issued against some Congress leaders who were forbidden to enter certain areas and districts. Far away in the Northwest Frontier province Khan Abdul Ghaffar Khan, later to be known as the Frontier Gandhi but at that time not a member of the Congress, was arrested for allegedly seditious activities and sentenced to three years' imprisonment.

Gandhi refused to be hustled. He adjured the people to have patience and to observe non-violence scrupulously. But the spirit of unrest which this mass movement generated was reflected in various forms of mass struggle and some acts of discipline in different parts of the country. Several hundreds of those who had earned decorations from the British Government returned them. Thousands of school and college students—inadvisedly, as events proved—left the government institutions they attended, only a small proportion of them being absorbed in the few national institutions hastily organised to meet this exodus. Rabindranath Tagore was among those who protested against any political interference with the education of the country's youth, and he opposed non-cooperation as a philosophy of negation and nihilism. "My prayer," wrote the poet, "is that India may represent the co-operation of all the peoples of the world. For India unity is truth, and division evil. Unity is that which embraces and understands everything; consequently it cannot be attained through negation."

Despite these powerful protests the movement gathered momentum and strength. In July, 1921, the All-India Congress Committee passed a resolution urging the need to boycott all foreign cloth and to encourage hand spinning and hand weaving in order to popularise *khadi*. Liquor shops were picketed. On the last day of July, Gandhi presided over a ceremonious bonfire of foreign cloth in Bombay, a gesture which moved an English sympathiser of India, the late Reverend Charles Fryer Andrews, a friend of both Gandhi and Tagore, and known popularly as Charlie Andrews, to protest vigorously:

I was supremely happy when you were dealing great giant blows at the great fundamental moral evils, drunkenness, drugtaking, untouchability, race arrogance, etc., and when you were, with such wonderful and beautiful tenderness, dealing with the hideous vice of prostitution. But lighting bonfires of foreign cloth and telling people it is a religious sin to wear it, destroying in the fire the noble handiwork of one's fellow men and women, one's brothers and sisters abroad, saying it would be "defiling" to wear it—I cannot tell you how different all this appears to me. Do you know I almost fear now to wear the *khadi* that you have given me lest I should be judging other people as a Pharisee would, saying "I am holier than thou." I never felt like this before.

It was a prophetic reproach, for the accusation of a "holier than thou" attitude was later to be directed at Nehru himself when independence came. Indeed, the reproach is often levelled at the Indian people today. Jawaharlal, while not sharing Gandhi's views on industrialisation, felt that the development of cottage industries such as *khadi*, besides having some economic value, had also a political use in so far as it enabled the Congress to keep in touch with the peasant masses.

Gandhi repudiated the accusation of being a Pharisee. "For a firm believer in *swadeshi*," he affirmed, "there need be no Pharisaical self-satisfaction in wearing *khadi*. A Pharisee is a patron of virtue. The wearer of *khadi* from a *swadeshi* standpoint is like a man making use of his lungs. A natural and obligatory act has got to be performed whether others do it out of impure motives or refrain altogether." In other words, Gandhi was arguing that the propagation of *khadi* by the Indian people was both natural and necessary.

All India noted with interest the contrast between the unreal debates solemnly waged in the newly established legislatures and Gandhi's mass movement which was sweeping the country like a prairie fire. Here and there the flames rose aggressively. In August the Moplahs, a militant Muslim community with an admixture of Arab blood who are settled in Malabar in South India, embarked on a reign of terror believing that the British Raj had collapsed. Their principal victims were the local moneylenders most of whom happened to be Hindus. The Government succeeded in quelling the uprising which unwittingly did great damage to Hindu-Muslim relations, although its effects were not immediately visible. When in 1924 Mustafa Kemal himself abolished the Khilafat and bundled the Khalif, the self-styled "Shadow of God on Earth," out of Turkey the Khilafat movement collapsed, and with it Hindu-Muslim relations deteriorated. But this was to come later.

Meanwhile, the British authorities betrayed increasing symptoms of suspicion and fear. On May 10th Jawaharlal's sister Sarup was married at Allahabad to a young lawyer, Ranjit Pandit, who was later to become Nehru's close friend. He was a man of unusual versatility, being a Sanskrit scholar, an accomplished linguist speaking several European and Indian languages, passionately fond of both Eastern and Western music, and gifted with a taste and talent for art. Their marriage day, according to Hindu custom, was fixed on an auspicious date after reference to the Samvat calendar which begins from 57 B.C., marking the era of a celebrated Hindu king, Vikramaditya. Soon there were whisperings among the local British community that an uprising would take place on the wedding day. Inquiries revealed that by an interesting if entertaining coincidence May 10th was the anniversary of the outbreak of the Mutiny in 1857!

Individual arrests of leaders of Congress continued throughout the year. Early in September the Ali brothers were arrested and sentenced to two years' rigorous imprisonment for inciting the Indian army to disaffection. Nehru was threatened with prosecution for some allegedly seditious speeches he had made, but no action was taken against him until later in the year.

In this potentially explosive situation the British Government arranged for the visit of the Prince of Wales, now the Duke of Windsor, to India. Misreading the Indian mind, the authorities believed that the Prince's presence would excite the imagination of the masses with their traditional reverence for royalty, and bind closer the ties between India and the British Crown. They erred grievously.

The Congress, while emphasising that it meant no disrespect to the British Crown, proclaimed a boycott of all functions connected with the Prince's visit on the ground that the authorities were exploiting his presence for political purposes. On November 17th the Prince of Wales landed in Bombay, and his arrival immediately touched off an orgy of rioting and arson extending over three days.

In these disturbances over fifty people were killed by police firing, and some four hundred injured.

"The *swaraj* I have witnessed for the past two days," said Gandhi, "has stunk in my nostrils."

He began a penitential fast, vowing he would break it only when peace was restored. This had the desired effect, and on November 22nd Gandhi broke his fast. But the spirit of civil disobedience was astir. A complete suspension of public life, including the closing of business houses and schools, followed the Prince wherever he went. Empty streets greeted him. The functions in his honour were boycotted. So far the Government had been content with individual arrests, but now, alarmed by the turn of events, it decided on mass detentions. On November 19th all Congress and Khilafat organisations were declared unlawful, and early in December Deshbandhu Das, President-elect of the annual Congress session, was arrested with many others. Das left his countrymen a stirring message: "The whole of India is a vast prison. The work of the Congress must be carried on. What matters it whether I am taken or left? What matters it whether I am dead or alive?"

Similar mass arrests followed in the Punjab, Bihar and Nehru's home State, the United Provinces. There, some fifty-five members of the provincial Congress committee were arrested *en bloc* while assembled for a meeting. The drama of these events moved many outside the Congress, and there were cases, as Nehru notes, of even "government clerks, returning from their offices in the evening, being swept away by this current and landing in gaol instead of their homes." If the Government wanted to fill its prisons there were many thousands willing to oblige.

Coming to Anand Bhawan late on the evening of December 6th after a crowded day of work, Jawaharlal found the police searching the place. They had come with warrants of arrest for his father and himself. Though Jawaharlal and Motilal were charged on different counts and tried the following day by different courts, the sentence was the same—six months' imprisonment. Motilal's offence was that he was a member of an illegal organisation, the Congress Volunteers. Jawaharlal was charged with distributing notices for a hartal.[3] Actually,

[3] Suspension of all activity by business houses, schools and other institutions as a form of protest.

this was no offence under the law as it then existed, but this was discovered only later by the authorities, who released him after three months in prison.

The trials were conducted haphazardly. To prove Motilal's offence it was necessary to produce a Congress membership form duly signed by him. One such form was produced, and a tattered, illiterate witness holding the form upside down swore solemnly that the signature was indeed Motilal's. Neither Motilal nor Jawaharlal offered any defence, for it was part of the Congress creed to boycott the law courts. Throughout Motilal's trial Indira, then a child of four, sat in her grandfather's arms. It was her first experience of the dock.

On being sentenced Motilal sent a message on behalf of his son and himself to their comrades outside prison:

Having served you to the best of my ability while working among you, it is now my high privilege to serve the motherland by going to jail with my only son. I am fully confident that we shall meet again at no distant date as free men. I have only one parting word to say—continue non-violent non-co-operation without a break until *swaraj* is attained. Enlist as volunteers in your tens and hundreds and thousands. Let the march of pilgrimage to the only temple of liberty now existing in India,—the jail, be kept in an uninterrupted stream, swelling in strength and volume as each day passes.

During the months of December, 1921, and January, 1922, some 30,000 persons were imprisoned for their political activities.

Prison in those days was an unknown place. But in the tension of the general atmosphere Jawaharlal confesses to a tingle of excitement as the iron gates clanged behind him. Prison-going was soon to become a habit. For the moment novelty gave it a sense of exhilaration.

Lucknow District Jail, where the Nehrus were imprisoned, consisted for the most part of a number of huge barracks where the majority of the political prisoners were confined. Motilal and Jawaharlal, however, along with sixteen others, were put in an old weaving shed which stood on a wide-open space. Father and son, along with two of Jawaharlal's cousins, occupied a small shed, about twenty feet by sixteen, in this enclosure.

If prison was a novelty to them, political prisoners in such numbers were equally a novelty to the jailors. They did not know what to make of them—the jail manual had nothing about it. In those early days the political inmates were allowed a certain degree of latitude, newspapers being permitted and interviews with relatives being granted freely. Later, life and movement were rigidly circumscribed. But these were the halcyon days.

Nehru spent much time in discussion and talk. Through the newspapers he could follow the progress of the movement outside. He read of the Congress session at Ahmedabad late in December over which Hakim Ajmal Khan, a noted Muslim leader, presided in the absence of Das who was in prison. Gandhi was still free. Wearing his famous loincloth at Ahmedabad for the first time at a Congress meeting—he had adopted it in September—the Mahatma sponsored a resolution calling for "aggressive civil disobedience to all government laws and constitutions, for non-violence, for the continuance of public meetings throughout India despite the government prohibition, and for all Indians to offer themselves peacefully for arrest by joining the volunteer corps."

Gandhi had not redeemed his promise to gain *swaraj* within a year. But his revolution had achieved one big thing. It had freed the mind of a people from old shackles and chains.

Life in prison proceeded placidly. In the mornings Jawaharlal would help clean and wash their little shed and do his daily quota of spinning. He found a strange relaxation in washing his own and his father's clothes. For a while the educated political prisoners conducted classes in Hindi and Urdu and other elementary subjects for the benefit of their illiterate colleagues, but these came to an end when the prison authorities forbade movement or communication between the various barracks.

In the coming years Nehru was to know the inside of many prisons under varied conditions. Prison brought with it two advantages to which Nehru was often to refer in the coming years. It gave him enforced leisure for relaxation and writing. Although often irked and irritated by petty restrictions and the oppression of prison walls, he learned to adjust himself to his cramped surroundings. Many of his jail companions have testified to his remarkable resilience, and his zest for mental and manual activities. "His varied interests and vitality," writes Acharya Kripalani, now a Congress dissident and not always benevolent in judgement, "were a source of strength and entertainment to our enforced communal existence."

In prison Nehru has always liked to indulge his love for gardening. He is proud of his culinary talent, though rumour alleges that it does not extend beyond frying eggs and making tea.

"He can laugh like a boy," says the wasp-tongued Kripalani writing of him as a jail companion, "and can appreciate a joke—except when it is aimed at him."

Jawaharlal has an exaggerated feminine sensitivity to ridicule, and during India's first general elections was particularly riled by Communist cartoonists who inflated his figure to portray him as a bloated plutocrat.

In prison, as outside, Nehru had a passion for order and cleanliness. Working and relaxing to a strictly regulated daily regimen, he liked to enforce his sense of discipline on his companions. On the other hand, no one was more solicitous over a sick comrade, and Nehru has been known while in jail to sit up all night tending an ill or ailing colleague.

During one of his later periods of imprisonment he was visited by an English Quaker friend, Muriel Lester, who found him looking pale and hot, with a bevy of hornets buzzing around his cell.

"Don't they worry you?" she asked.

Nehru looked up with his quick boyish smile as if some memory had amused him.

"Yes," he replied. "At first they bothered me a great deal. The window seemed alive with them. I kept killing them, but always new ones flew in to take the place of the slaughtered. After days of this warfare I decided to try non-violence. I pronounced a moratorium vowing to kill no more and telling them to keep to their part of the cell—the window." He smiled again. "It worked. I've had no further trouble."

The days passed slowly in Lucknow Jail.

Suddenly, out of the blue, in mid-February, 1922, Gandhi decided to suspend his campaign of mass civil disobedience. The reason which prompted this action was an outbreak of mass violence at the village of Chauri Chaura in the Gorakhpur district of the United Provinces. A number of villagers who were infuriated by the police firing on them after some disturbances which followed a procession besieged the local police station where some twenty-two constables had taken refuge and burnt the building, together with its inmates, to the ground.

Gandhi was horrified by this holocaust. Although then on the eve of himself launching a local campaign of mass civil disobedience at Bardoli in western India, he peremptorily called off the entire non-cooperation movement. Instead he advised the people to follow a constructive programme of spinning, temperance, the propagation of Hindu-Muslim unity, social reform and education.

Jawaharlal and his father were upset by this sudden decision. However deplorable the Chauri Chaura episode might be, would every sporadic outbreak mean a halt to the struggle for freedom? Who could guarantee against the occurrence of such incidents? If non-violence was to be an end in itself it would always fail as a means. Moreover, the initiative would remain with the Government, who would invariably have the power to create circumstances compelling enough to force the withdrawal of any non-violent movement. Why, asked Motilal, should a town at the foot of the Himalayas be penalised if a village at Cape Comorin failed to observe non-violence?

Gandhi remained impervious to these arguments. "Let the opponent glory in our humiliation or so-called defeat," he wrote. "It is better to be charged with cowardice and weakness than to be guilty of denial of our oath and sin against God. It is a million times better to appear untrue before the world than to be untrue to ourselves." When the All-India Congress Committee met on February 24th at Delhi, Gandhi was roundly assailed for calling off the movement. Imperturbably he read out letters from Motilal and Lala Lajpat Rai, both then in jail, condemning his action, and he went on to say gently but firmly that those who went to jail were civilly dead and could not claim or be expected to advise those outside. He asked the delegates to think for themselves. Although they finally endorsed his action, they made no secret that by and large they were unconvinced by his arguments.

Shortly after this, Jawaharlal was released on the technical ground that he was wrongly sentenced. For his mother and Kamala his imprisonment was the first of many enforced partings still to come. He spent a few days with them at Anand Bhawan and then decided to visit Gandhi at his ashram at Ahmedabad. On the night of Friday, March 10th, before Nehru's arrival, Gandhi was arrested and taken to the local Sabarmati Jail. With him Gandhi took to prison an extra loincloth, two blankets and five books, one of them a copy of the

Sermon on the Mount which some Californian schoolboys had sent him.

Nehru saw him at Sabarmati. Later he attended his trial which was presided over by a British judge, Sir Robert Broomfield, who treated the Mahatma chivalrously, with great dignity and good feeling. He was sentenced to six years' imprisonment, the same term to which Tilak had been sentenced thirteen years earlier.

"I believe," said Gandhi while pleading guilty, "that I have rendered a service to India and England by showing in non-cooperation the way out of the unnatural state in which both are living. In my opinion non-cooperation with evil is as much a duty as cooperation with good."

In sentencing him Sir Robert Broomfield observed:

The law is no respecter of persons. Nevertheless it is impossible to ignore the fact that you are in a different category from any person I have ever tried or am likely to have to try. It would be impossible to ignore the fact that in the eyes of millions of your countrymen you are a great patriot and a great leader. Even those who differ from you in politics look upon you as a man of high ideals and of noble, even saintly life. . . . There are probably few people in India who do not sincerely regret that you should have made it impossible for any government to leave you at liberty. But it is so. . . . I should like to say [in passing sentence] that if the course of events in India should make it possible for the Government to reduce the period and release you, no one will be better pleased than I.

Nehru came away emotionally stirred. He was struck as much by the courtesy of the judge as by Gandhi's cool and implacable courage. Sarojini Naidu, the poetess, who also attended the trial, saw it in different terms. She wrote:

My thoughts sped across the centuries to a different land and different age when a similar drama was enacted and another divine and gentle teacher was crucified for spreading a kindred gospel with a kindred courage. I realised now that the lowly Jesus of Nazareth, cradled in a manger, furnished the only parallel in history to this invincible apostle of Indian liberty who loved humanity with unsurpassed compassion, and to use his own beautiful phrase "approached the poor with the mind of the poor."

For Nehru barely five weeks of liberty remained. With his father and the vast majority of his colleagues in jail, he felt acutely unhappy outside. The machinery of Congress had deteriorated in the enforced absence of the leaders, and Jawaharlal tried to repair some of the damage. It was no easy task. Despite wide popular enthusiasm for the civil-disobedience movement, the masses had so far received little training to carry on by themselves, and much of the organisation and discipline carefully built up by the leaders was disappearing during their absence in jail. There existed in fact a very real danger that undesirable or reactionary elements might enter Congress's ranks and capture the organisation for their own purposes. Against this background Gandhi's decision to suspend civil disobedience was wise, courageous and timely.

Jawaharlal did not then see it in that light. But he remained loyal to Gandhi's behests. Outside prison he interested himself particularly in the propagation of *khadi* and the boycott of foreign cloth, a vital plank in the Mahatma's constructive programme. In doing so he fell foul of the authorities. He discovered that although nearly all the cloth merchants of Allahabad had vowed not to import or purchase foreign cloth, and had formed an association for the purpose, several of them, particularly the big dealers, were surreptitiously doing so. Remonstrations produced small results, and the association seemed powerless to intervene. Nehru then decided that the shops of the erring merchants should be picketed. This action proved effective but riled the Government, which issued a warrant for Jawaharlal's arrest along with some of his colleagues. The charge against them was criminal intimidation and extortion. In addition Nehru was accused of sedition.

He did not defend himself, but made a statement, more for the purpose of buoying up public morale than to justify his acts. He was sentenced on all three counts concurrently for a total period of one year and nine months. "Affection and loyalty," Nehru declared in the course of his statement, "are of the heart. They cannot be purchased in the market place, much less can they be extorted at the point of the bayonet. We are fighting for the freedom of our country and faith. I shall go to jail again most willingly and joyfully. Jail has indeed become a heaven for us, a holy place of pilgrimage. I marvel at my good fortune. To serve India in the battle of freedom is honour enough. To serve her under a leader like Mahatma Gandhi is doubly fortunate. But to suffer for the dear country! What greater good fortune can befall an Indian unless it is death for the cause or the full realisation of our glorious dream?"

He was to go to prison another seven times. Now he was back again for the second time after six weeks of freedom. He discovered that conditions inside the Lucknow District Jail had changed greatly. Shortly after Jawaharlal's release Motilal had been transferred to another prison, the hill jail of Naini Tal, and with his departure the prison rules at Lucknow became more rigid. Nehru now found himself one of about fifty persons huddled together in a barrack, each barrack being "a jail within a jail."

Although he knew the majority of his barrack companions, the absence of privacy irked him, and the daily round of bathing and washing one's clothes in public, exercising together by walking round the barrack, talking and arguing interminably until scope for intelligent conversation was reduced to the minimum jangled his nerves and frayed them. "It was," Nehru wrote, "the dull side of family life, magnified a hundred-fold, with few of its graces and compensations, and all this among people of all kinds and tastes."

The monsoon was not far off, and soon the rains came. Having almost exhausted his capacity for companionship, Jawaharlal retreated into himself, whiling away the hours by reading when he was not lying in the open watching the skies and clouds. He had always been sensitive to the beauty of nature, and now, bereft of the joy of watching a tropical sunrise or sunset, deprived of the sight of colour within the grey stone walls of his barrack, he derived a deep, almost sensuous pleasure in the contemplation of the monsoon skies. Time in prison was of no account. Lying in the open courtyard of the barrack, he would spend hours gazing at the rain clouds as they drifted slowly overhead, and the majesty of their movement and moods induced in him an almost trance-like ecstasy. "Sometimes," he wrote, "the clouds would break, and one saw through an opening in them that wonderful monsoon phenomenon, a dark blue of an amazing depth, which seemed to be a portion of infinity."

Nehru missed other things. For the first time he became acutely aware of the bliss and felicity of home. He thought of the agony of waiting which must overwhelm his mother and wife outside, of Indira, his four-year-old daughter of whom he saw so little. Her second name was Priyadarshini, which means Dear to the Sight; and, writing to her from prison some nine years later, he was to exclaim: "Priyadarshini— dear to the sight, but dearer still when sight is denied." He missed many things, but most of all, he says, he missed the sound of women's voices and the laughter of children. One day it suddenly struck him that he had not heard a dog bark for nearly eight months.

He read a great deal, widely and discursively as he always does. So addicted was he to this habit that his devotion to books somewhat irked and puzzled the British superintendent of the jail.

"Mr. Nehru," said that worthy, "I cannot understand your passion for reading. I finished all my reading at the age of twelve."

Gradually the prison rules became more stringent, and the manner of their enforcement led to frequent clashes between the prisoners and the jail authorities. Letters and interviews were restricted to one a month. Newspapers were barred. Such little news as Nehru and his companions got from the outside world came through the mysterious prison grapevine, and what they heard filled them with foreboding and dismay.

Following Gandhi's imprisonment the Congress had split into two factions—the No-Changers who stood by the old programme of non-cooperation and the Pro-Changers who wanted the Congress to take part in the new elections to the central and provincial legislatures and, if possible, to capture these bodies. Motilal and Deshbandhu Das led the latter school, while the No-Changers were headed by the subtle and astute Chakravarti Rajagopalachari, a Madras politician, who was to become the first Indian Governor-General when independence came. Nehru instinctively sided with the No-Changers, thereby finding himself again in political conflict with his father, and this added to the mental and emotional turmoil seething within him.

Increasing friction between the political prisoners and the jail authorities led the latter to segregate some seven suspected ringleaders, including Nehru, to a distant wing of the jail cut off from the main barracks. Among the seven were Gandhi's son, Devadas, and the Mahatma's secretary, Mahadev Desai. Such seclusion was not unwelcome to Nehru after his overcrowded barrack life. He and his companions devised a regular routine of work and exercise. Most of them did a little spinning daily. They tended a vegetable patch, watering it from a well in the yard, two of them drawing the water in a huge leather bucket by pulling at a yoke which ordinarily held two bullocks. Running around their little enclosure constituted the only other form of physical activity. And they read and talked.

"Prison has made a man of me," Nehru remarked many years later to the Socialist leader Acharya Narendra Deva, while they were both in jail for the last time in 1942. If nothing else, it gave him time to read and think, and hardened his physical and moral fibre.

On January 31, 1923, all the political inmates of Lucknow Jail were released. Some days earlier the United Provinces legislature had passed a resolution favouring a political amnesty; and the moment being propitious for such a gesture, the Government had acceded.

Nehru came out eager but not exultant. He was filled with vague forebodings, for the Congress was a divided camp and Gandhi was still in prison. On November 14th Jawaharlal had celebrated his thirty-third birthday anniversary in prison. It was the first birthday he celebrated in prison—but not the last.

7

THE LOTUS YEARS

How quickly India had changed! Barely a year before, there was thunder in the air. A storm had swept the skies, a gale had filled the heavens. Many landmarks were uprooted; but, unlike a wind from the sea which causes havoc but leaves an invigorating breath of freshness and life in its trail, the aftermath was dispiriting. A vast weariness seized the land.

Jawaharlal was depressed by the atmosphere. The Congress, split into two factions, was a house divided against itself, and intrigue had eased out idealism. Various cliques were manœuvring for power by attempting to capture the machinery of Congress. Nehru's heart and head were with the No-Changers because the programme of entering the councils or legislatures seemed to him dangerously like compromise, and compromise at this stage was an admission of defeat. It meant a watering down of objectives, and the idea was repugnant. But he found to his dismay that the No-Changers were animated by no resolute political purpose, their programme being one merely of social reform. It was a choice between Tweedledum and Tweedledee.

Faced with this dilemma Nehru decided to concentrate on his own State, where he was secretary of the United Provinces Congress Committee. He set about rehabilitating the organisation of Congress, which had suffered greatly in the shake-up. But he was mentally ill at ease, his inner doubts assailing the clarity and vigour of his actions. The eternal urge to do something was clouded by the political doubts around him, for the road wound like a maze and the signposts were unsure.

Municipal administration was one form of public activity which was still open to Congressmen, and in 1923 the municipal corporations of many big cities had Congress representatives as their mayors or presidents. Das was mayor of Calcutta, while in Bombay and Ahmedabad the two Patel brothers, Viththalbhai and Vallabhbhai, both destined to leave their mark on national affairs, ruled the civic roosts. About the same time Nehru was elected president of the Allahabad municipality.

He found here an outlet for his pent-up energy, and characteristically concentrated on his job. There were aspects of municipal administration which fascinated him and absorbed his attention, particularly its scope for social service, and for a time he felt that here were Augean stables worth the effort to cleanse them. He thought there was room for reform in the municipal machine. But he discovered soon that initiative and change—even in the narrow confines of local self-government—were not encouraged by the authorities. There was no room for radical reform, and civic development was conditioned by finance, which was the Government's perquisite. As usual, the wheels of bureaucracy ground slow and ground exceedingly small. Nehru characteristically suggested a tax on land values, but a horrified official was quick to point out that this would contravene a sacred clause of the land-tenure regulations. None the less Nehru persevered in the civic field, devoting to it that meticulous attention and study which distinguished him from most of his colleagues in the Congress.

The tendency to centralise authority in himself and to do things on his individual initiative is a trait very early evident in Nehru's career. Partly this arises from the fact that as a perfectionist he would rather have a thing not done than do it shoddily. His distrust of the ability of most of his colleagues to carry out an undertaking with the scrupulous and exacting efficiency he demands has often led Nehru to heap more on his plate than he can conveniently dispose of. This trait persists and finds vent in the petulance and impatience which seize him when a microphone breaks down at a meeting or a crowd shows signs of indiscipline.

So it was with his brief civic career which lasted two years. In this period he paid to municipal affairs the same meticulous care and attention which he brought to bear in the building up of organisations in the Congress. There is extant, among other records, a memorandum he wrote on "the treatment of prostitutes by the Allahabad municipality." It bristles with sentences which reflect his approach to more general problems: "The world would be a very different place if we could abolish prostitution and lying and cruelty and oppression and the thousand and one ills that flesh is heir to, by resolutions." He was referring to the municipality's attempt to abolish prostitution by passing a resolution and appointing a committee. And again, "Let us know what we are driving at and then we may be in a better position perhaps to achieve our purpose." As in politics, so in civic affairs, he insists on knowing the objectives.

Yet amid these generalisations is a hard core of practical suggestions. He states these point by point, and rounds off with a characteristic broadside: "I do not believe in issuing a fiat that prostitutes must not live in any part of the city of Allahabad except a remote corner. If this is done I would think it equally reasonable to reserve another part of Allahabad for the men who exploit women and because of whom prostitution flourishes."

Charlie Andrews recounts a comment made in his hearing by one of Nehru's most bitter political opponents in the United Provinces: "Whatever we may think of young Nehru's socialist doctrines," he said, "the efficient way in which he handled the Allahabad municipality as chairman, was beyond all praise."

At this time he was also elected secretary of the All-India Congress, and as a result his working day averaged fifteen hours. He was often limp with exhaustion by evening.

Nehru none the less remained acutely aware of the growing demoralisation in the political atmosphere. With the institution of legislatures and ministerships, the Government's power of patronage was considerably enlarged, and many one-time nationalists nibbled at the bait of office and moved into the calmer waters of cooperation with the authorities. Nehru himself was indirectly approached by an English acquaintance, Sir Grimwood Mears, then Chief Justice of the Allahabad High Court, with an offer of the Education Ministership in his province. The naïveté of this approach amused but did not impress him. Ministerships were a dime a dozen. But this drift away from non-cooperation was none the less "a demoralising dribble."

Nehru gave much time to thought on the fortunes of the country and the Congress. Gandhi, he had long felt, symbolised the confused desires of the people, and in so far as the Mahatma's leadership had not given these desires a clear form and purpose it had failed. If anything, the confusion was worse confounded. There seemed to him to be no clarity of objective, only a vague inchoate movement for freedom with no defined political, economic or social programmes and plans. Did *swaraj* mean merely self-government or complete independence? Would the peasantry still be left to the mercy of the landlords in a free India and the workers abandoned to the caprices of the new and growing capitalist class? Here were the first faint stirrings of socialist thought which were to achieve aggressive expression only after Nehru's visit to Europe in 1926.

Das, who was now working in active cooperation with Motilal, tried to influence Jawaharlal to support the so-called Swarajist creed of entering the legislatures which, he argued, was not designed to promote cooperation but to carry the nationalist battle a step further from the country into the councils. It was a plausible, even attractive argument, but it did not convince Nehru. He felt that to enter the legislatures would be to divert the people's attention from the single objective of independence through mass effort, and to dissipate and diffuse their already confused energies. If they must enter the legislatures let them do so as a symbolic gesture on the Sinn Fein pattern, by capturing seats in the councils and then refusing to occupy them. Nehru had actually put this proposal before Gandhi in 1920. But the Mahatma's reactions were not favourable. Gandhi felt that to get elected and then not go into the councils would only further confuse the mass mind. He was probably right.

From 1923 onwards Nehru found much solace and happiness in his family circle. The emptiness of prison life had made him aware of many things he had hitherto taken for granted—of Kamala's love and loneliness, her pride and sensitivity, and her passion, frustrated by ill-health, to share in his political work. "She wanted," he was to write many years later after her death, "to play her own part in the national struggle and not be merely a hanger-on and a shadow of her husband. She wanted to justify herself to her own self as well as to the world. Nothing in the world could have pleased me more than this, but I was far too busy to see beneath the surface and I was blind to what she looked for and so ardently desired." Of her eagerness to share in his political work he was to become consciously aware only during the non-cooperation movement of 1930. But already his subconscious mind felt the urge for a closer comradeship between them.

"Delicate to a degree, frail as a flower, she was a woman with a consuming sense of patriotism." That is how a friend of the family describes Kamala. What Jawaharlal did not then understand was his wife's intense desire to justify herself as a worthy political comrade in his eyes. Her health, never strong, had already begun to deteriorate, and her physical inability to share fully in the rigour and hardships of her husband's political life must have weighed heavily on the mind of this proud, ailing and acutely sensitive girl.

Jawaharlal's mother was also ill. Unlike her husband and son, she was orthodox in her habits and attitude to life, and her world gravitated around her husband, home and children. When Motilal made his decision to follow the Mahatma and abandon his luxurious way of life, his wife, although frail and ill, had readily adjusted herself to their new mode of living. There was something indomitable in this tiny fragile woman which sustained her spirit through recurring trials and tribulations.

It was typical of Motilal that although he would have liked Jawaharlal to join him and Das in their campaign to enter the legislatures, he did nothing to persuade or influence him. Perhaps he divined the mind of his son and, sharing a common end, refrained from quarrelling over the means. While aware that his new-formed Swaraj party would attract some careerists and opportunists along with many genuine patriots, Motilal was confident that he could sever "a diseased limb" if and when the occasion required. The Congress was politically baulked, and what could be more logical than to carry the fight from the country to the councils? So Motilal and Das argued and hoped.

If the spirit of the leaders was low, there was still fight in the people. In May a local flag satyagraha was held at Nagpur in the Central Provinces in which some two thousand people took part, and thereafter processions with the national flag were allowed without let or hindrance by the Government. But the Swarajists were steadily gaining ground, and in September, at a special session of the Congress in Delhi presided over by Maulana Abul Kalam Azad, the Congress gave them a mandate to enter the legislatures.

Shortly after, Nehru came into conflict with the authorities and was arrested for the third time. It happened that in the Punjab the Akalis, a reformist and advanced section of the Sikh community, were demonstrating against the allegedly corrupt *mahants* (guardians) of their *gurudwaras* (holy shrines). Their protest took the form of non-violent resistance, wave after wave of Sikh volunteers marching on the *gurudwaras* only to be brutally beaten back by the police who were guarding the shrines. The spectacle of these burly, normally aggressive Sikhs, many of them former soldiers, refraining from any retaliatory violence entranced Jawaharlal. They had learned, he reflected, the lesson which Gandhi had taught, and like him were attempting to shame the wrongdoer into doing right, not by using violence against him but by inviting suffering on themselves. Although the movement was declared illegal it ultimately triumphed, and the administration of the *gurudwaras* benefited as a result. But the agitation was to continue over some years.

Meanwhile, a similar demonstration, though for different reasons and on a smaller scale, was taking place in the Sikh State of Nabha, whose ruler had been deposed by the Government, who appointed a British administrator in his place. This action was resented by the Maharaja's Sikh subjects, who demonstrated against it. In the course of this non-violent demonstration a religious ceremony at a place called Jaito was stopped by the British administrator. As a result the agitation converged on Jaito, and batch after batch of non-violent Sikhs attempted to march on the place, only to be beaten back.

Jawaharlal was invited to watch one of these marches, and from Delhi—shortly after the special session of the Congress—he proceeded with two companions to Jaito where a batch of Sikh volunteers had collected. He had no intention of joining in the demonstration, and in fact kept apart. But on arriving at Jaito an order was served on him and his two companions by the British administrator requesting them not to enter the Nabha State territory, and if they had entered it, to leave it immediately. They were then in fact well inside the State boundaries, and in any case they could only leave by the next train, which was some hours later. Moreover, they had come, not as participants in the demonstrations, but as spectators. They explained these facts to the police officer who had served the notice on them. His reply was to arrest them and detain them in the local lock-up.

There Nehru with his two companions was kept for the day, and in the evening they were marched through the streets to the railway station. Nehru's left wrist was handcuffed to the right wrist of one of his companions, and a chain attached to the handcuff was held by the policeman leading them. Behind came his second companion, also handcuffed and chained. Although momentarily irritated by these extraordinary measures, Nehru and his companions were sufficiently lively to be amused by the quixotry of the situation, and it was in quite cheerful spirits that they arrived at the station.

Their subsequent experiences quickly dispelled this mood. At Jaito they were put, handcuffed and chained, into a crowded third-class compartment where they spent the night huddled together until they arrived at Nabha in the morning. Here, still handcuffed and chained, they were delivered to the local jail authorities and spent the next three days in a tiny insanitary cell with a low roof which they could almost touch. At night rats scurried over their faces as they slept on the floor.

From this cheerless habitat the trio were taken finally to a court-room where the proceedings were Gilbertian and prolonged. The judge knew no English and seemed unable to write in the language of the court, which was Urdu. Throughout the hearings, which lasted nearly a week, he wrote not a line. Nehru and his two companions did not defend themselves, but submitted a statement retailing the facts.

Of a sudden one day they were taken from the courtroom to another room presided over by another magistrate. On inquiry they learned that they were being tried on a new charge for conspiracy. Because this crime required a minimum of four persons acting in concert, a fourth man, a Sikh who had nothing whatever to do with them, was lodged in the dock along with them. The proceedings now deteriorated into broad farce, until about a fortnight after their arrest the two trials ended. In the conspiracy case Nehru and his companions were each awarded eighteen months' imprisonment and in addition received a sentence of six months for breach of the order to leave the Nabha territory.

On the same evening they were summoned by the superintendent of the jail, who showed them an order of the British administrator suspending their sentences under the criminal procedure code. The net result was that they were free to go, and almost immediately they were escorted to the railway station and released there. What happened to the unfortunate Sikh who was tacked on as the fourth accused in the criminal conspiracy case they were never able to discover.

One result of their stay in the insanitary cell in Nabha Jail was an attack of typhus which overcame all of them. Nehru's companions were for a while seriously ill, and he himself was bed-ridden for almost four weeks.

In December the elections for the Central Assembly and the Provincial Councils, in which the new Swaraj party under Motilal and Das contended, took place. The Swarajists staged an impressive triumph, winning forty-five seats in the Central Legislature, which enabled them, with the help of other nationalist groups, to command a working majority. But real power did not lie in the legislature but with the Viceroy. The Swaraj party's success stemmed from the remarkable teamwork of Motilal and Das, who, although temperamentally different, complemented each other's qualities and together made a formidable combination. Between the two men there existed a bond of mutual respect and affection. Das, also a successful lawyer, was a perfervid patriot with a gift for emotional oratory which dovetailed into Motilal's talent as an organiser and his zest for battle.

Shortly after the election the Congress held its annual session at Cocanada in South India which was presided over by the younger of the two Ali brothers, Maulana Mohamed Ali. A man of strong likes and dislikes, vitriolic of tongue and mercurial in temper, Mohamed Ali had a natural liking for the eager and high-mettled Jawaharlal. He insisted that Nehru should accept the All-India Congress secretaryship which he had relinquished earlier in the year, and Nehru consented to do so during Mohamed Ali's one year of Presidency. They were good friends, and the younger man relished as much the nimble mind and wit of his older colleague as the latter was drawn by the ardent, questing spirit of Jawaharlal.

Then and later they had many verbal jousts on religion and the Almighty. As with the meek and mild Hindu who was Gandhi, so also with the militant Muslim who was Mohamed Ali, Nehru felt that the attitude of both men was "irrationally religious." In his autobiography he writes, "Mohamed Ali had an extraordinary way of bringing in some reference to God even in Congress resolutions, either by way of expressing gratitude or some kind of prayer."

They argued good-humouredly over their differences, and Nehru records how Mohamed Ali once remarked to him that despite his superficial protestations he believed that Jawaharlal was fundamentally religious. Nehru's comment is interesting: "I have often wondered how much truth there was in his statement. Perhaps it depends on what is meant by religion and religious."

Much the same reaction to Nehru's widely bruited "lack of religion" came from the Mahatma. "While Jawaharlal always says he does not believe in God," remarked Gandhi, "he is nearer God than many who profess to be His worshippers." Gandhi instinctively recognised that in Nehru's vocabulary religion means service of humanity. As Sri Prakasa, an old friend of Jawaharlal, puts it: "He may not be 'religious' but he is a person truly devoted to duty. In Sanskrit we have one word, *dharma*, both for duty and religion."

Unhappily, the shadow of religious differences in the shape of mounting Hindu-Muslim tension lowered over the Congress session at Cocanada. The cloudburst was to descend shortly.

Divided as the Congress was, the Cocanada session had no alternative to seeking safety in compromise. While reaffirming the non-cooperation resolutions adopted at previous sessions, it permitted the Swarajists to enter the councils, simultaneously emphasising that "the principle and policy of that boycott remain unaltered." The people were called upon to carry out the constructive programme and prepare for the adoption of civil disobedience. In a way the resolution reflected faithfully the confused mind of the Congress. For Jawaharlal, unhappy over these shifts and stratagems, the Cocanada session was memorable for the foundation of a country-wide volunteer organisation, known as the Hindustani Seva Dal, which in time grew to be a sort of disciplined corps élite of the Congress. The initiator of this movement, Dr. N. S. Hardiker, had the enthusiastic support of Nehru.

The clouds were thickening on the political horizon, and in 1923 Hindu-Muslim goodwill slumped sharply. In November, 1922, Mustafa Kemal had exiled the Sultan of Turkey, who was also the Kaliph of the Muslim world, and with the virtual abolition of that office the Khilafat movement in India lost its mainspring. The lure of ministerships and other official perquisites generated a new rivalry between Hindus and Muslims. Militant Hinduism reared its head, and the Hindu Mahasabha, representing Hindu extremism, held its first significant session at Banaras in August, 1923, and embarked on the *shuddhi*, or reconversion movement. With Gandhi in prison the Swarajists held the field outside; and though they scored successive paper triumphs against the Government in the Central Assembly and provincial legislatures, it was clear that real power remained with the Viceroy and the provincal governors. In Bengal the virtual collapse of the non-cooperation movement brought the terrorists to the fore. There was talk again of the necessity of violence.

At this juncture, in mid-January, 1924, Gandhi was removed from prison to a hospital in Poona where he was successfully operated on by a British surgeon, Colonel Maddock, for appendicitis. Jawaharlal, with his father, visited the Mahatma in the hospital. On February 5th the Government unconditionally remitted the unexpired portion of his sentence, and Gandhi was free again. He had served about two years of his six-year sentence.

Early in March, Gandhi went to convalesce at Juhu, a seaside resort near Bombay, and in the first week of April he resumed the editorship of his two weeklies, *Young India* and *Navajivan*.[1] His first article, reiterating the need for non-violence, appeared on April 3rd. "My patriotism," he wrote, "is not exclusive; it is calculated not only not to hurt any other nation but to benefit all in the true sense of the word. India's freedom as conceived by me can never be a menace to the world."

He went on to reproach those who had been false to the movement's ideals:

We pledged ourselves to be non-violent towards each other and our opponents, whether administrators or co-operators. We were to appeal to their hearts and evoke the best in them, not play upon their fear to gain our end. Consciously or unconsciously the majority of us—the articulate portion—have not been true to our pledge. We have been intolerant towards our opponents. Our own countrymen are filled with distrust of us. They simply do not believe in our non-violence. Hindus and Muslims in many places have provided an object lesson not in non-violence but in

[1] New Life.

violence. Even the Changers and No-Changers have flung mud against one another. Each has claimed the monopoly of truth and with an ignorant certainty of conviction sworn at the other for his helpless stupidity.

But on the controversial issue of council-entry Gandhi for the moment held his peace.

In April, Das and Motilal went to Juhu to discuss developments with Gandhi. Jawaharlal, with his mother, wife and daughter, accompanied his father, the family staying in a tiny cottage by the sea. They found Gandhi in a cheerful, even playful mood, indulging, as was his wont, in the little jokes he loved; and Motilal, entering into the spirit of the company, sometimes chaffed the Mahatma mercilessly. Himself impeccable in dress, he found something incongruous in Gandhi's ascetic habits and his always spotless white *khadi* garments.

"You're a bit of a dandy," he teased him.

Gandhi laughed uproariously.

Motilal, realising the Mahatma's hold on Jawaharlal, tried to enlist his aid to restrain his son's ardour. He was disturbed by what he described as Jawaharlal's "monkey tricks"—his habit of living on parched rice and roasted gram, of travelling third class under the torrid summer sun.

"I appreciate sacrifice and endurance," said Motilal. "But this is just primitiveness. It hurts me. He listens to you. You must talk to him about it."

"Certainly I will do as you wish," Gandhi replied.

On the question of council-entry, which Motilal and Das discussed with him from day to day, at some length, Gandhi was adamant. He was friendly and courteous but implacable. As Jawaharlal discovered, there could sometimes be steel in that soft voice and the calm eyes could suddenly be stony. Gandhi insisted that council-entry was inconsistent with non-cooperation as he conceived it, and although he conceded that the Swarajists had a mandate from the Congress for their entry into the legislatures he made it clear that he could not actively help them so long as he was not convinced of the utility of their action.

"Let's agree to disagree," he said.

They parted on that note. Motilal on his side was equally unyielding, and though he admired Gandhi greatly, and cherished a strong

affection for him, he was the only man in the Congress who refused
to treat the Mahatma worshipfully, and dealt with him as an equal.
He too could be hard and flint-like.

Nehru relates how later in that year he showed Gandhi a photograph of Motilal taken when his father had no moustache. Until
then Gandhi had always seen Motilal with the moustache which
he wore in his later years. He looked at the picture for a long time.
Shorn of his moustache, Motilal's mouth was revealed in its hard firm
line.

"Now," said Gandhi, "I know what I have to contend against."

Watching the Mahatma and Motilal, Nehru was torn again by
contending urges. He agreed with Gandhi that the policy of council-
entry detracted from the spirit of non-cooperation. But Gandhi himself, he felt, was not clear about objectives. As always, the Mahatma
refused to lay down any long-term programme, preferring to grope
his way forward step by step. To Nehru "he seemed to be completely
at sea, unable to find his bearings." What the younger man in his
impatience did not then realise was Gandhi's real and profound distress that his message of non-violence had taken no deep roots in the
people.

The spirit of violence was very much in the air.

In Bengal political dacoities continued. Armed youths raided
armouries and banks, and attempted to murder officials. A police
officer was shot at Chittagong, and in Calcutta a European civilian,
mistaken for the local commissioner of police, was murdered in broad
daylight. As the cry of Hindu-Muslim unity lost its compelling urge
with the collapse of the Khilafat movement, sporadic conflicts broke
out between the two communities and a number of riots took place
in the bigger cities. The fanatics and die-hards were busy on both
sides, each objecting to the cohesive activities by the other, Hindus
denouncing Muslims for the slaughter of cows and Muslims in turn
accusing Hindus of disturbing their prayers by playing music before
mosques.

Gandhi, protesting against these outbreaks, urged non-violence on
both sides. He wrote:

The Hindus and Muslims prate about no compulsion in religion. What
is it but compulsion if Hindus will kill a Muslim for slaughtering a cow?
It is like wanting to convert a Muslim to Hinduism by force. Similarly,

what is it but compulsion if Muslims seek to prevent by force Hindus from playing music before mosques? Virtue lies in being absorbed in one's prayers in the presence of din and noise. We shall both be voted irreligious savages by posterity if we continue to compel one another to respect our religious wishes.

Gandhi's was the small voice of reason doomed to be lost for the time being in the mounting tumult and shouting which assailed both sides. Profiting by this turmoil, Hindu and Muslim reactionaries sought to consolidate their political position with the Government by inveigling appointments and by cooperating closely with the authorities.

Nehru was sick at heart. Where would this landslide end? Even a few Congressmen who had been to prison with him in 1921 and 1922 were now glad to bask in the official sunlight and serve as ministers in the Government. "Like the Nazis," he commented bitterly many years later, "they had flirted with revolutionary methods before changing sides."

The rot was spreading in the body politic, and to Nehru, Gandhi seemed to have lost the initiative. In June when the All-India Congress Committee met at Ahmedabad, Gandhi insisted that membership of the Congress should be limited to those who produced a prescribed quantity of self-spun yarn per month. Hitherto membership was confined to those who subscribed to the principles of the Congress and paid four annas a year. The proposal created considerable feeling as it entailed a fundamental change in the constitution of the Congress. Jawaharlal, greatly taken aback, offered his resignation as secretary. Motilal and Das vehemently opposed it, sensing that this unorthodox approach constituted a frontal attack on the amorphous policy of the Swarajists and was the signal for the cry of "Back to Gandhism." To register their disapproval the two leaders, accompanied by their supporters, withdrew from the meeting before the voting. Gandhi's proposal was endorsed by 67 to 37 votes, but the Mahatma realised that his was a Pyrrhic victory. It had not achieved his end of charging the ambiguous political atmosphere with a positive purpose.

Ultimately the resolution was withdrawn. What distressed Gandhi even more than this empty victory was the fate of another resolution he sponsored condemning the deed of a terrorist, Gopinath Saha, while expressing sympathy with his motives. Das opposed it, and the resolution was finally passed by a majority of only eight votes. To the Mahatma this indicated that not all of his colleagues in the Congress were serious about their professions of non-violence. "What preyed upon my mind," he wrote later, "was the fact of unconscious irresponsibility and disregard of the Congress creed or policy of non-violence. . . . That there were seventy Congress representatives to oppose the resolution was a staggering revelation."

Gandhi was acutely unhappy, and Nehru was quick to see the reason for his distress. The Mahatma, he realised, dealt only in absolutes. He could understand absolute war or absolute peace. "Anything in between he did not appreciate." He could not understand the attitude of the Swarajists, which seemed to him neither logical nor just. If they believed in non-cooperation they should boycott the legislatures. On the other hand, if they believed in cooperation, they should enter the legislatures and cooperate fully with the authorities for quicker reform and progress.

In September the mounting flames of Hindu-Muslim conflict flared into fury at Kohat in the Northwest Frontier Province where 155 persons were killed and vast damage was done to property. There followed a wholesale evacuation of the Hindu population of Kohat. To stun the country into sobriety Gandhi went on a twenty-one-day penitential fast; but though this momentarily calmed the atmosphere, and induced a unity conference between Hindu and Muslim leaders, its effects were short-lived.

In December the annual session of Congress was held at Belgaum with Gandhi in the chair. Nehru, who had hoped that the Mahatma might give a positive lead to the country in his presidential address, was disappointed. It was the shortest presidential address ever delivered before the Congress, and in it Gandhi merely reiterated his faith in the charka, Hindu-Muslim unity and the removal of untouchability. "I swear by civil disobedience," he declared. "But civil disobedience for the attainment of swaraj is an impossibility unless and until we have attained the power of achieving the boycott of foreign cloth." To Nehru this seemed uninspiring, nor was he enthused by Gandhi's definition of India's political goal as "a federation of friendly interdependent States rather than independence." This was cryptic and confusing.

None the less Nehru was persuaded to continue as the secretary of the Congress. It had become an almost permanent assignment. The Belgaum session also saw a formal healing of the breach between the Swarajists and No-Changers, thereby virtually giving quietus to the non-cooperation movement.

Political life was at an ebb and there was little mass activity during 1925, a year which Gandhi spent in incessant tours throughout the country. In the summer Jawaharlal with his father and family went to Dalhousie, a resort in the Himalayas, for a brief holiday. Motilal was troubled by asthma. They were at Chamba in the interior of the Himalayas when a telegram came announcing the death of Das. He had died suddenly on June 16th at Darjeeling, a hill station near Calcutta.

His death came as a heavy blow to Motilal, who, Jawaharlal relates, on learning the news, sat still for a long time without a word, bowed with grief. Das's death meant the passing away of a dearly loved comrade, and the burden of the Swaraj party now rested solely on the shoulders of Motilal. In his last letter to Motilal, Das had written: "The most critical time in our history is coming. There must be solid work done at the end of the year and the beginning of the next. Our resources will be taxed and here we are both of us ill. God knows what will happen."

In the autumn of 1925 Kamala, who had been ailing for some time with a tubercular infection, fell seriously ill. For many months she lay in a Lucknow hospital with no sign of improvement, and it was finally decided, on the advice of Jawaharlal's old friend Dr. M. A. Ansari, that she should be taken to Europe for treatment. That year the Congress was held at Kanpur, and Nehru spent many anxious, distracted days travelling between Allahabad, Kanpur and Lucknow.

Early in March, 1926, Jawaharlal, with Kamala and their eight-year-old daughter Indira, sailed from Bombay for Venice. Accompanying them were Nehru's brother-in-law, Ranjit Pandit, with his wife Vijayalakshmi. They were to stay in Europe for a year and nine months, and the period was to mark a decisive turning point in Nehru's opinions and outlook.

8

JOURNEY TO EUROPE

THEY had planned to stay in Europe for six to seven months. But the demands of Kamala's health, combined with the quiescent political situation at home and the tingle of new and exciting ideas abroad, lengthened their sojourn.

The major part of their twenty-one months abroad was spent at Geneva in Switzerland and in a mountain sanatorium at Montana. In the summer of 1926 Nehru's younger sister, Krishna, joined them and remained with them until the end of their tour. In September, 1927, Motilal came out to Europe, and it was in his company that Nehru with his family visited Moscow for about four days for the tenth anniversary celebrations of the Soviet Republic. Earlier, as Kamala's health improved, Jawaharlal had made brief visits to Britain, France and Germany, and in February, 1927, he went to Brussels as a representative of the Indian National Congress to the Congress of Oppressed Nationalities.

Much had happened in the fourteen years since Nehru was last in Europe. He had left it as a youth of twenty-three, "a bit of a prig," as he himself confessed, "a queer mixture of the East and West, out of place everywhere, at home nowhere." The years had seen him start on his discovery of India, but the pilgrim had still a long road to travel. Gandhism had given Nehru's nationalism a distinctive stamp. It had opened windows on a world far different from the sheltered ease of Anand Bhawan, and made him kin with the peasant and the worker. It had taken him inside prison walls. Yet it had not quite stilled the turmoil within him or answered completely the many questions, doubts and hesitations which plagued and pursued him. Surely independence was not an end in itself. And if it were not, what form of economic and social freedom would an independent India aspire to achieve? To that, Gandhism gave no definite answers. It was not even clear as to what *swaraj* meant. Was it a vague form of Dominion status or did it signify complete independence?

Europe also had changed—more volcanically than Nehru had. It had been the epicentre of a great global war which had altered both geography and history, shifting boundaries, creating new States, and sending thrones tottering and crowns crashing in its wake. Above all, with the emergence of Soviet Russia, the first Communist State in the world had come into being. The climate of European, even global thought, had changed.

Europe seemed in the uneasy process of settling down. But it was the lull before the storm, and the economic blizzard was not far away. During Nehru's stay in Europe, Germany was admitted to the League, and the United States Secretary of State, Frank Kellogg, proposed a pact for the renunciation of war which was to be signed in Paris in August, 1928. In Britain a general strike was precipitated by the coal miners, and London broke off diplomatic relations with Moscow. There was a revolution in Nicaragua. Thomas Masaryk was reelected President of Czechoslovakia, while far away in China, Chiang Kai-shek, overthrowing the Hankow régime, established himself in authority at Nanking. In Japan, Hirohito succeeded his father, Yoshohito, as Emperor. A soldier of fortune, Pilsudski, seized power in Poland.

Nehru, stimulated by his surroundings, had his mind receptively open to new ideas. "I found the vast political, economic and cultural changes going on in Europe and America a fascinating study," he wrote later. "Soviet Russia, despite certain unpleasant aspects, attracted me greatly and seemed to hold forth a message of hope to the world." Nationalism, he felt, was not enough. It was too narrow and inadequate a creed. Unless related to the wider urges and needs of humanity as a whole, it lacked content and meaning. India could operate in a vacuum only at her peril.

At the Villa Olga at Villeneuve lived Romain Rolland, whom Nehru saw with a letter of introduction from Gandhi. Three years earlier Rolland had published his biography of Gandhi and become the mouthpiece of the Mahatma in Europe. Nehru's pilgrimage was not without irony. Of Gandhi, Rolland had written: "I saw surging up on the plains of the Indus the citadel of the spirit which had been raised by the frail and unbreakable Mahatma. And I set myself to rebuild it in Europe." Now Nehru sought in Europe the answers to the riddles which had tormented him in India.

Rolland soothed but did not entirely satisfy. Of a more robust fibre was Ernst Toller, the German poet and dramatist, whom Nehru met in Brussels. Toller, then thirty-four, intense and often melancholy, seemed overwhelmed by a sense of tragedy. He was to be exiled from Germany by the Nazis, and to die by his own hand as the shadows of the Second World War crept over Europe.

Nehru was impressed by Toller's passion for truth and freedom, by his blazing courage and deep social conscience. Seven years later, in 1934, he met the German again, now an exile from his native land and living the distracted, uprooted life of a refugee. In 1939 Toller killed himself, and Nehru, in a surge of sorrow and anger, lamented his dead friend. The world of Fascism, he reflected, was too brutal for Toller's sensitive spirit, too coarse for his fine nature. "But it was democratic England and democratic France with their false promises and betrayals and stabs in the back that broke him."

At Brussels where he met Toller at the Congress of Oppressed Nationalities Nehru came in contact with many Asians, including Madame Sun Yat-sen, who were later to figure prominently in the nationalist movements of their countries. One elusive figure he did not meet but Motilal encountered him later. He was an Indo-Chinese, slim, with a waxen skin, gentle luminous eyes and a wispy beard. His name was Nguyen-Ai-Quoc, but the world was to know him as Ho Chi-minh. In November, 1954, on his way to Peking, Nehru met Ho at Hanoi in Indo-China.

There were many Communists present at the Brussels conference, and watching them at work alongside the socialists, who included George Lansbury of Britain, Nehru got an insight into the inner conflicts of the Western Labour world. The equivocal attitude of the British socialists to the question of Indian independence had irritated Nehru, who somewhat despised them. The Communists, he felt, were at least not hypocritical. Whatever their faults, they were not imperialistic. On seizing power, they had voluntarily liquidated the special privileges which the Tsarist Government had claimed in countries such as Persia. Towards Turkey their attitude was generous. They had not only renounced all claims on Constantinople, Turkish waters and Turkish territory in both Europe and Asia, but they had cultivated Turkish friendship with a view to defeating the postwar Allied aim of partitioning that country. In China, Lenin had waived such extra-territorial rights and other privileges as Tsarist Russia had enjoyed. The Bolshevik approach to America was exceptionally friendly. British imperialism was their public enemy Number One, and this attitude aroused an evocative echo in Asia, particularly in India. Nehru remembered how after the First World War Churchill had talked of British hegemony straddling the Middle East from Delhi to Constantinople.

"I welcomed the developments in Russia as a counterpoise to all this," he commented.

Nehru's reaction to the Communists must be appreciated in this context. In his autobiography he confesses that at this time he did not know much about "the fine points" of Communism—"my acquaintance being limited to its broad features." He was, like many Indian intellectuals, none the less impressed by the will and effort of the Russian people and Government to lift their country literally by their bootstraps to better conditions of life. On the other hand, he was then, as now, irritated by the Communists' dictatorial ways, their aggressive and rather vulgar methods, their habit of denouncing everyone who did not agree with them.

Some ten years later, in his autobiography, Nehru returns to the theme:

I am very far from being a Communist. My roots are still perhaps partly in the nineteenth century, and I have been too much influenced by the humanist liberal tradition to get out of it completely. This bourgeois background follows me about and is naturally a source of irritation to many Communists. I dislike dogmatism, and the treatment of Karl Marx's writings or any other books as revealed scripture which cannot be challenged, and the regimentation and heresy hunts which seem to be a feature of modern Communism. I dislike also much that has happened in Russia, and especially the excessive use of violence in normal times.

But there was no lack of violence either in the capitalist world, Nehru mused.

Marx's scientific method in evaluating social and economic phenomena undoubtedly influenced him. "I incline," he admits in his autobiography, "more and more towards a communist philosophy." The colouring of his thought is Marxist, but it permeates a mind which is modern, independent and nationalist. In a letter to his daughter Indira, written from prison and dated February 16, 1933, Nehru cites approvingly Lenin's warning not to consider Marxism as a dogma, and he quotes a passage from Lenin's writings—"We think that it is especially necessary for Russian Socialists to undertake an independent study of the Marxist theory, for that theory gives only general guiding ideas which can be applied differently in England for instance, than in France, differently in France than in Germany, differently in Germany than in Russia."

Nehru's criticism of India's Communists stems from the same approach. In his reckoning, Communism as Marx preached it is as outmoded as the capitalism of the *laissez faire* school. If there can be no such thing as the wholesale transplantation of Marxism in India, there is equally no room for uncontrolled private enterprise in the modern State, particularly in underdeveloped countries. The utilitarian ideal of ensuring the greatest good of the greatest number prevails, and since the common man signifies the greatest number it is in his interests largely that the national economy should be shaped.

Nehru's economic ideas were assuming a definite socialist pattern, and in his own mind he was now convinced that *swaraj* must be redefined in terms of the masses, giving to the purely political concept of freedom a social and economic content. That was the objective. Political independence was only a means to this end, but the political goal should also be defined. Nehru favoured complete independence.

These social and economic ideals, he felt, could be equated with Gandhism. They could be implemented through the Congress. True, as he reflected later, "ideologically he [Gandhi] was sometimes amazingly backward. . . . Yet in action he had been the greatest revolutionary of recent times in India." Gandhi's conception of democracy was metaphysical. He interpreted democracy not in terms of numbers or majority or representation but in terms of service or sacrifice. Whether he was a democrat or not in the conventional sense, he did represent the peasant masses of India. He was the quintessence of the conscious and subconscious will of those millions, Nehru affirmed. The Mahatma was "the beloved slave-driver."

At this period Nehru had read neither Marx nor Marxist literature carefully. He was to do this only in the early 1930's, when he spent much time in jail. The first Soviet Five-Year Plan was two years away. Trotsky was to be expelled from the Communist party in November, 1927, about the time Nehru with his father visited Moscow.

The Soviet Five-Year plans, beginning in 1929, later set Nehru's mind thinking along the lines of planned economy. Yet even then, stimulated though he was by their mammoth undertakings, made possible largely by American technical aid, he recoiled at the idea of transporting such ideas and projects in their entirety to Indian soil. It was absurd, he argued, to copy blindly what had taken place in Russia, for its application depended on the particular conditions prevailing in the country concerned and the stage of its historical development. India could learn equally from Russia's achievements and mistakes. It could, for instance, advance more cautiously. Here Nehru quotes Lloyd George approvingly—"There is no greater mistake than to leap the abyss in two jumps."

Nehru's interest in Soviet Russia stemmed from Kerensky's abortive attempt which signalised the prelude to the Bolshevik revolution.

"I had not read anything about Marxism then," Jawaharlal recalled much later. "But my sympathies were very much with Lenin and the others."

Two things in the Russian upsurge particularly fired his mind. He began to think much more of politics in terms of social change, and he was stirred also by reports of progress in the Asian regions north of Afghanistan, in the lyrically named States of Uzbekistan, Samarkand and Bokhara. But there was little of detailed news.

Nehru was, of course, more immediately and intensely occupied in India's own political struggle. The strategy to be pursued in India was conditioned by the country's circumstances, and Gandhi, he felt, was himself "a tremendous conditioning factor." But the idea of planning on a nationwide scale which Soviet Russia typified intrigued him.

As he remarked some years later, "The Soviet experiment didn't come in the way. On the contrary, it helped our thinking."

The Brussels conference, while it enabled him to watch the inner conflicts of the Western Labour world, also helped him to understand some of the problems of colonial and dependent countries. He saw that subjection was a state by no means peculiar to India, but belonging to a broader context. Just as capitalism provided its own grave-diggers, so its spawn, imperialism, nurtured within itself the seeds of conflict and decay, and both systems had their roots in global trends which affected East and West, the white and coloured, the privileged and dispossessed. Colonialism and capitalism were two faces of the same coin, capitalism, with its hankering after cheap labour and cheap raw materials, leading ultimately to colonialism. So at least Marx had taught.

Nehru's antipathy to capitalism, particularly in its uncontrolled form, springs from this ideological association of it with colonialism. In his mind capitalism is the head and fount of the vicious sin of colonialism. While admitting that both Communism and Fascism exalt the State and extinguish the individual, he is especially critical of Fascism as being the logical product of aggressive capitalism. He explains in a letter to his daughter:

Fascism thus appears when the class conflicts between an advancing socialism and an entrenched capitalism become bitter and critical. . . . So long as capitalism can use the machinery of democratic institutions to hold power and keep down labour, democracy is allowed to flourish. When this is not possible, then capitalism discards democracy and adopts the open Fascist method of violence and terror.

Nehru was influenced by the Marxist attitude to capitalism and colonialism but was by no means prepared to swallow it whole. The Congress movement for independence, he argued, was not a labour or proletarian movement but essentially a bourgeois movement more interested in political independence than in any change in the social order. Yet the dynamics of Gandhism had charged it with a revolutionary purpose, and until the nationalist urge gave place to a socio-economic plan its utility was not exhausted. Nehru felt that the time had come to give it that direction and stimulus.

On the purely anti-colonial plane the Brussels conference mobilised a new organisation, the League Against Imperialism. Among its patrons were Einstein, Madame Sun Yat-sen and Romain Rolland, although Einstein was to resign from it soon after in protest against its anti-Zionist views. Nehru was also a member, and notes that it appeared to work in close liaison with the Communists. He recalls, more with amusement than anger, that he was expelled from this body in 1931, without being called upon for an explanation, because of his approval of Gandhi's truce with the Government of Lord Halifax, then Lord Irwin, Viceroy of India.

Many Indian revolutionaries, exiled from their homeland for their political views and activities, resided in Europe during the interval between the two world wars.

Nehru took time to see some of them. While always happy to meet his countrymen abroad, he was disappointed by the intellectual calibre of these exiles. Not a few of them appeared to be no more than amiable eccentrics. The aged Shyamaji Krishnavarma who, although well off, lived with his wife in a musty dust-laden attic in Geneva was one of them. He had become something of a psychopath, was suspicious of strangers, and apt to regard most Indians who approached him as British spies—a melancholy relic of a past to which he clung pathetically.

Another revolutionary was Raja Mahendra Pratap, whose wanderings had taken him over the Far East and Central Asia, to Japan, China, Tibet and Afghanistan. He called to see Nehru garbed in an extraordinary composite costume, part military, embellished with high Russian boots, his jacket and trousers containing a complicated layer of pockets bristling with letters, papers, pictures, postcards and all manner of miscellaneous oddments.

"Long ago," he told Nehru solemnly, "I lost a valuable despatch box in China. Since then I have preferred to carry all my papers on my person."

Another exile whom Nehru met was Moulvi Obeidulla, who had spent a large part of his time in Turkey, and had worked out a scheme for a United States of India which he now propounded. It was an ingenious plan—on paper. There was also an Indian woman revolutionary, a Parsi known as Madame Cama, who resided in Paris and might have stepped out of the pages of the French Revolution. She was a gaunt haggard woman with blazing eyes, and in meeting her Nehru was a little taken aback when she strode towards him and peered fiercely into his face. At that time she was stone deaf and had a disconcerting habit of asking questions without waiting for replies. The replies, in any case, made no difference to her opinions, which were settled and well defined over the years.

In Berlin, Nehru came across Barkatulla, an ancient but still vivacious agitator anxious to stumble with the times. Of a nomadic disposition, he left for San Francisco while Nehru was in Europe, and died there very shortly after.

Berlin had a small colony of Indian revolutionaries who were a legacy of the First World War. They were a family divided among themselves, riven by schisms and suspicions, and some of them had abandoned their revolutionary activities for respectable, even sedate occupations. A few still kept the flag of revolution flying.

Among them were Virendranath Chattopadhyaya, a brother of the celebrated poetess and politician Sarojini Naidu, and Champakraman Pillai, one of the very few Indians who later worked with the Nazis. Pillai was an ardent nationalist obsessed only with achieving independence for his country, and quite undisturbed by the social or economic implications of freedom. He died in the mid–1930's in Berlin.

Of an altogether different genre was Virendranath Chattopadhyaya, who for many years had lived a hand-to-mouth existence abroad. He was able and charming, a delightful companion more often than not dressed in tattered clothes but never embittered, a truly beloved vagabond. "Chatto," as he was popularly known, died in extreme poverty in Moscow during the Second World War, friendless and alone.

Two visitors from America, one an Indian, the other an American, were also close to the Nehru household. The American was Roger Baldwin of the Civil Liberties Union of New York, whose liberal mind and idealism attracted Nehru. Dhan Gopal Mukerji, author of the much discussed *My Brother's Face* and writer of some delightful books for children, was the Indian. Although not a political exile, he had made his home in the United States. He, too, like Toller, was to die by his own hand.

Until Motilal arrived Nehru spent much of his time sight-seeing and skiing when Kamala's health permitted him to leave her. He had done some ice skating in his youth and, characteristically, he entered into the new sport enthusiastically and with thoroughness. It gave him, as mountaineering did, a sense of physical exhilaration and excitement.

One of his expeditions on the Col de Voza nearly ended in disaster. With a couple of companions Nehru was engaged in sliding down a slope when, on one of their tobogganing efforts, an over-enthusiastic companion pushed him before he was prepared, and Nehru found himself hurtling down a slope with a sheer precipice not far ahead. Luckily he was able to swerve to one side, landed on a rocky bed and escaped with a few scratches.

It was the third occasion on which Jawaharlal had escaped death in the open. Seventeen years earlier, as a student in Europe, Nehru was mountaineering in Norway with a British companion when they decided to bathe under a roaring torrent descending from a glacier. The stream was not deep, but on entering it Nehru found the water freezing and the bed of the stream extremely slippery. His limbs were numbed, and he slipped and fell, found himself unable to regain his foothold, and was swept rapidly along by the torrent. Luckily his companion managed to clamber out and, running along the bank, seized one of Nehru's legs and dragged him out. Later they discovered that the torrent tumbled over a sheer precipice some two hundred yards further.

The second incident occurred shortly after Nehru's marriage when he was holidaying in Kashmir in the Zoji-la pass. With a few companions, and accompanied by a local shepherd who served as a guide, Nehru was making his way to the cave of Amarnath some eight miles away. They crossed and climbed several glaciers, and after almost twelve hours' continuous trekking saw a huge ice-field burst into view. Across, on the other side, lay the cave. Negotiating the ice-field was a tricky business, for there were many crevasses, and deceptive fresh snow lay across their trail. Nehru stepped onto a snow patch which gave way under him and he found himself hurtling down a yawning crevasse. But the rope held and he was pulled out, shaken but safe.

Not long after his arrival in Europe a general strike precipitated by the coal miners broke out in Britain. Nehru followed its course interestedly, and in visiting England some months later he went for a brief period to a mining area in Derbyshire. The pinched, haggard faces of the miners, particularly of their wives and children, stirred him deeply. He was also moved to anger by the spectacle of the miners being tried and sentenced for trivial offences under the emergency regulations by magistrates who were often directors and managers of the coal mines. He thought this a travesty of justice, particularly British justice, which legitimately prided itself on its equity and impartiality.

While Nehru and his father were in Berlin during the fall of 1924, an invitation reached them requesting them to visit Moscow for the tenth anniversary celebrations of the Soviet Republic in November. The invitation came from the Soviet Society for Cultural Relations with Foreign Countries. Jawaharlal was eager to go, but Motilal was less enthusiastic. What was the point, he argued, in going all the way to Moscow when they had only a week to spare for the trip.

But Jawaharlal's persistence prevailed. With Kamala and Krishna the two Nehrus travelled by train from Berlin across the desolate waste of Poland, reaching the Russian frontier at Niegeroloje on the night of November 7th, some twenty-eight hours after leaving the German capital. The journey had been tedious, and Motilal was not in the best of tempers.

At the frontier station the Indian guests were accorded a reception by the railway staff and other officials. Although they had had their dinner, food was pressed on them. They conversed haltingly with their hosts through an interpreter whose French was more enthusiastic than accurate. They were shown around the station gay with flags and pictures of Lenin and were exposed to their first experience of Lenin worship.

Motilal watched the gush of adulation wryly.

"Just like the visit of a Congress deputation to a village in India," he remarked.

They clambered into a Russian train, occupying special sleeping cars, and arrived at Moscow the following afternoon. Among those waiting on the platform to receive them was Shapurji Saklatvala, a scion of the House of Tata, and a Communist member of the British House of Commons.

The Grand Hotel de Moscow where they stayed was a drab caravanserai despite lingering evidences of former grandeur and luxury. Moscow's streets were full, owing probably to the anniversary celebrations, and Nehru noted that near the Kremlin was an ancient chapel dedicated to the Virgin Mary which many people, mostly women, entered. On a wall adjoining the chapel was Marx's saying, "Religion is the opium of the masses."

Here was a city both Eastern and Western. Its streets were crowded with many Asian races, and Nehru felt the fascination of "this strange Eurasian country" of the hammer and sickle. "In Moscow," he wrote, "Asia peeps out from every corner, not tropical Asia but the Asia of the wide steppes and the cold regions of the north and east and centre. It has heavy boots on and every variety of long coat and hat."

They stayed in Moscow for four days observing closely the unusual tenor and tempo of the life around them. They visited the opera and were enthralled by the beauty of the ballet, and intrigued by the audience of workaday people in casual attire, without coats and in their shirt-sleeves. The Museum of the Revolution, which seemed shoddy, disappointed them.

Nehru was amused by the droshky, which he describes as a primitive conveyance, a kind of four-wheeled rickshaw drawn by a horse. "Why anyone should use this ancient mode of locomotion it was difficult to imagine," he pronounced. Momentarily he had forgotten India's bullock cart.

Both the Nehrus called on Kalinin, then President of the Soviet Union, and found that he lived in two or three simply furnished rooms with no evidence of luxury or ostentation. The Foreign Minister, Chicherin, proved more elusive. Motilal, who was impressed by the Russian's reputation as a remarkably clear-headed man with great linguistic talent, was eager to meet him but was irritated when a Foreign Office official informed him that the interview was fixed for four o'clock the next morning. Chicherin apparently worked throughout the night.

"And what am I supposed to do awake until four o'clock?" Motilal inquired peevishly.

The official compromised by fixing the interview at 1:00 A.M.

They visited Lenin's tomb in the Red Square under the shadow of the Kremlin. In life, Nehru remarks, Lenin was physically not over-attractive and about him was the smell of the Russian soil. But in death he felt there was a strange beauty in Lenin's countenance, and his brow was peaceful and unclouded. "On his lips," Nehru writes, "there hovers a smile and there is a suggestion of pugnacity, of work done and success achieved. He has a uniform on and one of his hands is tightly clenched. Even in death he is the dictator."

Motilal found it difficult to adjust his mind to the strange structure and workings of the Soviet State. The collectivist idea was foreign and especially repugnant to his upbringing. If he shared his son's enthusiasm for some aspects of Soviet progress, he recoiled at its regimentation.

Jawaharlal's own assessment of Soviet achievements was by no means uncritical, but he was impressed by the attitude and effort which the new rulers brought to bear on most problems. Going around a prison on the outskirts of Moscow, he is careful to qualify his generally favourable verdict by the proviso that their hosts were displaying to them only the brighter side of jail life and that outside Moscow such model institutions were probably more the exception than the rule. None the less the actual improvements they were shown were radical and a welcome departure from the dehumanising methods of old. Moreover, the mentality of the prison officials seemed neither sadistic nor punitive. The warders were unarmed, and only two men at the principal entrance had bayonets. The prison was a central jail for serious offenders who included some political prisoners guilty of high treason and whose sentences of death had been commuted to ten years.

"The idea underlying our prison system," explained the governor, "is not to punish or to make an example of the offender but to separate him from society and improve him by making him work in a disciplined manner."

This seemed to Jawaharlal, not unmindful of Soviet ruthlessness on the political plane, an eminently civilised attitude.

Conscious of growing Hindu-Muslim strife in India, he was particularly interested in the Soviet treatment of minorities. Russia was a country with numerous national minorities, different languages and cultures, with primary instruction given in sixty-two different languages and books and newspapers published in fifty-two languages. The progress registered over the past five years had by no means ensured complete equality, but compared to what the British had done in India over 150 years it was certainly encouraging and impressive. Perhaps, reflected Nehru, the British do not want the minorities problem to be solved.

It is interesting to see how Nehru applies the yardstick of Indo-British relations in his assessment of Soviet achievements. His views at this period derive much from the ugly fact of British overlordship in India. Thus in trying to work out the future relations of India and Russia, he complains of "the rigidity of the British Government that seeks to encircle and strangle Russia." The Russians, he felt, were eager to avoid war but determined not to be caught unprepared in the event of hostilities. "She [Russia] will not easily forgo the freedom she has achieved at the cost of tremendous effort and sacrifice," was Nehru's verdict in 1927. Even so, he is careful to point out that Russia as such has never known democracy. In 1917 she jumped from one form of autocracy, Tsarism, to another form of autocracy, Communism.

In view of Nehru's present policy of non-alignment with the power blocs, his attitude to the same issue as far back as 1927 acquires particular significance. He felt there was no economic motive for Russia to covet India because their economies, largely agricultural, were similar, not complementary, and the cry of Russian expansion he dubs a British-created bogey dating back to Tsarist days. "The continued friction that we see today," he writes, "is between England and Russia, not between India and Russia. Is there any reason why we in India should inherit the agelong rivalry of England against Russia?"

Significantly again, Nehru accepts the verdict of a British political commentator on Anglo-French plans to encircle Russia. According to this commentator, the growth of the League of Nations and the spirit of the Locarno Pact were expressions of a desire to combat Bolshevism. "We must make it clear," concludes Nehru, "that we shall not permit ourselves to be used as pawns in England's imperial game, to be moved hither and thither for her benefit." Although the principals and positions have somewhat altered, the hangover from those distant days persists.

The Indian political situation had seen no great change in the twenty-one months of Nehru's stay abroad. If anything, the reactionary forces, with mounting Hindu-Muslim tension, had gathered strength in India. The triennial elections to the Central Legislative Assembly and the Provincial Councils took place in November, 1926, and saw the emergence of a new party, the so-called Nationalist party, led by the communally militant-minded Lala Lajpat Rai and Pandit Madan Mohan Malaviya. One result of this was to weaken the truly national groups like Motilal's Swarajist party, which lost substantially to the new organisation.

The Hindu Mahasabhites on the one hand and the Muslim Leaguers on the other grew daily more vociferous. Many Muslims started drifting away from national to purely communal parties, while some Hindus moved from the Congress to the Hindu Mahasabha and the newly formed Nationalist party. Nehru, sick at heart, was not greatly interested in elections or electoral manœuvres. He recalled with some relish an American socialist's definition of politics as "the gentle art of getting votes from the poor and campaign funds from the rich by promising to protect each from the other." Now it was even worse, for Hindu and Muslim communalists each posed as protectors of their respective communities against the other.

In December, 1926, the whole of India was horrified at the murder of Swami Shraddhanand by a Muslim fanatic. Shraddhanand, who had played a magnificently inspiring role in the first days of non-cooperation in Delhi, was a magnetic personality, tall and erect, his giant frame always garbed in the orange robes of a *sanyasi*. Nehru, hearing the news, was both horrified and depressed. He remembered how seven years before in Delhi's ancient Street of Silver, known as Chandni Chowk, Shraddhanand—confronted by the drawn bayonets of a Gurkha platoon—had bared his great chest and invited them to kill him.

Gandhi meanwhile was touring the country content to feel its pulse until the moment was ripe for action. For the time being he was engaged in propagating the cult of *khadi* and preaching his message of anti-untouchability.

At this juncture Mr. Stanley Baldwin's Conservative Government announced the appointment of an all-British commission headed by Sir John Simon (later Lord Simon) to inquire into the working of the Indian Government and to propose further constitutional reforms, if necessary. The exclusion of Indians from this body, in a matter which affected them most intimately, infuriated public opinion in India and had two immediate consequences deleterious to the British Raj. It healed, albeit temporarily, the breach between the Congress and the Moderates and to some extent between Hindus and Muslims. Both the Congress and the Muslim League denounced the commission as a body deliberately packed with Britons for the purpose of sabotaging India's political advance. The Liberals and other moderate groups echoed this condemnation and called for a boycott of the commission. Secondly, the announcement had the effect of injecting new life into the body politic and of galvanising the country into activity again.

Why, when India's political life was seemingly at an ebb, did a Conservative Government choose to rear a new Frankenstein monster? The blame must rest with the then British Secretary of State for India, Lord Birkenhead, who mistakenly calculated that the appointment of the commission would prove an apple of discord and further dissipate and weaken the Swarajists. Additionally, a general election, with the possibility of Labour being returned to office, was not far off, and Lord Birkenhead felt he could not risk leaving the nomination of the commission's personnel in socialist hands. The Conservatives, he insisted, could not afford to "run the slightest risk that the nomination of the Commission should be in the hands of our successors." Some two years earlier, in a letter to Lord Reading, then Viceroy of India, Lord Birkenhead sought the Viceroy's advice "if at any time you discern an opportunity for making this [a commission] a useful bargaining counter or for further disintegrating the Swarajists." It was clear on what lines Birkenhead's mind was moving.

The commission was announced on November 8, 1927, Nehru learning of it for the first time from a newspaper he read in Moscow. Sir John Simon, an eminent lawyer, was well known to Motilal, and by a curious coincidence the two men were at that very time jointly briefed in an Indian appeal before the Privy Council [1] in London.

Not long after their Moscow visit, the Nehrus arrived in London, where Motilal was soon immersed in legal consultations with Simon. At one such consultation Simon invited Jawaharlal to accompany his father and, although not interested in the case, Nehru acceded to the invitation. While politically divided, their relations were personally cordial.

It was time, Nehru felt, to return to India. The annual Congress session was scheduled to be held in Madras in Christmas week, and India was simmering again. He himself, from his eyrie in Europe, had been able to see the picture whole and more clearly. Now he was

[1] Then the highest court of appeal from the judgements of courts in India.

returning with very definite ideas on what independence for India should mean politically, economically and socially.

The coming years were to see Nehru endeavouring to put these ideas into practice. India was to be free within another two decades, but no one discerned this at the time. Behind were many years of struggle. Ahead lay toil, tragedy, tears—and triumph.

9

FERMENT AND FIRE

Accompanied by his wife, daughter and younger sister, Nehru sailed from Marseilles for India early in December, 1927. They disembarked at Colombo in Ceylon and proceeded from there to Madras, where the Congress was to hold its annual session. A notable absentee at this meeting was Motilal, who had decided to stay on in Europe for another three months.

The Madras session was presided over by a Muslim nationalist, Dr. M. A. Ansari, whose opening speech was distinguished for a striking sentence: "Non-cooperation did not fail us, we failed non-cooperation." Ansari also called upon the Congress to boycott the Simon Commission and to summon a national convention to frame a constitution for India. He stressed the need for unity. The opposition of the Moderates to the Simon Commission was mainly on the score that Indian representatives had no place on it. Congress opposition went deeper. It resented the idea that India should be made the subject of periodical examination on her fitness for self-government; and, having always claimed for the country the right of self-determination, it refused to admit the right of the British Parliament to be the arbiter in this matter.

Nehru, returning from Europe with a vague idea of spending some months in the remote rural areas, found himself plunged almost immediately in the maelstrom of Congress politics. At the Madras Congress he presented a number of resolutions which reflected the new ideas seething in his mind.

One of these defined complete national independence as the goal of the Indian people, and to his embarrassed surprise this found almost unanimous support, even the veteran Irish theosophist Annie Besant lending it her imprimatur. Gandhi, who attended the open session of the Congress, took no public part in the proceedings; but it was obvious that the resolution was not to his liking, and later he delivered an oblique if characteristic broadside at it and some other resolutions, notably one urging the boycott of British goods.

Gandhi wrote:

The Congress stultifies itself by repeating year after year resolutions of this character when it knows it is not capable of carrying them into effect. By passing such resolutions we make an exhibition of our impotence, become the laughing stock of critics and involve the contempt of our adversary. The Congress cannot become the irresistible force it was and is intended to be, if its resolutions are ill conceived and are to remain paper resolutions. We have almost sunk to the level of a schoolboys' debating society.

Gandhi's rebuke, as Nehru quickly discovered, was justified. The same session which confirmed his independence resolution passed soon after another resolution boycotting the Simon Commission and suggesting the convening of an All-Parties conference which would include the Moderates whose political goal was Dominion status. In all probability the majority of Congressmen were not really interested in Nehru's proposals but felt that they must humour him by approving of his "harmless academic suggestions."

Equally still-born was a republican conference held as a sideshow to the Congress over which Nehru was persuaded to preside. This was its first and last session.

"There is much in the criticism that we are not a persevering lot," Nehru commented philosophically on this debacle.

The juxtaposition of the independence resolution which he sponsored and the republican conference over which he presided is interesting, for some twenty years later, as Prime Minister of an independent India, Jawaharlal was to keep India within the British Commonwealth but as a republic.

Gandhi was troubled by Jawaharlal's impetuousness, and with his uncanny instinct sensed that Nehru was moving away from him. In a letter dated January 4, 1928, he addressed the younger man more in terms of sorrow than of anger:

You are going too fast You should have taken time to think and become acclimatized. Most of the resolutions you framed and got carried could have been delayed for one year. Your plunging into the "republican army" was a hasty step. But I do not mind these acts of yours so much as I mind your encouraging mischief-makers and hooligans. I do not know whether you still believe in an unadulterated non-violence. But even if you have altered your views, you could not think that unlicensed and un-bridled violence is going to deliver the country. If after careful observation of the country in the light of your European experiences you are convinced of the error of the current ways and means, by all means enforce your own views, but do please form a disciplined party. . . . If I can advise you, now that you are the working secretary of the Indian National Congress, it is your duty to devote your whole energy to the central resolution, that is, unity, and the important but secondary resolution, that is, boycott of the Simon Commission. The unity resolution requires the use of all your great gifts of organization and persuasion.

About a fortnight later, in another letter, dated January 17th, the Mahatma repeats the rebuke:

The differences between you and me appear to be so vast and so radical that there seems to be no meeting ground between us. I cannot conceal from you my grief that I should lose a comrade so valiant, so faithful, so able and so honest, as you have always been; but in serving a cause, comradeships have got to be sacrificed. The cause must be held superior to all such considerations. But this dissolution of comradeship—if dissolution must come—in no way affects our personal intimacy. We have long become members of the same family, and we remain such, in spite of grave political differences.

To Gandhi it seemed as if they had come perilously near the parting of the ways. But it was a danger signal, no more. Jawaharlal's larger loyalty to the country and the Congress with which he identified Gandhi found him marching again alongside the Mahatma.

The year 1928 saw the country stirring to new life. To Nehru, who had left a sullenly quiescent India in 1926, the change appeared considerable and comprehensive. It seemed to affect every section of the people, giving to the peasantry, the industrial workers, middle-class youth and the intelligentsia generally the glow of a new impulse and resolve. Nehru felt that India was once more on the march. There was vitality in the people and a resilience which the heaviest repression could never completely crush.

"If I were convinced that the people of India were worthless I would not bother to work for them," Jawaharlal once remarked to a close colleague. "But my country's history tells me that India has been and is a great country. She has undergone vast historical changes and produced many great men."

Now history was in the making again.

Until this time Nehru had not interested himself actively in the trade-union movement, and his knowledge of the condition of industrial workers was meagre and largely academic. Trade unionism was of comparatively recent growth in India, for no real organisation among the industrial workers existed until the end of the First World War.

Towards the close of 1928, shortly before the Calcutta session of the Congress over which Motilal presided, Nehru attended for the first time a meeting of the All-India Trade Union Congress, a body then only eight years old but representative of the majority of organised labour. There had also recently come into being two other unions, both controlled by Communists or near-Communists. These were the Girni Kamgar Union at Bombay, comprising mainly the textile workers, and the Great Indian Peninsula Railway Union, composed of transport workers.

The T.U.C. met at Jharia in the heart of the coal-belt area of Bihar. Listening to the proceedings, Nehru sensed the same trends and divisions which characterised the political world. Here also was the old tussle between the reformists and revolutionaries, between the conservative elements and radicals. Nehru's heart was with the radicals but his mind counselled caution, and wisely he refrained from taking sides.

He was therefore not a little surprised when on returning to Calcutta he learned that in his absence he had been elected T.U.C. President for the following year. Ironically also, he discovered that he had been put up by the Moderates against a working-class candidate sponsored by the radicals. Discretion had yielded dividends, but Nehru was furious. He thought it "positively indecent" that a newcomer and a non-worker should be suddenly thrust into such eminence in the labour world. It reflected, he felt, the infancy and weakness of the trade-union movement in India. Nevertheless he decided to accept the nomination.

The peasantry was also astir. Touring the province of Orissa late in 1927, Gandhi had come upon rural ryots cowed by the intimidation of the *zamindars,* or landlords, who were supported in their oppression by the local police and administration. Gandhi called upon the peasants to shed their fear.

"Fear," he told them, "is worse than disease. The man who fears man falls from the estate of man. Fear God alone."

Gandhi, remarking on "the death-like quiet" of the Orissa country-side, characterised the peace of the British administration as "the peace of the grave."

But by 1928 the peasantry were no longer quiescent. Ground down by taxes and imposts, and harassed by the demands of the landlords' agents, they became increasingly restive, particularly in the United Provinces and in Gandhi's own district of Gujerat in western India where the small peasant proprietors of Bardoli rose in protest against the Government's enhanced tax assessments.

There came into the political picture at this juncture a man who was to leave a deep impress on the nationalist movement, and who with Gandhi and Nehru was to play a decisive role before and after independence. His name was Vallabhbhai Patel.

Patel, whose brother Viththalbhai was President of the Central Assembly, came, as Gandhi did, from Gujerat. A lawyer by training and at one time a noted "blood" in Ahmedabad [1] society who had scoffed at "the vapourings" of Gandhi, Patel soon shed his briefs, chips and cards to follow the Mahatma. Like Jawaharlal and his father, he was attracted by Gandhi's insistence on action in resisting a wrong. He had been impressed by the Mahatma's championship of the cause of the Champaran peasants against the indigo planters, and shortly after this he became Gandhi's principal lieutenant when the Mahatma launched a similar campaign on behalf of the peasants of Kheda in Gujerat.

Patel was nearing fifty-four at this time—a solidly built man with a large bald craggy skull and a face that might have been carved from granite. His countenance was strong and sombre. He was as he looked —rock-like, hard, immovable, unflinching. Six years had gone by since Patel had thrown up his lucrative practice at the Ahmedabad Bar and joined the Mahatma. He was a superb organiser with a genius for getting things done.

Like Gandhi, Patel had something of the earthiness of the peasant,

[1] Ahmedabad is the chief city of Gujerat.

and his roots were in the soil. He spoke in the racy idiom of peasant India. The protest of the Bardoli peasants who were landholders was directed mainly at the Bombay Government's arbitrary enhancement of the land tax by 22 per cent, on data which the peasant proprietors claimed was grossly inaccurate. Patel called upon the landholders to refuse payment of the revised assessment and urged the Government to appoint an impartial tribunal to investigate their grievances. He mobilised some 250 volunteers to help him and organised the peasants in sixteen camps.

The Government initially struck hard, arresting the volunteers, seizing the peasants' lands and auctioning them at fantastically low prices.

"Don't worry," Patel advised the peasants. "Let the Government take your land to England—if they can."

The peasants obeyed him to a man and christened him Sardar, which means Leader, a title by which Patel was to be known to the end of his life.

In the face of this unyielding but non-violent movement the Government was at last compelled to give way. An inquiry was ordered, and the rise in assessment was reduced from 22 per cent to 5.7 per cent.

Bardoli, as Nehru noted, became a sign and a symbol of hope and strength and victory to the Indian peasant.

Enthusiasm had also infected the country's youth, and Jawaharlal followed keenly the proceedings of youth leagues and youth conferences meeting in different parts of the country. They varied in character, some being almost semi-religious in complexion, while others revelled in discussing revolutionary ideology and technique. There was interest, not always informed, in the first Soviet Five-Year Plan. Above all, the Simon Commission provided a focus for organised opposition and crystallised, as it were, the country's latent passion and pride. The newly formed youth leagues took a prominent part in the boycott of the commission. Nehru was in great demand as a speaker on their platforms and in their forums, as was also Subhas Bose, who in the Second World War was to invoke the aid of the Germans and Japanese for freeing his country. Bose, bespectacled and cherubic, was then thirty.

India vibrated with suppressed energy. There was thunder in the air.

On the political plane, the arrival of the Simon Commission in Bombay on February 3, 1928, was the signal for hostile demonstrations which pursued that unfortunate body wherever it went. Black flags greeted its appearance in cities and towns, while the cry of "Simon, go back," reverberated in its wake. There was police firing in Bombay and Madras, scuffles and *lathi* [2] charges, notably in Lahore, where the sixty-four-year-old Lala Lajpat Rai, who was heading a procession of demonstrators, was beaten on his chest and shoulders by a British officer with a baton. Lajpat Rai died nine days later, and his death loosed a wave of bitter anger and resentment throughout the country. The demonstrators he was leading had indulged in no violence, and Lajpat Rai himself was standing quietly by the roadside when he was attacked.

Indian sensitiveness, as Nehru bitterly remarked, had not then been blunted by repeated police brutality. "To find," he wrote, "that even the greatest of our leaders, the foremost and most popular man in the Punjab, could be so treated seemed little short of monstrous, and a dull anger spread all over the country, especially in north India. How helpless we were, how despicable, when we could not even protect the honour of our chosen leaders."

Nehru himself was shortly to feel the weight of the baton and lathi blows of the police. This happened at Lucknow, where he had gone to organise the demonstrations against the commission. It had been decided, following a police ban on processions, that the demonstrators should converge in batches of sixteen on the scheduled meeting place. Nehru was leading one such batch when he heard the clatter of horses' hoofs behind him and, turning, saw a posse of mounted police, about three dozen strong, bearing down upon them.

The impact of the horses broke up the column of sixteen, some of whom sought refuge on the sidewalks, where they were pursued by the mounted police and beaten down. Nehru, after a preliminary moment of hesitation, decided to hold his ground. He found himself alone in the middle of the road. Although momentarily tempted to make himself less conspicuous, he stayed firm only to find a mounted policeman with a long baton charging towards him. Nehru received two resounding blows on his back.

"The bodily pain I felt," he wrote later, "was quite forgotten in a

[2] A bamboo stick wielded by the police.

feeling of exhilaration that I was physically strong enough to face and bear lathi blows. And a thing that surprised me was that right through the incident, even when I was being beaten, my mind was quite clear and I was consciously analysing my feelings."

A sterner ordeal awaited him and his companions the next day when the commission reached Lucknow. Far from cowing the people, the incidents of the previous day had the effect of stirring them to even more vigorous protest, and when the various groups joined the main procession on the following day the demonstrators numbered several thousands. The authorities meanwhile had thrown a strong cordon of foot and mounted police as well as the military around the railway station where the commission was expected. These forces barred the way of the demonstrators, who, however, were content to line up on one side of a huge open space and shout their slogans.

Suddenly Nehru and his companions perceived in the far distance a moving mass which soon revealed itself as mounted police. These came charging towards the processionists, belabouring on the way such stragglers as were moving in the no man's land between the police and the demonstrators. As batons and lathis descended on the Congress volunteers, the open space before the processionists soon had the appearance of a battlefield dotted with writhing figures nursing bruised and broken limbs and heads.

Meanwhile, the mounted police continued their charge on the main mass of demonstrators, who, following the example of Nehru and his immediate companions, held their ground. The horses, pulled to a sudden stop before the front line of the processionists, reared up on their hind legs, their front hoofs quivering in the air over the heads of the nearest demonstrators.

There followed a wild melee as the foot and mounted police wielded their batons and lathis. Nehru, half blinded and stunned by blows, was at one moment filled with an intense desire to hit back. "But long training and discipline held, and I did not raise a hand except to protect my face from a blow. Besides, I knew well enough that any aggression on our part would result in a ghastly tragedy, the firing and shooting down of large numbers of our men."

Writing of this experience many years later, Nehru recalled how the faces of the policemen, especially of the British officers who did most of the real beating and battering, were distorted with hate and fury. Probably, he reflects, the faces of the demonstrators also were charged with anger and hate. And he asks himself to what end all this would lead.

One immediate reaction, in the absence of an organised mass movement by the Congress, was a recrudescence of terrorism and violence. Among the first to be shot down and killed in Lahore was a young British police officer by the name of Saunders who was alleged to have hit Lala Lajpat Rai the fatal blows which shortly after led to the Punjab leader's death. On April 8, 1928, two crude bombs which did little damage and caused no fatalities were thrown from the visitors' gallery on to the Government front bench in the Central Assembly. Simon was at the time seated in the President's gallery. Two young men, Bhagat Singh from the Punjab and Batukeshwara Dutt from Bengal, who was then domiciled in Kanpur in the United Provinces, were arrested for this act, and on June 12th both were sentenced to transportation for life after a trial held in Delhi. Bhagat Singh, a nephew of Sardar Ajit Singh, a revolutionary who had been deported from India by the British Government in 1907, was a remarkable personality, an avowed terrorist, audaciously brave, with the attractive intellectual face of many agitators and an unusually gentle manner of speech. He was to be tried later in the so-called Lahore Conspiracy Case for the murder of Saunders, sentenced to death and executed early in 1931.

Bengal and the United Provinces were also the scenes of terrorist activity. To counter this wave of violence the Government launched a number of conspiracy cases and issued various ordinances empowering the authorities to arrest and detain suspects without trial. In Bengal the jails were being rapidly filled with political prisoners. But the spirit of violence was very much abroad, and not until Gandhi canalised the awakened mass fervour into non-violent channels by launching his civil-disobedience movement in March, 1930, did terrorism abate. Indeed, it reached its climax about the time when the movement was beginning, a number of terrorists carrying out a daring and spectacular raid on the armoury at Chittagong in Bengal.

Labour was growing restive. There were strikes in the Bengal Jute Mills, on the East Indian Railways, in the Tata Iron and Steel Works at Jamshedpur in Bihar, and among Calcutta's scavengers and municipal workers. Bombay's textile mills were paralysed for nearly six months when over 100,000 millhands, "miserable and militant," in Nehru's phrase, struck work in protest against retrenchment and a threatened reduction in wages. The economic depression was only just around the corner.

Alarmed by this aggressive turn of events, the Government struck at labour. On March 20, 1929, it arrested thirty-two of the more prominent leftist labour leaders, belonging principally to the Communist-dominated Girni Kamgar Union of Bombay and to some of the advanced groups in Bengal, the United Provinces and the Punjab. Thus began the celebrated Meerut [3] trial which was to conclude only in a storm of controversy four and a half years later.

Nehru, as President-elect of the Trade Union Congress, was naturally concerned with these developments. He organised a defence committee which was headed by his father and which included the Congress President, Dr. Ansari, and himself, but he found it difficult to collect money or to secure the professional services of lawyers, except his father and a few others, free of charge. Never having entertained a high opinion of the generosity of his legal colleagues— "men of my own profession," as he terms them—he was not surprised; nevertheless he was filled with chagrin at their "cupidity." Patriotism, he felt, should override pelf. He at least had no use for any Dodson and Fogg. His difficulties were partly solved by the fact that by 1930 the majority of the defence committee, including himself, found themselves in turn in jail!

At the Madras session of the Congress, Nehru was again persuaded —this time by his old friend Dr. Ansari—to take up the Congress secretaryship. Since the open session of the Congress had also passed his other two resolutions—one on the need for association with the League Against Imperialism and the other on the danger of a global war—he felt the pull of an added obligation.

The Madras Congress had authorised its executive committee, known as the Working Committee, to draw up a *swaraj* constitution in consultation with other parties, including the Moderates. This inevitably meant a Dominion-status constitution—at that time anath-

[3] A town in the United Provinces where the trial was staged.

ema in the eyes of Nehru. Moreover, since the conference also included communal organisations, the chances of an agreement on the minorities issue were small. So it proved.

Motilal, who had returned from Europe in the spring of 1928, was keenly interested in the All-Parties Conference. Along with many of his countrymen he regarded as a challenge Lord Birkenhead's taunt that he had twice in three years invited his Indian critics to put forward their own suggestions for a constitution but with no response. The conference met first in Bombay in May, when it was decided to appoint a committee headed by Motilal to draft the constitution and to make a full report on the minorities issue. This report was subsequently known as the Nehru report. While not a member of the committee, Jawaharlal was closely associated with its proceedings as secretary of the Congress.

On the communal issue the committee made several concessions to the minorities, although these were not regarded as entirely adequate by the Muslims who were headed by Mohamed Ali Jinnah. It is interesting to note that Jinnah, who was later to be the founder of Pakistan, did not press for separate electorates for the Muslims but accepted the principle of joint or common electorates with some reservations—for example, that residuary powers should vest in the provinces.

As far as the political goal of India was concerned, the committee plumped for Dominion status; but Dominion status was to be the next immediate step, not a remote stage of the country's evolution. Nehru fought this commitment fiercely, insisting that if all the groups could not accept independence as their objective, the Congress at least should do so. But Motilal, who had set his heart on the report as it stood, would not yield. Father and son found themselves at odds again, both being equally adamant in their views.

When the All-Parties Conference met at Lucknow in August to consider the committee's report, Nehru forcefully put forward his view, which was shared by Subhas Bose. But to no purpose. Thereupon the dissidents partly salved their wounded ego by founding the Independence for India League—a heroic but empty gesture.

Another shock awaited Nehru. While realising that the constitution, as devised by the committee, was based on the idea of private property, he was piqued by a clause under Fundamental Rights which guaranteed to the big landholders known as the Oudh [4] taluqdars their vested rights in their estates. Nehru did not appreciate the idea of displaying any tenderness to persons whom he regarded as semifeudal landholders. He offered his resignation as the Congress secretary on the ground that he was one of the founders of the Independence for India League. But the working committee were not impressed. They declined to accept it.

"And again," says Nehru, "I agreed. It was surprising how easy it was to win me over to a withdrawal of my resignation. This happened on many occasions and as neither party really liked the idea of a break, we clung to every pretext to avoid it."

Gandhi had taken no part in the proceedings of the All-Parties Conference or committee. He was not present at Lucknow. But he blessed their efforts in *Young India*, writing with an eye cocked affectionately on Jawaharlal:

If we are sure of the sanction we need not worry if swaraj is spelt dominion status or independence. Dominion status can easily become more than independence if we have the sanction to back it. Independence can easily become a farce if it lacks sanction. What is in a name if we have the reality? A rose smells just as sweet whether you know it by that name or any other. Let us therefore make up our minds whether it is to be non-violence or violence, and let the rank and file work for the sanction in real earnest even as the diplomats must work at constitution-making.

It was a clear call to the country, particularly its youth, to abjure the ways of violence, and some months later the Mahatma was to condemn in the same unequivocal terms the action of Bhagat Singh and Batukeshwara Dutt who threw two bombs into the chamber of the Central Assembly. Gandhi wrote:

The bomb-throwers have discredited the cause of freedom in whose name they threw the bombs. The Government would be foolish if they become nervous and resort to counter-madness. If they are wise, they will see that they are in no small measure to blame for the madness of the bomb-thrower. By their indifference to popular feeling, they are exasperating the nation and the exasperation is bound to lead some astray. Congressmen whose creed is non-violence will do well not to give even secret approval to the deed but pursue their own method with redoubled vigour, if they have faith in it. The bomb has no milieu in India.

Meanwhile, Gandhi was content to preach his message of *khadi*,

[4] A district in the United Provinces.

unity, abolition of untouchability and drink, and the boycott of foreign cloth. He set out on another of his Indian pilgrimages, this time through the southern region of Andhra.

During these two crucial years Nehru also spent many months roving around the country. Soon after the Madras session of the Congress he set out on various tours of the country in the course of which he addressed many meetings of peasants, workers, youths and political followers. During 1928, apart from his other activities, Jawaharlal presided over four provincial Congress conferences—in the Punjab, in Malabar in South India, in Delhi and in the United Provinces. He visited the rural areas in his own province and occasionally explored his new-found interest in the industrial workers by addressing them. In between he presided over a number of youth leagues and students' conferences in Bengal and Bombay.

Nehru was infected by the rumble of latent energy in the country which he felt would soon mount to a roar. Here was good ground for planting the ideas he had formed in his own mind during his visit to Europe. He discovered that his listeners were eagerly receptive. Like him, they were a little tired of politicians who grew magniloquent on the glories of the country's ancient past and who perorated on the sins of the alien rulers and the sacrifices demanded of the people without telling them exactly what they hoped to achieve. These speeches fostered emotion without encouraging thought.

Gandhi had set the mould, but Nehru felt that even within this fixed pattern it was possible to influence content and character. Everywhere he went he spoke on political independence and social freedom, making the former a step towards the attainment of the latter. "I wanted," he confesses, "to spread the ideology of socialism especially among Congress workers and the intelligentsia." This was as far back as 1928. Yet when twenty-six years later as Prime Minister, Nehru reiterated his objective for India as a socialist State there was a lifting of eyebrows in many quarters in and outside the country.

What many people do not realise is that Nehru's ideas on most political, economic and social matters have been fixed and consistent for at least a generation. Circumstances, particularly those created by Gandhi's predominant and pervasive influence, compelled him to zig-zag to his target. But in his mind the objectives were clear. Only the course towards them was impelled by existing conditions.

How often during these years must Nehru have recalled his favourite lines from Swinburne: "Grief a fixed star, and joy a vane that veers / These many years."

He was not a pioneer in socialist thought in India, for the progress of the Soviet State and the beginning of the first Five-Year Plan in Russia in 1927 had already provoked an interest in Marxist theory. What he did was to infuse this thinking with a political purpose by linking it to the nationalist movement inside the country and to international trends and happenings abroad. On the United Provinces Provincial Congress Committee were men like Acharya Narendra Deva and Sampurnanand,[5] whose minds had been moving for some time in a socialist direction. In 1926 this committee even tried to draw up a mild socialist programme for the province which was designed to deal with local agrarian problems. In 1929 it went a step further, making a recommendation on definitely socialist lines to the All-India Congress Committee which that body, meeting in Bombay later in the year, accepted so far as the preamble went, thus committing the Congress to the principle of socialism. Consideration of the detailed proposals was postponed to a later date. As with many Nehru-inspired proposals at this period, the All-India Congress Committee merely passed the resolution, "not realising," in Jawaharlal's words, "what they were doing." They were considerably surprised when some five years later they were confronted with a defined socialist programme. This was something novel, they protested.

In December, 1928, the Congress held its annual session in Calcutta with Motilal in the presidential chair. Between father and son the differences over the All-Parties Conference Report had meanwhile grown acute. Jawaharlal was not prepared to compromise on the independence issue, and Motilal, faced by his son's implacable front, was increasingly irritated. Tension in the house grew as tempers rose. But not even Motilal's explosive outbursts could quell his son's ardour.

Kamala, although lapsing into illness again, was firm in her husband's support. Her loyalty touched Jawaharlal, who, with his father, was miserable and unhappy over their differences. Perhaps Nehru recalled the earlier days when as a bride Kamala had watched him debate with Motilal his urge to join the Mahatma. Then too the

[5] Now Chief Minister in Uttar Pradesh, the former United Provinces.

father had exploded in wrath, on one occasion ordering Jawaharlal out of his house. Motilal at the time was ablaze with anger, but Jawaharlal's face was also set. For a crucial few moments the two men had faced each other. Then Jawaharlal felt a small cool hand slipping into his and clasping it firmly. It was Kamala standing by her husband's side, bringing him her comfort and loyalty. The old man, looking at the two, had relented.

Now he was firmly determined that the report he had fathered and fostered should receive the approval of the Congress as it stood. Ultimately the situation was saved by a characteristic compromise. The resolution accepted the All-Parties Report, but intimated that if the British Government did not agree to the Dominion status constitution within a year the Congress would revert to independence.

"It was," as Jawaharlal put it, "an offer of a year's grace and a polite ultimatum."

So they moved into the crucial year of 1929.

10

LAHORE—AND AFTER

"WHAT's the objection to a Nehru?" an acquaintance once asked.

Jawaharlal, puffing at a cigarette, watched the smoke clouds pensively. He smiled.

"We don't quite belong."

In a sense this is true, for although he is *for* the people Nehru is not *of* the people. Between Gandhi and the masses was a mystic communion of thought, even language. Nehru draws inspiration from the crowds; they stimulate him like a drug; but with the people as a whole, masses and classes, he is always a little above, ahead and beyond.

"We don't quite belong." Perhaps never was the wistful recognition of his existence as an individual apart more forcefully apparent than in the formative years of 1928–1929 when he found himself politically estranged both from his father and from Gandhi, and although close to the masses, always separate from and ahead of them.

Nehru was caught in that paradox with the closing of the Calcutta Congress session. He had opposed Gandhi's compromise resolution at the open session, albeit half-heartedly. And yet once again he persuaded himself to be identified with the Congress organisation as its general secretary.

"In the Congress sphere I seemed to act the part of the famous Vicar of Bray," he remembered.

Gandhi was annoyed by the persistence of Jawaharlal and Subhas Bose in opposing his compromise resolution, to which he assumed they were a party.

"You may take the name of independence on your lips," he declared at Calcutta, "as the Muslims utter the name of Allah or the pious Hindus utter the name of Krishna or Rama, but all that muttering will be an empty formula if there is no honour behind it. If you are not prepared to stand by your words, where will independence be? Independence is a thing made of sterner stuff. It is not made by the juggling of words. . . . If you want the Nehru report to fructify, the least you can do is to work out this resolution."

Motilal himself was less declamatory. "Both Subhas and Jawaharlal" he remarked good-humouredly in his closing speech, "have told you in their speeches that in their opinion we old men are no good, are not strong enough and are much behind the times. There is nothing new in this. It is common in this world that the young always regard aged men as behind the times. I would give you one word of advice. . . . Let us work for *swaraj* by whatever name we might call it. . . . One year is nothing in the history of the nation. I have not the least doubt that the next Congress will see us united and taking another step forward."

For both India and the British, 1929 was to be more than a year of grace. It was to be a year of testing, a year giving a new momentum and direction to the nationalist movement which would radically alter its character. The economic depression was on the horizon, and the next few months would witness the beginning of a global crisis.

In India both industrial labour and the peasantry were restive. Strikes became increasingly frequent. Terrorism had reared its head, and the intelligentsia, particularly the country's youth, followed closely the course of the conspiracy trials in Bengal and the Punjab. Protest against the treatment of political prisoners found a focus in the prolonged hunger strike of a young revolutionary, Jatindranath Das, who died after fasting for sixty-one days. He was hailed as India's MacSwiney, and his death brought mammoth mass demonstrations all over the country. Nehru, who visited him in prison, thought that he looked "soft and gentle like a young girl. He was in considerable pain when I saw him," he adds.

Gandhi was busy touring India. He was absorbed in propagating his cult of *khadi*. In May he came to Bombay for a meeting of the All-India Congress Committee, and outlined his plan for civil resistance should Dominion status not be granted by the end of the year.

He wanted the Congress to register at least 700,000 men and women volunteers on its rolls by August.

In June, Gandhi visited the United Provinces on a tour arranged for him by Jawaharlal. Nehru accompanied him on a part of his itinerary, and marvelled again at the vast masses which gathered to hear the Mahatma. They ranged from 25,000 to over 100,000, and since there were no broadcasting facilities it was obvious that the majority of them were content merely to see the Mahatma.

To Nehru it seemed that the propagation of *khadi* was a comparatively minor activity in the context of the developing political situation. Now, as often before, he found it difficult to understand Gandhi's mental processes and the background of his thought. Why was the Mahatma so preoccupied with non-political activities? Why did he want to glorify poverty, which was a hateful and an ugly thing? Gandhi often used the phrase *Daridranarayan*, which means "the Lord of the Poor" or "God that resides in the Poor." The phrase irritated Nehru. Were the rich and the poor always to be with us? And were the poor always to be regarded as God's chosen people to live eternally their wretched and degrading lives?

On the other hand Jawaharlal noted with pleasure that the legislatures had lost their lure for his father. Motilal, irked by the ineffectualness of parliamentary proceedings, circumscribed as these were in India, was waiting merely for a suitable opportunity to lead the swarajists out. That opportunity came with the Lahore session of the Congress in December, 1929. But before this, Motilal and Jawaharlal were to find themselves at cross-purposes again.

The son's politics were not always to his father's liking. To Motilal a creed like socialism was just another new-fangled idea, capable of providing some mental stimulation to the young, but irrelevant to the political situation as it existed in India. He did not very much mind Jawaharlal chasing these will-o'-the-wisps provided he did not damage himself in the process. Unlike his son, he was willing to compromise on ultimate objectives in order to register immediate practical gains. He was not particularly enamoured of independence as opposed to Dominion status.

As August approached, the provincial Congress committees put in their nominations for the President of the Lahore session of the

Congress. Ten of these committees plumped for Gandhi, while five voted for Vallabhbhai Patel and three for Jawaharlal. Gandhi, however, declined the honour even when pressed to take it by a meeting of the All-India Congress Committee in Lucknow late in September. Instead he put forward Jawaharlal's name, which was accepted. In doing so, Gandhi was probably influenced by the hope that the responsibility of high office would moderate the younger man's exuberance. Moreover, if the Congress were to adopt independence as its objective, who more worthy to usher in the new creed than the person who had steadfastly propagated it?

Jawaharlal was just forty when he assumed the Congress *gadi* (throne). He was not the youngest to occupy this office, Gokhale having achieved it at the same age, while Maulana Abul Kalam Azad was slightly under forty when he attained it.

Happiest and proudest over his election was Motilal. Never before in the history of the Congress had a son succeeded his father to the Presidency. Motilal, in handing over office to his son, must have felt that he was passing on to him his political legacy even as he would his personal estate.

A year earlier at the height of the controversy between father and son, the old man had confided to a colleague, "The one thing I am proudest of is that I am Jawaharlal's father." He had sired a son worthy of his own high exacting standards. Motilal often disagreed with Jawaharlal, and sometimes spoke his mind curtly to him. But woe betide the person who would criticise the son in the father's presence!

Gandhi had consulted Nehru before recommending him for the Presidency.

"Do you feel yourself strong enough to bear the weight?" he had asked him.

"If it is thrust upon me, I hope I shall not wince," was Jawaharlal's reply.

In commending him to the people, Gandhi wrote of him in terms of the highest praise: "He is undoubtedly an extremist thinking far ahead of his surroundings. But he is humble and practical enough not to force the pace to the breaking point. He is pure as crystal. He is truthful beyond suspicion. He is a knight *sans peur, sans reproche*. The nation is safe in his hands."

Gandhi also saw in Jawaharlal's election a challenge to the country's youth. "This appointment of Jawaharlal Nehru as the captain," he wrote, "is proof of the trust the nation reposes in its youth. Jawaharlal alone can do little. The youth of the country must be his arms and his eyes. Let them prove worthy of the trust."

The mounting tempo of events in India disturbed the British authorities in both Whitehall and New Delhi. Almost two years had passed since the appointment of the Simon Commission in the spring of 1927. The commission's two-volume report was to be published in two instalments on June 10 and June 24, 1930. Meanwhile, developments in India had stolen a march on the commission, whose ideas of constitutional progress, when they were finally published, proved woefully out of date. They were condemned to cold storage even before publication by a statement made by Lord Irwin,[1] who had succeeded Lord Reading as the Viceroy in 1926.

Irwin, lean, tall and angular—"that tall, thin Christian," as Mohamed Ali was later to call him—was a man of impressive personality, with gracious ways, deeply religious, and imbued with a humane outlook on life.

"We are in India to keep our tempers," was his first word of counsel to his military secretary.

He was as good as his word, keeping his temper in circumstances which might have tried a smaller man. In Indian eyes Irwin presented a striking contrast to his predecessor, who was notable for his sense of ceremony and excessive legal caution. Irwin was informal and human.

On October 31, 1929, after consultations with the Government at Whitehall and with their approval, Irwin made the following declaration: "I am authorised on behalf of His Majesty's Government to state clearly that in their judgement it is implicit in the declaration of 1917[2] that the natural issue of India's constitutional progress as there contemplated is the attainment of Dominion Status." With this, Irwin coupled an invitation to Indian leaders to meet representatives of the British Government at a round-table conference in London.

Clearly the declaration was made with an eye to the demand of

[1] Later Lord Halifax.
[2] Made by Mr. Edwin Montagu, then Secretary of State for India.

Congress for Dominion status by the end of 1929. It conceded the principle though not the immediate substance of Dominion status, and by inviting Indian leaders to meet British spokesmen it sought to break away from the old tradition which required each stage of Indian development to be investigated and dictated by London.

It did not wholly meet the demand of Congress, but in so far as it signalised a new approach it seemed worthy of consideration. A Leaders' Conference was accordingly summoned at the house of Viththalbhai Patel, President of the Central Assembly, and to it were invited representatives of various groups. Gandhi and Motilal were the principal Congress spokesmen, while Sir Tej Bahadur Sapru, an eminent lawyer who had been Law Member in Lord Reading's Executive Council, headed the Moderates. The joint resolution which emerged from their deliberations was drafted by Gandhi, who incorporated certain modifications suggested by Sapru.

As it finally stood, the joint manifesto accepted the Viceroy's declaration in principle subject to certain vital conditions. These stipulated that all discussions at the proposed Round Table Conference in London should be on the basis of full Dominion status for India, that there should be a predominant representation of Congressmen at the conference and a general amnesty of political prisoners. Additionally, as far as was possible under the existing conditions, the Government of India should from thenceforth be carried on on the lines of a Dominion government.

Nehru was unhappy over the declaration. He felt that to give up the demand for independence, "even in theory and even for a short while," was improper and dangerous because in effect it suggested that the objective of complete independence was a mere bargaining counter capable of being changed and whittled down to extract temporary advantages. Characteristically, he at first refused to sign the manifesto, and characteristically again, he later yielded.

Jawaharlal's reasons for signing the manifesto were rational and did him credit. He knew that the Congress could not afford to split on the eve of what might prove to be a decisive struggle. In any event, the British Government was hardly likely to accept the conditions laid down in the manifesto, and in that case the Moderates would be committed along with the Congress, since they were parties to the manifesto. Later, Nehru was to realise that these conditions—while

vital to the Congress—were regarded as mere bargaining append-
ages by the Moderates. They meant different things to different
people.

Yet his unhappiness over lending his signature to the manifesto
persisted. Subhas Bose, torn by none of the internal conflicts which
obsessed Jawaharlal, had refused to sign it. So had Dr. Kitchlew and
another Muslim leader, Maulana Abdul Bari. Brooding over the
matter, Nehru decided to unburden himself to Gandhi, and accordingly wrote to the Mahatma suggesting that he, Jawaharlal, should
withdraw from the Presidency of the Congress.

Gandhi's reply, dated November 4, 1929, is interesting as a revelation of the technique he invariably employed to soothe Nehru's
qualms and to win him over to his side. His letter combines solicitude
for Jawaharlal's feelings with a frank, direct appraisal of the practical
issues involved. It is an appeal at once to the heart and the head:

How shall I console you? Hearing others describe your state, I said to
myself, "Have I been guilty of putting undue pressure on you?" I have
always believed you to be above undue pressure. I have always honoured
your resistance. It has always been honourable. Acting under that belief,
I pressed my suit. Let this incident be a lesson. Resist me always, when
my suggestion does not appeal to your head or heart. I shall not love you
the less for that resistance. But why are you dejected? I hope there is no
fear of public opinion in you. If you have done nothing wrong, why dejection? The ideal of independence is not in conflict with greater freedom.
As an executive officer now and president for the coming year, you could
not keep yourself away from a collective act of the majority of your colleagues. I hope, therefore, that you will get over your dejection and resume
your unfailing cheerfulness.

Nehru was conquered. After three days of reflection he decided that
what he had done was for the best.

As Jawaharlal had foreseen, and as the Congress leaders had also
envisaged, the conditions attached to the joint manifesto proved
unacceptable to the British authorities.

Gandhi, with Motilal, Sapru, Jinnah and Viththalbhai Patel, was
scheduled to meet Lord Irwin at Viceroy's House in Delhi on December 23rd, on the eve of the Lahore Congress. On that day, while en
route from Hyderabad to the capital, the Viceregal train in which
Lord Irwin was travelling was damaged by a bomb explosion on the
railway line a mile from New Delhi. The bomb, which was worked

by a time fuse, damaged the Viceroy's dining saloon, injuring one attendant; but Lord Irwin was unhurt.

The Viceroy was in a cordial, even jovial mood when a few hours later he met Gandhi and his colleagues. For nearly forty-five minutes they discussed the bomb incident. Then Lord Irwin turned to the business on hand.

"Where shall we begin?" he inquired. "Here is your manifesto. Shall we begin with the political prisoners?"

Obviously the British Government were prepared to make concessions in this matter. But Gandhi demurred. He fastened immediately on the issue of Dominion status.

"Could Your Excellency," he inquired, "give us an assurance that the Round Table Conference in London will proceed on the basis of full Dominion status?"

"That," countered Lord Irwin, "I cannot. I would refer you to the Government's communiqué of October 31st. I have no authority to proceed beyond that. But on the other hand there is nothing to prevent you achieving a Dominion constitution for India in London."

Gandhi was not satisfied. He rose to leave. Not until February, 1931, was he to meet Lord Irwin again for a series of talks which were to culminate in the celebrated Gandhi-Irwin Pact. In between, the Mahatma was to launch another civil-disobedience campaign and to go to prison.

But now the country's eyes were focussed not on Delhi but on Lahore.

Jawaharlal, President-elect of the Congress, was also President-elect of the Trade Union Congress, whose meeting was scheduled to take place at Nagpur only a few weeks before the Lahore session. It was unusual for the same person to preside in the same year over the annual sessions of these two all-India bodies, and Nehru, conscious of the distinction, planned to be a bridge between them. He hoped to broaden the proletarian basis of the Congress and simultaneously to draw labour deeper into the national struggle. In neither objective was he entirely successful.

If Jawaharlal was instinctively at home with the peasants, he was less at ease with the urban proletariat, although a considerable proportion of them was drawn from the rural areas. The Congress was in close touch with the peasantry. Its affiliations with industrial labour were less direct, for labour leadership, then aggressively leftist, distrusted the Congress as essentially a bourgeois institution dominated by the middle class. Nehru, sharing this suspicion, inclined towards the more advanced labour elements but did not actively support them.

What he should have done at Nagpur was to support the centre group which still formed a strong core and might have held together the contending right and left wings, then divided over the question whether the T.U.C. should or should not cooperate with the Whitley Labour Commission [3] appointed by the Government. As it was, the right wing, finding itself in a minority at Nagpur, broke away from the T.U.C., thus greatly weakening that body. Three years later a Communist group was to secede from the parent organisation, leaving the trade-union movement split in three—the original T.U.C., the Moderates and the Communists—each pulling in its own direction and for its particular ideology.

One probable reason for Nehru's closer affinity with the peasant than with the worker was that bad as the position of the industrial worker was, it was better than the peasant's. Time and again he deplores the peasant's lot.

"What is the unhappy creature to do," Jawaharlal asks in his autobiography, "when life presents itself to him as a bitter and unceasing individual struggle with every man's hand raised against him? How he lives at all is an almost incredible wonder."

At Lahore [4] the Congress camp, pitched on the banks of the Ravi River, seethed with life. Over 30,000 delegates and spectators convened for the Congress session, and as Nehru rode at the head of the presidential procession, seated on a white charger, the crowds cheered tumultuously. If Motilal was elated at the scene, Jawaharlal's mother, Swaruprani, was ecstatic. The Presidency of the Congress was the highest honour which the country could bestow. As her son had taken his place in the procession, Swaruprani had showered flowers on him and watched his face, tense but still youthful, glance up at her and flush for a moment with emotion.

[3] So called after its chairman, Mr. J. H. Whitley, former Speaker of the House of Commons.
[4] Former capital of the undivided Punjab. Now chief city of West Punjab in Pakistan.

Nehru's presidential speech bespoke his mind. It was direct, forth-right and forceful, clear for the most part of the cloudy verbiage which so often encumbers his utterances today. But the ideas he expressed then are not far different from his present views, and show an extraordinarily stubborn continuity of thought and feeling. By and large, the central core of his ideas has hardened with the years. He declared:

I must frankly confess that I am a socialist and a republican, and am no believer in kings and princes, or in the order which produces the modern kings of industry who have greater power over the lives and fortunes of men than even the kings of old, and whose methods are as predatory as those of the feudal aristocracy. . . . The Congress, it is said, must hold the balance fairly between capital and labour, and zamindar and tenant But the balance has been and is terribly weighted to one side, and to maintain the status quo is to maintain injustice and exploitation. The only way to do right is to do away with the domination of any one class over another.

Twenty years later, as Prime Minister, Nehru's thoughts moved in the same groove when he declared with equal emphasis that the objective of his government was the transformation of India into a socialist State. Private enterprise would have its place in his scheme of things but only under "the strategic control" of the Government. In other words, the balance, tilted against the have-nots, would be righted by removing the harsher inequalities between the classes and the masses and by adjusting the returns for labour and capital on a more equitable basis. Social justice was the ideal, not social regimenta-tion. This envisaged a classless society, but more on the socialist than on the Marxist model, with the utilitarian motif predominating. It was Mazzini speaking through Marx.

Nehru's interpretation of independence as President of the Congress was again not far different from his interpretation of the same objective as Prime Minister of India. At Lahore he proclaimed: "Independence for us means complete freedom from British domination and British imperialism. Having attained our freedom, I have no doubt that India will welcome all attempts at world cooperation and federation and will even agree to give up part of her independence to a larger group of which she is an equal member." And Jawaharlal went on to say that "India could never be an equal member of the

Commonwealth unless imperialism and all that it implies is discarded."

Today one of the main props of India's foreign policy is the removal of colonialism and racial discrimination. India's attempts at world cooperation and federation persist, and her decision to remain within the British Commonwealth even while asserting her right to be a republic symbolises her willingness to give up part of her independence to a larger group of which she is an equal member.

At Lahore, Nehru also made it clear that his adherence to nonviolence was based on no doctrinal belief:

Violence too often brings reaction and demoralization in its train, and in our country especially it may lead to disruption. It is perfectly true that organised violence rules the world today and it may be that we could profit by its use. But we have not the material or the training for organised violence, and individual or sporadic violence is a confession of despair. The great majority of us, I take it, judge the issue not on moral but on practical grounds and if we reject the way of violence, it is because it promises no substantial results. Any great movement for liberation must necessarily be a mass movement, and a mass movement must essentially be peaceful, except in times of organised revolt.

Nehru characterised the country's three major problems as the minorities, the princes, and labour and the peasantry, and on each his words were inexorably prophetic. Had India's princes only troubled to scan his address, they would have read the writing on the wall.

Mindful of the suffering and sacrifices which lay ahead, Jawaharlal concluded his address with a tocsin call: "Success often comes to those who dare and act; it seldom goes to the timid who are ever afraid of the consequences. We play for high stakes; and if we seek to achieve great things it can only be through great dangers."

The resolutions passed by the Lahore Congress adhered strictly to the letter and spirit of Jawaharlal's presidential address. Inevitably the so-called Nehru report lapsed. Complete independence, or *Purna Swaraj*, was now the aim of the Congress, and Gandhi himself, having been responsible for postponing the demand for independence at Calcutta, now moved the main resolution, which among other things declared that the word *swaraj* in the first article of the constitution of the Congress meant complete independence.

At 10:00 P.M. on the night of December 31, 1929, the discussion on the independence resolution ended. The voting took another two hours, and on the stroke of midnight the resolution was declared carried. It was an historic occasion whose significance few present on the banks of the Ravi in that grey, bitter-sweet dawn of a numbly cold day fully realised. How many saw that independence would be achieved within less than two decades? Jawaharlal unfurled the tricolour amid a huge chorus of voices shouting, *"Inquilab Zindabad!"* (Long live the Revolution!). He read the independence pledge, and thirty thousand throats repeated it after him.

A logical corollary to this resolution was the boycott of the legislatures and all Government committees, a decision which formed the preamble to the independence declaration. These steps were described as preliminary "towards organising a campaign of independence," and the Congress authorised the All-India Congress Committee, which comprised provincial representatives, "to launch a programme of civil disobedience including non-payment of taxes, whether in selected areas or otherwise and under such safeguards as it may consider necessary." The tricolour of independence thus became the banner of peaceful resistance.

None the less there were a few who insisted on dissenting from the main conclusions of the Lahore session. They were spearheaded by the volatile Subhas Chandra Bose, a proved patriot who in this instance at least allowed his emotion to run away with his judgement and invoked in the process the blessings of the politically dormant Mrs. C. R. Das, whose benediction appeared more provincial than national.

In obedience to the Congress mandate Motilal called upon the Congress members of the Central Assembly and the Provincial Councils to resign their seats. Nearly all of them did, only a very few— the majority of whom later wandered into the alleyways of cooperation with the Government—refusing to do so.

On January 2, 1930, the Working Committee of the Congress passed a resolution fixing January 26th as Independence Day, when meetings would be held and the independence pledge taken all over the country. Since the achievement of independence, January 26th is celebrated as Republic Day.

The first Independence Day, January 26, 1930, saw great gatherings intoning the pledge whose opening lines read:

We believe that it is the inalienable right of the Indian people, as of any other people, to have freedom and to enjoy the fruits of their toil and have the necessities of life, so that they may have full opportunities of growth. We believe also that if any government deprives a people of these rights and oppresses them, the people have a further right to alter it or to abolish it.

On this note of challenge and resolve the country marched forward to another campaign of civil disobedience.

11

CIVIL DISOBEDIENCE

POLITICALLY, Jawaharlal had "arrived."

From the Lahore Congress onward, his place on the Indian political stage was preeminent, second only to Gandhi, who by insisting on Nehru's election as President of that session had virtually proclaimed him his political heir. Motilal was closer in the Mahatma's counsel. Gandhi respected the rugged common sense of Vallabhbhai Patel. But it was on younger shoulders that the Mahatma's mantle must fall, and to that there were only two aspirants. The other was Subhas Bose.

Bose, some nine years younger than Nehru, was in many ways dissimilar. He had come to the Congress by way of Cambridge and the Indian Civil Service, from which he had resigned in 1921 at the Mahatma's call. He had been a rebel from youth, and as an undergraduate in a Calcutta college had been suspended for nearly two years for leading a students' strike and threatening to thrash an English professor who had passed some disparaging remarks on Indians.

Bose's childhood coincided with the heyday of the teachings of the Hindu reformers, Ramakrishna Paramahansa [1] and his disciple Vivekananda, who in the last decade of the nineteenth century visited America and founded in San Francisco the headquarters of the Ramakrishna Mission. Both these reformers sought to free Hinduism from the trammels of outworn ritual and to intellectualise its teachings. Both men came from Bengal, Bose's home province.

From his mother, a woman of intense religious fervour, Subhas learned something of the precepts of these sages who fired his lively and imaginative mind. Meditating over them, he resolved, like

[1] Born in 1834. He preached that all creeds are only facets of the same Truth.

Buddha, to forsake his family and live a life of renunciation. While Jawaharlal was settling down to his work as a lawyer at Allahabad, Bose was wandering amid the foothills of the Himalayas, which are the traditional seat of Hindu spirituality. From there Bose trekked along the banks of the sacred Ganga, visiting the holy cities of Banaras and Mathura, Brindaban and Gaya, seeking vainly his own Holy Grail. He was disappointed in this pilgrimage, and, echoing Omar Khayyám, he realised that his quest had ended in disillusionment:

> Myself when young did eagerly frequent
> Doctor and Saint, and heard great Argument
>   About it and about: but evermore
> Came out by the same door where in I went.

The mystic strain in Bose's character survived and remained with him until his death in an air crash in Formosa on the eve of the Japanese surrender in World War II. Politics imbued with philosophy and religio-mystic thought lead to strange idealisations. They were to lead Subhas into an association with Fascism and Nazism for the liberation of his country.

Bose was not greatly influenced by Gandhi, with whose methods and philosophy he often vigorously disagreed. His only political guru was Deshbandhu Das, whose death in 1925 left him bereft of a secure anchorage. Bose had no patience with Gandhi's non-violence, and was irritated by the intricate permutations and combinations of the Mahatma's political processes. There he differed from Nehru, who by rationalising Gandhi's inconsistencies sought to reduce his teachings to an intellectual pattern of thinking. Temperamentally and intellectually Bose and Gandhi were poles apart. Eventually this was to influence Bose's place in the Congress hierarchy.

Nehru, while still critical of many phases in the Mahatma's political thought, found in him a lodestar that never ceased to attract. He found too that he was beginning to share with Gandhi an immense and unusual popularity with the masses. He could not but realise that he had become a national hero. Songs were written about him and legends grew around him. He was showered, as is the Indian way, with titles. He was hailed as Bharat Bhushan (Jewel of India) and Tyagamurti (Embodiment of Sacrifice).

If this adulation sometimes went to Nehru's head, as he confesses it did, he had his wife and sisters to provide the necessary corrective.

With them the extravagant new titles conferred on Jawaharlal were a subject for endless raillery and fun.

At the breakfast table he was often adjured by one of them, "O Jewel of India, pass me the butter," or sometimes even little Indira would pipe, "O Embodiment of Sacrifice, what is the time?"

Motilal watched the proceedings with affectionate amusement. But Jawaharlal's mother was not amused. To her the adulation showered on her son by the country seemed a perfectly natural reaction.

Following the Lahore session Motilal, at his son's suggestion and after consultation with Gandhi, decided to give over his house Anand Bhawan [2] to the nation, renaming it Swaraj Bhawan. The family moved across the road to a new house, christened after the old, which soon housed a Congress hospital and the offices of the All-India Congress Committee. Motilal did not live to complete the legal formalities of transfer, which were later done by Jawaharlal, who in accordance with his father's wishes created a trust of the property.

The country-wide response to the independence pledge-taking ceremony on January 26th demonstrated the depth and strength of popular feeling which only awaited the signal to launch on civil disobedience. As Nehru was to write in a letter [3] to his daughter three years later, 1930 opened "with the air dark with the shadow of coming events."

On January 31st Gandhi suddenly announced his so-called Eleven Points, expressing his willingness to put off civil disobedience if Britain, by conceding his Points, would grant the substance of independence. He demanded eleven things: (1) total prohibition of alcohol; (2) the restoration of the exchange rate of the rupee to 1s 4d; [4] (3) reduction of land revenue by 50 per cent; (4) abolition of the salt tax; (5) reduction of military expenditure by at least 50 per cent; (6) reduction of the salaries of civil servants by half; (7) a protective tariff against foreign cloth; (8) enactment of a coastal reservation bill in favour of Indian shipping; (9) release of all political prisoners not condemned for murder or attempted murder; (10) abolition or control of the Criminal Investigation Department, whose principal target

[2] The Abode of Happiness became, by its new name, the Abode of Independence.

[3] Dated May 17, 1933.

[4] It had been fixed three years before at 1s 6d.

was the Congress; and (11) issue of firearms for self-defence, subject to popular control.

"Let the Viceroy," declared Gandhi, "satisfy us with regard to these very simple but vital needs of India. He will then hear no talk of civil disobedience."

It was a startlingly miscellaneous list of demands designed obviously to appeal to various sections of the people—the masses, classes, businessmen and intellectuals. But to Nehru this curious mélange of social and political reforms seemed to bear no relation whatever to the basic demand for independence.

Once again he was peeved and puzzled. What, for instance, had the abolition of the salt tax to do with civil disobedience? Gandhi was soon to let the country and the Congress know.

"There is no article like salt, outside water, by taxing which the State can touch the starving millions, the sick, the maimed and the utterly helpless," Gandhi proclaimed. "The tax constitutes therefore the most inhuman poll tax the ingenuity of man can devise."

Like the hated *gabelle* which formed a rallying cry for the French peasantry before the onset of the French Revolution, salt suddenly became the symbol of revolt in India. By calling on the people deliberately to break the salt law and "manufacture" salt on the open beaches, Gandhi gave a dramatically rebellious significance to a simple act.

On March 2nd the Mahatma wrote a letter to the Viceroy, Lord Irwin, addressing him as "Dear Friend," in the course of which he said:

Even the salt he [the peasant] must use in order to live, is so taxed as to make the burden fall heaviest on him, if only because of the heartless impartiality of its incidence. The tax shows itself more burdensome to the poor man for salt is the one thing he must eat more than the rich, individually and collectively.

After enumerating the various burdens heaped on the Indian people, Gandhi went on to write:

if you cannot see your way to deal with these evils and my letter makes no appeal to your heart, on the eleventh day of this month I shall proceed with such co-workers of the ashram as I can take, to disregard the provisions of the salt laws. I regard this tax to be the most iniquitous of all from the poor man's standpoint. As the independence movement is essentially for the poorest in the land, a beginning will be made with this evil. The wonder is that we have submitted to the cruel monopoly for so long. It is, I know, open to you to frustrate my design by arresting me. I hope that there will be tens of thousands ready, in a disciplined manner, to take up the work after me, and, in the act of disobeying the Salt Act, to lay themselves open to the penalties of a law that should never have disfigured the statute book.

The letter was delivered to the Viceroy through an English messenger, a young Quaker by the name of Reginald Reynolds.

Lord Irwin's reply was formal, and merely regretted that the Mahatma should be "contemplating a course of action which is clearly bound to involve violation of the law, and danger to the public peace."

On March 12th, at 6:30 in the morning, Gandhi, accompanied by seventy-eight followers, set out on his famous march from his ashram at Sabarmati for the small sea-side village of Dandi, 241 miles away. He was then sixty-one. He strode briskly, staff in hand, speaking at wayside villages and towns to crowds which swelled progressively, and as he marched a fire of patriotic fervour flared through the land.

At Jambusar, about halfway between Sabarmati and Dandi, Motilal and Jawaharlal, on their way back to Allahabad from a meeting of the All-India Congress Committee at Ahmedabad, met the Mahatma. They spent a few hours with him there, and then walked a little distance with him. Father and son finally bade him farewell. "That," wrote Jawaharlal, "was my last glimpse of him then as I saw him, staff in hand, marching along at the head of his followers with firm step and a peaceful but undaunted look. It was a moving sight."

It was a spectacle which stirred Nehru deeply and brought welling to the surface again the ardour and impatience of his impetuous spirit. He longed to plunge into the struggle which had still to begin. At this juncture he turned to the country's youth, who, like him, were straining at the leash, and in a message to them even as the Mahatma marched onward he apostrophized: "The pilgrim marches onward. The field of battle lies before you, the flag of India beckons you, and freedom herself awaits your coming. Do you hesitate now, you who were but yesterday so loudly on her side? Will you be mere lookers-on in this glorious struggle and see your best and bravest face the might of a great empire which has crushed your country and her children? Who lives if India dies? Who dies if India lives?"

On March 21st the All-India Congress Committee meeting at

Ahmedabad prepared itself for the now inevitable struggle. It was arranged that as each successive President was arrested, his nominee should succeed him, appointing in turn a new Working Committee to replace those members who were also arrested. This applied not only to the Central Congress organisation but to provincial and local committees.

Earlier Gandhi had indicated that while a sporadic act of violence would not lead him to call off the movement as he had done in the last civil-disobedience campaign eight years earlier, he would not tolerate violence as in any way part of the movement. In his march towards Dandi he preached the message of non-violence incessantly, and as was his wont spoke frankly on the deficiencies of himself and the Indian people: "We are not angels. We are very weak, easily tempted. There are many lapses to our debit."

On April 5th Gandhi with his followers reached Dandi, and on the following day, after his morning prayers, the Mahatma walked to the beach and, picking up a lump of crude salt, symbolically broke the law. In the event of his arrest he nominated a veteran Muslim Congressman, the white-bearded Abbas Tyabji, to succeed him in the leadership, and on Tyabji's arrest he announced that Mrs. Sarojini Naidu should succeed.

Gandhi's action was the signal for a country-wide breaking of the salt law. "It seemed," wrote Nehru, "as though a spring had been suddenly released."

The British authorities, inclined at first to dismiss the Mahatma's march as a futile political pantomime, now took alarm. They resorted to firing and to lathi charges on demonstrators. Once again Gandhi adjured his people to remain steadfastly non-violent in the face of repression. "If we are to stand the final heat of the battle," he urged, "we must learn to stand our ground in the face of cavalry or baton charges and allow ourselves to be trampled under the horses' hoofs or be bruised in the charges."

On April 14th Nehru was arrested while entraining from Allahabad for Raipur in the then Central Provinces.[5] He had earlier, after addressing a huge meeting and leading a vast procession, ceremoniously "manufactured" some contraband salt. He was charged with breach of the salt law, tried summarily behind prison walls and sentenced to

[5] Now known as Madhya Pradesh.

six months, this being his fourth term of imprisonment. Jawaharlal was back in jail after nearly seven years, being detained this time in Naini Central Prison in his home province. He was to remain there, with an eight-day interval of freedom, until January 26, 1931.

Outside, the movement raged, with repression increasing on the one hand and determined defiance mounting on the other. Nehru had wanted Gandhi to succeed him as the Congress President during his absence in jail, but the Mahatma declined, and Jawaharlal then nominated his father as his successor. Although ailing and stricken by the first onset of the illness which ten months later was to end in his death, Motilal took over the reins of responsibility with his accustomed vigour, and directed the movement with determination and discipline.

Gandhi was arrested in the early hours of May 5th while sleeping peacefully in his hut at Dandi. "At the dead of night like thieves they came to steal him away," wrote Mira Ben, his English disciple.[6] "For 'when they sought to lay hands on him they feared the multitude because they took him for a prophet.' "

With Jawaharlal's arrest civil disobedience had acquired a new tempo, and arrests, firing on crowds and lathi charges grew to be ordinary everyday occurrences. From breach of the salt laws the movement fanned out into other directions. Foreign cloth shops were picketed, liquor booths boycotted.

A feature of the movement was the remarkable awakening of Indian women, who left their sheltered homes in thousands and took their place by their menfolk in the fight for freedom. Many hundreds of them were arrested and imprisoned. From this period derives the spirit of equality and emancipation which henceforth was increasingly to inspire feminine progress in India.

Not surprisingly, the women of the Nehru household were foremost in the fray. For many hours daily Jawaharlal's mother, sisters and wife stood under the hot summer sun picketing foreign cloth shops, sharing with others of their sex the rudeness and indignities to which they were sometimes subjected by the police. Motilal's patriarchal outlook could not easily accommodate itself to the idea of his wife, daughters and daughter-in-law participating in such activities. But he did not interfere, and secretly took pride in the courage and energy

[6] The former Miss Madeleine Slade, daughter of a British admiral.

which they displayed. Later, when he joined Jawaharlal in jail, he spoke with affectionate pride of their doings.

Most surprising of all was the spirit and ardour displayed by the ailing Kamala, whose determination—while it surprised Jawaharlal—also moved him deeply. In the early months of 1930, as civil disobedience loomed large on the horizon, he had sensed for the first time Kamala's eager desire to prove herself a worthy political comrade. Now, from behind prison walls, he followed with amazement his wife's efforts to galvanise the movement in Allahabad city and district, and her energy, will and organising capacity left him with a feeling of proud if baffled astonishment. Kamala, although ill and weak, was trying to justify herself in her husband's eyes.

"She made up for inexperience by her fire and energy," Nehru wrote much later, "and within a few months she became the pride of Allahabad." From then onwards he saw Kamala in a new light, and from this sense of political affinity grew a deeper personal communion between them. Prison and his own political preoccupations had so far prevented Jawaharlal from seeing that what Kamala wanted above all was not to be a mere shadow of her husband but his companion and helpmate. But now at long last he saw and understood.

Daily the movement gathered in strength. As prohibitive laws grew in number, the civil resisters discovered new foci for defiance. There were large-scale raids on salt pans and depots, resulting in the arrest of many top-ranking leaders of Congress; but despite their imprisonment the movement continued with unabated fervour. In the course of this peaceful and determined struggle in which vast masses participated in villages, towns and cities, nearly 100,000 persons went to prison.

The most spectacular demonstration of non-violence was seen in the hitherto turbulent Northwest Frontier Province, which is peopled largely by the Pathans and other martial tribesmen. Here Khan Abdul Ghaffar Khan, a brother of Nehru's old friend Dr. Khan Sahib, had organised the movement whose followers were known as Khudai Khidmatgars (Servants of God) and who were pledged to non-violent service. Because of the rough rust-coloured blouses they wore they were popularly called Red Shirts though they had no Communist affiliations whatever.

Khan Abdul Ghaffar Khan's father had been the chief of a clan

of tribesmen centred on a village in Peshawar district on the borderland of India as it then extended before Pakistan. Ghaffar Khan was
a man of abstemious, even austere habits, and had been associated
with the national movement since the days of the Rowlatt Act, though
until 1930 his Khudai Khidmatgars were not in active cooperation
with the Congress.

The Frontier Gandhi, as Ghaffar Khan came to be known, was
early attracted by the non-violent teachings of the Mahatma, and
sought to impart them to his followers. In an area such as the Northwest Frontier Province, where the rule of an eye for an eye and a
tooth for a tooth prevails, this was a highly ambitious undertaking. But
the Frontier Gandhi persisted in his message of non-violence, which
slowly percolated through the minds of the hitherto aggressive tribesmen.

Now they came out in their thousands to demonstrate peacefully
against the alien Raj. Armoured cars were moved against them, and
in certain districts the British authorities resorted to indiscriminate
firing. But the tribesmen were not easily cowed; and although there
were a few instances of violent retaliation, the Khudai Khidmatgars
generally held their peace and faced unflinchingly the bullets and bayonets of the military. So impressive was the forbearance and patience
of these normally unruly Muslim tribesmen that on one occasion in
Peshawar two platoons of British-led Hindu troops, the 18th Royal
Garhwali Rifles, refused to fire on them when ordered to do so, and
were hastily brought back to their barracks under arrest. The Frontier
Gandhi was imprisoned along with many hundreds of his followers.

From prison Nehru followed eagerly the trend of events outside. He
was seized with a sense of elation and pride. The bearing of Indian
women, particularly of his wife, mother and sisters, exhilarated him,
and he was moved also by the strangely peaceful behaviour of the
turbulent Pathans under the leadership of Khan Abdul Ghaffar Khan.
Sooner or later he knew his father would join him in prison. On June
30th Motilal was arrested in Allahabad shortly after he had been on
a visit to Bombay, one of the chief citadels of civil resistance in the
country. He was sentenced to six months' imprisonment, and joined
his son in his barrack in Naini Central Prison.

The barrack where Jawaharlal was confined, for the first time by
himself, was a small circular enclosure roughly one hundred feet in

diameter and ringed by a wall fifteen feet high. In the centre of this enclosure was a squat drab building containing four cells. Jawaharlal occupied two of these, using one of them as a bathroom and lavatory. The enclosure bore an elegant designation. It was known in the jail as Kuttaghar—the Doghouse.

Nehru found the circular wall of his prison-house more oppressive than the rectangular walls to which he had so far been accustomed in jail. The summer months were uncomfortably warm, and at night he slept in the open, in the narrow corridor between the inner building and the enclosing wall, his bed being heavily chained to the ground, probably to prevent its use as a ladder of escape! At night the jail, like a jungle, was full of strange sounds—the clatter of the sentries' footsteps, the clanking of keys, the weird shouts and cries of the watchmen on guard, and the hundred and one small noises that break the vast stillness of a prison asleep.

Lying on his bed, Nehru liked to watch the open sky and follow the clouds as they moved across the star-studded canopy of the heavens. Sometimes he would try to work out the approximate time from the position of a familiar constellation. A constant stellar companion was the pole star, which peeped cheerfully at him every night from just over the rim of the prison wall.

Nehru rose very early in the morning, about 3:30 or 4:00 A.M. As usual, he planned his day carefully, devoting nearly three hours to spinning on his own charkha, and another two or three hours to weaving. He read a great deal, exercised himself within the narrow ambits of his enclosure, washed his clothes, and generally tidied up the place.

Daily newspapers were not permitted, but a Hindi weekly journal carried accounts of the civil-disobedience movement, and Nehru often found this dramatic reading. Although the principal Congress leaders were in jail, the movement continued steadfastly. There were daily lathi charges, firing at demonstrators was not uncommon, and martial law was declared at a few places, including Sholapur in western India, where the penalty for carrying the national flag was ten years' imprisonment.

Many hundreds were arrested and imprisoned daily throughout the country. But their place was taken by many hundreds of others. Women, workers and students were prominent in the movement.

Prabhat pheris,[7] comprising groups of men, women and children who moved in procession at dawn from street to street singing patriotic songs, were a feature of civil resistance in 1930. Throughout the day women clad in saffron [8] saris picketed shops purveying foreign goods, particularly British textiles, and by the autumn of 1930 imports of cotton piecegoods had declined to between a third and a fourth of the previous year's figures. In Bombay sixteen British-owned mills closed down, and workers in the larger cities came out frequently in protest processions, thereby helping to paralyse production. By July 6th the London *Observer* was commenting caustically on the "defeatism" and "demoralization" of the Europeans in India, while the British-owned Calcutta *Statesman* conceded that "everybody admits the gravity of the situation, and all classes of traders are seriously affected by the situation."

Yet, oddly enough, the temper of the people if aroused was often good-humoured. Hikmet Bayur, former Turkish ambassador to Afghanistan, recalls that while touring India in 1930 when Gandhi and Nehru were in prison he was entertained to tea by an Indian superintendent of a jail in northern India. There were other Indian guests, and while they were having tea in the garden, loud cries of *Gandhiji ki jai* reached their ears. On inquiry he found that it was the habit of the political prisoners in that jail to greet the setting sun with this slogan.

"How many are there here?" he asked.

"Eight to nine thousand," they told him.

"And how many were there here in 1921?"

"About a thousand."

"And how many do you think there will be ten years hence?" he persisted.

The Indian guests laughed and pointed good-humouredly at the superintendent.

"Then *he* will be in."

Even inside jail Nehru discovered that the tingle and excitement of events outside were infecting some of the convict inmates.

"*Swaraj* is coming," they exclaimed. "Will *swaraj* take us out of this hell?"

[7] A squad singing devotional or patriotic songs in the morning.
[8] Saffron denotes sacrifice.

For a month Jawaharlal was alone in his barrack, and was then joined by another political prisoner, Narmada Prasad Singh, whose arrival was a relief. Two and a half months later, on the last day of June, 1930, he was pleasantly surprised when his father strode into the enclosure accompanied by Dr. Syed Mahmud, now Minister for External Affairs in Nehru's cabinet.

Motilal had been arrested early that morning while he was still in bed.

"And now we are together again," he remarked.

Seeing his son, he was in great good humour. Motilal had barely seven months to live, but neither father nor son realised it.

12

THE DEATH OF MOTILAL

In June in India the rains come.

As summer eased into the monsoon the political temperature also subsided. Motilal and Jawaharlal heard vague rumours of truce, of peace parleys and conferences. Nationalist leaders outside the Congress party, notably two lawyers, Sir Tej Bahadur Sapru, a former member of the Viceroy's Executive Council in Lord Reading's time, and Dr. M. R. Jayakar, a prominent lawyer from Bombay, were in touch with the British authorities with a view to effecting a compromise between the Government and the Congress.

Lord Irwin was not averse to a settlement. The civil-disobedience movement had proved far more pervasive and powerful than the Government had calculated, and the Viceroy was also anxious that the projected Round Table Conference in London should meet under peaceful auspices.

On July 9, 1930, Lord Irwin, addressing a joint session of the two legislatures at the Centre—the Council of State and the Legislative Assembly—declared, "It is the belief of His Majesty's Government that by way of the conference it should be possible to reach solutions that both countries and all parties and interests in them can honourably accept, and any such agreement at which the conference is able to arrive will form the basis of the proposals which His Majesty's Government will later submit to Parliament." The Viceroy also affirmed that the pledge of Dominion status as India's constitutional objective stood.

Soon after, a conference of certain nationalist members of the Central Legislature requested Sir Tej Bahadur Sapru and Dr. Jayakar to act as intermediaries between the Government and the Congress. Following an exchange of correspondence with the Viceroy, Sapru and Jayakar interviewed Gandhi at Yerawda Jail near Poona on July 23rd and 24th.

While not opposed to a truce, Gandhi was unwilling to commit the Congress to a decision without the consent of Motilal and Jawaharlal. He himself was inclined to attend the conference provided its discussions were limited to safeguards or such adjustments as were necessary in the transitional period before complete self-government. And while conceding the possibility of Dominion status as an objective, he was reluctant to rule out the ideal of complete independence. He also insisted that with the calling off of satyagraha the Government should release all political prisoners.

Accordingly, the Mahatma handed to Sapru and Jayakar a letter along with a note, embodying his ideas, which he asked them to hand over to the Nehrus. On July 27th the two intermediaries descended on Motilal and Jawaharlal in their jail at Allahabad.

Motilal, who was running a temperature, was not his usual self at the time. The talks continued desultorily for two days, concluding on July 28th. To Jawaharlal it seemed that there was little common ground between the Government and the Congress. Neither ideologically nor politically had he any close affinity with the two moderate nationalists who sought alternately to persuade and cajole him. "We talked and argued in a circle," he wrote, "hardly understanding each other's language or thought, so great was the difference in political outlook."

Gandhi had been cautious in his communications. "Jawaharlal's must be the final voice," he insisted in his letter to Motilal. He went on to promise that he himself "would have no hesitation in supporting any stronger position up to the letter of the Lahore resolution."

Sapru and Jayakar emerged from Naini with no positive commitments. All that the two Nehrus were prepared to say was that they could offer no proposals until they had consulted their colleagues on the Working Committee, particularly Gandhi. Father and son wrote to the Mahatma to this effect.

Would the Viceroy agree to such consultations? Lord Irwin sought refuge in a compromise. He was willing that the two Nehrus should interview Gandhi in Yerawda Jail, but he could not agree to the other members of the Working Committee, such as Vallabhbhai Patel and Maulana Abul Kalam Azad, who were both outside prison and still engaged in an active campaign against the Government, joining in these talks.

Sapru, who brought the Viceroy's reply to the Nehrus on August 8th, argued that they should not lose the chance of consulting with Gandhi at Yerawda. Jawaharlal and Motilal were not averse to this, although they pointed out that the three of them could not commit the entire Working Committee to their views. They also asked that Dr. Syed Mahmud, who was in prison with them at Naini and who was the Congress secretary, should accompany them to Yerawda. With this request the Government complied.

On August 10th Motilal and Jawaharlal, with Mahmud, were conveyed by a special train which took them to Kirkee, a wayside station near Poona. Although the train made no halt at the bigger stations, the news had travelled, and large crowds greeted them along the route. They reached Kirkee late on the night of August 11th.

To their surprise they were not conducted immediately to Gandhi's presence but were detained in a separate prison barracks that night, and for the next twenty-four hours. By dint of some subtle questioning of a British jail official, Motilal was able to deduce the reason for this unusual procedure. The Government did not want the Nehrus to meet the Mahatma for the first time except in the presence of Sapru and Jayakar, who had not yet arrived. Motilal, irritable and tired after the train journey, was not amused.

When on August 13th Sapru and Jayakar finally arrived, and the Nehrus were invited to meet them along with Gandhi in the prison office, Motilal declined. He insisted that they should first see Gandhi alone. This was conceded. The Government also agreed that Vallabhbhai Patel, who had been arrested in the interval, should join the talks along with another member of the Congress Working Committee, Jairamdas Daulatram, who was in prison.

The talks continued for three days, concluding on August 15th. Once again the Nehrus, with Gandhi, reiterated their inability to say anything authoritative without reference to a properly constituted meeting of the Congress Working Committee, but in their individual capacities they made three stipulations. India's right to secede at will from the British Empire should be recognised; the country should be given a complete national government responsible to the people, and this should cover Gandhi's eleven points; British claims, including India's so-called public debt, should be referred to an independent tribunal. The conditions were unacceptable to the Viceroy, and the negotiations were terminated.

Motilal was a tired and ailing man already in the grip of the illness which was to end in his death seven months later. Occasionally his vigour and forcefulness asserted themselves. Sometimes the old exuberance of spirit found vent in a renewed zest for life and living, and he could still astonish his jailors by the amplitude of his appetite for good food which he invariably described as "simple."

"Very probably," comments Nehru, "at the Ritz or the Savoy it would have been considered simple and ordinary food as father himself was convinced it was. But at Yerawda where India's greatest political leader made do on goat's milk, dates and an occasional orange, this was princely diet."

On August 16th they bade Gandhi goodbye and boarded their special train for their jail in Naini. This time the wayside crowds were, if anything, larger and more demonstrative.

At Naini, Motilal's health continued to deteriorate, and on September 8th the Government released him after he had served exactly ten weeks in prison. Some days later Jawaharlal was joined in jail by his brother-in-law, Ranjit Pandit, husband of his sister Vijayalakshmi. On October 11th Nehru, having served his six-month sentence, was also released. He was to be free for only eight days.

Outside, the non-cooperation movement had lost none of its momentum. The world slump in prices had hit the Indian agriculturist, and the Congress was considering whether a no-tax campaign in the rural areas should be started. Very soon the peasants would be called upon to pay their taxes.

Vallabhbhai Patel had already initiated a no-tax campaign on his favourite battleground of Bardoli in Gujerat. Mounting official repression drove the peasants from their homes into the neighbouring State of Baroda.

A British journalist meeting a crowd of peasant women camped in the open with their cattle and meagre goods asked them why they had left their homes.

"Because Mahatmaji is in prison," was the answer.

Jawaharlal, surveying the scene, felt that a similar movement should be initiated in the United Provinces. There was, however, one vital difference between the two areas. In Gujerat the *ryotwari* system prevailed whereunder the peasant was also proprietor of the soil, and thus dealt directly with the State. The United Provinces was a zamindari or taluqdari area where the peasant, only a tenant at will, paid his tax to the landlord, who in the role of middleman in turn paid his due to the State.

If the peasant alone were persuaded to withhold his tax, the landlord would be isolated politically and economically, and the class issue would pose itself sharply. This the Congress was anxious to avoid. On the other hand a tiredness had settled on the cities and the middle classes. If the movement were not to flag, the centre of political gravity should be shifted from the urban to the rural areas.

The Congress set about doing this in a characteristic way. Jawaharlal summoned a meeting of the United Provinces Congress Committee, and after a long debate it was decided that the call for a no-tax campaign should be given but that it should be permissive for any district within the province to take it up. The Congress appealed for support impartially to the landlord and the peasant.

On October 13th Nehru, with his wife, left for a brief holiday at the hill station of Mussoorie, where Motilal was recuperating. It was a joyous reunion enlivened by the presence of Indira and the three small daughters of Vijayalakshmi.

Jawaharlal played with the children, but even here the political motif intruded. They would march in procession around the house, led by the youngest child holding the national flag aloft, and singing in chorus the song of patriotic India, *Jhanda uncha rahe hamara* (Keep our flag flying high).

These were the last few days Jawaharlal spent with his father before the final onset of his illness took Motilal away.

On October 17th Nehru, with his wife, left Mussoorie for Allahabad to be in time for the Peasant Conference scheduled to be held there on October 19th. It was arranged that Motilal should follow them on October 18th.

En route to Allahabad, Nehru was served thrice with orders, under Section 144 of the Indian Criminal Procedure Code, forbidding him to speak in public. At Allahabad he found nearly two thousand peasants gathered to hear him. He addressed them, and the conference decided to start a no-tax campaign in Allahabad district itself.

That same evening Motilal arrived from Mussoorie, and Jawaharlal, after greeting him at the station, left hurriedly with Kamala for another meeting of peasants and urban workers. The meeting concluded after eight that night, and, weary from the day's excitement and toil, they motored to Anand Bhawan, where Nehru knew his father was staying up for him.

Almost within sight of Anand Bhawan their car was stopped. A police officer served a warrant of arrest on Nehru. Kamala was allowed to proceed on her way, but Jawaharlal was whisked across the Yamuna River to his old retreat in Naini Prison. The clock struck nine as the prison gates opened to receive him.

At home Kamala's tidings momentarily shook Motilal. The old man sat for a while in silence, with his head bent in grief. Then with an effort he roused himself.

"I am going to be well," he announced, "and do a man's work. Enough of these doctors and their advice!"

For a few brief days Motilal rallied. He worked with his old energy, and even seemed for a while to improve in health. He called on the country to observe November 14th, Jawaharlal's birthday, as a day of rejoicing and to celebrate it by reading at public meetings the offending passages from his son's speech which had led to his conviction. The old lion was having his last growl at the Government.

So enthusiastic was the country's response that the authorities had to resort to lathi charges to break up the processions and meetings. Nearly five thousand people were arrested on that day alone.

"It was a unique birthday celebration," Jawaharlal comments.

In jail Nehru rejoined his old comrades Syed Mahmud, Narmada Prasad and Ranjit Pandit, the three of them sharing the same barrack. It was his fifth term of imprisonment. He had been sentenced to a total of two years' rigorous imprisonment and a further term of five months in default of fines aggregating Rs. 700 (about $150) which he had refused to pay.

Meanwhile, the struggle continued outside. The peasant conference at Allahabad which Nehru had addressed on the day of his arrest proved the spearhead of a vigorous no-tax campaign in many districts of the United Provinces. Although the landlords did not join, few of them, in view of the country's political temper and the deepening economic slump, resisted the peasantry. For the same reasons the Government moved cautiously.

But inside the jails, behind the prison walls, repression grew. A number of political prisoners were flogged, and in protest Nehru and his three companions went on a fast for three days. Jawaharlal had fasted before, but never beyond twenty-four hours. It was seventy-two hours this time.

Motilal visited his son in jail, careful always to present a buoyant front, but Jawaharlal was distressed by the growing and visible decline in his father's health. At his urging Motilal finally consented to go to Calcutta for rest and medical treatment.

Inside Naini life proceeded fitfully but in comparative calm. Nehru's brother-in-law, Ranjit, proved a gay and resourceful companion. Being fond of flowers, and with a passion for horticulture, he soon had his two companions helping him to turn their drab prison courtyard into a blaze of colourful blooms and blossoms. Ranjit's ingenuity found unexpected outlets. Within the forbidding walls of their barrack, symbol of British authority, he contrived ironically to set up another British symbol—a miniature golf course.

Nehru returned to his old prison pastime of watching the stars march across the sky. Now and again planes passed overhead, for Allahabad was then on the route of most air lines operating between Europe and the East. Sometimes of an early winter morning he would watch an air liner with its cabins lit up fly majestically across the dark, sombre sky.

New Year's day brought him an unexpected gift. Kamala was arrested.

"I am happy beyond measure and proud to follow in the footsteps of my husband," she told a reporter who asked her for a message. "I hope the people will keep the flag flying."

If Nehru was proud at the thought that his wife had courted imprisonment, Motilal was disturbed. Because he knew that Kamala was far from well, and that jail would aggravate her ailment, he decided to cut short his stay in Calcutta and return to Allahabad.

On January 12th Motilal called at Naini to see his son. Jawaharlal was shocked at his father's appearance, but Motilal seemed unaware of the dismay he caused. He had aged greatly in the few weeks since his last visit. His erect frame was shrivelled and bent. He looked ill and weary, and his face was swollen with the ailment which gripped him. Yet he insisted that he felt better.

The first Round Table Conference had opened on November 12th in London. The Congress was absent; but, contrary to expectations, the miscellaneous elements which attended, comprising the Princes, the Liberals, Hindu and Muslim spokesmen, displayed some unity of purpose. The idea of Federation was welcomed, even the Princes supporting it. Both at Whitehall and in New Delhi the British authorities were hopeful that the Congress might be persuaded to attend the second session, which was scheduled for the autumn months of 1931. The first session concluded in January.

On January 25th the Viceroy, Lord Irwin, ordered the unconditional release of Gandhi and the members of the Congress Working Committee, including Nehru. They were released on January 26th, which is India's Republic Day.

In the forenoon of January 26th Nehru was told in prison that his father's illness had taken a serious turn and that he must hurry home. Only a fortnight had elapsed since he had last seen his father. As he put his things together, he thought of Motilal's puffed and pain-stricken face and the agony which must have tormented him despite his brave front.

"That face of his haunted me," Jawaharlal recalled.

At Anand Bhawan where he hurried from jail, Nehru, on entering his father's bedroom, was shocked by Motilal's appearance. For a brief moment he hesitated on the threshold, numbed by the sight of his suffering. Then he went forward to embrace his father. The old man rose from his pillow, and for a few moments father and son clung to each other without speaking.

There were tears in Jawaharlal's eyes as he sat by his father's side. Motilal's eyes glistened with joy and pride.

Gandhi also hurried straight from jail to Anand Bhawan, coming by train from his prison at Poona.

He arrived at Allahabad late at night, but Motilal kept awake to greet him.

For a few moments Gandhi looked silently at his dying friend and comrade-in-arms.

"We shall surely win *swaraj*," he said in his quiet persuasive voice, "if you survive this crisis."

"No," said Motilal firmly. "I am going soon, Mahatmaji, and I shall not be here to see *swaraj*. But I know you have won it and will soon have it."

Some of Gandhi's serenity seemed to communicate itself to the stricken but still spirited man. During the next few days he looked peaceful and composed, his thoughts obviously alternating between his country and his son. India's freedom seemed assured. Now he commended to Gandhi's charge, personal and political, his dearest and most precious possession—Jawaharlal.

There were days when Motilal seemed to rally, when an echo of his old ebullient high spirits was heard. Then he would joke with and tease Gandhi, who enjoyed his mild raillery. But these occasions were few and far between.

The house was full of relatives, friends and political comrades. Across the road, at Swaraj Bhawan which Motilal had donated to the nation, the Congress Working Committee held its deliberations. Motilal was too ill to participate in their proceedings, but the thought of India's freedom persisted in his mind. Off and on he would remark wistfully that he would like to die in an India which was free.

The end was near. Motilal's condition slumped sharply, and on February 4th it was decided to remove him by car for X-ray treatment to Lucknow. He himself was insistent that he should not leave Anand Bhawan, where he wished to die. But Gandhi supported the doctors' decision. And Motilal yielded.

They took him slowly by road to Lucknow, where he arrived exhausted. But the next day, February 5th, he seemed to rally. He was cheerful throughout the morning, but by the evening his condition had deteriorated again and he was placed on oxygen when difficulty in breathing set in.

Throughout that night Jawaharlal kept vigil by his father's bedside together with his mother and the doctors. Motilal tossed restlessly, and his sleep was fitful and disturbed.

As dawn broke and the first shafts of daylight stole into the room, Jawaharlal, watching his father's face, saw a sudden calm come on it and a strange peace, as if all sense of struggle had vanished, possess it. He thought his father had fallen asleep. But Swaruprani, also watching intently, knew better. She uttered a cry as she realised that her husband was dead.

They wrapped Motilal's body in the tricolour flag of India, and took it by car that day back to Allahabad. Ranjit drove, with Hari,[1] who was Motilal's favourite servant, seated beside him. Jawaharlal sat by his father's body.

People had assembled all along the route, and at Allahabad the crowd was dense. Motilal went back to his beloved Anand Bhawan where, covered with flowers, his body lay on a bier for a few hours in state. Then, as the shadows of evening fell, the bier was taken, accompanied by a tremendous concourse of people, to the banks of the holy Ganga where Jawaharlal lit the funeral pyre.

"The stars were out and shining brightly when we returned lonely and desolate," he wrote.

[1] Hari now serves Nehru at the Prime Minister's Residence, New Delhi.

13

TIME FOR TRUCE

From henceforth Nehru, bereft of his father, moved in the inner orbit of the Mahatma.

In a sense Jawaharlal stood between Motilal and Gandhi, for while Motilal followed politically in his son's footsteps Jawaharlal followed the Mahatma. The advent of Gandhi with his weapon of non-violent non-cooperation precipitated an inner conflict in Nehru. He was torn between loyalty and love for his father and an urge to march under the Mahatma's banner. Out of love for his son, the father resolved the conflict: he marched in his son's footsteps.

Because he was anxious above all things to check his son's impetuosity, Motilal was at times prepared, against his better judgement, to go some way with him. Gandhi, equally unwilling to move as fast as Jawaharlal, was also a restraining influence. While his father lived, Nehru's political ardour was subject to a double check, but Motilal's death removed one arm of the brake.

The relations between Gandhi and Nehru, because they derive from the original association with the father, can be understood only in that context. As the bond between the two was purified and strengthened through the common ordeal of trial and sacrifice, Nehru came to identify in Gandhi the leader image with the father image. The Mahatma became a blend of parent and political chief, and to disown him seemed in time an act almost of political patricide. So through the coming critical years, as the country moved painfully to freedom, Nehru, although he had many and occasionally deep differences with Gandhi, adjusted himself to the Mahatma's views, thereby giving the impression of an individual unable to make up his mind on vital issues.

There exists in Nehru's character, despite his eruptive and emotional outbursts, a strong strain of calculation. Even when he temporised with the Mahatma, subordinating his own views to the larger and more immediate interests of the country, he never shed or surrendered them. Beneath his mild exterior Gandhi concealed a will which could be hard and flintlike. More resilient than Gandhi in some ways, though less inclined to compromise, Nehru has the same unyielding, adamant core. He can bend but he will not break.

Gandhi, often acting more from intuition than from reason, liked to refer to his instinct as his "inner voice," thereby giving it a messianic motivation. The battle between heart and head, between thought and feeling in a man so intrinsically rational as Nehru lasted only as long as he remained under the tutelage of his father and Gandhi. Love for the two men contended with loyalty to his ideals. The head invariably surrendered to the heart, which gave Nehru in those long years until Gandhi's death on January 30, 1948, the appearance of a man of impulse with a hesitant and vacillating mind.

Nothing could have been further from the truth. "I have not consciously renounced anything that I really valued, but then values change," Nehru once remarked.

With Gandhi's death the battle between heart and head was over, and from that time Nehru has set out to implement his ideas boldly, brooking no opposition, and enabled by his immense prestige and the talisman of his name to carry the country as a whole with him.

In the twenty decisive years between December, 1927, when he returned from Europe convinced in his own mind that the political concept of freedom had no meaning without a defined social and economic content, until August, 1947, when India attained freedom, Nehru was busy, whenever he was out of jail, propagating the need for clear political and economic objectives. His own economic ideas were settling in a socialist mould. Despite the Mahatma's metaphysical approach to many problems, Nehru felt that his own modern ideas could be fulfilled through the Congress.

Even while his father lived, Jawaharlal had prevailed on the Congress to think of *swaraj* in terms of complete independence. On the economic front Nehru had also, though less successfully, prodded the Congress along the socialist path. He was in deadly earnest. But neither the country nor the Congress realised it at the time.

Over the remaining sixteen years of Gandhi's life Jawaharlal was to find himself constantly at loggerheads with the Mahatma. He liked the non-conformist streak in his leader; he admired his creative spirit and his ability to meet fresh challenges and embark on new experiments. But Gandhi's mind seemed tethered to ideas far removed from the radicalism of Nehru's, and he seemed not only to move in another world but to think on another plane.

In those early days some of Gandhi's most favoured projects, such as hand-spinning and hand-weaving, appeared to Nehru to be merely an intensification of individualism in production and therefore a throwback to the pre-industrial age. A projection of this programme was a revival of village industries. In Nehru's economic vocabulary, based largely on modern idioms, such enterprises signified the means to an end, not an end in themselves. Unless village industries were harnessed to modern industrial techniques they could never provide even the essential material goods which India needed. Gandhi appeared to think otherwise. He made it clear that he had no objection to machinery as such; but he felt that large-scale machinery was out of place in the India of his day. Nehru demurred. If India, he contended, had to have railways, bridges and transport facilities, it had either to produce them itself or depend for them on others. Certainly India could not be expected to liquidate such basic industries as iron and steel, nor the lighter small-scale ones.

Discussion on the Soviet Five-Year Plan which was introduced in 1929 was under way when Nehru visited Russia in 1927. The project stirred his imagination, and on his return he tried to popularise the idea of planning in India. Gandhi watched his efforts with benevolent curiosity, and even followed with interest the setting-up in 1938 of the National Planning Committee under Nehru's leadership and the auspices of the Congress. The British Raj might be functioning in India, but to Jawaharlal this national effort represented something more positive than economic theorists at play. In 1950 it was to fructify in independent India's first Five-Year Plan.

Apart from inuring the Congress to socialist ideas by exposing it occasionally to socialist resolutions, Nehru in the coming years was to refer time and again to "the evils of unrestricted and unplanned industrialisation." Many in and outside the Congress were to dismiss these utterances as talk in a heroic vacuum. But, as always, Nehru was in deadly earnest. The mixed economy, with its public and private sectors, which his government established when Nehru became Prime Minister was among the first fruits of this thinking.

Although Nehru had been hopeful that he could influence Gandhi continuously in a socialist direction, he was to discover soon that there were basic differences between the Mahatma's ideals and the socialist objective. Gandhi's view of property as a trust, his antipathy to heavy industrialisation and his fear that the rights of the human personality might be ignored in a collective organisation of economic life prevented him from identifying his own philosophy with socialism. He did not share Nehru's belief that there was no basic opposition between the yogi and the commissar, and that socialism was an equation between individual liberty and a planned economic order.

Yet significantly here again Nehru did not press his view to the point of breaking away from the Mahatma. While the Mahatma lived he was content to serve as a bridge between Gandhism and socialism, and although sympathetic to the Congress Socialist group [1] when it was formed in 1934, he never joined it. He preferred to be a democratic socialist, preserving both economic security and liberty. With Gandhi's death, and under the impulse of the new forces released in independent India, Nehru moved more rapidly in the socialist direction and finally stole the party's thunder. In January, 1955, the Avadi session of the Congress officially adopted a socialistic blueprint for India which was to become a welfare state on the socialistic pattern.

In the years to come, largely under Nehru's stimulus, the Congress was gradually to develop a foreign policy based in the initial stages on "the elimination of political and economic imperialism and the co-operation of free nations." As far back as 1920 the Congress had adopted a resolution in which India's desire to cooperate with other nations, and particularly to develop friendly relations with her neighbours, was stressed. Twelve years before the Second World War, in 1927, the Congress, on Nehru's persuasion, had proclaimed that India

[1] This group later seceded from the Congress to form a separate Socialist party in February, 1948.

would be no party to "an imperialist war" and that in no event should India be compelled to join a war without her people's consent.

Thus Nehru's much debated foreign policy is not the product of an overnight caprice. It flows as naturally from the Mahatma's teaching that violence and war solve nothing as from Nehru's educative pleas over the years for an India in close relationship with the countries of the East and West. Writing in prison during the Second World War, Jawaharlal recalls:

In particular, we thought of close relations with our neighbour countries in the east and west, with China, Afghanistan, Iran and the Soviet Union. Even with distant America we wanted closer relations for we could learn much from the United States as also from the Soviet Union.[2]

Within the family circle Motilal's death drew Jawaharlal closer to Kamala. The civil-disobedience movement of 1930 had revealed her to him in a new light, as friend and comrade, and in this experience Nehru found a new delight. Prison and their separation from each other intensified this feeling. Nehru has recorded how under the shadow of his father's last illness and death their relationship acquired a new basis of comradeship and understanding. Kamala was to die early in 1936, but the five brief years which remained for both of them were to see pain, prison, illness, tragedy and long partings.

On the very day of Motilal's death, on February 6, 1931, several prominent representatives to the Round Table Conference in London, including Sir Tej Bahadur Sapru and Dr. Jayakar, landed in Bombay. On February 8th some of them arrived in Allahabad for discussions with Gandhi and the Congress Working Committee. They had little to say that was new, but they urged the Congress to strengthen their hands by attending the second session.

Gandhi listened politely, but Nehru's reactions were less inhibited and restrained. In his heart and mind he rather despised these moderate counsellors who seemed to him to interpret politics more in terms of personalities than of principles. They were inordinately anxious that Gandhi should reopen negotiations with the Viceroy. Indeed, they had appealed to him on their arrival in Bombay to do nothing by word or deed to upset the precarious political balance,

[2] *The Discovery of India*, written between August 9, 1942, and March 28, 1945, when Nehru was in jail.

and in a statement the Mahatma had agreed to hold his hand until he had met them.

Now Sapru, Jayakar and the silver-tongued Srinivasa Sastri, who hailed from Madras, brought to bear on the Mahatma the full weight of their persuasive eloquence. What would be lost by Gandhi's writing to the Viceroy for an interview? they argued. Probing every avenue of peace was the first tenet in the creed of a satyagrahi. Gandhi, after some reflection, agreed. If he could change the heart of his opponent, perhaps he could change his mind.

On February 14th the Mahatma accordingly wrote to Lord Irwin seeking an interview in order to discuss the political situation. The Viceroy readily agreed. His reply was telegraphically transmitted, and on February 16th Gandhi left Allahabad for Delhi.

The historic Gandhi-Irwin talks commenced at two o'clock on the afternoon of February 17th. For Nehru this was a distressing, even painful phase, and often during the coming months he was to reflect whether the sacrifices of non-violent non-cooperation could so lightly be written away for a temporary truce with the opponent. He opened his mind to the Mahatma and argued with him.

"You are right in your doubts and hesitations," said Gandhi pensively. "But as a satyagrahi I must welcome above all a meeting with those who disagree with me."

Jawaharlal was not altogether convinced.

"True, I can understand your dealing with individuals in this way on personal or minor matters. But here you are up against an impersonal machine, the British Government."

Gandhi smiled.

"You must be patient. Let us wait and see."

The talks progressed, and Gandhi soon summoned the Congress Working Committee to Delhi. He had started the negotiations by proffering six minimum demands to Lord Irwin as earnest of the British Government's good intentions.

He wanted the Viceroy to declare a general amnesty for all political prisoners; the immediate cessation of repression; restitution of all confiscated property; the reinstatement of all Government employees punished on political grounds; liberty to manufacture salt and to picket liquor and foreign cloth shops; and the holding of an inquiry into police excesses.

As usual Gandhi's demands were a curious mélange of social and political pleas seemingly paying little attention to the basic political objectives.

Nehru, not for the first time, was puzzled by this moral-metaphysical approach. What had sin and salvation and the liberty to manufacture salt and to picket liquor shops to do with the country's freedom?

If Nehru was disturbed, a British politician he was later to come to know well was outraged. Addressing the West Essex Conservative Association on February 23, 1931, Winston Churchill declared: "It is alarming and nauseating to see Mr. Gandhi, a seditious Middle Temple lawyer, now posing as a fakir of a type well known in the East, striding half-naked up the steps of the Viceregal Palace, while he is still organising and conducting a defiant campaign of civil disobedience, to parley on equal terms with the representative of the King-Emperor."

Lord Irwin, the representative of the King-Emperor, had different ideas. Like Gandhi, he was essentially a peacemaker, and, like the Indian who wished to humanise politics, the Englishman was anxious to humanise his country's administrative machine. He was also, like Gandhi, deeply religious, although the ascetic strain was not so astringent in him. Irwin wanted an easing in the political tension between Britain and India, and he was eager that the Congress should be represented at the Round Table Conference. In both these objectives he was temporarily successful.

When the talks seemed at one stage on the verge of a breakdown, Irwin called for Gandhi, with whom he had a three-hour interview. They were both exhausted at the end. As Gandhi rose to leave, staff in hand, Irwin said kindly, "Good night, Mr. Gandhi, and my prayers go with you."

Off and on, the Mahatma consulted his colleagues on the Working Committee. He found them, particularly Jawaharlal, more adamant than he himself was inclined to be. Nehru deplored the acceptance of any basis for discussion with the Government save complete independence, while Vallabhbhai Patel, who had initiated a peasant no-tax campaign in Bardoli, was naturally insistent on the unconditional return of confiscated lands. None of them felt that the Government's undertaking on the release of political prisoners was sufficiently comprehensive.

But Gandhi had set his heart on a settlement. He was prepared to compromise, and at length the Working Committee reluctantly agreed. Gandhi's final meeting with the committee was held in eerie circumstances at two o'clock on the morning of March 5th. He came to it straight from the Viceroy's house with a draft copy of the settlement.

Glancing at it, Nehru noticed that Gandhi had accepted the principle of self-government with reservations or safeguards.[3] He was numbed by the discovery, being literally shocked into silence.

As Nehru lay in bed that night, his mind travelled back to the saga and sacrifices of the non-violent movement. Were all these sacrifices to be frittered away in this temporary provisional compromise? How could Gandhi have brought himself to surrender the position when victory seemed within his grasp? Were all their brave words and deeds to end in this?

Nehru wept. He was distressed beyond measure, and his grief and embitterment found vent in tears.

Gandhi was not unaware of Jawaharlal's state of mind. Early next morning he asked Nehru to accompany him on his usual daily walk. He spoke to him gently but earnestly, like a father attempting to persuade a wilful son.

"I have, believe me," he assured Jawaharlal, "surrendered nothing vital. There is no loss of principle involved." And he went on to explain that his acceptance of reservations or safeguards was, as the settlement admitted, "in the interests of India."

Nehru, while somewhat mollified, was not convinced.

"What frightens me," he protested, "is your way of springing surprises upon us."

Gandhi inclined his head meekly.

"Although I have known you for fourteen years," Jawaharlal continued, "there is something unknown about you which I cannot understand. It fills me with apprehension."

[3] Clause 2 of the Delhi Settlement (dated March 5, 1931): "As regards constitutional questions, the scope of future discussion is stated, with the assent of His Majesty's Government, to be with the object of considering further the scheme for the constitutional Government of India discussed at the Round Table Conference. Of the scheme there outlined, Federation is an essential part; so also are Indian responsibility and reservations or safeguards in the interests of India, for such matters, as, for instance, defence; external affairs; the position of minorities; the financial credit of India, the discharge of obligations."

"Yes," Gandhi agreed placidly. "I admit the presence of this un-known element and I confess that I myself cannot answer for it or foretell where it might lead to."

At noon that day the Gandhi-Irwin agreement was formally signed at the Viceroy's house. Both the Mahatma and the Viceroy were in a cheerful mood.

"We must drink each other's health," said Irwin, and, knowing Gandhi's abstemious ways, added quickly, "in tea."

Gandhi agreed. "But I shall drink the toast in water, lemon and a pinch of salt." He chuckled.

They joked over Churchill's references to the Mahatma as "a half-naked fakir," and Irwin, merry and mischievous, reminded Gandhi obliquely of this as he left.

"Gandhi," he called after the departing Mahatma, who had for-gotten his shawl, "here's your shawl. You haven't so much on, you know, that you can afford to leave this behind."

Gandhi laughed uproariously.

If the Congress Working Committee was disturbed by the terms of the settlement, many in the country were even more distressed. Under the settlement the amnesty to political prisoners did not in-clude those kept in detention without trial. Even more contentious was the issue of the death sentence on Bhagat Singh. Public opinion demanded that it should be commuted, but the Government was adamant. On March 23rd, despite Gandhi's desperate pleading, Bha-gat Singh was executed.

"The corpse of Bhagat Singh will stand between us and England," said Nehru, who had met Bhagat Singh and admired his spirit.

None the less the Congress set out faithfully to carry out the terms of the settlement, and civil disobedience was called off all over the country. The Congress, if generally resentful of the settlement, was by no means chastened. Naturally it took pride in the people's sacri-fices and courage; but this was interpreted in the more die-hard offi-cial quarters, smarting under a settlement reached on equal terms between the King's representative and a rebel, as a derisive gesture at the Raj. The majority of British civil servants, like the majority of the Congress, was resentful over the truce.

Gandhi summed up his own view of the settlement in a few terse sentences: "For a settlement of this character it is not possible nor wise to say which is the victorious party. If there is any victory I should say it belongs to both. The Congress has never made any bid for victory."

It was the satyagrahi's approach.

While in Delhi, on one of his daily morning walks, Gandhi surprised Nehru with his heterodox views. They were discussing the future of the Congress.

"My own view," said Jawaharlal, "is that the Congress should cease to exist with the coming of freedom."

"That is not my view," said the Mahatma. "I think the Congress should continue—but on one condition. It must pass a self-denying ordinance that none of its members should accept a paid job under the State. If any one of its members desired such a post he should resign."

At that time Gandhi visualised the Congress as a party which eschewed office, contenting itself with exercising moral pressure on the executive. When independence came sixteen years later, Gandhi thought that the Congress, having achieved its political objective, should dedicate itself to the country's social and economic progress. But he did not demur when the Congress assumed office.

Another annual session of the Congress was in the offing, and its President-elect was the sternly forthright Vallabhbhai Patel. The session convened at Karachi under the shadow of Bhagat Singh's execution, and Gandhi himself on arrival was greeted with black flags and shouts of: "Gandhi, go back. Your truce has sent Bhagat Singh to the gallows."

Gandhi, however, soon pacified the hostile crowd of young men. On March 26th, standing on a platform which was set up in the open air, he addressed a mammoth gathering of 50,000. He was listened to respectfully but in silence.

The open-air stadium at Karachi contained a strong contingent of the so-called Red Shirts from the Northwest Frontier province led by Khan Abdul Ghaffar Khan. They were mostly Pathans (frontier Muslims) who had played a conspicuous part in the civil-disobedience movement, and they drew cheers wherever they went.

The main resolution moved at the session related to the truce and the Round Table Conference. It was ingeniously drafted to accommodate conflicting views, and as it finally emerged from the Congress Working Committee it read:

This Congress, having considered the provisional settlement between the Working Committee and the Government of India, endorses it, and desires to make it clear, that the Congress goal of *Purna Swaraj* [4] remains still intact. In the event of the way being otherwise open to the Congress to be represented at any conference with the representatives of the British Government, the Congress delegation will work for this object, and in particular, so as to give the nation control over the army, external affairs, finance and fiscal and economic policy and to have scrutiny, by an impartial tribunal, of the financial transactions of the British Government of India, and to examine and assess the obligations to be undertaken by India or England, and the right to either party to end the partnership at will provided, however, that the Congress delegation will be free to accept such adjustments as may be demonstrably necessary in the interests of India. . . . The Congress authorizes Mahatma Gandhi to represent it at the conference with the addition of such other delegates as the Working Committee may appoint to act under his leadership.

Gandhi shrewdly requested Nehru, who had accepted the resolution, to move it, but Jawaharlal was initially hesitant. He had never been happy over the truce which he had accepted as a matter of discipline, not conviction. How could he commend it wholeheartedly to the open Congress? But as usual he rationalised these contradictions. He had accepted the resolution, and this being so, he must declare himself for it. He spoke briefly on the spur of the moment, but his extempore speech sounded more convincing than any elaborately prepared address.

"One thing is certain," declared Nehru, "that we cannot afford to be here or there and do two things at the same time. Because of this, I implore you to decide once for all. So far we have decided to abide by Gandhiji, and let us do so until we see the way blocked for further progress."

There was opposition from some quarters and a few amendments were moved, but after Gandhi and Abdul Ghaffar Khan had spoken the resolution was passed.

Nehru also moved a resolution on Bhagat Singh and his two comrades who had been executed, and here he spoke with real fervour and conviction. They did not know, he said, how many Bhagat Singhs

[4] Complete independence.

they might have to sacrifice before India was free. The lesson which they should learn from Bhagat Singh was to die in a manly and bold manner so that India might live.

Gandhi had drafted the resolution, which, while paying tribute to the bravery and sacrifice of Bhagat Singh and his two colleagues, began with the significant line, "This Congress, while dissociating itself from and disapproving of political violence in any shape or form, places on record . . ." Thus only could the Congress creed of non-violence be reconciled with admiration for a patriot who believed in violence.

A resolution in which Nehru was particularly interested concerned Fundamental Rights and Economic Policy. Ever since his return from Europe in December, 1927, Jawaharlal had been anxious to broaden the objective of Congress from the attainment of political freedom to the consideration of economic and social plans and policies. As early as 1926, the United Provinces Congress Committee had drawn up a mild socialist programme aimed primarily at removing all intermediaries between the State and the cultivator. Three years later the same committee put forward a more detailed socialist plan which the All-India Congress Committee, meeting at Bombay, considered. The Bombay meeting adopted the preamble of this plan, thus committing itself to the principle of socialism but without either fully examining or understanding its implications.

"Another of Jawaharlal's whims," was the general verdict. "Let's humour him and pass it."

Nehru, however, was not so easily pacified. He was determined to create a new outlook in the Congress. While at Delhi earlier in the year he had broached the subject to Gandhi during one of their morning walks. Gandhi welcomed the idea of having a resolution on economic matters put before the Congress.

"Why don't you draft it?" he suggested to Jawaharlal. "You can then show it to me at Karachi."

Nehru set about drafting a resolution on Fundamental Rights and Economic Policy. These were on the broad basis of ideas which he generally endorsed and propagated, but Gandhi was not satisfied with the mere enunciation of principles. He wanted items like the duty on salt, the protection of indigenous cloth and a ban on intoxicating drinks and drugs to be included in the programme.

They argued back and forth, Nehru making several drafts until Gandhi and he were agreed. This draft was finally passed by the Congress and referred to the All-India Congress Committee which was scheduled to meet in Bombay in August. With some minor revisions the committee approved the resolution.[5]

One question remained to be finally settled—should Gandhi attend the Round Table Conference? Not long after the Gandhi-Irwin agreement, Irwin had left India to be succeeded by Lord Willingdon, who earlier had been Governor of two Indian provinces, Bombay and Madras, and was also a former Governor-General of Canada.

Willingdon, a man of considerable personal charm, with a reputation of being friendly to Indian aspirations, was bitterly hostile to the Congress and antipathetic to Gandhi, to whom he always referred as "the little man." There could in fact have been no greater contrast than between this lean tall aristocrat in his impeccable clothes, a well known cricketer in his day, and a product of Eton and Cambridge, and the slight, shrivelled toothless figure of the Mahatma in his loincloth and with his spinning wheel. Willingdon, along with his British official advisers, tended to underrate Gandhi's power and the influence of the Congress.

From London came disturbing reports that Whitehall regarded the question of safeguards as settled and closed. In August, 1931, the Socialist Government in Britain had been replaced by a National Government comprising the three parties [6] headed by the former Socialist Prime Minister, Ramsay MacDonald. Gandhi was worried by the reports. "The question is vital," he insisted. "The British Government at any conference must be open not merely to discussion on these questions, but to conviction."

In India itself, with a hostile civil service and a suspicious Congress, it was not easy to implement the terms of the Delhi Pact, as the Gandhi-Irwin agreement came to be known. In the more politically sensitive provinces such as Bengal, the Northwest Frontier Province and the United Provinces tension was not perceptibly eased. The Government's remissions of land revenue disappointed both the peasants and the Congress, and in the United Provinces the agrarian situation, far from improving, deteriorated.

[5] Cf. Appendix, page 493.
[6] Including the rump of the Labour party.

Resentful of the Delhi Pact for transferring the initiative from the Government to the Congress, and in a sense undermining the authority of the services, British officials saw in every Congress move to implement the agreement a drift towards dual authority. Like Willingdon, they were anxious to put the Congress in its place.

The Hindu-Muslim situation also disturbed Gandhi, much of his time after the Karachi session being taken up in improving relations between the two communities. He addressed them jointly and separately, urging them individually and collectively to fight communalism not by counter-communalism but by adopting a national approach.

Late in August, Gandhi left for Simla to see the new Viceroy, Lord Willingdon, who had succeeded Lord Irwin in April. Nehru joined him there and, with Vallabhbhai Patel, Khan Abdul Ghaffar Khan and Dr. M. A. Ansari, had several conversations with various British officials. The latter were courteous, but beneath their polite talk was a veiled threat that the next time the Congress embarked on non-cooperation the Government would come down on it with a heavy hand. Jawaharlal listened with amused interest. He sensed that, like him, the British officials regarded the truce merely as a breathing space.

Gandhi's talks with the Viceroy ended in the Mahatma's deciding finally to leave for London. An agreement was arrived at, with the Government on the one hand promising to investigate the Congress complaints and the Congress reserving to itself, should relief not be forthcoming, the right to take "defensive direct action."

From Simla, Gandhi on August 27th hurried by train to Bombay where the Peninsular and Oriental liner *Rajputana* was due to sail for London on August 29th. Nehru accompanied him, and at Bombay bade his chief farewell.

"I go to London with God as my only guide," declared Gandhi.

From the pier Nehru, a slim tense boyish figure, waved the Mahatma goodbye. Jawaharlal was to go to prison before Gandhi returned. He was not to see his leader for another two years.

14

IN PRISON AGAIN

GANDHI landed at Folkestone on Saturday, September 12th, and drove to London. There he stayed in the East End at Kingsley Hall with Miss Muriel Lester, an English friend of India, as his hostess.

Gandhi was the sole representative of the Congress party. Yet despite his presence in London, Nehru felt that the centre of political gravity still lay in India. What happened there would influence materially the course of events in Britain, and the most that Gandhi could do at the Round Table Conference was to explain the Congress point of view and hope thereby to convince the British public and the world of its reasonableness. He had no illusions about the National Government's acceptance of the plea of Congress.

If Gandhi himself had any illusions, these were quickly dispelled by the frank opinions expressed by the Conservative Secretary of State for India, Sir Samuel Hoare, who is now Lord Templewood.

At their first meeting at the India Office, Hoare politely but forthrightly explained that in his view there could be no question of immediate independence for India, or even of Dominion status, but he was prepared to move slowly towards the latter.

Gandhi, who appreciated frankness, reacted immediately.

"I can meet you, Sir Samuel," he said. "I shake hands with you over that. It's a point of unity between us, your truthfulness. Thank you."

Thereafter, though they disagreed often on many issues, they retained their mutual respect for each other.

The Hindu-Muslim issue dominated the Round Table Conference, and not surprisingly the British Government, holding the ring, real-

188

ised its potentialities. In the motley gathering which comprised the conference it was comparatively easy to set Hindu against Muslim, complicating this tangle by the intrusion of the Sikhs and so-called Untouchables.

Lord Willingdon had refused to accept a nationalist Muslim, Dr. M. A. Ansari, as part of the Congress team which was now represented by Gandhi alone, although a Congresswoman, the poetess Sarojini Naidu, was included in the conference, but as a representative of Indian women. Gandhi's task was not made easier by the Hindu extremists such as Pandit Madan Mohan Malaviya, Dr. Jayakar and the militant Dr. B. S. Moonjee, who staked their communal[1] claims as high as possible in an effort to sabotage any agreement with the Muslims. On the other hand, Jinnah, who was to be the founder of Pakistan, played an intermediary role in these proceedings. His failure to get the two communities together intensified his latent suspicion of the Congress and of Gandhi, and led him ultimately to chalk out the separate path which ended with Pakistan.

Looking back at the conference, it is impossible to absolve Gandhi entirely of blame for the subsequent deepening fissure between Hindus and Muslims. He should have set his face as sternly against the Hindu extremists as he did against the Muslim intransigents, and, by refusing to countenance the high-pitched demands of Malaviya, Moonjee and Jayakar, achieved a settlement with the Muslims and other minorities who now sat sheltered incongruously under the broad feudal umbrella of the Aga Khan.

Not that the Muslim and other minority demands were reasonable. With the exception of the Sikhs, all the other minorities, including the Untouchables, plumped for separate electorates; and the demand for their representation in the legislatures, even allowing for weightage, was out of all proportion to their numerical strength. But the approach of Congress, as represented by the Mahatma, lacked reality.

In effect the Mahatma finally said to the minorities, "Join with me on the political issue of independence, and I shall accept your communal demands."

To that, of course, the obvious answer was: "In order to get inde-

---

[1] In India the term, because of its political implications, implies "religious" or "sectarian," contrary to its broader connotation in the West.

pendence communal unity is essential. Why do you not first concede our claims and we shall then join you in securing independence?"

The negotiations between Gandhi on the one hand and the minorities headed by the Aga Khan on the other finally broke down. Matters were not improved by the minorities [2] banding themselves together and presenting both Gandhi and the British Government with a *fait accompli* in the form of a memorandum. This claimed for the minorities, in addition to their statutory rights, representation through separate electorates and a declaration of civil rights. It was, as Gandhi characterised it, undoubtedly a scheme designed to share power with the bureaucracy by a large-scale division of jobs and the plums of office. Nehru noted sadly that, although masked as "Indianisation," it was really jobbery on behalf of certain elements of the population.

Gandhi refused to have anything to do with it.

"The Congress," he declared, "will wander, no matter how many years, in the wilderness rather than lend itself to a proposal under which the hardy tree of freedom and responsible government can never grow."

Most of all he resented the demand of the Untouchables for separate electorates outside the Hindu register, describing this as "the unkindest cut of all." It would mean, he pointed out, the recognition of untouchability in perpetuity, a "perpetual bar sinister."

Meanwhile, the political situation in India was deteriorating, and the remissions granted by the Government to the peasantry of the United Provinces were specially disappointing, the remissions related to the current tax demand not taking into account arrears or debts. Even so, the peasants were in no position to meet the entire bill. Nehru and his Congress colleagues advised them to pay as much as they could; but this was a counsel of perfection, since the marginal ability of the peasant to pay was small in any case. The number of ejected peasants grew, and simultaneously the slump in agricultural prices aggravated the misery of the countryside.

The collection of the new taxes was to start in October. Since Gandhi's departure Nehru had written to him regularly once every week by air and sea mail, and kept him informed of the deteriorating

[2] These included the Muslims, Sikhs, Untouchables, Anglo-Indians, Europeans and the Catholic section of the Indian Christians.

agrarian situation in the United Provinces. Sooner or later the Congress hands would be forced, although Nehru and his associates had no desire to come into collision with the Government.

From England, Gandhi counselled patience. According to his initial schedule he should have been back in November, but it appeared now as if his return would be delayed. What were they to do, demanded Nehru and his colleagues.

"Act according to your lights," was Gandhi's cabled reply.

On December 1st the second session of the Round Table Conference ended, and Gandhi prepared to leave for India after paying a visit to his biographer, Romain Rolland, at Villeneuve. Politically his mission had failed, and Hindu-Muslim divisions on the constitutional plane had, if anything, intensified.

This did not disturb Nehru unduly, for in his calculation the conference, constituted as it was, was bound to fail. It was a talk-shop where scheming and opportunism had full play. At the same time he recognised that the Indian case, by the projection of internal differences on an international plane, had suffered badly in the eyes of the world. In India itself the tale of failure and divisions in London had produced a sense of humiliation, of frustration and despondency. The glow of the last civil-disobedience movement, with its climax of the Delhi Pact, flickered wanly.

Here, Nehru felt, was an opportunity for the reactionaries to raise their heads. He was not far wrong.

Temporarily on the retreat, they now mobilised their forces at home and abroad. Hindu-Muslim tension was to increase in the coming years as the privileged members of both communities scrambled for the prizes of office. British officials in India, the majority of whom had never reconciled themselves to the "humiliation" of the Gandhi-Irwin agreement, were eager for a "showdown" with the Congress. In Lord Willingdon they had a Viceroy who shared their mood. Abroad, in London, Churchill continued to bay for the blood of the Congress.

The general elections in England in October, 1931, saw the Tories returned to power with an overwhelming majority, and on November 5th a second National Government, with Ramsay MacDonald as Prime Minister, was announced. In his final speech to the Second

Round Table Conference MacDonald declared that if a communal settlement acceptable to all the Indian parties was not forthcoming the British Government would announce its own communal award.

In this depressing atmosphere Gandhi wended his way home. He left London for Folkestone on December 5th, stopping en route at Villeneuve for the long-planned meeting with Rolland. As he disembarked at Bombay on December 28th, the first news which greeted him was the arrest of Nehru and Khan Abdul Ghaffar Khan, and the imposition of ordinances which enabled the Government summarily to arrest and detain suspects.

"Christmas gifts from Lord Willingdon, our Christian Viceroy," Gandhi characterised them.

What had happened?

The peasants in the United Provinces, unable to pay their dues even after the remissions granted them, and faced with renewed demands for payment of taxes in October, had turned to the Congress for advice. It was a difficult situation. The Congress knew that many local officials were sensitive over the remissions already granted, regarding this as yet another surrender to Congress demands. On the other hand, to advise the peasants to pay was to ask the impossible of them. Even if the peasants paid the current demand, what guarantee was there that they might not be dispossessed of their land on the ground that they still owed past arrears?

Some months earlier, while with Gandhi at Simla, Nehru had posed this problem to a British official and had asked him what he would do if a peasant were to seek his advice.

"I would simply refuse to answer him," said the official.

But this the Congress could not do.

Matters came to a head when the Allahabad District Congress Committee, which contained a strong leavening of peasants, decided that it could not possibly advise the peasants to pay. Even then the United Provinces Provincial Congress Committee warned it to take no aggressive step without its approval and that of the All-India Congress Working Committee.

The Provincial Congress Committee accordingly deputised its president, Tassaduk Ahmad Khan Sherwani, ironically the scion of a prominent Muslim landowning family, to present the issue before the Working Committee. He was accompanied by Purushottam Das

Tandon,[3] a straggly-bearded Congressman who looked like a tattered prophet from the Old Testament. Nehru, as he wryly admits, "was not considered a very safe person to advise on social and economic matters." The Working Committee itself was straining every nerve to avoid a conflict with the Government.

But Sherwani and Tandon proved most persuasive advocates of the peasants' cause. The Working Committee had no strong economic or social predilections, although it was politically advanced. Above all, it was reluctant to aggravate the landlord-tenant issue. None the less the committee found it hard to escape the implications of Sherwani's sturdy pleading.

Reluctantly it gave the United Provinces Provincial Committee authority to permit the suspension of payment of rent and revenue in any area. But simultaneously it advised the committee not to force the issue, and to carry on negotiations with the Government while these were possible.

For some short while the committee sought to parley with the authorities. But the feeling of inevitable conflict overwhelmed both sides, and each parried with the other rather like two contestants in a bout of shadow boxing. On their side the local authorities, obsessed with official notions of prestige, manœuvred for the "kill." The Congress on its part was also eager to save face.

At this juncture, a peasants' conference held under the auspices of the Allahabad District Congress Committee rang what in official ears sounded suspiciously like a tocsin call to action. It passed a tentative resolution declaring that if better terms were not obtained it would have to advise the peasants to withhold payment of rent and revenue, a move which brought not only the provincial committee but the provincial government to the alert.

The United Provinces Government, making this a *casus belli*, broke off negotiations with the Congress, which in turn prepared itself for the inevitable blow. Both sides were manœuvring for position, the Congress anxious to avoid a showdown until Gandhi came back, the Government determined to strike while it had the initiative.

Inevitably the Government struck first. It announced a series of ready-made ordinances permitting arrest and detention on suspicion

[3] He was later President of the Congress, and is now a member of the Lok Sabha (People's Assembly), the lower house of India's Parliament.

without trial. These measures applied not only to the United Provinces but to Bengal and the Northwest Frontier, where discontent had been simmering for some time.

In Bengal, long the centre of terrorist activities, the Delhi Pact had never been popular, particularly in youth and labour circles. As in the United Provinces so also in Bengal, the vicious circle of unredressed popular grievances, official repression, protest and counter-action generated an uneasy and, because of the terrorist movement, explosive situation. A special prison camp for détenus had been set up by the Bengal Government at a place called Hijli, about seventy miles from Calcutta, and here the guards, on the plea of the prisoners' rioting, opened fire on them, killing two and seriously injuring twenty of the inmates. Public protest compelled the appointment of a judicial inquiry, which held that the firing was unjustified.

The terrorists were active again. Not long after the Hijli episode a terrorist in Chittagong [4] shot down a police officer who happened to be a Muslim, thereby precipitating a Hindu-Muslim riot. Police reprisals took the form of letting loose hooligans on the town who looted in broad daylight while the authorities remained passive. In November a veiled form of martial law was introduced in the district of Chittagong, being extended later to Midnapore (where three British magistrates had been shot down in quick succession) and to Dacca. A curfew order was introduced, young men were forbidden to use bicycles, people were ordered to carry identification cards, collective fines were imposed on villages suspected of harbouring revolutionaries, and political suspects were required to remain indoors for weeks at a time.

During this period a number of revolutionaries were condemned to death and hanged. The Bengal Congress, faced with mounting public indignation, found itself in an invidious position. Officially the Delhi Pact imposed a truce, but the breach between the Government and the people was widened daily.

In November, Nehru visited Calcutta, where he addressed a number of mass meetings and discussed the situation privately with individuals and groups. Most of all he was anxious to convince those he met of the futility of terrorist methods and of the harm they were doing to the cause of freedom.

[4] A port in East Bengal.

On the last evening of his stay in Calcutta, shortly before he was leaving for the railway station, Nehru was told that two young Bengalis were waiting to see him. They were terrorists, and Nehru, on entering the room where they waited, found himself confronted by two tense youths barely twenty years old. Their faces were taut and nervous, but Jawaharlal was fascinated by their blazing brilliant eyes.

"We have come to warn you," said one of them. "Your propaganda against terrorism is harming the country. It is keeping away the young men from us."

Nehru spoke to them forthrightly, stressing his view that the activities of the terrorists injured the cause of freedom and made difficult the process of building up national unity and discipline. Terrorism, he argued, would encourage sporadic violence, and the habit of indiscriminate murder would deepen fissures inside the country. It would breed communal violence.

The two boys were not convinced. They argued and expostulated angrily. But Nehru held firmly to his view, and in turn spoke sharply.

"We warn you," they repeated as they left: "if you continue your criticism we shall deal with you as we have done with some others."

In the train on his way back to Allahabad, Nehru found his thoughts turning often to the two boys. Had he spoken more gently and quietly he might perhaps have been able to convince them. But he had been in a hurry to catch his train, and their shrill, angry protests had irritated him. He never saw them again.

In December the Bengal Congress summoned a special provincial session at Berhampur and accused the Government of virtually violating the Delhi Pact. It urged that the All-India Congress should give formal notice to the Government and revive the civil-disobedience campaign, with special emphasis on the boycott of British goods. The revival of the non-cooperation movement, it argued, might help to divert the energy of the country's youth to non-violent forms of protest. The Bengal Congress was preparing to strike back.

Away on the other side of India, on the Northwest Frontier, the Red Shirts under Khan Abdul Ghaffar Khan were causing the local authorities concern. Early in December they set up a camp in the Peshawar district to train volunteers for the national movement. The Frontier Provincial Congress Committee characterised the British Prime Minister's announcement at the Round Table Conference as unsatisfactory, and delegated Ghaffar Khan to proceed to Bombay to discuss the situation with Gandhi on his arrival. Disturbed by these developments the Frontier authorities invited Ghaffar Khan and his brother, Dr. Khan Sahib, to talk over matters with them. The two brothers refused to parley with the Government behind the back of the Congress.

Ordinances were immediately clamped on the province, and the Khan brothers, with their more prominent colleagues, were summarily arrested and imprisoned on December 24th, four days before Gandhi's arrival.

Jawaharlal himself had only another two days of freedom.

Early in December he had left Allahabad to tour the Karnatak district of Bombay, his primary purpose being to inspect the headquarters of the Congress volunteer body known as the Hindustani Seva Dal. Kamala was ill again, and Jawaharlal, on his way to the Karnatak, arranged for her stay and treatment in Bombay. Here he heard of the comprehensive ordinances introduced by the United Provinces Government, one of them providing for the punishment of parents and guardians for the political sins of their children and wards.

"A reversal of the old biblical practice," Nehru noted grimly.

From Allahabad shortly after came the news of the arrest of Purushottam Das Tandon. The Government had struck; and Nehru, realising that his place was in his own province, hurried there, leaving Kamala bed-ridden in Bombay.

At Chheoki railway station, a few miles from Allahabad, Nehru was served with an order interning him within the municipal limits of Allahabad and forbidding him to attend any public meeting or function, speak in public, or write anything in a newspaper or leaflet. The order was served on him at midnight while he was alighting from the Bombay train to take the shuttle to Allahabad. At the time, amusingly enough, he had still one foot in the Bombay train.

Similar orders were served on such of Nehru's colleagues as were still free, including Tassaduk Sherwani.

On reaching Allahabad, Nehru wrote to the district magistrate who had issued the order on him, informing him curtly that he did not propose taking any orders from him as to what he should or should not do. He went on to say that he proposed carrying on with his normal work in the ordinary way and that he intended leaving shortly for Bombay in order to meet Gandhi and attend a session of the Congress Working Committee of which he was the secretary.

The magistrate had spelt Nehru's name incorrectly as Jawahir Lal, and this annoyed Nehru intensely. In his letter to that official he pointed out the mistake and expressed the hope that it would not recur.

"What do you think of my letter?" Nehru asked some of his colleagues after reading it to them.

"It is too curt," said one of them, Sri Prakasa, who is now Governor of Madras. "If that letter goes in its present form you will not go to Bombay."

Jawaharlal smiled.

"I am going," he insisted, "and nobody will stop me."

But Sri Prakasa was right.

On the morning of December 26th Nehru and Sherwani boarded the train at Allahabad station for Bombay. Soon after leaving Chheoki, the train pulled up on the border of Allahabad district at a small wayside station called Iradatganj.

Looking out of the window Nehru saw a police wagon by the railway line. A few moments later a number of police officials mounted up to the compartment and put Nehru and Sherwani under arrest. The wagon trundled its way to Naini Prison. It was Boxing Day, and the British police superintendent who had arrested them, deprived of his holiday, looked solemn and glum.

Their trial took place on January 4, 1932, inside the prison. Early that morning Gandhi, with the President of the Congress, Vallabhbhai Patel. had been arrested, and both were detained without trial as State prisoners.

Shortly after his arrival in Bombay the Mahatma had telegraphically sought an interview with the Viceroy, and Lord Willingdon, in a long telegram from Delhi, had agreed provided Gandhi did not discuss the ordinances introduced by the Government in Bengal, the United Provinces and the Frontier nor the official action taken under them.

Since that was precisely what Gandhi wished to discuss, he wired to the Viceroy accordingly, adding that the ordinances were legalised Government terrorism. He went on to say that the Congress Working Committee, on his advice, had tentatively passed a resolution sketching a plan of civil disobedience. "If His Excellency thinks it worth while to see me," concluded Gandhi, "the operation of the resolution will be suspended pending our discussion in the hope that it may result in the resolution being finally given up."

Lord Willingdon in his reply stated the Government's inability to negotiate "under the threat of the resumption of civil disobedience." Gandhi's rejoinder implied that the launching of civil disobedience was in any case inevitable and imminent but went on to say, "I wish to assure the Government that every endeavour will be made on the part of the Congress to carry on the campaign without malice and in a strictly non-violent manner."

Early the next morning, on January 4th, Gandhi was arrested. "Infinite is God's mercy," he said in a message to his countrymen. "Never swerve from truth and non-violence, never turn your back, and sacrifice your lives and all to win *swaraj*."

Nehru and Sherwani were tried under the United Provinces Emergency Powers Ordinance for the identical offence—disobeying an order served on them not to leave the limits of Allahabad city. But whereas Sherwani was sentenced to six months' rigorous imprisonment and a fine of Rs.150 ($30), Nehru was sentenced to two years' rigorous imprisonment and a fine of Rs.500 (in default, six months more).

Sherwani, a Muslim, on hearing these disparate sentences, inquired of the magistrate, "Is there religious discrimination even in judicial judgements?"

What had rankled with the magistrate was Nehru's curt letter to him, which he characterised as "offensive."

The Government had declared the Congress illegal, and by January 10th the leading Congressmen from all over India were in jail. Gandhi had actually been arrested under a Bombay ordinance of 1827 which the Government had revived. Ordinance rule was extended throughout India, and in March the British Secretary of State for India, Sir Samuel Hoare, speaking in the House of Commons, admitted that the ordinances "cover almost every activity of Indian life."

Within the first four months some 80,000 people found themselves behind bars. Although deprived of their leaders the Congress rank and file fought on, offering various forms of civil disobedience, including the boycott of foreign goods and refusal to pay taxes. But the mammoth machinery of official repression ground its way inexorably.

Many Indian women, including Nehru's mother and his two sisters, Vijayalakshmi and Krishna, took part in the movement, and Vijayalakshmi and Krishna were soon in jail with a sentence of one year apiece. In order to deter widespread feminine participation, the Government took a perverse pleasure in making the conditions of jail life for women political prisoners unduly harsh. Girls of fifteen or sixteen, not out of their teens, were often sentenced to two years' rigorous imprisonment for merely shouting slogans or gathering in assembly.

"This time," said Sir Samuel Hoare in Parliament, "there will be no drawn battle."

In April came National Week when processions were held despite police prohibition, to be followed by lathi charges. In one of these, Jawaharlal's mother was badly hurt. Although by no means in the best of health, Swaruprani had insisted on participating in a procession which was halted by the police. The processionists stood in a long file, and a kindly Congressman obtained a chair on which Swaruprani sat at the head of the procession. Several persons, including some in Swaruprani's immediate entourage, were arrested by the police, but she was left alone.

Soon afterward the police made a fierce lathi charge on the processionists and, converging on Swaruprani, knocked the old lady from her chair to the ground, where she was beaten repeatedly with heavy canes. Blood streamed from an open wound in her forehead and she fainted. When the road had been cleared of the processionists, Swaruprani was found lying by the wayside. She was picked up by a police officer, who brought her in his car to Anand Bhawan.

Angry crowds, on hearing a false report of Swaruprani's death, shed their non-violence temporarily and attacked the police, who fired on the demonstrators, killing a few.

Reading newspaper reports of the incident a few days later, Nehru (who was only allowed a weekly paper) was deeply distressed and angered.

"The thought of my frail old mother lying bleeding on the dusty road obsessed me," he wrote, "and I wondered how I would have behaved if I had been there."

About a month later Swaruprani, her head still swathed in bandages, came to see her son, who in the meanwhile had been removed from Naini Prison to the jail at Bareilly. She wore her bandages proudly, as though they were badges of distinction, and her talk was glad and spirited. The mother in her saw in her bruises a tribute to her son.

Nehru's own health deteriorated in this period. For many months in 1932 his temperature registered a daily rise. Inclined to exult in his good health, he was peeved by these aberrations, and tried to counter them by long sunbaths in the winter when the crisp cold of North India conspires with the richness of the sun. It filled him with a new effulgence, lighting his body with a glow of friendly warmth, even rapture.

In prison, too, his dietetic habits changed. Like nearly all Kashmiri Brahmins, he had eaten meat since childhood; but in 1920, in the fervour of non-cooperation, he took to a strictly vegetarian diet. He had never been excessively fond of meat, and the change was to his liking. In 1926, on his journey to Europe, he reverted to meat-eating, but on his return became again virtually a vegetarian, with meat having a microscopic share in his diet. This habit persists.

Nehru proffers a curious reason for his antipathy to meat, its basis being more aesthetic than dietetic. Meat-eating, he says, "gives me a feeling of coarseness."

Under Gandhi's stimulus Jawaharlal had earlier given up smoking, a gesture of renunciation which he observed for five or six years not because of any sense of moral elevation it gave him but in order primarily to simplify his mode of living. It was also, he felt, a measure of self-discipline.

Bareilly's summer heat was enervating, and in view of Nehru's indifferent health the authorities decided to move him and Pandit Govind Ballabh Pant, also from the United Provinces and now Home Minister in the Central Cabinet, to the more salubrious climate of Dehra Dun, which nestles in the foothills of the Himalayas.

He had spent six weeks at Naini and four months at Bareilly. Now for another fourteen and a half months, almost to the end of his two-year term, he was to stay in Dehra Dun jail.

As Nehru and Pant left Bareilly, the local superintendent of police, an Englishman, came shyly forward, and as Nehru entered the police car handed him a package.

"It contains old German illustrated magazines," he explained. "I hear you are learning German. So I thought you might like to have a look at these."

It was a kindly thought and the gesture moved Nehru. Pant and he drove in the car through the cool night air to a wayside station fifty miles from Bareilly where they boarded the train for Dehra Dun. The prison authorities, fearing the possibility of a public demonstration, had decided on this course.

This comparatively long prison term gave Nehru time for thought and appraisal.

Outside, the civil-disobedience movement went on fitfully, but it was clear that the initiative rested with the Government and that the Congress was on the defensive. The Government had sequestrated Swaraj Bhawan, Motilal's old residence which he had deeded to the Congress and which this organisation used as its headquarters. In prison Nehru heard that his own house, Anand Bhawan, might also be seized against his father's income-tax dues, part of which he had paid and the remainder of which he had withheld when he had advised the United Provinces peasants not to pay their taxes. He felt that to pay his own taxes while counselling the peasants to withhold theirs would be incongruous and inequitable. The idea of having his mother turned out of the house and the Union Jack replacing the national tricolour on the masthead disturbed him. But mulling over the matter in prison, he felt that on a nationalist basis it would be no bad thing if his house were seized, for it would bring him nearer the peasantry who were being dispossessed. As events transpired, his house was not seized, for the Government came upon certain railway shares he held and these were attached. But Nehru's motor car, and Ranjit's also were attached and sold.

Nehru read eagerly the weekly newspaper allowed him in jail and from it learned something of the happenings outside. Off and on, his mother visited him, and the sight of her frail frame and indomitable spirit cheered while it also saddened him. Then one day he read that his mother, with his wife and daughter—Kamala was back in Allahabad—had called to see Ranjit in the Allahabad District Jail. The caprice of a peevish warder had turned on them, and for no fault of their own they were insulted and hustled summarily out of the jail. The United Provinces Government, far from inquiring into the matter, chose to treat it with lofty disdain.

Jawaharlal was angered and hurt. To avoid exposing those near and dear to him to similar official outbursts he gave up his interviews for nearly seven months. It was as hard for him as for those outside, but it was the only form of protest he could make.

Civil disobedience continued sporadically, having lost its momentum. There were fitful no-tax agrarian campaigns in the United Provinces and in Bombay, centred largely in Gujerat and the Karnatak. They were brief flashes in the pan. Attempts were made in April, 1932, to hold a Congress session in Delhi; but this again was no more than a symbolic demonstration, being confined to about five hundred persons, most of whom were arrested by the police.

Gandhi meanwhile, although in jail, had not been inactive. The impending communal award which the British Prime Minister had threatened weighed heavily on his mind, particularly the possibility of separate electorates being granted to the Untouchables. He wrote to Sir Samuel Hoare early in March.

"In the event of the decision creating separate electorates for the Depressed Classes I must fast unto death," Gandhi warned.

Nehru knew nothing of this correspondence, Gandhi's only confidantes being his secretary, Mahadev Desai, and Vallabhbhai Patel, both of whom were in prison with him.

In London the third session of the Round Table Conference ended after being five weeks in conclave. On August 17, 1932, Ramsay Mac-Donald announced the British Government's provisional scheme of minority representation known as the Communal Award. Not only were the Depressed Classes (the so-called Untouchables) given separate electorates, but they were also conceded the additional right of contesting seats in the general constituencies, it being stipulated that separate electorates were to lapse automatically at the end of twenty years.

To Gandhi the news came as no bombshell. He had expected some such manœuvre calculated to drive an additional wedge between the caste Hindus and the Untouchables in yet another effort by the British Government to offset the weight of the majority community. He lost no time in reiterating his views. On August 18th Gandhi wrote to the British Prime Minister that in protest against the award he would begin his "fast unto death" on September 20th. MacDonald, in a letter dated September 8th, regretted that the British Government's decision could not be changed unless the various Indian groups and communities agreed to an alternative as between themselves. Gandhi's reply was to repeat his determination to fast.

The release of this correspondence on September 12th produced widespread concern and dismay in India, but had the good result of galvanising all sections of the Hindu community, including the die-hard elements, to find a way out of the impasse.

As Rajendra Prasad, now President of India, declared: "Hindu society is on trial. If it has any life in it, it must now respond with a great and magnificent act."

Several orthodox Hindu temples were thrown open to the Untouchables, but this gesture did not solve the basic constitutional problem. Leaders of the orthodox and liberal elements, including some representatives of the Untouchables, waited on the Mahatma in prison.

At 11:30 A.M. on Tuesday, September 20th, Gandhi took his last meal of lemon juice and honey with water, before commencing his fast.

Once again Nehru, hearing the news in jail, brooded over the Mahatma's infinite capacity for giving shocks. Following some initial moments of anguish at the thought that he might never see Gandhi again, Jawaharlal was piqued by the feeling that here again Gandhi had characteristically chosen not a basic political issue but a side issue dealing with electorates. What was the practical value, he wondered, in immolating oneself for something so insignificant?

"He even seemed to suggest," mused Nehru, "that God had indicated the very date of the fast. What a terrible example to set!"

But anger soon gave way to concern. Nehru sat down to rationalise his mood of irritation. Thinking over Gandhi's decision, he recalled his wonderful uncanny knack of doing the right thing at the right moment. Maybe this too would work out in the right way. One must face death—even Gandhi's death—without flinching. A strange calm settled on him.

Gandhi's thoughts were also with Nehru, for instinctively he divined the feelings of the younger man. In a telegram sent to Nehru shortly after the Mahatma started his fast, Gandhi's tone was affectionate and intimate. The first three sentences of his message read: "During all these days of agony you have been before my mind's eye. I am most anxious to know your opinion. You know how I value your opinion."

On the fifth day of the fast, September 24th, after many comings and goings, an agreement was reached which was acceptable both to Gandhi and to Dr. B. R. Ambedkar, the most vocal and intelligent of the Depressed Class leaders, who agreed to forego separate electorates but at a heavy price. MacDonald's communal award had given the Untouchables a total of 71 seats in the provincial legislatures on the basis of separate electorates; this the Poona agreement [5] lifted to a total of 148 seats on the basis of general electorates. In the federal legislature visualised under the White Paper (embodying the recommendations of the Third Round Table Conference), the Depressed Classes were conceded 18 per cent of the total number of seats. MacDonald lost no time in telegraphically communicating the British Government's acceptance of the agreement, and on September 26th Gandhi terminated his fast.

Nehru, although congenitally allergic to pacts and agreements, heaved a sigh of relief. He sent Gandhi a congratulatory telegram of which the relevant sentences read:

No sacrifice too great for suppressed downtrodden classes. Freedom must be judged by freedom of lowest but feel danger of other issues obscuring only goal. Am unable to judge from religious viewpoint. Danger your methods being exploited by others but how can I presume to advise a magician. Love.

Nehru was clearly cautious in his reactions, for he sensed that one immediate result of Gandhi's fast would be to provide Congressmen, who were wearying of civil disobedience, with a convenient loophole. The Poona agreement constituted a respectable escape clause through which the movement would die of induced inaction.

There he was less than fair, for civil disobedience, such as it was, was at its last gasp. Nehru none the less was disturbed by the special facilities which the Government was giving Gandhi to meet people

[5] Named from the fact that Yerawda Prison, where Gandhi was lodged, is near Poona.

and to issue instructions from jail to the leaders of the Harijan [6] movement outside. His suspicions were borne out by a remark Sir Samuel Hoare made in Parliament in December. "The interest of many Congress workers," he observed, "has now been diverted to Mr. Gandhi's campaign against untouchability."

South India became the storm centre of anti-untouchability work. With Gandhi conducting the campaign from jail, interest in civil disobedience languished. Yet the movement continued its fitful course.

January 4, 1933, signalised its first anniversary, and an attempt was made under the instructions of the acting Congress President, Rajendra Prasad, to hold meetings all over the country. Prasad was arrested. In March another effort was made to hold the annual session of the Congress at Calcutta; Swaruprani, despite her ill health, insisted on attending. She was arrested at Asansol on her way to Calcutta, and detained for a few days. In all, about a thousand delegates were arrested en route to the session; but another thousand managed to escape police vigilance, and gathered at Calcutta. They were dispersed by repeated lathi charges but not before they had passed a number of resolutions. Many of them were arrested but released after a few days of detention.

Meanwhile, the success of Gandhi's untouchability campaign was beginning to rouse the ire of some orthodox Hindus. Dr. Ambedkar, on second thoughts, was also opposed to the proposed panel system of elections for the Harijans. To mobilise public opinion strongly behind him Gandhi decided to go on a twenty-one-day "self-purificatory" fast beginning on May 8th.

To Nehru the fast seemed an incomprehensible gesture; nevertheless, feeling that Gandhi was determined to undergo it, he sent the Mahatma a telegram in reply to a letter Gandhi had written to him.

"Whatever happens," Nehru wrote, "my love and thoughts will be with you."

On May 8th, the first day of his fast, the Government released Gandhi, and the Mahatma reciprocated by announcing the suspension of civil disobedience for a month, simultaneously calling on the Gov-

[6] Harijan means Child of God, a name bestowed by Gandhi on the Untouchables.

ernment to release all political prisoners and to withdraw the ordinances. Later Mr. M. S. Aney,[7] the acting President of Congress, extended the suspension period to six weeks. The Congress was proffering the olive branch.

Gandhi continued, and completed, his fast in the house of an old friend in Poona. To Nehru the mass emotionalism aroused by the fast seemed to be sheer revivalism which put clear thinking at a discount. Why was Gandhi always harping on purity and sacrifice? Surely the right thing was to get the people to think.

So Nehru mused in jail as the summer months evaporated into the monsoon and autumn. He knew that the suspension of civil disobedience, however temporary, was a death blow to the movement. One could not play fast and loose with the people. In mid-June civil disobedience was suspended for another six weeks, an attempt to give a semblance of life to a corpse only awaiting interment.

The end was not far. In mid-July, at a conference summoned in Poona, Gandhi received a mandate to reopen negotiations with the Viceroy "with a view to exploring the possibilities of peace." Nehru was disconcerted by the news. The Viceroy's refusal to grant Gandhi an interview came as no surprise, but further dampened the country's spirit. Another effort by Gandhi met with the same response.

Thereupon Gandhi announced the suspension of mass civil disobedience but permitted civil disobedience by individuals, in itself a meaningless gesture which the Government rightly construed as the virtual hoisting of the white flag. The mass civil-disobedience movement had lasted for eighteen months, in the course of which nearly 100,000 persons were imprisoned.

In prison Nehru heard of Gandhi's decision to disband his ashram at Sabarmati near Ahmedabad and to head the movement of individual civil disobedience. The Mahatma fixed August 1st as the date when he would leave the ashram, never to return to it until freedom was achieved. On the night of July 31st Gandhi was arrested, along with thirty-four other inmates of the ashram. He was removed from Sabarmati to Yerawda Jail near Poona, but released on August 4th after being served with an order to leave the village of Yerawda and live within the city limits of Poona. This he declined to do, and was again arrested and sentenced to a year's imprisonment.

[7] Later Governor of Bihar.

In jail Gandhi asked for the privilege he had formerly enjoyed of directing the Harijan movement from behind prison walls. But the situation had changed, and civil disobedience was virtually dead. The Government was prepared to allow him only limited facilities, and in protest the Mahatma embarked on another "fast unto death" on August 16th. On August 18th the Government offered to release him conditionally if he was prepared while outside "to abandon all civil disobedience activities and incitements." Gandhi refused a conditional release. On August 21st he was removed to a local hospital, and two days later, when his condition grew dangerous, the Government released him unconditionally.

In this period Nehru was transferred once again from Dehra Dun to Naini Prison. While there he heard that his mother had been taken suddenly ill and had been removed to hospital. His own two-year term of imprisonment was drawing to a close. But on August 30, 1933, the authorities decided to release him in view of Swaruprani's serious illness. Ordinarily he should have been released on September 12th.

Nehru emerged from his sixth term of imprisonment to see the changing face of India, exultant and defiant when he went to jail nearly two years before, now sombre and sullen and tired. Repression had taken its toll. He was to be free for exactly five months and thirteen days.

15

—AND AGAIN

"ONE begins to appreciate the value of the little things of life in prison," Nehru wrote while in one of the many prisons he has occupied.

In the four years from December 26, 1931, when he was arrested on his way to Bombay, to September 4, 1935, when he was released from Almora Jail after his seventh term of imprisonment, Jawaharlal was at liberty for barely nine months. If prison gave him time for thought it also deepened his sense of melancholy and intensified the mood of loneliness. In his eyes there settled the now familiar far-away look as of a dreamer scanning distant hills or horizons.

At this period Nehru, hovering in the mid-forties, found much time to resolve more clearly for himself his already formulated views and ideas. He was older in body and mind, with his intellectual curiosity still abundant and insatiable; and, save for a brief spell of ill health in 1932, which he quickly mastered, he was physically resilient and fit. Any bodily ailment, as he confesses, hurts his conceit of good health.

A favourite yoga exercise in this prison phase was the *shirshasana*, which consists in standing on one's head with the interlocked fingers of the hands supporting the back of the head, keeping the elbows on the floor, and the body vertically sustained upside down. It is meant primarily to stimulate the spine, and Nehru started his day with this exercise, as he still does, spending five to ten minutes early every morning in this inverted posture.

In prison he found the *shirshasana* not only physically invigorating but also a form of psychological stimulus. The slightly comic position increased his good humour.

"It made me a little more tolerant of life's vagaries," he recalls.

To Edgar Snow, the American journalist, who called on him shortly after he was Prime Minister, Nehru explained its physical advantages.

"It's a complete reversal of the normal situation," he told Snow. "The body is forced to adapt itself to new conditions. One sits or walks about all day and forgets about giving the spine a change."

Nehru is keenly interested in yoga exercises, which he still carries out for a few minutes on waking up every morning. An English journalist, Ian Stephens, who was in India for some years as editor of the British-owned *Statesman* and who is also a keen devotee of yoga, once found himself during an interview with Nehru seated on the same settee with India's future Prime Minister, both men tranquilly doing *pranayam,* or breathing exercises.

"It was much more fun than politics," observed Stephens.

In his early forties Nehru still retained a great deal of his boyish charm and enthusiasm. His face, always pale, suggested an inner tenseness; but the brown eyes, reflective and often brooding, could light up in response to something that pleased or amused him, and the mobile mouth flash a smile, gay, teasing, sometimes wistful and tender.

Nehru's face reflects the bundle of contrary emotions he is, and betrays both the masculine and feminine traits which constitute his character. In repose his face has an almost feminine delicacy of line, with the mouth carrying a curious impression of purposefulness and petulance. Already in his early forties, Nehru's hair was greying and thinning rapidly; today the bald dome of his well proportioned head conveys intellect and authority. There is ambition in the strong upper lip. The eyes, usually grave and sunken, sometimes seem to protrude from his pallid countenance, darting under dark eyebrows in moods of animation; but they are the sombre, sensitive eyes of a thinker and scholar.

Something of this sensitivity was seen in Nehru's reactions to prison life, of which the last term was until then the longest. If non-violence was in the air outside, violence grew in official circles and behind prison walls. Apart from what seemed a deliberate policy of ill-treating women prisoners in an attempt to deter women from joining the nationalist movement, political prisoners, particularly the younger and more spirited, were flogged on the slightest pretext. In April, 1933, an official spokesman in the British Parliament admitted that over five hundred individuals were whipped during 1932 for offences connected with the civil-disobedience movement, and a provincial inspector-general of prisons, in a circular dated June 30, 1932, impressed "upon superintendents and jail subordinates the fact that there is no justification for preferential treatment in favour of civil disobedience prisoners as such. This class require to be kept in their places and dealt with grimly."

From man's brutality to man against which, prisoner as he himself was, he felt helpless, Nehru turned to the birds and animals which brought a breath of civilised life to the jungle of political imprisonment. In Naini Prison and Bareilly Jail he had several companions, but in Dehra Dun, beginning with two companions, he found himself for nearly eight months, from January until his release in August, 1933, a solitary prisoner with no one to talk to except an occasional warder. In all three prisons he discovered some relief in watching the bird and animal life around him.

He found companionship in the pigeons abounding in Bareilly, and in Naini he often watched the green-feathered red-billed parrots as they swarmed through the prison and nested cheerfully in the crevices of the barrack walls. How human and elemental were their emotions! One day he was amused by a fierce fight between two male parrots for the favours of a female who sat calmly by, unruffled and cool, awaiting the outcome of the battle.

The woods and hills around Dehra Dun teemed with birds, and Nehru, of a late evening, often listened to their gay cacophonous twittering. High above their lively chorus there sometimes came the plaintive call of a koel, the Indian equivalent of the common cuckoo, whose weirdly exciting call is as well known in India as the cuckoo's is in Europe. Not so welcome was that other species of cuckoo, the brain-fever bird with its shrill, insistent whirring ascending trill. Sometimes eagles and kites would fly high up in the air, tracing spiral and gliding movements as they soared gracefully overhead. Nehru never tired of watching them. The symmetry of wild duck as they made their way across the sky also attracted him, and he liked to follow a flock as they swept past with a patterned beat of wings.

There were monkeys, too, in Bareilly; and Nehru, his heart being always with the underdog, once watched with relish the simians triumph over the unthinking cruelty of man. A baby monkey, losing its way in the barrack enclosure, was captured by a group of convicts and warders, who tethered it to a post with a string around its neck. Its cries attracted its elders; and one of them, a huge monkey, ignoring the captors, who were brandishing sticks, leaped on them, sent them scattering, and, gathering the tiny monkey in its arms, made away. Here was poetic if not legal justice. Nehru was delighted.

Not all the animal world attracted him equally. He liked to watch the antics of the lively friendly squirrels, whose trustful natures often led them to approach him as he sat reading. He would sometimes sit very still and allow a squirrel to clamber lightly up his leg and rest for a fleeting moment on his knee, blinking black inquisitive eyes.

One day in Dehra Dun, standing near the prison gate and talking to a warder, Nehru saw a man outside carrying a strange animal tied to a pole which looked a cross between a lizard and a crocodile.

"What animal is that?" asked the warder.

"It's a *bo*," said the man, calling it by a local name, "and I intend making a curry of it for myself tonight." He was an aboriginal forest-dweller.

Nehru puzzled for some years over this animal. Later, thumbing through a zoological volume, he discovered its identity. It was a pangolin.

Some of the other prisoners, especially the long-term convicts, kept animals as pets. In Dehra Dun, Nehru for a while adopted a neglected dog, a bitch who later gave birth to a litter of puppies. Three of these he also adopted and tended. When one of them acquired a violent distemper Nehru's natural solicitude for the sick projected itself to the puppy. He nursed it carefully, often getting up a dozen times in the course of a night to see to its wants. Happily, it recovered.

To this day his love for animals persists, and among the prize exhibits in the garden of the Prime Minister's residence in Delhi are two pandas. Nehru daily takes time off to see them.

He has never been able to abide reptiles, and the only unwelcome visitors to his cells were snakes, scorpions and centipedes, to the last of whom he is specially allergic. One night, feeling something crawling over his feet, he flashed his torch and saw a centipede. The next instant he had vaulted out of bed.

He read a great deal in jail—for instruction, largely, but also, it would seem, subconsciously to escape from the cramped environment of the prison walls. He liked to read travel books and, sitting in his tiny cell, to roam the world and see it through the eyes of the Chinese traveller Hiuen Tsang (who had visited India in the seventh century after Christ in the reign of the emperor Harsha), of Marco Polo, of ibn-Batuta, of Sven Hedin and Nicolas Roerich. With them he travelled the steppes of Central Asia, the seas and mountains, mysterious hinterlands and vast deserts. When the temperature rose in summer and the heat was oppressive, Jawaharlal would take out his pictorial volumes and gaze at the glaciers, the precipitous slopes and the snow-capped ranges of the Himalayas and the Alps, finding in this escapist exercise relief from his surroundings. He discovered that an atlas "could be an exciting affair."

Novels, he says, left him "mentally slack." But he read avidly a great many serious books, political, historical, economic and sociological. He was amused when the prison censors held up Spengler's *Decline of the West*, for which he had asked, characterising it as a dangerous and seditious book, judged apparently by its title. But then in Banaras Jail even the British Government's White Paper, containing its constitutional proposals for India, was withheld as "a political document"!

Nehru found Reinhold Niebuhr's *Moral Man and Immoral Society* specially invigorating, since it reinforced many of his own views on religion. While in prison, a Roman Catholic friend had sent him several Catholic publications and papal encyclicals, which he read closely. In the restricted formal sense of the word "religion," Catholicism seemed to him to be the only living religion in the West, offering, as Hinduism and Islam do, "a safe anchorage from doubt and mental conflict, an assurance for a future life which will make up for the deficiencies of this life." On the other hand, he thought that Protestantism, by wanting to have the best of both worlds, had failed to register in either.

Nehru's own view of religion, as he explains in his autobiography, approximates most closely to the Chinese cult of Taoism, to the path to be followed and the way of life. Parenthetically it is interesting to note that Mo-tzu, apostle of Taoism, was the first pacifist known to history. A man's way of life, Jawaharlal argues, should concern itself more with ethics than with religion, with the good of society rather than with his own personal salvation after death. Morality, as organised religions preach it, is often based more on metaphysical concepts like sin than on social needs, while organised religions, in Nehru's view, tend in time to become vested interests which, on getting entrenched, oppose progress.

Religion clouds men's minds because it rests on doctrine and dogma, and thereby discourages clear thinking. So Nehru feels. Religion in its formal sense, with its worshipping, temple-going and prayer-saying, has no appeal for him, but he likes to read the Gita with its gospel of action, and the writings of Swami Vivekananda who shares the same robust philosophy.

While on a visit to Ceylon in 1939, an Indian acquaintance organised a dinner for Nehru in the Indian style, served, as it occasionally is, on plantain leaves. Because of the unusual style of the dinner, it had to be held in a hall attached to a temple in Colombo.

As dinnertime approached, the host innocently suggested that they should go to the temple.

Nehru bristled. "Temple!" he stormed. "What temple? Why?"

Only after the circumstances had been explained to him was he pacified.

Nehru has more than once publicly denounced the habit of certain Indian politicians of importing too frequent references to the Almighty in their speeches. It is not that he is godless; but he feels that religion is a purely personal and private affair which has no place in politics, particularly Indian politics, which have always been sensitive to fanatical religious appeals.

In the stress of the moment Nehru has been known to give vent to utterances suggesting a profound scepticism in the existence of the Almighty.

During the individual satyagraha campaign of 1940, Jawaharlal came to see Gandhi at his ashram at Sewagram [1] shortly before offering individual satyagraha himself. It was a farewell call, and a feeling of sadness hung in the air. As Nehru rose to leave, Gandhi's wife,

[1] In Madhya Pradesh State, formerly known as the Central Provinces.

Kasturba, known popularly as Ba (mother), blessed him, saying, "God will look after you."

Jawaharlal turned to her with his quick smile. He asked teasingly: "Where is God, Ba? If he exists, he must be fast asleep."

Kasturba was a little taken aback, but Gandhi, who understood Nehru, chuckled heartily.

"He is nearer God," he remarked to Amrit Kaur,[2] "than many who profess to be His worshippers."

A friend of Nehru's, Dr. K. N. Katju, now Defence Minister in the Union Cabinet, has elaborated on the same view, expressing it in what might be described as a Hindu equation or ellipsis:

In the higher sense of the word, he [Nehru] is definitely a religious man. In the terms of the Bhagavad-Gita, devotion to incessant action for the welfare of others, unmindfulness of one's own personal care, comfort and ambitions, disinterested action without attachment to the fruit of action are the essence of the highest religion, and in that sense Jawaharlal is a religious man. He is incessant action personified.

Nehru's own view of religion seems to approximate to the above, for he likes to quote approvingly the definition of religion by the American philosopher the late Dr. John Dewey. "Any activity," wrote Dewey, "pursued in behalf of an ideal end against obstacles and in spite of threats of personal loss, because of conviction of its general and enduring value is religious in quality."

If this, comments Jawaharlal, is religion, then surely no one can have the slightest objection to it.

Aside from religion, more mundane philosophies occupied Nehru's thoughts in prison. The Bolshevik Revolution of 1917 had created some stir among educated Indians, and Nehru's visit to Europe and to Russia, where he had attended the tenth anniversary celebrations of the revolution, had stimulated his own interest further. He knew little at the time of the theory of Communism, and to his ears dialectical materialism sounded an exotic phrase. But on his return to India, particularly while he was in prison, he studied Marxist literature, read it copiously and pondered deeply.

Nehru's antipathy to the nineteenth century concept of formal democracy which gave a semblance of political equality but cloaked many social and economic inequalities had been growing steadily.

[2] Now Health Minister in the Union Cabinet, and its only woman member.

He was impressed by the Communist criticism that this type of government was only a democratic shell to hide the fact that one class ruled over the others. In reality it was plutocracy, the government of the privileged and the wealthy. To appreciate Nehru's attitude and approach to Marxism, one must take this basis into account.

The liberal *laissez faire* economists seemed to Jawaharlal to be more concerned with reducing economics to vague academic theories than with discussing it in a practical context. Marx was different. He was, as Nehru noted appreciatively, "a practical philosopher" with a scientific method of thought which he brought to bear on political and economic problems. Philosophy, Marx had contended, must not merely explain the world; it must set out to change it. In that sense, Marx was "dynamic," a favourite word of Jawaharlal's.

In prison Nehru read the *Communist Manifesto* of Marx and Engels. He also read Marx's *Das Kapital*; and its scientific attitude to history, with its attempt to interpret logically the development of human society, stimulated and excited him. The *Communist Manifesto*, while decrying the egalitarian principles of the French Revolution as expressed in the ideas of liberty, equality and fraternity, developed its own theory of socialism, calling upon the workers of the world to unite, and impressing upon them the fact that they had nothing to lose but their chains. *Das Kapital* carried Marx's thinking a considerable stage further, crystallising it in a new scientific socialism. Marx seemed to Nehru clear-cut in his ideas and ideals, Nehru being especially interested in Marx's discussion of the growth of industrial civilisation as represented by the big machine. Marx was not an infallible prophet. He had been proved wrong, particularly about the impending revolution in Europe. But Nehru first read him in the early thirties, against the background of the economic blizzard which then assailed the world, and in that context many of Marx's arguments seemed not only cogent and persuasive but convincing.

In a letter to Indira written from prison on February 16, 1933, Nehru asks and answers the question, What then is Marxism?

It is a way of interpreting history and politics and economics and human life and human desires. It is a theory as well as a call to action. It is a philosophy which has something to say about most of the activities of man's life. It is an attempt at reducing human history, past, present, and future, to a rigid logical system with something of the inevitability of fate or *kismet* about it. Whether life is so very logical, after all, and so dependent on hard-and-fast rules and systems, does not seem very obvious and many have doubted this. But Marx surveyed past history as a scientist and drew certain conclusions from it. He saw from the earliest days man struggling for a living; it was a struggle against nature as well as against brother-man.

Marx, Nehru insists, did not preach or create class conflict, because this had been endemic in human society long before Marx wrote a line. But his statement of "the economic law of motion of modern society" undoubtedly made the doctrine of class conflict a weapon for future Marxists to wield. Nehru also refuses to accept Marxism as a dogma which cannot be varied, quoting Lenin in support.[3] He would probably agree with Engels, echoing his cry, "Thank God, Marx was not a Marxist."

Similarly, while admiring much that had happened in the Soviet State, particularly the massive Five-Year plans which enabled the Bolsheviks to industrialise their country and improve the people's standard of living, Nehru was almost pathologically averse to adopting wholesale for India the methods employed successfully in another country. That is common sense. In prison he had felt that only a revolutionary plan could solve India's two related problems of land and industry, but the plan must accord with the country's peculiar conditions, development and needs.

Marx's is a dynamic, revolutionary concept of history. But Marx is being confuted in Asia, never more so than in India. Gandhi, with British approval and acquiescence in the final phases, proved that a political revolution was possible without violence. In independent India, Nehru is attempting to prove that an economic and social revolution, built on the utilitarian principle of the greatest good of the greatest number, is equally possible without violence or class conflict. There is to be no intermediate stage of the dictatorship of the proletariat, as Marx conceived it. Instead the State, by holding the ring, will ensure that there is no exploitation of the workers or any one class for the benefit of another. "There is no exploiting class left," Nehru wrote, analysing Marxist possibilities as far back as June, 1933. "If there is any exploitation it is done by the State for the benefit of all."

This is precisely what Nehru is endeavouring to do in India today, thereby demonstrating what in fact he really is—a Marxist by

[3] Cf. quotation in Chapter VIII, page 111.

intellectual conviction who wishes to bring in the socialist millennium by democratic means and methods. In this process he carries both Marxism and democracy a step further, hoping to prove, in another favourite phrase, that they can co-exist as partners in a politico-economic revolution. Here Nehru represents a type unique in the history of his time—a Marxist theorist wedded to democratic practices.

Other, and more personal matters preoccupied Nehru's thoughts. The health of both his wife and his mother had received a sharp setback while he was in jail. He had left Kamala in Bombay ailing with a recurrence of her old malady when he was arrested in December, 1931, and the thought of her was ever present. Despite her ill health she had taken an active part in the previous movement and been arrested on New Year's Day of 1931. This time, however, her fast weakening frame was in no condition to meet the challenge of her ardent spirit. Illness forced her to stay in bed, and for a while to leave Allahabad for medical treatment in Calcutta.

Swaruprani, though aged and delicate, insisted on taking a part in the movement, leading processions and addressing meetings in the towns and sometimes in adjoining villages. "Though her body was frail," wrote one of her daughters in commenting on this period, "her heart was as proud and strong as that of a lioness." The brutal beating which had been inflicted on her in April, 1932, had left its after-effects and impaired seriously her always delicate health. She was gravely ill when Nehru was released in August, 1933, but the sight of him by her bedside rallied and cheered her wonderfully. Slowly she recovered.

Indira was now a growing child. The thought that he had so little time to devote to her harassed Nehru with a gnawing sense of neglect. He had tried to remedy matters partly by educating her through a series of letters [4] he wrote to her from jail. They were written in different prisons over a period of three years between October, 1930, and August, 1933, the first of them being entitled "For Indira Priyadarshini on her thirteenth birthday." The day was October 26th,[5] the jail being Naini. Nehru's opening paragraph is a wistful greeting:

[4] Subsequently published in 1934 as *Glimpses of World History*.

[5] Indira's birthday takes place on November 19th according to the Gregorian calendar, but is observed on October 26th according to the *Samvat*, or Hindu reckoning.

On your birthday you have been in the habit of receiving presents and good wishes. Good wishes you will still have in full measure, but what present can I give you from Naini prison? My presents cannot be very material or solid. They can only be of the air and of the mind and spirit, such as a good fairy might have bestowed on you—something that even the high walls of prison cannot stop.

The last letter of this prison series was written on August 9, 1933, three weeks before Nehru emerged again from jail. It ends with the Persian invocation *Tamam Shud!* (It is finished).

Written in prison, the letters suffer in some respects from this limitation, being at time repetitious, diffuse and discursive. But as a panorama of world history, limned with few reference volumes and only some scattered notebooks within reach, the achievement is impressive, reflecting in its volume and quality the unusual range and capaciousness of the writer's mind. Inevitably there runs through them a strain of warm intimacy and affection.

Having stayed for some days by his mother's bedside in Lucknow, Nehru, once he was satisfied that she was on the road to recovery, left for Poona, where Gandhi was residing. It was over two years since he had waved him goodbye from the pier at Bombay when Gandhi had sailed for the Round Table Conference on August 29, 1931.

The Mahatma greeted him tenderly, realising that Nehru had been disturbed, at times distressed, by some of his attitudes and actions. Between them was no wall of mistrust but a cobweb of vague doubts which must be cleared. Gandhi had no conscious use for ideologies, having reached his own conclusions, political, economic, social and moral, on the pragmatic basis of personal experience. No wonder Nehru found him ideologically backward. And yet the Mahatma was essentially a rebel and a revolutionary, with much that was at once creative and non-conformist.

"What irks you, Jawaharlal?" he asked the younger man.

Nehru opened his heart and mind to him. He was anxious that India should tread the socialist path, and that the economic programme of the Congress as enshrined in the resolution on Fundamental Rights and Economic Policy passed at the Karachi session should hold the field. There must be no whittling down of objectives, economic or political, nor any display of undue tenderness.

The two men had many and long conversations. Nehru soon realised that ideologically a gap separated them both on the political and on the economic planes. Gandhi, as always, was prepared to go some way with his favourite disciple, but his milestones were marked and his signposts pointed rigidly in a definite direction on the road.

"Why are you bothered about stressing a precise political objective?" Gandhi asked, referring to Nehru's insistence on keeping complete independence as the goal.

"Because," explained Nehru, "the masses need an inspiring political ideal if they are to continue the struggle."

"I agree, but having fixed the goal, why repeat it? Surely the important and immediate need is to devise ways and means of realising it."

They argued back and forth.

"There must be a definite de-vesting of vested interests," Nehru urged, shifting the argument to the economic plane.

"Again, I agree," said Gandhi. "Without a material revision of vested interests the condition of the masses can never be improved. But it must be by conversion, not compulsion."

Nehru felt at the end of these prolonged talks that the Mahatma had been generous in his attitude. He had gone as far as he could to meet Jawaharlal's point of view. And, after all, in Gandhi's vocabulary conversion was not far removed from courteous and considerate compulsion. The Mahatma had a way of his own.

Later they were to elaborate and clarify their ideas in a series of letters. Writing to Nehru from Poona in a letter dated September 13, 1933, Gandhi affirms his optimism:

I would like to say that I have no sense of defeat in me, and the hope in me that this country of ours is fast marching towards its goal is burning as bright as it did in 1920; for I have an undying faith in the efficacy of civil disobedience.

Nehru was reassured. He felt, however, even while he talked with Gandhi, that the Mahatma was uncertain about what he should do himself. Should he offer individual civil disobedience, go to jail again, and demand the same privileges for conducting the Harijan movement, and if these were refused, fast again "unto death"? Or should he refrain from courting imprisonment and conduct the

Harijan movement as a free man? Or, again, should he retire from the Congress altogether and let the "younger generation" take his place?

Nehru saw no particular virtue or advantage in resurrecting the cat-and-mouse tactics which the first alternative envisaged. It was undesirable for Gandhi to withdraw from the Congress while it was still an illegal organisation. This left them with the second alternative, which Nehru and his colleagues reluctantly accepted. For the time being the Mahatma should not court imprisonment by offering individual civil disobedience.

In the course of his talk with Gandhi, Nehru had argued that there was no fundamental difference between individual civil resistance and mass civil resistance, the principle underlying both forms of resistance being a deliberate challenge to the authority of the Government. But Gandhi saw something more in it than that. He wrote:

I think that the fundamental difference is implied in your own admission that "it is essentially an individual affair." The chief distinction between mass civil resistance and individual civil resistance is that in the latter everyone is a complete independent unit and his fall does not affect the others; in mass civil resistance the fall of one generally adversely affects the rest. Again in mass civil resistance leadership is essential, in individual civil resistance every resister is his own leader. Then again in mass civil resistance, there is a possibility of failure; in individual civil resistance failure is an impossibility. Finally, a state may cope with mass civil resistance, but no state has yet been found able to cope with individual civil resistance.

It is a characteristic and engaging piece of Gandhian logic, postulating an inexorable conclusion based on largely hypothetical premises. Failure, according to the Mahatma, would not lie in results but in the capacity or incapacity of each individual to perform an ordained task. Individuals, en masse, might fail, but not the single person inspired with a single purpose. Means, to the Mahatma, were often more important than ends.

In September, 1933, Gandhi moved to the satyagraha ashram at Wardha, where he recuperated for six weeks before starting out in November on his Harijan tour, a pilgrimage which took him to every corner of the country, north, east, south and west, until his roving mission concluded at Banaras on July 29, 1934. In this tour, which occupied approximately nine months, the Mahatma covered some 12,500 miles, trekking at times on foot, travelling on other occasions by train, car and bullock cart, and collecting in the course of his journey about Rs.800,000 ($160,000) for the Harijan cause.

To Nehru, after twenty months of isolation, India seemed overcome by a vast ennui and exhaustion. It was the weariness not of despair but of repressive rule. Though there was spring in the muscle of Indian nationalism, physically it was tired, though its spirit flickered and stirred. The country lived in the shadow of ordinance rule, and Nehru himself was always conscious of the imminence of rearrest.

This feeling of insecurity made it difficult for him to settle down, and infused in him a sense of hustle. He was by no means anxious to return to jail, for the gesture in the prevailing conditions was meaningless, and he had certain urgent matters to attend to, domestic and national.

His younger sister, Krishna, had become engaged to be married to an Oxford-educated barrister, G. P. Hutheesing, a Gujerati from Gandhi's home province, and Nehru was anxious that the marriage should take place before he was imprisoned again. The marriage took place very simply at Allahabad in the third week of October.

In the middle of October Congress workers of the United Provinces met in Allahabad to consider the political situation. The Provincial Congress Committee being illegal, it was not officially convened, but the meetings of the Congress workers were not shrouded in secrecy. These meetings showed Nehru what he had sensed since he came out of jail—the nationalist movement had reached an impasse. It was not possible to plan immediate steps because a stalemate prevailed. The only thing they could do was to keep their long-term objectives clear.

Thus the Allahabad meetings contented themselves with accepting socialism as their economic objective. Politically they expressed themselves against the withdrawal of civil disobedience, in itself an empty gesture because the movement was at a dead end and because ordinance rule prevailed throughout the country. On the economic plane it is doubtful if many of them knew what socialism implied, apart from a vague belief that it would diminish the gap between the haves and have-nots by ensuring the greatest good of the greatest number.

At this stage Nehru's purpose was twofold. He wanted to keep the objectives, political and economic, clear and defined before his colleagues, and by educating the Congressmen in their implications, to make them realise their value and importance.

Socialism was vaguely in the air, and in the following year a socialist group led by Jayaprakash Narayan, and including veterans like Narendra Deva, along with the younger elements represented by Yusuf Meherally, Asoka Mehta, Dr. Ram Manohar Lohia and Minoo Masani, came into being. Jawaharlal, while in sympathy with this group, did not join them as a member, perhaps because he resented their occasionally sharp criticism of Gandhi as a reactionary. Gandhi, he felt, despite his metaphysical and mystical approach to things, was a more realistic revolutionary than these "parlour socialists."

Yet, paradoxically enough, he remained eager to spread the cult of Marxist socialism by cajoling, even compelling, his colleagues to study Marxist literature.

Sri Prakasa, now Governor of Madras, and no socialist, was once called upon to talk to a group Nehru had convened to discuss socialism. He expressed as eloquently as he could his cautious thoughts.

"What sort of socialist are you?" Nehru inquired brusquely.

Sri Prakasa was nonplussed.

"Certainly not a Marxist," he answered boldly. "Perhaps a Fabian." Jawaharlal was riled.

In November, Nehru visited the Banaras Hindu University, where he castigated his Hindu audience for the reactionary overtones in the preaching and practice of Hindu communalism. True, there was also Muslim communalism, but what was the point, Nehru argued, in denouncing this type of communalism before a Hindu audience? His broadside, however, was resented.

Partly in reparation, partly in explanation, he decided to write a series of articles on the evil of communalism, Hindu and Muslim. His main point was that since communalism was allied to vested interests it could not but work in conjunction with reactionary forces. The articles created wide interest, and stimulated some discussion. In the course of this series Nehru for the first time propounded the idea of a constituent assembly to iron out and settle political and communal differences, a proposal which was to be put into practice later, as India approached freedom.

There was little that Jawaharlal could do at this stage except to attempt to educate his countrymen through his speeches and writings. This he was determined to do until prison claimed him again.

Gandhi, away on his Harijan tour, was drawing vast crowds. Early in December Nehru met him at Jabalpur in the Central Provinces, where members of the Congress Working Committee had been informally invited to foregather. Here, and shortly afterward in Delhi where he met Gandhi and his colleagues again, Nehru perceived that the Congress was groping in the dark. The Working Committee were divided in their opinion as to whether civil disobedience should or should not be withdrawn. Gandhi favoured its continuance, which meant the prolongation of the prevailing impasse, with the country marking time politically while the Mahatma pursued his Harijan campaign.

Neither Gandhi nor his colleagues on the Working Committee viewed Nehru's propagation of socialistic ideas kindly. Toward the end of December, in an interview with a Madras newspaper, Gandhi obliquely chided Nehru, expressing his belief that Jawaharlal would not commit the Congress to "novel ways." The Mahatma went on to defend the zamindari system as a desirable part of the country's rural and national economy. Gandhi in this characteristic fashion was attempting to right the balance inside the Congress, but to Nehru the Mahatma's attitude seemed antediluvian, and far removed from his own views on the subject. He was angry and hurt, and for a while even contemplated resignation from the Working Committee. But in a calmer mood he realised that his duty was to carry on, and his arrest shortly afterward, on February 12, 1934, summarily resolved this particular dilemma.

January came, and with it another conundrum. Independence Day was on January 26th, and since the Congress was still an illegal organisation, to celebrate the day was to invite widespread arrests. Jawaharlal was planning to leave for Calcutta, partly to meet old colleagues there but primarily for medical consultations with Kamala's doctors. Before leaving, he and his colleagues in the United Provinces reached a compromise on the Independence Day celebrations which reflected their own and the country's divided mind. It was agreed that something should be done, but there was no agreement as to what this should be.

Nature intervened to divert them for a time from their perplexities. On the afternoon of January 15, 1934, while standing on the verandah of his house in Allahabad, Nehru was thrown off balance by a rumbling movement which shook the floor and set doors and windows banging. Looking across the road, he saw several tiles sliding down the roof of Swaraj Bhawan. This terrestrial disturbance lasted for two or three minutes, and Nehru, while appreciating that it was an earthquake, did not then realise its magnitude. He left with Kamala for Calcutta on the evening of the same day.

Bihar in northeast India was the epicentre of this tremendous upheaval which in a matter of a few minutes reduced towns and villages in the northern districts to a shambles, destroying or damaging over a million houses, and killing several thousands of people. In all, an area of 30,000 square miles, containing a population of 10,000,000, was devastated.

Rajendra Prasad, now President of India and then the foremost Congress leader in Bihar, was in jail, but on January 17th the provincial government released him. Without the help of public workers the administrative machinery found it difficult to cope with the catastrophe, nor was it over-enterprising or efficient in devising relief measures. On the other hand, the Government, chary of the Congress, was nervous that if its workers were allowed a free hand they would make political capital out of the situation.

Jawaharlal, after spending four days at Calcutta, paid a fleeting visit to the venerable Rabindranath Tagore at his open-air university of Santiniketan. He had been there twice, but it was Kamala's first visit to the poet. They were then planning to send Indira, who would shortly be completing her school studies, to Santiniketan.

Between Nehru and Tagore, separated by a gap of nearly thirty years, existed a bond of affection and understanding. Although an ardent nationalist, there was much in Gandhi's philosophy which the poet did not accept, particularly the Mahatma's creed of abnegation and asceticism. Tagore believed in a full and joyous life. But poet and Mahatma also understood each other.

"You're getting ready for another arrest cure," Tagore had once twitted Gandhi. "I wish they'd give me one."

"But," retorted Gandhi, "you don't behave yourself."

The Bihar earthquake induced another controversy between the two men. Gandhi saw in this dire visitation the wrath of God, a form of divine chastisement for men's cruelties against the Untouchables. "The Bihar calamity," he wrote in *Harijan*, "is due to the sin of untouchability."

Tagore protested. He called this "an unscientific view of phenomena," and deplored the danger of its ready acceptance by large sections of the people. He referred to "the indignity" of it all. But Gandhi would not relent. Nehru, of course, agreed entirely with Tagore.

On his way back from Calcutta Nehru stopped at Patna to discuss with Rajendra Prasad measures for non-official relief work. Forty miles north of Patna he surveyed the town of Muzaffarpur, littered with debris and containing survivors demoralised by their awe-inspiring experiences. Nehru returned to Allahabad to devote himself entirely to the work of organising funds and aid for Bihar.

Not long afterwards the Allahabad Earthquake Relief Committee deputised Jawaharlal to visit the stricken areas, and for ten days he toured these torn and tragic districts. The green plains of North Bihar had been scorched and uprooted as if by a wayward giant hand. Eighty miles below Patna the city of Monghyr on the banks of the Ganga lay desolate, destroyed and forlorn. Here Nehru, by seizing spade and shovel and working with them, set others to follow his example in an effort to accelerate relief. Bihar is primarily a peasant province, and non-official relief work was concentrated largely in the rural areas.

On February 11th Nehru returned to Allahabad limp and weary from the accumulated strain of sheer physical exhaustion. So haggard was his appearance that his family and intimates were shocked by it. He tried to write a report of his tour, but weariness and sleep overcame him. Of the next twenty-four hours he spent at least twelve in sleep.

In the late afternoon of the next day, as Kamala and he had

just finished tea, a car drove up with an inspector of police. Jawaharlal, realising his freedom had ended, went forward to greet him.

"I have been waiting for you for a long time," he remarked.

The police officer was embarrassed and apologetic.

"The warrant is from Calcutta," he explained shame-facedly.

During his four-day stay in Calcutta, Nehru had addressed three meetings, devoting himself primarily to condemnation of the terrorist movement but also vigorously criticising the recent actions of the Bengal Government. These provided the three main counts against him in his subsequent trial.

Now he turned from the police officer to see Kamala looking at him intently. A moment later she left the verandah to go upstairs to collect some clothes for him. Jail had become part of their normal routine. But when Jawaharlal went upstairs to bid her goodbye she clung to him feverishly, and for the first time in his jail-going experience fainted and collapsed. He held her in his arms, taken aback at her reaction. A few moments later she revived. Had Kamala a premonition that the end was near?

That night Nehru was taken from Allahabad to Calcutta. On February 16th he was sentenced by the Chief Presidency magistrate to two years' imprisonment, his seventh term in jail.

The real burden, he reflected, was not his. "It had to be shouldered, as always, by womenfolk—by my ailing mother, my wife, my sisters."

Kamala was dying, but Jawaharlal did not then realise it.

16

"GRIEF, A FIXED STAR"

FROM the Presidency Jail where he was lodged during his trial, Nehru was taken to the Alipore Central Jail, also in Calcutta, and there placed in a tiny cell, about ten feet by nine.

The cell overlooked the chimneys of the jail kitchen, which belched smoke through the greater part of the day. Comparing Alipore with his other prison abodes, Nehru was struck by the drabness of his surroundings with their sullen stare of red brick walls and the unending fumes of smoke. No tree or greenery cheered him, but over the walls of his bare prison yard he could just see the tops of two trees in a more fortunate neighbour's yard. They were dry and stark, devoid of foliage. But slowly the leaves budded along the thin branches and made a tracery of green above the prison wall.

Nehru was not allowed at first to go out of his yard. For the greater part of the evening and night, from sunset to sunrise, he was locked up in his cell. Pacing back and forth in that cramped space, he was amused by the recollection of a bear he had once watched tramping up and down his cage in the zoo. To relieve his tedium he read, and sometimes practised *shirshasana*, standing on his head and contemplating the topsy-turvy world around him. It was one way of righting the balance.

Restrictions were relaxed after a month, Nehru being then allowed to walk up and down under the main wall every morning and evening. The sounds and noises of a big industrial city like Calcutta occasionally percolated into the prison—the jangle of trams, the hum of voices, music from a gramophone in a neighbouring house, and now and then the plaintive threnody of a Bengali song. A few birds nested within the prison walls, and Nehru was specially interested in a kite's nest which was full of new-born fledglings. Their home was on one of the trees which peeped over the wall of his neighbour's yard. Nehru spent time watching the tiny kites grow up.

For news in India he was dependent largely on an English weekly published in Calcutta, with the prison grapevine and visitors supplementing this meagre fare. He also read the *Manchester Guardian Weekly* to keep in touch with European and international affairs. Both at home and abroad the tidings were gloomy.

Hitler, appointed Chancellor of the German Republic on January 30, 1933, had been in power for a little over a year when Nehru was arrested. The Führer's arrival on the international scene saw the dictators helping themselves as the shadow of Nazism lengthened over Europe. About the time Nehru was imprisoned, Fascist riots broke out in France, where a National Government was formed. Parliamentary rule had died in Austria in March, 1933, the same month in which it had died in Germany. Dollfuss, Austria's pocket dictator, seemed to think that the Austrian socialists were a greater menace than the Nazis. In February, 1934, his artillery bombarded the workers in their new block of flats in Vienna, perhaps the best workers' dwellings in the world, and in the four-day battle that ensued nearly a thousand men, women and children were killed. Dollfuss was to be killed by the Austrian Nazis in July.

In Spain, whence King Alfonso XIII had been driven out in 1931, Manuel Azaña, attempting feebly to keep the Rights at bay, was forced out of office in the autumn of 1933. Gil Robles, with Alejandro Lerroux, assumed power, and terror struck Spain, a workers' government in the Asturias being put down in a bath of blood by Moorish troops. The pendulum was to swing again in February, 1936, when the Left won a sweeping victory. Five months later, in July, Spain was to plunge into civil war.

Japan had launched on her expansionist career in September, 1931, when she invaded Manchuria, and despite the protests of the enfeebled League of Nations she had succeeded in converting Manchuria into the "independent" republic of Manchukuo. Aggression was beginning to pay dividends. The melancholy farce of the disarmament conference which met in Geneva in February, 1932, dragged its weary length into 1935, but it was dead when Hitler ordered the withdrawal of the German delegation in October, 1933.

Between 1929 and 1933 the world was also economically ill. Prices fell, currencies wobbled, there were widespread unemployment and want. The slump struck the New World and the Old. In 1933 over 15,000,000 people were out of work in America. In June, 1933, the world economic conference had met, appropriately in the Geological Museum in London, but, failing to reach any positive decision, had dispersed in July.

War was still five years away, but its shadow lowered over Europe.

The news from abroad depressed Nehru, who since his visit to Europe in 1927 had studied international affairs closely. At home it was equally gloomy.

Gandhi had followed Nehru into Bihar, enjoining on the Congress workers and people to cooperate with the Government in the work of relief. Congress estimates placed the number of earthquake victims at about 20,000, but the Government, unable to compute it exactly, put the total lower, though no official figures were released.

While Gandhi toured Bihar a number of Congressmen gathered in Delhi to consider some way out of the political stalemate. The meeting was presided over by Dr. M. A. Ansari, and those who took a prominent part in the discussions included Dr. B. C. Roy, now chief minister of West Bengal, and Mr. Bhulabhai Desai, a leading lawyer of Bombay who was later to head the Congress Parliamentary party [1] in the Assembly. The conference tentatively decided, subject to the approval of Gandhi and the Working Committee, that the time had come to revive Motilal's old Swaraj party and to contest the elections for the Central Assembly which were scheduled for November, 1934. In the attempt to break the stalemate the switching off of civil disobedience must be accompanied by the switching on of a national effort to capture the Central Assembly.

The dual policy of the British Government of repressing the nationalist movement on the one hand and moving cautiously towards self-government on the other had brought the Congress machine temporarily to a standstill. The White Paper embodying the Government's recommendations following the three Round Table conferences had already been published, and despite Churchill's opposition, it was

[1] Also known as the Swaraj party.

endorsed by the British Parliament in March, 1933. This was followed by the setting up of a Joint Select Committee drawn from members of the House of Commons and the House of Lords presided over by Lord Linlithgow, who was to succeed Lord Willingdon as Viceroy. The committee, sitting almost continuously from April, 1933, to November, 1934, held 159 meetings and examined 120 witnesses, the bill embodying its report reaching the Statute Book on July 24, 1935. It contained 473 clauses and 16 schedules, its passage through Parliament being stormy and contentious. The debates covered four thousand pages of Hansard, totalling over 15,500,000 words. Never has so much been said by so many to such small effect. The Government of India Act of 1935 was never fully implemented.

Broadly, the Act, which came into operation on April 1, 1937, envisaged an all-India federation, comprising the Princely States and the autonomous Governors' Provinces, on certain terms and conditions which were never fulfilled. It also conferred autonomy on the provinces, with the provincial governor exercising a supervisory role and with authority to dismiss summarily a provincial administration, thus suspending provincial autonomy at his will. Provincial autonomy was to start functioning in the provinces by the end of July, 1937.

Meanwhile, the elections to the Central Assembly were scheduled for November, 1934. On April 4th Ansari, Desai and Roy arrived at Patna to canvass Gandhi's support for their decision to enter the legislatures. Unknown to them the Mahatma on April 2nd had already reached a decision to call off civil disobedience, leaving himself alone "to bear the responsibility of civil resistance if it is to succeed as a means of achieving Purna Swaraj."

He listened, as was his habit, patiently to his visitors, and discussed with them his own decision taken on April 2nd. On April 5th, in a letter to Ansari, Gandhi, while reiterating that his views on the utility of the legislatures "remain, on the whole, what they were in 1920," approved of their move to contest the elections for the Central Assembly. On April 7th the Mahatma released a statement announcing his decision to call off civil resistance and advising Congressmen to devote themselves to "nation-building" activities such as the removal of untouchability, the propagation of hand-spinning and the spread of communal unity.

The decision was hailed by Ansari and his colleagues as signifying a dual programme designed to carry on the national struggle both within and outside the legislatures. But Nehru thought otherwise. The first news of Gandhi's decision reached him through the jail superintendent, who disclosed to him casually that the Mahatma had withdrawn civil disobedience.

Though disappointed Nehru was not surprised. The news was unpleasant but it could only have been a matter of time before civil resistance petered out. Inside jail he was less advantageously placed than Gandhi to assess the situation which the Mahatma must have sized up with his instinctive understanding. Nor was Nehru happy over the decision to enter the legislatures, which he had always felt were unreal and unrelated to the urgent needs and problems of the country. But even this move, with the vast political depression weighing over the people, was inevitable, and it might have some educative value.

When some days later Nehru, scanning the weekly newspaper allowed him, came upon Gandhi's statement of April 7th, he was filled with dismay and amazement. He read the statement over and over again. With Gandhi's decision to suspend civil disobedience he did not quarrel, but what strange reasons the Mahatma gave for his decision! He had apparently had a chat with some inmates and associates in his ashram. From them he had learned of "a valued companion of long standing," a staunch satyagrahi who had wearied of prison and now preferred his private activities to a negative life in jail. Gandhi was taken aback but impressed by the example. In this attitude there was nothing new, for his approach to problems was always pragmatic, deriving general principles from personal or individual experience and observation.

"I was blind," he confessed. "Blindness in a leader is unpardonable. I saw at once that I must for the time being remain the sole representative of civil resistance in action."

To Nehru this seemed absurdly metaphysical and mystical. What had the Congress and he to do with the foibles or failings of one of Gandhi's ashramites, and was a national movement to be conducted on the basis of an individual's whim? He was indignant and outraged.

"It seemed to me," he wrote in a burst of angry candour, "an insult to the intelligence and an amazing performance for the leader of a national movement."

So deep and turbulent were his reactions that he felt as if the cords of allegiance which had bound him to Gandhi for many years had snapped. Loneliness oppressed him, and in the desert of his prison cell his mind once again probed his curious relationship with Gandhi, tender but also febrile, near and yet at times so far.

The Mahatma, aware of these differences, had once advised Nehru to dismiss them as temperamental. But to Nehru their divergences in outlook seemed much more than temperamental. It was a difference not only in outlook but in methods. Nehru liked to have his objectives clear and defined. One step is enough for me, was Gandhi's philosophy. He seemed more concerned with means than ends, because in his reckoning ends flowed from means. Right means produced right ends.

"Look after the means," the Mahatma was fond of repeating, "and the end will take care of itself."

Yet to Jawaharlal clarity of thought was the prime prerequisite, and to him vagueness about an objective seemed not only deplorable but a cardinal sin. It hinted at a confused mind too ready to compromise, and more concerned with achieving the next immediate step than with consolidating effort in order to attain the final objective. Where mysticism and emotion reigned there could be neither clearness of thought nor fixity of purpose.

At this time Jawaharlal, in jail, was reading Bernard Shaw's new plays, and he found an analogy which comforted him in the preface to *On the Rocks* with its dramatic high-light in the debate between Christ and Pilate, representing respectively the eternal and the transient values of life. Over and over again he read the speech wherein Christ chides Pilate for fear and lack of faith:

Fear of Imperial Caesar, the idol you have yourself created, and fear of me, the penniless vagrant, buffeted and mocked, fear of everything except the rule of God; faith in nothing but blood and iron and gold. You, standing for Rome, are the universal coward; I, standing for the Kingdom of God, have braved everything, lost everything and won an eternal crown.

Might not, Nehru contemplated as he read this, might not Gandhi stand for values less transient and more elementally powerful than his own? The thought chastened him, but the uneasiness and some of the bitterness lingered.

The crisis, posing as it did many problems and queries, led Nehru characteristically to rationalise his position. He felt at the time as if he were living in "a very wilderness of desolation." To whom should he cling?

"Of the many hard lessons that I had learnt," he recalls, "the hardest and the most painful now faced me: that it is not possible in any vital matter to rely on any one. One must journey through life alone; to rely on others is to invite heartbreak."

The reflection is important, for it marks the beginning of the philosophy of life which now governs Nehru. Obsessed as he is with a sense of history and hustle, he agrees (of all persons with Kipling!) that "he travels fastest who travels alone." As Prime Minister and the idol of millions, with his mind fixed clearly on definite objectives, Nehru realises that he is in a position to implement his ideas, and is obviously anxious to achieve this in his lifetime. Hence, his overwhelming self-confidence and self-centredness, his tendency to do things himself and thus concentrate power in his hands, his impatience with many of the men around him, his mistrust of some, his intolerance with others, his habit of keeping his own counsels which sometimes verges on secretiveness. Part of this may be ascribed to a not unpleasing vanity which leads him to have a good opinion and assessment of himself. But largely and primarily it springs from a sense of dedicated service to the people he loves passionately and in whom he has an abiding faith. Leaders and colleagues might fail him. But the Indian people never will.

Alone with his thoughts he brooded for many hours on events outside. Had he been free, the impact of events and individuals would soon have taken him out of himself and immersed him in new activities. In jail, he found it hard to shake off the doubts and depression that seized him. But slowly his natural resilience of mind and body asserted itself, dispersing the feeling of isolation.

And then Kamala came to see him. She had been far from well and was in Calcutta for medical treatment. There were shadows under her eyes; she had always looked frail, but her illness—although gnawing its way remorselessly in her—had barely altered her outward appearance. She was animated, full of tales of happenings outside, and her love and cheerfulness communicated themselves to Jawaharlal. He felt that she brought a radiance with her, and its warmth lighted up his heart and mind. His spirit grew buoyant again. He had never felt closer to her than he did that day in jail.

Calcutta's humid climate did not suit Jawaharlal, who wilted under its clammy touch. As summer advanced, the increasing heat depressed him and he began to lose weight.

Early one day in May he was asked to pack up his belongings, as he was to be transferred elsewhere.

"Where do I go?" he asked.

"To Dehra Dun," they told him.

Nehru was not displeased. He had liked Dehra Dun, which nestled in the hills, and he would be nearer Kamala. The cool night air of Calcutta felt like a balm as he drove to the station. The huge crowds fascinated him.

It was nine months since he had left Dehra Dun, but he returned to find conditions inside the prison altered. This time a disused cattle shed, cleaned for his habitation, served as his cell. It had a little verandah and an adjoining yard fifty feet in length. But the walls, recently raised against his arrival, were about fifteen feet high, and completely blocked his old view of the mountains whose sight had been his major compensation in Dehra Dun Jail. This time he was not allowed to step out of the yard.

Nehru missed the mountains. During his last stay at Dehra Dun he had often, while looking at them, recalled the lines of the Chinese poet, Li T'ai-po, bard to a Ming emperor:

> Flocks of birds have flown high and away;
> A solitary drift of cloud, too, has gone, wandering on,
> And I sit alone with Ching-ting peak, towering beyond.
> We never grow tired of each other, the mountain and I.

Confined in his cell and yard, Nehru could yet conjure up the fragrance of the green grass outside, the tender, tired earth and the white gleaming silhouette of the mountains beyond. He was kept alone, and he craved the company of men and nature.

The rains came. There was a refreshing drop in the temperature, and the air was full with the whisper of new life. Sometimes, as the iron door of his yard swung open to admit a warder, Nehru caught a glimpse, brief and tantalising, of a verdant sweep of grass, of flowers, and of trees with their leaves glistening with raindrops in the sunshine. Whenever possible he had liked to grow and tend flowers in prison, cheering his dismal cell with a posy of gay blooms.

Nehru was worried by two things—by Kamala's illness, which he now realised was more serious than he had suspected, and by the turn of political events. He was allowed a daily newspaper in Dehra Dun, and his distress over the drift in the nationalist tide was real and acute.

Aside from the Congressmen who planned to resuscitate the Swaraj party, another group, mainly comprising the younger elements, set out to organise a Socialist party, also within the Congress. Thus Gandhi was left controlling an in-between group which, while it did not relish a return to constitutionalism with its implication of co-operation, was not enamoured greatly of socialism. Nehru's description of this middle group as "moderately constitutional" was not inapt.

The Government reciprocated Gandhi's gesture by lifting the ban on Congress organisations with some exceptions. These exceptions affected the Frontier Province and Bengal, while certain allied or affiliated units like the Khudai Khidmatgars,[2] or Frontier Red Shirts, and the Hindustan Seva Dal were still under an embargo in some of the provinces. By mid-June of 1934 the ban was lifted in most of the provinces, the Government also expediting the release of political prisoners.

Outside prison the only group reflecting Nehru's opinion was the Socialist party which was formed in May, 1934.[3] That month at Patna the All-India Congress Committee met to discuss the Swarajists' programme of council entry which the Socialists, led by Narendra Deva and Jayaprakash Narayan opposed strenuously. But Gandhi carried the day, the Swarajists' programme being endorsed, and his own decision suspending civil disobedience, while reserving the right of satyagraha to himself on behalf of the Congress, also receiving approval.

Nehru, reading the Patna proceedings, was again assailed by doubts. It was Gandhi's speech which had quelled the opposition, and to Nehru its tone seemed to be dictatorial. He felt that Gandhi was in

[2] This had become a regular organisation of the Congress in 1931.
[3] It held its first all-India conference at Patna on May 17, 1934. Later, branches of the party were formed in several provinces.

effect saying, "If you choose to follow my lead you have to accept my conditions." Moreover, Nehru was hurt by the fact that Gandhi had not waited for the committee's decision but, unceremoniously gathering up his belongings, marched away on his Harijan tour. There was too much imposition from above, Nehru thought, too little free and intelligent discussion from below.

Subsequent events depressed him further. Communalism and reaction were very much in the air. Inside the Congress itself were elements represented by Pandit Madan Mohan Malaviya and Mr. M. S. Aney, who were bitterly opposed to the Communal Award even as modified by Gandhi on behalf of the Harijans. They had some justification for their attitude, for the award as embodied in the Government of India Act of 1935 tilted the scales heavily in favour of the minorities against the Hindu majority. Not only were the minorities given representation out of all proportion to their numbers, but the electorate was divided into as many as nineteen religious and social categories— Muslims, Sikhs, Christians, Depressed Classes, Europeans, Anglo-Indians, landholders, commerce and industry, and so on—and each of them was given separate representation in the provincial legislatures. It was "divide and rule" with a vengeance. On the other hand the Hindus, where they were in a minority, as in the Punjab and Bengal, were given representation below their numerical strength. For example, in the Punjab the Hindus, comprising 28.3 per cent of the population, were allotted 24.6 per cent of the seats in the provincial legislature. Similarly in Bengal, where they were 44.8 per cent of the population, they had only 32 per cent of the seats as compared to the Europeans, a microscopic minority in the province, who had 25 out of 250 seats.

Hindu-Muslim tension grew. So sadly had feeling between the two communities slumped that a prominent member of the Hindu Mahasabha [4] actually congratulated the Government for not lifting the ban on the Muslim Red Shirts and their leader Khan Abdul Ghaffar Khan. Reading this, Nehru was deeply angered, the helplessness of his situation intensifying his rage.

He was also upset by a resolution of the Congress Working Committee, directed at the new Socialist party, which deprecated "loose talk about the confiscation of private property and the necessity of

[4] A militant Hindu organisation.

class war." Nehru felt that the charge was unjustified because no responsible Socialist had advocated confiscation, although members of the party had made frequent references to the existence but not to the desirability of class war. The resolution implied that persons holding these views had no place in the Congress organisation. "The Working Committee," it noted, "is further of the opinion that confiscation and class war are contrary to the Congress creed of non-violence." Nehru, it is interesting to note, saw no reason why such persons should not be members of Congress.

The frustration induced by imprisonment created in him a sense of political and personal claustrophobia. Nehru was assailed by dreams. He dreamt once that Abdul Ghaffar Khan was being attacked on all sides and that he, Nehru, was fighting to defend him. He woke up limp and exhausted. His pillow was wet with tears.

Evidently his nervous condition was none too good. He was disturbed by nightmares, and sometimes woke up to find himself shouting in his sleep. One night he dreamt he was being strangled, and his shouts brought two warders scurrying anxiously to his cell.

News of Kamala's health was bad and distressed him further, aggravating his sense of helplessness. In June, 1934, Nehru had begun writing his autobiography, partly to clear his own mental cobwebs by putting down his thoughts on paper, partly to divert his mind from the depression which enveloped him. He was to complete it in February, 1935, writing the entire book, with the exception of the postscript [5] and a few minor textual changes, in jail.

Throughout 1934 Kamala's health had been failing, and towards the end of July it slumped sharply and her condition grew critical. On the night of August 11th Nehru was brought from Dehra Dun under police escort to Allahabad and there informed that he was to be temporarily released in order to see his ailing wife. He was to be at liberty for eleven days.

He found Kamala a wan shadow of her self, frail, exhausted and weak. The thought that she might die entered his mind for the first time, and he discovered himself recalling the days when as a young bride she had come from Delhi to Allahabad. How virginal was the freshness of her looks! She was girlish but had a mind of her own, with strong likes and dislikes and opinions which she always expressed

[5] Written at Badenweiler in the Black Forest on October 25, 1935.

frankly, sometimes forthrightly. In the early years of their marriage, young as they both were—Nehru was twenty-six when he married and Kamala seventeen—they had quarrelled often with the impetuousness and sharp dogmatism of youth. Looking at her, Jawaharlal reflected that she had changed little through the years. Kamala had never been matronly, and as Indira grew to womanhood they had often been mistaken for sisters. But Nehru realised that he himself had changed greatly in the eighteen years since their marriage.

Indira had also come from her school at Santiniketan. She was now nearly seventeen, the same age as Kamala was at her marriage, and like her mother, of a quiet, serious disposition but with something too of her father's reflectiveness and purposefulness.

There was another invalid in the house. Swaruprani, now in her mid-sixties, was ailing. With her son in jail during the greater part of the past three years, and her daughters intermittently in and out of prison while her daughter-in-law's health languished slowly, Swaruprani led a lonely and exacting existence. About the only moments of solace she experienced were when Jawaharlal, out of jail, could spend some days with her. The fact that the Government had set no definite limit on his latest lease of freedom and might take him back to prison any day intruded an element of uncertainty into the lives of mother and son, and made it difficult for either to adjust to this peculiar position.

Nehru had given the Government no undertaking when he came out of jail, but he felt it would be improper to engage in political activities during the respite they had allowed him. Many things had happened while he was in jail which had disturbed, even distressed, him. Gandhi was at Wardha, and Nehru lost no time in writing his thoughts to him. The letter, dated August 13, 1934, contains nearly two thousand words, but they crystallise the doubts, fears and hesitations of the past three years, and some of the passages are revealing as a reflection of Jawaharlal's own political philosophy. He wrote:

When I heard that you had called off the C.D. movement I felt unhappy. Only the brief announcement reached me at first. Much later I read your statement and this gave me one of the biggest shocks I have ever had. I was prepared to reconcile myself to the withdrawal of C.D. But the reasons you gave for doing so and the suggestions you made for future work astounded me. I had a sudden and intense feeling, that something broke inside me, a bond that I had valued very greatly had snapped. I felt terribly lonely in this wide world. I have always felt a little lonely almost from childhood up. But a few bonds strengthened me, a few strong supports held me up. That loneliness never went, but it was lessened. But now I felt absolutely alone, left high and dry on a desert island.

Human beings have an enormous capacity for adapting themselves and so I too adapted myself to some extent to the new conditions. The keenness of my feelings on the subject, which amounted almost to physical pain, passed off; the edge was dulled. But shock after shock, a succession of events sharpened the edge to a fine point, and allowed my mind or feelings no peace or rest. Again I felt that sensation of spiritual isolation, of being a perfect stranger out of harmony, not only with the crowds that passed me, but also with those whom I had valued as dear and close comrades. My stay in prison this time became a greater ordeal for my nerves than any previous visit had been. I almost wished that all newspapers might be kept away from me so that I might be spared these repeated shocks.

The Working Committee is not directly responsible for this state of affairs. But none the less the Working Committee must shoulder the responsibility. It is the leaders and their policy that shape the activities of the followers. It is neither fair nor just to throw blame on the followers. Every language has some saying about the workman blaming his tools. The committee had deliberately encouraged vagueness in the definition of our ideals and objectives and this was bound to lead not only to confusion but to demoralisation during periods of reaction, and to the emergence of the demagogue and the reactionary.

I am referring especially to the political objectives which are the special province of the Congress. I feel that the time is overdue for the Congress to think clearly on social and economic issues but I recognise that education on these issues takes time and the Congress as a whole may not be able to go as far at present as I would like it to. But it appears that whether the Working Committee knows anything about the subject or not it is perfectly willing to denounce and to excommunicate people who happen to have made a special study of the subject and hold certain views. No attempt is made to understand those views, which it is notorious are held by a very large number of the ablest and most self-sacrificing people in the world. Those views may be right or wrong but they deserve at least some understanding before the Working Committee sets out to denounce them. It is hardly becoming for a reasoned argument to be answered by sentimental appeals or by the cheap remark that the conditions in India are different and the economic laws that apply elsewhere do not function here. The resolution of the Working Committee on the subject showed such an astounding ignorance of the elements of socialism that it was painful to read it and to realise that it might be read outside India. It seemed that the overmastering desire of the committee was somehow to assure various vested interests even at the risk of talking nonsense.

A strange way of dealing with the subject of socialism is to use the word, which has a clearly defined meaning in the English language, in a totally different sense. For individuals to use words in a sense peculiar to themselves is not helpful in the commerce of ideas. A person who declares himself to be an engine-driver and then adds that his engine is of wood and is drawn by bullocks is misusing the word engine-driver.

Gandhi's reply, dated August 17th, is written in a tone of gentle chiding:

Your passionate and touching letter deserves a much longer reply than my strength will permit.

I had expected fuller grace from the Government. However, your presence has done for Kamala and incidentally for Mama what no drugs or doctors could have done. I hope that you will be allowed to remain longer than the very few days you expect.

I understand your deep sorrow. You were quite right in giving full and free expression to your feelings. But I am quite sure that from our common standpoint a closer study of the written word will show you that there is not enough reason for all the grief and disappointment you have felt. Let me assure you that you have not lost a comrade in me. I am the same as you knew me in 1917 and after. I have the same passion that you know me to possess for the common good. I want complete independence for the country in the full English sense of the term. And every resolution that has pained you has been framed with that end in view. I must take full responsibility for the resolutions and the whole conception surrounding them.

But I fancy that I have the knack for knowing the need of the time. And the resolutions are a response thereto. Of course, here comes in the difference of our emphasis on the methods or the means which to me are just as important as the goal, and in a sense more important in that we have some control over them; whereas we have none over the goal, if we lose control over the means.

Do read the resolution about "loose talk" dispassionately. There is not a word in it about socialism. The greatest consideration has been paid to the socialists, some of whom I know so intimately. Do I not know their sacrifice? But I have found them as a body to be in a hurry. Why should they not be? Only if I cannot march as quick, I must ask them to halt and take me along with them. That is literally my attitude. I have looked up the dictionary meaning of socialism. It takes me no further than where I was before. I read the definition. What will you have me read to know its full content? I have read one of the books

Masani gave me, and now I am devoting all my spare time to reading the book recommended by Narendra Deva.

You are hard on the members of the Working Committee. They are our colleagues as they are. After all we are a free institution. They must be displaced, if they do not deserve confidence. But it is wrong to blame them for their inability to undergo the sufferings that some others have gone through.

After the explosion I want construction. Therefore, now, lest we do not meet, tell me exactly what will you have me do and who you think will best represent your views.

But for that there was no time.

Kamala had improved slightly with Jawaharlal's coming, and the doctors attending her were required to send a daily bulletin of her condition to the Government. On August 23rd, on the eleventh day after Nehru's release, the familiar police car drove up and a police officer informed him that his respite was over and that the time had come to return to prison. He took up his few belongings and said goodbye to Kamala, to his sisters, to the friends and relatives who were there, and lastly to his mother. As he got into the police car, Swaruprani, unable to conceal her anguish, came running up to him with her arms outstretched, her face tortured by agony and emotion.

"That face of hers haunted me for long," Jawaharlal wrote.

He was taken this time not to Dehra Dun but to Naini Jail in Allahabad so as to be near his wife. The old cell he had occupied was now tenanted by a détenu who was kept confined without trial or conviction. Jawaharlal found himself placed in another part of the jail. During his last imprisonment at Naini his brother-in-law Ranjit, who was with him, had planted a flower bed, and Nehru had been looking forward to seeing it again. But his new habitat was devoid of flowers or greenery.

Not that this mattered, for his mind was full of Kamala and he had a foreboding that the slight improvement in her health would not be maintained. For two weeks he received a daily bulletin from the doctors attending her; but then these ceased, although Kamala's health was deteriorating. Thereafter every hour in prison, with its uncertainty, was an agony.

There were two reasons why the British authorities were reluctant to release Nehru at this time. In October the Congress was holding its annual session in Bombay, and in November the Assembly elections which the Swarajists were contesting were to take place. Nehru would be a disturbing element outside jail.

A month after his re-arrest Jawaharlal was taken home for a brief visit to his wife. Kamala's condition was serious. The prison officials informed him that he would be allowed to visit his wife twice every week, even specifying the days. But when the days came nothing was done, and Nehru's anxiety grew to anguish under the strain of this casual and cruel attitude.

Early in October they took him out again to visit Kamala. In the intervening period of waiting, various intermediaries had hinted that if only Jawaharlal gave assurances to keep away from politics for the rest of his term he would be released. But Nehru was unwilling.

Some report of these moves had evidently reached Kamala, whom Jawaharlal found in a dazed condition and running a high temperature. As he prepared to leave her after his brief visit, she smiled at him and signalled to him to bend down nearer her.

Her voice was a whisper. "What is this I hear about your giving an assurance to the Government? Don't do it!"

It was decided to move Kamala to a sanatorium in the hills at a place called Bhowali. The day before she left, Nehru was again taken out of jail to pay her a fleeting visit. She was bright and cheerful, and the change in her condition made Jawaharlal buoyant. But when, he wondered, would he see her again?

Some three weeks later Nehru was transferred from Naini to Almora Prison so as to be nearer Kamala. Bhowali was on the way; and, Nehru stopping there en route, the improvement in Kamala's health cheered him, lifting his heart as he journeyed onward with the mountains high around him and the tang of the mountain air on his face.

The prison stood on a ridge with the glistening peaks of the Himalayas in the far distance, and a range of softly wooded mountains in between. Here Nehru occupied one of his more lordly prison habitats —a hall of fifty-one feet by seventeen, marred only by a moth-eaten roof and a crude, broken, uneven floor. Some twoscore sparrows nesting precariously in the eaves kept him company. Occasionally a drifting cloud crept through the crevices of the roof and the tattered coir matting covering the fifteen barred windows, leaving in its trail a damp chilling mist.

But there was grandeur around him. He spent many hours in his dilapidated barrack or in an adjoining yard watching the clouds sail by, marvelling at the intricacy of the patterns they traced and the shapes they took, curiously animal-like at times, moving on other occasions in massive formation, wave upon wave of them, like an on-coming sea or ocean. Sometimes the wind whistled through the deodar trees just outside the jail walls, giving the impression of a tide coming in along the sea front.

There was enchantment in the air but also tragedy. News of Kamala was bad, and the ups and downs of her condition were a constant fret and worry. Nehru longed to be free.

In September, Gandhi announced his decision to retire from the Congress after the October session. He explained his differences with his colleagues, not all of whom, he confessed, agreed wholeheartedly with his views, although they were reluctant to oppose him openly. In the circumstances he felt that by withdrawing from the Congress his colleagues would be free "to give effect to the dictates of their reason" and he could pursue unhampered his own experiments in satyagraha. His statement implied that if they wanted him to stay as the leader, they must follow his lead "faithfully, ungrudgingly and intelligently."

From prison Nehru followed the proceedings of the Bombay session which opened on October 26th under the Presidency of Dr. Rajendra Prasad, who called upon the Congress to hold to its sheet anchor of non-violent non-cooperation. Jawaharlal was not over-enthusiastic about the proceedings, but he was glad when the Congress adopted the idea of a Constituent Assembly for settling the constitution of the country, an idea which he had canvassed in writing during his brief spell of freedom in 1933. While doing this, the Congress rejected the British Government's White Paper.

For the rest, the Congress endorsed the decisions taken by the All-India Congress Committee at Patna, especially those regarding the Parliamentary Board and the promulgation of *swadeshi*. It forbade candidates fighting the elections on the Congress ticket from making the communal issue a plank in their electioneering campaign. Members elected to the legislature were also required to be neutral on questions relating to the Communal Award, which the Congress would try to modify by agreement among all the parties. This attitude towards the Communal Award led to the resignation of Pandit Mala-viya and Mr. Aney, who wanted the Congress to make the award an electoral issue. They formed a separate group known as the Congress Nationalists to fight the elections on the issue of the Communal Award.

On October 28th Gandhi officially announced his retirement from the Congress, having failed to persuade it to change its creed to "truthful and non-violent" methods instead of "peaceful and legitimate" methods. In his speech, severing his connection with this body, he accused himself of negligence. "My retirement from the Congress," he declared, "may be regarded as a penance for this negligence although it was wholly unconscious. What I am aiming at is the development of the capacity for civil disobedience. Disobedience that is wholly civil should not provoke rataliation."

So Gandhi took his bow temporarily from the Congress. To Nehru it seemed, rightly, that the step was of no great significance, for Gandhi could never, even if he wanted to, really rid himself of his dominating position in that organisation. He must carry his burden to the end.

In November came the elections to the Central Assembly where the Congress succeeded in winning 44 seats in a house of nearly 130. The Congress Nationalists under Malaviya and Aney gained 11 seats while the Independents, who included Jinnah, secured 22. The Europeans, and nominated non-officials, on whom the Government could rely, totalled 11 and 13 respectively. The official element totalled 26. Thus the Congress with the support of the other nationalist groups could invariably beat the Government on a vote.

With the elections and the meeting of the Congress in Bombay over, Nehru, never more anxious to be out of jail, half expected that he would be released. But this was not to be.

Shortly after the Bombay Congress session, the Frontier leader Khan Abdul Ghaffar Khan was arrested for a speech he had made in that city and sentenced to two years' imprisonment. Subhas Chandra Bose, hurrying home from Europe to his father's deathbed—he arrived too late—found his movements subject to the most humiliating restrictions.

These were hardly portents of peace. Nehru realised with a heavy heart that the Government were determined to keep him in jail despite

Kamala's critical condition, and not long afterward the authorities made it clear that such indeed was their intention. On November 14th he spent his second birthday in jail. He was forty-five.

After he had been a month in Almora Jail, Nehru was taken to Bhowali to see Kamala, and thereafter he was permitted to see her approximately once every third week until May, 1935, when she left for Europe for treatment. To Jawaharlal these visits, brief though they were, were precious. He could have fairly long talks with Kamala, and both were cheered by the meetings. But the imminence of death hovered over her, and the thought that a day might come when they must part for good racked him.

January came, and with it the snow which mantled the deodar trees in a garment of white so that in the sunlight they looked glistening and ethereal with a touch of faun and fairy. One morning in mid-January a telegram arrived from Bombay, where Swaruprani had gone to convalesce, informing Jawaharlal that his mother had been stricken with paralysis. For many anxious days and nights she hovered between life and death, recovering finally; but she was never to be herself again.

Kamala's condition was worsening, and it was decided that she should go to Europe for further treatment. On the May morning fixed for her departure Jawaharlal was allowed to come to Bhowali to bid her farewell, which each did with a brave smile. Swaruprani was there with her younger daughter Krishna. Nehru watched the car taking his wife wend its way down the hill. Then he turned to bid his mother and sister goodbye. His eyes were sad but dry. As he walked away from them to the waiting car which was to take him to Almora Jail, his face seemed suddenly tired and haggard and his step slow and weary. He looked as if he had aged in a few hours.

Back in Almora Prison Nehru, deprived of his intermittent visits to Bhowali, found prison life more oppressive than ever. On June 1st came the news of an earthquake in Quetta on the previous day in which about 25,000 people perished. Gandhi, who had interpreted the earlier earthquake in Bihar as a punishment for the sin of untouchability, saw in the latest calamity a call to prayer. "Let us pray," Gandhi advised the people in Harijan.

Inexplicably the Government refused to allow Congress relief workers to enter Quetta, and this led to a spate of rumours by no means creditable to the authorities. It seemed as if the military-police mentality had come to stay.

"Almost it would seem," wrote Nehru, "that the British Government in India is permanently at war with large sections of the Indian people."

On September 4, 1935, Nehru was suddenly discharged from Almora, five and a half months before his term was to expire. Kamala, who was at Badenweiler in the Black Forest in Germany, was critically ill again. Jawaharlal hurried to Allahabad, which he reached the next day, and on the same afternoon he set out by air for Europe, journeying by way of Karachi, Baghdad, Cairo, Alexandria, to Brindisi and Basle. On the evening of September 9th he reached Badenweiler.

Kamala greeted him with her old brave smile. She looked desperately ill, and it was evident that she was in great pain. They could say little to each other. Although she brightened somewhat on the following day, it seemed as if her life was slowly ebbing. She grew weaker but she survived the immediate crisis.

Kamala's helpless condition tortured Jawaharlal. He could do little to help. Off and on, he read to her, and she liked to have him do so, but the effort of listening tired her. One of the books he read and which she enjoyed was Pearl Buck's *The Good Earth*. Occasionally he read to her, and discussed with her, chapters from the manuscript of his autobiography.

As the days progressed she seemed to improve. Her wan, emaciated face and frame bespoke illness and suffering, but a visitor looking at her bright smiling face might be deceived into thinking that her condition was not too critical.

Jawaharlal stayed in a small pension in town, and every day, morning and afternoon, he walked to the sanatorium to spend some hours by Kamala's bedside. Sometimes they recalled old memories and talked of far-off forgotten things. In Jawaharlal's heart was a great eagerness to make up for past omissions, and he would have liked to tell her the deeper things that disturbed his being. But Kamala talked also of the future, clinging to life with the illusive hope of the desperately ill. Jawaharlal, restraining himself, held his peace. "Sometimes, looking into her eyes," he mused, "I would find a stranger peeping out at me."

He thought of the times when Kamala had stood by his side in the political clashes with his father whenever Motilal's temper had flared in an outburst of verbal wrath; of his father's death, their brief holiday in Ceylon and of the growing strength and understanding of their relationship. Kamala had proved her mettle even before Motilal's death, in the great upheaval of 1930 when, although ill and running a temperature, she had gone out night after night into the cold, wind-swept streets of Allahabad, sometimes sitting for hours at the head of a procession brought to a halt by the police. On one such night a friend had got her a blanket and, returning an hour later, had found Kamala shivering in her sari with the blanket snuggly wrapped around an old lady who sat near her.

She wanted to justify herself, Jawaharlal mused, to her own self as well as to the world. Not understanding fully her mind, he had been of little help. But Kamala had justified herself in both ways. He had only realised in the past five years that she had wanted to play her own part in the national movement and not be a mere shadow of her husband. Within her slim, wraith-like frame she had a spark of vitality, even dynamism, but illness had dimmed it.

For a month Nehru stayed in Badenweiler, and in that period Kamala rallied sufficiently for the doctors to advise him that he could leave safely for a brief visit to England, which he had not visited for eight years and where friends were pressing him to come. Indira was at school at Bex in Switzerland. He decided to take her with him to England.

They stayed twelve days in London, a period which coincided with Nehru's election as President-elect of the Congress for 1936–1937, and this in turn perhaps enhanced the importance of Nehru's visit and contacts. He had always been happy to visit England, and the welcome and cordiality which greeted him, even among those who disagreed with him politically, pleased and touched him. Almost he sensed in England "a vague pricking of conscience" at the doings of British authority in India.

But behind it all British opinion, intelligent as well as unintelligent, seemed a little tired and bored by India. The Government of India Act of 1935, with its promise of constitutional advance, served as a salve to some consciences. Why did the Congress not cooperate? Although the views of the Tories, Liberals and Socialists differed somewhat, they seemed to Nehru rooted in the narrow grooves of party predilections and objectives. Only a major upheaval in India, he felt, or an international conflagration would shake them out of their mental lethargy.

War was nearer than many of them suspected. In January, 1935, a plebiscite had restored the Saar to Germany, and by March Hitler was emboldened to repudiate the military clauses of the Versailles Treaty and occupy the Rhineland. In May the Nazis under Konrad Henlein became the strongest German party in Czechoslovakia. Five months later, on October 2nd, the Italians invaded Abyssinia, flaunting the League, which belatedly applied economic sanctions against the aggressor. On May 1, 1936, the armies of the Duce were to enter Addis Ababa in the wake of the fleeing Haile Selassie, and the King of Italy was to become the Emperor of Ethiopia.

Nehru returned to Badenweiler from London cheered by the contacts he had made but disturbed by the drift of events in Europe.

Winter had come to the Black Forest. The trees were swathed in white, but as Christmas drew near Kamala's condition again deteriorated, and another crisis loomed before them. The calm and chill of the atmosphere affected Nehru. The winter scene, he reflected, "seemed so like the peace of cold death to me, and I lost all my past hopeful optimism."

But Kamala rallied, and asked that she be taken away from Badenweiler. It was not only the long stay that depressed her but the death of another patient—an Irish boy who had sometimes sent flowers to her and occasionally visited her. His passing away made her melancholy and thoughtful.

The session of Congress was to be held in April, 1936, and Nehru, who had heard the news of his election as President while in London, was faced with a dilemma. Should he return to India or resign the Presidency? He talked it over with Kamala.

"You must go," she pressed him. "There is no question of your resigning. After April you can come back to me."

At the end of January they moved Kamala from Badenweiler to a sanatorium near Lausanne in Switzerland. Earlier Nehru had paid another fleeting visit to London and Paris.

Kamala seemed to improve in her new surroundings. Although there was no conspicuous change in her condition, there seemed no likelihood of any immediate crisis ahead. The doctors felt that her condition would continue as it was for some time, possibly registering some slow progress. Should Jawaharlal return or stay? Friends in India were pressing for his return, but his own mind, torn by doubts, was uncertain.

Once again he talked the matter over with Kamala and consulted the doctor. It was decided that he should return to India by air, leaving Lausanne on February 28th. When it had all been settled, Jawaharlal had the feeling that Kamala was uneasy. She did not say anything, but he sensed that his imminent departure was worrying her. He tried to reassure her. He would be away for only two or three months. If she needed him urgently, a cable would bring him back to her within a week.

Four or five days before the date of Jawaharlal's departure, the doctor took him aside and urged him to postpone his departure by a week or ten days. He would not say more. Indira had just then come from her school at Bex to spend a few days with her parents. Nehru lost no time in rearranging his schedule.

He thought a subtle change had come over Kamala, and although physically her condition did not alter, her mind appeared to rove between the vague borderland of life and the hereafter. She seemed to be shedding the coils which bound her to her earthly existence, and grew more and more detached from her immediate environment. Kamala was dying.

During the last few days, as Jawaharlal sat watching by her bedside, she would tell him that someone was calling to her. Now and again she would point at a door or corner of her bedroom and speak of a figure or shadow or shape she saw entering the room. Jawaharlal could see no one.

Early on the morning of February 28th, as Indira and her father watched beside her, Kamala sighed softly and breathed her last. The doctor was also with them.

A few friends came from neighbouring towns, and that day they took Kamala's body to the crematorium where within a few minutes it was reduced to ashes. These were placed in an urn for the journey home.

Flying back from Europe to India accompanied by the urn containing Kamala's ashes, Jawaharlal was overcome by an overwhelming sense of loneliness and exhaustion. She is no more; Kamala is no more, was the recurring refrain in his mind.

While in London he had put the complete manuscript of his autobiography in the hands of his publishers. He thought of the times when he had read odd chapters and portions of the manuscript to Kamala. She would never read it in full.

The plane touched down at Baghdad. Nehru, seized by a sudden impulse, went to the cable desk. He sent a cable to his London publishers giving them the dedication for his book. It read: "To Kamala who is no more."

17

PRELUDE TO WAR

In March, 1936, after spending a few days at Montreux with Indira, Nehru returned to India.

A curious episode marked his journey back. At Montreux he had a visit from the Italian Consul at Lausanne who came over especially to convey Signor Mussolini's deep sympathy at the death of his wife. Jawaharlal was a little surprised because he had never met the Fascist dictator nor had any communication with him.

Thinking over this strange gesture he recalled that some weeks earlier a friend in Rome had written to say that Mussolini would like to meet him. At that time Rome was not on Nehru's itinerary, but now he realised that his plane would be passing through the Italian capital. Was there a purpose in Mussolini's mannered courtesy? Jawaharlal's suspicions were confirmed when a few days later the invitation to see the Duce was repeated—this time with slightly more insistence. Though he did not wish to appear discourteous, he had no great anxiety to see Mussolini, and in any case the Italian war against Abyssinia would expose the meeting to invidious interpretations. The Fascists might make political capital out of it. Nehru politely declined.

He was therefore somewhat taken aback when on landing in Rome in the late afternoon en route to India he was met by a high Italian official who handed him a letter from Mussolini's Chief of Cabinet. The letter stated that the Duce would be glad to receive him at six that evening. Nehru courteously demurred, arguing that his reaction to the invitation had already been conveyed. The official insisted, pleading finally that his job was at stake. Nehru need see the Duce only for a few minutes. All that Mussolini wanted was to convey his personal condolences. Nothing would appear about the interview in the Press.

They argued for an hour, politely on both sides but with an increasing sense of strain. Nehru at last had his way. A telephone message was despatched to the Duce's palace to inform him that the Indian leader regretted he could not come. Later that evening Nehru wrote a personal letter to Mussolini thanking him for his message of condolence and regretting that he could not accept his invitation. So the encounter closed, courteously but on a note of challenge.

Nehru got back to India with the firm conviction that both at home and abroad the time had come for a revaluation of ideas. Europe was in turmoil, and the twilight of barbarism deepened as the shadow of the swastika lengthened over the world. The tramp of the Nazi jack boot echoed around Europe even while the Fascist armies, deploying poison gas, closed on Addis Ababa. Japan was preparing to launch her second and more extensive attack on China within a few months. Eden had displaced Hoare at the British Foreign Office, but both London and Paris were committed to a policy of non-intervention. "A war postponed may be a war averted," declared Eden in the House of Commons. But war was not to be averted, and Eden was to realise this as Neville Chamberlain with his umbrella paid court to the Duce in Rome.

To Nehru it seemed that Nazism was the embodiment and intensification of the two things against which the Congress was fighting—imperialism and racialism. Progressive forces therefore must align themselves with those who opposed imperialism and racial reaction. But here Nehru, together with India, was caught in the cleft of a dilemma. In the eyes of a subjugated country there was no greater imperialism than the one which ruled it. If therefore India was to align itself with Britain against the evil things Fascism represented, Britain must shed her imperialism. It was only as a free nation, of her own free will, that India could join with Britain and France in a war against Fascism and Nazism. This view, which Nehru was to express in his presidential address to the Congress was to become the cornerstone of the foreign policy of the Congress during the war years.

The long terms he had spent in prison over the past five years had made Jawaharlal a spectator of the Indian scene. They had given him time to watch, study, analyse and assess the developments in the country. By and large the picture depressed him, for the Congress politically seemed to have come to a dead end with only entry into the legislatures offering an escapist avenue of activity. The advent of the Socialist group, far from galvanising his colleagues, had divided them, and even Gandhi seemed to look askance at the activities of the Socialists. Never in recent years was the British Raj so firmly in the saddle. At home, as abroad, reaction reigned as the vested interests entrenched themselves, and communal tensions grew in India with the widening field for office and opportunism which the prospect of provincial autonomy offered.

While the all-India federation, which envisaged the princely States and the Provinces joined in a single federal government, was conditional on cooperation between these two components and subject to various checks and safeguards, provincial autonomy was to come into operation as from April 1, 1937. Here again, while the ministers were responsible to a popularly elected legislature, the pivot of the entire provincial administration was not the Chief Minister but the Governor appointed by the Crown and acting as the Crown's representative. In this capacity he could intervene, veto or legislate on his own authority. He could even suspend the ministry or dismiss it. In theory all the provincial portfolios were held by the popularly elected ministers. In practice it was open to the Governor to overrule a minister's decisions, though in that event the entire ministry might resign.

Similarly at the centre, even under federal rule,[1] all real power was concentrated in the Viceroy or Governor-General as representative of the Crown. Power in fact derived from the Crown, which through its representatives, central and provincial, could in any event effectively exercise it. Moreover, the Federal Legislature at the centre was so conceived as to make of the Princes' nominees a solid counterweight to nationalist aspirations. As the Act stood, the Federal Legislature was to consist of an upper house known as the Council of State and a lower house known as the Assembly. Although the States ruled by the Princes contained only one-fourth of India's total population, they were given two-fifths of the seats in the Council of

[1] This was never enacted.

State (104 out of 260), and one-third of the seats in the Assembly (125 out of 375).

Actually, the federal structure never came into being, owing partly to popular opposition, including that of the Princes, and partly to the outbreak of the war. The result was that at the centre the old bicameral legislature, also consisting of a Council of State and an Assembly, continued almost until the advent of independence.

In 1936 popular attention was concentrated primarily on the coming provincial autonomy. Should the Congress contest the elections to the legislatures which were scheduled for the opening months of 1937, and if successful should they accept office and form governments in the provinces? Nehru was of the opinion that the Congress should contest the elections, but he felt that on no account should Congressmen take office. He expressed these views in his presidential address at the Lucknow session which met in April, 1936. He warned:

It is always dangerous to assume responsibility without power. It will be far worse with this constitution hedged in with safeguards and reserved powers and mortgaged funds, where we have to follow the rules and regulations of our opponents' making. Imperialism sometimes talks of co-operation, but the kind of co-operation it wants is usually known as surrender, and the ministers who accept office will have to do so at the price of surrender of much that they might have stood for in public. That is a humiliating position which self-respect itself should prevent one from accepting. For our great national organization to be party to it is to give up the very basis and background of our existence.

Not all of his colleagues were enamoured of this outlook, which many felt was too categorical and didactic. Lucknow brought neither solace nor vindication to Nehru. The Congress as a whole was not prepared to take an uncompromising attitude. It preferred to wait on events, and neither politically, economically nor socially did it assume the firm, defined, rigid, unyielding front which Jawaharlal would have liked it to achieve.

Fascism had left him sick at heart, repelling him by its crudity, vulgarity and violence. Nehru came back from Europe with his faith in socialism reinforced, regarding it not as a vague humanitarian creed but as a robust scientific economic philosophy capable of being translated in practical terms, in vast and revolutionary changes in India's political and social structure. While affirming his own faith, he was prepared to recognise that the Congress as a whole was not ready to march with him. He declared at Lucknow:

Socialism is thus for me not merely an economic doctrine which I favour; it is a vital creed which I hold with all my head and heart. I work for Indian independence because the nationalist in me cannot tolerate alien domination; I work for it even more because for me it is the inevitable step to social and economic change. I should like the Congress to become a Socialist organization and to join hands with the other forces in the world who are working for the new civilization. But I realize that the majority in the Congress, as it is constituted today, may not be prepared to go thus far.

At the same time Nehru affirmed his belief in the need for industrialisation, and while recognising that *khadi* and village industries had a place in India's economy he felt they were temporary expedients of a transition period rather than solutions of the country's vital problems. Their role, though important, was subsidiary.

Once more he affirmed his belief in the machinery of a constituent assembly as the only proper and democratic method for framing a constitution, leaving its delegates free to negotiate a treaty after that with the representatives of the British Government. But for the time being he would have the Congress contest the elections if only to carry its message to the masses, some 35,000,000 [2] of whom were now enfranchised.

In his presidential address Nehru bitterly deplored the torpor which had overcome the Congress. "We have largely lost touch with the masses," he confessed. "Congress membership stands at below half a million, registering 457,000."

While listening to him respectfully the Congress was not prepared to follow his lead in every detail. It joined with him in condemning the Government of India Act and in resolving to contest the elections. But on the question of office acceptance it kept the issue open, leaving the All-India Congress Committee to decide it at the proper moment.

Nor did the Congress approach economic problems with the revolutionary outlook which Jawaharlal favoured. Its resolution on the agrarian programme merely reiterated large and unexceptionable principles such as "freedom for the peasant from oppression and harass-

[2] This constituted roughly 14 per cent of the total population, and was mainly based on property qualifications. Under the Government of India Act, 1919, the number of voters was 8,744,000.

ment at the hands of Government officials and landlords" and "emancipation of the peasant from feudal and semi-feudal levies."

It was clear that a majority of Congressmen supported the old leadership and was not prepared to move as fast or as far as Nehru would have liked. Gandhi, although he had officially retired from the Congress, was present at the session. He took no part in the proceedings, but he was careful to see that the majority of members in the Working or Executive Committee reflected his views. The President of Congress had theoretically the right to nominate his own committee. Jawaharlal, however, soon discovered that the Old Guard were solidly massed against him, and they could not be ignored for membership of the executive. Of the fifteen members of the committee, one (Subhas Bose) was in prison while ten represented the Old Guard. Nehru found himself in a minority along with the three Socialists, Narendra Deva, Jayaprakash Narayan and Achyut Patwardhan, whom he was able to bring on to the executive. He offered to resign but was pressed to stay on, which he did more from a sense of duty than from conviction.

"Some day," Mohamed Ali had warned him way back in 1929, "your present colleagues will desert you, Jawahar." And he had added theatrically, "Your own Congressmen will send you to the gallows!"

Nehru had thought it a dismal prophecy, and laughed.

Within the Congress he was now virtually a captive of the Working Committee, but in the country the magic of his presence and name could still influence public opinion, particularly among the younger elements. Although not a member of the Socialist group, Nehru was by now firmly convinced that the objective to work for in India was a socialist State. Thenceforward he preached this creed persistently even though he was not yet clear in his own mind how to apply socialism to Indian conditions and how to interpret this philosophy in terms which the masses would understand.

He was attracted by Marx but disliked the dogmatism of the Marxists, their intolerance and violence. Something of the humanist liberal tradition in which he was bred still clung to him, although in time he was to shed its outer habiliments.

"You will end your days like Trotsky," a friend had prophesied. Nehru had smiled wanly.

Though a capable and exacting administrator, as his secretaryship of the Congress proved, Jawaharlal at this period was not interested in controlling the Congress machine. He attached no importance at the time to organisational control, and the thought never entered his mind. He had a prodigious capacity for work, which he lavished on the country and on the Congress, a stern sense of discipline and punctuality; and, despite his explosive temper, which evaporated quickly, he could infect co-workers with his enthusiasm and make them work as a team. He revelled in activity, and crowds were a spur and a stimulus.

"I like to be at the storm centre of life," Nehru has often remarked.

He was a socialist, but he respected the Individual Man as opposed to the Mass Man which his friend Ernst Toller had dramatised. The State, he agreed, must step in to protect the underprivileged, but it must do so within a democratic framework where the individual was not submerged by the leviathan of an omnipotent government.

What mattered were the people.

"The people," he has often repeated, "will go as far as you can take them. It is only vested interests which block the path of progress. These, and confused, selfish thinking."

If Nehru returned from his brief sojourn abroad with his faith in socialism reinforced, he was now more convinced than ever that India should see herself in an international context, divorce from which was unreality. Isolation meant insulation, the cutting off of a country from currents of international thought, progress and activities. It was vital that the Indian problem should be set and seen against an international background.

India's struggle against imperialism was part of the liberal world's fight against Fascism. It was a common struggle. In his presidential address at Lucknow he urged that a message of admiration and sympathy be sent to the Ethiopians, who were desperately resisting Mussolini's Fascist forces. This was done, and May 9th was observed as Abyssinia Day, when resolutions were passed expressing sympathy with Abyssinia and condemning Italy.

Prison had intensified his introspective bent, and his last term in jail, with its trials, worries and disappointments, had strengthened the introvert in him.

"I was not an introvert," he wrote while he was in jail in 1935, "but prison life, like strong coffee and strychnine, leads to introversion."

He used to while away the hours in jail by drawing an outline of McDougall's cube for the measurement of introversion and extroversion.

"I gaze at it to find out how frequent are the changes from one interpretation and another," he mused. "They seem to be rapid."

The introvert and extrovert were reflected in an article about himself that he wrote about this time and published under the pseudonym "Chanakya" [3] in a Bengal journal, *Modern Review*. It is an engaging and revealing essay in self-analysis, referring to his flashes of temper, his overmastering desire to get things done, his impatience with the slow processes of democracy, his conceit and pride, the former of which he describes as "already formidable."

"He cannot rest, for he who rides a tiger cannot dismount," he reflects.

Looking into the future and projecting himself into it, Jawaharlal writes of himself, "In normal times he would just be an efficient and successful executive, but in this revolutionary epoch Caesarism is always at the door, and is it not possible that Jawaharlal might fancy himself as a Caesar? Therein lies the danger for Jawaharlal and India."

A prophetic warning. Yet the frankness of the analysis reveals an awareness of and insight into his qualities and defects. He might not be able to dismount from the tiger, but he seems determined not to let it run away with him.

Jawaharlal's unhappiness over the Lucknow session continued. Chafing at the majority in the Working Committee who were opposed to his views, he persisted in propagating his socialist ideas, and this in turn led to a crisis, some members offering their resignation. Gandhi's intervention brought a temporary truce.

Nehru had been advised to go slow on the plea that the country was demoralised, a verdict he did not share. In a letter written to Gandhi in June he dissented from this view. "My own little experience during the past months," he wrote, "has not confirmed

[3] Chanakya was the chancellor of the emperor Chandragupta Maurya, and is sometimes called the Machiavelli of India.

this impression. Indeed I have found a bubbling vitality wherever I have gone and I have been surprised at the public response."

At this juncture the views of Nehru and of his more conservative colleagues on the Working Committee differed sharply. On July 17th and 18th the outbreak of civil war in Spain, which was spearheaded on the rebel side by General Franco, saw Nehru urging the Congress to establish a united front with the progressive forces. His socialistic utterances continued to disturb many Congressmen. It was whispered that the gulf between the Mahatma and Nehru was widening, and Gandhi was alleged to have said, "My life work is being ruined by Jawaharlal's utterances."

Gandhi was quick to deny this allegation in an article in *Harijan* of July 25th entitled "Are We Rivals?" He wrote:

So far as I am aware, Jawaharlal has come to the conclusion that India's freedom cannot be gained by violent means and that it can be gained by non-violent means. And I know for a fact that he did not in Lucknow "come out for the use of violence in the struggle for independence." No doubt there are differences of opinion between us. They were clearly set forth in the letters we exchanged some years ago. But they do not affect our personal relations in any way whatsoever. We remain the same adherents to the Congress goal, that we have ever been. My life-work is not, cannot be ruined by Jawaharlal's programme, nor have I ever believed for that matter that it has been harmed even by "the firmness and repression of the British Government." My philosophy, if I can be said to have any, excludes the possibility of harm to one's cause by outside agencies. The harm comes deservedly and only when the cause itself is bad, or being good its champions are untrue, faint-hearted, or unclean.

Heading the conservative bloc inside the Working Committee was the rugged, blunt-spoken Vallabhbhai Patel, who until his death in December, 1950, worked as a brake on Nehru's socialistic ideas and programmes. Like Gandhi, Patel came from Gujerat; although a London-trained lawyer he had the canny earthiness of the peasant, in no way interested or impressed by academic theories.

The main task before the Congress after the Lucknow session of April, 1936, was to prepare for the election, and late in August the Working Committee met in Bombay to draft the election manifesto of the Congress. This document, which was later adopted by the All-India Congress Committee, reiterated the political goal as complete independence, condemned the British-imposed constitution, and emphasised its belief in a constituent assembly as the only medium for devising a charter and constitution of independence. It insisted on respect for equal rights and civil liberties, and enunciated a broad economic and social programme for the benefit of the masses. Congressmen, it promised, would enter the legislatures "not to cooperate in any way with the Act, but to combat it and seek to end it."

Although at one time Nehru had planned to resign from the Presidency of the Congress and devote himself to the electoral campaign, he now realised that Gandhi wanted him to remain. Patel was also among the nominees for Presidency of the next Congress at Faizpur, a village in the East Khandesh district of Bombay Province. Nehru felt he must make his position clear. As the session drew near he issued a statement expressing his willingness to be President if the Congress so desired, but his countrymen, he added, must "realise what I stand for, what thoughts move me and what the springs of action are for me."

Gandhi kept clear of politics and took no part in the electoral campaign, but his advice was readily available to his colleagues. The differences between Nehru and Vallabhbhai Patel—though temporarily breached—remained, but Gandhi wisely mollified Nehru, restraining him good-humouredly from any precipitate action or gesture.

When late one day in September, Jawaharlal, Patel and Rajendra Prasad called on Gandhi at Sewagram, the village near Wardha in the Central Provinces where he now had his ashram, they found him engrossed in treating two patients ill with enteric. They waited for some time, but Gandhi continued his nursing.

"If you have no time," remarked Patel at last, "we had better go."

Gandhi smilingly dissented. "I must finish treating my patients," he explained.

"But isn't it like King Canute trying to stop the waves?" Nehru expostulated.

Gandhi laughed. "That is why we have made you King Canute," he said good-humouredly. "So that you can stop the waves."

Patel withdrew his candidature for the Presidency, but in doing so stressed that his gesture did not imply that he endorsed all of Jawaharlal's views. "On some vital matters," he confessed, "my views are in conflict with those held by Jawaharlal." Patel added: "The President has no dictatorial powers. . . . The Congress does not part with its powers by electing any individual, no matter who he is. I ask the delegates to plump for Jawaharlal as being the best person to represent the nation and guide in the right channel the different forces that are at work in the country." It was a plain hint to Nehru to adjust his views more accommodatingly with those of his colleagues. The hint was not lost on Jawaharlal. In his presidential address, after deploring "the triumphant course of Fascism in Europe," Nehru went on to say: "The Congress today stands for full democracy in India and fights for a democratic state, not for socialism. It is anti-imperialist and strives for great changes in our political and economic structure. I hope the logic of events will lead to socialism; for, that seems to me the only remedy for India's economic ills." Congressmen, he insisted, were going to the legislatures not to cooperate with the Government of India Act but to combat it. But he reiterated his personal view that the only logical consequence of the policy of the Congress was to have nothing to do with acceptance of office.

Soon after the outbreak of civil war in Spain in July, Nehru had pleaded for a united front with all progressive forces, and he now clarified his proposal:

The real objective before us is to build up a powerful joint front of all the anti-imperialistic forces in the country. The Congress has been indeed in the past, and is today such a united popular front, and inevitably the Congress must be the basis and pivot of united action. The active participation of the organised workers and peasants in such a front would add to its strength and must be welcomed. Cooperation between them and the Congress organisations has been growing and has been a marked feature of the past year. This tendency must be encouraged. The most urgent and vital need of India today is this united national front of all the forces and elements that are ranged against imperialism. Within the Congress itself most of the forces are represented, and in spite of their diversity and difference in outlook, they have cooperated and worked together for the common good.

Clearly this was a bid for broadening and strengthening the structure of Congress on the basis of closer cooperation with the peasants and workers—an oblique proposal for "socialising" the Congress.

Once again the general session deferred a decision on office acceptance, the meeting being of the opinion that such a decision was best made after the elections.

Following the Faizpur session, the leaders of Congress concentrated on the electoral campaign. Nehru had been busy on this since April. Between then and February, 1937, he spent at varied intervals about 130 days stumping the country, covering nearly 65,000 miles. His means of transport included planes, trains, motor cars, lorries, various types of horse-driven and bullock-drawn vehicles, steamers, paddle-boats, canoes, elephants, camels, bicycles and horses. Off and on, he trekked through the villages on foot.

His working day sometimes extended over twenty hours, in the course of which he was known to address as many as twelve meetings ranging from one thousand to over a hundred thousand people. In the south and in certain districts such as Maharashtra women formed a large part of the audience. He talked to peasants, industrial workers, merchants, traders, businessmen, students, lawyers, doctors, artisans and scavengers. In all, his voice and presence reached out to some 20,000,000 people.

One day in a Punjab village Jawaharlal was surrounded by a crowd of about a thousand villagers who greeted him with the cry *Bharat Mata ki jai!* [4]

"What does it all mean?" he asked them.

They did not know.

"Who is this *mata* you salute?" Nehru persisted.

"It is *dharti*" (the earth), said a peasant.

"Whose earth?" Nehru questioned. "Your village earth? Your province? India? The world?"

They were silent again, and then some voices suggested that Nehru himself should explain it to them.

Nehru did. He told them that Bharat Mata was Mother India and that they were all her children, they and other Indians who resided in the north, south, east and west. When they said *jai* they were hailing the people of India, Bharat Mata's sons and daughters.

"Who are these sons and daughters?" Nehru asked them. "They are you, all of you, and I. So when you cry *jai*, you are shouting your own *jai* as well as the *jai* of all our brothers and sisters throughout Hindustan. Remember this. *Bharat Mata* is you, and it is your own *jai*."

[4] Hail to Mother India! (Bharat is India, and Mata, Mother.)

"You are right," they said after listening to him intently. A glow suffused their faces and a light seemed to dawn on their slow, heavy peasant minds.

The success of Congress at the polls was spectacular. Out of a total of 1,585 seats, of which only 657 were open to general and not sectional competition, the Congress secured as many as 715. It gained absolute majorities in five provinces—Madras, the United Provinces, the Central Provinces, Bihar and Orissa. In Bombay it won nearly half the seats, and with the support of other nationalist groups was able to constitute a majority. In Assam it emerged as the strongest party, securing 35 seats out of 108, and here again it was in a position, with extraneous support, to form later a coalition ministry. Of 50 seats in the predominantly Muslim Northwest Frontier Province the Congress won 19, of which 15 were from Muslim constituencies, and with the help of some Muslim nationalists it was successful in forming a ministry. Thus the Congress controlled eight of India's eleven provinces. Only in the Punjab, Sind and Bengal was it in a minority, and in Bengal it did better than expected, winning 60 seats out of 250. The most striking success of the Congress was registered in Madras, where it pushed out of office the Justice party [5] which had enjoyed power since 1922. As against 159 seats won by the Congress, the Justice party could obtain only 21.

Jinnah, later the creator of Pakistan, had also entered the political lists as head of the Muslim League. There is reason to believe that at this stage Jinnah honestly hoped to join in cooperation and coalition with the Congress to work provincial autonomy "for what it was worth." With the Congress, the League condemned federation, though possibly for different reasons. A strong federal government at the centre might render nugatory the autonomy of the Muslim majority provinces.

Addressing his followers in Delhi in March, Jinnah had declared: "The Hindus and Muslims must be organized separately, and once they are organized they will understand each other better, and then we will not have to wait for years for an understanding. . . . I am helping eighty million people, and if they are more organized they will be all the more useful for the national struggle."

[5] This party was non-Brahmin.

In the next ten years the differences between the Congress and the Muslim League were to congeal into implacable conflict and division, the fissures hardening with the League's declaration in December, 1940, of Pakistan or a partitioned India as the political goal of Indian Muslims. In August, 1947, the achievement of independence saw Pakistan come into being.

When the time arrived for forming the provincial ministries, the Congress refused to do so unless the Government made it clear that there would be no interference by the Governor or Viceroy in the realm of provincial autonomy. This view was embodied in a resolution passed by the All-India Congress Committee in March, 1936, which laid down that while the Congress should assume office in those provinces where it commanded a legislative majority it should not do so unless the leader of the Congress party in the legislature was satisfied and able to state publicly that the Governor would not use his special powers of interference "or set aside the office of ministers in regard to their constitutional activities."

There was much parleying to and fro between the Congress and the Government, the deadlock being finally ended by a vague assurance given by the Viceroy, Lord Linlithgow, who had succeeded Lord Willingdon in 1936. Linlithgow, in a statement issued in June, 1937, accepted Gandhi's suggestion that "it is only when the issue between a Governor and his minister constitutes a serious disagreement that any question of the severing of their partnership need arise."

Shortly afterward ministries of Congress were formed in six provinces, Bombay, Madras, the United Provinces, Bihar, the Central Provinces and Orissa, and later the rule of Congress was extended to Assam and the Frontier Province. These ministries were to remain in office until early in November, 1939, when the Congress withdrew from the administrative field in protest against the British Government's commitment of India in the war without any reference to Indian representatives.

Nehru was not happy over the decision to accept office. With Subhas Bose he had opposed the right-wing leaders who had argued that by forming ministries the Congress could improve its position in the fight against the new constitution. But as usual he accepted the decision of Congress loyally when it was made.

"Acceptance of office," said Nehru, rationalising the decision to himself, "does not mean by an iota acceptance of the slave constitution. It means fight against the coming of federation by all means in our power, inside as well as outside the legislatures. We have taken a new step involving new responsibilities and some risk. But if we are true to our objectives and are ever vigilant, we shall overcome these risks and gain strength and power from this step also. Eternal vigilance is the price of liberty."

In Jawaharlal's reckoning the Congress was now committed to a dual policy—to carry on the struggle for independence and simultaneously to carry through those provincial legislatures where the Congress was in power constructive measures of economic reform. He was particularly interested in agrarian relief for the peasant involving a reform in the system itself. Planning also absorbed his attention. Real power, he recognised, was still in the hands of the British Governors and ultimately in the hands of the Viceroy as the supreme representative of the Crown. He had no illusions about the limitations on Congress authority.

In 1936 Nehru started on his whirlwind tours of India, visiting remote villages and hamlets, travelling deep into the heart of the countryside, looking at the many-visaged face of India mirrored in Tamil and Punjabi, Maratha, Sikh, Gujerati, Sindhi, Assamese and Oriya, and reflected in layers of disparate culture infinite in their variegation and form—"like some ancient palimpsest," Jawaharlal reflected.

He was discovering India. In these ten years before independence Nehru was to sink his roots deeper in the Indian soil, and in giving to his people the message of duty, discipline and service was to receive from them not only boundless love but a new insight into the ancient vivid story of their common country. How timeless and unbroken was the flow of life and culture! The vast mass of peasant India was illiterate, yet it was moving and exciting to find that even the most ignorant among them often carried a picture gallery in his mind drawn from the old myths, traditions and epics and going way back to the *Ramayana* and the *Mahabharata*. They were downtrodden, miserable, steeped in poverty. Yet there was a mellowness and a gentleness, at times even a living grace about them. "Sometimes," writes Nehru, "as I was passing along a country road or through a village, I would start with surprise on seeing a fine type of a man, or a beautiful woman who reminded me of some fresco of ancient times." The type endured.

In these country-wide journeyings Nehru addressed crowds ranging from small groups to a multitude of one hundred thousand. The peasants' problems were rooted in their poverty; and the shadows of debt, the moneylender, oppressive rents and taxes and harassment by the police were always with them. Primarily Nehru was concerned in making them think of India not in terms of their village alone but of the country as a whole. At times he even talked to them of the world outside India, of China ravaged by Japan, of the Italian atrocities in Abyssinia, of Spain, of the menace of Fascism in Europe, of Russia's progress, of the wonderful economic advance of America.

He found the countryside excited by the news of popular administrations in the province. Provincial autonomy might not signify real power, but it had wrought a psychological change throughout the land. The peasants in the villages, as also the workers in the towns and cities, seemed to have acquired a new confidence and to look forward to better things.

Moved though they were by a sense of urgency and a realisation that their days in office might not be extensive, the administrations of Congress were not able for various reasons to accomplish all they had planned. They were new to office, and inevitably there were some inefficiency and incompetence. But there were also a great deal of energy and enthusiasm and a willingness to learn from mistakes. Planning and reform often called for coordination not merely within a single province but between two or more provinces. Here the rigidity of the central government could be a major deterrent. The conservatism of the entrenched bureaucracy, Indian and British, was another obstacle.

None the less the more urgent problems, such as rural indebtedness, were tackled, and legislation was passed to lighten the burden of debt on the harassed peasantry. Labour conditions in factories were improved, while attempts were made to extend sanitation and public health. A system of mass education known as basic education was introduced. Not all of these reforms survived the exit of the ministries of Congress, lack of finance and other handicaps also preventing the completion of many schemes.

Nehru, while probing the possibilities of reform and general amelioration, was struck by the absence of reliable statistics and other relevant data. In August, 1937, shortly after the formation of the Congress provincial governments, the Working Committee had passed a resolution recommending the ministers of Congress to set up an interprovincial committee of experts to investigate the nature of the major problems confronting the country and to devise ways and means of tackling them. With insufficient data and no reliable statistics this was a formidable task, but the effort was significant of the concern of Congress for large-scale planning, primarily under Jawaharlal's stimulus and encouragement.

Toward the end of 1938 the idea germinated in the appointment of a National Planning Committee at the instance of the Congress. Nehru was chairman of this body, which comprised representatives of provincial governments and certain princely states along with fifteen members drawn from the ranks of industrialists, labour leaders and economists. The committee suffered from the fact that there was no popular government at the centre and hence no national direction at the pivot. Cooperation was not forthcoming from the authorities at New Delhi.

Despite the lukewarm, even hostile, attitude of the central government, the committee under Nehru's direction set out to form a ten-year plan for the country. The general aim of the plan was to ensure an adequate standard of living for the masses by stepping up production, industrial and agricultural, and also by ensuring a more equitable distribution of wealth. It was calculated that the national wealth would have to be increased by 500 to 600 per cent if the standard of living was to be really progressive. This, however, seemed too ambitious a target, and the committee aimed at a 200 to 300 per cent increase within ten years.

The Planning Committee never completed its task, for even while it was considering the reports of its various sub-committees, Nehru was arrested in October, 1940, and sentenced to four years' imprisonment. He was released in December, 1941, to be arrested again in August, 1942, and detained without trial until June 15, 1945. This was his last term of imprisonment. The crowded sweep of events left the work of planning unfinished. Nehru was only able to pick up the threads in 1950 when, as Prime Minister, he initiated independent India's first five-year plan. But the earlier infructuouse venture had an educative value, for it helped to promote interest in planning all over the country.

One unfortunate result of provincial autonomy was to divert the nationalist effort from a country-wide into a provincial groove. Internal conflicts grew, particularly on the communal front where the Congress party's refusal to form coalition governments with the Muslim League infuriated Jinnah and his followers. The Congress pleaded that it was willing to invite Muslim representatives, including members of the League, to join its provincial ministries provided they became members of the Congress party. Jinnah cleverly interpreted this as an attempt by the "Hindu Congress" to suborn Muslims from their League loyalties with the bait of office. Whatever the motives of Congress might have been, this policy was a grave tactical blunder because it aggravated a sense of grievance, frustration and isolation among the Muslim leaders and masses. By exploiting this feeling Jinnah was able to sharpen religious differences and lead his co-religionists like a Muslim Moses into the promised land of Pakistan.

Had the Congress handled the League more tactfully after the elections Pakistan might never have come into being. A divided Hindu and Muslim India represented a gospel of frustration. Jinnah certainly created Pakistan. But the Congress by its sins of commission and omission also helped to make it possible. Misreading the poor showing of the Muslim League at the polls—the League candidates secured less than 5 per cent of the total Muslim votes cast and were not able to gain a single seat in the overwhelmingly Muslim province of the Northwest Frontier—the Congress spurned Muslim League overtures for a coalition. The result was not to drive the League into the political wilderness but to strengthen Jinnah's hands as the foremost champion of Muslim claims and rights.

"There are only two parties in the country," Nehru affirmed soon after the elections: "the Congress and the British."

"No," retorted Jinnah. "There is a third—the Muslims."

Temperamentally there was much in common between the two men, both being combative, explosive, proud, sensitive and assertive. But Jinnah was the more calculating and canny. As a political tactician he was superlative—ready to pounce upon and capitalise on every mistake of Congress. And in this period the Congress made several mistakes.

In October, 1937, Jinnah, addressing the League in Lucknow, declared that "the majority community have clearly shown their hand that Hindustan is for the Hindus."

Gandhi was moved to protest. "As I read it, the whole of your speech is a declaration of war," he wrote. It was.

In the succeeding months an acrimonious correspondence developed between Jinnah and Nehru which only widened the breach between the Congress and the League. To Nehru the controversy appeared unreal, for to him it seemed that the League under Jinnah's leadership was more interested in claiming special privileges for the Muslims than in pressing for the country's independence. But Jinnah was astutely manœuvring himself into the position of holding the balance between the nationalists and the British Government. In the process he was building up the Muslim League into a mass organisation like the Congress.

"Quit India," Gandhi was to say to the British in 1942.

"Divide and quit," was Jinnah's advice.

If he would not help the British, he would not hamper them. He would not be used as a cat's-paw to draw Britain's chestnuts out of the Congress fire, but he hinted cleverly that he was willing to do so if he were left master of the fireside. Both Jinnah and the British Government were engaged in the same game—to isolate the Congress and thereby to weaken it.

Both felt that in the last round the other could be eliminated. Both were to realise too late that each had created a Frankenstein's monster from whose grip neither could entirely escape. The British were to find themselves confronted suddenly with the reality, not the phantom of Pakistan. And Pakistan in turn was to find itself a truncated spectre of the robust image it had thought it would be. But the Congress would also pay the price in a divided India.

Meanwhile, the war clouds were gathering in Europe. In the summer of 1936 Hitler had sent aid to Franco's Fascist rebels, and in September of the following year he came to terms with Mussolini and founded the Rome-Berlin Axis. The long agony of Spain's civil war dragged its tragic course. Guernica was destroyed in April, 1937, and two years later Göring could boast that "all the important victories of General Franco were obtained with the help of German volunteers." There were Italian mercenaries also, but the prowess of Fascist arms was exposed at Guadalajara in March, 1937, when the Spanish Government forces routed Mussolini's soldiery.

Totalitarianism was running amuck. In July, 1937, Japan mounted its second offensive against China, in defiance of the dying League of Nations, and by the end of the year it had seized Nanking and was master of the Yangtse from the coast to Wuhu. With the signing of the Anti-Comintern Pact Japan joined the Rome-Berlin Axis.

In March, 1938, Hitler seized Austria; and not long after Czechoslovakia, that "far-away country" of Neville Chamberlain fantasy, crept into world headlines as Hitler demanded the return of the Sudeten Germans to the Reich. There followed Munich in September, and the twilight before the long night of war descended on Europe.

Nehru watched these tragic happenings with increased foreboding.

The year 1938 had also brought him a personal affliction with the death of his mother. Swaruprani had been ailing for a long time, and two paralytic strokes had crippled her, although she continued in her undaunted way to maintain her interest in the things that concerned her. Her solicitude for her children, particularly her son, was the dominant interest that sustained her. She was struck by a third paralytic stroke one night while her son and two daughters were around her, and early the next morning, as they watched by her bed, she passed peacefully away.

"She's gone too," said Jawaharlal in a whisper to his sisters as Swaruprani breathed her last.

It was seven years since with his mother he had sat by his dying father's bedside.

Abroad, the war clouds thickened. In the summer before Munich the Nazi Government had extended him an invitation to visit Germany, prefacing its gesture with the assurance that it was well aware of his opposition to Nazism. Jawaharlal declined, and instead visited Czechoslovakia and Spain, with an interlude in Britain.

He arrived in Barcelona in mid-June, 1938, and after seeing some of the ministers—Negrín, the Prime Minister, was away in Madrid—he left for the front accompanied by Krishna Menon, who was then the moving spirit behind the India League in London. They were received at headquarters by General Lister who was in command of that sector. Lister, a former stonemason, impressed Nehru greatly as a good example of the new officers of the popular army. Looking at him and at his colleagues, Jawaharlal reflected that the gibe of the British professional soldier in India that it would take years to train Indians to assume senior military command was without substance. "Alas for this old type which shines so much at polo and bridge and on the parade ground, but is so out of place today," Nehru apostrophized the British Blimp. He was to remember this experience when as Prime Minister of independent India the question of Indianising the army came up.

Nehru visited the International Brigade, 60 per cent of whom were Spaniards, and talked to many of the volunteers. At the headquarters of another brigade a Spanish officer drank a toast to India and Indian freedom.

Aside from Lister, Nehru met Del Vayo, then the Foreign Minister of the Republic, in Barcelona. He took to him immediately, being struck by his vitality and determination. Like Lister, Del Vayo was not a professional. He had been a journalist before the Revolution made him Foreign Minister. Nehru had several talks with the Spaniard, and presented him with the national flag. Several months later, in September, he met Del Vayo again, this time in Geneva. Del Vayo asked Nehru whether it was possible for India to send food supplies to Republican Spain, and Jawaharlal did this immediately on his return to India. He was emotionally stirred by Spain, and in Bombay, when he pleaded for food ships to go there, the tears streamed down his face.

Another personality whom he met and thought arresting was the celebrated woman leader La Passionara, daughter of a Basque miner, "middle-aged and homely looking, the mother of grown-up children." He met her first in a little room where she spoke fiercely and ardently in a torrent of lilting Spanish, only part of which Jawaharlal understood. He was moved by her spirit and passion. "She was the symbol," he wrote, "of the common man and woman who had suffered and been exploited for ages and were now determined to be free."

Spain enthralled Nehru with its valour and determination, its gay courage and defiance. The so-called Non-Intervention Committee comprised five Powers, Britain, France, Germany, Italy and Russia, the last three of whom were giving aid to one side or the other. The civil war was to end in March, 1939, with Franco's victory, but to Nehru it seemed in that golden June of 1938 that the Republicans might win.

If he was excited by Spain he was depressed by the mood in Britain and Czechoslovakia, and in Europe. In July, in London and Paris, he addressed meetings on behalf of Republican Spain, appearing in Paris on the same platform as La Passionara. Less than two months after the annexation of Austria, in May, 1938, Hitler had massed his troops on the Czech frontier; and although these were later withdrawn following a Franco-British *détente*, the smell of aggression was again very much in the air.

During these autumn months Nehru gravitated between London, Paris, Geneva, the Sudetenland and Prague, following events with a sense of pained dismay. In Czechoslovakia he watched the devious strategy of Lord Runciman, who was endeavouring simultaneously to soften up Henlein and, as Nehru put it, "to break the back of the Czechs." The way was being prepared for Munich.

He spoke in London with Eden, now out of office, with Lord Halifax, Atlee and with some of the more prominent politicians of all parties. Their attitude chilled him, for they met his anti-Fascist and anti-Nazi views with polite evasions and an air of slight deprecation.

"There are many other considerations to be borne in mind," they reminded him.

There were. But when he tried to tell the British Labour party that to be anti-Fascist was equally to be anti-Imperialist, and that their approach to Indian independence must also be unequivocal he was met with the same verbal detours.

Nehru took time to make his attitude clear in a letter to the *Manchester Guardian* dated September 8, 1938. Its concluding paragraphs epitomise the Congress approach to events abroad:

We in India want no Fascism or imperialism, and we are more convinced than ever that both are closely akin and dangers to world peace and freedom. India resents British foreign policy and will be no party to it, and we shall endeavour with all our strength to sever the bond that unites us to this pillar of reaction. The British Government has given us an additional and unanswerable argument for complete independence. All our sympathies are with Czecho-Slovakia. If war comes, the British people, in spite of their pro-Fascist Government, will inevitably be dragged into it. But, even then, how will this Government, with its patent sympathies for the Fascist and Nazi States, advance the cause of democracy and freedom? So long as this Government endures, Fascism will always be at the doorstep.

The people of India have no intention of submitting to any foreign decision on war. They alone can decide and certainly they will not accept the dictation of the British Government, which they distrust utterly. India would willingly throw her entire weight on the side of democracy and freedom, but we heard these words often twenty years ago and more. Only free and democratic countries can help freedom and democracy elsewhere. If Britain is on the side of democracy, then its first task is to eliminate empire from India. That is the sequence of events in Indian eyes, and to that sequence the people of India will adhere.

Nehru returned to India in November two months after the betrayal of Czechoslovakia at Munich, conscious that war was merely a matter of time. On September 28th, from the visitors' galleries in the House of Commons, he had heard Neville Chamberlain announce dramatically that he had received an eleventh-hour invitation from Hitler to meet him and Mussolini and Daladier at Munich. Chamberlain, intense, narrow, opinionated and seemingly overwhelmed by his previous meetings with Hitler, impressed Nehru unfavourably. A week earlier Jawaharlal had listened to the League of Nations as it debated on Czechoslovakia, and in the process intoned its own and that country's obsequies.

India, Nehru realised, must now define its attitude in the event of a war breaking out between Britain and Germany, between a decaying but still stubborn imperialism and arrogant Nazism. Although Gandhi understood little of the nuances of international politics he had already provided a basis for the thinking of Congress by stressing that international interdependence rather than national independence was his goal. Independence was primarily the means to an end. The Mahatma had stressed:

My service of India includes the service of humanity. . . . Isolated independence is not the goal of the world States. It is voluntary inter-dependence. The better mind of the world desires today not absolutely independent States, warring one against another, but a federation of friendly, inter-dependent States. The consummation of that event may be far off. I want to make no grand claim for our country. But I see nothing grand or impossible about our expressing our readiness for universal independence. I desire the ability to be totally independent without asserting the independence.

Nehru set out to mould the thinking of Congress on this basis, and by and large Congress policy followed the lines indicated by him in his letter to the *Manchester Guardian*. In Asia India's sympathies, again under Nehru's inspiration, were with China in its fight against the brutal onslaught of Japan. But not all leaders of Congress were sympathetic to China's cause, the most outstanding among these being Subhas Bose, who at the time was President of the Congress, having been elected to preside over the annual session held at Haripura in Gujerat in February, 1938.[6]

When in 1938 the Congress sent a medical unit consisting of a number of doctors with material and equipment to China, Bose disapproved on the ground that India should do nothing to alienate Japan. But Jawaharlal's will, backed by the people's support, prevailed. Bose was equally lukewarm to Nehru's speeches and activities against the Nazis and Fascists whose ruthless strong-arm methods he rather admired. In his presidential address at Haripura in February, 1938, Bose urged that India should do nothing to alienate any country or people. "We shall find in every country, men and women who will sympathise with Indian freedom, no matter what their own political views may be," he declared. "In this matter I should take a leaf out of Soviet diplomacy."

Nehru thought differently, the Congress and the country as a whole following his lead. Bose was soon to come into open conflict with the High Command of Congress. Contrary to its wishes, he challenged the official candidate for the Presidency of the next annual session at Tripuri, and emerged triumphant as President for the second successive year. But Bose's triumph was short-lived, and although he presided over the Tripuri session in March, 1939, his rebel activities compelled the Congress Executive to take disciplinary action against him. In August, 1939, the Working Committee passed a resolution declaring Bose ineligible for any elective office for three years.

Over Europe the war clouds were gathering. On March 15, 1939,

[6] There was no annual session of the Congress in 1937.

German troops marched into Prague, and Czechoslovakia ceased to exist. On April 7th, which was Good Friday, Mussolini invaded Albania. Hitler turned his attention next to Danzig and Poland, and Europe trembled on the brink of war. In August, Germany made terms with Russia, Berlin entering into a non-aggression pact with Moscow. The stage was set for the invasion of Poland. On the morning of September 1, 1939, Hitler struck.

Nehru was in Chungking when the war began in Europe. He had left for China's war-time capital in mid-August by way of Calcutta and Kunming, planning to spend some time in the northwest with the Eighth Route Army and also to visit the Congress medical unit which was working in that area. The outbreak of war compelled him to cut his visit short and return to India, having spent only thirteen days in China, most of them in Chungking.

They were crowded days spaced by five air raids which Nehru watched from a darkened dugout. The grim, immobile calm of the Chinese impressed him, as also did their prodigious industry. He thought them "a singularly grown-up people." He visited factories, summer schools, military academies, youth camps and make-shift universities. He was particularly interested in China's development of cottage industries and the village cooperative movement.

His hosts were the Generalissimo and Madame Chiang Kai-shek, both of whom received him graciously, and he had many conversations with them and with other Chinese leaders and notabilities. Nehru was charmed by the vivacity of Madame Chiang, and, wearing a Chinese gown, he posed for a photograph with her and the Generalissimo. One person whom he was eager to meet was not available in Chungking. Madame Sun Yat-sen was then in Hongkong.

Nehru returned to find India committed to war. On the very day that Hitler had invaded Poland, the Viceroy, Lord Linlithgow, without consulting any of the Indian leaders or legislatures, had announced that India was at war. Clearly the British, while fighting Nazism, were not prepared to shed their own imperialism. The British Government had declared that it was fighting for democracy and freedom.

"Whose freedom?" Nehru asked. The question was to echo around India.

18

IN THE WILDERNESS

EARLY in August, before his departure for Chungking, Nehru had attended a meeting of the Working Committee at which the attitude of the Congress to war was defined. The resolution which the committee adopted was very largely his handiwork. It stated:

> In this world crisis the sympathies of the Working Committee are entirely with the peoples who stand for democracy and freedom, and the Congress has repeatedly condemned fascist aggression in Europe, Africa and the Far East of Asia, as well as the betrayal of democracy by British imperialism in Czechoslovakia and Spain.
>
> The past policy of the British Government as well as recent developments demonstrated abundantly that this Government does not stand for freedom and democracy and may at any time betray these ideals. India cannot associate itself with such a Government or be asked to give her resources for democratic freedom which is denied to her and which is likely to be betrayed.

In other words, only a free India could participate in a war against those who threatened freedom and democracy. It was incongruous for an India shackled to one imperialism to fight other brands of imperialism and militarism.

Nehru returned to India in time to participate in a Working Committee meeting on September 14th, and here again his was the hand which drafted the main resolution on the war. Characteristically, he viewed it not only as a conflict of armed forces but as an international crisis which had overtaken humanity, and he persuaded the committee to embody this in its resolution. It was four days before this took final shape.

Gandhi alone demurred, arguing that whatever support was given to the British should be given unconditionally and it should be of a non-violent character. This was not Nehru's view. In his mind there was no question of the doctrine of non-violence coming in the way of armed conflict for defence or against aggression. India should support Britain in a war against Nazism but it could do so only as a free nation.

In the resolution which he drafted it is interesting to see Nehru's prophetic vision of a free India. It stated:

If this war is to defend the *status quo*, imperialist possessions, colonies, vested interests and privilege, then India can have nothing to do with it. If, however, the issue is democracy and a world order based on democracy, then India is intensely interested in it. And if Great Britain fights for the maintenance and extension of democracy then she must necessarily end imperialism in her own possessions, establish full democracy in India, and the Indian people must have the right of self-determination by framing their own constitution through a constituent assembly without any external interference, and must guide their own policy. . . . The crisis that has overtaken Europe is not of Europe only but of humanity and will not pass like other crises or wars, leaving the essential structure of the present-day world intact. It is likely to refashion the world for good or ill. India is the crux of the problem, for India has been the outstanding example of modern imperialism, and no refashioning of the world can succeed, which ignores this vital problem. With her vast resources, India must play an important part in any scheme of world reorganization. But India can only do so as a free nation, whose energies have been released to work for this great end. Freedom today is indivisible and every attempt to retain imperialist domination in any part of the world will lead inevitably to a fresh disaster.

At the same meeting the Working Committee appointed a subcommittee consisting of Nehru, Azad and Patel to deal with all the issues arising out of the changing war situation. Because Gandhi's views did not command the support of the Working Committee, the Mahatma felt that Nehru, who was the clearest expositor of the attitude of Congress, should be given the widest freedom to define and canvass it. Actually, the sub-committee only functioned for six months until March, 1940, when the Ramgarh session met. Its first action was to advise the provincial Congress committees not to act or speak hastily, "precipitating a development before its proper time." Meanwhile, the Congress was prepared to negotiate, if there was room for negotiation. But the British Government's rigid front narrowed the ground for manœuvre. In the view of both the Viceroy, Lord Linlithgow, and of the British authorities in London the present was not the appropriate time for India to press its claim for freedom. Thus a breach between the two parties was inevitable.

"We have not put forward any demand in the spirit of the market place," countered Nehru.

He elaborated on this plea, urging:

We must be convinced of that world freedom, and we must see India in the picture of that world freedom. Then only will war have meaning for us and more, our minds and hearts, for then we shall be struggling and suffering for a cause that is worthwhile not only for us but for all the peoples of the world. Because we feel that as a large number of British people have the same world ideals as many of us possess in India, we have offered them our cooperation in the realisation of these ideals. But if these ideals are not there, what do we fight for? Only a free and consenting India can throw her weight for ideals that are openly proclaimed and acted upon.

In the last week of September Lord Linlithgow invited more than fifty Indian political leaders, including Gandhi and Nehru, to meet him "for a full and frank discussion." Most of the discussions were full and frank, but as between the Government and the Congress there was no yielding of ground.

Nehru reiterated his views to the Viceroy with his usual forthrightness.

"A little more slowly, Mr. Nehru," Linlithgow protested at one stage. "My slow Anglo-Saxon mind cannot keep pace with your quick intellect."

Nothing positive followed from these talks, and early in October the Congress Working Committee reiterated its views. Not surprisingly, the British authorities concentrated on playing up the Princes and the minorities, more particularly the Muslims, against the Congress, pleading that political advance was impracticable without communal unity. In doing so, they strengthened the hands of Jinnah, who in the coming years was to capitalise cleverly on his opportunities.

In this situation of growing tension it became increasingly difficult for the Congress to maintain its eight provincial ministries in office. But here it was guilty of a tactical error. Instead of compelling the Government to dismiss the ministries, the Congress on its own initiative withdrew them, thereby casting itself out in the wilderness and leaving the field free—to Jinnah and the British.

With the resignation of the ministries of Congress by November, 1939, Governors' rule operated in eight provinces. In the remaining three, coalition governments, largely Muslim (though not Muslim League), were in power. Jinnah was quick to swoop on his opportunity. He called upon Muslims and all those opposed to the Congress to celebrate the departure of the Congress ministries as a Day of Deliverance, and fixed December 22nd for the celebration. The Muslim masses, who by now largely followed him, responded with enthusiasm.

"Democracy," Jinnah proclaimed, "can only mean Hindu Raj all over India." And he repeated approvingly Lord Morley's dictum that "the fur coat of Canada will not do for the extremely tropical climate of India."

In January, 1940, Gandhi made another attempt to secure Jinnah's cooperation "in building up the Indian Nation."

Jinnah's reply was a sneer.

"You start," he said, "with the theory of an Indian nation that does not exist."

He was preening himself for the declaration of Pakistan which the Muslim League was shortly to make at its Lahore session in March, 1940. Presiding over this session, Jinnah repeated his newly discovered doctrine that Hindus and Muslims constituted two separate nations and that therefore India should be divided to contain separate homelands for each. At Lahore the League raised the banner of Pakistan.

"No power on earth," declared Jinnah, "can prevent Pakistan."

The Congress met at Ramgarh in March, almost simultaneously with the session of the Muslim League at Lahore. Maulana Abul Kalam Azad, who presided, stressed the need for a firm decision either in favour of cooperation with the war effort or non-cooperation.

"As we stand today," said Azad, "we have to decide whether we should march forward in this direction or go backward. When once a step is taken there is no stopping. To cry halt is to go back and we refuse to go back. We can only, therefore, go forward."

But how? Nehru shared with Gandhi the feeling that the Congress should as far as possible avoid any large-scale embarrassment to the British authorities during the war. But he did not share Gandhi's view that if support were to be given it should be non-conditional and non-violent. Even at this juncture Gandhi was thinking in terms of individual satyagraha, arguing that non-violent action on a limited, organised scale would mobilise world opinion in India's favour.

Civil disobedience was virtually decided upon at Ramgarh, but the Congress kept the door open, refraining from any positive step to implement it and awaiting a gesture from the Government. As Gandhi put it: "The question has come from London whether the Congress has closed the door to negotiation and compromise. My interpretation of the resolution is that the Congress has not closed the door. It has been closed by Lord Zetland." [1]

Shortly after, in May, 1940, came Hitler's blitzkrieg against the Scandinavian countries, Holland, Belgium and France. The epic of Dunkirk left the British poised perilously on the brink of extinction, and in the circumstances it was impossible for the Congress to take craven advantage of the situation. It could only hold its hand.

Some felt differently, among them Subhas Bose, who had seceded from the Congress to form his Forward Bloc party. England's peril, he insisted, was India's opportunity. Bose, a resolute if ruthless patriot, was soon to leave India, visit Berlin and later Singapore, where he was to ally himself with the Japanese militarists and Nazis. He had no qualms about his allies provided their help enabled him to free his country. In this he emulated Winston Churchill, who about the same time was declaring that he was willing to shake hands with the devil if it meant England's salvation.

Early in July the Congress Working Committee assembled at Delhi and, under the sobering influence of the moderate Mr. C. Rajagopalachari, toned down its demand. It asked for a recognition of Indian freedom, and as a token of this called upon the British authorities to establish a National Government, which would comprise various parties, at the centre. This could be done by agreement and convention, and would involve no immediate legislative changes likely to embarrass the proceedings of the British Parliament in London. Later, of course, the required statutory changes would have to be made; but, given this token gesture, the Congress expressed its willingness to cooperate fully in the war effort.

[1] The British Secretary of State for India.

Had there been a more imaginative Viceroy in Delhi and a more responsive Government in London, history might well have taken a different turn. But Lord Linlithgow, well intentioned though he was, was incapable of adopting the bold long view. Nehru describes the Viceroy faithfully if also cruelly:

Heavy of body and slow of mind, solid as a rock and with almost a rock's lack of awareness, possessing the qualities and failings of an old-fashioned British aristocrat, he sought with integrity and honesty of purpose to find a way out of the tangle. But his limitations were too many; his mind worked in the old groove and shrank back from any innovations; his vision was limited by the traditions of the ruling class out of which he came; he saw and heard through the eyes and ears of the civil service and others who surrounded him; he distrusted people who talked of fundamental political and social changes; he disliked those who did not show a becoming appreciation of the high mission of the British Empire and its chief representative in India.

In London Mr. L. S. Amery had replaced Lord Zetland as Secretary of State for India, and although mentally more resilient and robust than his predecessor he was unable to mellow Churchill's uncompromising attitude to India. Nehru recalled that as far back as January, 1930, Churchill had declared, "Sooner or later you will have to crush Gandhi and the Indian Congress and all they stand for." The British Prime Minister was a resolute opponent of Indian freedom. "England, apart from her empire in India, ceases for ever to exist as a great power," he had warned.

On August 8, 1940, Lord Linlithgow disclosed the British Government's reaction to the Congress resolution. The Viceroy would invite a certain number of representative Indians to join his executive council and to form a war advisory council. But there was no question of the transfer of government to any organisation or group whose authority was directly denied by large sections of the minorities. In any case this was not a time for the decision of constitutional issues which must await the end of the war.

Not only was the British Government unwilling to part with power, but it appeared as if it were resolved to encourage division by using the dead weight of the minorities and Princes against the nationalists. So the Congress construed the Viceroy's declaration. Even to Nehru, who had been none too happy over the Delhi resolution, the reaction of the British Government came as a rude shock. He had long felt that freedom would only follow a period of struggle and travail and sorrow, and he had spoken his mind soon after the Delhi meeting: "In this world of war and conflict, we may not escape the price of freedom. To expect otherwise is to delude oneself. The future will ultimately depend on the strength of the Indian people and on the organised power of the Congress. To the increasing of that organised strength, therefore, all our energies must be directed."

Now that the British Government had shown its hand, they had come to the parting of the ways. Conflict seemed inevitable. Nehru's mind travelled back over the past few fateful months. He thought of his own denunciations of Nazism and Fascism and of how the Indian people had instinctively recoiled against that gospel of hate and race, of blood and iron. How deeply they had been moved when horror enveloped Holland and Belgium, and France fell! Dunkirk had followed, and the Congress, conscious of England's imminent peril, had resolutely set its face against those who urged that England's peril was India's opportunity. Although, Nehru reflected, England's ruling classes had treated his people badly, in their hearts the Indian people had no ill will for the British, who were bravely facing danger, even extinction. Britain's rulers had been imaginative enough to propose a union of England and France on the eve of the French collapse. But to India their mind was closed and their heart chilled. Why should that be?

Soon after the Viceroy's declaration, Nehru wrote:

I am sorry, for in spite of my hostility to British imperialism and all imperialisms, I have loved much that was England, and I should have liked to keep the silken bonds of the spirit between India and England. Those bonds can only exist in freedom. I wanted India's freedom for India's sake, of course; but I also wanted it for England's sake. That hope is shattered, and fate seems to have fashioned a different future for us; the hundred-year-old hostility will remain and grow in future conflicts, and the breach, when it comes, as come it must, will also not be in friendship, but in hostility.

There he was wrong.

Gandhi had retired from participation in the politics of Congress after the Delhi resolution. At Delhi he had pleaded again that the support of Congress to the war effort should be strictly non-violent and confined only to "moral help." But neither Nehru nor his other colleagues were prepared to accept his view, and they had gone to the length of offering full cooperation in a violent war effort if the fact of Indian freedom were conceded and recognised.

Having broken with its leader and been rebuffed by the British Government for its pains, the Congress realised that it could no longer remain passive. As Nehru put it, "Positive action became inevitable, for sometimes the only failure is in failing to act." On August 18th the Working Committee, meeting at Wardha, placed on record that "the rejection of the Congress proposals is a proof of the British Government's determination to continue to hold India by the sword." A month later, presiding over the All-India Congress Committee meeting at Bombay, Maulana Azad declared that the Viceroy's offer was "not worth looking at." The committee later passed a resolution, drafted by Gandhi, affirming its belief in non-violence, and declaring its intention to persuade the Indian people to dissociate themselves from the war in a non-violent way. It should be noted that the Bombay resolution, while it accepted the principle and practice of non-violence in its application to India's internal struggle for freedom, had not gone beyond that position to extend non-violence to defence from external aggression or indeed internal disorder. But that remained Gandhi's view, and as subsequent events were to show he interpreted the resolution so.

The Congress had returned to Gandhi. In effect the Bombay resolution was a call to the people to refuse to cooperate in any way with the war effort. "Self-imposed restraint," said the resolution, "cannot be taken to the extent of self-extinction." Late in September, Gandhi saw the Viceroy at Simla, and letters were subsequently exchanged between them. Lord Linlithgow explained the treatment of pacifists in England and the limitations on their freedom of speech and action:

While the conscientious objector is absolved from the duty of fighting and is allowed even to profess his own faith in public, he is not allowed to carry his opposition to the length of endeavouring to persuade the others, whether soldiers or munition workers, to abandon their allegiance or to discontinue their effort. It would clearly not be possible, in the interests of India herself to acquiesce in interference with the war effort which would be involved in freedom of speech as wide as that for which you have asked.

Gandhi, in a statement issued from Sewagram, commented:

The Viceroy was all courtesy, but he was unbending and he believed in
the correctness of his judgement, and as usual had no faith in that of
nationalist India. The Britisher is showing extraordinary bravery on the
battlefield in a marvellous manner. But he lacks bravery to take risks in
the moral domain. I often wonder, whether the latter has any place in
British politics.

The courtesy of language could not disguise the breach in relations.
Some form of civil disobedience seemed inevitable, and since the
Congress had declared that it was not its intention to embarrass the
Government such a demonstration would have to be conducted on an
individual, not a mass basis. This is what Gandhi actually suggested
when the Working Committee met at Wardha on October 13th.
The first volunteer selected to offer individual satyagraha was Vinoba
Bhave, who was later to inspire and lead the Bhoodan movement.[2]

On October 17, 1940, Vinoba inaugurated the individual satyagraha campaign by delivering an anti-war speech at a small village a
few miles from Wardha in the then Central Provinces. He was arrested four days later and sentenced to three months' imprisonment.
The campaign was to be carried on through various defined stages,
spanning a little over a year, and in the process some 30,000 men and
women were to be jailed.

But the movement had little use beyond a symbolic value, and
was essentially negative. Its limited character was conditioned primarily by the Congress's desire not to embarrass the Government; but,
as Gandhi confessed, the unhappy state of communal relations in the
country also counselled caution. Under Jinnah's leadership the Muslim League, while not cooperating directly in the war effort, was careful to do nothing against it. Jinnah welcomed the Government's
implied assurance that no future constitution, interim or final, would
be adopted without the League's consent; meanwhile, he propagated
his two-nation doctrine, the field being open and clear for him.

By the end of the year 1940, eleven members of the Congress
Working Committee, including Nehru; 176 members of the All-
India Congress Committee, 29 former Ministers and over 400 mem-
bers of the central and provincial legislatures were in jail. Azad was

[2] The Bhoodan movement aims at the surrender of land by voluntary donation. Bhoodan means literally "gift land."

arrested on New Year's Eve, and sentenced to eighteen months' imprisonment.

It had been arranged that Nehru should offer individual satyagraha from November 7th in the district of Allahabad in his home province. But the authorities anticipated events by arresting him on October 31st at Chheoki railway station as he was returning from Wardha after visiting Gandhi. His offence apparently lay in three speeches which he had delivered to the peasants in the Gorakhpur district earlier that month.

Nehru's trial took place in Gorakhpur Prison before a British magistrate who sentenced him to four years' imprisonment. Jawaharlal's speech is a moving and memorable statement, being more an indictment of the rulers than a defence of himself. Here are its concluding passages:

I stand before you, sir, as an individual being tried for certain offences against the State. You are a symbol of that State. But I am something more than an individual also; I, too, am a symbol at the present moment, a symbol of Indian nationalism, resolved to break away from the British Empire and achieve the independence of India. It is not me that you are seeking to judge and condemn, but rather the hundreds of millions of the people of India, and that is a large task even for a proud Empire. Perhaps it may be that, though I am standing before you on my trial, it is the British Empire itself that is on its trial before the bar of the world. There are more powerful forces at work in the world today than courts of law; there are elemental urges for freedom and food and security which are moving vast masses of people, and history is being moulded by them. The future recorder of this history might well say that in the hour of supreme trial the Government of Britain and the people of Britain failed because they could not adapt themselves to a changing world. He may muse over the fate of empires which have always fallen because of this weakness and call it destiny. Certain causes inevitably produce certain results. We know the causes; the results are inexorably in their train.

It is a small matter to me what happens to me in this trial or subsequently. Individuals count for little; they come and go, as I shall go when my time is up. Seven times I have been tried and convicted by British authority in India, and many years of my life lie buried within prison walls. An eighth time or a ninth, and a few more years, make little difference.

But it is no small matter what happens to India and her millions of sons and daughters. That is the issue before me, and that ultimately is the issue before you, sir. If the British Government imagines it can continue to exploit them and play about with them against their will, as it has done for so long in the past, then it is grievously mistaken. It has misjudged their present temper and read history in vain.

I should like to add that I am happy to be tried in Gorakhpur. The peasantry of Gorakhpur are the poorest and the most long-suffering in my Province. I am glad that it was my visit to the Gorakhpur district and my attempt to serve its people that has led to this trial.

Nehru's eighth term in jail was to last a little over a year, for on December 4, 1941, three days before Pearl Harbor, the British Government released all satyagraha prisoners whose offences were "formal or symbolic in character," including Nehru and Azad. In this period Jawaharlal, with such newspapers and books as were available to him, followed the course of the war and of events in India. There was little happening on the home front apart from the individual satyagraha campaign. But abroad the tempo of the war had heightened.

The Battle of Britain was virtually over at the time of Nehru's arrest, and German plans for the destruction of Britain were baulked. On October 28, 1940, Italian troops invaded Greece, and Nehru followed closely the fortunes of the gallant Greeks as they fought the invader. The Duce had embarked on the first of his inglorious adventures. Hungary and Rumania were drawn into the Axis orbit, and it was plain that Hitler was contemplating a move in the Balkans. On April 6, 1941, the Nazi army invaded Yugoslavia for the purpose of mounting an offensive from there on Greece. By the end of May the Germans were in Crete.

British arms advanced in North Africa as the Italians retreated. Tobruk fell on January 22nd, and Benghazi was captured on February 6th. Almost simultaneously the Italians laid down their arms in Somaliland, and in May, Haile Selassie returned to Addis Ababa: Mussolini's North African Empire was shattered.

But once more the Allied fortunes waned. Late in March Rommel took over the Libyan command, and as in Greece so in North Africa: the Germans retrieved what the Italians had lost. On June 22, 1941, Hitler struck at Russia. "We followed with anxious interest the dramatic changes in the war situation," Nehru recalls.

Other important if less dramatic events were also taking place. Nehru read of Roosevelt's Four Freedoms and not long after came news of the signing of the Atlantic Charter between Churchill and Roosevelt in August, 1941. One of its eight points stipulated that all

peoples should have the right to choose their own form of government, and that sovereign rights and self-government should be restored to those who had been forcibly deprived of them. Nehru read
the point with amused scepticism. Did it apply to India? He was
soon to know. From Churchill came a bland, blunt and resounding
No.

Nehru left prison to be plunged soon in a new atmosphere of tension, for the bombing of Pearl Harbor on December 7th signalised
not only the entry of America and Japan into the war but was shortly
to bring hostilities to the frontiers of India. From a distant spectacle
war became a close reality. Would Britain now resile from her rigid
attitude and open the door to honourable cooperation by India with
the formation of a national government at the centre? But of this
there was still no sign.

Shortly after Nehru's release on December 23rd, when the Working Committee met at Bardoli, it was faced with an altered external
situation; but internally the situation was the same. Thus it could
do no more than reiterate its "sympathies with the peoples who are
the subject of aggression and who are fighting for their freedom,"
and endorse the Bombay resolution of September 16, 1940, as the
watchword of Congress policy.

In the course of the discussions at Bardoli, Gandhi discovered that
the general interpretation by Congress of the Bombay resolution
was somewhat different from his own. He had thought that the resolution committed the Congress to non-violence even in regard to
external war, whereas in the view of his colleagues, notably Nehru,
Azad and Patel, the principle of non-violence was accepted only in
relation to their internal political struggle, and was never intended
to be extended to external war. Indeed, as they pointed out to him,
the Congress had never applied that principle even in relation to the
Indian armed services and police. Congressmen had frequently urged
more rapid Indianisation of the army, and Jawaharlal's father had
himself been a member of the Skeen Committee which had examined
the possibilities of Indianising and reorganising the army. But Gandhi,
while he admitted that he had misread the Bombay resolution, was
eager that his view should prevail. "It is my certain belief," he affirmed, "that only non-violence can save India and the world from
self-extinction." This view, however, was not wholly acceptable to

his colleagues, who agreed to disagree. Once again, Gandhi relinquished the leadership of the Congress.

Meanwhile, the Japanese were advancing rapidly in Southeast Asia, and on the Pacific front Hongkong fell on Christmas Day; less than two months later, on February 15th, Singapore surrendered. The way was open for the Japanese to infiltrate into the Dutch Empire, into Sumatra, Borneo, Java and Indonesia. Before the end of January the Japanese had landed in New Guinea.

Earlier, in mid-December, the Japanese turned their attention to Burma, moving insect-like through the jungle, burrowing, crawling, fanning out in unexpected directions as the British forces and the Chinese retreated before them. Rangoon fell on March 8, 1942, and as refugees and troops streamed over the Indo-Burma border India realised that the war had come to her doors.

In February Marshal Chiang Kai-shek, accompanied by his wife, visited India and, while appealing to the British to grant real political power to the Indians, also urged India to join the common cause of freedom, "for only in a free world can the Chinese and Indian peoples obtain their freedom."

Nehru, who had met the celebrated couple at Chungking, saw them frequently at Delhi and again at Calcutta, where the Generalissimo and his wife called on Gandhi. Chiang tried to dissuade Gandhi from extending non-violence to the war.

"Your civil resistance," he said, "is not mere passivity, I'm sure. But the Japanese may not listen to active civil resistance, and may even make the preaching of non-violence impossible."

Gandhi would not be dissuaded.

With Nehru's exposition of the view of Congress the Chiangs were more impressed. But if the British had calculated on the Generalissimo and his decorative wife persuading the Congress to alter their basic attitude to cooperation with the war effort they were to be disappointed.

The fall of Burma had cut the direct supply route from India to China, and India now became the keystone of allied defence in the Indian Ocean while remaining a reservoir of man power and war materials for the democratic forces in the Near and Far East. Three days after the surrender of Rangoon, on March 11th, Churchill announced that the British Government had decided to send Sir Stafford Cripps to India with a plan which the War Cabinet had approved. It would be Sir Stafford's mission to ascertain whether this plan would secure a "reasonable and practical" measure of acceptance and "thus promote the concentration of all Indian thought and energies" on the war against Japan.

Cripps was well known to Indian leaders, including Gandhi, Nehru and Jinnah. He had visited India in 1939 to canvass the prospects for a tour by an all-party parliamentary delegation in India. Congress leaders—as also Jinnah—respected his integrity and ability, and Gandhi was drawn to him as a man of deep religious conviction. His radical socialism was a link with Nehru.

Cripps, who at that time was Leader of the House of Commons, had returned earlier in the year from Russia, where he had been appointed ambassador in dramatic if unorthodox circumstances. His political prestige was high. If anybody could convince the Congress of the British Government's good intentions, he was the man.

Yet Cripps's mission laboured under several limitations, some of them serious. He would be negotiating with the Indian leaders not alongside the Viceroy but independently of him, and it was well known that Lord Linlithgow resented his exclusion. As a result, the Government of India did not look kindly on the mission. Moreover, Britain was negotiating from a position of weakness, not strength, which made both her bona fides and her generosity suspect in Indian eyes. Cripps also came out with a cut-and-dried plan incapable of amendment, to be accepted or rejected as a whole. And he seemed throughout to be in an unconscionable hurry to get away. He had come with a rigid scheme which he felt he could persuade the Indian leaders to accept within a defined time schedule. Sir Stafford arrived with his assistants at New Delhi on March 22nd and his mission was over on April 11th. It almost seemed as if he were Buzfuz arguing to his brief.

An obvious major limitation in the scheme was that it represented a compromise between the Congress dream of a unified India and the Muslim League's demand for a partitioned India. As far as the future was concerned, the War Cabinet pledged itself to grant Dominion status at the end of the war, and suggested that an Indian constituent assembly should itself then frame the new constitution. Thus the plea of Congress for a unified India was seemingly satisfied. But simultaneously the scheme provided for the right of individual provinces to contract out of the India which would arise under the new constitution. This was the olive branch waved at the Muslim League.

What of the immediate present? Here the Congress desired at the centre a national government or an executive council composed of representative Indians of various parties with the Viceroy enjoying the status of a constitutional monarch. "We are not interested in Congress as such gaining power," said Azad, "but we are interested in the Indian people as a whole having freedom and power."

Discussion revealed that all that the plan visualised for the immediate future was an extension of the Viceroy's executive council with the appointment of a few additional Indians representative of various parties. But neither these additional members nor the executive council as a whole would exercise any real authority. All power would continue to vest in the Viceroy, who would be responsible solely to the India Office in London.

It was agreed at one stage that there should be an Indian Minister of Defence, but he again would have his functions limited to such innocuous subjects as canteens, stationery and printing, public relations, social arrangements for foreign missions and amenities for troops.

"This," said Nehru in exasperation, "is simply ludicrous."

The Congress did not press for any restrictions on the normal powers of the British Commander-in-Chief. If anything it was prepared to extend them and give him additional powers as War Minister. But it insisted that the real political power should be wholly in Indian hands.

"The Government of India," wrote Azad in a final letter to Cripps, "do not realise that the war can only be fought on a popular basis."

It was not the Congress alone which finally rejected the scheme. Every other party consulted, including the Moderates and the Muslim League, repudiated the plan, though for differing reasons.

Even as Sir Stafford was preparing to leave, Nehru, who all along had hoped desperately that the mission would succeed, issued a statement urging the Indian people to adopt guerrilla tactics if the Japanese invaded their soil.

"We are not going to surrender to the invader," he declared. "In spite of all that has happened we are not going to embarrass the British war effort in India."

But events were to prove too strong for him. The bitter disappointment caused by the failure of the Cripps mission was a reaction to the high hopes it had aroused. A sense of indignant frustration seized many millions in the country, and even the victories of the Japanese were hailed by many for the humiliation they inflicted on British arms. In January, 1941, Subhas Bose had eluded the policemen holding him in detention in his house in Calcutta and had slipped across the northwest frontier into Russia and from there to Berlin. Many thousands in India tuned in to listen to him over the Azad Hind (Free India) radio operating first in Berlin and later in Malaya.

Nehru found it difficult to fight the emotional complexes which the failure of the Cripps mission, on the one hand, and the spectacular success of Japanese arms, on the other, had generated. None the less the All-India Congress Committee, when it met late in April at Allahabad, warned the country against these trends:

The committee repudiates the idea that freedom can come to India through interference or invasion by any foreign nation, whatever the professions of that nation may be. In case an invasion takes place, it must be resisted. Such resistance can only take place in the form of non-violent non-co-operation as the British Government have prevented the organization of the national defence by the people in any other way. The committee would, therefore, expect the people of India to offer complete non-violent non-co-operation to the invading forces and not to render any assistance to them. We may not bend the knee to the aggressor nor obey any of his orders. We may not look to him for favours nor fall to his bribes. If he wishes to take possession of our homes and our fields, we will refuse to give them up even if we have to die in the effort to resist them. The success of such a policy of non-co-operation and of non-violent resistance to the invader will largely depend on the intensive working out of the Congress constructive programme, and more especially the programme of self-sufficiency and self-protection in all parts of the country.

The draft of this resolution was Nehru's handiwork but it embodied Gandhi's ideas. Some days before the meeting, the Mahatma had expressed the hope "that the forthcoming A.-I.C.C. will revert to the non-violent method and give the clearest possible instructions about non-violent non-co-operation." Hitherto Nehru had resisted the idea that non-violence should be projected to the plane of defence against external aggression. Now he had surrendered. The Congress, as it had done earlier after the rebuff contained in Linlithgow's August offer, once again turned to Gandhi after the failure of the Cripps mission.

From henceforth until August, when the entire Congress Working Committee, including Gandhi and Nehru, were to be jailed, the initiative and leadership were to lie in Gandhi's hands. Early in May the Mahatma, writing in the columns of *Harijan*, invited the British to withdraw from India, thereby giving the signal for the "Quit India" campaign which followed.

Although couched in less peremptory language the sentiment, to some extent the phraseology of Gandhi's injunction, echoed the imperious words of Cromwell to the Long Parliament: "You have sat too long here for any good you have been doing. Depart, I say, and let us have done with you. In the name of God, go!" Leave us to God, said Gandhi, and it may be anarchy. But go.

Never in their long history of nearly two hundred years were the British rulers so divided and estranged from the people. The "steel frame" of the British services which Lloyd George had eulogised soon after the First World War had seen its shining heyday in the reign of Curzon. Rust had begun to set in, and in some places, rot. As communications grew and political consciousness spread, even the lowly villager had ceased to bow before the majesty of a white face, and Gandhi's message of satyagraha with its simple appeal to human dignity and independence, lit a fire in millions of minds.

Now, under the stress of war and the strain of political turmoil, the administrative services were showing signs of distinct wear and tear. The governmental machinery was too wooden to adjust itself easily to the alarums and excursions of the time. In the city of Madras, a vague rumour of the approach of a Japanese fleet—subsequently proved false—sent many high officials scurrying for safety and led to the panic-stricken demolition of some of the harbour facilities. As Nehru remarked, "It seemed as if the civilian administration of India was suffering from a nervous breakdown."

Similarly in Bengal, village homesteads were summarily cleared of their occupants by administrators "in a flap." In eastern Bengal, where economic life depends largely on trade and traffic by river boats, the destruction of thousands of these crafts by the authorities for fear they should fall into the hands of the Japanese caused widespread distress and was one of the major factors which later aggravated the Bengal famine. "For a Bengali to part with his canoe," said Gandhi, "is almost like parting with his life. So those who take away his canoe he regards as his enemy."

In this period Nehru was acutely unhappy. He did not want the Axis Powers to win, for he knew that that would lead to certain disaster. As he had said from the dock during his last trial, "There are very few persons in India, I suppose, whether they are Indians or Englishmen, who for years past have so consistently raised their voices against Fascism and Nazism as I have done." The thought of a Japanese invasion of India troubled him, but in a curious way it also thrilled him. Anything, he sometimes felt, that would shake up my people's immemorial calm, so like the peace of the grave, would be preferable to the dank torpor which engulfs us. If the Japanese came, they would be resisted, and the Congress had called upon the people to do so. Nehru would have liked that resistance to be forthright and violent; but, having accepted the Mahatma's view, he characteristically rationalised it by asking himself what other means was left to an unarmed civilian population to defend itself save non-violent non-cooperation.

He was tired and his mind was troubled. In May he decided to get away from the problems which beset him and seek peace and rest in the foothills of his beloved Himalayas. One of Nehru's favourite pieces of poetry is a verse of Walter de la Mare which he likes to quote:

> Yea, in my mind these mountains rise,
> Their perils dyed with evening's rose;
> And still my ghost sits at my eyes
> And thirsts for their untroubled snows.

He went to Kulu in the green fragrant inner valleys of the Himalayas, where he spent a fortnight trekking and climbing in that wilderness of enchantment. He was not to know another such holiday for a long time.

Returning to Allahabad, Nehru discovered that the Government had arrested some of his close colleagues, including Rafi Ahmed Kidwai,[3] who was later to be Food Minister in the Union Cabinet.

[3] He died on October 10, 1954.

The President of the United Provinces Provincial Congress Committee, Krishnadat Paliwal, was also in detention. They were among many whom the Government drew into their dragnet under the Defence of India Act which gave the authorities powers of summary arrest and imprisonment.

Gandhi's articles in *Harijan* and his "Quit India" slogan were beginning to create a stir in the country. Nehru detected in the Mahatma's speech and writing a new urgency and passion, and realised that it must eventually lead to some form of action. But what, Nehru wondered, was the type of action Gandhi contemplated?

He was disturbed by this development, for the only effective action was mass civil disobedience, and that would hamper the war effort at a time when India herself stood in grave peril of invasion. Nor did Nehru entirely approve of the strong nationalist overtones in Gandhi's utterances in the context of a world in flames. It seemed to him that the Mahatma's approach was too narrow, and ignored the larger international considerations which in this time of common peril could not humanly be overlooked.

He went to Sewagram several times and discussed his doubts and fears with the Mahatma.

Gandhi agreed with him that perhaps he had tended to ignore certain international factors, and promised to remedy this omission, which he subsequently did. But on the basic issue of action he would not be shaken.

"We cannot passively submit to Britain's autocratic and repressive policy in our country," Gandhi explained earnestly. "If we do not do something to challenge it, our people will be completely demoralised, and whatever the end of the war might be, we shall have put back the clock of freedom for many years. Besides, if we submit to our rulers we shall also submit to the invaders. Inaction will paralyse us. Action will strengthen our fibre."

Confronted with the sullen passivity of the people, Jawaharlal was inclined to agree.

"But," he argued, "however justified action or conflict with the British Raj might be on moral grounds, would it not seriously hamper the war effort? And at a time when India is in danger?"

"You must trust in God," Gandhi adjured him. "What you and I want to change is the moral basis of the war. India is the symbol of colonial domination. If we remain unfree, what hope is there for the other enslaved countries of the world? Then indeed this war will have been fought in vain."

As often before, they argued back and forth.

On July 6th the Working Committee met at Wardha; Gandhi was present. Largely as a result of his talks with Jawaharlal, whom he was anxious to carry with him in his plans, Gandhi went to the point of agreeing that if India were declared free and a Provisional Government set up, that Government would throw all its resources in the struggle for freedom and against aggression and cooperate fully with the United Nations in the defence of India. This implied that the Mahatma had reconciled himself to the use of force in resisting external aggression.

This view was embodied in the resolution passed by the Working Committee on July 11th which referred to "the widespread increase of ill will against Britain and a growing satisfaction in the success of Japanese arms." The resolution declared:

The Congress Working Committee view this development with grave apprehension, as this, unless checked, will inevitably lead to a passive acceptance of aggression. The committee hold that all aggression must be resisted, for any submission to it must mean the degradation of the Indian people and the continuation of their subjection. The Congress is anxious to avoid the experience of Malaya, Singapore and Burma and desires to build up resistance to any aggression on, or any invasion of, India by the Japanese or any foreign power. The Congress would change the present ill will against Britain into goodwill, and make India a willing partner in a joint enterprise securing freedom for the nations and peoples of the world and in the trials and tribulations which accompany it. This is only possible, if India feels the glow of freedom.

The resolution went on to explain the "Quit India" slogan:

In making the proposal for the withdrawal of British rule from India, the Congress has no desire whatsoever to embarrass Great Britain or the allied powers in their prosecution of the war, or in any way to encourage aggression on India, or increase the pressure on China by the Japanese or any other power associated with the Axis group. Nor does the Congress intend to jeopardise the defensive capacity of the allied powers. The Congress is, therefore, agreeable to the stationing of the armed forces of the allies in India, should they so desire, in order to ward off and resist the Japanese or other aggression and to protect and help China.

The proposal of withdrawal of the British power from India was never intended to mean the physical withdrawal of all Britishers from India, and certainly not of those who would make India their home and live there as citizens and as equals with the others. If such a withdrawal takes place with goodwill, it would result in the establishing of a stable provisional government in India, and co-operation between this Government and the United Nations in resisting aggression and helping China.

The last paragraph of the resolution warned that the Congress would be compelled to act if its appeal failed, and clearly indicated the possibility of mass satyagraha:

The Congress will then be reluctantly compelled to utilize all the non-violent strength it might have gathered since 1920, when it adopted non-violence as part of its policy for the vindication of the country's political rights and liberty. Such a widespread struggle would inevitably be under the leadership of Mahatma Gandhi.

It was now evident that the Congress was not prepared to remain indefinitely in a state of passive quiescence, and that unless the British Government responded quickly mass satyagraha was inevitable, although Gandhi himself had not defined the form of action he contemplated.

"I am not ready with a planned programme as yet," Gandhi explained to a British newspaper correspondent shortly after the meeting. "But it will be my biggest movement."

To the country he gave no specific advice, but his mind was moving on the lines of mass satyagraha. Narendra Deva, the Socialist leader, recalls how he met Gandhi at Sewagram about this time when Gandhi was awaiting a visit by Nehru.

"How," asked the Mahatma, "will Jawahar react to the idea of satyagraha?"

"In my opinion," replied Narendra Deva, "if satyagraha is decided upon Jawahar will not stay out."

Gandhi agreed.

But Narendra Deva goes on to state that Nehru's intellect never really approved of the decision. When they were later in detention together in Ahmednagar Fort,[4] the Socialist leader reveals that Jawaharlal expressed the opinion that the step had been taken too hurriedly.

"It might have been possible to bring Britain to terms with the help of American pressure," Nehru remarked.

[4] In the State of Bombay.

This reading of possibilities is confounded by Churchill's war memoirs, which disclose that the British Prime Minister remained adamantly obtuse to President Roosevelt's appeals on behalf of India.

On August 7, 1942, the All-India Congress Committee met in Bombay to consider what is now historically known as the "Quit India" resolution. After urging the immediate recognition of Indian freedom and the ending of British rule in India "both for the sake of India and for the success of the cause of the United Nations," the resolution specifically declared that the primary object of a provisional government representative of all important sections of the people "must be to defend India and resist aggression with all the armed as well as the non-violent forces at its command, together with the Allied Powers."

"Freedom," the resolution emphasised, "will enable India to resist aggression effectively with the people's united will and strength behind it." Gandhi, in accepting the use of force to resist external aggression, had marched some way further with Jawaharlal.

But the core of the resolution lay in its concluding paragraphs, which repeated the demand for the withdrawal of British powers from India. Lastly, the resolution declared that

the Committee is no longer justified in holding the nation back from endeavouring to assert its will against an imperialist and authoritarian Government which dominates over it and prevents it from functioning in its own interest and in the interest of humanity. The Committee resolves therefore to sanction, for the vindication of India's inalienable right to freedom and independence, the starting of a mass struggle on non-violent lines under the inevitable leadership of Gandhiji.

It was left to the Mahatma to decide when such action should be taken.

"By embarking on mass struggle, it [the committee] has no intention of gaining powers for the Congress. The power, when it comes, will belong to the whole people of India," the resolution emphasised.

Nehru, moving the resolution, explained at some length the background from which it had emanated. Both Gandhi and he had travelled a long road in reaching this milestone. "The resolution," Nehru affirmed, "is in no sense a challenge to anyone. If the British Government accepts the proposal it will change the position for the better, both internal and international, from every point of view. You know that Gandhiji has agreed that British and other armed forces stationed in India might continue."

Azad, who presided, and Gandhi were careful to strike a sober but firm note. Both emphasised that their next step would be to approach the Viceroy, as representing the British Government, and to appeal to the heads of the principal United Nations for an honourable settlement which while recognising India's freedom would also help the cause of the United Nations in the war against the aggressors.

"We must look the world in the face with calm and clear eyes even though the eyes of the world are bloodshot today," Gandhi pleaded.

Even at this late stage the Mahatma clung to the belief that a settlement could be reached with the British Government. On the morning of August 9th, the day after the committee concluded its session, Gandhi remarked to his secretary, Mahadev Desai, "After my speech of last night, they will never arrest me."

They arrested him not an hour later, at early dawn, shortly after he had wakened for his usual morning prayers. Simultaneously the police were arresting the other members of the Congress Working Committee, including Nehru, who was taken into custody at the house of his younger sister, Krishna. He had gone to bed well after midnight, and was drowsy with sleep when his sister woke him up to tell him that the police had arrived.

Gandhi's last instructions were conveyed through another of his secretaries, Pyarelal.

"Let every non-violent soldier of freedom," said the Mahatma, "write out the slogan 'Do or Die' on a piece of paper or cloth, and pin it on his clothes, so that in case he died in the course of offering satyagraha, he might be distinguished by that sign from other elements who do not subscribe to non-violence."

The entire Working Committee, including Gandhi, were taken in a heavily guarded special train from Bombay to Chinchwad, a wayside station not far from Poona, whence Gandhi was whisked away in a motor car to be detained at His Majesty's pleasure in a residence owned by the Aga Khan at Poona. Nehru, with the other members of the Working Committee except Mrs. Sarojini Naidu, who was later detained with the Mahatma at Poona, was taken to Ahmednagar Fort.

It was to be Jawaharlal's longest term of detention, for he was not to be free again until June 15, 1945.

19

BLOOD AND TEARS

AHMEDNAGAR, a military station, lies a little over two hundred miles from Bombay, and its fort, dating to the sixteenth century, was the scene of a shining epic in Indian history when the woman warrior Chand Bibi defended it heroically against a Mogul army.

The twelve members of the Working Committee were housed in a number of rooms ringing three sides of a large quadrangle which contained a dilapidated, ill-kept lawn. A number of convict warders looked after their wants.

For Jawaharlal, as for his companions, this was a new experience, for while they had at one time or another all been in jail they had never before been kept together in this fashion. They were a variegated band, their ages ranging from forty-four to sixty-eight, politically akin but differing from one another in temperament, tastes, habits and outlook. The youngest was Hare Krushna Mahtab, later to be Governor of Bombay, while the oldest was Sardar Vallabhbhai Patel. Nehru was to spend his next three birthdays in jail.

They lived a companionable if drab existence, spending their time in various chores such as organising meals and trying to make themselves and one another as comfortable as they could, in cultivating their patch of garden, digging, reading, playing games, talking and indulging in badinage, anecdote and argument. At times the discussions were lively and controversial enough to ruffle some tempers.

But on the whole their life was equable and agreeable, and they learned to know and understand one another much better. Azad, with his vast store of scholarship, was an engaging conversationalist with a richness of lore and learning, and Nehru found special delight in his company. There was Vallabhbhai, master of a mordant wit, who would often mischievously cap the rarefied conversation of others with a rustic proverb. Others included Asaf Ali, fastidious and always neat as a new pin; the self-taught Shankerrao Dev, whose energy found vent in fierce games of badminton, bouts of cooking and the singing of *bhajans*;[1] and Dr. Syed Mahmud, who was gently ruminative, with an interesting turn of talk and reminiscence. In this diversified company were a chemist, Dr. Prafulla C. Ghosh from Bengal; the lean and argumentative Acharya Kripalani, today a Congress rebel and a leader of the Praja Socialist party; and the Socialist Narendra Deva. A loquacious companion was Dr. Pattabhi Sitaramayya, who was to become Governor of Madhya Pradesh. Govind Ballabh Pant, later to be Home Minister in Nehru's cabinet, enlivened their discussions, his nimble thought contrasting strangely with his heavy body. Mahtab's heartiness could be infectious.

As he had accustomed himself to do in jail, Jawaharlal kept to a regulated regimen, waking early to do his yogi exercises, busying himself in the garden or in the pantry, where he revelled in frying eggs for their breakfast or in showing his companions to what precise degree water should be boiled for tea or how a slice of bread should be toasted. He was meticulous and exacting, sometimes displaying a trace of old-maidish fussiness. But he was also vital, energetic, alive and entertaining, bringing to whatever he did a sense of hustle and bustle.

For almost three weeks they were deprived of newspapers and of all contact with the outside world. But gradually this rigidity was relaxed. Jawaharlal received many newspapers, Indian and foreign, and was always getting new books. After breakfast he worked usually in the garden—digging, sowing, planting and pruning, weeding out the lawn and watering the flower beds. He read voraciously, making notes of the things that interested him, and he also wrote. On April 13, 1944, some twenty months after he came to Ahmednagar, Nehru began his book *The Discovery of India*, which he completed about five months later. It is diffuse and rambling, and discursive in parts, but it reflects eloquently his deep, awakened interest in the culture and thought of India, which long discussions with his companions, notably Azad and Narendra Deva, had illumined and enriched.

[1] Religious songs.

From outside, the news was depressing. As the details seeped slowly into their prison, Nehru and his companions were able to piece together a fairly composite picture of the people's reactions to the events of August 9th. A hot gush of mass anger had welled to the surface and overflowed in violent and non-violent protest. Despite the country-wide arrests which had left them leaderless, thousands of Indians had demonstrated against the repression of the Raj. Confined at first to Bombay, Ahmedabad and Poona, these demonstrations soon spread throughout the country, and in certain districts, notably in Bihar, in the Midnapur area of Bengal and in the southeastern tracts of the United Provinces, the long arm of British authority had ceased to function for several days.

There were peaceful hartals [2] and protest meetings, but there were also outbreaks of mob violence, arson, murder and sabotage. Students and workers were prominent in these demonstrations, which were sometimes dispersed by tear gas and baton charges and sometimes fired upon. In Ballia in the United Provinces crowds were machine-gunned from the air. According to the Government of India's own figures for the period from August to December, 1942, the police and military had opened fire on demonstrating crowds, some of them violent, as many as 538 times, killing 940 and wounding 1,630 persons. Nehru, who thought these figures grossly underestimated, later put the number of those killed at about 10,000. By the end of 1942 over 60,000 had been arrested.

The initial damage and destruction done by violent mobs were considerable. Official statements for this period give the following statistics: 250 railway stations damaged or destroyed; 550 post offices attacked; 50 post offices burned; 200 post offices damaged; telegram and telephone wires cut at 3,500 places; 70 police stations burned and 85 other government buildings destroyed. In addition the military casualties were 11 dead and 7 wounded, while the number of police killed was 31, the total of those injured being described as "very large."

The public reaction was undoubtedly strong, widespread and in many places violent. But the authorities also struck ruthlessly and with a heavy hand. Apart from the aerial machine-gunning of crowds in Ballia, there were harrowing tales of repression in Midnapur and

[2] Suspension of work on the scale of a general strike.

of military excesses on villagers in the hamlets of Ashti and Chimur in the Central Provinces. Nehru recalls cases where whole villages were reported to have been sentenced to all manner of punishment from flogging to death. The Banaras Hindu University was closed and occupied by the military. In Bengal the local government admitted that "Government forces burnt 193 Congress camps and houses in the subdivisions of Tamluk and Contai before and after the cyclone of 1942." Collective fines were imposed on towns and villages, and in the British House of Commons Mr. Amery declared that these amounted to 9,000,000 rupees ($1,800,000), to be recovered mainly from indigent, often starving villagers.

By January, 1943, the uprising—for it was an uprising—was quelled. Much earlier, in September, 1942, Churchill had boasted: "The disturbances were crushed with all the weight of the Government. . . . Large reinforcements have reached India and the number of white troops in that country is larger than at any time in the British connection." Mr. Churchill was back to his days as a subaltern in Bangalore. But the empire over whose liquidation he later refused to preside was on the highroad to dissolution.

Gandhi meanwhile had been in communication with the Viceroy, writing his first letter on December 31, 1942, but of this Nehru and his colleagues were not aware. Linlithgow held that the August resolution was responsible for the outbreak of popular violence and called upon Gandhi "to retrace your steps and dissociate yourself from the policy of last summer." If he did so, the Viceroy promised to "consider the matter further."

Gandhi's reply was to announce that he proposed, as a satyagraha, to go on a twenty-one-day fast, "according to capacity," beginning on February 9th and ending on March 2nd. He made it clear that "my wish is not to fast unto death but to survive the ordeal if God so wills. The fast can be ended sooner by the Government giving the needed relief." What the Mahatma possibly visualised was the release of the Working Committee and himself.

But the Government was adamant, Lord Linlithgow in his reply stating: "I hope and pray that wiser counsels may yet prevail with you. But the decision whether or not to undertake a fast with its attendant risks is clearly one that must be taken by you alone and the responsibility for which and for its consequences must rest on you alone." The Viceroy went on to describe the Mahatma's contemplated action as "political blackmail."

On February 8th the Government of India, through its Home Secretary, Sir Richard Tottenham, offered Gandhi a temporary release for the duration of his fast, which it hoped he would carry out away from the Aga Khan's residence. But Gandhi declined. He began his fast on February 9th, and although he experienced some critical periods during his ordeal he survived.

To Nehru and his companions, isolated from Gandhi and unable to decipher the deeper motivations of his mind, the fast seemed as mystifying as to many members of the public. They had heard of it only on February 11th, but were aware that Gandhi had been contemplating some such action since his arrest. Jawaharlal had an intellectual antipathy to fasts as a political weapon, but in the present crisis he was torn between love for the Mahatma and doubt as to the wisdom of his action. Often in the past he had felt that Gandhi's methods of conversion were not far removed from courteous and considerate compulsion, and he had never reconciled himself to the rationale behind them. But on the other hand were Gandhi's unerring instinct and his choice of the right means. Indeed, Nehru himself had written of the Mahatma some years ago: "Which way he might turn in a crisis it was difficult to say but whichever way it was, it would make a difference. He might go the wrong way according to our thinking but it would always be a straight way." According to his own lights, Gandhi had used a moral weapon and had survived the ordeal. With millions of his countrymen, Nehru breathed a sigh of relief.

From Ahmednagar Fort, Azad as President of the Congress had addressed on February 13th a protest to Lord Linlithgow against the accusations contained in his correspondence with Gandhi. The letter was sent on behalf of the Working Committee, and bears evidence of Nehru's penmanship. Azad wrote:

I wish to confine myself more especially to one issue and to make it clear that so far as we are concerned both as individuals and in our corporate capacity speaking on behalf of our organisation, your charge that the Congress had organised a secret movement of violence is wholly false and without foundation. As an English patriot and a lover of British freedom, it should not be impossible for you to appreciate how Indian patriots and lovers of India's freedom might feel, and it should be possible for some element of fair-play and square dealing to be kept up in our relation to each other. To make serious charges against those who are prevented from replying to them, to make those charges (without producing evidence to support them) by the vast propaganda machine of a powerful Government and at the same time to supply news and views which are contrary to them are not evidence either of fair-play or a strong case.

The Congress was calling on Linlithgow to play cricket, but no answer was vouchsafed to this missive.

In September, 1943, Lord Linlithgow left India after having served as Viceroy for seven and a half years, and leaving in his wake a famine which his policy of negativism had done much to engender. The terrible Bengal famine, which claimed nearly 3,500,000 lives, had reached its peak in the last quarter of 1943; but it is typical of Linlithgow's curious insensitivity that he saw no reason, as Viceroy, to visit that stricken area before he went. One of the first acts of his successor, Lord Wavell, was to tour Bengal.

The famine was very largely man-made. Official complacency went to the extent of denying its existence even while hundreds of starving villagers who were trekking for food into the capital died on the streets of Calcutta. But a time arrived when the truth could not be concealed. "Corpses," said Nehru, "cannot easily be overlooked. They come in the way."

India, which was dependent largely for her rice supplies from Burma, was cut off from that source by the Japanese. Yet the Central Government had not troubled to start a Food Department even over a year after the Japanese war had begun. Others also were to blame, including the provincial government of Bengal and the Indian black marketeers who battened on the misery of their fellow men.

"In an independent India," Nehru declared in one of the first speeches he made on his release from prison in June, 1945, "such black marketeers will be hung from the lamp posts."

On February 22, 1944, Gandhi's wife, Kasturba, died while in detention with her husband. They had been married sixty-two years. Gandhi's own health deteriorated shortly after, and on April 16th a communiqué announced that he was suffering from malaria. His condition soon gave cause for anxiety as his blood pressure dropped and his anaemia worsened. On May 5th Gandhi was released, and left his place of detention next morning to stay at a friend's house at Poona. Six days later he arrived in Bombay, whence he left for the seaside resort of Juhu where over twenty years before Jawaharlal had visited him with his father.

From his prison in Ahmednagar, Nehru had been keenly following events at home and abroad.

In March, 1943, Montgomery had launched his attack on the Mareth Line which was to take his forces, together with the American and French contingents, to Tunis and Bizerte by May. The whole of North Africa was now clear of the enemy, the stage being set for the invasion of Europe. Sicily, the outpost most threatened by the African victory, fell to Allied arms in August. Even earlier, on July 25th, Mussolini had crashed from his dictatorship, and six weeks later the Italian mainland was invaded, while across the Adriatic Sea Tito was soon to feel himself strong enough to emerge from his underground lair.

Most of all, the Soviet campaign absorbed Nehru, for Stalingrad had stirred his admiration as it had that of the entire Allied world. In the summer of 1943 the Russians launched their great offensive across the Dnieper, driving the German armies before them. By the first week of October Soviet arms had regained the entire Caucasus, and by November all possibilities of the German forces escaping from the Crimea were ended. By the spring of 1944 it was clear that the German armies could no longer hold or contain the Russian advance.

If progress on the Pacific front against Japan seemed slower, this was because Germany was the primary target of the Allies. By July, 1944, with the Allied advance on New Guinea and the neighbouring islands, the initiative had passed from the Japanese. Earlier in March three Japanese divisions had crossed the Chindwin River in Burma, and in a frontal attack on the Manipur sector had infiltrated into India and invested Imphal. The invaders were badly mauled, and by August the Japanese had retreated from Indian soil.

Watching the sweep of Allied victories in the East and West, Nehru wondered what the British reaction on India would be. True, the Mahatma was released, even if "on medical grounds," and a new Viceroy, Lord Wavell, was in Delhi. It mattered little, however, whether Willingdon succeeded Irwin or Wavell followed Linlithgow. The virus lay in the system, and though an individual Viceroy might accelerate or retard the pace of progress he could do little unless the basic system itself were altered. Would victory leave the British more arrogant than before, oblivious, like Churchill, to the aims for which the war was fought, anxious only to preserve the status quo and extend it? Had not the leaders of even the British Labour party, echoing Churchill, "stressed the resolve of the British people to keep the empire together after the war"?

Gandhi, outside jail, realised that the first thing to do was to break the political stalemate, and he set about doing it. A request to meet the Working Committee in prison was refused, and Wavell also courteously expressed his inability to meet the Mahatma. "I feel," the Viceroy wrote, "that a meeting between us at present could have no value and could only raise hopes which would be disappointed. If after your convalescence and on further reflection, you have a definite and constructive policy to propose for the furtherance of India's welfare, I shall be glad to consider it."

Further correspondence with Wavell proved equally fruitless, the Viceroy merely reiterating his view. It was evident that with the initiative in its hands the British Government was content to await the outcome of the war, whose issue now could only be victory for the Allies.

Gandhi, rebuffed by the Government, turned to Jinnah to discover whether what he called "a heart-to-heart agreement between us" might not lead the British authorities to revise their attitude. But Jinnah also realised that he, like the British, was in a position of strength. Gandhi was manœuvring from a position of weakness. Between them there was no common ground; for while Gandhi argued on the basis of a united India, Jinnah began from the axiom that because the Hindus and Muslims were two distinct nations India must be divided.

The meetings which took place at Jinnah's house in Bombay lasted for eighteen days, beginning on September 9th. Gandhi expressed his willingness to discuss the partition of India, and Jinnah set out to persuade him to accept the principle of Pakistan. Their talks each day were reduced to letters which they exchanged with each other. By September 15th it was clear that a wide gulf separated their views.

"The more your argument progresses," Gandhi wrote, "the more alarming your picture appears to me. It would be alluring if it were true but my fear is that it is wholly unreal. . . . You do not claim to be a separate nation by right of conquest but by reason of acceptance of Islam. Will the two nations become one if the whole of India accepted Islam?"

Jinnah's reply claimed that "Muslims and Hindus are two major nations by any definition or test as a nation. . . . By all the canons of international law we are a nation."

Their talks ended on September 26th, and on the following day their correspondence was released. As Gandhi said, "The talks and correspondence seem to run in parallel lines, and never touch one another."

Nehru and his companions followed the progress of the talks in the newspapers which were now permitted them freely. Knowing the minds of both the participants, they were not surprised at the outcome. But the fact that the talks took place on Gandhi's initiative and at Jinnah's house pointed to the leeway which the League had made up while the Congress was immobilised.

The war in Europe was drawing to a close. In June, 1944, the Allies had landed in Normandy, and as their armies advanced through western Europe the Russians marched through the Balkans. By the end of the year the Germans were retreating across the Rhine. Hitler's Reich was collapsing around him, and by May Day, 1945, the Red flag of the Soviet flew over the site of the Reichstag in Berlin. The war in Europe was over.

Even while the Working Committee languished in jail, Congressmen outside had not been inactive. The Congress group in the Central Assembly, led by Bhulabhai Desai, a celebrated lawyer from Bombay, still formed the major opposition to the Government in the legislature, while Gandhi, although checkmated temporarily on the political front, continued his constructive activities, propagating village industries and the cause of the Harijans.

During March and April, 1945, the members of the Congress Working Committee who were interned at Ahmednagar were dispersed and sent to their respective provinces preparatory to their release. On March 28th Nehru, with Govind Ballabh Pant and Narendra Deva, was taken to Naini Central Prison in the United Provinces, where they met some of their old colleagues, notably Rafi

Ahmed Kidwai, who was later to be a prominent member of Nehru's cabinet. From Naini, after a short stay, Nehru, Pant and Narendra Deva were moved to Izatnagar Jail near Bareilly, where Pant, who was ill, was released shortly afterward. For over two months Nehru shared a barrack with Narendra Deva until early in June when they were both transferred to Almora Prison, where Nehru had been an inmate ten years earlier.

In the last week of May, Churchill announced his intention of holding a general election, and this projected India again into the political picture. "If we are returned," declared Ernest Bevin, "we shall close the India Office and transfer this business to the Dominions." British Labour thereby pledged itself to give India Dominion status.

Lord Wavell meanwhile had been summoned to London for consultations. He returned to India on June 5th with instructions to make a constitutional offer on behalf of the British Government, which at that time was Churchill's National Government and which included Labour representatives. The offer was described as "an agreed national offer on the part of this country [Britain] to the people of India."

The Wavell offer proposed a reconstitution of the Viceroy's Executive Council so that all its members except the Viceroy and the Commander-in-Chief would be Indian political leaders. Muslims and what were described as Caste Hindus [3] were to have equal representation. The portfolio of External Affairs, which the Viceroy had hitherto held, would be transferred from him to an Indian member, and fully accredited persons would be appointed to represent India abroad. The Viceroy expressed the hope that with reconstitution at the centre the provincial ministries which had withdrawn would resume office. To enable him to proceed with this plan Lord Wavell announced that he would call a conference of party leaders, provincial premiers and former premiers who would be asked to submit to him lists of names from which he could select the personnel of the new Executive Council. The Viceroy said that these proposals embodied "the utmost progress possible within the present constitution," but that none of them would "in any way prejudice or prejudge the essential form of the future permanent constitution

[3] This implied an additional seat for a Scheduled Caste Hindu or Harijan.

or constitutions for India," which would be a matter for Indians themselves to frame.

Lord Wavell's broadcast was accompanied by a statement by Mr. Amery in the House of Commons that the members of the Congress Working Committee, who were still in custody, would be released. On June 15th Nehru was released from Almora. It had been his longest term of imprisonment—1,041 days.

Ranjit, his favourite brother-in-law, had died [4] while he was in jail, and Jawaharlal's first act was to spend his first night at Ranjit's estate at Khali, not far from Almora, where in the past he had spent so many pleasant days. It was in the nature of a pilgrimage.

That afternoon, at Almora, he went to lunch with an American friend, Gertrude Emerson Sen (who represented a United States Journal [5] in India), and her Indian husband, Dr. Sen, who is a scientist.

He had a slight fever, says Gertrude Sen, and he looked almost transparent as he sat back in a corner of a couch.

"It seems so strange to be free," he said quietly, looking slowly up and down the room. "I don't mean physically but psychologically."

She had asked the wife of a British official who was eager to meet Nehru to drop in for ten minutes before lunch. The Englishwoman came, and Nehru talked to her pleasantly and graciously. As she rose to go, he insisted that she take with her some mangoes he had brought along with him from jail. They were from his garden in Allahabad.

"It would be a pity to leave them behind," he said.

From Khali, Nehru went to Allahabad, where he spent a night before hurrying to Bombay, where the Congress Working Committee was meeting. Gandhi was there, and the reunion was affectionate. Though it was good to meet old friends and comrades, Nehru felt curiously like an outsider, free on a friendly but strange planet amid men and women eager to shower their affection on him but withal distant and unfamiliar.

The Working Committee decided to accept the Viceroy's invitation, and on June 25th the conference assembled at Viceregal Lodge, Simla.

[4] On January 14, 1944.
[5] *Asia*, now defunct.

Azad, a Muslim, was the Congress representative in his capacity as President of the Congress. Jinnah represented the Muslim League, and each was assisted by his respective Working Committee who convened at Simla. Nehru was there.

The conference almost immediately ran into difficulties, for Azad and Jinnah were unable to agree on the strength and composition of the Viceroy's Executive Council. Thereupon, on June 29th, Wavell adjourned the conference until July 14th for further informal consultations, requesting the party leaders to furnish him with their lists of nominees in order to enable him to make the final choice. The Congress complied, its list of five Congressmen including two Muslims, Azad and Asaf Ali, who was later to be the first Indian ambassador to the United States. Jinnah, however, insisted that the League was the sole representative of the Muslims, and as such only those Muslims it approved of should be included in the Executive Council.

The Congress was not alone in objecting to this monopolistic claim, for the Punjab's Muslim premier, Malik Khizr Hyat Khan, demanded that one of the Muslim seats be given to his nominee from the Punjab. Wavell, too, was unable to concede Jinnah's claim.

Had the Viceroy proceeded to form the new Executive Council on the basis he had outlined, irrespective of the League, the political history of India might have been different. He had assured Azad earlier that "no party to the conference would be allowed to obstruct a settlement out of wilfulness." But, faced with Jinnah's wilfulness, Wavell hesitated. His advisers both in India and Britain counselled him to end the conference, confessing a breakdown. He did so on July 14th. By doing this, and bowing to Jinnah's truculence, the British Government virtually conceded to the League a power of veto on the country's constitutional advancement. It allowed Jinnah to hold India's freedom to ransom. Well meaning and anxious to placate both parties in an endeavour to carry both with him, Wavell finally ended by alienating both.

Azad regretted the Viceroy's weakness, as did Nehru and his colleagues. But Labour had come into power in Britain a few days before the conclusion of the Simla conference, and Nehru and Azad realised that freedom was not far away.

"We are very near our goal," said Azad, "and the next stage is the goal itself. It does not matter at all what the intentions of the British Government are."

From Simla, Nehru hurried for a holiday in the hills and vales of Kashmir. He spent most of the one month he was there on a trek to the higher regions and passes, amid the glaciers and snow, and returned to India exhilarated in heart and spirits.

Like a man groping in a grey dimness, he tried slowly to piece together the Indian scene as it emerged from the haze which enveloped it. He sensed a feeling of suppressed excitement in the country, a mammoth urge to be up and doing in the fight for freedom, and the tang and tingle of their awakened desire infected him. India would be free soon—of that he felt certain.

In August the horror of the atom bomb was loosed on Hiroshima and Nagasaki, and on August 15, 1945, Japan surrendered. The Second World War was over. In the last days of Japan's downfall news came of the death of Subhas Bose in an air crash in Taiwan. Bose had organised the Indian National Army with the remnants of the Indian soldiers and officers captured by the Japanese in Burma and Malaya, and with the cry of "Chalo Delhi" (On to Delhi) had dreamed of marching into an awakened and independent India. Hindus, Muslims, Sikhs and Christians were represented in the army, and in Indian eyes it seemed as if they posed a challenge to the separatist forces at work in the homeland. The Indian National Army became a dramatic symbol of national unity. Bose had lived his finest hour.

On August 21st the Government of India announced that the general elections to the central and provincial legislatures would take place at the earliest possible date, and simultaneously it was divulged that Wavell was leaving for London for further consultations. On September 19th Clement Attlee, speaking from London and Wavell from India, announced that the British Government intended as soon as possible after the elections and after consultation with representatives of the legislative assemblies to bring into being a constitution-making body, and that meanwhile immediate consideration would be given to the contents of a treaty "which will require to be concluded between Britain and India." The Viceroy, it was declared, had been authorised, as soon as the election results were known, to take steps to bring into being a reconstituted Executive Council.

What the Congress was primarily anxious to preserve at this stage was the unity of India, and in September the Working Committee, responding obliquely to the Government's announcement, affirmed that the constitution should be federal, with the residuary powers vested in the units. As a corollary a resolution was moved later by Sardar Patel which characterised the Government's proposals as "vague and inadequate and unsatisfactory." None the less the Congress declared its intention of contesting the elections.

At this time Gandhi was in indifferent health—he entered a Nature Cure clinic at Poona shortly after—and the direction of Congress affairs was left in the hands of Azad, Patel and Nehru.

In October the Congress published its election manifesto which, again with an eye on the League's campaign for Pakistan, declared its faith in a federal constitution "leaving a great deal of autonomy for its constituent units." In the following months the trial of three Indian National Army officers was held in Delhi's Red Fort. Because the Congress had interested itself in their defence, Nehru appeared formally in court wearing his barrister's gown which he had discarded thirty years earlier. Bhulabhai Desai, who was the chief defence counsel, rose to his superb best, and his brilliant scorching advocacy and cross-examination rang a bell throughout India. The three officers on trial were a Hindu, Muslim and Sikh, and this again gave their appearance a symbolic significance. The accused were convicted, but were released almost immediately by order of the then Commander-in-Chief, General Sir Claude Auchinleck. New Delhi was on the retreat.

It was claimed at the trial that there was no ideological link between the army and Japanese fascism, and that the only idea inspiring the army was the winning of India's freedom. The British contended that the officers had disclaimed their allegiance to the British Crown and thereby broken their oath.

"Unless you sell your own soul," retorted Bhulabhai Desai, "how can you ever say, when you are fighting to liberate your own country, that there is some other allegiance which prevents you from doing so? If that were so, there would be nothing but permanent slavery."

The trial dealt a deadly blow to British prestige, canalising the country's mass fervour into the fight for freedom. "It became," said

Nehru, "a trial of strength between the will of the Indian people and the will of those who held power in India, and it was the will of the people that triumphed in the end."

The elections for the central and provincial legislatures took place in January, 1946; and although the Congress fared well, the elections were notable for the impressive advance registered by the Muslim League, which at the centre and in the provinces captured quite 75 per cent of the Muslim votes. On the part of both the Congress and the League was an awareness that freedom was near, and the stepping up of political pressures on both sides aggravated the tension in the atmosphere. It needed only a spark to set things alight.

The spark came from an unexpected quarter. On February 19, 1946, Bombay was the scene of demonstrations by some three thousand naval ratings of the Royal Indian Navy who rose in violent protest against differential treatment, food and living conditions. A number of British officers and men of the fighting services were attacked by the demonstrators, and trouble spread rapidly. The Congress tricolour was hoisted on some naval sloops in the harbour, and British personnel were forced off the ships. Batches of ratings roamed the city in lorries.

By the next day the trouble had spread to other naval establishments in the suburbs. Slogans such as "Quit India" and *Jai Hind* (Hail India) were chalked by the ratings on walls and public places. Congress, League and even Communist flags fluttered from Royal Indian Navy lorries, and naval establishments in Karachi, Calcutta, Delhi and Madras were affected, military police opening fire on the strikers at the first centre and being fired upon in return by the ratings. In the first of several encounters, nine were injured and one killed.

On February 21st the British military police opened fire on the naval demonstrators in Bombay, and feeling ran high. An attempt by the ratings to capture an armoury inside a barracks was foiled. British troops fired on the ratings elsewhere in the city, the demonstrators retaliating with hand grenades. The situation grew more explosive when over a thousand men in the Royal Indian Air Force camps in Bombay came out on a sympathetic strike.

By February 22nd the mutineers were in control of nearly twenty naval vessels in Bombay harbour, including the flagship of the

British vice-admiral, and trained the ships' guns on the city. On the previous day Sardar Patel, who was in Bombay, appealed for a peaceful settlement and advised workers in the factories, as well as students, not to strike. "Such a thing," he counselled, "is not likely to help the unfortunate naval ratings in their efforts to get redress of their legitimate grievances or in the great difficulty in which they find themselves." Privately he advised the demonstrators to surrender, promising that the Congress would do its best to prevent unduly severe punishment or victimisation. On February 23rd the Royal Indian Navy ships under the control of the rebel ratings surrendered. Earlier that day Jinnah had also unreservedly offered his services to the navy men to see that justice was done. Simultaneously he had appealed to the ratings to call off the mutiny and to the public not to add to the difficulties of the situation.

So inflammable, however, was the public mood that these appeals to the masses went unheeded. There were widespread rioting in Bombay and Calcutta, and disturbances in Karachi and Madras. Mass violence on an unprecedented scale broke out in Bombay, where an orgy of arson and looting continued for almost four days. Both the military and the police opened fire on several occasions, inflicting heavy casualties. On February 24th the casualty figures were officially placed at 187 killed and over 1,000 injured.

Nehru visited Bombay, and after a tour of the wreckage-strewn city in the company of Sardar Patel addressed a large meeting where he denounced the violence of the anti-social elements who had exploited the public indignation. "What has happened in Bombay," he said, "clearly demonstrates how anti-social elements in a vast city like Bombay exploit a situation. In every free country there is this problem, but in our country this is complicated by our fight for freedom. The time has come when we should direct our energies along the channel of constructive work. What happened in Bombay shows that the constructive tendency is lacking."

Freedom was not far off, and Nehru impressed this on his audience. "For the past twenty-five years," he continued, "the people of India have made tremendous sacrifices in the cause of winning our national independence. Our freedom is near at hand today. We have all the virtues for winning our freedom, but I confess that we lack the discipline which is essential for a free country."

The country's view of the naval mutiny was reflected in the speeches made by Congress and League speakers in the Central Assembly, who joined in ascribing it to racial discrimination and resentment at foreign rule. "Why," asked a Congress spokesman, Minoo Masani, "do the people of Bombay unanimously support the mutineers? It is because Indians do not differ. We do not accept the moral basis of your authority. Your law is not law to us. It has not got the consent of the people behind it. That is why when your military or civil law is broken every one instinctively regards the rebellion with sympathy. In other words, the real cause of this mutiny is the existence of British rule in this country. . . . The ratings who surrendered in the interests of their country were the moral victors of the struggle."

Masani's sentiments were echoed by a Muslim Leaguer, Abdur Rahman Siddiqui. "Those boys," said Siddiqui, "did not go mad overnight when they committed acts to which exception is taken. Whether in Bombay or Karachi these boys have behaved as any group of young folk would have done. My boys had a larger justification to do what they did than the men of the American or British forces." And turning to the Government benches, he concluded: "Your age is finished and a new age has dawned. Unless you go with the spirit of the age there will be trouble and misery for my own countrymen as well as for those who would like to crush them."

Consciousness of this fact was seeping through the minds of Britain's Socialist leaders. The Great Rebellion of 1857, which was touched off by a mutiny of Indian soldiers, had seen India transferred from the rule of the East India Company to that of the Crown. Now, by a queer irony, a mutiny of the navy was to signalise the transfer of India from foreign dependence to freedom. Britain was preparing to quit India, but before quitting she was to divide.

On February 19th, the day which saw the outbreak of the naval mutiny in Bombay, Lord Pethick-Lawrence, Secretary of State for India, announced the decision of the British Government to send a Cabinet Mission to India to discuss with the Indian leaders how political power could best be transferred to Indian hands. In January an all-party Parliamentary delegation from Britain had toured India, discovering to their genuine surprise the country's deep and widespread feeling against British rule. They were impressed by the explosive potentialities of the situation, and on returning home, their report did much to accelerate the Government's decision.

The Cabinet Mission comprising Lord Pethick-Lawrence, Sir Stafford Cripps (President of the Board of Trade), and Mr. A. V. Alexander (First Lord of the Admiralty) arrived in India on March 23rd. Its first duty, as the British Prime Minister, Mr. Attlee, explained in Parliament, was to set up "a machinery of decision" that would enable Indian leaders to receive political power in no way incompatible with the sovereign dignity of India.

Until April 27th the Mission was engaged in separate conversations with the leaders of various political and communal parties, notably the Congress and the League, in an endeavour to find a basis of agreement between the two latter parties. The talks proving fruitless, the Mission then invited the Congress and the League to nominate four representatives each who along with the Mission and the Viceroy would discuss the possibility of agreement on a tentative scheme put forward by the Mission.

The scheme visualised a Union Government at the centre dealing with foreign affairs, defence and communications. There would be two groups of provinces, the one of the predominantly Hindu provinces and the other of the predominantly Muslim provinces dealing with all the subjects which the provinces in the respective groups desired to be dealt with in common. The provincial governments would deal with the remaining subjects and have all the residuary sovereign rights. At some later stage the princely States would enter into this three-tier structure on terms to be negotiated with them.

Subject to certain reservations both the Congress and the League agreed to meet in conference with the Mission and the Viceroy to discuss the scheme. Azad, as President of the Congress, nominated Nehru, Patel and Khan Abdul Ghaffar Khan as his colleagues. Jinnah was accompanied by Liaquat Ali Khan, later to be Prime Minister of Pakistan, Nawab Mohammad Ismail Khan from the United Provinces and Abdur Rab Nishtar from the Frontier province.

The conference which met at Simla on May 5th ended without reaching an agreement on May 12th, and the venue was thereupon shifted to Delhi. Prior to this, both the Congress and the League submitted memoranda containing their respective views of a constitutional settlement. The League memorandum visualised a Paki-

stan group comprising the six Muslim majority provinces of the Punjab, Northwest Frontier, Baluchistan, Sind, Bengal and Assam, formed as one group and dealing with all subjects except foreign affairs, defence, and communications necessary for defence, these three to be dealt with by the constitution-making bodies of the two groups—Pakistan and "Hindu India"—sitting together. The Congress memorandum suggested the formation of a Constituent Assembly consisting of representatives from the provincial assemblies and the Princely States to frame a constitution for a Federal Union, the Union Government dealing with Foreign Affairs, Defence, Communications, Fundamental Rights, Currency, Customs and Planning, "as well as such other subjects as, on closer scrutiny, may be found to be intimately allied with them," with the provinces enjoying all the remaining powers. Under this scheme groups of provinces might be formed, and such groups would determine the provincial subjects which they desired to take in common.

Obviously the Congress memorandum was nearer to the proposals of the Cabinet Mission and the Viceroy than was the League scheme. It was therefore not surprising that when on May 16th the Mission announced its own recommendation it ruled out Pakistan and favoured an All-India Union on the old three-tier basis of a Union government at the centre, groups of provinces and provinces; but the three groups it visualised included one comprising all the six Muslim provinces earmarked by Jinnah with the additional proviso that any of the provinces in a group could opt out of a particular group. Simultaneously it announced the Viceroy's intention to form an interim government having the support of the major political parties. The Mission's announcement was in no way an award but a recommendation, as Lord Pethick-Lawrence emphasised at a press conference. It was for Indians meeting in a constituent assembly to devise their own constitution for a free India. "The Government and people of Britain are not only willing, they are anxious to play their full part in achieving this result," said Lord Pethick-Lawrence.

Nehru and his colleagues, mindful of the earlier Cripps debacle, had approached the Cabinet Mission cautiously, unwilling to take on trust declarations which were not supported by positive action. They recalled how on the failure of his earlier mission Cripps had turned and rent the Congress as if it had desecrated some sanctuary.

They remembered how Wavell, after promising that no party would be allowed to obstruct a settlement out of wilfulness, had truckled to Jinnah's wilfulness. Even now, although their views on the constitutional position were very near those of the Cabinet Mission, the latter was unwilling to make an award, and the Congress particularly disliked the compulsory banding into one group of the six Muslim provinces as the Mission's plan envisaged.

What Nehru and his colleagues did not sufficiently appreciate was that the British Government, while willing to accept a constitution agreed to by the major political parties in India, was unwilling to impose one. The British view was honest and logical, for if they imposed a constitution they would have to stay in order to implement it. And they wanted to withdraw—and withdraw gracefully. Hence the onus of devising a constitution for free India devolved on the Indians.

Jinnah also eyed the Mission's statement suspiciously. It had categorically rejected Pakistan, although the compulsory grouping plan might, he felt, be described as a halfway house to that ideal. But Jinnah calculated that the Congress would refuse to join the Interim Government, and Wavell, as he had earlier assured Azad during the first Simla conference, now assured Jinnah that he would go ahead with the plan as far as circumstances permitted "if either party accepted." Wavell had offered the Congress and the League equal representation in the Interim Government with the addition of two members, one representing the Sikhs and one the Untouchables. Later Wavell decided to add representatives of the Parsis and the Anglo-Indian community.

On June 6th the Council of the Muslim League, meeting in Delhi, accepted the Cabinet Mission's plan "inasmuch as the basis and foundation of Pakistan" were "inherent in the Mission plan by virtue of the compulsory grouping of the six Muslim provinces." The Congress Working Committee meeting on May 24th adopted a more cautious approach, describing the picture as "incomplete and vague" and insisting that the Interim Government could only be the precursor to full independence.

Nehru meanwhile had been elected President of the Congress for the ensuing year, and in this capacity he entered into correspondence with the Viceroy requesting that the proposed Interim Government should in practice function like a Dominion Cabinet. Wavell was unable to agree. On June 16th the Viceroy announced that he was issuing invitations to fourteen individuals to join the Interim Government "on the basis that the constitution-making will proceed in accordance with the statement of May 16." There were to be five representatives each from the Congress and the League, the Congress invitees being Nehru, Patel, Rajendra Prasad, Rajagopalachari and Hare Krushna Mahtab. On June 24th the Working Committee expressed the inability of the Congress to join the Interim Government.

Jinnah chuckled with triumph. On the basis of the Viceroy's assurance he was confident that Wavell would go forward with the formation of the Interim Government without the Congress. But Wavell thought otherwise. Instead, on June 26th, to Jinnah's unconcealed chagrin, the Cabinet Mission announced that its plan had been shelved, and Wavell proceeded to form a Caretaker Government of permanent officials. "You have chosen to go back on your pledged word," Jinnah wrote angrily to Wavell.

It cannot be said that the Viceroy emerged impressively from these negotiations. By constantly shifting his ground he exposed himself to a charge of bad faith from both sides, and when on July 22nd he wrote to the League leader that the Muslim League should agree to a revised distribution of seats in the Interim Government which he still hoped to set up, on the basis of six seats for the Congress, five for the League and three for members representing other minorities, Jinnah was exceedingly wrath. His indignation was intensified by statements made by Cripps and Pethick-Lawrence in London that Jinnah had "no monopoly of Muslim appointments."

The elections to the Constituent Assembly saw both the League and the Congress triumphant, the League capturing 74 out of the 79 Muslim seats while the Congress with its supporters controlled 292 seats. On July 10th Nehru declared that there was a "big probability" that there would be no grouping, a statement which further exasperated Jinnah.

On July 29th, at a meeting of the League Council in Bombay, the Muslim League withdrew its acceptance of the Cabinet proposals and sanctioned Direct Action to enforce Pakistan.

"Why do you expect me alone to sit with folded hands?" Jinnah asked rhetorically at a press conference. "I also am going to make trouble."

Direct Action was to set in train massacres, violence and bloody riots which were to extend beyond August 15, 1947, culminating in the mass migration of 11,500,000 souls, Hindu, Muslim and Sikh, in a two-way trail of blood between India and Pakistan.

Nehru watched events with foreboding, for although Jinnah had refused to indicate what form Direct Action would take it was clear that the League contemplated some form of violence. Unless there was a mass upsurge by the Muslims, Jinnah plainly feared that Pakistan would slip rapidly below the horizon. He would give the British and the Congress a demonstration of "bloodshed and civil war," thereby blackmailing and bludgeoning both into acceptance of Pakistan.

Direct Action Day was set for August 16th. Ostensibly designed to explain to the Muslim masses the meaning of the resolutions passed by the Council of the League in Bombay, it had a sinister purpose. Jinnah had himself indicated the shape that these demonstrations might take. On July 29th in Bombay, speaking on the Direct Action resolution, the Qaid-i-Azam (Saviour of the People), as Jinnah was now known, roundly declared, "Never have we in the whole history of the League done anything except by constitutional methods and by constitutionalism. But now we are forced into this position. This day we bid goodbye to constitutional methods."

There could be only one meaning to this threat. Jinnah was calling upon the Muslim masses to react with violence. On August 16th they did, letting loose in Calcutta and at Sylhet in Assam an orgy of violence which cost about six thousand lives and thousands of casualties in Bengal alone. The gutters of Calcutta ran with blood during what a British-owned daily, *The Statesman*, described as "The Great Killing." Thousands of Hindus fled from the capital city, leaving behind them a metropolis red with carnage, grey with the pall of smoke from burning buildings and black with the wings of vultures hovering over the dead, a veritable witches' cauldron of death and destruction.

Calcutta was only the beginning of a chain of violence which spread like a bush fire throughout the country, burning its way into the villages of the interior, particularly in the Noakhali area of southeastern Bengal, and in adjoining Bihar and Assam. On August 15, 1947, as an American correspondent was to put it, a bleeding Pakistan was to be carved out of the body of a bleeding India. But already in August, 1946, Jinnah had begun his surgical operation.

On July 22nd Nehru had seen Wavell, who had handed him a letter extending an invitation to the Congress to nominate six members (including one scheduled caste representative) to the proposed Interim Government of fourteen members. Simultaneously the League was invited to nominate five representatives, but Jinnah declined. The Congress accepted the invitation, and Nehru in his capacity as the Congress President wrote to Jinnah suggesting a coalition government. Jinnah was adamant, his reply stating that events did not call for a revision of the League decision.

On August 17th, on the second day of the Calcutta blood bath, Nehru saw the Viceroy, and soon afterward, having consulted his colleagues, prepared a list of the proposed members of the Interim Government. They included Nehru, Patel, Rajendra Prasad, C. Rajagopalachari, Asaf Ali, Dr. John Matthai [6] and a scheduled caste member, Jagjiwan Ram. Sarat Chandra Bose, elder brother of Subhas Bose, was included. Besides Asaf Ali two non-League Muslims were appointed with a promise that two more would be added, and a Parsi and a Sikh completed the list. The Government was announced on August 24th and took office on September 2nd.

On August 24th Wavell, broadcasting from Delhi, appealed to the Muslim League to reconsider its decision and join the Interim Government and enter the Constituent Assembly which Jinnah now threatened to boycott. The Viceroy also advised the League to desist from violent words and actions. That very night Sir Shafaat Ahmed Khan, a non-League nominee to the Interim Government, was stabbed by some Muslims at Simla.

In Delhi a Muslim League member, Ghazanfar Ali Khan, bitterly denounced "Nehru's Government" at a meeting of Muslims who passed a resolution condemning the formation of the Interim Government without the League. "Muslims will resist such a Government with their blood," it warned. The League was on the warpath.

Nehru was deeply disturbed by the Calcutta killings, which he realised was a tocsin call by the League to further violence. In this

[6] Representing the Christians.

inflammatory situation the position of the Interim Government was delicate and peculiarly vulnerable, for any stern measures against further outbreaks would inevitably be exploited by the League as an effort by Nehru's "Hindu Government" to suppress the Muslims. Hindus too, Nehru realised, were capable and guilty of mob violence, and they had indeed retaliated in Calcutta and elsewhere, in addition to taking the initiative at other places. Nehru felt that the only way to tackle the problem was to regard it not as a communal but as a human issue impinging on the sensitivities and feelings of all men, irrespective of their religion or politics. Shortly before entering the Interim Government, Nehru uttered a note of warning. "This new development of violence," he said, "has ceased to be communal or political. It has become a challenge to every decent instinct of humanity and it should be treated as such." But by now his was a voice in a wilderness of hate and fury.

Jinnah and the League were in no mood for appeasement. On the eve of the Interim Government's assuming office the Qaid-i-Azam's chief lieutenant, Liaquat Ali Khan, called on all Muslims to observe September 2nd as a "Black Day" by hoisting black flags on their residences and places of business "to register the Muslim nation's silent contempt at the installation in office of the Hindu Congress and its satellites." From Bombay, Jinnah thundered, "India stands on the brink of ruinous civil war." He was doing everything to make that possible.

In September Hindu-Muslim clashes and rioting took place in Bombay and Dacca, and there was a further recrudescence of violence in Calcutta. But waves of hate and terror, however well organised, could not on their own momentum achieve far-reaching results. "Pakistan is the only solution," repeated Jinnah with the menacing monotony of a Greek chorus.

But, clever tactician that he was, he soon realised that by keeping the League out of the Interim Government he had allowed the Congress to assume a position of vantage which might end in the League's isolation and drive it to sterile opposition against an administration which could count on the support of the British authorities. He now manœuvred to enter the Interim Government to paralyse and break it from within, thereby hoping to demonstrate that Hindus and Muslims could not work in office together. If the Interim Government succeeded, it would be a demonstration that Pakistan was a provocative myth, and at all cost the Interim Government must be undermined.

Jinnah first put out a "feeler" in a press interview that if the British Government were to invite him to London to start a new series of conferences "on an equal footing with other Indian negotiators" he would accept the invitation. Wavell thereupon invited him to Delhi for discussions, but Nehru quite rightly protested that this would once again reduce settled issues to a state of flux and make the task of government difficult. The Congress realised that the operative words in Jinnah's offer were "on an equal footing," which if accepted implied that the League would have the same number of representatives in the Interim Government as the Congress. The British Cabinet accordingly expressed its inability to invite Jinnah to London.

The Qaid-i-Azam had now no alternative to securing the entry of the League into the Interim Government on the old basis. He would have to be content with five representatives as against six for the Congress. Early in October he met Nehru twice within three days at the house of the Nawab of Bhopal, their first conversation lasting three hours, and their second extending for well over an hour. Though Nehru was not unaware of the deeper motivations behind Jinnah's move, he was conciliatory, though cautious and firm. He realised that the lawyer in Jinnah was trying to trip him into some admission or concession. The letters exchanged between them and subsequently released show that he resisted all of Jinnah's demands save one which, after consultation with his colleagues, he substantially accepted. This expressed the willingness of the Congress, "as a result of the elections to accept the Muslim League as the authoritative representative organisation of an overwhelming majority of the Muslims of India provided that for identical reasons the League recognises the Congress as the authoritative organisation representing all non-Muslims and such Muslims as have thrown in their lot with the Congress." Jinnah protested, trying vainly to enlarge this recognition by a concession that the Muslim League was the sole representative of the Muslims in India. Gandhi, he said, had accepted it. Perhaps, said Nehru and his colleagues, but Gandhi could not and did not commit either them or the Congress.

Jinnah continued to argue with Nehru, but before their correspondence had ceased he had seen the Viceroy twice, and on October 13th had assured Wavell that the Muslim League would enter the Interim Government. It did so on October 26th, its five representatives being Liaquat Ali Khan, I. I. Chundrigar, Abdur Rab Nishtar, Ghazanfar Ali Khan and Jogendra Nath Mandal, the last being a member of the scheduled castes. This was Jinnah's way of deriding the Congress.

The Qaid-i-Azam, having achieved his objective, now set about to sabotage the Interim Government from within, a comparatively easy task because the administration until August, 1947 (when partition came), functioned against a background of widespread communal rioting, particularly in East Bengal and Bihar. Jinnah's reaction to the conflagration he had done so much to kindle was to reiterate his cry. "There is no possibility of an end to India's civil strife unless Pakistan is absolutely achieved," he threatened.

The five Muslim League members of the Government worked as a separate and distinct wing—a Cabinet within a Cabinet—which made cohesive or purposeful administration impossible. Wavell had neither the temperament, inclination nor political perceptiveness to ensure more effective coordination. He presided uneasily over a house divided against itself.

Jinnah next set about undermining the Constituent Assembly which, it was announced, would convene on December 9th. On November 21st the Qaid-i-Azam issued a ukase to his followers forbidding any of them to take his seat. By now a creeping paralysis had set into the governmental machinery and cramped constitutional progress. It was what Jinnah had planned to achieve.

In London it was realised more clearly than in Delhi that such intransigence, if allowed to have its way, could only end in explosive disaster. The situation had mounted to proportions clearly beyond Wavell's capacity. The British Government thereupon invited the Viceroy and the Indian leaders to come to Britain for consultation. "The purpose of the proposed discussion," it was announced, "is to endeavour to reach a common understanding between the two major parties on which the work of the Constituent Assembly can proceed with the cooperation of all parties." On December 3rd Wavell, accompanied by Nehru, Jinnah, Liaquat Ali Khan and Sardar Baldev Singh, the Sikh representative, left for London.

The Congress and the League had come finally to the parting of the ways. But ahead lay a grim and blood-drenched road.

20

FREEDOM COMES

"MR. NEHRU," said Lord Mountbatten at the conclusion of their first interview at Viceregal House, "I want you to regard me not as the last Viceroy winding up the British Raj but as the first to lead the way to the new India."

Nehru flashed a friendly smile.

"Now," he said, "I know what they mean when they speak of your charm being so dangerous."

With Lady Mountbatten, who was also to play a decisive if supplementary role, Mountbatten had arrived at New Delhi on March 22, 1947. His appointment had been announced on February 20th, though Attlee had offered him the Viceroyalty as far back as December 18th, while Wavell was still in London.

The Socialist Government's fears that India was heading towards a civil war were reinforced by their conversations with the four Indian leaders who arrived with Wavell in London on December 3rd. When the invitation for these talks had been first extended, Nehru had expressed his reluctance to attend because the Congress suspected that the British Cabinet wished to reopen the whole question of the Interim Government and the Constituent Assembly which the Muslim League had announced it would boycott. It was only on Attlee's assurance that his Government had no such intention that Nehru had consented to go, but on the understanding that he, with Baldev Singh, must be back in India for the Constituent Assembly which was to meet on December 9th. To this proviso Attlee had also agreed.

Not only were Congress-League relations gravely embittered when Wavell with the four Indian leaders left for London; the Congress was also deeply suspicious of the actions of the Viceroy himself and of senior British officials.

In an aggressively outspoken speech to the Subjects (or Agenda) Committee of the Congress at Meerut on November 21st, Nehru had bluntly declared, "There is a mental alliance between the League and senior British officials," and he went on to reveal that the atmosphere in the Interim Government after the League's entry had become so vitiated that Congress members had twice threatened to resign. Nehru had openly accused Wavell of failure to carry on the Government in the spirit in which he had started. "He is gradually removing the wheels of the car, and this is leading to a critical situation," he charged.

In the circumstances it became imperative to replace Wavell, whose mind and outlook in any case could not easily adjust themselves to the Socialist Government's plans for the transfer of power to India. Wavell had been asked by London to work out a blueprint for this purpose.

"All that he brought back," Attlee complained to Mountbatten, "was a military evacuation plan."

The London talks failed in their object of securing the participation and cooperation of all parties in the Constituent Assembly, the point at issue being whether or not the decisions of the groups of provinces should be taken group-wise or province-wise. The League, supported by the British Government, took the former view, the Congress held to the latter, but it was willing to refer the issue to the Federal Court [1] and abide by its verdict. To this, however, the League would not agree.

The talks ended on December 6th to enable Nehru and Baldev Singh to attend the opening of the Constituent Assembly on December 9th. When the Assembly met, not a single one of the seventy-four Muslim League delegates was present. It is noteworthy that in his inaugural address the President, Dr. Sachchidananda Sinha, in his day a celebrated journalist and public worker, referred to the United States Constitution as a fitting model for India's constitution-makers because it was based "on a series of agreements as well as a series of compromises."

[1] The highest judicial body then in India.

Dr. Rajendra Prasad was elected permanent chairman of the Constituent Assembly two days later. In his opening address, while acknowledging the limitations placed on that body by the absence of the League, he declared: "But I also know that despite these limitations the Assembly is a self-governing and self-determining independent body in whose proceedings no outside authority can interfere and whose decisions no one outside can upset or alter or modify." It was a plain hint to the British Government to keep clear. At the end of December, in a speech at Bareilly, Prasad declared that "the constitution that was being evolved by the Constituent Assembly would be so framed as to be acceptable to all groups in India." Despite the boycott of the League, the Assembly was going ahead with its work.

In this tense, tenuous atmosphere Mountbatten assumed the Viceroyalty. He came to India charged with a specific task to be accomplished by a prescribed deadline—the transfer of political power to India by June, 1948. When some ninety years earlier India had come under the British Crown, Queen Victoria had reigned; and now, by a strange quirk of history, her great-grandson was entrusted with the job of ending that association. India was to be a republic by her own choice, and also by her own choice to remain in the Commonwealth.

Mountbatten had many glittering qualities, but he had also some sober assets. Purposeful, ambitious and determined, with a resolute will once his mind was made up, he was a man of prodigious industry and irresistible drive, capable of marshalling facts as well as men, and mobilising both to achieve the end in view. Politics to him was a military operation where the separate pieces of an uneasy, complicated puzzle had first to be sorted out, persuaded into place, rearranged gently but with firmness and eased into an ordered pattern.

Mountbatten was only forty-six when his appointment as Viceroy was announced. His wife—a goddaughter of Edward VII who was a close friend of her grandfather, Sir Ernest Cassel—was a year younger. They had become engaged in Delhi in 1921 while Mountbatten was touring India on the staff of the Prince of Wales (later the Duke of Windsor) and were married in the following year. On July 18, 1947, they celebrated their silver wedding in Delhi.

Until the eve of the Second World War the Mountbattens had

lived the gay gilded life of the set which gravitated around the Prince of Wales up to the time of his abdication as Edward VIII in 1936. The war had wrought far-reaching changes in both of them, and they emerged with their character and outlook transmuted and inspired by a new sense of duty and service. Edwina Mountbatten had matched her husband's spectacular war record with her own odyssey of devoted service to the ill and wounded on many war fronts. She came to India resolved to make her husband's mission succeed and to serve the country as best she could, but it is doubtful if she visualised the very important and influential role she was to play before and after independence.

On Nehru particularly Edwina Mountbatten made an immediate impact. She had known few Indians well before coming to India, but for many years she had known and admired greatly Sarojini Naidu, the poetess and politician, who had been to school with her mother. Sarojini, a bubbling effervescent woman, was a brilliant if malicious conversationalist, a devastating mimic with a personality which was flamboyant, but lovable, often explosive and sometimes irascible, and with a wit composed equally of arsenic and old lace. She was not a person in whose presence one relaxed. But Edwina Mountbatten could be such a person. She sensed that what Nehru most wanted and did not know how to achieve was to relax. And in the coming months, at the height of many tense grave crises, she was able to coax him into a few moments of relaxation, in company, or along with her husband or daughter or by herself. More than any other person she was able to soothe his strained, tired, overwrought nerves, and Nehru soon found in her an understanding and intelligent companion, able to reinforce some of his views, to persuade him away from others, to take his mind momentarily from the things which obsessed or irritated him, a companion always willing to help but never to intrude.

Even before Mountbatten's arrival the political atmosphere, embittered by the deepening cleavage between the Congress and the League, had exploded in an outbreak of fierce rioting in the Punjab involving Hindus, Muslims and Sikhs. For some weeks before these happenings Gandhi had been touring eastern India where there had been similar Hindu-Muslim outbreaks, particularly in the Noakhali area of southeast Bengal. The Punjab conflagration which began on

March 4th was not to subside until after independence, reaching its peak in the immediate aftermath of partition.

On March 4th thirteen persons were killed and 105 injured in communal clashes in the Punjab's capital, Lahore, and the trouble soon spread to other important cities and towns such as Amritsar, Attock, Multan and Rawalpindi. The immediate cause of the flare-up was the resignation of the Muslim Premier, Malik Khizr Hyat Khan, who was opposed to the politics of the Muslim League and whose coalition cabinet was based on Hindu-Sikh-Muslim cooperation. Had the British authorities headed by the Governor, Sir Evan Jenkins, acted more decisively and stepped into the breach created by the resignation of the Ministry, the situation might have been brought more promptly under control. But the days of the British Raj in India were drawing to a close, and few British officials had their hearts fully in the primary job of maintaining law and order. In the minds of some of them, the prospect of civil chaos in India on the eve of independence was not without its allurement. What better testimony to the inability of Indian rulers and administrators to control the communal situation once the strong arm of British authority was withdrawn! Nearly a century before, Lord Lawrence of Mutiny fame had preached the gospel of "masterly inactivity," and its echoes were to linger and reverberate in the Punjab and elsewhere as the British prepared to leave India.

On March 5th the death toll mounted in Lahore, with seven persons killed and eighty-two wounded by police firing. The disturbances in Lahore were brought under control by March 11th, but elsewhere the conflagration continued. Nehru, accompanied by three Punjab leaders, visited the riot-affected areas of Rawalpindi, where the Sikhs made strong representations for more adequate protection. The scene of carnage and destruction, a grim foretaste of things to come, shocked Nehru. "I have seen ghastly sights and I have heard of behaviour by human beings which would degrade brutes," he said on his return to Delhi. "All that has happened in the Punjab is intimately connected with political affairs. If there is a grain of intelligence in any person he must realise that whatever political objective he may aim at, this is not the way to attain it. Any such attempt must bring, as it has in a measure brought, ruin and destruction."

Even the London *Times*, normally tender to the Muslim League, was moved to rebuke it. Deprecating attempts to enforce a communal dictatorship by unconstitutional agitation, it warned:

The danger is in no way lessened if the agitation claims to be based on democratic principles. It is a curious feature of the campaign conducted in the Punjab by the Muslim League that a 56 per cent. majority in the province enables it to invoke these [democratic] principles while it fiercely controverts them in other parts of India.

On March 20th, on the eve of Mountbatten's arrival in India, it was officially announced that 2,049 persons had been killed in the Punjab and over 1,000 seriously injured. Two days after he had assumed office, on March 26th, there was another flare-up in Calcutta, and shortly after an outbreak of Hindu-Muslim violence in Bombay. The train of violence lighted by Jinnah's call for a Direct Action day showed no signs of subsiding.

Nehru had been among the first to interview the new Viceroy. He was acquainted with Mountbatten, having met him and Lady Mountbatten a little over a year earlier at Singapore in the closing phases of the Southeast Asia Command. They had liked each other and got on well together.

"Did Mountbatten try to indoctrinate you?" an acquaintance had asked Nehru on his return from Malaya.

Nehru laughed. "We did a bit of mutual indoctrination."

The process was to continue in India.

At their first meeting Mountbatten, greatly daring, asked Nehru his opinion of Jinnah.

"Success," said Nehru, "came to Jinnah very late—when he was past sixty. The secret of his success has been to take up a permanently negative attitude."

He did not add that the British attitude to the League's campaign for Pakistan had not a little to do with this success. But Mountbatten, always impressively briefed, doubtless appreciated this. Nor did Nehru add that success in his own case had come too soon.

Nehru made two other points in this conversation which are significant in view of his policy as Prime Minister.

"What do you think is the biggest single problem facing India?" asked Mountbatten.

Nehru's answer came without hesitation. "The economic one."

Discussing India's connection with the Commonwealth, Mountbatten inquired what form it should take, and was surprised when Nehru suggested that it should take the form of an Indo-Anglian union with both countries enjoying common citizenship.

To Mountbatten this seemed a closer bond than the Commonwealth status, but that was not how Nehru saw it. Over the past few days Jawaharlal had been turning this problem over in his mind, and had discussed it with Krishna Menon, whose opinion on matters, political and constitutional, he was beginning to value greatly. Menon had accompanied him on his tour of Republican Spain ten years earlier, and over a long period had done useful work as a Congress publicist in London. He had an agile, resourceful mind and an astute understanding, and his value to Nehru lay in his ability to rationalise Jawaharlal's instinctive, often emotional ideas. Lean, stringy and saturnine, with a caustic tongue and a look of imperious disdain, he suggests (too easily perhaps) the Grey Eminence hovering balefully in the background. Actually he is not that sinister. Menon knew that Nehru had been stirred by Churchill's offer of an Anglo-French Union when France lay mortally stricken. Why could India not remain a member of the Commonwealth on the basis of common citizenship, not Dominion status? It would entail a two-way traffic and ensure reciprocity.

From Gandhi, Mountbatten was to hear what he felt was an even more startling suggestion, for in the midst of several genial interviews he had with the Viceroy, the Mahatma blandly proposed that the Interim Government should resign and that Jinnah should be invited to form a cabinet. Gandhi felt that this was the only way in which to end the communal blood bath.

"I am absolutely sincere," he assured Mountbatten.

With Jinnah, Mountbatten's contacts were less cordial. The Qaid-i-Azam at that time was seventy, an ailing man, obsessed with a mission, who was to die a little over a year later. Jinnah had always been cold, formal and precise, his pencil-thin body encased in elegant clothes, with a slight touch of the theatrical in his manner enhanced by his monocle and the greying hair in which a white lock stood aggressively like a plume.

Jinnah was icily courteous, and his manner did not thaw when his opening gambit was abruptly checkmated by the Viceroy.

"I will enter into discussion on one condition only," he loftily insisted when they sat down to talk.

"Mr. Jinnah," said Mountbatten, "I am not prepared to discuss conditions or indeed the present situation until I have had the chance of making your acquaintance and knowing more about yourself."

The interview ended on a courteous but formal note.

"My God!" was Mountbatten's reaction to a member of his staff. "He was cold. It took most of the interview to unfreeze him."

What was Jinnah's reaction?

"The Viceroy does not understand," he told his secretary.

The purpose of these talks was to ascertain whether it was still possible for the Congress and the League to reach an agreement on the basis of the Cabinet Mission Plan. Such a task would have been difficult of achievement in normal circumstances. But circumstances were far from normal, for the talks were conducted against a turbulent background of strife and disorder, with riots and bloodshed at various points punctuating a civil-disobedience movement which the League had launched against the Congress Ministry in the Frontier province, where 97 per cent of the population was Muslim.

By mid-April the situation had grown so incendiary that on Mountbatten's persuasion Gandhi and Jinnah made a joint appeal calling on Hindus and Muslims to return to reason, to avoid, both in speech and in writing, any incitements to acts of violence and disorder. The appeal, released on April 15th, called upon all the communities in India, "to whatever persuasion they may belong, not only to refrain from all acts of violence and disorder but also to avoid both in speech and writing, any words which might be construed as an incitement to such acts."

It was a counsel of perfection inspired by the highest motives and directed especially at the two storm centres of the Punjab and the Frontier, both of which contained Muslim majorities. But in neither province did the fires of hate show signs of dying.

Clearly there was no chance of the Congress and the League reaching an agreement on the basis of the Cabinet Mission Plan. Now it was either partition or chaos, and even that surgical operation would entail much blood-letting.

To delay partition would be to increase and intensify the orgy of civil war. The Interim Government at Delhi containing nine members with Congress affiliations or sympathies and five Muslim League representatives was a house divided against itself. There was no positive initiative or direction from the centre.

Gandhi was still implacably opposed to the idea of partition, but to Nehru and Vallabhbhai Patel it now seemed that Pakistan was preferable to chaos and to an India drowned irrevocably in a sea of anarchy. But the Congress was insistent that the British Government, having set a deadline for their departure, should reveal their blueprint of Operation Withdrawal. British motives were still suspect.

"This simply cannot go on," Nehru complained to Mountbatten. "If you do not produce a plan I shall resign."

Patel was more positive and didactic.

"You won't govern yourself," he accused the Viceroy, "and you won't let us govern."

On April 19th Mountbatten revealed to his immediate entourage that he was beginning to think that Pakistan was inevitable. Not many days later he charged Lord Ismay, his chief of staff, who knew India well and was said to be sympathetic to Muslim aspirations, to sound Jinnah on his reactions to a Pakistan based on a divided Bengal and Punjab, both Muslim majority provinces but with considerable non-Muslim elements.

"Better a moth-eaten Pakistan," said Jinnah bitterly, "than no Pakistan at all."

This view the Qaid-i-Azam confirmed in an interview with Mountbatten on April 23rd. The Viceroy's press attaché, Alan Campbell-Johnson, notes of the meeting, "His mood was . . . accommodating. He seemed to be resigned to the partition of the Punjab and Bengal."

But Jinnah's mood of resignation was transient. Not a week later he was again on the warpath, demanding a Pakistan with an undivided Punjab and Bengal. As usual, he had a difficulty for every solution.

At this juncture Mountbatten sensed that speed was the essence of the situation, and that the deadline of June, 1948, would have to be accelerated to an earlier date if the transfer of power was to be effected with the minimum of chaos and bloodshed. He accordingly set out to devise a Draft Plan which after considerable discussion in India and London allowed for the principle of partition but provided

for early Dominion status as an interim arrangement based upon the
Government of India Act of 1935 with modifications. It envisaged
one or two sovereign States, and if one, stipulated that power should
be transferred to the existing Central Government at Delhi.

Nehru, shown an earlier draft by Mountbatten at Simla, had reacted strongly. In his view such a plan had clearly to recognise that
India and the Constituent Assembly were the successors to British
India, while Pakistan and the Muslim League were the seceders. The
concept of India as a continuing entity should be preserved, he persisted. Nehru's view was that India must carry on in every way as
before, Pakistan being merely the outcome of permission to dissident
provinces to secede. The work of the Central Government at Delhi
must not be interrupted. Primarily as a result of his insistence, the
original Mountbatten Plan as modified by London was further modified to soothe the susceptibilities of Congress.

Jinnah meanwhile had been declaring that if the British Government decided that India should be divided, the Central Government
at Delhi must be dissolved and all powers should be transferred to the
Constituent Assemblies formed to represent Pakistan and Hindustan. But on the successor-seceder principle Nehru's view was to prevail.

Within the Congress it had been obvious since the release of the
Working Committee in June, 1945, that the Mahatma had politically receded into the background. Authority was henceforth concentrated mainly in the hands of Nehru and Patel, who took the
major decisions, many of them including the vital decision on Pakistan, contrary to the Mahatma's own views and inclinations.

Of the two, Patel was the more authoritarian but also the more
practical. Behind a seemingly hard, inflexible mind and will Vallabhbhai concealed a capacity for resilience and realistic compromise. He
might never know when he was beaten, but he knew what to do
when he was checkmated. Intellectually and temperamentally he was
poles apart from Nehru, to whom he was also at times personally
antipathetic. His loyalty and devotion were bounded by India, and
with the verbal irony of which he was capable Patel was wont on
occasions to dwell sarcastically on Nehru's international incursions.
He liked to call himself a peasant, although his academic background
was by no means unimpressive. He sneered, with a droop of his heavy-

lidded eyes, at "cultured intellectuals," and listening to him one sensed the chief victim at whom his sneer was aimed.

The miracle of the Mahatma is that he could attract to himself such bewilderingly disparate personalities as those typified by Nehru and Patel. The two men were to work closely together until the coming of independence and after, each complementing or compensating for the qualities or quirks in the other. Nehru's emotionalism and strong exhibitionist streak—a lingering legacy of the spoilt child—often irritated the Sardar who asserted himself at times by administering a stern verbal spanking to the offender.

But like Jawaharlal, Vallabhbhai also recognised the outstanding qualities of his colleague. He realised the supreme patriotism of the younger man, whose vanity and susceptibility to flattery, however exuberant, would never yield to the blandishments of those who might seek to gain his political support by probing the chinks in his personal armour. He was, Vallabhbhai conceded—perhaps reluctantly—the Galahad of Indian politics—as the Mahatma had described him years before, "a knight *sans peur, sans reproche.*" Flattery might dent his armour but could not pierce it.

On May 18th Mountbatten, accompanied by his wife, left for London in response to "a courteous but firm summons" by the Socialist Government, who awaited the Viceroy's personal elucidation of the Congress and League reactions to the Draft Plan before proceeding further. The Viceroy had barely arrived in London when Jinnah in India loosed a calculated time bomb demanding an 800-mile corridor to link the eastern and western wings of Pakistan. Nehru's reaction was sharp. In an interview to the United Press of America he described the demand as "fantastic and absurd," a characteristic phrase which Jawaharlal employs when confronted with what he deems is the height of perversity.

"We stand for a union of India with the right to particular areas to opt out," Nehru explained. "We envisage no compulsion. If there is no proper settlement on this basis without further claims being advanced, then we shall proceed with making and implementing the constitution for the Union of India."

Mountbatten returned to Delhi on May 31st and immediately set about securing the consent of the Congress and League leaders to the Draft Plan as approved by Whitehall. The Plan accepted the principle of partition, leaving the Congress and the League to devise the details, the British Government undertaking to transfer power to the two States on the basis of full Dominion status with power to secede from the Commonwealth. The date of this transfer was advanced from June, 1948 to August 15, 1947.

Both Nehru and Patel were reconciled to the idea of partition, realising that with the advent of Pakistan, Jinnah could no longer block the progress of India.

"By cutting off the head," said Nehru, "we shall get rid of the headache."

On June 3rd Mountbatten secured the consent of the Congress and League leaders to the Plan which was announced the same day. That evening Mountbatten, Nehru, Jinnah and the Sikh leader Baldev Singh broadcast their acceptance to the country.

Nehru's was the most thoughtful of the four broadcasts, and couched in language reflective, restrained and wistful.

"We are little men serving great causes," he observed. "But because the cause is great something of that greatness falls upon us also."

They all disliked the vivisection of India, he said, but they could not let India bleed continuously. A surgical operation was preferable in the circumstances.

Gandhi was still adamantly opposed to partition. Speaking after his evening prayer meeting, shortly before Nehru broadcast, he levelled an indirect rebuke at him.

"He is our King," said the Mahatma. "But we should not be impressed by everything the King does or does not do. If he has devised something good for us we should praise him. If he has not, then we shall say so."

Independence was only three months away, but India in the birth pangs of freedom endured an agonising travail. In the City of Kings, which is Delhi, the two parties sat down to divide the spoils of political power, from the armed and civilian services and police, to aircraft, ships, guns, money, desks, chairs and typewriters. A boundary commission pronounced its award through its British chairman, Sir Cyril Radcliffe, who was compelled to declare his view following a deadlock between the Indian and Pakistani members. In Bengal and the Punjab the provincial legislatures decided on the partition of their respective areas. A referendum in the Frontier province resulted in an overwhelming majority for the Muslim League, which also secured Sylhet district in Assam. In Delhi also the Princes met to decide to which of the two States they should accede, wandering around the vast reception rooms of Viceroy's House "like a letter without a stamp"—as one of the more cynical Dewans or princely Prime Ministers observed of his erstwhile master. Feudalism was dying with the passing of the British Raj.

Outside Delhi the two-way exodus of Muslims, Sikhs and Hindus to and from India and the Pakistan of tomorrow had begun. Not since the migration of the Israelites had history witnessed so mammoth a movement of the human race as started to cross the Punjab borders from late June until nearly a year later. In that period some ten million human beings were on the march, while away in the East, on the borders of divided Bengal, another odd million trekked their way to safety.

In the Punjab, soon to be sliced like an apple into an eastern and western sector, belonging respectively to India and Pakistan, the situation was serious. As the deadline of August 15th approached, both sectors erupted into carnage and flame, and it was against this grim backdrop of frenzy and slaughter that the curtain rose on partition, and on the freedom of India and Pakistan.

Jinnah had left Delhi for Karachi on August 7th to become the first Governor-General of Pakistan. It had earlier been understood that Mountbatten would remain as the Governor-General of both the Dominions; but at the last moment Jinnah had staked his own claim. At the invitation of the Congress Government Mountbatten decided to stay on as Governor-General of India.

Gandhi too had left Delhi for Calcutta on August 7th en route to Noakhali, where Hindu-Muslim conflicts, accompanied by killing, pillage and arson, had raged for some days. He was not in Delhi on the night of the declaration of independence. But inside the massive pile of red and white sandstone where India's Constituent Assembly met to witness the birth of independence, he was remembered.

Rajendra Prasad, as President of the Assembly, paid a tribute to the Mahatma "who has been our beacon light, our guide and philosopher, during the last thirty years," and the tribute was echoed in Nehru's message to the nation. He declared:

On this day our first thoughts go to the architect of this freedom, the Father of our Nation, who, embodying the old spirit of India, held aloft the torch of freedom and lighted up the darkness that surrounded us. We have often been unworthy followers of his and have strayed from his message, but not only we, but the succeeding generations, will remember this message and bear the imprint in their hearts of this great son of India, magnificent in his faith and strength, courage and humility. We shall never allow that torch of freedom to be blown out, however high the wind or stormy the tempest.

In the Constituent Assembly Nehru ended his moving speech with memorable and prophetic words:

And so we have to labour and to work and work hard, to make our dreams real. These dreams are for India, but they are also for the world, for all nations and peoples are too closely knit together today, for any one of them to imagine that it can live apart. Peace has been said to be indivisible, so is freedom, so is prosperity now, and so also is disaster in this one world, that can no longer be split into isolated fragments.

Shortly after midnight Nehru intoned the text of the pledge to which every member of the Constituent Assembly dedicated himself. It read:

At this solemn moment, when the people of India, through suffering and sacrifice, have secured freedom, I, a member of the Constituent Assembly of India, do dedicate myself in all humility to the service of India and her people to the end that this ancient land attain her rightful place in the world and make her full and willing contribution to the promotion of world peace and the welfare of mankind.

The proceedings inside the Chamber ended on a formal note, but there was a touch of anti-climax when, according to the prescribed ritual, Nehru and Prasad proceeded to Viceroy's House where Mountbatten was awaiting them. The two leaders were charged with the duty of informing the Viceroy that the Constituent Assembly had assumed power for the governance of India, and of inviting him to be the first Governor-General.

The ceremony, which took place amid a barrage of flash bulbs, ended with Nehru elaborately handing over to the Governor-General a long parchment envelope with the words, "May I submit to you the portfolios of the new Cabinet?"

When the two Indian leaders had left, Mountbatten, surrounded by his entourage, carefully opened the envelope to discover its contents. It was empty! Someone had forgotten to insert the enclosure.

* * *

The Appointed Day had come, the day which Nehru himself described in his message to the nation as the day appointed by destiny.

When freedom came Nehru was three months short of his fifty-eighth birthday. Patel, who was to share with Jawaharlal the major burden of office until his death in December, 1950, was fourteen years his senior, while Gandhi, destined to die at the hands of an assassin before six months had passed, was approaching his seventy-eighth year.

Behind the three men lay nearly three decades of tumultuous toil for the freedom of India. Gandhi's political influence in the councils of the Congress had waned perceptibly during the past two years, but his personal influence was still considerable, and the moral authority he wielded was potent enough to alter political decisions of which he disapproved.

To both Nehru and Patel he was Bapu, which means Father, and like a father he was capable of exciting love along with reverence and awe. Though he had a parental kindliness, he also had a sternness which could be steely. Nehru and Patel were disparate beings, but both had been attracted to the Mahatma as a man of action, as an individual who believed in doing things, in energising men's minds into action but action based on peaceful methods and directed not only against foreign rule but against the evils, economic and social, which encumbered India. They were impressed by his instinctive communion with the people and his complete identification with them. "He did not descend from the top," wrote Nehru. "He seemed to emerge from the millions of India."

Often he baffled and exasperated them both. Believing in absolutes, the Mahatma could not be easily shaken from a point of view, and sometimes his mental processes were difficult to follow or understand. But the greatest lesson he taught his countrymen—to shed fear and hate—was embedded deeply in the hearts and minds of both men. Patel, it is true, had always had the reputation of being a good hater, but even his hatred was tinged on occasion by a touch of magnanimity. There was a core of serenity in the character of this tough, turbulent and turgid man.

Fearlessness—that was the clue to Gandhi's character, and the greatest gift he had given India. So Nehru often reflected in those days and the coming years. It was a teaching in line with Indian tradition, for the gospel of *abhaya* (fearlessness of mind and body) had been preached in the ancient books and repeated by some of India's wisest sages, by Yagnavalkya who flourished at the court of Janaka, father of Sita, heroine of the *Ramayana*, and by Chanakya, adviser to the Emperor Chandragupta.

And yet Gandhi's philosophy, personal and political, was not one of quietism or even of pietism but of action—firm, resolute and often rebellious. If he drove others he also drove himself. The Mahatma, Nehru recalled, was the beloved slave-driver, a phrase which one of Gandhi's Muslim disciples had often used in describing him in the past.

Fearlessness, Action, Freedom from Hate—these were to be Nehru's guiding stars in the critical years ahead just as in the years gone by they had been the stars to blazon Gandhi's message across the tired and troubled sky of India. But at the moment the omens were unpropitious. Even as the country emerged from subjection into freedom, the flames of civil conflagration raged fiercely around them. India was reenacting the drama of Cain and Abel, but on a monstrous, gargantuan scale, with brother slaying brother in a fit of religious frenzy and hate on a dimension unequalled in the history of any fratricidal clash; for this, ironically enough, was officially described not as armed warfare but as civil conflict.

India was being partitioned. Was the freedom of India and Pakistan to perish in a holocaust of fire and blood? Gandhi, even before the proclamation of independence, had left Delhi for distant Noakhali but was persuaded to stay in strife-torn Calcutta, where he laboured for a month to dispel hate with love, calling on all people, Hindus and Muslims, to shed their fear and to canalise their energy into peaceful action for the building up of India and Pakistan.

In Delhi, as the refugees from Pakistan converged on the capital, on foot, by train, in bullock carts and by plane, the full horror of the hate lust loosed by partition dawned on the people. The refugees came on an endless tide, the dead borne in litters, the ill, the maimed, the wounded, children orphaned or lost during the long trek, widows bereft of their husbands, carrying with them the pathetic debris of their belongings, homeless, starved, impoverished, embittered, victims of a fear and hate which now also seized them. As they poured in with their tales of suffering and woe, visible victims of a madness unleashed by both sides, Delhi's Hindus and Sikhs fell upon the Muslims in reprisal.

In India itself forty million Muslims had decided to remain, and Delhi, once the proud capital of the Moguls, contained many thousands of the Islamic faith. Despoiled of their houses and farms in the Punjab, the Hindu and Sikh refugees found themselves homeless in Delhi, and it was not long before they proceeded forcibly to evict Muslim families from their houses and even turned their sacred mosques into dwelling places. On the other side of the border in Pakistan the same things were happening, Hindu temples and Sikh *gurudwaras* [2] being desecrated and turned to domestic use. Amid this terrible carnage and conflict there were in both India and Pakistan many instances where Muslims safeguarded Hindus and Sikhs, while the latter in turn protected their Muslim brethren.

To Nehru the first days of freedom were as gall and wormwood. In the madness which had seized both sides he felt that the first fruits of the independence for which they had struggled for so long had rotted ere they were ripe. Within two days after the declaration of independence he was on his way to the Punjab, accompanied by Pakistan's Prime Minister, Liaquat Ali Khan, their principal objectives being the towns of Ambala and Amritsar, where the Sikhs and Muslims had indulged in mutual and indiscriminate slaughter. Nehru was shocked by the "terrible orgy" he witnessed. He rebuked the Sikhs roundly.

"India," he declared in a broadcast, "is not a communal State but a democratic State in which every citizen has equal rights. The Government is determined to protect these rights."

He announced that the Governments of the two Punjabs, with the resolute help of the Governments of India and Pakistan, were determined to put a stop to this frenzy.

But the situation with the two-way trail of blood was mounting to monstrous proportions. Within an area of barely 30,000 square miles some 10,000,000 people were on the move between India and Pakistan, and from the air, through a white fog of dust, one could

[2] Centres of worship in which are kept the *Granth*, or Bible, of the Sikhs.

sometimes discern a single one-way "crocodile" of carts, cattle and human beings snaking their way in a murky file fifty miles long.

The caprice of nature conspired with the hate of man. Floods came, covering the rich crowded plains of the Punjab—as the five rivers of the province overflowed their banks, marooning in their pitiless wake thousands of these miserable folk, drowning men, women, children and cattle, and entrapping entire encampments of refugees already numb with terror, weariness and want.

Unless this insane carnage could be contained and controlled Nehru realised that the poison must spread to Delhi and beyond. During the next few days he strained every nerve to prevent it from seeping into the capital. But by then the frenzy had assumed the dimensions of a tidal wave.

This was Nehru's shining hour. Sad and dispirited though he seemed outwardly, he continued to display his extraordinary physical energy, resilience and courage, often driving or walking alone into a crowd of enraged Hindus and Sikhs while they were attacking and pillaging Muslim homes, himself personally chastising looters and other more unruly and menacing elements. In this crisis his courage and example were superb.

"He vindicates," wrote a British observer at that time,[3] "one's faith in the humanist and the civilised intellect. Almost alone in the turmoil of communalism, with all its variations from individual intrigue to mass madness, he speaks with the voice of reason and charity." Not only did he speak. He acted.

There was another voice to reinforce his. On September 9th Gandhi arrived in Delhi after a month's stay in Calcutta, and was horrified by the gory spectacle which the capital presented.

"I am prepared," said the Mahatma, "to understand the anger of the refugees whom fate has driven from West Punjab. But anger is little short of madness. It can only make matters worse in every way. Retaliation is no remedy. It makes the original disease much worse. I, therefore, ask all those who are engaged in these senseless murders, arson and loot to stay their hands."

That same night Nehru in a speech broadcast from Delhi appealed to the sanity and civilised instincts of his countrymen, now in danger of being lost in a fit of frenzied hate:

[3] Alan Campbell-Johnson in *Mission with Mountbatten* (Robert Hale, 1951).

During the last few weeks I have wandered about West Punjab and East Punjab and my mind is full with the horror of the things that I saw and that I heard. During these last few days in the Punjab and in Delhi, I have supped my fill of horror. That, indeed, is the only feast that we can have now. . . .

This morning our leader, our master, Mahatma Gandhi, came to Delhi, and I went to see him and I sat by his side, for a while, and wondered how low we had fallen from the great ideals that he had placed before us.

I go to the country-side, and people with spikes and all sorts of destructive weapons, when they see me, shout "Mahatma Gandhi ki jai! Jawaharlal ki jai!" I feel ashamed to hear these cries from these people, who might have committed murder, loot and arson, in the name of Mahatma Gandhi. It is not by shouting slogans that they will wash off the evil deeds that they have done. And even we will not get over these evil deeds by just honouring the Mahatma in name, and not following what he had told us all these long years.

What is happening now is something directly inimical, and so directly opposed to these ideals. The very thought of it shames me, and makes me sometimes doubt if all the good work that we have done in these many years is not going to bear fruit at all. And yet that doubt cannot remain for long. For I do believe that good work must bear good results just as I do believe that evil must bear evil consequences. There has been enough of evil work in this country. Let us put an end to it, and start good work, and try to follow the great lessons that the Mahatma has taught us.

Nehru, like Gandhi, visited the camps of Hindu and Sikh refugees, where they were sometimes greeted with hostile, even threatening, cries and demonstrations, but he also made it a point to visit the refugee camps for Muslims in Delhi, the largest of which was in the Purana Qila,[4] while another was housed near the historic tomb of Humayun, second of the Mogul emperors.

From across the border came reports of similar atrocities committed in Pakistan—at Lahore, Karachi, Quetta, Nawabshah, Bannu and Peshawar—where the Hindu and Sikh minorities were left helpless. Nehru, with Gandhi, raised his voice with equal firmness against these outrages. Both men appealed to Hindus, Sikhs and Muslims to live and let live, to forget the past and not to dwell unduly on their sufferings but to extend the hand of fellowship to each other and to resolve to live at peace with each other. It was wrong, both

[4] Old Fort.

men insisted, that a single Muslim should feel unsafe in India's capital, as it was wrong that Hindus and Sikhs should be in fear of their lives in Pakistan.

At one of his prayer meetings during these critical days Gandhi described a visit he had paid to a Muslim refugee camp where an old Muslim in tattered clothes had stood quietly in a row with his wife beside him to greet the Mahatma. Gandhi noticed that they both bore knife wounds.

"I hung my head in shame when I saw them," he confessed to his startled audience.

How many perished in the two-way trek between India and Pakistan no one can compute with any certainty. The more responsible estimates place the figure at 200,000, roughly 20 for every thousand on the basis of the total stream of refugees being approximately 10,000,000. Compared with the Bengal famine of 1943, which claimed some 3,500,000 lives, this seems a small figure, but in terms of area and population it entailed a turmoil far in excess of what the Bengal famine provoked.

The rehabilitation of refugees was a major priority on the constructive programme of independent India because it was vitally linked with the two imperatives of unity and stability. That all three were achieved within five years of independence when the princely States were liquidated, the constitution enacted and India's first general elections (involving 160,000,000 voters, the vast majority of them illiterate) peacefully held is a remarkable tribute to Nehru as an administrator and political leader. He was to achieve this in a troubled, even stormy context, against the background of Kashmir, Hyderabad and Junagadh at home and of Korea abroad, to say nothing of other vexations, domestic and foreign.

Jawaharlal had learned well the lessons which the Mahatma had taught him, grafting on them the outlook and attitude which his Western upbringing and continued contacts abroad had helped him to appreciate. In him, therefore, as a leader at a particular juncture India was especially fortunate, for, like India, a bridge between the Occident and the Orient, Jawaharlal represents as perhaps no other living statesman does a finely tempered synthesis of the East and the West.

Nehru would echo without self-consciousness or affectation the words which an Englishman, Lord Halifax, who was also Viceroy of India, held up as an ideal for the country. The spirit these words represent is also his: "In thought, faith; in deed, courage; in life, service. So may India be great."

The past nine years in India have been moulded on that pattern of effort and achievement.

21

END OF AN EPOCH

OVER Delhi's chill winter air came the lilt of Gandhi's favourite chant, a song of praise to God with which his evening prayer meeting always ended:

> Raghupati, Raghava Raja Ram,
> Patita Pavana Sita Ram,
> Ishvara Allah tērē nam
> Sab ko sammati dē bhagvan.
>
> (Rama, King of the Universe,
> Who makes the sinner pure,
> Who is both Ishvara and Allah [1]
> Who gives his blessing to all.)

It was the evening of January 29, 1948, the last day on which Gandhi was to be present at evening prayers.

On January 20th, two days after he had broken his last fast which he had undertaken in an agonised attempt to induce all Indians—Hindus, Sikhs and Muslims—"to live like brothers," Gandhi's prayer meeting had been disturbed by a crude bomb exploding some fifty yards from where he was seated. A Hindu youth, Madan Lal, described as a refugee from West Punjab, was arrested for the offence. In his pocket was a hand grenade.

Gandhi was unruffled, and at his prayer meeting the next day he gently rebuked the offender. Probably the young man, he said, looked upon him as an enemy of Hinduism. The Mahatma had ended his

---

[1] Hindu and Muslim names for God, respectively.

fast only when he had received assurances that the Muslims would be allowed to move freely and unharmed in Delhi and that their mosques, forcibly occupied by Hindu and Sikh refugees, would be returned to them. Many Hindu and Sikh extremists resented this.

Nehru, who had also started a sympathetic fast, was asked by the Mahatma on January 18th to end it. "May you long remain Jawahar,[2] the jewel of India," wrote Gandhi in a painfully scribbled note.

The bomb incident of January 20th disturbed both Nehru and Patel, who insisted that the Mahatma should be adequately protected by policemen in plain clothes. But Gandhi would have none of it.

"Were there any noises at your prayer meeting today, Bapu?" Rajkumari Amrit Kaur, Health Minister and ardent disciple of the Mahatma, inquired of him on January 28th.

"No," said Gandhi. "But your question means that you are worrying about me. If I am to die by the bullet of a madman I must do so smiling. There must be no anger within me. God must be in my heart and on my lips."

He was to die within less than forty-eight hours. A fact that disturbed Gandhi during the last few days of his life was the widening rift between Nehru and Patel. Angered by the massacre of Hindus and Sikhs in Pakistan, Patel was nettled by what he felt was undue solicitude on the part of Nehru—as also of the Mahatma—for the Muslims in India. With characteristic bluntness Patel had proclaimed in a public speech that Muslims were not to be trusted unless they specifically declared their loyalty to India.

It was Patel who had the last interview with Gandhi on the evening of January 30th before the Mahatma left for his prayer meeting on the lawn by the house of Mr. G. D. Birla, the well known industrialist, with whom he was staying. Nehru and Azad were scheduled to see him after the prayer meeting.

He walked slowly across the lawn, his hands resting, as was his wont, on the shoulders of his two granddaughters, Manu and Abha, who flanked him. As they made their way to the meeting place, a short thick-set man darted forward and saluted Gandhi with folded hands in the Indian gesture of *namasthe*. He bent as if to touch the Mahatma's feet.

Gandhi returned the greeting, his hands also folded in *namasthe*.

[2] Jawahar means "jewel."

Suddenly the man produced a revolver and fired three shots at point-blank range into Gandhi's slight body. Two shots entered his chest while the third lodged in his abdomen.

The Mahatma's hands, folded in friendly greeting, sagged slowly to his sides. His knees bent and he collapsed in a small heap to the ground.

"Hé Ram," [3] he said, and sighed softly as he fell.

His eyes closed and a grey ashen pallor spread over his face. As he lay on the ground a trickle of blood ran in a crimson stain on his spotless white *khadi* garment.

They carried him inside but he was already unconscious. Within a few moments he was dead.

Nehru heard the news at his residence and hurried to Birla House, his mind numb with the horror of this overwhelming tragedy. They had laid Gandhi on a mattress on the floor where he was accustomed to sit every day transacting his work. He lay there in his last sleep, the dome of his head cushioned in flowers, his face pale but serene with a look that was calm and peaceful and noble.

Nehru knelt by the side of his dead master, and clasped the Mahatma's hand, clutching it like a child. He wept unrestrainedly, his body racked by sobs.

"The greatest treasure that we possessed we failed to protect," he was to accuse himself and his Government before the Constituent Assembly three days later.

Patel was also there, like Nehru overcome with grief but outwardly calm. The fragrance of incense filled the room. Alongside the mattress which was the Mahatma's bier, women knelt in prayer chanting softly the name of God—"Ram, Ram"—as Gandhi had spoken it when the hand of the assassin had felled him. [4]

Mountbatten, on hearing the news, came immediately. He was concerned for Nehru's safety since Jawaharlal's views on the treatment of the minorities were known to coincide with those of the Mahatma, and his life had also been threatened. Mountbatten knew of the rift between Nehru and Patel and, seeing both of them

---

[3] Invocation to God.

[4] The assassin's name was Nathuram Vinayak Godse, a member of a militant Hindu group and editor of a small provincial paper. He was subsequently tried and hanged.

together in the room, he acted with his instinctive sense of drama and timing.

"At my last interview with Gandhiji," he said looking at both of them, "he told me that his dearest wish was to bring about a full reconciliation between the two of you."

Nehru and Patel looked at each other, and then at Gandhi lying on the floor wrapped in his shroud of white homespun. They moved towards each other and embraced in a gesture of reconciliation.

Vast crowds had gathered around Birla House, and it was vital that they should be told authoritatively of Gandhi's death. Nehru came out to tell them. Thousands of people milled on the road outside the barred gates. Nehru, climbing on the gate, his wan, haggard face illuminated by a street lamp, addressed them.

"Mahatmaji," he said, "is gone."

His voice was choked with emotion and, having uttered a few sentences, he broke down, weeping openly. From the great crowd on the other side of the gate there came a sound like the moan and murmur of the sea as a wind carries the waves shorewards. The crowd wept. But Nehru recovered himself sufficiently to impress on them an urgent message.

"We can best serve Bapu," he declared, "by dedicating ourselves to the ideals for which he lived and the cause for which he died."

The hushed silence of his audience carried its affirmation.

It was decided that Jawaharlal and Patel should address the nation over the air, and the speeches of both men, unrehearsed and unprepared, were moving and dramatic. Despite their sense of numb sorrow both rose magnificently to the responsibility of the occasion. Nehru said:

The light has gone out of our lives, and there is darkness everywhere. I do not know what to tell you and how to say it. Our beloved leader, Bapu as we called him, the Father of the Nation, is no more. Perhaps I am wrong to say that. Nevertheless, we will not see him again as we have seen him for these many years. We will not run to him for advice and seek solace from him, and that is a terrible blow, not to me only, but to millions and millions in this country. And it is a little difficult to soften the blow by any other advice that I or anyone else can give you.

The light has gone out, I said, and yet I was wrong. For the light that shone in this country was no ordinary light. The light that has illumined this country for these many, many years will illumine this country for many more years, and a thousand years later, that light will still be seen in this country and the world will see it and it will give solace to innumerable hearts. For that light represented something more than the immediate present, it represented the living, the eternal truths, reminding us of the right path, drawing us from error, taking this ancient country to freedom.

All this has happened when there was so much more for him to do. We could never think that he was unnecessary or that he had done his task. But now, particularly, when we are faced with so many difficulties, his not being with us is a blow most terrible to bear.

A madman has put an end to his life, for I can only call him mad who did it, and yet there has been enough of poison spread in this country during the past years and months, and this poison has had an effect on people's minds. We must face this poison, we must root out this poison, and we must face all the perils that encompass us, and face them not madly or badly, but rather in the way that our beloved teacher taught us to face them.

The first thing to remember now is that none of us dare misbehave because he is angry. We have to behave like strong and determined people, determined to face all the perils that surround us, determined to carry out the mandate that our great teacher and our great leader has given us, remembering always that if, as I believe, his spirit looks upon us and sees us, nothing would displease his soul so much as to see that we have indulged in any small behaviour or any violence.

So we must not do that. But that does not mean that we should be weak, but rather that we should, in strength and in unity, face all the troubles that are in front of us. We must hold together and all our petty troubles and difficulties and conflicts must be ended in the face of this great disaster. A great disaster is a symbol to us to remember all the big things of life and forget the small things of which we have thought too much. In his death he has reminded us of the big things of life, that living truth, and if we remember that, then it will be well with India.

India mourned. The cremation took place the next day—a day of national fasting and prayer—when they bore Gandhi's body from Birla House to the banks of the Jumna where some 700,000 people awaited the cortege. Here was India, the India of contrasts and confusion, of strength, weakness, glory and spirit, with its poverty, its squalor, its filth, misery and dirt but also an India mighty and majestic.

There was little of ceremonial preparation in the final rite of cremation. Gandhi would have liked it so. As they bore his body and laid it tenderly on the funeral pyre—a pile of sandalwood logs banked high—Nehru paid his last homage to his master. He knelt and kissed the Mahatma's feet.

The great crowd pressed around the pyre as the chant of the priests rose like the thin lament of violins in the evening air, and Gandhi's son lit the logwood with a blazing brand. The flames, red and gold, leaped into the air reaching out to the sky as they consumed the mortal remains of the greatest man India had known since the Buddha.

From the vast crowd massed in a bowl of darkness and silhouetted by the flames rose a deep-throated cry, "Amar hogeye" (He is rendered immortal).

So instinctively the people echoed the age-old invocation contained in the Vedas:

Holy soul, may sun, air and fire be auspicious unto thee. Thy dear ones on the earth do not bewail their lot at thy departure for they know that thou art gone to the radiant regions of the blessed. May the waters of all rivers and oceans be helpful unto thee, and serve thee ever in thy good deeds for the welfare of all beings. May all space and its four quarters be open unto thee for thy good deeds.

Nehru returned to Rajghat, scene of the cremation, on the following morning. His face, still haggard, was inexpressibly sad and lined with care. He came with flowers which he laid by the charred remnants of the pyre.

"Bapuji," he said, "here are flowers. Today, at least, I can offer them to your bones and ashes. Where shall I offer them tomorrow, and to whom?"

He seemed to be seized with a sense of unutterable loneliness, and in the coming months, as the cares of office pressed heavily on him, he aged visibly, his shoulders, until then erect, wilting slightly with the stoop of years. But Gandhi, as he often recalled, would not have wanted it so.

Nehru, addressing the Constituent Assembly on February 2nd, said:

We mourn him; we shall always mourn him, because we are human and cannot forget our valued master; but I know that he would not like us to mourn him. No tears came to his eyes when his dearest and closest went away, only the firm resolve to persevere, to serve the great cause that he had chosen. So he would chide us if we merely mourn. That is a poor way of doing homage to him. The only way is to express our determination, to pledge ourselves anew, to conduct ourselves so and to dedicate ourselves to the great task which he undertook and which he accomplished to such a large extent. So we have to work, we have to labour, we have to sacrifice, and thus prove to some extent at least worthy followers of his. . . .

During the next twelve critical months when problems piled high on the Prime Minister's desk, Nehru was constantly to recall the Mahatma's injunctions and example, and remind the country that only by following them and working hard could India survive and endure.

Most of all Jawaharlal stressed the need for unity and tolerance, the urgency of bettering the lot of the common man, of rehabilitating the refugees and of harnessing and utilising for the general good the mighty resources of India. They must all work together and work hard to "change the face of India and make her great and prosperous."

"If we forget these lessons and ideals," he warned, "we betray our cause and our country."

He thought back over the years during which Gandhi had wandered about the country, clad only in his loincloth and with a staff, talking to the poor and the humble, to starving villagers, to dispossessed peasants, to hungry children clamouring for food in dusty hovels and on mud heaps, to angry and aggressive workers in mills and factories. Gandhi had trekked and traversed India from the Himalayas to the hills of the Northwest Frontier, from the Brahmaputra in the northeast and the green tea gardens of Assam to the palm groves and the paddy fields of the south, verdant and lush, as India tapers into the sea at Cape Comorin, which the country knows as Kanya Kumari.

Gandhi had always preached the gospel of returning good for evil, and had practised it. He had believed that the meek should inherit the earth, for he thought of India in terms of the poor and the oppressed and the downtrodden. To Nehru it now seemed that the first task for India, shocked into sobriety by the Mahatma's murder, was to find itself again, to rediscover the old values and place them in the new setting of a free country.

According to Gandhi's teachings this meant that the weight of the age-old burdens on the masses must be lifted and that their standards of living must improve. National wealth did not signify the concentration of riches in a few hands, for that way lay conflict and instability. If the meek were to inherit the earth, the dispossessed who were also the disinherited must find a better and freer place in it. India should concentrate on the things that united and strengthened it, for democracy meant discipline and tolerance and mutual regard just as freedom meant respect for the freedom of others.

Nehru's speeches in this period reiterate this theme. In a broadcast talk on the first anniversary of independence he posed a provocative question.

"All of us," he remarked, "talk of India and all of us demand many things from India. What do we give her in return? We can take nothing from her beyond what we give her. India will ultimately give us what we give her of love and service and productive and creative work. India will be what we are: our thoughts and actions will shape her. Born of her fruitful womb, we are children of hers, little bits of the India of today, and yet we are also the parents of the India of tomorrow. If we are big, so will India be, and if we grow little minded and narrow in outlook, so also will India be."

He was determined that the legacy of Gandhism should not perish with the death of its creator, and not only the statesman but the artist, thinker and scholar came to life in the beautiful and deeply moving speeches and statements he made at this time. In one such speech he observed how the generation whom Gandhi had done so much to uplift and inspire had in the end crucified him.

"He must have suffered," Nehru recalled of Gandhi, "suffered for the failing of this generation whom he had trained, suffered because we went away from the path that he had shown us, and ultimately the hand of a child of his—for he, after all, is as much a child of his as any other Indian—the hand of that child of his struck him down."

Yet Nehru adjured the nation not to mourn unduly but rather to strive to follow faithfully in their father's footsteps, for the Mahatma's death was in a sense the fulfilment of his life. Nehru insisted:

Even in his death there was a magnificence and complete artistry. It was from every point of view a fitting climax to the man and to the life he had lived. Indeed it heightened the lesson of his life. He died in the fullness of his powers and as he would no doubt have liked to die, at the moment of prayer. He died a martyr to the cause of unity to which he had always been devoted and for which he had worked unceasingly, more especially during the past year or more. He died suddenly as all men should wish to die. There was no fading away of the body or a long illness or the forgetfulness of the mind that comes with age. Why then should we grieve for him? Our memories of him will be of the Master, whose step was light to the end, whose smile was infectious, and whose eyes were full of laughter. We shall associate no failing powers with him of body or mind. He lived and he died at the top of his strength and powers, leaving a picture in our minds and in the mind of the age that we live in that can never fade away.

That picture will not fade. But he did something much more than that, for he entered into the very stuff of our minds and spirits and changed them and moulded them. The Gandhi generation will pass away, but that stuff will remain and will affect each succeeding generation, for it has become a part of India's spirit. Just when we were growing poor in spirit in this country, Bapu came to enrich us and make us strong, and the strength he gave us was not for a moment or a day or a year but it was something added on to our national inheritance.

Six years earlier, at a meeting of the All-India Congress Committee at Wardha, Gandhi had publicly designated Nehru as his political heir. It was at a time when the Mahatma disagreed with him on India's attitude to the war. The Mahatma said:

Somebody has suggested that Jawaharlal and I are estranged. It will require much more than differences of opinion to estrange us. We have had differences from the moment we became co-workers, and yet I have said for some years and say now that not Rajaji [5] but Jawaharlal will be my successor. He says that he does not understand my language, and that he speaks a language foreign to me. This may or may not be true. But language is no bar to a union of hearts. And I know this, that when I am gone he will speak my language.

Gandhi's prophecy was to come true, for more and more in the coming months and years Nehru was to speak the Mahatma's language. He was to preach Gandhi's gospel of fearlessness, action and freedom from hate. Love and forgive, the Mahatma had said, love and create, love and be free. In Delhi at the Inter-Asian Relations Conference in April, 1947, Gandhi had visualised the creation of One World. "I would not like to live in this world if it is not to be one," he had remarked. "I should like to see this dream realised in my lifetime."

[5] C. Rajagopalachari, former Governor-General.

They could not, Nehru reflected, achieve all of Gandhi's lofty ideals but they could at least walk faithfully in his footsteps. Had not Gokhale many years before said, "We have to serve India by our failures"? Now as never before Nehru felt the weight of the Mahatma's mantle and realised how heavy was the burden Gandhi had carried in his lifetime. India was free, and freedom brought with it added responsibilities and obligations.

Power corrupts some men; it coarsens others. Power was to coarsen slightly the fine fibre of Nehru's being, but it was also to toughen his spirit and will. Like Gandhi he was to become the beloved slave-driver, hustling India into activity, inspiring, urging and prodding his people up paths, steep, hard and stony, to broader uplands and richer fields. He was to praise and scold, allowing himself no rest and others little leisure, to galvanise the people with his own effort and example, gearing up the country and the administration to a new and quicker tempo.

In the process he was so to identify himself with the country and the administration as to merge himself in both, impregnating each with the distinctive stamp of his personality. India was to become Nehru, and so was the Government—a phenomenon which not only his own country but the world acknowledged.

The dangers implicit in such a situation are obvious. For one man to be simultaneously a talisman at home and a symbol abroad is to carry the weight of national existence on a thin-spun thread. But there are advantages in this situation from which India has benefited. Nehru's voice has enabled the Government to carry through unpopular policies such as the embargo on the use of armed force in Goa. It has helped to preserve unity at a time when fissiparous trends like linguistic urges, caste, provincialism, communalism and Communism tried to assert themselves. It won acceptance, despite opposition, for a socialistic blueprint and for a mixed economy broad based on the public (or governmental) and private sectors. It reconciled the country to a method of Robin Hood finance, the rich being mulcted by heavy taxation for the benefit of the poor. The doctrine of *panchshila* [6] rang a bell from Kashmir to Cape Comorin.

[6] Literally, "five tenets." These are: (1) non-aggression, (2) non-interference, (3) recognition of each other's sovereignty, (4) mutual help, and (5) peaceful coexistence.

Inside eight years the face of India—political, economic and social—was to be changed.

Under the British Raj the political map comprised about eighteen units directly administered by the Government along with 562 princely States. Within a year of independence this conglomeration of nearly 600 units was reduced to 26 States by the absorption of feudal India into the democratic framework. This meant that an area of over 587,000 square miles (about 48 per cent of India's total area) containing a population of nearly 80,000,000, or 27 per cent of the entire population, passed within twelve months from authoritarian to democratic rule. More recently [7] the States Reorganisation Commission has redrawn the political map, reducing the number of States from twenty-seven to sixteen, with three additional districts administered by the Central Government.

Patel's was the guiding spirit in the merging of princely with democratic India. He had able assistants, notably the energetic and resourceful V. P. Menon, an official who skilfully deployed blandishment and bludgeoning, never permitting the initiative to pass from New Delhi to the Princes. Although he was not directly concerned with these matters Nehru's support for Patel was whole-hearted. His views on princely India were well known, and he had expressed them long before independence, taking if anything a more extreme attitude than either Gandhi or Patel, who had urged Congress workers in the princely States "to work within their limitations" and make every effort to maintain cordial relations between the ruler and the ruled. To Nehru such tenderness seemed unjustified because the Princes in his view represented "probably the extremest type of autocracy existing in the world." Protected in their authoritarian rule by the strong arm of the British Raj, they were "Britain's fifth column in India," knowing neither competence nor benevolence, for the most part feudal, their rule rooted in medieval traditions mildewed with time. Very rightly, Nehru argued, autocracy should be the first casualty in a democracy.

India's new constitution made the country a republic within the British Commonwealth and was inaugurated on January 26, 1950, the day being celebrated as Republic Day. It had taken the Constituent Assembly four years to complete its prodigious task. Drawing its

[7] In September, 1955.

inspiration from the democratic countries of the United States, Canada, Britain, France and Switzerland, this document made the practice of untouchability an offence and appropriately was piloted through the Constituent Assembly by a Harijan, Dr. B. R. Ambedkar, the then Law Minister. The late Sir Benegal Narsing Rau, who was to represent India at the United Nations, had much to do in devising its form.

Under the constitution the elections to the central House of the People (now known as Lok Sabha) and to the Legislative assemblies in the States were held on the basis of adult franchise with every man and woman of twenty-one years and over entitled to vote. In India's first general elections in January, 1952, 176,600,000 voters figured on the electoral rolls of whom over 160,000,000 went to the polls. Of this mammoth number—the largest to take part in a democratic election anywhere in the world—quite 80 per cent were illiterate. Yet the elections were held peacefully, with no major incident. The number of polling booths was about 224,000, the number of representatives chosen being over 4,400. As an object lesson, the elections contributed somewhat to the political advancement of other underdeveloped peoples, Asian and African, whose claims to self-government could not now be denied on the score of illiteracy alone.

In the shaping of India's constitution, as also of the form and spirit animating the country's first general elections, Nehru's leadership was bold, positive and constructive. Unity and stability were the two vital needs of an India newly free; knowing how much hinged on these ideals Nehru concentrated on hammering them into the minds of the people.

Many Congressmen were opposed to the continuance of India's link with the Commonwealth. Yet others regretted that neither the word "democratic" nor "socialist" appeared before the term Republic. Some of the Indian Princes protested against the idea of the sovereignty of the people being enshrined in the Objectives Resolution passed by the Constituent Assembly in January, 1947, complaining that they were unrepresented in that chamber when the Resolution was discussed.

Nehru answered these comments and criticisms, justifying his decisions, notably the decision that India should remain as a republic in the Commonwealth. Basically, he said, India remained in the

Commonwealth because it was beneficial to her as well as to certain causes she wished to advance. He stressed that each country in the Commonwealth was free to go its own way, even to the point of breaking away from the Commonwealth. He said:

I wanted the world to see that India did not lack faith in herself, and that India was prepared to cooperate even with those with whom she had been fighting in the past; provided the basis of cooperation today was honourable, that it was a free basis, a basis which would lead to the good not only of ourselves, but of the world also. That is to say, we would not deny that cooperation, simply because in the past we had fought, and thus carry on the trail of our past *karma* along with us. We have to wash out the past with all its evil. I wanted, if I may say so in all humility, to help in letting the world look at things in a slightly different perspective, or rather try to see how vital questions could be approached and dealt with. We have seen too often in the arguments that go on in the assemblies of the world, this bitter approach, this cursing of each other, this desire, not in the least to understand the other, but deliberately to misunderstand the other, and to make clever points. Now, it may be a satisfying performance for some of us on occasions to make clever points and be applauded by our people or by some other people. But in the state of the world today, it is a poor thing for any responsible person to do, when we live on the verge of catastrophic wars, when national passions are roused, and, when even a casually spoken word might make all the difference.

He stressed the same points more vividly in a second speech to the Constituent Assembly:

We have to be careful in any business not to lose a thing which is advantageous to the nation. At the same time, we have to look at this problem in a big way. We are a big nation. If we are a big nation in size, that will not bring bigness to us unless we are big in mind, big in heart, big in understanding and big in action also. You may lose perhaps a little here or there with your bargainers and hagglers in the market place. If you act in a big way, the response to you is very big in the world and their reaction is also big. Because good always brings good and draws good from others and a big action which shows generosity of spirit brings generosity from the other side.

Nehru was expounding Gandhi's doctrine of means and ends, that the means mattered and that the right means always led to the right ends. He was also underlining the motivations which were later to guide his foreign policy.

Why did the word "democratic" or "socialist" not appear before the term Republic? Well, said Nehru, the whole of India's past was witness to the fact that it stood for democratic traditions.

"We stand for democracy," he affirmed. But democracy was not a static system of government and might evolve to fuller and more vigorous expression. "It will be for this House," said Nehru, "to determine what shape to give to that democracy, the fullest democracy, I hope."

Equally, he went on to argue, the word "socialist" would be redundant before the term Republic, for the content of economic democracy was contained in the Resolution. Nehru confessed:

I stand for socialism, and, I hope, India will stand for socialism and that India will go towards the constitution of a socialist State and I do believe that the whole world will have to go that way. What form of socialism again is another matter for your consideration. But the main thing is that in such a Resolution, if, in accordance with my own desire, I had put in that we wanted a socialist State, we would have put in something which might be agreeable to many and might not be agreeable to some and we wanted this Resolution not to be controversial in regard to such matters. Therefore, we have laid down, not theoretical words and formulas, but rather the content of the thing we desire. This is important and I take it there can be no dispute about it. Some people have pointed out to me that our mentioning a Republic may somewhat displease the rulers of Indian States. It is possible that this may displease them. But I want to make it clear personally, and the House knows, that I do not believe in the monarchial system anywhere, and that in the world today monarchy is a fast disappearing institution. Nevertheless, it is not a question of my personal belief in this matter. Our view in regard to the Indian States has been, for many years, first of all that the people of those States must share completely in the freedom to come. It is quite inconceivable to me that there should be different standards and degrees of freedom as between the people of the States and the people outside the States. In what manner the States will be parts of that Union is a matter for this House to consider with the representatives of the States. And I hope that, in all matters relating to the States, this House will deal with the real representatives of the States. We are perfectly willing, I take it, to deal in such matters as appertain to them, with the rulers or their representatives also, but finally when we make a Constitution for India, it must be through the representatives of the people of the States as with the rest of India, who are present here.

He was sorry that the States were not as yet represented in the House. But whose fault was it? The Government had made efforts during the past six weeks to get in touch with the committee representing the States rulers to find a way for their proper representation. It was not the Government's fault that there was delay. They were anxious "to get everyone in." "But," asked Nehru, "are we to postpone our work because some people cannot be here?"

This note of practicality and common sense, of history and hustle was to distinguish Jawaharlal's work in the coming critical years when India with its unity and stability virtually assured was to be moulded into a welfare state on a socialistic pattern.

Communism in India was to be resisted and fought, its violence ruthlessly crushed, though time and again it was to attempt to rear its hydra head and spit its venom on those it sought vainly to destroy. Partly its strength was to be undermined by its own inherent stupidities but basically it was to be weakened by the pace at which Nehru was to force his socialistic programme on the country and simultaneously to urge a policy of independence between the two power blocs outside. Thus cleverly he seemed to contrive to cut the ground under the feet of the Indian Communists at home and abroad.

In his own mind Nehru was certain of the intrinsic rightness of his domestic and foreign policies, rooted as these were not in a short-term plan to overcome indigenous Communism but on a long-range basis of thinking which went back over the years. He had for long felt that State planning with a socialistic bias was vital for the economic uplift of an underdeveloped country which because of its geographical situation, its political necessities and economic urgencies also needed a generation of peace for its development. Peace meant internal and international stability and goodwill for all men. It was the only guarantee for the continuance of civilised values and ideals.

The pattern of this thinking was to impress itself on Nehru's India. In the two years between Gandhi's death in January, 1948, and the passing away of Patel in December, 1950, Nehru was to reflect in his personality and policies the dim haze of an India oppressed with many tremendous burdens—the running sore of partition with the ensuing canker of Indo-Pakistan hostility, the problems of refugee rehabilitation, a disorganised and weakened economy, widespread unemployment, turmoil in Kashmir, trouble over Hyderabad and Junagadh, Kore, and the vague restive feeling that independence was exacting a heavy—at times it seemed a too heavy—price from the Government and the people. India, like Nehru, appeared in those two crucial years to symbolise a stricken cause, unpopular and forlorn, groping in a darkness which enveloped both and threatened to engulf them.

But India, like Nehru, was soon to reveal a hard core of unyielding faith and resolution. The Nehru legend grew with the legend of India as both stepped purposefully into a future largely of their own making. India was to respond nobly to the call of Nehru to tighten its belt and lift the country by its bootstraps to happier and bigger things.

The end of the Korean War brought a change in the cycle of trade, with India helping itself to capitalise on this turn in economic fortune. The first five-year plan, to be followed by the second, was under way; a beginning had been made with the ambitious programme of dams, irrigation projects and power works; community projects were slowly changing the face of the countryside, and a spirit of buoyant self-help was evident throughout the land. Abroad, Nehru's foreign policy, by projecting a new dimension into current international thinking, while it aroused controversy, was also inducing reflection.

All this lay ahead. But in the early months of 1948 the feeling that an epoch had ended with Gandhi's death and that the future seemed dark and uncertain weighed on India's mind. It weighed also on Jawaharlal's, though on the lone pinnacle upon which he now felt elevated a sense of duty, of mission and destiny seized him. It is the last lap of our long journey, he declared to his countrymen while addressing them through the Constituent Assembly. Perhaps, he confessed, they were all actors in some terrible Greek tragedy which was moving on to its inevitable climax of disaster. Yet, he adjured them to look at the picture in perspective and see "the rising star of India far above the horizon." He was convinced that destiny had cast a special role on their country. He declared:

Whether anyone of us present here can be called men or women of destiny or not I do not know. That is a big word which does not apply to average human beings, but whether we are men or women of destiny or not, India is a country of destiny and so far as we represent this great country with a great destiny stretching out in front of her, we also have to act as men and women of destiny, viewing all our problems in that long perspective of destiny and of the world and of Asia, never forgetting the great responsibility that freedom, that this great destiny of our country has cast upon us, not losing ourselves in petty controversies and debates which might be useful, but which would in this context be either out of place or out of tune.

Theirs, he said in a speech addressed in December, 1948, primarily to a gathering of engineers and technicians, was a generation sentenced to hard labour. Before India lay a road of toil and travail, but the goal was worthy of the effort.

22

JUNAGADH AND HYDERABAD

"Prakasa, what do you think of this *swaraj* and Pakistan?" Nehru inquired of his friend Sri Prakasa during one of the dark early days of freedom.

Sri Prakasa, who was lost in gloomy meditation, was silent. It was at the height of the partition killings.

With the feminine sensitivity which is part of his being Nehru divined the depth of his companion's gloom. He came and sat by Prakasa's side, his manner at once earnest and affectionate.

"There are only two things left for us now, Prakasa," he observed gently. "To go under or overcome our difficulties. And we are not going under."

In this mood every crisis posed a challenge. And crisis was to pile thick on crisis, like clouds drifting across a grey, angry sky.

The first impact of freedom touched two classes which were widely disparate—the people and the Princes, the former caught in the maelstrom of partition with its train of horrors, the second bereft suddenly of their oligarchic moorings and wandering like lost children afraid of the dark.

Nehru cherished for the Princes no great love or respect. While a few among them were progressive, the overwhelming majority, in his opinion, were no better than feudal tyrants. Like the Puranic Urvasi, nymph of Indra's [1] heaven, they had emerged from the churning of the ocean by the spirits of good and evil. But long years of over-protection and underdevelopment had stunted and enervated them.

[1] Indra is god of the firmament.

When freedom came the princely domains covered 562 units or States varying in size and resources and collectively containing in pre-partitioned India a population of about 90,000,000. They ranged in area from Kashmir, nearly as large as Great Britain, which before the Indo-Pakistan cleavage covered some 84,000 square miles, to the titular estate of Bilbari in Gujerat with an area of under two square miles and a population of less than thirty.

With the withdrawal of British power the doctrine of paramountcy, which placed the Indian Princes in special treaty relations with the British Crown, lapsed. They were now free to choose their future constitutional status by acceding to one or other of the two new Dominions, India and Pakistan, who were the effective successor Powers to the British Raj. On July 25, 1947, Mountbatten, addressing the Princes for the last time in his capacity as the Crown Representative, had advised them to make up their minds and individually accede either to India or to Pakistan. Although the discretion in this matter lay with the ruler, certain factors, such as the geographical contiguity of the State to the successor Dominion, the communal composition of its people and the holding of a plebiscite where necessary had to be taken into account.

"You cannot run away from the Dominion Government which is your neighbour any more than you can run away from the subjects for whose welfare you are responsible," Mountbatten advised the Princes.

A special States Department headed by Sardar Vallabhbhai Patel was accordingly formed in India early in July, 1947, to deal with the problem of the Princes. Patel handled his task with consummate skill, blending firmness with tact and generosity. He appealed to the Princes for cooperation, pleading with them to act as patriots and warning them that the alternative would be "anarchy and chaos which will overwhelm great and small in a common ruin." He assured them of generous privy purses guaranteed by the constitution and full ownership, use and enjoyment of all their personal properties as distinct from State properties. Alongside these concessions to the rulers Patel guaranteed to their subjects the same rights, liberties and privileges as those enjoyed by India's citizens.

The response was electric. Prince after prince signed the Instrument of Accession [2] and sent his State's accredited representative to the Constituent Assembly. By August 15, 1947, when India became independent, all but three States within its geographical limits had acceded to the Indian Dominion.[3] The exceptions were Kashmir, Hyderabad and Junagadh.

Kashmir, being contiguous to both Dominions, refrained from acceding to either, an ambiguous attitude which was to cost the State and its people dearly in the coming months and years. Junagadh, although geographically contiguous to India, unwisely chose to accede to Pakistan, a decision which its ruler was compelled to reverse when confronted with his subjects' opposition and the protest of the Indian Government. Hyderabad, like Kashmir, attempted to mark time by entering into a so-called Standstill Agreement with India for a year. But before the year ended the militant activities of the Razakars, a volunteer military corps of Muslim extremists, led the Government of India to launch a police action against the State. The result was Hyderabad's accession to India.

Junagadh provided a curtain raiser to a problem which was to find its climax in Kashmir. In mid-September, a month after the coming of independence, V. P. Menon, the resourceful right-hand man of Patel in the States Ministry, visited Junagadh in order to interview its Muslim ruler, the Nawab. Menon was informed by the Dewan, or Prime Minister, that the Nawab was indisposed and could not see him.

Junagadh, a small State covering some 4,000 square miles, had a predominantly Hindu population although ruled by a Muslim Nawab, and Muslims formed barely 18 per cent of its population. It lay in the Gujerat division of Bombay extending inland from the southern coast of the peninsula of Kathiawar. If Kashmir was Nehru's homeland Junagadh was in Patel's patrimony.

While a feudatory of the larger State of Baroda, to which it paid tribute, Junagadh in turn received tribute from minor feudatories within its territory such as the Sheikh of Mangrol and the ruler of

[2] The Instrument of Accession provided that the States should surrender to the Central Government the three subjects of defence, external affairs and communications without any financial liability and subject to a final settlement.

[3] Until formally declared a Republic on January 26, 1950, India was a Dominion.

Babariawad. While Menon was at Junagadh the Sheikh of Mangrol announced his accession to India. Babariawad had already done so.

Menon's return to Delhi coincided with Mangrol's renunciation of its accession to India, the Sheikh being forced into this reversal of policy. Simultaneously the Nawab of Junagadh, who had acceded to Pakistan, sent his troops into Babariawad.

Patel, infuriated by this *démarche* which amounted virtually to deriding India, demanded action.

"Unless there is a show of strength and a readiness to use force I shall resign," he warned.

Junagadh's action was contrary to the spirit of the understanding between India and Pakistan on the principles governing the accession of the States, for these had stipulated that while geographical contiguity was a major factor, the will of the people should be ascertained where the majority of the State's subjects were of a different religion or opinion from the ruler's. Junagadh's Nawab had not merely flouted the principle of geographical contiguity, since Junagadh was part of Indian territory: he had ignored the wishes of his predominantly Hindu subjects, whom he had not consulted.

"Where accession is in dispute," said Mountbatten, "the verdict of the popular will must prevail."

Nehru concurred with this doctrine, thereby committing himself to a plebiscite in Kashmir.

Not a month later, in October, the Pakistan Prime Minister, Liaquat Ali Khan,[4] at a meeting with Nehru in Delhi was to deliver himself of a sentiment on Junagadh which hardly squared with Pakistan's later attitude on Kashmir.

"Why should we not accept Junagadh's accession?" he asked. "After all, the ruler has the absolute right to accede without reference to the moral or ethnic aspects of the case."

He was to adopt a somewhat different approach when Kashmir's ruler acceded to India.

Meanwhile, the Nawab of Junagadh had followed his détente in Babariawad by despatching troops to Mangrol. Nehru sent no fewer than three requests to Karachi for the withdrawal of Junagadh troops from Babariawad and Mangrol, which by virtue of their accession to

[4] He was assassinated on October 16, 1951.

India were part of the Indian Union. But Pakistan continued to ignore his pleas.

On October 21st it was decided that Mangrol and Babariawad would have to be cleared of the Junagadh invaders. Accordingly, on November 1st Indian troops entered the two territories, and not long after the Nawab of Junagadh fled his State for Pakistan, leaving the administration in the hands of his Dewan and chief of police.

On November 8th the Dewan formally invited the Indian Government to take over the administration of the State in order to save it from a complete administrative collapse, and the Indian Government requested its regional commissioner in Rajkot, a town some sixty miles north of Junagadh, to comply with the request. It is noteworthy that the Dewan in informing the Pakistan authorities of his decision stressed that he was acting not only with the support of public opinion and the authority of the State Council but at the request of the Nawab himself before that embarrassed gentleman had winged his way to Karachi.

One of the first acts of the Indian Government on taking over the administration was to proclaim its intention to refer the Junagadh issue to a popular plebiscite. This was done between February 12 and 20, 1948, and resulted in an overwhelming vote in favour of accession to India. In Junagadh, out of 190,870 votes polled, 190,779 were for India, while in the feudatory territories of Mangrol, Babariawad and Manavadar, Pakistan polled less than 1 per cent of the total poll.

Hyderabad posed a more serious problem. Here was a large State, the premier State of India, with a population of over 17,000,000, covering some 83,000 square miles, as large as France and situated deep in the heart of India. Its ruler, a direct descendant of a Viceroy of the Mogul Emperor, was known as the Nizam from his title Nizam-ul-Mulk (Regulator of the State), and alone of all the Indian Princes he rejoiced in the honorific of His Exalted Highness. He was also described as Faithful Ally of the British Government.

Hyderabad represented Kashmir in reverse, for while in Kashmir a Hindu Prince ruled over a predominantly Muslim State, in Hyderabad a Muslim Prince headed a State in which Muslims constituted only 14 per cent of the total population. Its government, however, was controlled largely by a small Muslim oligarchy of which the Nizam was the fount and symbol.

Hyderabad had claimed a special status of independence for many years, but Britain had never recognised its title to independence, and in 1926 the then Viceroy, Lord Reading, had categorically rejected the Nizam's claim and reiterated Britain's status as the paramount Power. With the coming of freedom to India, the Nizam, who had virtually retired into his royal shell after the rebuff he received from Reading, began to toy anew with the idea of a special independent status for Hyderabad. He was encouraged in this by the Ittehad-ul-Muslimeen, a militant Muslim organisation which had its storm troopers in the Razakars who were headed by Kasim Razvi, a fanatical Muslim educated at Aligarh University who claimed that Hyderabad was a Muslim State and that Muslim supremacy was based upon the right of conquest.

Although he made various overtures to Pakistan, the Nizam, who revelled in diplomatic sleight of hand, felt himself sufficiently well situated to commit Hyderabad to neither Dominion. In doing so he misinterpreted the constitutional nexus created by the partition of India. With no geographical contiguity to Pakistan, Hyderabad could not accede to that Dominion. On the other hand, the Nizam made the mistake of believing that he need not accede to India either.

Even before August 15, 1947, the Indian Government had approached Hyderabad with a view to securing its accession to India. The Nizam, playing for time and high stakes, had refused to commit himself, but shortly after independence the negotiations were resumed. At the end of October, 1947, a duly accredited delegation, including Hyderabad's Prime Minister, the Nawab of Chattari, and the Nizam's constitutional adviser, Sir Walter Monckton, visited Delhi and returned with the draft of a Standstill Agreement for a year which the Nizam promised to sign on October 28th.

At dawn on that day Muslim crowds, incited by the Razakars, surrounded the residences of Monckton and Chattari and of the third member of the delegation, Sir Sultan Ahmed, and prevented them from leaving. Later on the same day the members of the delegation met the Nizam, who still seemed inclined to sign the agreement; but on the following day he changed his mind. Thereupon the members of the delegation resigned, being replaced at the Nizam's instance with a delegation composed entirely of Ittehad members.

To Nehru, as to Patel, this seemed like adding insult to injury. Patel was particularly wrathful. But Mountbatten's powers of persuasion prevailed, and he was able to persuade the Government of India to continue negotiations with the new delegation.

"I will not support the change of a single comma," he promised in a reference to the draft of the Standstill Agreement.

The new delegation, led by Nawab Moin Nawaz Jung, began on an obstreperous note, claiming association with, instead of accession to, India on the ground that the Nizam wished Hyderabad to be an independent sovereign State with a foreign policy in general alignment with India's.

Mountbatten's toughness paid, and in Patel the Hyderabad delegation found a man of steel. On November 24th the Nizam signed a Standstill Agreement for a year, giving to the Indian Government for that period control over defence, external affairs and communications.

Razvi had visited Delhi while the delegation was there, and Patel had been persuaded to see him. Their meeting was stormy.

"I shall return to the Red Fort [5] as a victor," Razvi was to boast later. He did return—as a captive.

The Nizam's devious diplomacy had made him suspect in the eyes of the Indian Government, which watched his subsequent manœuvres in and outside Hyderabad uneasily. During the next ten months, which were to culminate in New Delhi's police action, charges and counter-charges were made by both Governments.

The Hyderabad administration was now headed by Mir Laik Ali, a wealthy industrialist with business interests in both Hyderabad and Pakistan, and a brother-in-law of Moin Nawaz Jung. Initially the Nizam had offered the Prime Minister's post to Mr. Ghulam Mahommed, then Pakistan's Finance Minister and later its Governor-General. Ghulam Mahommed had declined the invitation, and Mir Laik Ali himself had accepted it after considerable hesitation and only after consulting Jinnah, whose permission he first obtained. He could

[5] The Red Fort was built by the Mogul Emperor Shah Jehan in the seventeenth century.

therefore hardly be described as an impartial administrator concerned only with Hyderabad's good.

Indeed, he lost no time in indicating where his sympathies lay. A loan was offered to Pakistan, and a currency ordinance discriminatory towards India was proclaimed. Several Congress leaders in the State were imprisoned without trial, while the Razakars were allowed free rein not only to propagate their virulent campaign of hate but to intimidate and attack the non-Muslim elements.

India replied with a vigorous economic blockade, which included a ban on the inflow of medical supplies. Early in 1948 the Indian High Commissioner in London had reported that Hyderabad was actively engaged in deals for the importation of modern weapons of war into the State. A clandestine traffic in arms by way of Pakistan was already under way, and a tall flaxen-haired Australian named Sydney Cotton was Hyderabad's chief gun-runner, violating international air conventions in the process of flying arms between Karachi and Hyderabad.

The Razakar hordes clamoured for war. Complaints were heard on both sides of the Indo-Hyderabad border of forays and raids. In Hyderabad one day a Razakar, echoing Kasim Razvi, boasted that his legions would soon march on Delhi and plant the Asafia flag of the Nizam's dynasty on the Red Fort. The waters of the Bay of Bengal, declared this orator, would wash the feet of the Nizam. Sea and land were to be mobilised against India.

In this explosive atmosphere it was not surprising that the negotiations to replace the Standstill Agreement of November, 1947, should have broken down in June, 1948. Earlier in May, a month before his departure from India, Mountbatten had tried to persuade the Nizam to visit Delhi for discussions and had even sent a personal emissary, his press attaché, Alan Campbell-Johnson, to Hyderabad to invite its ruler. His Exalted Highness was unwilling.

"What can Lord Mountbatten do within a month?" he asked querulously in his thin high-pitched voice.

Campbell-Johnson was taken aback by the tawdry appearance of this man reputed to be among the richest in the world. The Nizam was untidily dressed in a white cotton gown with loose white trousers, and his feet were encased in cotton socks and a venerable pair of slippers. His hands fidgeted. His knees seemed to knock together. He was small, with a stoop, and wore a brown fez set on the back of his head. This was the last ruling scion of the house of Asaf Jah, exulting in a sonorous string of titles which now seemed to mock him like echoes in an empty cave. This was His Exalted Highness, Rustam-e-Dauran, Arastu-e-Zaman, Lieutenant-General Muzaffar-ul-Mulk Wal Mamalik, Nawab Mir Osman Ali Khan Bahadur, Fateh Jung, Sipah Salar, Faithful Ally of the British Government, Nizam-ud-Daula, Nizam-ul-Mulk, Asaf Jah.

Campbell-Johnson attempted to explain to him that Mountbatten was a firm believer in constitutional monarchy.

"That," said the Nizam with a characteristic wave of the hand, "is where I join issue with him. Constitutional monarchy may be all very well in Europe and the West. It has no meaning in the East."

Like the Bourbons His Exalted Highness seemed determined to learn nothing and forget nothing. Despite the Razakars he appeared to his British visitor to be still politically master of the situation. He was to lose that eminence within four months.

The Razakars continued their hymn of hate. If hands are raised against the State, warned Razvi, they will be cut down—those hands and the hands controlling them. Was he referring to the Nizam? Shortly after, a Muslim editor, Shoiabullah Khan, whose paper was critical of the Razakars and urged integration with India, was assassinated. One of his hands was found cut by a sword.

From the beginning of 1948 the Razakars had extended their activities from Hyderabad city into the towns and rural areas, murdering Hindus, abducting women, pillaging houses and fields and looting non-Muslim property in a widespread reign of terror. In August the cumulative weight of their atrocities led to the resignation of two Hindu members from Mir Laik Ali's government.

The position was complicated for the Indian Government by the incursion of Communists into this area of terror and insecurity. The Communists at first allied themselves with the Hyderabad State Congress, but when the Razakar-dominated government lifted the ban on them they characteristically switched sides and raised the slogan of "Independent Hyderabad." Ostensibly siding with the Muslim farmers and labourers they called upon them to join their ranks, at the same time demanding that the Razakars "should forthwith submit themselves and also their arms to the guerrilla bands of the Communist party." "It is only then," they promised, "that the Communist party can support and safeguard them."

Abutting on Hyderabad State were the districts of Bombay, Madras and Madhya Pradesh,[6] with few natural barriers between the villages of Hyderabad and those of India. Thus the Razakars, often aided and abetted by Arab mercenaries in the Nizam's State Service and by armed soldiers of the Hyderabad State forces, could indulge in hit-and-run tactics, making frequent forays into Indian territory along the border. In the course of these incursions they murdered several people, besides damaging and destroying property. In July a party of about fifty Razakars, helped by some Hyderabad policemen, ambushed an Indian military convoy which was on its routine duty of exchanging patrols. The encounter took place near the Hyderabad village of Hanaj, and in the course of it five Indian soldiers were killed and five wounded. These troops had been stationed along the border for the protection of the terrorised Indian villagers.

Speaking in the Constituent Assembly on September 7th, Nehru gave a brief account of some of the depredations of the Razakars, which included incursions into over seventy villages inside Hyderabad, about 150 raids and forays into Indian territory and attacks on twelve trains on the border. The number of killed ran into hundreds, and many women had been raped or abducted. Property worth over Rs.10,000,000 (a little over $2,000,000) had been looted. Nehru also referred to Razakar attacks on Indian troops who were stationed along the border or in enclaves of Indian territory within Hyderabad. Nehru declared:

No civilised Government can permit such atrocities to continue to be perpetrated with impunity within the geographical heart of India; for this affects not only the security, honour, life and property of the law-abiding inhabitants of Hyderabad, but also the internal peace and order of India. We cannot have a campaign of murder, arson, rape and loot going on in Hyderabad without rousing communal passion in India and jeopardising the peace of the Dominion. Let the House consider what our predecessors in the Government of India would have done in these circumstances. For far less, they would have intervened drastically; the lapse of the Paramountcy of the British Crown cannot alter the organic inter-relation of Hyderabad and the Power whose responsibility for the security of India as a whole is, and should continue to be, unquestioned,

[6] Madhya Pradesh was formerly known as the Central Provinces and Berar.

or the mutual obligations of the one to the other. We have been patient and forbearing in the hope that good sense would prevail and a peaceful solution be found. This hope has proved to be vain and not only is peace inside the State or in its borders nowhere in sight, but peace elsewhere in India is seriously threatened.

What particularly perturbed the Prime Minister were the possible repercussions which Razakar attacks on Hindus inside Hyderabad might have on the safety of the 40,000,000 Muslims in India. In both the Junagadh and Hyderabad crises the thought of communal or religious passions being roused was uppermost in Nehru's mind, and he asked India to look at the problem dispassionately in a secular spirit. He urged:

It should be the business of all of us, to whatever religion or community we may belong, to lift this question away from the communal plane and to consider it from other, and, I think, more valid and more basic points of view. We wish to send our troops to Secunderabad to ensure security in Hyderabad, the security of all the people there, whether they are Hindus or Muslims, or they belong to any other religion or group. If subsequently freedom comes to Hyderabad, it must come to all equally and not to add to the flow of refugees, however grave their peril inside the State. They must face a serious situation and not run away from it.

The Prime Minister announced that the Indian Government had called upon the Nizam to disband the Razakars immediately and to facilitate the return of Indian troops to Hyderabad, since the State Government was either unwilling or unable to put down the terrorist activities which menaced law and order. These troops had previously been stationed at Secunderabad but had been withdrawn under the terms of the Standstill Agreement.

New Delhi, accused by many quarters of being too patient and too forbearing, was reaching the end of its tether. In the face of the intransigence of the State Government and the violence of the Razakars, early action was imperative, but even at this late hour the Nizam was hinting at an independent status for Hyderabad and was pressing for a plebiscite to decide the question of accession to India. In New Delhi's view a fair and comprehensive plebiscite was not possible in the context of Razakar terrorism, which had to be put down before the people's will was consulted. So far as Hyderabad's claim to an independent status was concerned, it was untenable, and Nehru made clear the Government's attitude in this regard. He said:

As for accession, it is equally clear to us that a territory like Hyderabad, surrounded on all sides by the Indian Union and with no outlet to the rest of the world, must necessarily be part of that Indian Union. Historically and culturally, it had to be a part, but geographic and economic reasons were even more peremptory in this matter and they could not be ignored, whatever the wishes of particular individuals or groups of individuals. Any other relationship between Hyderabad and the rest of India would have involved continuing suspicion and, therefore, an ever-present fear of conflict. A State does not become independent by merely declaring itself to be so. Independence connotes certain relationships with independent States and recognition by them. India could never agree to Hyderabad having independent relations with any other Power for that would endanger her own security. Historically, Hyderabad has at no time been independent. Practically, in the circumstances of today, it cannot be independent.

The Nizam was living in a dream world largely of his own creation. Prodded by the Razakar-dominated Government His Exalted Highness, albeit unwillingly and against Sir Walter Monckton's advice, had decided to take Hyderabad's case to the United Nations. It was well known that Pakistan had counselled this course, presumably in an effort to embarrass India, which itself had earlier referred the Kashmir issue to Lake Success.

Meanwhile, Hyderabad continued to maintain contact with Pakistan, and early in July its Prime Minister, Mir Laik Ali, flew secretly to the hill station of Ziarat where Jinnah, seriously ill and in the last stage of his tubercular infection, was resting. The Qaid-i-Azam was to die within two months.

What transpired between him and Mir Laik Ali is not known, but it is believed that Jinnah, while sympathetic, was not inclined to embroil Pakistan in the Hyderabad dispute. His own mind was absorbed with Kashmir. What would Pakistan do if Hyderabad found itself engaged in armed conflict with India?

"Let us wait and see," the dying Qaid-i-Azam is said to have murmured. Some, including Mir Laik Ali himself, spoke of Jinnah having given a vague assurance of intervention if Hyderabad could hold out militarily for a period which varied from fifteen days to three months.

By the first week of September it was known that a police action by India was imminent. What Indian Army Headquarters described as Operation Polo was being mounted, and an armoured division with one armoured brigade and another infantry brigade in reserve was mobilised for the purpose. The division was commanded by Major-General J. N. Chaudhuri, who was later to be the military governor of Hyderabad.

Hyderabad's regular military strength was rated at 20,000 supported by about 16,000 Arab irregulars and a horde of armed Razakars who despite the Nizam's pledge under the Standstill Agreement had not been disbanded within the three months specified but had in fact been increased and militarily equipped. So high was their own estimation of their strength and so low their opinion of the Indian Army's morale and fighting capacity that the Ittehad leaders boasted that the Indian forces could be held up for any period from three to nine months. In the interval Hyderabad hoped for the intervention of Pakistan and the sympathy of her friends, high among whom the Nizam rated Mr. Churchill.

As the imminence of armed conflict faced Hyderabad the Nizam appears to have been troubled by second thoughts. For Mir Laik Ali, caught between the cross-fire of the fanatical Razakars and the now hesitant Nizam, the position was invidious.

"What hope is there of any result but defeat and disaster?" His Exalted Highness demanded of his Prime Minister.

But Mir Laik Ali was still optimistic.

On the night of September 10th his brother-in-law, Moin Nawaz Jung, who was to lead the Hyderabad delegation before the United Nations, left for Karachi on his way to Paris. Around Hyderabad the Indian troops were awaiting the signal which was to launch Operation Polo.

The following night Jinnah, who had been brought that evening by plane from Quetta [7] to Karachi, suddenly passed away. The Indian Government was faced with a problem. Should Operation Polo, timed to begin on September 13th, be postponed? Nehru was hesitant but Patel was adamant. The Operation, he insisted, must proceed according to plan.

On September 13th the Indian troops converged on Hyderabad in a three-pronged attack, and after a brief encounter with the Hyderabad forces at Naldurg met with little resistance. The Razakars who had done so much to incite the conflict were not conspicuous in

[7] Quetta is about seventy miles from the hill station of Ziarat.

battle, although Razvi, who took no part in the actual fighting, bravely called upon Hyderabad's women to immolate themselves under the Indian tanks.

On September 16th, with Indian troops barely fifty miles from the cities of Hyderabad and Secunderabad, the Hyderabad commander, General El Edroos, a soldier of Arab stock, advised the Nizam to surrender. Earlier the Indian over-all commander, Lieutenant-General Maharaj Shri Rajendrasinhji, had broadcast an ultimatum calling upon the Hyderabad forces to surrender and thereby avoid unnecessary and useless loss of life.

Belatedly, the Nizam acted, ordering his ministers to proclaim a cease-fire, disband the Razakars and tender their resignations. This they did on the morning of September 17th, and at five o'clock that afternoon Hyderabad Radio announced the surrender of the State forces. Operation Polo was over.

In the last stages of the action Razvi had distributed arms and ammunition to some six thousand of his followers and had advised the Razakars either to stage a holocaust or to join the Communists. The majority did the latter, turning over their arms to the Communists and themselves going underground. Their action was to create a serious problem for the Indian military government in Hyderabad, particularly in the Telengana district, where for over two years the Communists incited and terrorised the peasants into acts of violence, murder, arson and rape, all directed against the landlords and the civil, police and military authorities in the area.

Hyderabad's surrender was followed by the appointment as military governor of General Chaudhuri, who had commanded the Indian armoured division in Operation Polo. On the night of September 19th Chaudhuri spoke for the first time over the radio to the people of Hyderabad, and the genuine sincerity of his tone, as well as the friendliness of his message, did much to reassure them. The chief task of the Indian army, he said, was to restore law and order, and he reminded them that India was a secular State with an army which made no distinction between different religions. He was speaking in the spirit which Nehru had enjoined upon India to observe.

Nehru himself, broadcasting on September 18th, emphasised again India's secular outlook and her desire for peace.

"We are men of peace," he proclaimed, "hating war, and the last thing we desire is to come into armed conflict with anyone. Nevertheless, circumstances which you know well, compelled us to take this action in Hyderabad. Fortunately it was brief and we return with relief to the paths of peace again."

The Prime Minister paid a tribute to the people both of India and Hyderabad for their calm in the crisis:

What has pleased me most during these past six days is the splendid response of our people, both Muslim and non-Muslim, to the call of restraint and discipline and the test of unity. It is a remarkable thing, and one which is full of good augury for the future, that not a single communal incident occurred in the whole length and breadth of this great country. I am deeply grateful for this. I should also like to congratulate the people of Hyderabad, who, during these days of trial, kept calm and helped the cause of peace. Many persons warned us of the risks and dangers that we faced and of the communal trouble that might besmirch our land. But our people have proved these prophets false and demonstrated that when crisis faced them, they could face it with courage, dignity and calm. Let this be an example and a pledge for the future.

Nehru went on to say that the military governor's primary task would be to restore normal conditions, and he had been instructed to interfere as little as possible with the ordinary life of the people of the State. As soon as normal conditions were restored, other administrative arrangements would be made and steps would be taken later for the election of a constituent assembly which would determine the constitutional structure of Hyderabad.

India redeemed these promises. On February 1, 1949, the Nizam entered into an agreement with the Indian Union which guaranteed His Exalted Highness all the personal privileges, dignities and titles enjoyed by him within or outside the territories of the State before August 15, 1947, the day of Indian independence. The Nizam was further guaranteed an annual privy purse of Rs.5,000,000 (a little over $1,000,000) and an additional sum of Rs.2,500,000 (over $500,000) to be paid yearly for the upkeep of his palaces besides a further Rs.2,500,000 to be given annually as compensation for income which he had lost from the Crown lands, now merged in the State. Generous monetary provision was also guaranteed for some of his relatives, including his two sons.

On November 23, 1949, His Exalted Highness issued a proclamation accepting the constitution framed by the Constituent Assembly of India as the constitution for Hyderabad subject to ratification by the State's people. In January, 1952, India held her first general elections under the new constitution in which Hyderabad participated. In the interim period, with the end of the military governor's rule, a mixed cabinet with four representatives of the State Congress had been functioning under an official Chief Minister. Following the elections a legislative assembly comprising 175 members came into being, and a popular government was established. The people's verdict endorsed that of the Nizam who meanwhile had been recognised as Rajpramukh or Governor of Hyderabad.

In neither Junagadh nor Hyderabad was Nehru interested as closely as Patel. The shadow of Kashmir obsessed him. By no principle as accepted by India and Pakistan, neither by virtue of contiguity of territory, of the State's communal composition or a popular verdict could either Hyderabad or Junagadh claim to have acted rightly.

Junagadh was a brief flash in the political pan, extinguished almost as soon as it arose. Here Pakistan was fishing in troubled waters from which it was relieved finally to extricate itself. Here also Pakistan's Prime Minister, Liaquat Ali Khan, by insisting that the mere accession of a State ruler was valid and sufficient weakened his subsequent objection to the Kashmir ruler's accession to India.

Hyderabad because of its size and status as the premier State of pre-divided India proved a more difficult obstacle to overcome, but its case for independence was as untenable as Junagadh's accession to Pakistan. Hyderabad had never in its history enjoyed an independent status, for since its creation in 1724 it had either relied on the Mogul emperor's support or had leaned heavily on the British. "There was only one King in India, the King of Delhi." In its early days Hyderabad had claimed a titular independence which British historians and administrators had contemptuously dismissed. "Its importance," writes Edward Thompson,[8] "was trivial in the extreme, and its independence completely fictitious in the half century before the Mutiny and perhaps most of all in Lord Wellesley's time (1798–1805). No one deviated from an attitude of steady contempt for it." Respect was to replace contempt, but the British attitude to the fiction of Hyderabad's independence never wavered. In 1926 the British Gov-

[8] *The Making of the Indian Princes* (London, Oxford University Press, 1943).

ernment had peremptorily and categorically rejected Hyderabad's claim to an independent status. It could not fairly be expected of the Indian successor Government that it should automatically accept a position which its predecessor had rejected for good reason. Hyderabad, lying deep in the heart of India, stretches almost from sea to sea across the peninsula. A huge independent enclave of this type with a Muslim ruler heading a predominantly Hindu population, whose sympathies, if not loyalties, would be divided from his, was a possibility too explosive for the Indian Government to contemplate or accept. Theoretically the Nizam, like every State ruler on the lapse of British paramountcy, might have claimed to be independent. But the realities of the situation, with the practical obligations it laid on both the two Dominions and the 562 States involved, were too far-reaching to be lightly ignored.

"There are certain geographical compulsions which cannot be evaded," Mountbatten had warned the Princes even before independence.

Kashmir posed for India and Nehru a more difficult and intractable problem.

23

THE SHADOW OF KASHMIR

To Nehru, Kashmir has always been a land of enchantment, and in writing of it he betrays a rapture of mood and thought which has led many people into thinking that his political attitude to it is coloured by this emotional glow.

Visiting Kashmir in the summer of 1940, after an absence of many years, Nehru was enthralled by the loveliness of the land, and wrote ecstatically about it.

Like some supremely beautiful woman, whose beauty is almost impersonal and above human desire, such was Kashmir in all its feminine beauty of river and valley and lake and graceful trees. And then another aspect of this magic beauty would come to view, a masculine one, of hard mountains and precipices, and snow-capped peaks and glaciers, and cruel and fierce torrents rushing down to the valleys below. It had a hundred faces and innumerable aspects, everchanging, sometimes smiling, sometimes sad and full of sorrow. . . . As I gazed at it, it seemed to me dreamlike and unreal, like the hopes and desires that fill us and so seldom find fulfilment. It was like the face of the beloved that one sees in a dream and that fades away on awakening.

Here is the ardour and intensity of a lover. Yet on that occasion, as on the many subsequent visits he was to pay Kashmir, Jawaharlal was to note with sorrow another of Kashmir's "hundred faces"—the misery and degradation of its downtrodden masses and the sadness mirrored in their sombre eyes.

He is aware that many people both in and outside India equate his political attitude to Kashmir with his emotional attitude to the homeland of his fathers. In a speech in Parliament on August 7, 1952, he referred to it.

"I am called a Kashmiri in the sense that ten generations ago my people came down from Kashmir to India," he remarked. "That is not the bond I have in mind when I think of Kashmir, but other bonds which have tied us much closer."

What those bonds are, the long chain of events starting from October, 1947, was to reveal.

Unlike Hyderabad with a Muslim ruler and a predominantly Hindu population, Kashmir had a Hindu ruler and a population which was predominantly Muslim. Larger in area than Hyderabad—Kashmir covers 84,471 square miles—this northern State has a population of about 4,500,000, of whom 77.11 per cent are Muslims, a little over 20 per cent Hindus, and under 2 per cent Sikhs. In the eastern province of Ladakh are nearly 50,000 Buddhists.

Kashmir's boundaries abut on five countries—the U.S.S.R., China, Afghanistan, Pakistan and India—although many miles of its borders, particularly the 900 miles which run along Sinkiang and Tibet, are not internationally defined. It touches Soviet territory along a short strip of land and is screened from Russia and China by the Himalayas and the Pamirs.

"You can climb to the top of the mountains and shout to us," said the ebullient Khrushchev during the Russian leaders' visit to Kashmir in December, 1955.

The famous Valley of Kashmir, 120 miles long and about 75 miles wide, is the heart of the State. Through it flows the Jhelum, which with the Indus and the Chenab are the three principal waterways of Kashmir.

To the north of the Valley lies Baltistan, and beyond it the regions of Hunza and Nagir, which in turn touch Gilgit. South is the province of Jammu with Ladakh to the east and on the west the districts of Muzaffarabad, Riasi, Poonch and Mirpur.

India's frontier with Kashmir runs along the Gurdaspur district ceded to India under the Radcliffe Award which partitioned the Punjab and Bengal. The Pakistan border ranges from west of Pathankot to Swat and Chitral and beyond to the Hindu Kush range.

Thus Kashmir, abutting as it does on Russia, China and Afghanistan, poses more than an Indo-Pakistan problem, a consideration very much in the forefront of Nehru's mind. In a broadcast to the nation on November 2, 1947, less than a week after India's intervention in

Kashmir, he referred to Kashmir as "a frontier territory adjoining great nations and therefore we were bound to take an interest in the developments there." Some three weeks later he elaborated on the same theme in the first official statement he made to the Constituent Assembly: "Kashmir because of her geographical position with her frontiers with three countries, namely the Soviet Union, China and Afghanistan, is intimately connected with the history and international contacts of India."

Many centuries ago, the freebooters of Central Asia, including the Scythians, had descended on the Indian plains through Kashmir along a trail not very different from that taken by the tribal marauders who came through the Northwest Frontier Province in October, 1947. Some say that the soldiery of Alexander the Macedonian moved along much the same route on their way to India following the course of the Kabul River and crossing the Indus to enter Taxila, some twenty miles northwest of Rawalpindi. This was around 325 B.C.

Beyond the strategic importance which geography gives it, Kashmir embodies in Nehru's eyes the secular spirit which he cherishes. That a State with a Muslim majority should cast its ties with India has always seemed to him a refutation of the two-nation theory on which Pakistan was founded. It is this bond more than any other which gives his utterances on Kashmir an almost apocalyptic fervour.

The theme recurs over and again in his speeches. Speaking to the Constituent Assembly in March, 1948, he touched on it forcefully:

We have become too used in India unfortunately to thinking of every problem or many problems in terms of communalism, of Hindu versus Muslim or Hindu and Sikh versus Muslim and so on. . . . Now, in this context of communal conflict the case of Kashmir stands apart, because Kashmir is not a case of communal conflict; it may be a case of political conflict, if you like; it may be a case of any other conflict, but it is essentially not a case of communal conflict. Therefore, this struggle in Kashmir, although it has brought great suffering in its train to the people of Kashmir and placed a burden on the Government of India and the people of India, nevertheless stands out as a sign of hope that we see a certain cooperation, combination and coordination of certain elements, Hindu and Muslim and Sikh and others on an equal level, and for a political fight for their own freedom. I wish to stress this because it is continually being said by our opponents and critics on the other side that this is a communal affair and that we are there to support the Hindus or the Sikh minorities as against the Muslim masses of Kashmir. Nothing can be more fantastically untrue. We could not for instance send our armies and we would not be there if we were not supported by very large sections of the population, which means the Muslims of Kashmir. We would not have gone there in spite of the invitation of the Maharaja of Kashmir, if that invitation had not been backed by the representatives of the people of Kashmir and may I say to the House that in spite of our armies having functioned with great gallantry, even our armies could not have succeeded except with the help and cooperation of the people of Kashmir.

In the same speech Nehru emphasised the dual objectives which had moved India to intervene in Kashmir:

We have only two objectives in the Jammu and Kashmir State. To ensure the freedom and progress of the people there, and to prevent anything happening that might endanger the security of India. We have nothing else to gain from Kashmir, though Kashmir may profit much by our assistance. If those two objectives are assured to us, we are content.

Kashmir's misfortune was its Hindu ruler, Maharaja Sir Hari Singh Bahadur, an autocrat who combined indolence with vast incompetence. He was a descendant of Raja Gulab Singh, a Dogra [1] who in the early years of the nineteenth century had established himself as the ruler of Jammu Province. In 1846 the Sikhs who earlier had dislodged Kashmir's Afghan ruler were in turn dislodged by the British, who made over Kashmir to Gulab Singh on payment of a sum of approximately $1,500,000.

The Dogra dynasty, almost without exception, was notorious for its cruelty and rapacity, its victims being mainly the helpless Muslim population who eked out a precarious living as peasants and artisans. Over 90 per cent of them were illiterate.

Hari Singh came to the throne in 1925, and continued in his forebears' traditions of unenlightened tyranny. In this land of chronic poverty the Maharaja mulcted his poor subjects mercilessly, the average tax per head for the Muslim peasants and workers, whose per capita income was about $3.00, rating at $0.11. While some Rs.4,000,000 (about $1,000,000) were expended on the ruler's court and another Rs.5,000,000 devoted to the army, the collective expenditure on public health, education, roads, irrigation, agriculture and industry was only a little over Rs.3,000,000.

[1] The Dogras, who include Hindus, Sikhs and Muslims, are among the best soldiers in the Indian Army.

Illiterate and downtrodden, the masses of Kashmir had very little political consciousness, and it was not until the Congress session at Lahore in 1929, over which Nehru presided and which proclaimed complete independence as India's goal, that the first faint stirrings of political awareness seeped into the State. The movement was led by Sheikh Mohammad Abdullah, then a young man of twenty-five and an unemployed teacher. Abdullah, a giant of a man standing six feet four in his sandals, was soon to be christened Sher-e-Kashmir, which means Lion of Kashmir. He was fearless, direct and outspoken, but with a strong streak of rustic shrewdness and guile.

In 1931 the Kashmiri masses led by Abdullah staged a minor, comparatively feeble revolt and Abdullah was thrown into prison for several weeks. Thereafter a number of abortive protests and revolts were staged, spearheaded by Abdullah's organisation, the All-Jammu and Kashmir Muslim Conference which he had founded in October, 1932.

Abdullah, who was early attracted by the secular politics of the Indian National Congress, was especially drawn towards Nehru, who in turn admired and approved of his national outlook, and the two men grew to be close friends. Consistent with this outlook Abdullah persuaded the Kashmir Muslim Conference to shed its communal label, and in June, 1939, it changed its name to the All-Jammu and Kashmir National Conference. A dissident minority led by Abdullah's nearest political associate, Chaudhri Ghulam Abbas, who was later to cast his lot with Pakistan, continued as the Muslim Conference. Inevitably this body drew closer to the Muslim League, while Abdullah's National Conference aligned itself with the Congress.

In May, 1946, while the British Cabinet Mission was in Delhi, Abdullah launched a "Quit Kashmir" campaign against the Maharaja and in consequence was sentenced to nine years' imprisonment. Nehru, defying the ruler's ban, entered Kashmir about this time and was arrested but released shortly after, being kept in detention for a few hours. Abdullah was to languish in jail until September, 1947.

A month earlier independence had come to the Indian sub-continent with the partition of India and Pakistan. Although with the lapse of paramountcy consequent on the British withdrawal the Princes were theoretically free to be independent, Mountbatten had advised them that practical considerations left them only with the choice of accession either to India or to Pakistan.

In June, 1947, he had visited Kashmir to impress the same advice personally on the Maharaja, who seemed congenitally incapable of arriving at a decision. Before going to Kashmir, Mountbatten had secured an assurance from the then newly created States Department in India, headed by Vallabhbhai Patel, that the Indian Government was prepared to give an undertaking to the Maharaja that if Kashmir acceded to Pakistan this would not be regarded as an unfriendly act by New Delhi, which recognised that the State was free to accede to whichever Dominion it chose. The Indian Government, however, was not prepared to entertain the prospect of an independent Kashmir.

Mountbatten accordingly advised the Maharaja on these lines.

"Ascertain the will of your people by any means," he counselled, "and join whichever Dominion your people wish you to join by August 14 this year."

But Hari Singh was incapable either of knowing or of making up his mind. He excused himself from a final meeting with Mountbatten where he was to have made known his decision on the plea that his royal person had been suddenly seized with an attack of colic.

In a speech to the East India Association in London in June, 1948, after his return from India, Mountbatten publicly deplored the indecision of Kashmir's Maharaja.

"Had he acceded to Pakistan before August 14," he recalled, "the future Government of India had allowed me to give His Highness an assurance that no objection whatever would be raised by them. Had His Highness acceded to India by August 14, Pakistan did not then exist, and therefore could not have interfered. The only trouble that could have been raised was by non-accession to either side, and this was unfortunately the very course followed by the Maharaja."

That procrastinating Prince hoped to triumph by delay. But events caught up with him. For the time being he sought a brief respite by approaching both India and Pakistan with the offer of a Standstill Agreement, hoping thereby to stave off the evil day of decision and meanwhile to preserve his precarious independence.

On August 14th the Pakistan Government signed a Standstill Agreement with Kashmir under which it assumed the responsibilities it held as part of British India and undertook to continue to run the communications, postal and telegraph services. The agreement came into effect on August 15th. India, unwilling to encourage the Maharaja in his efforts to make of Kashmir an independent State, desisted from entering into this commitment. It should be noted here that the Pakistan Government, judging from Jinnah's view expressed shortly before independence, had encouraged, even incited, the Princes into declaring their independence, for it calculated that since the overwhelming majority of the Princely States were in Indian territory such a declaration could not but gravely embarrass the Indian Dominion and, by dismembering and dividing it further, weaken its already precarious unity and stability. The gospel of independence for the Princely and autocratic States was a luxury India could not afford. On the other hand it was a weapon which Pakistan could effectively employ.

Nehru's opposition to the assumption of independence by any of the Princes was also based on a constitutional theory he had advanced long before the Kashmir conflict, at a time when negotiations for independence were proceeding between India and Britain. In May, 1947, he had insisted that India and the Constituent Assembly were the successors to, and Pakistan and the Muslim League the seceders from, British India.

On May 24th, in an interview to the United Press of America, he had explained the Congress point of view: "We stand for a union of India with the right to particular areas to opt out. We envisaged no compulsion."

This principle of India as a continuing entity he was to apply later and quite logically to the invidious status which Kashmir's Maharaja sought to secure for his State. The point was developed at some length in a speech he made in the Indian Parliament in August, 1952:

When the British Power established itself in India, it became evident that no other power in India could remain independent. Of course, these powers could remain semi-independent or as protectorates or in some other subordinate capacity. Accordingly, the Princely States were gradually brought under the domain and suzerainty of the British power. Similarly, when the British left India, it was just as impossible for odd bits of Indian territory to remain independent as it had been during their régime. At that time Pakistan was, of course, out of the picture. For the rest, it was inevitable that the princes and others, whoever they might be and whether they wanted it or not, must acknowledge the suze-rainty, the sovereign domain of the Republic of India. Therefore, the fact that Kashmir did not immediately decide whether to accede to Pakistan or to India did not make Kashmir independent for the interven-ing period. Since she was not independent, it was our responsibility as the continuing entity to see that Kashmir's interests were protected. I wish to say this, because it was undeniably our duty to come to Kashmir's aid, irrespective of whether she had acceded to India or not. On account of the continuing entity, India's responsibility to all the other States remained unchanged except in the case of those that had definitely and deliberately parted company.

In other words, the Indian Government's view was that so long as Kashmir did not accede to either Dominion it did not enjoy an inde-pendent status but was part of Indian territory and therefore India's responsibility.

Independence with the volcanic upheaval caused by partition was soon to jolt even Hari Singh in the ivory tower in which he had encased himself. The award of the Radcliffe Boundary Commission placed Kashmir's borders contiguous to both India and Pakistan with a divided Punjab wedged dangerously in the underbelly of Kashmir. The flames of the Punjab conflagration as the refugees, Hindus, Sikhs and Muslims, moved across the neighbouring tracts of Kashmir, particularly through the southern province of Jammu, which includes Chenani and Poonch, reached out into the State and threatened to engulf it. Here in Jammu province were concentrated nearly 2,000,000 of the State's 4,500,000 population, the majority of them being Hindus and Sikhs. But in Poonch and adjacent Mirpur resided a strong core of Muslim peasants, many of them former soldiers who had seen service in the Second World War.

In the spring of 1947 a no-tax campaign in Poonch was suppressed with great brutality by the Maharaja's forces, and as the fires of partition lit new hates Muslims attacked Sikhs and Hindus and were in turn attacked by them. From the two wings of divided Punjab their co-religionists poured into Jammu and Poonch to aid them.

Meanwhile, the Pakistan Government, having secured a Standstill Agreement with Kashmir, appeared to be anxious to force accession by economic and political pressures. Kashmir was not directly accessi-ble to India, and such merchandise as it possessed had always drifted down its three principal waterways—the Indus, Jhelum and Chenab rivers—to ports and centres in what was now Pakistan. In British days India had exported to Kashmir coal and steel, metal, cotton products, sugar, tea, oilseeds and tobacco. But now, despite the slim frontier along the Gurdaspur district line, India had no worth-while road link with the State. Moreover, even the tenuous air communication between Delhi and Srinagar extended over treacherous mountain passes and traversed some five hundred miles.

Admittedly, communications and traffic were badly disrupted in the upheaval following partition, but the sudden curtailment at this juncture of essential supplies from Pakistan to Kashmir (which was contrary to the Standstill Agreement) is difficult to explain save as purposeful economic pressure. At a time when Kashmir most needed these imports, the inflow of petrol, salt, sugar, cloth and other consumer commodities suddenly ceased or dwindled to a trickle. At Domei, the frontier post between Kashmir and Pakistan, the customs revenue dwindled from Rs.30,000 a day to a few hundred rupees.

If disruption of communications and traffic was the reason for this curtailment, how could Karachi explain the simultaneous organised incursion of tribesmen from the No Man's Land between Afghanistan and Pakistan across the Northwest Frontier into Kashmir? These men, armed and equipped with rifles, bren and sten guns, two- and three-inch mortars, anti-tank rifles, Mark-V mines and man-pack walkie-talkie sets—most of this equipment being obviously supplied by Pakistan—were given transit through Pakistan territory by motor transport and railway trains, provided petrol, food and accommodation and rendered every possible aid and comfort on their way to Kashmir.[2] Pakistan's spokesman, Sir Mohammad Zafrullah Khan, later denied these charges before the United Nations Organisation. Equally he repudiated the accusation that Pakistan army personnel had actively assisted the raiders. Yet on the U.N. Commission's first visit to Karachi in July, 1948, when it was no longer possible to conceal their presence in Kashmir, Sir Mohammad Zafrullah Khan, with the same suavity and blandness, confessed that they were there.

[2] The Pir of Manki Sharif, a prominent Muslim divine and politician, along with other notabilities in the Frontier province openly admitted to me during a visit I paid to Peshawar in August, 1953, that they had organised and helped these tribal raiders, and even took me to some Frontier villages and introduced me to several of them.

A major reason for Pakistan's active connivance with and assistance to these tribal marauders was possibly to divert their attention from the immediate internal problems created by partition to the promise of quick loot and plenty in the unravished land of Kashmir. Throughout their rule the British had curbed these restive frontiermen by a shrewd mixture of bribery and bludgeoning, expending lavish subsidies on the tribal chiefs in exchange for personal guarantees of peace. Soon after partition Karachi was faced with the threat of Pakhtoonistan, a movement for a separate homeland for the tribal Pathans led by Khan Abdul Ghaffar Khan, the Frontier Gandhi. In the circumstances what could be more natural or appropriate than to turn the tribesmen's attention elsewhere?

Whatever the motivations behind these incursions, the fact remains that by early September armed gangs, some of them in Pakistani army uniforms, and employing Pakistani military codes, were converging on the Kashmir border.

Life's photographer and correspondent, Margaret Bourke-White, who was in Pakistan when the Kashmir invasion was beginning, reports an encounter with a band of these tribesmen on the road between Rawalpindi and Baramula.[3]

"Are you going into Kashmir?" she asked them.

"Why not?" they said. "We are all Muslims. We are going to help our Muslim brothers in Kashmir."

Once inside the borders of the State, these freebooters made little or no distinction between Hindus, Muslims and Sikhs, looting all indiscriminately, killing, raping and destroying property. Within Kashmir itself the folly and excesses of the Dogras had roused Muslim resentment, and mass killings took place on both sides, particularly in Poonch.

By mid-October the Maharaja was sufficiently perturbed to protest on the one hand to Pakistan and on the other to appeal to India for arms. New Delhi took no urgent notice of this appeal, although sanction was formally given by the States and Defence Ministries, but no arms were actually sent. Earlier, on September 29th, the Maharaja had ordered the release of Sheikh Abdullah in a belated effort to overcome internal revolt and external invasion.

[3] *Halfway to Freedom*, by Margaret Bourke-White (New York, Simon and Schuster).

By mid-October a considerable part of the Poonch and Mirpur areas were in the possession of the invaders, who now moved down the Abbottabad-Mansara road which enters Kashmir near Muzaffarabad. Here the tribal raiders indulged in an orgy of looting and then proceeded along the Domel road which debouched down the Jhelum Valley to Kashmir's capital, Srinagar. Within four days of crossing the border they had covered more than half the distance to the capital. Uri was the next scene of slaughter, and on October 26th, leaving behind them a fearful trail of destruction and horror, the tribesmen entered Baramula, some thirty-five miles from Srinagar.

Had the invaders not dallied there, sating their lust for blood and plunder, the story of Kashmir might have been different. Within a matter of hours Baramula was turned into a blood-bath, only 3,000 out of its 14,000 inhabitants surviving. Hundreds were slaughtered in cold blood, the tribesmen in their frenzy making no distinction between Hindus, Muslims, Christians or Sikhs. A Catholic Franciscan convent, church and school were ransacked and burned to the ground while the Assistant Mother Superior, three nuns and a British officer's wife who happened to be there with her husband were raped and then butchered along with two men, one being the British officer. The young Muslim leader of the local National Conference, Maqbool Sherwani, after being tortured for several hours was crucified with nails on a post in the centre of the town.

By October 24th even the chronic indecision of Hari Singh had given place to deep-seated alarm and to a genuine concern for his personal safety. That night he sent an urgent message to New Delhi asking for armed assistance and offering to accede to India. On the morning of October 25th the Defence Committee considered the appeal, which was supported by Sheikh Abdullah, but no decision was taken, Mountbatten wisely advising that it would be impolitic and improper to give military aid unless Kashmir first acceded to India. The act of accession, he insisted, must precede the despatch of troops. His counsel was accepted and it was agreed that Vallabhbhai Patel's right-hand man, the States Secretary, V. P. Menon, should fly to Srinagar and investigate the situation.

Menon found the Maharaja completely unnerved by the turn of events. He explained to Hari Singh that India could not with propriety send troops to Kashmir's aid unless the State acceded to India.

Only thirty-five miles of a smooth tarmac road separated the invading hordes at Baramula from Srinagar, and even Hari Singh was beginning to realise that there was no time to be lost.

In a letter dated October 26th and addressed to Mountbatten the Maharaja signified his decision to accede to India, and this decision was supported by Abdullah's National Conference. None the less the Indian Government of its own volition did not deem this form of accession sufficient, and when on Menon's return to Delhi the Maharaja's letter was considered by the Defence Committee, it was decided that the Governor-General's reply should clearly stipulate that the Indian Government's acceptance of the Maharaja's act of accession was conditional on the will of the people being ascertained as soon as law and order were restored. Nothing provides clearer proof of India's bona fides in this matter. Nehru explained later to the Constituent Assembly:

We decided to accept this accession and to send troops by air, but we made a condition that the accession would have to be considered by the people of Kashmir later when peace and order were established. We were anxious not to finalise anything in a moment of crisis and without the fullest opportunity being given to the people of Kashmir to have their say. It was for them ultimately to decide. And here let me make clear that it has been our policy all along that where there is a dispute about the accession of a State to either Dominion, the decision must be made by the people of that State. It was in accordance with this policy that we added a proviso to the Instrument of Accession of Kashmir.

The military situation in Srinagar was desperate, for the troops in the capital consisted of only one squadron of cavalry. On Menon's advice the Maharaja had left Srinagar with his wife and son after setting up an interim government and inviting Abdullah to work with the Prime Minister, Mr. Mehr Chand Mahajan.

Since October 24th, when news of the tribesmen's invasion of Kashmir had reached Delhi, the Defence Committee had been probing the possibilities of sending Indian troops into Kashmir. On the testimony of the three commanding officers of the Indian armed forces who were then all British,[4] it was on the morning of October 25th that they received a directive to examine and prepare plans for send-

[4] They were General R. M. Lockhart (Commander-in-Chief, Indian Army); Air Marshal T. W. Elmhirst (Indian Air Force); and Rear-Admiral J. T. S. Hall (Indian Navy).

ing troops to Kashmir by air and road "in case this should be necessary to stop the tribal incursions."

Plans were hastily improvised and finalised on the afternoon of October 26th when the Indian Government decided to send military aid. Early on the morning of October 27th a battalion of the Sikh Regiment under Lieutenant-Colonel D. R. Rai, who was to be killed in action later that day, was flown out from Palam airport in Delhi to Srinagar.

The 330 men who comprised the air-borne battalion arrived barely in time to save Srinagar, for at the moment of their landing a small advance group of tribesmen was less than five miles from the capital. In their first encounter with the invaders on the outskirts of Baramula, the Indian troops quickly discovered that the enemy was far better armed than they had imagined and moreover was intelligently led. The tribesmen, organised in units and sub-units, were equipped with light and medium machine guns and mortars, and leading them was a Pakistani army officer, General Akbar Khan, who was later to become Chief of Staff of the Pakistan Army and still later was to be imprisoned for organising a plot against the Government. In Kashmir he was known by the pseudonym of General Tariq.

In this first action with the invaders Lieutenant-Colonel Rai was killed by a sniper's bullet, and his troops, left without a commander, fell back temporarily to a point only three and a half miles from Srinagar. But that same night they moved forward, and with the arrival of reinforcements from India the tide of battle turned and Srinagar was saved.

It was a remarkable military achievement, for the logistic obstacles against which the Indian armed forces had to contend were considerable. The five-hundred-mile air route between Delhi and Srinagar was over tricky mountain defiles where visibility in bad weather was practically nil. Winter at that time was only just around the corner. Yet the Indian Air Force, assisted by over a hundred civilian aircraft which were mobilised for the purpose, worked day and night on this precarious ferry service, which continued at the same furious tempo until November 17th, during which time 704 sorties were flown from Delhi. "It left our own SEAF efforts in the war standing," Mountbatten admitted to an aide.

Srinagar was saved; but Pakistan, baulked of its prey, was understandably bitter. It had grievously underrated the resourcefulness of the Indian armed forces. On October 26th, two days after news had reached Jinnah that the tribal raiders whom his Government had helped to transport, arm and feed had crossed into Kashmir, the Qaid-i-Azam flew from Karachi to Lahore, the better to witness at close quarters the triumph of this Muslim jehad. His rage on learning of the Maharaja's accession to India and of the arrival of Indian troops in Kashmir was unbounded. For a day or two he toyed with the idea of sending Pakistani forces openly into the State but was dissuaded from doing so by the timely intervention of Field-Marshal Sir Claude Auchinleck, who was then Supreme Commander administering the partition of the Indian Army and who threatened to withdraw all British officers, including the two commanders-in-chief, from the Indian and Pakistan armies if Jinnah persisted. Pakistan had proportionately more British personnel in her armed forces than India, and the point weighed with Jinnah.

Instead, the Pakistan Government contented itself by issuing an angry communiqué describing the Maharaja's accession to India as an act "based on fraud and violence, and as such cannot be recognised." On Nehru the tragic chain of events in Kashmir, weighted by disquieting developments in Hyderabad and Junagadh, pressed heavily. He aged in those critical days, but as the position in Kashmir grew more stable his old resilience of mind and spirit returned.

Once Srinagar was freed from the threat of the invader, the Indian Government's efforts were concentrated on persuading Karachi to desist from giving active aid, transport and equipment to the tribesmen. The Pakistan Government, while continuing to disclaim responsibility for the tribal incursions, suggested that if the Indian forces withdrew from Kashmir the raiders would withdraw simultaneously, thereby admitting by implication Karachi's control over these marauders.

When Jinnah made this suggestion to Mountbatten at a meeting at Lahore on October 30th, the Governor-General of India somewhat mischievously inquired, "How can the tribesmen be induced to remove themselves?"

"If you withdraw your troops," said the Qaid-i-Azam, "I will call the whole thing off."

As Nehru remarked later in the Constituent Assembly:

The Pakistan Government have proposed a simultaneous withdrawal of our forces and the raiders from Kashmir. This is a strange proposal and could only mean that the raiders were there at the instance of the Pakistan Government. We cannot treat with freebooters who have murdered large numbers of people and tried to ruin Kashmir. They are not a State, although a State may be behind them.

A State was in fact behind them, and the fact could no longer be concealed. For two months Nehru was in correspondence with the Pakistan Prime Minister, Liaqat Ali Khan, requesting him to desist from allowing the tribesmen to use Pakistan territory as a base for the invasion of Indian territory. On December 22, 1947, a letter from the Indian Prime Minister addressed to his Pakistan counterpart briefly enumerated the acts of aggression of Pakistan and the forms of aid given by Pakistan to the invaders. It called upon Pakistan nationals to cease participating in the attack on the Jammu and Kashmir State and to deny the invaders (1) all access to and use of Pakistan territory for operations against the Kashmir State; (2) all military and other supplies; and (3) all other kinds of aid that might tend to prolong the struggle.

In the same communication the Government of India once again expressed its earnest desire to live on terms of friendship with Pakistan and hoped that its request would be acceded to promptly and without reserve. Failing this response the Indian Government stated that it would be compelled to take such action, with due regard to its rights and obligations as a member of the U.N.O., as it might consider necessary to protect its own interests and those of the Government and people of Kashmir.

No reply was received from Karachi, and two reminders elicited the same reaction. On December 30th India referred the matter to the Security Council of the U.N., recalling articles 34 and 35 of the Charter, according to which any member may bring any situation whose continuance is likely to endanger the international peace and security to the attention of the Security Council.

From the beginning of the Kashmir imbroglio, Nehru had visualised the holding of a plebiscite under U.N. auspices, and Mountbatten had mooted the idea to Jinnah when he had met him at Lahore in October. Jinnah, however, suggested the holding of a plebiscite under the joint auspices of the two Governors-General. This was impracticable unless the fighting ended. As Nehru subsequently insisted, peace was a condition precedent to a plebiscite. He declared on November 21st:

I have repeatedly stated that as soon as the raiders have been driven out of Kashmir or have withdrawn, and peace and order have been established, the people of Kashmir should decide the question of accession by plebiscite or referendum under international auspices such as those of the United Nations. It is very clear that no such reference to the people can be made when large bodies of raiders are despoiling the country and military operations against them are being carried on. By this declaration I stand.

The point is of importance since India seems to have erred technically by recalling articles 34 and 35 which come under Chapter 6 of the Charter entitled "Pacific Settlement of Disputes." A more appropriate head for invoking the Security Council's intervention would have been Chapter 7, which is specifically concerned with "Acts of Aggression." By invoking Chapter 6 India enabled the Council to traverse a field which included charges by Pakistan of genocide against India instead of pin-pointing the issue to Pakistan's aggression against Kashmir.

India's reference of the Kashmir issue to the Security Council was, as Nehru described it, "an act of faith." India had nothing to conceal. She had acted with scrupulous rectitude and propriety, sending her troops to Kashmir only after the Maharaja, supported by Abdullah's National Conference, had acceded to India and with the pledge, given unilaterally and voluntarily, that it would be for the people of Kashmir to decide finally whether they wished to accede to India or Pakistan.

"We have indeed been overscrupulous in this matter so that nothing may be done in the passion of the moment which might be wrong," Nehru declared.

The fact of aggression by Pakistan, of her abetment of and aid to the tribal invaders was too patent to be denied, nor could any honest and reasonable observer gainsay the truth that Pakistan, despite India's protests and pleas, had continued to let her territory be used as a base for invasion on a neighbouring State. Nehru had more than once publicly admitted and deplored the attacks by non-Muslims on Muslims in Jammu. But India, as he reminded the world, had had no hand in this.

Nehru, addressing the Constituent Assembly on November 25, 1947, said:

I regret deeply that in parts of the Jammu province Muslims were killed and driven out. This of course has had nothing to do with our Government or our forces. But this mutual killing has been a very tragic feature during these past months in the Punjab, and Jammu was powerfully affected by this. We have sufficient evidence in our possession to demonstrate that the whole business of the Kashmir raids both in the Jammu province and in Kashmir proper was deliberately organized by high officials of the Pakistan Government. They helped the tribesmen and ex-servicemen to collect, they supplied them with the implements of war, with lorries, with petrol and with officers. They are continuing to do so. Indeed, their high officials openly declare so. It is obvious that no large body of men could cross Pakistan territory in armed groups without the goodwill, connivance and active help of the authorities there. It is impossible to escape the conclusion that the raids on Kashmir were carefully planned and well organized by the Pakistan authorities with the deliberate object of seizing the State by force and then declaring accession to Pakistan. This was an act of hostility not only to Kashmir but to the Indian Union.

India's case against Pakistan thus rested not only on legal but moral grounds, and to India as to Nehru the primary duty of the Security Council when faced with the facts was clear—to put a stop to the fighting by calling upon the invaders to withdraw and by requesting Pakistan to desist from letting her territory be employed as a base for invasion and attack. Only then could a plebiscite be held.

"It must be remembered," Nehru pointed out, "that all the fighting has taken place on Indian Union territory, and it is the inherent right of the Government of India to drive back any invaders on its territory."

The long and protracted wrangle which followed India's reference to the U.N.O., and which still continues, makes sad and sorry reading. Neither India nor Pakistan emerges creditably from this story. Patience the U.N. Commission certainly displayed, and its efforts culminated in the cease fire which became effective one minute before midnight on January 1, 1949. Kashmir was not completely freed of the invader, for on the other side of the Indian cease-fire line Pakistan, still rated in India's eyes as the aggressor, controls the so-called Azad

Kashmir [5] area of 5,000 square miles, Gilgit, northern Ladakh and Baltistan. If the U.N. Commission had patience, the mediators, Sir Owen Dixon and Dr. Frank Graham, who were subsequently and separately sent, showed equal perseverance and perhaps a greater degree of understanding. But their efforts, based on the initial U.N. line of equating aggressor with aggressed, foundered on that implacable rock.

Looking back, it is clear that the first doubts in Nehru's mind over Western policy and motivations in international affairs were implanted by what seemed to him and India the wholly inexplicable attitude of the Security Council on Kashmir. Instead of attempting to stop the fighting by directing Pakistan to cease giving aid to the raiders, the Council wasted many precious weeks by allowing this primary issue to be obscured and clouded by the problem of the plebiscite and by the absurd charge of genocide which Pakistan's spokesman, Sir Mohammad Zafrullah Khan, brazenly levelled against India. It almost looked as if the Security Council was anxious not only to treat aggressor and aggressed on the same basis but to put India rather than Pakistan in the dock. If, as India's spokesman Sir Gopalaswami Ayyangar asked, the Security Council could condemn Yugoslavia, Albania and Bulgaria for giving assistance to the rebels fighting the Government forces in Greece, what prevented it from condemning and compelling Pakistan to make the tribesmen withdraw?

The answer, whispered widely throughout India and elsewhere, was "power politics." To Nehru it seemed as if the bigger Western powers, more particularly the United States and Britain, were interested in evading the primary issue and in converting the Kashmir question into one of Indo-Pakistan relations as a whole.

He has never quite erased from his mind this lingering suspicion, and subsequent events, culminating in the promise of United States military assistance to Pakistan in February, 1954, have unfortunately deepened his doubts. Simultaneously his own attitude to the Kashmir problem has hardened until it now seems almost ossified into a wilful determination to congeal the position on the cease-fire line allowing only for some minor local adjustments. He appears no longer prepared to trust the holding of a plebiscite to the tender mercies of countries whose basic bona fides on Kashmir he distrusts.

"It [Kashmir] was only a plaything for them while it was very

[5] Azad means "free."

much in our hearts," he declared in a moment of bitter indignation in August, 1952. "They had the audacity to talk of imperialism to us when they were imperialists themselves and were carrying on their own wars and themselves preparing for future wars. Just because India tried to protect Kashmir from territorial invasion, people had the temerity to talk of India's imperialism!"

On Kashmir, it must be confessed, Nehru's mind is now virtually a closed book. Yet the fault is not entirely his. He sees Kashmir not only emotionally as his homeland but realistically in terms of India's security, abutting as that land does on China, Russia, Afghanistan and Pakistan. He sees it as the embodiment of the secular creed he cherishes with its Muslim majority but containing also Hindus, Sikhs and others.

Very early in the development of events in Kashmir, on November 2, 1947, Nehru reminded his countrymen: "It would be well if this lesson [of communal unity and organisation] were understood by the whole of India which has been poisoned by communal strife. Under the inspiration of a great leader, Sheikh Abdullah, the people of the valley, Muslim and Hindu and Sikh, were brought together for the defence of their common country against the invader. Our troops could have done little without this popular support and co-operation."

Abdullah has gone, a victim to his own grandiose dreams, and another man, Bakshi Ghulam Muhammad, rules in his stead. By a strange irony Abdullah, like Hari Singh whom he had fought and virtually replaced, nurtured visions of an independent Kashmir, a position India has consistently declined to concede. Meanwhile, the State's accession to India has been ratified by the Kashmir Constituent Assembly, although this does not strictly constitute the verdict of the people. On the Pakistan side of the cease-fire line, in the so-called Azad territory, live some 900,000 people with about another 100,000 scattered in the northern areas including Gilgit; and their verdict has not been sought. Nor will it be easy to register the verdict of the thousands of Hindus and Sikhs originally resident in Kashmir but driven by the early Pakistan onslaught into India.

Kashmir thus threatens to develop into something far more than an Indo-Pakistan problem, as Nehru predicted and feared it would. If India initially made some tactical mistakes both in Kashmir and at

Lake Success, the attitude of some of the bigger countries represented on the Security Council was unfortunately open to more than one interpretation and has boomeranged on themselves. Two years after India had referred the Kashmir issue to the Security Council, that same body, on America's initiative, was called upon to pronounce its verdict on the invasion of the North Koreans who crossed the 38th Parallel. India was interested to note the difference. If the North Koreans had invaded South Korea, so had Pakistan invaded Kashmir. Yet the United Nations Organisation was quick to brand the North Koreans as aggressors but has still to make up its mind on Pakistan.

Kashmir is now very definitely in the arena of the cold war, Marshal Bulganin and Mr. Khrushchev having seen to this during their visit to Srinagar in December, 1955, when they provocatively proclaimed their support of India's stand on Kashmir and declared that the problem had been successfully and rightly settled by the State's people. Impliedly this suggests Soviet approval of the status quo. It means a congealment on the cease-fire line, and Nehru, speaking in January, 1956, publicly welcomed the Soviet leaders' statement, declaring that he was in no way embarrassed by it.

To him obviously this seems a way out of the tangle created by what he believes was "power politics." If the world's leading Powers wanted to bring Kashmir into the cold-war arena the purpose has been achieved in a dramatic and highly unexpected manner. They are now hoist with their own petard.

On the cease-fire line itself not only India and Pakistan mark time. The world marks time.

24

UNITY AND STABILITY

"I have had to put up with a great deal which might have embittered me and filled me with hate," Nehru wrote to an English friend in Delhi some years before independence, "and yet I have survived. I feel pretty lonely often enough, but not bitter against anybody. Why should you succumb to this bitterness and hate? I suppose Delhi, imperial Delhi, is particularly responsible for it. It is not easy to remain sane there, and even I cannot stand it for long."

He could not have foreseen when he wrote this letter that within ten years he would be doomed to stay in Delhi, a Delhi, it is true, no longer imperial but democratic.

One of the first manifestations of the new spirit was the swift disappearance of the princely order, for which Vallabhbhai Patel, who headed the States Ministry, was primarily responsible. In doing this Patel took his cue from the manner in which Mountbatten had stampeded India into independence, leaving the leaders of the Congress and the Muslim League little time to think, plan or plot. Patel pressed the Princes into presiding over their own obsequies, and one by one these hapless autocrats accommodated themselves to the new democratic order by acceding to India.

"India in March, 1947, was a ship on fire in mid-ocean with ammunition in the hold," Mountbatten had said.

Speedy action was therefore imperative.

The situation was no less precarious or urgent in August, 1947, when the upheaval of partition brought many fissiparous forces to the fore. On July 5, 1947, the day on which the States Department came into being, Patel issued a statement assuring the princely States that no more was asked of them than accession on the three subjects of defence, foreign affairs and communications, since the larger common interests of the country were vitally bound up with these. He pleaded with the Princes to bear in mind that the alternative to cooperation in the general interest was anarchy and chaos, which would involve great and small in a common ruin if the States and Provinces were unable to cooperate and work together. Mountbatten buttressed this advice by himself counselling the Princes to exercise their free choice and accede either to India or to Pakistan.

By August 14, 1947, all but three States—Hyderabad, Kashmir and Junagadh—had made up their minds and acceded.

Accession established a new and organic relationship between the States and the Indian Government. In the immediate stresses following independence this relationship was to make for stability and cohesion. Accession, however, was only the first step in the cumulative process of integration. The next move was merger.

The States varied greatly in size and resources, and if they had to be fitted smoothly into the constitutional framework a process of integration was necessary. In turn this took two forms—external integration, which implied the consolidation of the smaller States into sizable administrative units, and internal integration, which meant the growth of democratic institutions and responsible government inside the States.

As Nehru had said in a speech in the Constituent Assembly in December, 1946:

The measure of freedom must be the same in the States as elsewhere. . . . If the people of a particular State desire to have a certain form of administration, even though it might be monarchical, it is open to them to have it. . . . If monarchical figure-heads are approved of by the people of the State, of a particular State, whether I like it or not, I certainly would not interfere.

The people of the princely States were unlikely in any case to favour the continuance of autocratic rule, and realistically, as also patriotically, the Princes, recognising the turn of events, moved with them.

Several large princely blocs were formed by the consolidation of small States and emerged as new composite States such as Saurashtra in the Kathiawar district of Bombay. Here some two hundred States with varying territories and jurisdictions were consolidated into one unit and administered as a single bloc of territory. A similar process saw the creation of Rajasthan, Vindhya Pradesh, Madhya Bharat and PEPSU.[1]

Alongside this development other princely States merged into the democratic provinces and lost their separate identity, although the rulers were guaranteed their succession rights, civil list, personal property, dignities and titles. Some of the Princes were created Raj Pramukhs, or Governors of the new units, among them being the Maharaja of Patiala, Raj Pramukh of PEPSU, the Jam Saheb of Nawanagar, Raj Pramukh of Saurashtra, and the Maharaja of Gwalior, Raj Pramukh of Madhya Bharat.[2] A few Princes, such as the Raja of Mandi, assumed diplomatic assignments.

With integration came democratisation as the people of the princely States demanded popular government and the transfer of power from the rulers to themselves. Nearly thirty years earlier, the authors of the Montagu-Chelmsford Report had warned, "Hopes and aspirations may overlap frontier lines like sparks across a street." This is what happened in Princely India soon after independence, and the rulers, reading the signs of the times, wisely bowed to the popular will.

Within a year India from a conglomeration of some six hundred units, comprising numerous provinces and States, became a compact area of twenty-six States. The primary credit for this prodigious performance must go to Vallabhbhai Patel.

In the three critical years between Gandhi's death in January, 1948, and the passing away of Patel in December, 1950, Vallabhbhai was to provide the ballast for Nehru's ebullience. During Gandhi's lifetime many in India had rated Patel as second in the Congress hierarchy, although the Mahatma had publicly designated Jawaharlal as his political heir. Patel lacked the mass magnetism of the younger man, though being himself no mean orator and, endowed with a vitriolic tongue and a penetrating mind, he could draw and hold the attention of huge audiences. He had a tremendous capacity for organisation, controlling the Congress party machine with the ruthless

---

[1] Patiala and East Punjab States Union, which is an overwhelmingly Sikh unit.
[2] In September, 1955, the States Reorganisation Commission suggested the discontinuance of the Raj Pramukhs.

efficiency of a Tammany Hall boss. His manner was uncompromising and his exterior tough, but he could be resilient, as his final acceptance of Pakistan proved. Above all, he was realistic with a clarity and serenity of mind which enabled him to see into the heart of a problem, reach a firm decision and act quickly. He was resolute of purpose.

Patel worked on a narrower plane than Nehru, with only India as his universe. But on that plane he was formidable. He had no patience with theories or theorists, being conservative in his economic and political outlook. Just as he had taken away power from the Princes but left them with their dignities and privileges, he had over many years mulcted India's industrialists and businessmen of heavy contributions for the Congress party coffers, dangling before them the bait of rich economic dividends when freedom came. Patel was no socialist. He liked to say that Gandhi was the greatest socialist of them all. Riches, he agreed with Gandhi, were a trust to be dispensed wisely but never to be forcibly appropriated by the people.

Politically Nehru moved on a wider plane, seeing India not as an isolated unit but within a global context. Economically his thinking was coloured by his Marxist reading; but progress to him meant, as he felt it did to Gandhi, the uplifting of the downtrodden and the oppressed. The State, particularly in an underdeveloped country, had a major economic role to play, and State planning implied State control. It meant the intrusion of the Government into the world of finance and industry, and the limitation of private enterprise within defined bounds. The manner in which Patel and Nehru separately drew strength from Gandhism for their respective economic creeds is interesting and illuminating. Gandhism was to prove all things to all men.

That a mental and temperamental gulf separated the two men is undeniable. While Gandhi lived, the intellectual tug-of-war between them had been kept under control largely by the Mahatma's overpowering influence over both and also by the intrinsic patriotism of the two men, who realised that while the struggle for independence lasted, strength lay in unity. The oppressive, often overwhelming problems which freedom brought in its immediate train preserved that bond. With Patel's death Nehru was freed from many mental inhibitions and some administrative and party restraints.

In India this juxtaposition of relationships at the highest level produced what might be described as a type of political schizophrenia with the politicians, the administrators and people bringing split minds and personalities to bear on most problems. Before he died Patel, old and weary but still resolute and purposeful, was to realise that Nehru's magic with the masses far outweighed the influence of his own practical and realistic policies. In the summer of 1950 the resignation of Congress President Babu Purushottam Das Tandon, a social and political conservative closely aligned with the Patel school of thought, threatened a major crisis in the party. The annual Congress session at Nasik that year was the last one which Patel attended. As his tired eyes rested on the huge crowds of peasants and villagers who had turned out to greet Nehru, the old man, realistic to the last, sensed who was master.

"I could not bring them out," he confessed with characteristic frankness. "They have come to see Jawahar."

Yet in those three critical years before December, 1950, when Patel died, the two men strove to work together and to bury their antipathies for the good of the India they both passionately loved.

Perhaps Nehru's verbal restraint was the greater, for Patel with his vitriolic, often venomous sarcasm could sometimes lash out bitterly —and did.

A foreign correspondent, an American,[3] asked Nehru shortly after Gandhi's death whether it was correct to represent him and Patel as political duellists, and whether the future depended upon who won.

"We differ sharply on details of concrete measures and often find ourselves at opposite poles," Nehru admitted. "And yet, it's odd, but the memory of Gandhiji keeps us together. In death he is stronger even than when he was alive."

Jawaharlal went on to elaborate his reply. Patel and he, Nehru felt, had a mutual confidence in each other's integrity, and the strong belief that neither was avid for power in itself.

"A nod from me and Patel will resign. I know that. He knows the same thing about me," said Nehru.

Both men, however much they might have differed on administrative details, were joined in a common resolve—to preserve and strengthen the unity and stability of India. The integration of the

[3] Edgar Snow.

princely States into the country's democratic framework was the first step in this process and helped to cushion the series of critical situations and shocks which followed freedom. Of these the most urgent was the absorption and rehabilitation of the 8,100,000 people who were forced to migrate to India from their homes in West and East Pakistan.

During the explosive and, later, unsettled period which continued until June, 1948, over 5,000,000 non-Muslims moved into India from West Pakistan, while another stream of nearly 3,000,000 refugees poured in from East Pakistan. In the reverse direction over 4,000,000 Muslims migrated from India to Pakistan. India, writhing in the toils of partition, was thus faced with the problem of coping with a constant influx of displaced persons whose total number roughly constituted half the population of Canada.

Nehru had himself witnessed the tragic two-way trek and had seen some of the ghastly atrocities and the degradation of the human spirit which it had incited on both sides. While the refugees from West Pakistan were equally divided into urban and rural categories, a large majority of displaced persons from East Pakistan came from the rural areas. The primary problem therefore, after evacuating them to safety and providing them with relief, was to rehabilitate them in the environment, urban or rural, to which they were accustomed and help to find them suitable employment or some means of livelihood. It was a stupendous task, complicated by the fact that the refugees included many thousands of women and children, a considerable number of them being widows and orphans.

All types of vehicles and transport from bullock carts to planes were pressed into service to evacuate this vast mass of fleeing and frightened humanity, but a majority of them trekked the greater part of their fearful journey on foot. Reception camps were hastily organised along the route where arrangements were made for providing food, shelter and medical aid, and skeleton staffs of volunteers aided the few officials who worked day and night to cope with the Herculean job which threatened at times to overwhelm them. As the camps settled down and grew more organised, recreational and educational facilities were made available and workshops were set up for minor trades such as weaving, spinning, dyeing, tailoring, woodwork, soap making and handicrafts.

Gradually the rural workers were placed on evacuee land in different parts of India, including East Punjab, PEPSU, Delhi, Rajasthan, Bombay and Uttar Pradesh. To tide over the initial difficulties loans were provided to them. Similarly the urban population were as far as possible established in the cities and towns and were found employment in industries, business houses, vocational crafts and the various professions. Everywhere refugees were accorded priority for Government employment, and a number of new townships for displaced persons came into being in different parts of the country.

Naturally it was not possible to rehabilitate and find employment for all the displaced persons. But on the whole the results achieved by this mammoth, country-wide cooperation between the authorities, the refugees and their more fortunate countrymen in India were impressive and a compliment to the spirit of community and self-help animating the Government and the people. In the case of the refugees from East Pakistan the results were not as impressive, and rehabilitation remains a major problem in eastern India, aggravated as it is by spasmodic migrations between the two Bengals which still continue.

By the end of 1950, however, the problem was under control, and in the six years since then progress has been sufficiently marked and consistent to reduce rehabilitation from being a top priority to a place far lower down the scale of national urgencies.

In November, 1950, Nehru could address Parliament on this question with confidence and with a justifiable pride in achievement against tremendous odds:

We have had to face a refugee problem of such magnitude that I doubt whether any other country in the world has had to face anything similar. I submit—for the moment I am talking about the refugees from Western Pakistan—that compared with the way in which the refugee problem has been dealt with in other countries, our results have been creditable. I do not say that they are satisfactory; that is a different thing. I only say that they compare well. There have been refugee problems in the past and there are refugee problems even today in many countries of the world—Germany, Japan and many countries of Europe after the war. Refugees from the last war still continue to live in camps in many countries of Europe.

Nehru also lost no opportunity to use this unhappy situation to impress on India's people the danger of allying religion with politics, appealing to both the majority and minority communities to live and let live. Early in April, 1948, in a speech to the Constituent Assembly, he recalled how Indians talked a great deal about politics being allied to ethics but invariably also made the hideous and costly error of combining and confusing religion with politics. Had the bloodstained past taught them nothing?

"We must have it clearly in our minds and in the mind of the country," he warned, "that the alliance of religion and politics in the shape of communalism is a most dangerous alliance, and it yields the most abnormal kind of illegitimate brood."

In the framing of the constitution which lasted a little over three years, Nehru emphasised the same secular note.

Democracy, as he recalled, was no exotic growth in India, and for centuries, long before the advent of British or Mogul rule, the stress was on self-governing institutions and a corporate life. In Vedic days the people were represented by a system of vote in the *Samiti*, or House of the People, which was the highest political institution, and alongside it was the *Sabha*, or Council of Elders. Law, called *dharma*, was sovereign, and the King or *rajan* was elected by the *Samiti*. He was regarded as embodying the *danda*, or executive power, which upheld and enforced *dharma*. For centuries sayings such as *janata janardana* (the people are God), and *Panchamukhi Parameshwara* (the voice of the people is the voice of God) were current throughout the country.

India had also its full measure of tyrants and autocrats who ruled by the sword. She had known both kings and republics, some enlightened like the great Asoka, many of them cruel despots. But always associated with the king were the wise men to whose counsel the ruler paid heed. The Indian tradition of reverence for the man of learning and authority derives largely from this. Even among the common people in the villages, democratic rule was expressed in the *panchayat*, or village council, which preserved the community's ordered and corporate life. The *panchayats* in fact survived to British days, and into independence.

On these democratic foundations and traditions India reared her independent constitution. Although the Constituent Assembly had first convened under unhappy auspices in December, 1946, with the Muslim League stubbornly boycotting it, it lost no time, once freedom came, in getting under way. On August 14, 1947, it assembled as a sovereign body to assume power on behalf of the Government of India.

The faint lineaments of the India which was to emerge with independence are discernible from its first session when its President, Dr. Rajendra Prasad, spoke of a classless society which was to grow into a cooperative commonwealth. These ideals were enshrined in the Resolution on Objectives which Nehru moved in a vigorous and eloquent speech. The resolution visualised an India

Wherein all power and authority of the sovereign, independent India, its constituent parts and organs of government are derived from the people; and

Wherein shall be guaranteed and secured to all the people of India justice, social, economic and political; equality of status, of opportunity and before the law; freedom of thought, expression, belief, faith, worship, vocation, and action, subject to law and public morality; and

Wherein adequate safeguards shall be provided for minorities, backward and tribal areas, and depressed and other backward classes; and

Wherein shall be maintained the integrity of the territory of the Republic and its sovereign rights on land, sea and air according to justice and the law of civilized nations, and this ancient land attain its rightful and honoured place in the world and make its full and willing contributions to the promotion of world peace and the welfare of mankind.

Once more the secular light shone brightly in the Prime Minister's oration. He declared:

The one thing that should be obvious to all of us is this, that there is no group in India, no party, no religious community, which can prosper if India does not prosper. If India goes down, we go down, all of us, whether we have a few seats more or less, whether we get a slight advantage or we do not. But if it is well with India, if India lives as a vital, free country then it is well with all of us to whatever community or religion we may belong.

And he ended on an evocative note with one of the earliest references he made to a theme which was later to recur often—the atom bomb:

We hear a lot about the atom bomb and the various kinds of energy that it represents, and in essence today there is a conflict in the world between two things, the atom bomb and what it represents and the spirit of humanity. I hope that while India will no doubt play a great part in all the material spheres, she will always lay stress on the spirit of humanity and I have no doubt in my mind that ultimately in this conflict that is confronting the world the human spirit will prevail over the atom bomb. May this Resolution bear fruit and may the time come when in the words of this Resolution this ancient land will attain its rightful and honoured place in the world and make its full and willing contribution to the promotion of world peace and the welfare of mankind.

India's constitution, declaring her a sovereign democratic republic, is rooted in the idea that this sovereignty vests ultimately in the people, with the people exercising freely and unfettered their right to select their representatives, with the vote conferred on all adults, irrespective of creed, community or sex, with the State pledged to a secular way of life, with every citizen, high or low, Brahmin or Untouchable assured of the fundamental rights to equality, freedom, property and to constitutional remedies, freedom of religion and cultural and educational rights. It is a constitution which because it guarantees the rule of law, with all that that implies, is a truly democratic document.

Appropriately, one of its principal draftsmen was Dr. B. R. Ambedkar, an Untouchable who as the Law Minister had the privilege of piloting the draft bill. The Constituent Assembly considered the measure clause by clause, and on November 26, 1949, in the name of the people of India it adopted and enacted it. Exactly two years, eleven months and eighteen days were expended in formulating, devising, drafting, discussing and approving of the constitution. When this historic document emerged finally from the Constituent Assembly it comprised 395 articles and eight schedules.

India being a republic, its constitution drew primarily from the republican constitutions of the United States, Switzerland, Eire and France, although, being wedded to the Commonwealth concept, it also drew copiously from the constitutions of the United Kingdom, Canada and Australia. The form of government it prescribes is, like Britain's, a parliamentary government with the executive responsible and subject to the legislature. It ensures an independent judiciary and independent public service commissions for the selection of officials. Like the American constitution it provides for a strong centre but goes beyond the United States constitution by allowing the President in the event of an emergency to supersede the powers of a State or States. In India there is only one constitution applicable to the entire country, but in America the States have the right to make their own local constitutions. Moreover, in the United States of America each State has the freedom to grant its citizens or residents a number of special rights which it may deny or grant on more difficult terms to non-residents. This state of affairs does not operate in India. Like the American constitution again, India's constitution is written.

As it emerged finally from the Convention at Philadelphia in September, 1787, the United States constitution was divided into seven articles each being subdivided into sections, and as with India's constitution the main agency of change was by amendment, though the Philadelphia document is also subject to alteration by interpretation and by the growth of conventions. There are other interesting parallels and contrasts. In the first 150 years of its life, between 1787 and 1937, the United States constitution was amended twenty-one times, and the first ten of these changes came en masse only two years after the constitution was inaugurated. These ten amendments were concerned with consolidating what might be described as the fundamental freedoms—of religion, speech, assembly and petition. Similarly within the first five years of the inauguration of the Indian constitution there have been as many as six amendments, nearly all of them concerned with defining more precisely the ambit of fundamental rights.

Broadly the same principles govern both the United States and Indian constitutions. For example, Article 2 of the American constitution provides for a strong executive, which makes for vigour and efficiency in government; Articles 1 and 3 define the separation of powers between the executive, legislature and judiciary and devise a system of checks and balances, while in Hamilton's opinion the preamble constituted a sufficient bill of rights, though ten amendments were necessary to ensure this. These principles are also reflected in the articles of the Indian constitution.

A peculiar feature of the Indian constitution is the chapter dealing with directive principles of State policy which enjoin generally and specifically that if democracy is to be real and effective it must have both an economic and a political content. The only parallel is the constitution of republican Eire, which also embodies similar directives. Part III of the Indian constitution broadly groups fundamental rights as rights to equality, freedom, property, constitutional remedies, cultural and educational rights and rights against exploitation and freedom of religion.

Nehru was specially interested in the enumeration and drafting of these directive principles, since it had always been an article of faith with him that political democracy was incomplete without economic and social democracy. Significantly, in his speech on the Objectives Resolution he recalled the revolutionary examples of only three countries—America, France and Soviet Russia.

"Our mind," he declared, "goes back to these great examples and we seek to learn from their success and to avoid their failures."

In effect the directive principles are designed to be codes of constitutional propriety determining the relation of the Government with the people. Among the economic rights and principles of social security which the constitution specifically requires the State to ensure for its people are adequate means of livelihood, fair distribution of wealth, equal pay for equal work, protection of child and adult labour, employment and free and compulsory education for children up to the age of fourteen. It also provides for public assistance in the event of unemployment, old age, sickness, disability and other cases of undeserved want, a living wage, conditions of work assuring a decent standard of life, full enjoyment of leisure, and social and cultural opportunities, and raising the level of nutrition, as also of health. Special emphasis is laid on the promotion of the educational and economic interests of the Scheduled Castes and Tribes and other weaker sections of the people.

The directive principles also enjoin that, consistent with India's desire for world peace, the country's foreign policy should promote international peace and security. It should do this by maintaining just and honourable relations between nations, by fostering respect for international law and treaty obligations in the dealings of organised peoples with one another, and by encouraging the settlement of international disputes by arbitration.

A logical epilogue to the constitution was the holding of India's first general elections, which were staggered over a hundred days and completed in early February, 1952. Never before had the democratic world witnessed so mammoth an election involving over 160 million voters, the vast majority of whom were illiterate, exercising their franchise in nearly 500 national parliamentary districts equipped with over 224,000 polling booths. The number of ballot papers printed exceeded 620 million. Over 1,800 candidates contested the 497 seats in the Lok Sabha, or House of the People, while another 15,000 candidates vied with one another to secure the 3,283 seats in the State Assemblies.

Taking the most microscopic groups into account, there were initially some 77 political organisations in the field. But these were gradually whittled down to five parties—the Congress, Communists, Socialists, the K.M.P.P. (Kisan Mazdoor Praja Party) [4] and the Jan Sangh, which represented extremist Hindu opinion. The Socialists and the K.M.P.P. were dissident Congress groups whose dissatisfaction with that party's economic policies had led them to break away from the parent body. At that time the Communists had been declared illegal in certain States such as Andhra, Kerala [5] and Hyderabad where their violence some months previously had forced the local governments to ban them. But this did not prevent the Communist party from running candidates under different labels such as the United Front of Leftists and the People's Democratic Front.

Broadcasting on the eve of the elections on November 22, 1951, Nehru appealed to the people for discipline and order:

Hundreds of millions of people in India will determine the future of this country. They will put their voting papers in terms of thousands of ballot boxes indicating their choice, and will or should do so peacefully. Out of these voting papers will emerge the Members of the Parliament of India and of the State Assemblies and we shall accept the result of this election without question.

That is the essence of democracy. All of us naturally want the cause we represent to triumph and we strive for that end. In a democracy, we have to know how to win and also how to lose with grace. Those who win should not allow this to go to their heads; those who lose should not feel dejected.

The manner of winning or losing is even more important than the result. It is better to lose in the right way than to win in the wrong way. Indeed, if success comes through misconceived effort or wrong means, then the value of that success itself is lost.

There have been interminable arguments about ends and means in India. Do wrong means justify right ends? So far as we, in India, are concerned we decided long ago that no end, for which wrong means were employed, could be right. If we apply that principle to the elections, we

[4] Peasants, Workers and People's party.
[5] This is made up of Travancore and Cochin.

must come to the conclusion that it is far better that the person with wrong ends in view be elected than that the person whose aims are worthy should win through dubious methods. If dubious methods are employed, then the rightness of the aims becomes meaningless.

I lay stress upon this because it is important and because there is a tendency, during election time, to disregard all standards of behaviour. I earnestly hope that every candidate along with his supporters will remember that to some extent he has the honour of India in his keeping and conduct himself accordingly.

Nehru himself plunged into the elections with his old passion and fervour, and wherever he went, north, south, east and west, millions came to listen to him. He travelled by all means of locomotion, on foot and by air, covering some 70,000 miles in his triumphal tour, fighting the elections on a dual plane by concentrating his verbal fire against the totalitarian Communists on the one hand, the reactionary communalists on the other.

Greeted at one centre by a parade of red flags, he turned angrily on the shouting, gesticulating Communists.

"Why don't you go and live in the country whose flag you are carrying?" he asked.

"Why don't you go to New York and live with the Wall Street imperialists?" they shouted back.

Nehru's opponent whom he defeated was a Hindu revivalist, and many of the Prime Minister's speeches in his own constituency, as elsewhere in India, echoed the appeal contained in his eve-of-the-election broadcast.

"We owe a special duty," he had then said, "to our minority communities and to those who are backward economically or educationally and who form the largest part of the population of India. We are all clamouring for our rights and privileges. It is more important to remember our duties and responsibilities."

The elections ended in a triumph for the Congress party, which captured 364 out of the 399 seats in the House of the People. It also won over 2,200 assembly seats in the various States, in all of which it was eventually able to form Congress administrations.

Roughly the votes cast for the Congress were four times those given to the Socialists and almost ten times those cast for the Communists. The Communists, who had hoped to capture Kerala State, came out second best, winning about 25 per cent of the seats. It was Nehru's last-minute visit to this Red stronghold which turned the tide. In the two days he was there he made seventy-six speeches, addressing huge crowds in the major villages, towns and cities.

India's first general elections were a tribute to the people's democratic outlook and sense of discipline. Despite the fact that the election campaign was vigorously waged by all parties, the actual elections were remarkable for the orderly and peaceful spirit which characterised them. They were a major education in government not only to India's people but to many countries in Asia and Africa. In only six polling stations out of a total of 224,000 had polling to be adjourned due to local incidents. The average poll was from 50 to 60 per cent, and in some States more women exercised their franchise than men. Villages displayed greater keenness and enthusiasm than towns, polling in the rural areas averaging 60 per cent of the electorate compared to 40 per cent in the towns. An interesting feature of the elections was that fourteen Princes were elected to various State assemblies and two to the House of the People, six of them standing on the Congress ticket. Democracy was infecting the princely order.

The integration of the princely States into the democratic framework, the rehabilitation of the 8,000,000 refugees, the drawing up of a constitution for independent India and the holding of the first general elections were four major steps in the country's progress towards unity and stability. Two other steps reinforced this process. They were India's decision to remain as a republic within the British Commonwealth and the Government's firm resolve to counter and crush Communist terrorism inside the country.

"At last, after two hundred years, Britain has conquered India," said a hard-boiled Indian newspaperman on the morrow of independence. Britain had indeed conquered India, for nothing became her so much as the manner of her leaving.

One manifestation of this was India's decision to remain within the Commonwealth. This had not always been Nehru's view, and as President of the Lahore Congress session in 1929 he had resolutely advocated complete independence for India outside the Commonwealth. Nearly twenty years later, on April 27, 1949, he agreed to a declaration issued at the conclusion of a conference of the Commonwealth Prime Ministers in London that India, as a republic, would remain within the British Commonwealth of Nations.

Speaking in the Constituent Assembly on May 16, 1949, when he moved for the ratification of this decision, Nehru recalled

that day 19 years ago when we took a pledge on the bank of the river Ravi, at the midnight hour, and I remembered the 26th January the first time and that oft-repeated pledge year after year in spite of difficulty and obstruction, and finally I remembered that day when standing at this very place, I placed a resolution before this House. That was one of the earliest resolutions placed before this Honourable House, a resolution that is known as the Objectives Resolution.

Two years and five months have elapsed since that happened. In that resolution we defined more or less the type of free Government or Republic that we were going to have. Later in another place and on a famous occasion, this subject also came up, that was at the Jaipur session of the Congress, because not only my mind, but many minds were struggling with this problem, trying to find a way out that was in keeping with the honour and dignity and independence of India, and yet also in keeping with the changing world and with the facts as they were. Something that would advance the cause of India would help us, something that would advance the cause of peace in the world, and yet something which would be strictly and absolutely true to every single pledge that we had taken. It was clear to me that whatever the advantages might be of any association with the Commonwealth or with any other group, no single advantage, however great, could be purchased by giving up a single iota of our pledges, because no country can make progress by playing fast and loose with the principles which it has declared.

Since the promise of independence Nehru had given close thought to the continuance of India's link with Britain on a basis somewhat different from that which had hitherto bound the countries of the Commonwealth. In India's own interest as also in the larger interest of international goodwill he felt that that bond should continue, though on a different nexus. Hitherto the binding link among members of the Commonwealth had been their common allegiance to the British monarch, which in a sense created among them a common nationality. But India had decided to be a republic and, while remaining within the Commonwealth, desired to enjoy a status which according to Nehru was "something between being completely foreign and being of one nationality." He had long been attracted by the idea contained in Churchill's war-time offer of an Anglo-French Union wherein the French and British peoples would maintain their separate identities, one country being a monarchy and the other a republic, and yet march in step.

In Krishna Menon, who was anxious that India should remain within the Commonwealth, Nehru found an ardent ally. The Mount-battens also influenced him in the same direction, and the realism of Vallabhbhai Patel pointed the same way. Within the Congress party opinion was divided, the more extreme elements reacting strongly against the idea of an association in which countries like South Africa were partners. The Communists, of course, were vehe-mently vocal in their denunciation.

Nehru defended his decision vigorously on his return from London both in the Constituent Assembly and outside. In a broadcast to the nation on May 10, 1949, he asked whether a country lost its independence by an alliance with another country, and he spoke of the strength of the Commonwealth which lay in its flexibility and its complete freedom. He declared:

I have naturally looked to the interests of India, for that is my first duty. I have always conceived that duty in terms of the larger good of the world. That is the lesson that our Master taught us and he told us also to pursue the ways of peace and of friendship with others, always maintaining the freedom and dignity of India. The world is full of strife today and disaster looms on the horizon. In men's hearts there is hatred and fear and suspicion which cloud their vision. Every step, therefore, which leads to a lessening of this tension in the world, should be a wel-come step. I think it is a good augury for the future that the old con-flict between India and England should be resolved in this friendly way which is honourable to both countries. There are too many disruptive forces in the world for us to throw our weight in favour of further dis-ruption, and any opportunity that offers itself to heal old wounds and to further the cause of cooperation should be welcomed.

He returned to the theme in the Constituent Assembly a week later. Nehru explained:

We join the Commonwealth obviously because we think it is bene-ficial to us and to certain causes in the world that we wish to advance. The other countries of the Commonwealth want us to remain, because they think it is beneficial to them. It is mutually understood that it is to the advantage of the nations in the Commonwealth and therefore they join. At the same time, it is made perfectly clear that each country is completely free to go its own way; it may be that they may go, some-times so far as to break away from the Commonwealth. In the world today where there are so many disruptive forces at work, where we are often on the verge of war, I think it is not a safe thing to encourage the breaking up of any association that one has. Break up the evil part of it; break up anything that may come in the way of your growth, because nobody dare agree to anything which comes in the way of a nation's growth. Otherwise, apart from breaking the evil parts of the association, it is better to keep a cooperative association going which may do good in this world rather than break it.

The Communists' vehement opposition to India's membership in the Commonwealth still persists, but Indian opinion as a whole now recognises the wisdom of Nehru's decision which has been of mutual advantage to Britain and India.

At that time the Indian Communist party was in open hostility to the Government, which described the attitude of the Reds as "bordering on open revolt." This policy, which expressed itself in violence, strikes, sabotage, murder, arson and looting, stemmed from the resolution adopted by the second congress of the Indian Communist party at Calcutta in February, 1948. Until then the Reds under the leadership of Puran Chand Joshi had maintained a united, if uneasy, front with Nehru's Government. Now, adopting the so-called Zhdanov line, they emerged as a party of violence, openly shedding "the reformist policy pursued by the former party leadership." Inevitably Joshi was overthrown along with his policy.

The prevailing economic situation, with acute food shortage, unemployment, rising prices and the influx of refugees, helped the Reds, who launched on a campaign of widespread strikes and sabotage on the industrial front with the primary object of paralysing production and communications. They also preached and planned violence on the political plane, particularly in Telengana, a pocket of territory inside Hyderabad. Here they incited the local peasants to mount a reign of terror against the landlords, and in certain villages in this area the Communists succeeded for a time in setting up their own administrations. Aside from this they were virulently active in the southern tracts of Kerala and Andhra and in the east in Bengal.

The Government of India and the State Governments reacted strongly to the Red challenge. Vallabhbhai Patel in his capacity as Home Minister [6] moved with his accustomed vigour, and the Communist party was proscribed in Hyderabad, Kerala and Bengal.

In the Madras State Assembly the then Chief Minister, C. Rajagopalachari, warned the Communists in opposition.

[6] He combined this with his office of States Minister.

"I am your enemy Number One," he told them bluntly. "May I say you are my enemy Number One? That is my policy from A to Z."

Nehru, who in a parliamentary speech had described the Indian Communist party as "the most stupid party among the Communist parties of the world," not only utilised the full force of the governmental machinery against the Reds but also called upon the people to resist their call to violence. Several Communist leaders were summarily arrested and held in detention, and where necessary the army reinforced the police in quelling violence and lawlessness.

In July, 1949, Nehru visited the storm-centre of Calcutta, where the Communists called on the masses to boycott a meeting he had planned to address. But more than a million people assembled to hear him. The Prime Minister urged them not to tolerate lawlessness, not to be afraid of the law-breakers but instead to use their own efforts to restore law and order.

As Nehru started to speak, a bomb was thrown into the crowd, killing a policeman and two spectators and injuring others, including the bomb-thrower. The Prime Minister asked the people not to panic, and the crowd, responding to his call, remained calm.

Speaking some time later in the Constituent Assembly, Nehru recalled the incident. His speech was made during a debate on the Preventive Detention Bill by which the Government sought to strengthen their powers of summary arrest and detention. A member of the opposition had attempted to dismiss the Calcutta disturbances as "the sweep of history which had forced the broad masses into action," a phrase which moved the Prime Minister to abrupt and angry retort. He remarked:

Speaking of Calcutta, another incident comes to my mind; this took place two or three years ago. Calcutta was then faced with grave and unprecedented problems because of the large influx of displaced persons from East Bengal. A state of semi-terror prevailed in the city and bombs were thrown at policemen, shops and tram-cars. It was about this time that I went to Calcutta and addressed these "broad masses." A million of them came to my meeting and at that meeting a bomb was thrown, resulting in the killing of a police inspector and two or three others; the man who threw the bomb was himself wounded. Anticipating some disturbance of this kind, I had requested them at the outset that, even in the event of a murder in their midst, they should remain calm and disciplined. And they did behave with discipline. As I was still speaking, the "broad masses" wanted to deal with the bomb thrower and restore order. They were clearly not willing to be imposed upon by the terrorists and some of them said so. Eventually, order was restored. The "broad masses" went into action against the trouble-makers. This seems to me to be a more plausible instance of the "broad masses in action."

If in the name of democracy you want people to be incited to do wrong and the structure of a democratic State we have built up undermined, you are welcome to it. Only it is not my conception of democracy.

By the middle of 1950 the back of the Red movement was broken and party morale was visibly cracking. Internal dissensions within the Communist hierarchy had meanwhile intensified, and with the outbreak of the Korean War in June, 1950, the party's tactics underwent a change. For the past five years India's Reds have been noticeably quiescent.

Nehru's firm policy had yielded good dividends. His Government's resolute reaction to the Communist campaign of hate and violence had demonstrated two things. It had shown the Government's determination to use all its resources in maintaining law and order and it had helped to inculcate in the people a will to resist violence.

By 1952, five years after independence, India was slowly settling down to a pattern of unity and stability.

25

THE WELFARE STATE

NEHRU would agree with Gandhi that independence is an ideal first to be won and then forgotten for the higher ideal of cooperation and brotherhood. This is evident in his political and economic thinking. It influenced his decision to keep India within the Commonwealth and it emerges clearly in his much-debated foreign policy. On the economic plane it expresses itself in his endeavour to make a welfare state of India.

Ever since his first visit to Soviet Russia in 1927, the idea of national planning had gripped his mind. In his autobiography Nehru writes of the change which his twenty-one-month stay in Europe, after an absence of thirteen years, wrought on him:

My outlook was wider, and nationalism by itself seemed to me definitely a narrow and insufficient creed. Political freedom, independence, were no doubt essential, but they were steps only in the right direction; without social freedom and a socialistic structure of society and the State, neither the country nor the individual could develop much. I felt I had a clearer perception of world affairs, more grip on the present day, ever changing as it was. I had read largely, not only on current affairs and politics, but on many other subjects that interested me, cultural and scientific. I found the vast political, economic, and cultural changes going on in Europe and America a fascinating study. Soviet Russia, despite certain unpleasant aspects, attracted me greatly, and seemed to hold forth a message of hope to the world.

In the eleven years between his return from Europe and the outbreak of the Second World War Nehru had occasion to reflect deeply on these matters, particularly during his enforced leisure in jail. He read Marx and followed closely the progress of the Soviet

Five-Year plans. In 1938, when the Congress party controlled the governments in all but three of India's provinces—Bengal, Punjab and Sind—Nehru was able to persuade the Congress to set up a Planning Committee which secured the cooperation of both the Congress and non-Congress provinces, some princely States (including Hyderabad, Mysore, Baroda, Travancore and Bhopal) and industrialists as well as labour representatives and economists.

Nehru was chairman of this body, but it was soon obvious to him as to his colleagues that national planning on a comprehensive scale could only take place under a free national government prepared to introduce fundamental changes in the country's social and economic structure. Nevertheless the Committee persevered with its task, guided by the primary objective of trying to ensure in its ten-year plan an adequate standard of living for the masses by stepping up agricultural and industrial production as well as by improving the social services.

Nehru's own reactions to this effort in planning are interesting in view of the Five-Year plan he was later to inspire and inaugurate as Prime Minister of an independent India. He wrote:

Constituted as we were, not only in our Committee but in the larger field of India, we could not then plan for socialism as such. Yet it became clear to me that our Plan, as it developed, was inevitably leading us towards establishing some of the fundamentals of the socialist structure. It was limiting the acquisitive factor in society, removing many of the barriers to growth, and thus leading to a rapidly expanding social structure. It was based on planning for the benefit of the common man, raising his standards greatly, giving him opportunities of growth, and releasing an enormous amount of latent talent and capacity. And all this was to be attempted in the context of democratic freedom and with a large measure of cooperation of some at least of the groups who were normally opposed to socialistic doctrine. That cooperation seemed to me worth while even if it involved toning down or weakening the Plan in some respects. Probably I was too optimistic. But so long as a big step in the right direction was taken, I felt that the very dynamics involved in the process of change would facilitate further adaptation and progress. If conflict was inevitable, it had to be faced. But if it could be avoided or minimized that was an obvious gain.

Class conflict was not a discovery of Marx, Nehru has often insisted. It was endemic in society long before *Das Kapital* was written. But violence, suppression and force are not, as the Communists think, the only solvent to this conflict. You cannot, Nehru affirms, equalise men by levelling down different socio-economic groups or individuals to one plane. The important thing is that there should be no suppression of equal opportunities to develop, which should be ensured to all. But obviously in a democratic society this calls for a system of checks and balances if exploitation is to be curbed so that the weak are not driven to the wall.

A welfare state, of a socialist pattern, has been Nehru's ideal for India for many years, certainly since 1927. But from the beginning he has held that the socialist pattern of society he envisages should be achieved not by coercion but by consent, by a process of free discussion—in short that it should be planning by persuasion, for the people and by the people. These democratic processes his government has scrupulously observed in initiating the Five-Year plans whose ideal of a welfare state is enshrined among the objectives of the Indian Constitution.

The first of these plans emanated from a Planning Commission appointed by the Government in March, 1950, and presided over by Nehru. For fifteen months this body investigated carefully the country's economic conditions, potentialities and needs, setting up for this purpose an advisory board with various panels. In 1951 a draft outline of the First Five-Year Plan was published, comprising a brochure of some three hundred printed pages, and this was widely distributed throughout the country for discussion and comment. Eighteen months later, in the light of public criticism and comment, a revised summary was released on which the First Five-Year Plan was based. The target date was set for April 1, 1956.

In a broadcast to the nation Nehru explained both the purpose and the policy of the plan which was produced approximately after two and a half years of inquiry, discussion and thought. He explained:

Our economy and social structure have outlived their day, and it has become a matter of urgent necessity for us to refashion them so that they may promote the happiness of all our people in things material and spiritual. We have to aim deliberately at a social philosophy which seeks a fundamental transformation of this structure, at a society which is not dominated by the urge for private profit and by individual greed and in which there is a fair distribution of political and economic power. We must aim at a classless society, based on cooperative effort, with opportunities for all. To realise this we have to pursue peaceful methods in a democratic way.

Democratic planning means the utilization of all our available resources and, in particular, the maximum quantity of labour willingly given and rightly directed so as to promote the good of the community and the individual.

Although the plan endeavoured to integrate various activities—agriculture, industry and social services—the stress was on the improvement of agriculture. Basically, the plan was divided into two sectors—public or governmental, and private, thus allowing both the State and private enterprise to share in the common task of national development, although the private sector, working within the framework of a plan, was necessarily subject to what the Prime Minister described as "strategic control."

Self-sufficiency in food was a major target, the aim being to increase the production of food grains by about 14 per cent at the end of five years. This would make for economic self-reliance, since India's annual imports of food and cotton at the time were from 5 to 10 per cent of her needs, signifying an outlay of over $400,000,000 in foreign exchange every year. Blessed by good rains for two successive years and aided by improved agricultural methods, including the intelligent use of tractors and fertilisers, buttressed by an extension of irrigated tracts, the output of food grains in 1955 was 20 per cent higher than it was in 1951. Similarly, cotton production during 1954–1955 reached a level of 4.3 million bales, exceeding the target of the plan, while the output of agricultural commodities, notably sugar cane and oil seeds, was also stepped up.

In 1956 increased irrigation becomes available, and this should help not only to maintain but to expand rural production. According to the Planning Commission about half the present increase in agricultural output could be ascribed to developmental methods, and of these the plan gives irrigation a high priority. In 1951 some 50,000,000 of India's 250,000,000 cultivated acres were irrigated by various means including wells, artificial lakes, dams and canals. Through multi-purpose projects of irrigation and power, some of which are still in process of construction, the plan aimed at adding 19,000,000 acres to the present irrigated land by the target date of April 1, 1956. In the closing months of 1955 about 12,000,000 acres, or nearly 25 per cent, of the present acreage under irrigation were brought into the irrigation system, and by the target date it is expected that the total will reach a little over 16,000,000 acres, larger than the total amount of land now under cultivation in Japan and only a little less than all the irrigated land in the United States.

High among the multi-purpose projects are the great river-valley development schemes which apart from expanding the irrigated tracts will step up India's electric power capacity. The per capita consumption in India when the plan started was 14 kilowatt hours compared with 3,536 in Canada, 2,400 in Sweden and 2,290 in the United States of America. Thus the leeway to be made up is considerable. Over the past three years the country's electric generating capacity has risen from 2.3 million kilowatts to three million kilowatts. The plan visualises a total increase of 55 per cent, or roughly a little over a million kilowatts.

"Power," said Nehru in a broadcast he made in December, 1952, "is the foundation of all development today."

Although keenly interested in multi-purpose projects, large and small, he continues to emphasise the major importance to India of minor works of irrigation. "They yield quicker and more widespread results." Water, he has always felt, is India's lifeblood, and water provides the common link between agriculture and industry, giving irrigation to the first and power to the second.

The largest of the multi-purpose projects is the Bhakra-Nangal project in East Punjab which draws on the waters of the Sutlej, and when completed will irrigate and provide power to the Punjab, PEPSU, Delhi and parts of Rajasthan. About 100,000 persons are working on the project under the supervision of over forty American technicians, two of whom, G. L. Savage and Harvey Slocum, have built some of America's greatest dams.

When completed the Bhakra Dam will rise 690 feet above the river bed, being the second highest in the world, ranking only after Hoover (Boulder) Dam. Meanwhile, the entire flow of the Sutlej has been canalised into two diversion channels, each fifty feet in diameter and half a mile in length. About eight miles below the Bhakra Dam is the Nangal Dam, which regulates the supply of water from the Bhakra Dam into the forty-mile-long Nangal Hydel canal feeding two power houses before it joins the Sirhind irrigation canal.

The irrigation canal system of this giant project extends nearly 3,000 miles, some 520 miles comprising main and branch canals with another 2,000 miles of distributaries. Work on the canals is ahead of schedule, and when completed the canals will irrigate over 3,500,000 acres of land,[1] promising an annual output of 1.3 million tons of wheat and other food grains, 800,000 bales of cotton, nearly 550,000 tons of sugar cane, 100,000 tons of pulses and oil seeds and 1,500,000 tons of green and dry fodder. Half the cotton which India imports will come from this resuscitated area, and about one-third of the present imported wheat.

Below the Bhakra Dam a hydroelectric station with an installed capacity of 400,000 kilowatts is to be constructed. Its power will be distributed for private consumption as well as to railways, tube wells, cottage industries and to the larger industries such as textiles, cement, sugar, chemicals and fertilisers. In time, new towns will spring up in the river valley as power and irrigation bring plenty to the people.

Produce or perish, Nehru had warned the nation soon after independence. India's greatest wealth was her man power and this she should utilise fully.

Nehru had adjured his countrymen in January, 1948:

Let us get on with work, hard work. Let us produce, but what we are producing is not for individual pockets but for the nation, to raise the standard of the people and the common man. If we do that we shall see India progressing rapidly and many of the problems that face us today will be solved. It is not an easy task for us to rebuild India. It is a very big problem, though we are a numerous people, and there is no lack of resources in India, there is no lack of human beings, capable, intelligent and hard working. We have to use these resources, this man power in India.

Besides the Bhakra-Nangal project, which should be completed in 1959, are other mammoth multi-purpose projects many of which should see completion within a year or two. They include the Hirakud project in Orissa with its three-mile-long dam, the longest in the world, which will irrigate 1,500,000 acres of rice land when it is completed in August, 1956. Among the 30,000 persons working on the project are some technical experts supplied under the British

[1] About two and a half times the area irrigated by Grand Coulee.

Commonwealth's Colombo Plan. The Damodar Valley project, servicing Bihar and Bengal, will take longer to complete, but the First Five-Year Plan envisages the construction of four dams, one each at Tilaiya, Konar, Maithon and Panchet Hill with an installed hydroelectric capacity for 104,000 kilowatts, a barrage at Durgapur with an irrigation-cum-navigation canal, a thermal power station of 200,000 kilowatts at Bokaro, and the requisite transmission. Work on these undertakings is proceeding to schedule. Like the T.V.A., the Damodar valley project is run by an autonomous government corporation. Other projects include the Tungabhadra project abutting on Andhra, Hyderabad and Mysore, which is planned to benefit an area of 2,000,000 acres of which 700,000 are now under irrigation. The project also envisages the generation of hydroelectric power. Yet other projects include the Kakrapara weirs and canals project in Bombay, the Machkund hydroelectric project between Andhra and Orissa, the completed Mayurakshi project in West Bengal and the Kosi project in Bihar on which work started in January, 1955.

In all, some 46 per cent of the public investment of the First Five-Year Plan was earmarked for increasing agricultural output and extending India's irrigation and power projects. In a country where the overwhelming majority of the people live in villages and work on the land the accent in economic development must inevitably be on agriculture. This was so in the First Five-Year Plan, whose primary aim was the achievement of economic stability.

Just as he planned that India politically should move from stability to progress, so also economically Nehru visualised the process in the same idiom and terms. The First Five-Year Plan represented stability. The Second represents progress.

Speaking on the First Five-Year Plan in 1952, he remarked:

Our ideals are high and our objectives great. Compared with them, the Five-Year Plan appears to be a modest beginning. But, let us remember that this is the first great effort of its kind and that it is based on the realities of today and not on our wishes. It must, therefore, be related to our present resources or else it will remain unreal. It is designed to be the foundation of a bigger and better plan of progress in the future. Let us lay the foundations well and the rest will inevitably follow.

Agriculture, he argued, was bound to continue to be India's greatest activity. The strongest stress should therefore be laid on it because it was only on the basis of agricultural prosperity that India could make industrial progress.

"But agriculture," he pointed out, "has to be fitted into the larger economy of the nation. The growth of industry, big and small, is essential for the growth of any modern nation. Indeed without industrial development there cannot be any higher standard of living for our people or even enough strength in the nation for it to preserve its freedom."

Hence the larger stress on industrial development in the blueprint or framework of the Second Five-Year Plan, which was released for public discussion and comment in March, 1955. On the economic as on the political plane it is illuminating to see how Nehru moves logically and purposefully step by step.

Not that the First Five-Year Plan ignored industrial development. But it was necessarily circumscribed, a little less than 10 per cent of the public investment being devoted to this sector, which included cottage and small-scale industries. In addition, some forty-two industries under private management participated in the development programme.

Nehru has never been against industrialisation. On the contrary he has always actively advocated it. Nor for that matter has the Congress party opposed it, although doctrinaire interpreters of the Gandhian creed of the spinning wheel tend to see omniscient economic virtues and values in the development of handicrafts and cottage industries. Gandhi was not against the machine as such. He was against the big machine, which he felt had led to the concentration of power and riches in the hands of the few. "What I object to," the Mahatma once wrote, "is the craze for machinery, not machinery as such. . . . If we could have electricity in every village home I should not mind villagers plying their implements and tools with electricity."

Nehru's views on industrialisation go much further. As chairman of the National Planning Committee which the Congress had sponsored as far back as 1938, nine years before independence, he had felt that it was not a mere question of adjustment between heavy industrialisation and cottage industries: one must dominate the other. And he had faced and answered the question boldly. He had concluded:

The economy based on the latest technical achievements of the day must necessarily be the dominating one. If technology demands the big machine, as it does today in a large measure, then the big machine with all its implications and consequences must be accepted. Where it is possible, in terms of that technology, to decentralize production, this would be desirable. But, in any event, the latest technique has to be followed, and to adhere to out-worn and out-of-date methods of production, except as a temporary and stop-gap measure, is to arrest growth and development.

In his own mind he has never questioned that India should be industrialised rapidly, but what he is anxious to curb are the evils of industrialisation, particularly in a country of arrested economic growth like India, where certain industrialists and politicians have, according to Nehru, "thought too much in terms of the nineteenth century development of capitalist industry in Europe and ignored many of the evil consequences that were obvious in the twentieth century." In India, because of arrested economic growth, these consequences are likely to be more far-reaching.

The simple or rather simpleton remedy is to do away with the big machine and thereby hope to minimise unemployment. That is not Nehru's view. The problem of India, as he sees it, is one of scarcity of capital and abundance of labour—how to utilise this wasted labour, this manpower that is producing nothing. Nehru believes that machinery should be introduced on the largest scale provided it is used primarily for absorbing labour and not for creating fresh unemployment.

In an under-developed country such as India planning with fixed priorities and on a basis of regulation and coordination becomes imperative. No planning could thus ignore agriculture, which is the mainstay of the people, nor the social services, which are woefully deficient for their needs. At the same time, writing in jail during his last term of imprisonment, Nehru emphasised: "The three fundamental requirements of India if she is to develop industrially and otherwise are: a heavy engineering and machine-making industry, scientific research institutions, and electric power. These must be the foundations of all planning."

Under the stimulus of the First Five-Year Plan several new major industries came into being. In the public sector these include the fertiliser factory at Sindri in Bihar, a plant which has been in production for nearly three years, and has a daily output of 1,000 tons of ammonium sulphate. Simultaneously fertiliser consumption has increased from less than 200,000 tons of ammonium sulphate per annum to nearly 600,000 tons in 1955. A locomotive workshop now operates at Chittaranjan in West Bengal, and India's locomotive works produce about a hundred locomotives per year. More recently penicillin and D.D.T. factories have gone into production, as has also a newsprint factory which is expected to meet nearly 40 per cent of India's internal requirements. Late in 1955 a factory for making railway passenger coaches and another for the manufacture of machine tools commenced to operate. Governmental enterprise under the First Five-Year Plan includes the nationalisation of internal air transport and the development of a modern shipbuilding industry in which both the Government and private enterprise cooperate.

Alongside these State or governmental undertakings private enterprise has responded to the national call, and in several fields output exceeds the targets. With her cotton textile industry producing over 6,000,000 yards of cloth per annum, India now ranks as the world's second largest producer and exporter of cotton textiles. Between 1951 and 1955 the output of cement went up from 2.7 million tons per year to well over four million tons in 1954–1955, while in the same period the paper industry has stepped up production by 50 per cent. Steel plants showed an annual output of 1.5 million tons towards the end of 1955, a figure which it is hoped to step up to about 5,000,000 tons under the Second Five-Year Plan, when three large State plants are additionally expected to function. Even now Americans, Britons, Russians and Germans are helping India to build new plants or draw up plans for them. The new target for cement, which it is hoped to achieve by 1961, is set at 10,000,000 tons per annum. Factories manufacturing a variety of light engineering products are working almost to capacity, while private enterprise is now able to meet more than half the requirements of rayon yarn.

Private foreign investment and technical skill have also contributed to the fruition of the plan, these including three oil refinery projects, two of which are in production. Meanwhile, foreign capital and technical skill are assisting in developing new lines of production such as the manufacture of dyes, chemicals, pharmaceuticals, industrial explosives, engineering products and various types of machinery. The refineries represent investments totalling $106,000,000, the largest foreign investments in independent India. According to a census of foreign investments recently produced by the Reserve Bank of India, private investment of a long-term character increased in net by a little over $250,000,000—not a large amount as an addition to capital resources but indicative of the measure of confidence reposed by the informed foreign investor.

Typical of the progress achieved under the First Five-Year Plan is the rise in the over-all index of industrial production and the fall in commodity prices. As compared to 1950, when the over-all index stood at 105, the figure for the first quarter of 1955 was 157.9, and the upward trend continues. The price index has dropped from 399.6 at the beginning of 1954 to 358.6 at the end of August, 1955. During 1954–1955 development expenditure in the public sector totalled about 1.1 billion dollars, and in 1955–1956 it is expected to reach 1.5 billion dollars. In the field of private enterprise, during the twelve months ending July, 1955, over 370 permits were granted to entrepreneurs to establish new industries or expand existing ones. Over 100 of these were for new undertakings. Thus stable conditions have been restored in trade and industry, and self-sufficiency has been attained in a number of consumer goods. The drive is now on for self-sufficiency in capital goods.

In terms of American and European development this effort is modest. As with the National Planning Committee of 1938–1939, the object of the First Five-Year Plan was to mitigate and in time eliminate the appalling poverty of India's people by lifting their standard of living and carrying it higher and higher. When the plan was initiated India's national income was $20,000,000,000 a year, and it was hoped in the five-year period to raise it by 11 per cent. Within three years, however, in terms of constant prices, the national income has risen by 12.4 per cent, which even allowing for favourable factors such as two good monsoons, exceeds the rate of population growth. India's planners and economists are well aware that this does not permit of complacency even if in India the density of population is less than half that of Japan, Germany and the United Kingdom. But on a civilised calculus, if there are more stomachs to feed there are also more brains to think and more bodies to work.

India's Prime Minister in a speech in Parliament in December, 1952, warned against undue complacency in this respect:

However rapid our industrialisation may be, it cannot possibly absorb more than a small part of the population of this country in the next ten, twenty or even thirty years. Hundreds of millions will remain who have to be employed chiefly in agriculture. These people must, in addition, be given employment in smaller industries like cottage industries and so on. Hence, the importance of village and cottage industries. I think the argument one often hears about big industry versus cottage and village industry is misconceived. I have no doubt that we cannot raise the people's level of existence without the development of major industries in this country; in fact, I will go further and say that we cannot even remain a free country without them. Certain things, like adequate defence, are essential to freedom and these cannot be had unless we develop industry in a major way. But we must always remember that the development of heavy industry does not by itself solve the problem of the millions in this country. We have to develop the village and cottage industry in a big way, at the same time making sure that in trying to develop industry, big and small, we do not forget the human factor. We are not merely out to get more money and more production. We ultimately want better human beings. We want our people to have greater opportunities, not only from an economic or material point of view but at other levels also.

Nehru's strong interest in the community projects which are an important feature of the First Five-Year Plan derives from this concern. Unless material advancement is fortified by progress in education and the social services, he fears that national development will be lopsided.

The per capita income of India's people has risen over the past five years from $53 to $58 per annum, and the long-range goal is to double this figure to roughly $100 a year, a target which on the present basis should take another four Five-Year plans. But the pressure of population on land is depressingly heavy, since urban employment accounts for only about 5 per cent of the workers. The consequence is considerable unemployment and underemployment in the villages and towns. Some time ago the Finance Minister, Mr. C. D. Deshmukh, placed the number of fully unemployed people at 15,000,000. Reliable statistics are hard to come by or are unavailable, but some informed observers place the total number of those unemployed or employed only for two or three months in the year at as much as 40,000,000. Against this, the rate of India's population growth is nearly 5,000,000 a year, signifying an annual increase of between 1.5 and 2 million more persons seeking employment annually.

Appropriately the village programme of Community Development was launched on the anniversary of Gandhi's birthday, October 2, 1952, a beginning being made with fifty-five development projects spread over India's States and covering some 25,000 villages with over 16,000,000 people.

"The work which has started here today," said Nehru, addressing a huge crowd of peasants, "spells the revolution about which some people have been shouting for so long. This is not a revolution based on chaos and the breaking of heads but on a sustained effort to eradicate poverty. This is no time for speeches. We must make India great by our toil."

Saying which, Nehru seized a spade and, heading a covey of officials, inaugurated the first effort in voluntary road building.

This attempt in rural self-help covers many spheres of village life, including the building of local roads, embankments, schools and hospitals, reclamation of virgin and waste lands, helping the grow-more-food campaign and encouraging public health, education and literacy. It is intended to be a people's programme with Government participation, although in the initial stages the inspiration and initiative came from the Government. Valuable aid has been extended by the United States Government in the way of monetary assistance, equipment, supplies and experts, and also by the Ford Foundation.

The success of Community Development led to the National Extension Service which now functions alongside it with a view to creating a permanent organisation for rural development which is linked with the administrative set-up. The roots of the welfare state of Nehru's dream are here. During the First Five-Year Plan 1,200 blocks comprising 120,000 villages with a population of about 80,000,000 out of India's 550,000 villages were covered by this scheme. Of the 1,200 blocks 700 were taken under the intensive community programme and 500 under the N.E.S.

History, according to Nehru, had selected India as one of democracy's chief testing grounds, and in Community Development and the N.E.S. it found concrete and constructive examples of the democratic spirit at work.

"All over India," proclaimed the Prime Minister, "there are now centres of human activity that are like lamps spreading their light more and more in the surrounding darkness. This light must grow and grow until it covers the land."

By the summer of 1955 the village development programme covered some 100,000 villages with a population of nearly 80,000,000, roughly one-fifth of India's population. In other words, one out of every five villagers is now receiving expert community advice on diverse matters which affect him and his family closely—on better agricultural methods, on the use of fertilisers, on the value of literacy and education, on building schools and hospitals through voluntary labour, on maintaining a basic standard of public health and sanitation, on curbing malaria, and on fighting the jungle and recovering land for cultivation.

By June, 1955, over 400,000 acres of forest and waste land were reclaimed and over 750,000 acres were brought under irrigation. In addition some 155,000 acres were cultivated with fruit and vegetables. During the same period about 12,000 miles of roads, in which the land as well as the earthwork was contributed almost exclusively by the villagers, were constructed, besides 600 miles of essential drains.

The spread of literacy is another matter in which rural India is absorbed. Dr. Frank Laubach, the celebrated American expert on literacy programmes, has been of invaluable help here, and his slogan "Each one teach one" has proved widely infectious in the campaign to spread adult literacy. Less dramatic though no less useful has been the extension of formal education for children with the emphasis on craft training. By the summer of 1955 over 14,400 adult education centres had been started along with nearly 6,000 new schools while another 1,600 old schools had been given over to basic and craft training.

Perhaps the most remarkable effort in community cooperation has been the successful drive against malaria, a scourge which at one time annually afflicted 100,000,000 victims. Until 1951 a million people died directly of the disease every year, while another million died indirectly. The Plan aims to reduce the actual incidence of the disease, which is particularly virulent in the rural areas, to less than a million a year, thereby bringing the death rate proportionately lower. In the rural areas the initial accent is on prevention rather than on cure. D.D.T., supplied by American Point Four, has proved particularly effective, and in 1955 the incidence of the disease had been reduced from an annual average of 100,000,000 cases to 25,000,000.

With improved health, better education and a growing sense of social service, rural India is slowly stirring to new life and reaching out to broader horizons. Land is the crux of the problem, for to the landless or impoverished peasant land is the symbol of new opportunities and better livelihood. A considerable proportion of these landless labourers are Untouchables, a fact which is urgently present in Nehru's mind. Speaking at the Community Projects Conference in May, 1952, he referred to it. He said:

Really what we are committed to is not a few community centres but to working for the biggest community of all and that is the community of the people of India, more especially those who are down and out, those who are backward. There are far too many backward people in this country. Besides the Scheduled Castes and the Scheduled Tribe organizations, there is an organization called the Backward Classes League. As a matter of fact, you can safely say that 96 per cent. of the people of India are economically very backward. Indeed, apart from a handful of men, most of the people are backward. Anyhow, we have to think more of those who are more backward because we must aim at progressively producing a measure of equality in opportunity and other things. In the modern world today, you cannot go on for long having big gaps between those who are at the top and those who are at the bottom. You cannot make all men equal, of course. But we must at least give them equality of opportunity.

Land reform, beginning with the abolition of large estates, was a major method in this process. It is no new-fangled theory, for it has been the Congress policy since the Karachi session of 1931 when under Nehru's inspiration and with Gandhi's support the Congress adopted a resolution on Fundamental Rights and Economic Programme. "In order to end the exploitation of the masses," it declared, "political freedom must include real economic freedom for the starving masses." The resolution stipulated that the system of land tenure and revenue and rent "should be reformed." Even earlier, in 1928, the satyagraha struggle launched successfully by the peasants of Bardoli under the leadership of Sardar Vallabhbhai Patel had focussed country-wide attention on the plight of the Indian peasantry. In 1929 the United Provinces Provincial Congress Committee, again under Nehru's inspiration, had drawn up a socialist programme which declared that the existing land system should go, and that there should be no intermediaries between the State and the cultivator. In other words, the big landlords known variously as zamindars or taluqdars

should be replaced by peasant proprietors. The preamble of this resolution, endorsing the principle of socialism, was adopted by the All-
India Congress Committee, although as Nehru frankly conceded later,
"the A.-I.C.C. passed that resolution without giving much thought
to it and most members probably did not realise what they were
doing."

But Nehru realised and remembered. That was important. Through
the years before independence and after he was constantly to remind
his countrymen of the land hunger of the peasants, their misery and
indebtedness, and the paramount need for land reform. In the early
years of freedom, around 1948, the Communists, capitalising on the
peasants' discontent, raised Lenin's cry of "Land to the Tiller," and in
certain areas, such as the Telengana district of Hyderabad, they were
successful in inciting the peasantry against the landlords, even depriv-
ing them forcibly of their land.

The Fundamental Rights enshrined in the Indian Constitution
include the right of property, and Nehru's Government could not
constitutionally expropriate land without compensation, nor was this
in its mind. Inside the Congress itself were vested landed interests
opposed to any change; outside, the bigger landlords resisted the
reform by demanding compensation on a fantastic scale. It therefore
became necessary to amend the constitution so that while altering the
procedure of compensation in case of acquisition, no landlord would
be deprived of his property except by process of law and save on
grounds of public interest. But a fair compensation had to be paid.

Even so there remain formidable obstacles in the way of the speedy
achievement of land reform reared largely on the peasant's ignorance
and gullibility which make him an easy prey for a rapacious landlord
who is also rich and literate. The responsibility for implementing
land reform rests on the State Governments not all of whom have
shown adequate vigour. For the most part tenancy legislation, grant-
ing occupancy rights to the present tillers and limiting their rent,
has been adopted. But even in places where the legal title has been
transferred to the tiller he is often, despite well spread-out instalments, unable to pay the five or ten years' rent he must give to the
landlord as compensation. For the greater part, however, the old
system of zamindari landlordism whereby hereditary tax collectors
for the old British Government gradually assumed ownership of the

land itself has been abolished. But even here generous compensation has had to be paid.

Admittedly Nehru's Government has not succeeded as well as it had hoped in implementing its policy of land reform. Progress has been slow. It is the price democracy and democratic methods must pay, and Nehru realises this.[2] He warned:

We in this country must not think of approaching our objectives through conflict and force. We have achieved many things by peaceful means and there is no reason why we should suddenly abandon that method and take to violence. There is a very special reason why we should not do so. I am quite convinced that, if we try to attain our ideals and objectives, however high they may be, by violent methods we shall delay matters greatly and help the growth of the very evils we are fighting. India is not only a big country with a good deal of variety; and if any one takes to the sword, he will inevitably be faced with the sword of someone else. This clash between swords will degenerate into fruitless violence and, in the process, the limited energies of the nation will be dissipated or, at any rate, greatly undermined. The method of peaceful progress is ultimately the method of democratic progress.

Broadly the First Five-Year Plan has achieved nearly 90 per cent of its objectives, agricultural and industrial. The Second Five-Year Plan, which at the moment of writing is still in its formative stage, is cast in the same democratic mould as the first, the blueprint being thrown open to public discussion, its approach being pragmatic, not doctrinaire, and conceived on the principle of trial and error with a view to relating and reconciling the idealistic and the realistic. Consistent with its objective to ensure a more rapid increase of national income, stepping it up from 3 to 5 per cent annually, and to provide a greater volume of employment, the Second Five-Year Plan lays stress on greater industrialisation. Its investment targets considerably exceed those of the First Plan.

But in between the first and the second plans occurred developments such as the Prime Minister's visits to China and Russia, the visits of Chou En-lai, Bulganin and Khrushchev and the definite enunciation by the Congress at its session at Avadi in January, 1955,

[2] Supplementing the Government's land reform through legislation is Vinoba Bhave's Bhoodan movement which aims at the surrender of land by voluntary donation. Vinoba is still far from the target of 50,000,000 acres he had set himself to collect by the end of 1955. To date he has collected nearly 4,000,000 acres.

of a socialist pattern of society as the party's economic objective for India.

Emphasis on a mixed economy is now more marked, and the private sector seems to be shrinking as the public sector encroaches on its domain. Taxation is on the upgrade, with the threat of a ceiling on incomes and of deficit financing, the Government's fiscal policy being based on the Robin Hood principle of mulcting the rich in order to help the poor. Somebody must pay for India's development projects. By American standards the outlay of $4,000,000,000 for the First Plan is small, but it is large and burdensome by Indian norms. India's total national income is only about 6 per cent of that of the U.S.A. Moreover, India has more than double America's population. Over 90 per cent of the money for the First Plan was raised by internal financing, primarily by heavy taxation. Grants from the Colombo Plan, the American Point Four programme and World Bank loans have made up the remainder. For the Second Plan, whose goals are more ambitious, India will have to find $1,700,000,000 from abroad, or else curtail her targets.

Private enterprise looks like beating a strategic retreat before "the wild men" of the Congress party who press for wholesale nationalisation as the only method of accelerating industrial output. Oddly enough, other Congress followers simultaneously clamour for an extension of the domain of handicrafts, hand looms and cottage industries as the only quick solvent of unemployment. The mixed economy which Nehru preaches as a panacea for the country's economic ills finds a curious reflection in his own party. There it is mixed more than somewhat.

In the confused and complicated texture of thought of Congress, Nehru's economic thinking runs consistently like a firm thread. Over the past thirty years his economic views have not altered their course appreciably, although occasionally they have broadened or narrowed their emphasis. With the sole exception of Gandhi, Nehru was the only Indian leader when independence came who had thought out and worked out for himself a definite political, economic and social philosophy which power gave him a unique opportunity to implement.

Less doctrinaire than the Gandhism which influenced their shape and direction, Nehru's beliefs are equally inflexible and purposeful.

They might bend but they will not break. Within their flexible framework they attempt to accommodate and reconcile Gandhi's non-violence, his love for the small man and acceptance of the small machine, his simple democracy where the gulf between the rich and the poor would not be marked, his gospel of the charkha and village India with Nehru's own rational scientific outlook, his eagerness for technological and industrial advancement on the most modern lines and his dream of a world where the peasant, the technician, the worker, the industrialist, the scholar, scientist and intellectual would together share the fruits of their toil and thought. Nehru envisages for India a type of economic life distinctive in itself, conditioned to its own ways of living, and identified neither with the *laissez faire* economics of the nineteenth century nor the patterned totalitarianism of Soviet Russia or Nazi Germany.

Marxism has undoubtedly influenced his economic thinking but has not captured it. Although Nehru feels that Marx was wrong in some of his statements he admires him for what he describes as his insight into social phenomena and his scientific approach to problems. On the other hand, India's Prime Minister rarely troubles to conceal his contempt for Communists *qua* Communists whether in or outside India. Like Engels he would probably thank God that Marx was not a Marxist.

On March 5, 1955, Nehru addressed the Federation of Indian Chambers of Commerce and Industry, which represents indigenous Big Business, and explained to them the motivations of the Avadi resolution for the establishment of a socialistic pattern of society:

The slogans of yesterday have very little meaning in the present day, whether the slogans are capitalistic, socialistic or communistic. All these have to be fitted into the nuclear age. Not that they are all wrong. They have some elements of truth but they have to be refitted and rethought of. Capitalism, socialism, Marxism, all these are children of the Industrial Revolution. We are on the eve of at least something as great as the Industrial Revolution, perhaps something bigger. It is affecting everything—production, distribution, thinking, and everything else. In this context, why was this decision for a socialistic pattern of society taken? It was taken to give an indication of the objective and the approach. We have to fit India into the nuclear age and do it quickly. While learning from other countries, we should also remember that each country is conditioned by its past. All the factors that have conditioned India have to be remembered.

Elsewhere, in a speech in Parliament, Nehru repudiated the charge that his Government would confiscate foreign property in India:

We as a self-respecting nation will never tolerate any plea from any quarter to confiscate any foreigner's property in India. From any point of view, this attitude of snatching away property of foreigners in India to increase the country's wealth is totally wrong. We want to establish a socialistic pattern of society and it is an utterly wrong approach to suggest that in doing this, we should forcibly take over other people's property. Our laws should be such that more and more equality is brought about among people.

Nehru also explained in another speech, delivered in November, 1954, the place of private enterprise in national planning:

Undoubtedly private enterprise is useful so far as our country is concerned. We wish to encourage it, but the dominance which private enterprise had throughout the world during a certain period is no more. It is out of date in that sense of the word. For a planner, it has now a secondary place. Any system which is based on what is called the acquisitiveness of society is absolutely out of date; in modern thinking it is also considered immoral. That does not mean that we are doing away with private enterprise. I think there is much scope for it, and where you allow private enterprise, you should give scope, freedom and encouragement to it to develop, but we must realise that the day of the acquisitive element in society has not passed but is passing.

More recently he has vigorously denied that his Government plans to nationalise all industries in its efforts to achieve a socialistic pattern of society. Nehru's Government, while showing no undue favour to private enterprise, has helped it in various ways—by loan or capital subscription, export promotion and tariff protection. In 1955 the Industrial Investment and Credit Corporation of India with shareholders from three countries was established. It is entirely under private management and the Indian Government has helped it with a long-term interest-free loan. More recently India has joined the International Finance Corporation, which is designed to assist private enterprise. During the past few years the Government and private industry, including foreign capital, have cooperated in mixed enterprises such as shipping and shipbuilding, the manufacture of locomotives and coaches, machinery and machine tools and the exploration of oil.

The Avadi session of the Congress followed only two and a half months after Nehru's visit to China which took place in the latter half of October, 1954. He came back impressed with the Chinese Communists' economic efforts, prepared to concede that their progress on the agricultural front had been quicker than India's but with the strong belief that industrially India was more advanced, and he did not disguise his conviction that India, given a socialist objective and planned guidance, could and would move faster.

An authoritarian régime, Nehru points out, might take less time for constructive achievement than a democratic government. But authoritarian régimes such as that in Russia have actually taken considerable time in registering economic progress.

"I think," Nehru once remarked, "that the difference in the time limit is not so great as people imagine. Indeed it need not be if the people of a democratic country are eager enough for change and are prepared to work for it."

He was impressed also by the discovery that China was no pale imitation of Russia but was conditioning her plans to her circumstances. "They are supposed to be Marxists in China, but the way they are interpreting Marxism is very different from the way the Russians did. I don't say there is a conflict. That is for them to say." [3]

Nehru also came back conscious of the fact that in a regimented economy such as China's the Government could act faster and might possibly secure quicker results. But he was careful to emphasise that India had chosen the democratic way and that the Avadi resolution was a shining beacon of that democratic resolve and faith. His visit to China, as his later visit to Russia, roused in him a competitive spirit. India could go one better along the democratic path.

"They can pass a law overnight if they want to," he remarked in a reference to the Chinese. "Nevertheless they go on saying that it will take them twenty years to lay the socialist basis of their society."

To Khrushchev and Bulganin, who boasted of Russia's "wonderful achievements," he said, chiding them gently: "After all Soviet Russia took forty years to get the machines running. Give us thirty years!"

[3] In a speech at the Avadi session of the Congress in January, 1955.

26

INDIA AND ASIA

"I have learned that a Prime Minister cannot afford to be sensitive," Nehru remarked to an American journalist not long after he assumed office.

Over the years, as India has acquired a place on the international stage and Nehru himself has won international stature as a world statesman with a distinctive foreign policy which simultaneously draws angry criticism and warm approval, the lesson he learned has in all probability been reinforced.

Nehru's foreign policy is rooted primarily in what might be described as the principle of enlightened self-interest. He has said so openly more than once, and in December, 1947, speaking in the Constituent Assembly, he boldly proclaimed it:

Whatever policy you may lay down, the art of conducting the foreign affairs of a country lies in finding out what is most advantageous to the country. We may talk about peace and freedom and earnestly mean what we say. But in the ultimate analysis a government functions for the good of the country it governs and no government dare do anything which in the short or long run is manifestly to the disadvantage of that country. Therefore whether a country is imperialistic or socialist or communist its Foreign Minister thinks primarily of the interests of that country.

To India as to most of the newly independent countries of Asia peace is a vital imperative, for without peace it is not possible to give political freedom economic content and reality. The choice for pre-war Europe lay between guns and butter. The choice for post-war Asia lies between guns and bread. Unless Asia's economic conditions are improved and its standard of living stepped up, there will be no meaning or reality in its independence. That is how India and many Asian countries view the international scene. Progress to them means peace which means stability which means strength which in turn spells plenty and prosperity.

But Nehru's foreign policy, although necessarily conditioned by India's needs, derives also from a long history and background. If it suits his country's immediate requirements it also fits into the framework of India's thought and tradition. The doctrine of *panchshila* might claim to be as old as the Buddha whose precepts of peace were enshrined in the rock edicts of Asoka and echoed more than two thousand years later in Gandhi's teachings. Through the thought of these three teachers runs the recurring theme of means and ends. Buddha taught that through the Noble Eightfold Path—right views, right intention, right speech, right action, right livelihood, right effort, right mindfulness, right concentration—lay the road to nirvana wherein he who attains nirvana attains all knowledge of the truths and is emancipated. Good means make for good ends, Gandhi constantly preached.

Yet Nehru, while acknowledging the influence of his master's ethical and moral teachings, has pointed out the practical difficulties in applying them wholesale to given situations. In a speech he made in March, 1949, he warned:

There is always a great difference between a prophet and a politician in their approach to a problem. We had the combination of a prophet and a great statesman; but then we are not prophets nor are we very great in our statesmanship. All we can say is that we should do our utmost to live up as far as we can to that standard, but always judging a problem by the light of our own intelligence, otherwise we will fail. There is the grave danger, on the one hand, of denying the message of the prophet, and on the other, of blindly following it and missing all its vitality. We have, therefore, to steer a middle course through these.

Against this background it is possible to understand why Nehru on the international stage appears to zig-zag to his target, for while he considers each issue on its intrinsic merit he also views it in relation to the interests of his country. If he talks constantly of moral and ethical values it is not for the benefit of the world so much as for the understanding of his countrymen, reared as they are in an ancient tradition of means and ends. The end here is peace, and the means, though they may alter with the situation, must be right and good. India is paramount in Nehru's foreign thinking.

He has never seen independence for India in terms of isolation, which is why the description of his foreign policy as "neutralism" irritates him. Neutralism implies a refusal to express positive views on specific issues and a reluctance to pursue the expression of these views with positive action. But on no important issue, from her first appearance as an independent nation in the U.N., has India refrained from expressing a definite point of view or helping to implement it.

Thus in 1946 when India was on the threshold of independence, she sent "a more or less independent delegation," to quote Nehru's words, to the U.N., where it took an attitude on the Palestine problem which initially was shared neither by the Russians, the British nor the Americans, who either favoured partition or the creation of a unitary State. India proposed the establishment of a federal State with an Arab majority at the centre and with autonomy for the Jewish and Arab regions, a solution broadly contained in the minority report of the Palestine Committee. The proposal was looked upon at first with suspicion by both sides, but in the last forty-eight hours of the debate, when it seemed that partition was inevitable, those who originally had wanted a unitary State favoured the Indian suggestion. Then it was too late, partition being decided upon by a two-thirds majority.

Similarly when the North Koreans crossed the 38th Parallel in June, 1950, India was among the first to join with the democratic countries in denouncing it as aggression, and promptly sent an Indian Army hospital unit to South Korea. "Any military assistance is beyond India's capacity and would make little difference," Nehru explained subsequently in an interview with an American news magazine.[1] "India's defence forces have been organized essentially for home defence and not for service in distant theatres of war." In the same interview he declared, "It is perfectly clear that North Korea launched a full-scale and well-planned invasion and this, in the context of the United Nations Charter, has already been described as aggression by the Security Council." Later, in carrying out the armistice terms in Korea, India contributed five thousand troops who supervised the repatriation of the prisoners.

[1] *U.S. News and World Report*, September 15, 1950.

A call for a "cease fire" in Indo-China was first made by Nehru in February, 1954, with a view to creating a suitable atmosphere for the conference at Geneva. Although it was immediately scoffed at as impracticable, a cease-fire line was eventually established, but only after the French Army, stunned by the disaster of Dienbienphu, virtually faced military extinction in the Red River delta. The then American ambassador to India, Mr. George Allen, has gone on record as saying that when he pointed out to Nehru that the Communists had stepped up the fighting directly in the face of his appeal for relaxation (by their attack on Dienbienphu), the Indian Prime Minister publicly criticised the Communists as the side responsible for the flare-up in the fighting. He also criticised the Americans for threatening to extend the war to the Chinese mainland. On the announcement of the cease fire, India sent army and civilian personnel to Indo-China to assist the U.N. Commission in carrying through the terms of the armistice.

Similarly in the autumn of 1950, after MacArthur's victory at Inchon, Nehru urged a cease fire in Korea along the 38th Parallel. He did this in order to avoid the enlargement of the war and further waste of blood. The Chinese Government had warned the Indian ambassador in Peking that China would enter the war if the U.N. forces crossed the 38th Parallel. Peking is bluffing, said Washington, and MacArthur talked of having his boys home by Christmas. Three years later, after sustaining some 96,000 additional casualties in American dead and wounded, the U.N. accepted a truce along approximately the same line as the 38th Parallel.

India, it is true, refrained from naming China as the aggressor after the People's Army had crossed the Yalu. But in China's eyes, as Peking had warned New Delhi, MacArthur's advance on the Yalu, not the Chinese reaction to it, was an act of aggression. China has long regarded Korea as a dagger pointed at her flank. Was it aggression for China to cross the threshold in order to protect the door? Moreover, as India argued, the recrossing of the 38th Parallel from the south would be a violation of the very principle on which the U.N. named the North Koreans as aggressors when they crossed it from the north. In either case it was open to the construction of an attempt to achieve Korea's unity by force.

Other examples of India's positive intervention can be cited. In

April, 1955, Nehru urged moderation in the explosive talk and threats about Quemoy and Matsu, a plea which President Eisenhower wisely heeded. India's good offices were also available in helping to secure the release of the captive American flyers in China. And at Bandung, as earlier, Nehru urged on Chou En-lai the need for a peaceful settlement on Formosa.

These proposals and actions hardly accord with neutralism as the world understands it. India's foreign policy therefore, as Nehru has often insisted, is independent and not neutral. It is not isolationist in the sense that India wishes to retreat and encase herself in an ivory tower of her own devising. In his speech to Congress during his visit to the United States in October, 1949, Nehru stressed the point. "Whether we want to or not," he declared, "we realize that we simply cannot exist in isolation. No country can. Certainly we cannot. Our geography, our history, the present events, all drag us into a wider picture."

India thus neither seeks to evade her international responsibilities nor to refrain from expressing boldly her opinion on various issues. The pattern of Indian history has in fact followed closely the pattern of American history in the early decades after 1787. Like America, India began internally with the consolidation of the States. Externally she is anxious to avoid foreign entanglements much as America did in the long years ending with the two world wars.

Emerging as the strongest of the major Powers after the Second World War, the United States cannot escape its new international obligations, and looks on the world with altered eyes. The foreign policy she pursues is, like India's, motivated primarily by enlightened self-interest. Which is why Indians, conscious of American history between 1787 and 1947, are puzzled by America's allergy to their own country's foreign policy.

India wants peace but not peace at any price, as Nehru has made plain on more than one occasion. He explained it while addressing the House of Representatives during his visit to America:

We have to achieve freedom and defend it. We have to meet aggression and to resist it and the force employed must be adequate to the purpose. But even when preparing to resist aggression, the ultimate objective, the objective of peace and reconciliation, must never be lost sight of, and heart and mind must be attuned to this supreme aim, and not swayed or clouded by hatred or fear. This is the basis and the goal of our foreign policy. We are neither blind to reality nor do we propose to acquiesce in any challenge to man's freedom, from whatever quarter it may come. Where freedom is menaced, or justice threatened, or where aggression takes place, we cannot be and shall not be neutral. What we plead for, and endeavour to practice in our own important way, is a binding faith in peace, and an unfailing endeavour of thought and action to ensure it. The great democracy of the United States of America will, I feel sure, understand and appreciate our approach to life's problems because it could not have any other aim or a different ideal. Friendship and cooperation between our two countries are, therefore, natural. I stand here to offer both in the pursuit of justice, liberty and peace.

India, as Nehru has often declared, was vitally interested in Korea because the peace of Asia was involved. This is a facet of his foreign policy which the West has still to understand and appreciate fully, for it is one of the basic influences which motivates India's international dealings. Although he has always sternly discountenanced talk of India as the leader of Asia, Nehru is intensely conscious of the fact that geography has given his country a pivotal place on that continent.

There might not, as he explained in his speech to Congress in the United States in October, 1949, be very much in common between the Chinese and the people of the Middle East or West Asia, as India now terms this region. So also there are cultural, historical and other differences between the lands of the Far East, of Arabia, Iran and Southeast Asia.

"But whichever region you may take," he went on to declare, "India inevitably comes into the picture."

The problems of Southeast Asia impinge on India, as do those of the Far East. While the Middle East may not be directly connected with Southeast Asia, both are connected with India. So also India's foreign policy must be viewed in terms of the country's relations with her neighbours, who include Pakistan, Afghanistan, Tibet, China, Nepal, Burma, Malaya, Indonesia and Ceylon.

As Nehru has said in a reference to India's place in Asia:

Whatever regions you have in mind the importance of India cannot be ignored. . . . Whether it is a problem of defence or trade or industry or economic policy India cannot be ignored. Even culturally speaking our bonds are very great with all those parts of Asia, whether it is Western

Asia or the Far East or Southeast Asia, and these bonds are very old and very persistent.

From this pivotal position which India occupies certain consequences flow, and are reflected in the country's foreign policy. The first of these is that with the independence of India and other Asian countries and their emergence as free territories on the international plane there is need for a readjustment of the relations between Asia and Europe. The political and economic domination of the second over the first must end. Hence the removal of the last vestige of colonialism in Asia as in Africa is a major plank of India's foreign policy. Nehru has always insisted that decisions concerning Asia should be taken only after close consultation with the free countries of that continent.

In the Prime Minister's opinion, many factors join the countries of Asia together, apart from geography. Foremost among these is the lingering remembrance of European domination over the peoples of this continent. The approach of Asia also differs from the approach of Europe, for Asia's concern is primarily with the immediate human problems of underdeveloped countries, such as food, clothing, education and health. Unlike the countries of Europe, the countries of Asia are not directly concerned with problems of power politics. Nehru has explained:

I do not mean to say that we in Asia are in any way superior, ethically or morally, to the people of Europe. In some ways I imagine we are worse. There is, however, a legacy of conflict in Europe. In Asia, at the present moment at least, there is no such legacy. The countries of Asia may have their quarrels with their neighbours here and there, but there is no basic legacy of conflict such as the countries of Europe possess. That is a very great advantage for Asia and it would be folly in the extreme for the countries of Asia, for India to be dragged in the wake of the conflicts in Europe.

Asia and Europe can and must co-exist, but only on the basis of equality and friendship. Here again, in the global context, Nehru sees India as peculiarly positioned to be the link between Asia and Europe, between the East and the West. Himself an epitome of the cultures of both continents, he is the representative of a country which has adopted many of the political and economic systems of the West without losing its own intrinsic personality and is in some ways an epitome of the world, containing all cultures from the most primitive to the most modern.

Geographically India again is well positioned to be the link between the New World and the Old. Westward she looks out to Europe and the Atlantic Ocean; eastward her gaze rests on the sprawling earth of China with, beyond, the Pacific and the Americas; northward she scans the lands of the Soviet Asian republic, while to the southwest lies the vast bulk of Africa. Southeast across the Indian Ocean are the new civilizations of Australia and New Zealand.

"India," Nehru notes, "becomes a kind of meeting ground for various trends and forces and a meeting ground for what might roughly be called the East and the West."

Despite the strong Asian consciousness which activates certain aspects of his foreign policy, Nehru still gropes on the international plane for the one world of his and Gandhi's dreams. But just as in India, echoing Gandhi, he wants the cultures of all lands to be blown about in his house as freely as possible but refuses to be blown off his feet by any, so also he would not have Asia's people live in other people's houses as interlopers, beggars or slaves.

"We should work for that ideal," he said, "and not for any grouping which comes in the way of this larger world group. We, therefore, support the United Nations structure which is painfully emerging from its infancy. But in order to have One World, we must also, in Asia, think of the countries of Asia cooperating together for that larger ideal."

Just as large masses of indigent, discontented people are a dead weight on a community or a country, so also the backward underdeveloped countries of Asia and Africa constitute a drag on the progress of the world. Only by helping them to develop economically and socially, and by enabling them to rise to their full stature, can the human race as a whole progress in peace, brotherhood, dignity and freedom. Asia and Africa must help themselves to rise, and even while India trembled on the brink of freedom, Nehru was exploring ways and means to resuscitate the spirit of Asia, and in doing so to lift the burden from the giant but tired back of Africa.

In March, 1947, about five months before independence came, the first All-Asian Relations Conference assembled at Delhi under the auspices of the Indian Council of World Affairs and was attended by the representatives of practically all the Asian countries except Japan, but including the Soviet Republics of Central Asia. Its purpose was to consider the common problems which all Asian countries had to face, such as national movements for freedom, racial discrimination, industrial development and cultural cooperation. Although no positive results emerged from the conference, its significance as the first assembly of Asian representatives in history was not lost on the delegates. In inaugurating the conference Nehru expressed the hope that it would stand out as a landmark dividing the past of Asia from the future.

"Strong winds are blowing all over Asia," said Nehru. "Let us not be afraid of them, but rather welcome them, for only with their help can we build the new Asia of our dreams. Let us have faith in these great new forces and the dream which is taking shape. Let us, above all, have faith in the human spirit which Asia has symbolized for those long ages past."

Within the next two years five Asian countries—India, Pakistan, Burma, Ceylon and the Philippines—were to achieve their independence. In this altered context another Asian conference was summoned by Nehru in January, 1949, to consider the crisis in Indonesia created by the second Dutch "police action" against the infant republic. Nineteen countries were represented, including Australia, which sent a delegate, and New Zealand, which had an observer. In a vigorous but restrained speech Nehru explained that the primary purpose of the meeting was "to consider how best we can help the Security Council to bring about a rapid and peaceful solution of the Indonesian problem." Their intention was to work within the framework of the United Nations. "We meet to supplement the efforts of the Security Council, not to supplant that body. We meet in no spirit of hostility to any nation or group of nations, but in an endeavour to promote peace through the extension of freedom. It must be realised that both freedom and peace are indivisible."

The resolution condemning the Dutch military action broadly echoed these sentiments. It also endorsed Nehru's suggestion that the free countries of Asia should begin to think of some more permanent arrangement for effective mutual consultation and concerted effort in the pursuit of common aims. This assembly yielded more positive results than the first, the end of the year 1949 being marked by the successful conclusion of the Round Table Conference at The Hague and the subsequent transfer of power to the Indonesian people.

Meanwhile, the cold war was growing in intensity, and India followed with close concern and interest the war in Indo-China where India's sympathies were with the people of Viet Nam in their struggle for freedom. The two Governments of Viet Minh and Viet Nam claimed to represent the people's nationalist aspirations, and in accordance with India's policy the Government decided to recognise neither. But a consul-general was stationed at Saigon.

Nehru was criticised by some quarters at home, as well as by others abroad, for sitting on the fence.

"India will sit there as long as she finds it comfortable," he retorted. "Anyhow, nobody is going to order us about."

In May, 1950, some of the South and Southeast Asian countries, including Australia, met at Baguio in the Philippines, where the suggestion was mooted that these countries might consider forming a non-Communist bloc to operate within the U.N. India, committed to a policy of non-alignment, resisted this suggestion. Instead the conference recommended that the countries concerned should consult each other to further the interests of the peoples of the region and to ensure that in any consideration of the special problems of South and Southeast Asia the point of view of the peoples of this area should be kept prominently in mind.

This was consistent with Nehru's view that the voice of Asia should be heard and could no longer be ignored. Since India's independence he had insisted that in all matters concerning Asia, decisions should be taken only after close consultation with the free countries of Asia, and in addressing the U.N. General Assembly at Paris in November, 1948, he had reiterated this plea:

May I say, as a representative from Asia, that we honour Europe for its culture and for the great advance in human civilisation which it represents? May I say that we are equally interested in the solution of European problems; but may I also say that the world is something bigger than Europe, and you will not solve your problems by thinking that the problems of the world are mainly European problems? There are vast tracts of the world which may not in the past, for a few generations, have taken much part in world affairs. But they are awake; their people are moving and they have no intention whatever of being ignored or of being passed by. It is a simple fact that I think we have to remember, because unless you have the full picture of the world before you, you will not even understand the problem, and if you isolate any single problem in the world from the rest, you do not understand the problem. Today I do venture to submit that Asia counts in world affairs. Tomorrow it will count much more than today.

It was preposterous and impertinent for non-Asian governments, he urged, to decide on the fate and future of various parts of Asia without even troubling to consult the independent countries of that continent. This applied as much to Indo-China as to Korea and Formosa. In the case of the two last-named areas the exclusion from the U.N. of Communist China, which was vitally concerned with both, rendered the proceedings of that body illogical and anomalous. Moreover, the United Nations was never intended to be a group of nations thinking only one way and excluding other nations. The basic principle of universality had been abandoned by the United Nations, said Nehru. "This is a return to the attitude that caused the League of Nations to fail."

Not until April, 1954, was another Asian conference convened, and this time it was at Colombo when Burma, Ceylon, India, Indonesia and Pakistan—the so-called Colombo Powers—met to discuss such subjects of common interest as peace in Indo-China, the recognition of Mao Tse-tung's régime by the United Nations, and the ending of colonialism in Tunisia and Morocco. In between, the war in Korea, opening in June, 1950, had halted in July, 1953, with the beginning of the truce talks at Panmunjom. The Indo-Chinese struggle was drawing to its sordid close. In February, 1954, America had agreed to extend military aid to Pakistan, which was shortly to join the Middle East Defence Organisation along with Greece, Turkey, Iraq and Iran. Late in 1949 India had withdrawn her recognition of the Kuomintang régime and instead had proceeded to recognise the new People's Government primarily for the reason that the Communists had established a sound and stable rule over the entire mainland. China had invaded Tibet in order to "liberate" her despite the Indian Government's appeal to Peking to settle the question peacefully through negotiations.

Thus in the five years between the second Asian conference at Delhi and the Colombo conference the two Power blocs had encroached considerably on the "area of peace" which Nehru had sought to extend as a buttress and buffer throughout South Asia. For India as for Asia an independent policy built on a delicate but stable balance of forces in this region was vital. So Nehru argued. But the war in Korea, the fighting in Indo-China, Peking's incursion into Tibet, the studied exclusion of Red China from the United Nations and the United States threat to extend the war to the Chinese mainland if aggression continued, and above all the American promise of armed aid to Pakistan, had hemmed in and contracted the "area of peace" and in Nehru's words had brought the possibility of world war "right up to our door." He thought that the importation of Western arms into Asia was "a reversal of the process of liberation." It was re-entering Asia militarily by the back door.

During this period about the only credit item on the ledger of India's international relations was the creation of an Asian-Arab bloc, later described as the Afro-Asian bloc, in the United Nations. Even this was on a nebulous and limited basis. The Colombo conference was inspired, among other things, by the idea of giving this form of Afro-Asian cooperation more body and content and of making it more compact and consolidated. Bandung was to mark the first flowering of this process.

The Afro-Asian conference at Bandung which was convened under the sponsorship of the Colombo Powers should be viewed against this background. Its purposes, according to the Bogor [2] communiqué, were fourfold—to promote goodwill and cooperation between the nations of Asia and Africa, to explore and advance their mutual as well as common interests, and to establish and further friendliness and neighbourly relations; to consider social, economic and cultural problems and the relations of the countries represented; to consider problems of special interest to Asian and African peoples—for example, problems affecting national sovereignty, racialism and colonialism; and to view the position of Asia and Africa and their peoples in the world of today and the contribution they can make to the promotion of world peace and cooperation. In seeking to convene the Afro-Asian conference there was no desire for exclusiveness in respect

[2] The final decision to summon the Afro-Asian conference was taken at Bogor in Indonesia in December, 1954. Prior to this there had been consultations between the Prime Ministers of India, Indonesia and Burma.

of membership or for the building up of a regional bloc among the participating countries.

Nehru was of the opinion that the decisions of the Colombo Powers had some influence on the Geneva conference in the summer of 1954, and although India took no direct part in it, Nehru's Harry Hopkins, the angular and intense Krishna Menon, played a positive role behind the scenes. This thought was also in the minds of many of the delegates present at Bandung and was reflected in the speech of President Soekarno, who inaugurated the conference on April 18, 1955.

"I think," he observed, "it is generally recognised that the activity of the Prime Ministers of the sponsoring countries which invited you here had a not unimportant role to play in ending the fighting in Indo-China. Look, the people of Asia raised their voices and the world listened. It was no small victory and no negligible precedent."

Of the twenty-five independent governments of Asia and Africa invited to attend by the five Colombo Powers, only one—the Central African Federation—excused itself. The twenty-nine participants included countries as varied as China and the Philippines, Ethiopia and Japan, Laos and Liberia, while apart from Nehru, Chou En-lai and Soekarno there were outstanding personalities such as Carlos Romulo of the Philippines, General Nasser of Egypt and Prince Wan of Thailand. Between them these countries represented more than half the population of the world.

By agreeing that there should be no voting but only a consensus of opinion taken, the differences in views among the delegates were not allowed to crystallise. This method also made for compromise, the resolutions passed at the end of the conference reflecting this spirit. It had never been the intention of the sponsors to promote an Asian-African bloc in hostility to any other bloc, and indeed this would have been contrary to India's foreign policy. But it was Nehru's hope to extend through the Afro-Asian countries the "area of peace."

On innocuous matters such as the need for cultural and economic cooperation and on human rights and self-determination no acute differences of opinion arose. Controversy, however, was sharp on two heads of discussion—colonialism, and the promotion of world peace and cooperation. Did the term colonialism embrace all forms of imperialism, the old Western type of exploitation and the new type of Soviet imperialism resorting to force, infiltration and subversion? Ceylon's Prime Minister, Sir John Kotelawala, posed the question sharply, and following a lively, often acrimonious debate the conference resolution declared that colonialism in all its manifestations was an evil which should speedily be ended.

Similarly, discussion under the head of promotion of world peace and cooperation developed into a heated debate whether coexistence provided the answer or whether the panacea should be sought on more defined lines. Was the solution passive resistance or military pacts or the enlargement of the unaligned area of peace? One delegate calculated that at least fourteen of the twenty-nine participating countries had entered into military pacts. As it finally emerged, the resolution was a compromise between the contending views, satisfying itself with the declaration that the problem of peace was correlated with the problem of international security, that it was dependent as much on security as on international goodwill and confidence, and that the participating countries should respect such security arrangements as were in conformity with the Charter of the United Nations as well as other peaceful means of the parties' own choice, also in conformity with the Charter. Arrangements for collective defence, it was emphasised, must not be used to serve the particular interests of the big Powers. The resolution embodied the so-called Bandung Peace Declaration of Ten Principles, incorporating among them, though not mentioning specifically, Nehru's doctrine of *panchshila*, or Five Principles for promotion of world peace.

The Five Principles were first enunciated in the preamble to the Sino-Indian agreement on trade with Tibet in April, 1954. Later in June, 1954, they appeared in the course of a joint statement signed by Nehru and Chou En-lai when the Chinese Prime Minister visited Delhi that month. The Five Principles are: (1) mutual respect for each other's territorial integrity and sovereignty; (2) non-aggression; (3) non-interference in each other's internal affairs; (4) equality and mutual advantage; and (5) peaceful coexistence and economic cooperation. "If these principles," said the statement, "are applied not only between various countries but also in international relations generally, they would form a solid foundation for peace and security, and the fears and apprehensions that exist today would give place to a feeling of confidence."

It was another way of extending the "area of peace"—through the hearts and minds of peoples and rulers. *Panchshila*, with its underlying faith in human goodness and moral values, was Nehru's answer to the doctrine of security pacts and arrangements. Moral resolve was the counterpart to massive retaliation. Since then nine more countries —Indonesia, North Viet Nam, Yugoslavia, Egypt, Cambodia, Soviet Russia, Poland, Laos and Nepal—have signed *panchshila* declarations with India, while Burma is among the countries which have commended it as "worthy of universal respect."

Chou En-lai played his hand more skilfully than Nehru did at Bandung. While the Indian leader in moments of exasperation indulged in bouts of temper and tantrums as is his habit—understood and forgiven in India but less easily excused abroad—Chou presented a bland suave front and an air of sweet reasonableness. He was out to make Communist China respectable, and succeeded to a remarkable extent. The small nations of Asia, he declared, had nothing to fear from their great neighbour China, and he invited all the delegations present at the conference, particularly China's neighbours, Thailand and the Philippines, to visit Peking. Where the border line between China and a neighbouring country had not yet been fixed, Chou declared his country's willingness to do so by peaceful means. He dramatised the equally "peaceful intentions" of the large Chinese minorities residing in many Southeast Asian countries by signing an agreement during the conference with the Indonesian Government on their Chinese minority.

Chou sought to reduce the international tension by inviting the United States Government to settle the question of Taiwan through peaceful negotiations. In this also he was temporarily successful, Mr. Dulles expressing the view that "the situation in the Formosa area was becoming less hazardous—there was less danger of war—than in the past few months." The United States Secretary of State went on to explain that "that was the result of a number of causes, one of the most important being the Bandung Conference where Asian nations had made it clear that they did not feel that the Formosa issue should be resolved by a resort to war by one side or the other."

In this sense Nehru was at least successful in extending the climate if not the area of peace. Chou En-lai might have played his cards skilfully, but it was Nehru who made it possible. Just as the Colombo conference led to a lowering of international tension, bringing about the Geneva conference and helping to end the war in Indo-China, so also Bandung was followed by the summit conference at Geneva when Khrushchev and Bulganin ventured out of Moscow into the democratic world. The Indian Prime Minister's sensitivity to the international atmosphere and his sense of timing were never displayed more dramatically or to better advantage than in the three Asian conferences that have met, primarily at his initiative, since the first gathering of Asian representatives assembled at New Delhi in March, 1947.

Almost it seems as if in international matters Nehru thinks a jump ahead of his contemporaries, Asian and European. Perhaps that is why they feel he is out of step!

27

BETWEEN TWO WORLDS

Nehru had come to Bandung fresh from a visit to China in the latter half of October, 1954. It had been a triumphal tour, and Nehru went back to India impressed with the vigour and vitality of the Chinese people. In a farewell broadcast from Peking on October 27th he had referred to the Communists' Long March and compared it with India's long march to freedom:

Both [countries], I feel, can learn something from each other. Both can cooperate in many ways, even though their problems may differ to some extent and their methods might not be the same. The essential thing between two nations and two peoples is tolerance and friendly feelings. If these are present, then other things follow. I am convinced that these are present in China and India.

Nehru himself had travelled a long way since his last visit to China on the eve of the Second World War when Generalissimo and Madame Chiang Kai-shek had been his hosts. In the new China he was struck by the purposefulness of the leaders, and though alive to the methods by which Communism achieved its objectives, he was especially impressed by the progress of the women, and the care lavished on the country's children and youth. He referred to it in the last speech he made on Chinese soil at the Canton airport on October 30th: "I have seen this ancient country in new garb, and it is the faces of youth here that I shall especially remember, the vital, active, joyful faces of young men and young women, boys and girls and children, that is the memory especially that I shall carry away with me and my ears will ring with your voices."

They were Asian voices, and for Nehru they carried a special message. He had met Madame Sun Yat-sen, now known by her maiden name of Ching Ling-soong, at the Brussels Congress of the League Against Imperialism back in 1927, but his memory of China travelled remotely to ancient days, to the first cultural links built between India and China by Hiuen Tsang, the pilgrim from Cathay who had roamed Hindustan in the seventh century after Christ when Harsha had reigned as Emperor of the Five Indies.

China was a part, a big part, of Asia. Like India she had suffered for many generations from exploitation by the West, and that fact had forged a bond between them. China had reached independence by a route far different from that of India's. Whether one liked or did not like the Communist régime, it represented a stable government exercising authority over the entire mainland.

If Communism had taken root in China and prevailed, it was because the nationalist movement had failed dismally to progress on its own momentum and fulfil itself. India might have gone the same way had Gandhi not appeared on the scene at the right moment.

"The birth of Communism in Asia," Nehru once remarked, "is largely due to its alliance with nationalist movements fighting for independence from foreign domination. . . . The tendency of Asian nationalist movements to follow the leadership of the Communist party is dependent on the degree to which their deep-rooted anti-colonial impulse is ignored by the Western powers."

Was it not significant that while Communism was strong in dependent countries like Indo-China, it was comparatively weak in independent countries such as India, Pakistan and Ceylon?

For nearly two hundred years before independence India had been the prey of a single imperialist power, but China had been the victim simultaneously of several imperialist forces, being ravished by the British, French, Germans and Portuguese, to say nothing of the Japanese. There, Nehru reflected, but for the grace of God and Gandhi goes India.

The political thought and systems of the two countries contrasted strongly. Yet to Nehru, reared on the gentle teaching of Gandhi, there was nothing incongruous in the belief that Communism and democracy could subsist side by side at peace with each other. Had Gandhi during the war not appealed simultaneously to Roosevelt and

Hitler? That was the civilised approach. Why should China and India not live as good neighbours?

Moreover, practical considerations—in other words a policy of enlightened self-interest—reinforced such an attitude. On India's two thousand-mile northern border pressed the huge land mass of Communist Asia, separated only by the vast buffer of the Himalayas. The Chinese incursion into Tibet could bring effective Communist power to the borders of India along the old caravan route to Lhasa. Aid from the democratic countries was many thousands of miles away.

Realism, not fear, has influenced this approach, for fear does not enter into the calculus of Nehru's political thinking. In his view, to accept foreign military bases in the country or military aid from abroad, quite apart from negativing India's independent policy, would envelop her in the larger psychosis of fear which he has consistently condemned.

The Prime Minister declared, soon after independence, in March, 1948:

> We are not citizens of a weak or mean country, and I think it is foolish for us to get frightened, even from a military point of view, of the greatest of the Powers today. Not that I delude myself about what can happen to us if a great Power in a military sense goes against us; I have no doubt it can injure us. But after all in the past, as a national movement, we opposed one of the greatest of World Powers. We opposed it in a particular way and in a large measure succeeded in that way, and I have no doubt that if the worst comes to the worst—and in a military sense we cannot meet these great Powers—it is far better for us to fight in our own way than submit to them and lose all the ideals we have. Therefore, let us not be frightened too much of the military might of this or that group. I am not frightened and I want to tell the world on behalf of this country that we are not frightened of the military might of this Power or that. Our policy is not a passive policy or a negative policy.

Despite the sense of Asian communion which draws India and China together against evils such as colonialism and racial discrimination and infuses both with the desire to step up not only their own economic standards but those of the underdeveloped countries of the Orient and Africa, Nehru is acutely alive to the differences in the political thought and methods of the two countries and is inspired by a strong competitive urge that India should forge ahead.

A speech he made in February, 1953, reveals this feeling strongly:

Between us [China and India] there is a very big difference, the effects of which it remains for history to show. The difference is that we [in India] are trying to function in a democratic set-up. It is no good saying that we are better or more virtuous than others. No question of virtue is involved in this. Ultimately, it is a question of which set-up and which structure of government—political or economic—pays the highest dividends. When I say highest dividends, I do not mean merely material dividends, although they are important, but cultural and spiritual dividends also. Intellectual freedom is an important factor, certainly; but the future will show its worth. We have deliberately chosen a democratic set-up and we feel that it is good for our people and for our country in the ultimate analysis. Nevertheless, it sometimes slows down the pace of growth, for we have to weigh the demands of tomorrow with the needs of today in the building up of our country.

It is here that Communism has its greatest attraction to an Asian people, for the pace of progress can sometimes make the vital difference between survival and extinction. A Communist system more often than not produces results more quickly than the slow-moving millstones of democracy can. On the other hand the reaction of India, as of many Asian countries, to Communist governments such as those of China and Russia is a mixture of admiration and revulsion, admiration for the speed with which they have transformed their economics, revulsion at some of the methods by which they have achieved it. Hungry men think more often through their stomachs than through their minds, and a loaf of bread means more to a beggar than the freedom to express his opinions. Of what use is intellectual freedom in a gnawing world of hunger and pain? Therein lies the danger of a large democracy like India, genuinely trying by democratic means to improve her economic conditions, losing to Communism because of the latter's speedier pace of progress. Hence Nehru's attempts to build up a political democracy in India which while safeguarding democracy ensures to its hungry masses a priority in the economic scheme of things. Hence also his sense of history and hustle.

Independent India has had its differences with Communist China, notably on Tibet. India's policy on Tibet was in line with the old British policy; she recognised both China's historic claim to suzerainty (not sovereignty) and Tibet's claim to autonomy. At the first Asian Relations Conference in March, 1947, the Indian sponsors in New Delhi had set up a huge map of Asia in the auditorium showing the boundaries of Tibet clearly demarcated from those of China.

The Kuomintang representative had protested vigorously against this, insisting that Tibet was a part of China, and in order not to wound his susceptibilities the Sino-Tibetan boundaries as shown in the map were actually erased. It would thus seem that Communist China's attitude to Tibet is as much a legacy from the Kuomintang régime as India's is from the British.

When in the autumn of 1950 the People's Government of China disclosed its intention of "liberating" Tibet, New Delhi took a temperate but a firm line. It earnestly counselled the Chinese to settle the matter with the Tibetans by peaceful negotiations. For many months the authorities at Lhasa had unsuccessfully tried to make diplomatic contact with Peking in order to negotiate a peaceful settlement. The arrival in August, 1950, of the first Chinese Communist ambassador to India provided them with this opportunity, and in September a seven-man Tibetan delegation that had been waiting at Kalimpong for a summons to Delhi got in touch with the Chinese envoy. The talks failed, and Peking demanded that the delegation come to the Chinese capital. Owing to the difficulty of obtaining visas for Hong Kong, and also owing to the inexperience of the Tibetan delegation, there was considerable delay in their departure, which Peking construed as due to hostile foreign intrigue and interference.

On October 25th the delegation left Delhi, and almost simultaneously came the news that the "People's army units have been ordered to advance into Tibet." India protested strongly. In a note dated October 26, 1950, and addressed to the Chinese Foreign Minister, the Government of India declared:

In the present context of world events, the invasion by Chinese troops of Tibet cannot but be regarded as deplorable, and in the considered judgement of the Government of India, not in the interest of China or of peace. The Government of India can only express their deep regret that in spite of the friendly and disinterested advice repeatedly tendered by them, the Chinese Government should have decided to seek a solution of the problem of their relations with Tibet by force instead of by the slower and more enduring method of peaceful approach.

Peking reacted sharply, in effect telling India to mind her own business. In a reply dated October 30th the Chinese Foreign Minister affirmed:

The Central People's Government of the People's Republic of China would like to make it clear: Tibet is an integral part of Chinese territory, the problem of Tibet is entirely a domestic problem of China. The Chinese People's Liberation army must enter Tibet, liberate the Tibetan people, and defend the frontiers of China. This is the resolved policy of the Central People's Government.

The note went on to allege that "under outside instigation" the Tibetan delegation "had intentionally delayed the date of its departure for Peking." It declared again that "the problem of Tibet is a domestic problem of the People's Republic of China and no foreign interference shall be tolerated." It also alleged that the Indian Government had been influenced in its views "by foreign influences hostile to China in Tibet."

India, in a firm reply, categorically repudiated the allegation that her representation to China was affected by foreign influences hostile to Peking. "At no time," it emphasised, "has any foreign influence been brought to bear upon India in regard to Tibet." It declared that the Chinese Government was equally mistaken in thinking that the Tibetan delegation's departure for Peking was delayed by outside instigation. It regretted China's action:

There has been no allegation that there has been any provocation or any resort to non-peaceful methods on the part of the Tibetans. Hence there is no justification whatever for such military operations against them. Such a step involving an attempt to impose a decision by force, could not possibly be reconciled with a peaceful settlement. In view of these developments, the Government of India are no longer in a position to advise the Tibetan delegation to proceed to Peking unless the Chinese Government think it fit to order their troops to halt their advance into Tibet and thus give a chance for peaceful negotiations.

Shortly afterward Nehru declared that any transgression of the Indo-Tibetan border would be resisted. The same principle would apply to the Nepalese-Tibetan border. India proclaimed her determination to do this by guaranteeing the integrity of the Himalayan border States of Nepal, Sikkim and Bhutan. There could be only one transgressor—China.

Nepal, like Tibet, was a legacy from British days and, like Tibet, it was of international interest because it lay across the path of Communist infiltration into India.

Nehru said in a speech in October, 1950:

We have inherited both good things and bad from the British. Our relations with some of our neighbouring countries developed during an expansive phase of British imperial policy. Nepal was an independent country when India was under British rule; but strictly speaking, her independence was only formal. The test of the independence of a country is that it should be able to have relations with other countries without endangering that independence. Nepal's foreign relations were strictly limited to her relations with the Government functioning in India at the time. That was an indication that Nepal's approach to international relations was a very limited one.

Despite this, India went further than the old British Government had done in encouraging Nepal to develop foreign relations, which now include ties with the United States, Britain and France. But geography gives Nepal a peculiar relationship with India, for access to this land-locked kingdom, bounded by the high mountain passes leading to Tibet on the north, lies only across India.

Nehru declared in the same speech:

We recognise Nepal as an independent country and wish her well. But even a child knows that one cannot go to Nepal without passing through India. Therefore, no other country can have as intimate a relationship with Nepal as ours is. We would like every other country to appreciate the intimate geographical and cultural relationship that exists between India and Nepal.

For generations Nepal had been under the rule of an oligarchy of autocratic Ranas or princelings who constituted the ruling clan, the king enjoying only titular authority, with all power concentrated in the Prime Minister, who headed the Ranas. Proximity to India had exposed Nepal to the invigorating breeze of new and democratic ideas, and when India attained independence these ideas created a ferment and generated a spirit of revolt against the Ranas. Nehru's position was difficult. India wished to treat Nepal as an independent country; but at the same time she was well aware that unless some steps were taken to democratise the régime, difficulties and embarrassments would arise which Nepal's northern neighbours were certain to exploit.

These thoughts were uppermost in Nehru's mind, and he made no secret of them. Speaking shortly after China's invasion of Tibet, he expressed his doubts and fears openly:

Our interest in the internal conditions of Nepal has become still more acute and personal, because of the developments across our borders, to be frank, especially those in China and Tibet. Besides our sympathetic interest in Nepal, we were also interested in the security of our own country. From time immemorial, the Himalayas have provided us with a magnificent frontier. Of course, they are no longer as impassable as they used to be but are still fairly effective. The Himalayas lie mostly on the northern border of Nepal. We cannot allow that barrier to be penetrated because it is also the principal barrier to India. Therefore, much as we appreciate the independence of Nepal, we cannot allow anything to go wrong in Nepal or permit that barrier to be crossed or weakened, because that would be a risk to our own security. The recent developments have made us ponder more deeply over the Nepal situation than we had done previously. All this time, however, we had functioned in our own patient way, advising in a friendly way and pointing out the difficulties inherent in the situation in a spirit of cooperation.

The Ranas, like the Bourbons, were determined to learn nothing and to forget nothing. On the other hand, the then Nepalese monarch, King Tribhuwan, associated himself with the popular struggle against the Ranas, and late in 1950 brought the situation to an unexpected head by taking refuge from the Ranas in the Indian embassy at Khatmandu. His Majesty was flown to New Delhi along with two of his Ministers, and shortly afterward the popular revolt against the Ranas in Nepal acquired a new pitch, culminating in the overthrow of their century-old autocracy in January, 1951.

King Tribhuwan returned to Nepal after an absence of 101 days with the intention and hope of guiding the democratic movement on stable lines. In this he was not successful, owing principally to the wranglings between the Koirala brothers, M. P. and B. P., which weakened the Nepalese Congress party and simultaneously strengthened extremist groups like the Gorkha Dal on the right and the Communists on the left.

King Tribhuwan died on March 13, 1955. His successor, King Mahendra, abler than his father, has since tried to induce a measure of political equilibrium by taking a more direct hand in the administration, but the volatile politics of Nepal render this difficult. The Communist party, outlawed shortly after the revolution, appears to be gaining ground; and the return of its leader, K. I. Singh, who earlier had taken refuge in Tibet, adds uncertainty to a situation already enigmatic and equivocal as well as potentially explosive.

India is sometimes accused of accelerating too hastily the pace of democratic progress in Nepal. The contrary is the case, for New Delhi is as vitally interested in maintaining stability in Nepal as Khatmandu is, knowing full well that failure to do so will throw the country into the lap of the Communists on the left or into the outstretched arms of the extreme reactionaries on the right.

After the revolution Nehru explained:

We have tried for what it is worth to advise Nepal to act in a manner so as to prevent any major upheaval. We have tried to find a way, a middle way, if you like, which will ensure the progress of Nepal and the introduction of or some advance in the ways of democracy in Nepal. We have searched for a way which would, at the same time, avoid the total uprooting of the ancient order. Whether or not it is possible to find such a way, I do not know. We are a patient Government. Perhaps, we are too patient sometimes. I feel, however, that if this matter drags on, it will not be good for Nepal and it might even make it more difficult to find the middle way we have been advocating.

Unhappily Nepal shows no signs of settling down to stable democratic conditions. India, say some Nepalese, is attempting to "colonise" their country, a charge perhaps inevitable in the peculiar circumstances which obtain, but unjustified. New Delhi's primary interest, as Nehru has explained, is to prevent anything going wrong in Nepal and to ensure that the barrier dividing Nepal from Tibet is not crossed or weakened, "because that would be a risk to our own security." An Indian military mission is now at Khatmandu helping to reorganise the Nepalese forces, and Indian engineers have extended and strengthened communications along the Indo-Nepalese border. Nehru is taking no chances.

Apart from the Asian link which leads many Indians to remember China's Asianism and forget her Communism, the other bond is Peking's unequivocal hostility to colonialism as Asia and Africa understand it. Quite frankly, the concept of Soviet imperialism or colonialism makes little impact on the Asian mind, which has always equated colonialism with colour. Colonialism, to Asia and Africa, spells the domination of white Powers over the coloured countries of the earth. The Japanese, it is true, were also condemned by India as colonialists in China. But pre-war Japan, according to the Asian thesis, was so wedded to Western techniques of production and power that her imperialism was a parallel projection on the political plane. Moreover, the traditional concept of colonialism fixes its main motivations in an urge for sources of cheap raw materials and for cheap and plentiful manpower.

In Asian eyes no one of these tests applies to Soviet imperialism or colonialism. The countries behind the Iron Curtain are European and white with the exception of the Soviet Asian republics which claim to be equal and autonomous units of the U.S.S.R. Colour does not enter into this form of imperialism which most Asians equate with the old wars and struggles of European countries for political or economic domination. Nor are the Iron Curtain nations reservoirs of cheap manpower or sources of cheap raw materials, countries such as Czechoslovakia enjoying proportionately a higher industrial level than Soviet Russia.

If it is imperialism, says the average Asian, for Russia to have a base at Helsinki, 600 miles from Moscow, is it not equally imperialism for Britain to have a base at Singapore, 9,000 miles from London? Why condemn the one and condone the other?

Here is where Communism, opposed equally to colour and colonialism (in the sense in which Asia and Africa understand it), scores against Western countries whose attitude to both is equivocal. So at least India thinks, judging by the statements of Mr. Dulles on Goa, particularly the unfortunate reference in the Dulles-Cunha statement to Goa as "a province of Portugal." Legalistically that is Lisbon's view but to accept the phrase is to seem to subscribe to the view. And Washington's subsequent embellishments have done little to improve matters.

China and Russia cashed in heavily on the Dulles contretemps, both countries coming out strongly against the continuance of Portuguese dominion over Goa. While the French, after protracted negotiations, had yielded gracefully, ceding Chandernagore in West Bengal early in 1951 and transferring Pondicherry with Karikal, Yanam and Mahe three years later, the Portuguese took up a consistently stubborn attitude, claiming Goa, Damaun and Diu to be part of metropolitan Portugal and hence the internal concern of Lisbon. The Portuguese attitude is not dissimilar to that of Britain vis-à-vis Cyprus except that Britain claims this eastern Mediterranean island as a Crown colony.

Like the former French possessions the Portuguese territories in

India have no economic importance or military significance, but Mormugão is an all-weather harbour capable of development. India's view on the Portuguese possessions, as it was on the French possessions, is that they are enclaves peopled by blood brethren in no way different from the Indians in independent India except that their outlook has necessarily been coloured by long years under Portuguese and French domain. The continued presence of these pimples on the Indian map, symbolising a colonial status from which India had emerged, was construed as an affront to nationalistic sensibilities. France has yielded, but Portugal remains obdurate.

The satyagraha campaign culminating in the events of August 15, 1955, when Portuguese soldiers wantonly opened fire on unarmed Indian satyagrahis, killing nearly thirty of them, might easily have erupted into violence had not Nehru intervened and ordered the cessation of the campaign. His voice was authoritative enough to restore peace and order. Other means, such as an intensification of the economic blockade and the closing of land and rail communications between India and Goa, were instead enforced.

In the context of the larger objective of Nehru's foreign policy India was left with no alternative. As the Prime Minister pointed out in Parliament shortly after the events of August 15th, the imperative of a peaceful approach can have no meaning if India itself abandons that approach in a flush of anger. To his critics who suggested that Goa militarily was a smaller problem than Hyderabad, Nehru retorted, "The fact that a war is a little war does not make it less of a war." India had no doctrinaire attachment to non-violence, and had resorted to force in Kashmir and Hyderabad either when threatened with aggression or with a situation calculated to endanger the peace and security of her territory. But every peaceful effort, she believes, should be explored before venturing on force.

Here Nehru obviously relies on the good offices of the Western democracies, more particularly Britain and the United States, to persuade Lisbon to see reason. That is why the Dulles-Cunha statement in December, 1955, while Khrushchev and Bulganin were in India, took both India and her Prime Minister aback, precipitating an unhappy situation on which both China and Russia were quick to capitalise.

Speaking in Calcutta shortly afterward, Nehru made a pointed reference to Goa, describing it as "a touchstone by which people's ideas and professions of freedom will be tested." Plainly this rebuke was directed at the West. Both the Indian people and the Indian Government, as Nehru reminded his audience, are still committed to liquidate these colonial outposts.

If Lisbon's claim that Goa is part of Portugal is genuine, how, India asks, was Lisbon prepared in 1947 to discuss its transfer to Hyderabad State for an agreed payment, and in fact even ready to associate Hyderabad with Goa's administration? This disclosure, which was made by Sir Mirza Ismail, Dewan or Prime Minister of Hyderabad at the time, refutes Portugal's pretensions. Nor, as Lisbon's apologists claim, would the merger of Goa endanger the status of its small Catholic minority of 200,000 inhabitants. In India today there reside peacefully some 8,000,000 Christians of whom 4,500,000 are Catholic.[1] Christianity incidentally came to India long before Islam, Thomas the Apostle landing on the Malabar coast in A.D. 52.

On his way back from Russia in July, 1955, Nehru called on the Vatican, where the Pope in a public statement officially declared that there was no religious issue involved in Goa. His Holiness paid a tribute to India's tolerant treatment of her Catholic minority. The Indian Prime Minister was the first major statesman to fly almost directly from the Kremlin to the Vatican, where he was extended the same courtesy and cordiality. Nehru did this without a trace of self-consciousness. His visit was in its way symbolic of the coexistence he urged. It was *panchshila* in practice.

Soviet spokesmen, particularly Khrushchev and Bulganin, have repeatedly declared since their tour of India in the winter of 1955 that Portugal should quit Goa and that India's action in Kashmir was valid and justified. Nehru's annoyance with the West for being equivocal over both these issues was expressed in a speech in which he stated with marked deliberation that far from being embarrassed by the Soviet declarations he agreed with and approved of them. His peevishness was reflected in a further statement that India was friendly to all nations but more friendly to those who were more friendly to her.

Does this imply that he leans closer to Russia and China than to Britain and the United States? It would be reading too much into

---

[1] The author of this book is a Catholic.

his statements to deduce this; moreover, Nehru is well aware that the strength of his foreign policy derives from his steadfast refusal to hitch India to either bloc. Over the years he has developed sufficient acumen and calculation to thread his way skilfully, now veering to this side and then to that, but keeping always between the two worlds which contend for supremacy and power. The stakes he plays for are India's survival, stability and strength.

Nehru is in fact now projecting his *panchshila* doctrine from the political to the economic, scientific and cultural planes. The cultural exchanges of dancers, painters, artists, musicians and writers have probably been on a more spectacular scale with China and Russia than with Britain or the United States. But while the number of students and technicians studying and working in the first two countries could be counted on the fingers of one's hands their number in the second two runs to several hundreds. Over 1,500 Indian students are in the United States, while the number of permanent American residents in India, including businessmen, technicians, farm-extension workers, missionaries, officials and students exceeds 5,000. There is no comparable movement between India and the Communist world. Trade between the United States of America and India annually averages $350,000,000, America's largest supply of manganese and jute coming from India. Until recently there were no Russian technicians in the country, though with the likely erection of a Soviet steel plant and other works a number plan to come. Indo-Soviet economic relations are on the basis of trade, not aid. On the other hand India received as economic aid and technical assistance some $70,000,000 last year from the United States. Similarly, there have been far more Western scientists and experts in India than their counterparts from Russia or China. Knowledge of English and the orientation of the educated Indian mind to the West more than to the East partly account for this.

The big gravitational pull of Communism, apart from colonialism and colour, is its professed passion for peace, an aim which coincides with India's objective in the international sphere. The overtones of the cold war, highly publicised in the American and Western press and released for global consumption by Western news agencies, too often depict the democracies in bellicose mood making warlike noises off and on the stage. Moscow, like Peking, can coo as gently as any sucking dove, and India, with many Asian countries, forgets the plans for atomic control emanating from American sources such as Acheson, Lilienthal and Baruch, while remembering only the loud-voiced Soviet demands for more disarmament and for the banning of nuclear warfare. Asia, including India, does not understand the mechanics of U.S. politics which enables civilians and servicemen to speak out of turn, leaving the outsider wondering who really represents the voice of America. Is it Eisenhower or Dulles, or Knowland or Radford?

War is a luxury which a country seized with growing political and economic pains cannot afford. But war, judging by the bellicose post-war utterances of some American politicians, seemed not only an urgency but a necessity. It was a point of view India found difficult to understand, particularly when it was reinforced by security and military pacts which contracted the "area of peace" and brought the cold war to India's doorstep. The American decision in February, 1954, to give military aid to Pakistan marked a decisive turning point. On India it forced two decisions, both of which were disagreeable and contrary. It compelled her at a time when she could ill afford it to step up her military expenditure and simultaneously to tighten her belt in order to maintain the pace of her planned economic development.

The new phase of courtship with China and Russia dates from this period. Nehru had visited the United States in October, 1949. Almost exactly five years later he was to visit China and a few months later, in July, 1955, he went to Soviet Russia. In the winter of 1955 he welcomed Khrushchev and Bulganin to India. In between Tito had received him warmly in Yugoslavia and was an honoured guest in India. The doctrine of *panchshila* was affirmed in turn by China, Yugoslavia and Russia. It was Nehru's answer to the doctrine of massive retaliation which had brought the hot war into Asia and the cold war to India's threshold. It almost seemed as if the West believed that Asia was expendable.

Nehru had gone to America in a spirit of discovery. "No person engaged in public affairs can understand the modern world unless he understands the United States," he had then said; and even earlier, reflecting on India's foreign policy during his last term of imprisonment in Ahmednagar, he had written, "Even with distant America we wanted closer relations, for we could learn much from the United States as also from the Soviet Union." The polarization of his international thinking was even then apparent, although later many in America were to denounce his foreign policy as being altogether too ambivalent.

He enjoyed many things he saw in the United States—the warm homely friendliness of the farmers in Illinois, the pertness of the newsboys, the uninhibited conversation of New York's taxicab drivers, the zest and vitality of the people going about their chores in the streets. One thing in particular he wanted to see in America was its universities. He visited Princeton, where he met Dr. Albert Einstein, whom he had always greatly admired, and the atom physicist Dr. Robert Oppenheimer. He took time to pay a call on the late Dr. John Dewey, then in his ninetieth year, and also participated in his birthday dinner. At Columbia he was greeted by General Eisenhower, who at that time was president of the University, and who conferred on him the honorary degree of Doctor of Laws. Nehru particularly enjoyed his visit to Columbia, and was impressed by Eisenhower, who he felt was more thoughtful and reflective than many of the politicians. But he liked Truman's informality and genuine fellow feeling. Of the political executives he was particularly struck by Secretary of State Dean Acheson.

He was interested also in America's technological and material development, whose mammoth proportions overwhelmed him. But he was not amused when at a dinner party in New York with a group of businessmen one of them turned to him and innocently remarked, "Do you realise, Mr. Prime Minister, that you are eating dinner tonight with at least $20,000,000,000?" Nehru thought the remark unnecessarily brash and vulgar, and typical of America's undue preoccupation with materialism.

At the National Press Club in Washington the Indian Prime Minister was asked if he found any signs of cultural, philosophical and social progress in the United States. He side-stepped the question.

"I do not think," he replied, "that the great technological and material development made by the United States can go far or endure for long without progress along cultural, philosophical or social lines."

Not everyone in America was satisfied with the result of Nehru's visit. In his conversations with the political executives India's Prime Minister was careful to explain his policies wherever these impinged on mutual interests and problems, and was especially concerned to elaborate on his foreign policy. But simultaneously he refrained scrupulously from being drawn into any commitments. His utterances, public and private, were equally cautious on the economic plane whether in the way of aid, technical assistance or private investment.

In fact, he made this clear very early during his tour, for speaking to the National Press Club he declared, "There is no question of any deal." He had wanted, he said, to visit the United States for the past thirty-five years but his political activities had prevented him. "I have read a fair amount of early American history and became interested and wished to see the country and its people. Even when I was a university student, I could see the U.S. forging ahead of all other countries technically and scientifically. During the tour, I shall go from place to place and form innumerable pictures in my mind, but the difficulty in a crowded schedule is not meeting individuals for leisurely talks."

Nehru's idea in going to the United States was threefold—to demonstrate India's friendship for America as well as her gratitude for America's sympathy in India's struggle for independence; to learn more about America; and to make Americans more conscious of India as a factor in world affairs.

The cold war was intensifying and was to erupt eight month later in the Korean devastation. Despite the kindliness and warmth displayed on all sides, Nehru felt that American political and business circles were not sufficiently receptive to his ideas. He sensed, as many Indians do, a rigidity in their outlook curiously akin to the closed minds of totalitarian countries who denounce those who are not with them as against them, and question their motives.

What is good for the United States or Russia, Nehru argued, was not necessarily good for India. Besides, the foreign policy of neither of these two countries was so successful that India should willy-nilly follow them. In the coming months and years he was often to remark that in her zeal to destroy totalitarianism America was unconsciously shaping herself in the image of her opponents and detractors.

The differences between India and America, he reflected and sometimes expressed aloud, were caused more often by the actions of third nations and by the reactions, varying at times, of India and the United States to them. But India in her own interests, as also in the general interests of world peace, must steer a middle course.

By July, 1955, when the Indian Prime Minister visited Russia, he had grown greatly in international stature and was the centre of world-wide controversy. America's offer of military aid to Pakistan was a little over a year old, and had been followed almost immediately after, in June, 1954, by the first *panchshila* agreement, signed with China when Chou En-lai visited New Delhi en route to Peking from Geneva. Nehru's own visit to China was made in October. His reception in Russia was as tremendous, tumultuous and carefully organised as his welcome in China. It was nearly twenty-eight years since he had visited the U.S.S.R.

In that time he studied Marxism closely, and while he was not attracted by all its facets he was impressed by its spirit of scientific inquiry. He had followed the Soviet Five-Year plans, often with en-thusiasm, noting with approval the spread of education, literacy, health and economic development in Russia. But his idea was to make of India a state representative of a synthesis between the Western concept of democracy and socialism as the Marxists conceived it. "In regard to individual and political rights and civil liberties," Nehru had written during the Second World War, "we were influenced by the ideas of the French and American revolutions as also by the constitutional history of the British Parliament. Socialistic ideas, and the influence of the Soviet revolution came in later to give a powerful economic turn to our thoughts."

Nehru returned from Russia in July, 1955, with no illusions but some ideas.

"The thing you've got to remember about the Russians," he said in a conversation, "is that they have never known democracy. When the Bolsheviks came to power nearly forty years ago the Russians jumped from one autocracy to another—from Tsarism to Com-munism. In fact the Russians throughout their history have never known democracy as Western Europe understands it. Therefore to talk to them of democracy and individual liberty is like trying to explain to a blind man what the colour white means. Once you understand this you begin to understand the Russian mind, though you might not agree with it."

Asked what he thought would be the course of the Soviet revolution after Stalin's death, Nehru commented: "Stalin was a dictator, and gave Russia yet another taste of dictatorship. But even he zig-zagged to his objective, being alternately tyrannical and temporising. When it was a question of preserving his country's existence, he was prepared, like Churchill, to shake hands with the devil. He even shook hands with Hitler."

Russia's present leadership, Nehru feels, does not vest in the hands of a single man whose writ runs throughout the country. Even if Khrushchev appears to be in command, he is one of a small team. And when men work together, whether as tyrants or democrats, compromises must ensue. Therefore Soviet rule, as long as the present apparatus of power functions, must operate through compromise. Russia's present political technique, both at home and abroad, is one of seeming compromise. The end remains but the means alter.

Nehru explains the new phase in Soviet strategy as impelled by the Kremlin's recognition that it can no longer hope to impose Communism on the entire world and therefore must beat a strategic retreat. In the Indian Prime Minister's view, two factors are building up to end the cold war, the first being the mass destructive power of nuclear weapons and the second being the narrowing East-West economic gap. Thus the new Soviet strategy appears to be based upon a more realistic appreciation by the Kremlin of the present world situation. It represents a process of adaptation and adjustment which in Nehru's view must culminate in thawing out the cold war as the warm breezes of peaceful coexistence blow in mounting strength.

According to India's Prime Minister, Communism in the pure Marxist sense, with the rule of the proletariat ultimately withering away to make room for a true classless society or State, has still to be achieved in Russia as in China.

"The Soviet leaders," Nehru disclosed after they had left India, "told me that it would take them anything from another ten to fifteen years to achieve Communism in their own country."

Apart from his eagerness to know something of the methods of Russia's technological development, India's Prime Minister was especially interested in the status and treatment of the Soviet minorities, particularly in the Asian republics which he visited. A process of assimilation was obviously under way, but he was interested to notice that for the time being Moscow respected the minorities' cultural and religious susceptibilities.

Nehru came back from Moscow with the strong conviction that

what Russia could achieve in forty years India could do in less. The same sentiments had earlier stirred him in China.

On the way home he visited Yugoslavia, where he compared his impressions of Russia with Marshal Tito. This exchange of views was especially instructive.

"Tito," he remarked later, "knows his Russia better than most non-Russians. He understands their language. He's lived there for years. He knows their mind."

Like Nehru, Tito believes in the virtues of coexistence, though like the Indian Prime Minister the Yugoslav leader has made it plain that aggression, from wherever it comes, will be resisted.

After Nehru's departure from Moscow the Kremlin probably calculated that with a few deft manœuvres it could tip India into the Communist-dominated camp. There the Russians were wrong, for identification with Moscow, as Nehru knows, would negative and make nonsense of his foreign policy. Moreover, as the Indian Prime Minister also realises, any such move would leave Russia as the decisive factor between China and India, enabling Moscow to counterbalance Asia's two leading countries and act as the fulcrum of a seesaw on which India and China could only move alternately up and down. The battle for Asia, as Nehru knows, is not between Russia and America but between India and China.

The broad strategy of Khrushchev and Bulganin was planned in Moscow before their departure for New Delhi. The welcome they received was massive and tumultuous. Partly it reciprocated the hospitality shown to India's Prime Minister in the U.S.S.R., partly it reflected the exotic interest which attaches to a Russian far more than to a Chinese in India. To the great mass of the Indian people a Communist leader from Russia is almost as novel and exciting as an interplanetary visitor from Mars.

Khrushchev and Bulganin were both exuberantly friendly, donning Gandhi caps, threatening to climb up cocoanut trees, quipping gaily with all manner of people, and back-slapping farmers, workers, students and officials in a truly *tovarisch* trauma. To the masses this was better than a circus even if to the more sophisticated Indians the exhibitionism of the Soviet guests seemed crude. But the reception which the Russians received was everywhere warm and enthusiastic.

Kashmir as the focus of power politics in Indian eyes and Goa as a raw colonial sore were the two obvious points to plug. The Russians concentrated all their verbal fire and venom on them. Where they erred in their tactics was in their vehement attacks on Britain, for whom India has no hostility, and on the United States, who, however provocative some of her actions might seem to the Indian Government and people, was engaged in no direct quarrel with them. These attacks embarrassed the Indian Government, which found it difficult in its capacity as host to administer a direct rebuke to its guests. None the less Nehru on more than one occasion, in the presence of Khrushchev and Bulganin, obliquely rebuked them by affirming that India considered all countries her friends and was the enemy of none.

The Russian move to draw India into her orbit has failed as it was bound to fail, but that does not mean that India has thereby moved closer to the West. Nehru still keeps India poised on the razor edge of his foreign policy. Such a policy, he affirms, with peace as its primary objective, is in India's interest and in line with her tradition and thought. "I am on my own side and on nobody else's," he once brusquely exclaimed in a Parliamentary debate.

It is also consistent with the foreign policy visualised by the Indian National Congress as far back as 1920. In that year a resolution was passed affirming India's desire to cooperate with other nations and especially to develop friendly relations with neighbouring countries. Seven years later, at Madras, the Congress passed another resolution declaring that India could be no party to an imperialist war and that in no event should India be made to join any war without the consent of her people. This was twenty years before independence, and before Japan's aggression in Manchuria and Hitler's rise to power.

Nehru has often described this resolution as the foundation of India's foreign policy. Referring to it in January, 1955, he remarked: "India's foreign policy of non-alignment and friendly relations with all nations, as well as our general outlook about freedom of all countries and anti-colonialism started from that period. It is well to remember this, because it means that our foreign policy is not a sudden growth, but a natural outcome of our thinking for many years past."

Nehru himself on joining the Interim Government reaffirmed this policy at a press conference in September, 1946, almost a year before independence and before he became Prime Minister.

"In the sphere of foreign affairs," he said, "India will follow an independent policy, keeping away from the power politics of groups aligned one against another. She will uphold the principle of freedom for dependent peoples and will oppose racial discrimination wherever it may occur. She will work with the other peace-loving nations for international cooperation and goodwill without exploitation of one nation by another."

From that policy he has not deviated, and the apparent zig-zags in the course he has pursued between the two power blocs have been influenced by the actions of one or the other of the two groups. His own course, as traced retrospectively, is consistent with his policy.

Because of her democratic background and the fact that she has accepted the democratic way of life, India marches alongside the Western democracies on long and vital paths. Her destiny lies in and with democracy.

28

JAWAHARLAL

"How lonely he must feel!"

The thought was uppermost in the minds of some Swiss friends of Jawaharlal when the news of Gandhi's assassination reached Geneva.

Nehru, it is true, was seized at that time with a sense of unutterable loneliness. But loneliness had lived with him as a companion almost all his life—from his boyhood days when as the only child for a decade in his household he had sought for companionship among his elders, his mother and aunt and older cousins and the Muslim major domo with the silver locks and beard, Mubarak Ali. As a boy and even when older his favourite dream was of himself flying high above the earth with the eerie ecstasy of a being apart.

Loneliness had followed him into later life. The seven years abroad at Harrow and Cambridge, though interesting and formative, were years of comparative exile. He had returned to India to be caught in the toil and turmoil of politics, in the great surge of the struggle for independence with its exhilaration and depression, its misery and joy, the setbacks, disappointments and suffering, the long years entombed in prison.

With the coming of independence and his assumption of the Prime Ministership, Nehru's sense of loneliness has, if anything, been enhanced. He stands apart from and above his immediate colleagues, his main communion with the country being through its vast masses, with whom he loves to mingle and talk. From quite early in his political career he has felt at home with crowds, drawing from them strength, exhilaration, even exultation, and in turn communicating the same feelings to them. Even as a child he recalls how bathing in the Ganga he felt no religious sentiment as a devout Hindu does but "an element of community with the crowd." Nehru describes this feeling as an "emotional phenomenon." Is this hunger for communion with crowds a reflex of his own inner loneliness? His occasional youthful light-hearted exuberance when in the company of intimates or persons he likes probably derives from the same urge and is a device to cover the same feeling of desolation.

"The lonely eagle in a flock of birds," is how a socialist friend described him in earlier days. The parallel persists, and power highlights the peculiar relationship existing between the Prime Minister and his immediate political and administrative entourage. In recent years he has rarely shared his confidences fully with any one of them, preferring to seek their counsel separately on separate issues but sometimes taking more than one of them into his confidence in order to assess and compare their individual opinions. The mass as a vital conglomeration of people, he trusts. He is less sure of individuals, however near they are to him. As a worker and leader in the Congress he was in the habit of concerning himself with the tiniest minutiae of organisation. The habit remains, and often he will spend time on details which could safely be left for decision and execution at much lower echelons.

"The Indian masses," Nehru observed long ago, "have the ingrained habit of expecting everything to be done from the top. Therefore, presumably, action will have to take place at the top. But our effort will be to train the masses to act for themselves. The village and its panchayat will be the starting point." Perhaps over the years he has equated this thinking from the mass to the personal plane. At the highest administrative level there are few who could claim to be his confidants today. To each he will open a compartment of his mind, and look out on each through a window of his choosing. To none will he disclose his complete mind.

"I have continually had a feeling of growing up," Nehru writes in his autobiography. "Dynamic" and "dynamism" are among his favourite words. In the process of growing up he has left some of his old companions far behind him temperamentally and intellectually. Despite his personal solicitude for and charm, even tenderness, towards those for whom he entertains a deep regard or affection, there is something impersonal in his most intimate relations which leads him suddenly to draw down the blinds of his mind and enclose himself in a shuttered world.

"He talked to me at one moment as a brother and at another as the Prime Minister of India," remarked one of his sisters, to both of whom he is deeply attached.

The light of his eye, of course, is his daughter Indira, who now acts as her father's chatelaine at the Prime Minister's Residence in New Delhi. Educated at Tagore's university of Santiniketan, in Switzerland and later in Oxford, she was married in March, 1942, to Pheroze Gandhi, a Parsi by religion [1] and no relative of the Mahatma. They have two sons, Rajiv and Sanjaya, and to them, aged respectively thirteen and eleven, the Prime Minister is a fond and understanding grandfather. He plays and gambols with them with the zest of a juvenile but keeps a careful and solicitous eye on their upbringing.

Indira shares her parents' qualities which in fact were strongly similar—their spirited approach to life, their directness of speech, their sense of dedicated service, their volatile temper, their friendliness and reserve. In her public appearances she is apt at times to be cold, almost glacial, with more than a hint of self-consciousness in her bearing. This gives her a misleading look of hauteur. But privately, among relatives, friends and intimates, she relaxes with something of the spirit of her mother and the charm of her father. She was barely four years old when Nehru was first arrested, and the story goes that on hearing of it she mounted her nursery table and addressed her assembly of dolls, calling upon them to court imprisonment with her father.

Is Nehru a good judge of men? Some complain that he is apt to be excessively influenced by his immediate circle, and it was said in pre-independence days that he was more at home and more easily impressed by Indians with a Western upbringing than by those who had their social, cultural and educational roots in the indigenous soil. If true, the charge is no longer valid. Over the past two decades or more, persuaded originally by his favourite brother-in-law, Ranjit Pandit (the husband of Nehru's sister, Vijayalakshmi), Jawaharlal has drawn closer to his Indian affinities, and his book The Discovery of India,

---

[1] The Parsis of Persian origin are followers of the prophet Zoroaster, and number a little over 100,000 in India.

written during his last imprisonment and first published in March, 1946, is proof of this newly awakened awareness.

He has a habit of approaching and assessing persons, as he does problems, more by the yardstick of vision than that of analysis, more by instinct and imagination than by cold-blooded reason and evaluation. Today those around him consist largely of those who have grown up with him—men like Maulana Azad, Govind Ballabh Pant and the late Rafi Ahmed Kidwai, though even among these he has not hesitated to ring the changes, keeping now one, now the other nearest to him.

Sometimes he has drawn from less familiar sources. He relied greatly over a period on the sage and sober counsel of the late Sir Gopalaswami Ayyangar and carried on a prolonged honeymoon, which was abruptly ended, with the astute C. Rajagopalachari of Madras. Off and on he is wont to consult the Vice-President, Dr. Radhakrishnan, but it is noticeable that these intermittent counsellors are requisitioned only when he wants his own opinions reinforced. The closest to him today is probably the didactic and controversial V. K. Krishna Menon, with whom he visited Spain during the civil war some twenty years ago. Menon has an aptitude for rationalising Nehru's instincts and impulses, particularly in the field of foreign affairs, and of clothing them in clear, precise language and logical thought. He is also a superb draftsman, able to capture the consensus of opinion in a committee or assembly and reduce it to a formula or resolution acceptable to all or most.

By and large the men around Nehru are men of talent and aptitude, including some not always or only recently associated with the Congress. These include the Finance Minister, the able Sir Chintaman Deshmukh, a former Governor of the Reserve Bank and member of the Indian Civil Service, and T. T. Krishnamachari, the Commerce Minister, a businessman whose affiliations with the Congress are of older though also of comparatively recent date. Because a cabinet must be composite and cohesive, those who comprise it are necessarily of the Prime Minister's outlook and share most if not all of his predilections and views. But Nehru is careful always to follow democratic processes, and the Congress Parliamentary party, whose chief he is, is always scrupulously briefed in his policies and plans.

Within his own party and Government the Prime Minister is ready to compromise on details and on minor disputes and casuistries, but on the big issues and on the basic principles he is rarely, if ever, prepared to yield. About the only two instances are the Hindu Marriage bill and the 1955 report of the States Reorganisation Commission, both of which have come in for heavy revision.

Perhaps he is inclined to trade too much on the talisman of his name, expecting thereby to carry through measures not acceptable to certain sections of the people. He erred badly in encouraging the appointment of the States Reorganisation Commission, hoping through it to satisfy certain urges for linguistic States and in the process to strengthen the unity and integration of the country. Instead the Commission's recommendations submitted in September, 1955, set off a chain reaction for linguistic units which found explosive expression in certain areas, notably Bombay, Orissa and East Punjab. This certainly surprised Nehru, who intensified his initial mistake by insisting that the recommendations should go through the democratic process of being submitted to the opinion of all parties and persons before the Government made up its own mind. It would have been wiser had he accepted the recommendations straightaway, for they were the considered proposals of a non-partisan commission comprising three eminent individuals with no party affiliations.

Herein lies the danger of his splendid isolation. Had Vallabhbhai Patel, who by his swift incorporation of the princely States laid the foundations of independent India's unity, been alive, he might have served as a restraining and guiding hand. But in India today there is no one to restrain or guide Nehru. He is Caesar. And from Caesar one can appeal only to Caesar.

The fact of his close communion with the people, with the vast naked hungry masses of India who strive for better things and better days, gives Nehru a sense of almost omnipotent power. That he takes no undue advantage of it, insists on respecting what he likes to call the people's democratic urges and often readily admits his mistake, as on the States Reorganisation Commission, proves how deeply rooted is his regard for the common people. Of the unchallenged rulers of the world he is perhaps the only one whose strength and stability stem from the genuinely deep affection of the masses. He rules by love, not fear. He has often, quite sincerely, discounted the notion that there will be no leadership compared to his once he quits the political stage. The Indian people, he declares, are strong enough to go forward on their own momentum without being slaves to a single man, for no individual is indispensable.

Shortly after Gandhi's death an Englishwoman, Miss Muriel Lester, who was the Mahatma's hostess in London in 1932, posed the question, "On whom does the mantle of Bapu fall?" and answered, "On no one in particular—but on every one of us."

Jawaharlal would enthusiastically endorse that answer both in relation to the Mahatma and to himself. His mantle, he hopes, will fall on the Indian people.

Yet the fact of his unchallenged political supremacy, while it has served India well in the initial period of stress and strain, leaves several disquieting questions in its train. A great tree, it is said, dries up the soil around it. Who will succeed Nehru? And how will India fare without his overriding authority, drive and voice?

The answers to these questions depend on the time and manner of Nehru's demission from the political scene. In normal circumstances, it is likely that power will remain with the Congress party but will be shared by a group who will possibly veer from left to right of centre. Should the circumstances be abnormal, the immediate possibility is a swing to the extreme right, but instinct in this is the very real danger of a pendulum swing to the extreme left. Not merely for the preservation but continuance of Indian unity and stability the presence of Nehru at the helm of national affairs is vital for at least another seven years.

Approaching sixty-seven the Prime Minister still maintains an astonishing resilience of body and mind. He packs into twenty-four hours a bewildering range of activities. Rising a little after dawn, he works at his office through scores of telegrams, files and letters, finding time in between for interviews, speeches, attendance at various gatherings, the legislature while it is in session, conferences with his colleagues and officials, conversations with foreign diplomats, a cabinet meeting when that is on the schedule, and the normal and varied chores which go with his responsibilities. He does his yoga exercises every morning, standing on his head for five or ten minutes in his favourite yogic pose, and when time and the weather permit he likes to take a brisk morning canter on his horse. Swimming in the pool attached to his residence is another favourite exercise. It is rarely that the Prime Minister goes to bed before one in the morning, for it is his practice to work at his desk every night after dinner. He sleeps for about five hours. Almost the only time he gets nowadays for recreational reading is in the fifteen or twenty minutes before he falls asleep. His favourite books are on politics, poetry, philosophy, exploration and the wonders of modern science.

The interest in science which his private tutor Brooks first kindled in him as a boy has lingered over the years and grown. Nehru likes meeting scientists and talking and listening to them. He personally heads the Ministry of Atomic Energy, while he is also chairman of the Board of Scientific and Industrial Research. Long before independence he had declared that the three fundamental requirements of India if she was to develop industrially were a heavy engineering and machine-making industry, electric power and scientific research institutes. As Prime Minister, he has set about initiating and developing all three. Thought with him is invariably action.

The network of laboratories now studding India includes the National Physical Laboratory at New Delhi, the National Chemical Laboratory at Poona near Bombay, and the National Metallurgical Laboratory at Jamshedpur, along with research institutes in various parts of the country concerned with subjects as diverse as agriculture, industrial technology, fuel, drugs, tropical medicine, nutrition, malaria, cancer, leather, glass and ceramics. Nuclear research is also carried on under the auspices of the Indian National Atomic Energy Commission assisted by two nuclear-research institutes at Bombay and Calcutta. A factory for processing mozanite operates in Travancore-Cochin, while at Trombay near Bombay a plant for extracting uranium will soon be functioning. Plans for setting up a medium-powered atomic reactor are almost complete.

Nehru is excited by science not only as a form of intellectual activity but also as a means of furthering human progress. In December, 1937, almost ten years before independence, he recalled nostalgically in a speech to the Indian Science Congress the days when as a student he had haunted the laboratories of Cambridge. Science, he said, was of the very texture of life. Politics had led him to economics and in turn to science, for "science alone could solve the problems of hunger and poverty, of insanitation and illiteracy, of superstition and deadening custom and tradition, of vast resources running to waste, of a rich country inhabited by starving people." The thrill and ecstasy of science and things scientific survive.

In Nehru, despite a strong streak of the intuitive and the impulsive, there also resides a core of calculation and realism. Like Gandhi he likes to call himself a practical idealist.

"How impossible in this shifting world," remarked an American journalist, "to answer the question, 'What shall we do?'"

Nehru looked up from the book he was inscribing.

"That," he commented, "is the difference between the Indian and the Western mind. The Indian would not ask what he should do but what he should *be*."

And, having signed the book, he concluded, "For centuries we've been asking ourselves this question, 'What should we be?' I think that now in the new free India the time has come to ask ourselves the new question, 'What should we do?'"

The capacity to adjust himself and his thinking to altered circumstances accounts for and explains his unusual resilience of body and mind. Very often this is visibly conditioned by his environment. Just as a crowd acts on him as a tonic, so also the tired lines on his face momentarily vanish if a remark or observation made in a drawing-room conversation interests or amuses him. But the effect more often than not is transient.

This capacity for adjustment explains his efficiency as an organiser. The popular view of Nehru as a political Hamlet seized with doubts and often incapable of making up his mind is far from the real picture of the man. Nehru, having thought deeply over most matters, knows his mind on the big basic issues. Where he hesitates and fumbles, often appearing to run away from a decision, is on comparatively minor matters which are apt to irritate him. But even here, both before independence as Secretary-General of the Congress and later as Prime Minister of India, he has revealed a meticulous eye for the details of administration.

As Secretary-General he insisted on attention to the smallest detail, which cumulatively made for good organisation. Similarly as Prime Minister, his notes on the files are precise, and models of clarity. No official can doubt what the Prime Minister has in his mind. Nehru disposes of files quickly, never letting them accumulate on his desk. As long as he is in New Delhi the wheels of Government move fast and smooth. His tremendous energy can galvanise even the slow-moving machinery of bureaucracy, while his obvious devotion to work and service animate those around him with something of his dedicated spirit.

The legend that Nehru lacks organisational talent sprang from his seeming indifference to any control over the party machine. He could not, his colleagues therefore argued, be a practical politician. "Whatever you are tempted to do in politics, be sure you have the party machine behind you," was the advice of the wily Joseph Chamberlain to Lloyd George. In the lifetime of Gandhi and Vallabhbhai Patel, Nehru was supremely indifferent to such advice, but since Patel's death Nehru has shown an adroit capacity for managing and guiding the machine. He combined for a while the functions of Prime Minister and President of the Congress, threatened at one time to resign both offices but subsequently ensured that as Prime Minister the President was no more than his dutiful nominee. Today he is in supreme control of both the party and the State.

These meticulous mental methods are reflected in his personal habits. He has a passion for order and cleanliness, setting right a picture gone awry or personally dusting an untidy table in a friend's house and carefully rearranging the various papers, books and bric-a-brac on it. In his youth, particularly during the Westernized or "cyrenaic" phase of his life, Jawaharlal was wont to be somewhat fastidious in dress. Although now simple in his attire and mode of life, he is never sloppy or shabby, wearing even in the old days before independence his often frayed *achkhan* like a garb of royalty. "He is the only man I have seen," remarked a British friend at that time, "on whom a *khaddar* cap, worn by all the devotees of the Congress, becomes something princely."

The artist and the scholar are pronounced in Nehru. He loves flowers, children and animals, delights in the open sky and stars, in waterfalls, running brooks, trees and mountains. On his birthday and other festive occasions children have the run of his garden where Nehru's two pandas, Bhimsa and Pashi, whom he visits every day, are among the more exotic attractions. His eye for painting is by no means sure, but he is fond of listening to music and song and can be enthralled by a folk dance. His almost feminine feeling for the delicate is revealed in the fine yarn he spins on his charkha—a sure sign, as the late Mahadev Desai, Gandhi's faithful secretary, used to say, of a sensitive and artistic nature.

Nehru's scholarship is more comprehensive than erudite, his mind roving vast horizons. Because he equates thought with activity the amplitude of his thought is often reflected in the amplitude of his activity. As India's philosopher Vice-President has remarked, "He knows a good deal about a good many things." In his conversation, as in his public speeches, Jawaharlal is sometimes apt to be prolix, but in both modes of communication the feeling that he is thinking aloud is strong in his hearers. His thought, invariably diffuse, is not always disciplined, and strays down odd avenues, giving the curious impression of a stroll down a rambling but picturesque country lane. The sun shines, but sometimes there is thunder in the air.

Nehru is no great orator by classical or even conventional standards. But when the mood and occasion move him his eloquence takes wing in limpid, often moving prose. His broadcast speech announcing Gandhi's death to the nation was inspired in its tone and utterance, as were the various tributes to the Mahatma which he delivered shortly afterward. The famous "tryst with destiny" speech which he made on the night of August 14, 1947, ushering independence, was worthy of that memorable occasion, and there was natural eloquence in his inaugural address to the first Asian Relations Conference in November, 1946.

In his writings Nehru reflects two characteristic qualities of his mind, grace and strength. Here again he can be prolix, as the many discursive passages in *The Discovery of India* reveal; but at its best, as in most of his autobiography, particularly in the reflective, politico-philosophical parts, Nehru's style shows a vigour and clarity as pleasing and compelling to the ear as to the mind. A deep sincerity infuses his speech and writing. Sincerity is the dominant keynote of both.

Some of Nehru's most vigorous writing has been done for the columns of newspapers and journals, both at home and abroad, notably the articles and editorials which appeared at the time of the Munich crisis and during the early years of the war in the *National Herald* of Lucknow. This newspaper, which he helped to found in September, 1938, has a special place in his interest and affection. The first editorial which appeared in it was written by him from Prague on the eve of Munich, and he has subsequently contributed several articles and editorials to its columns.

"Whatever you might write," he used to advise the staff, "never write out of fear."

This was not Nehru's first association with a newspaper, for in his father's lifetime he had assisted at the birth of a newspaper called the *Independent* which Motilal had started on February 9, 1919, primarily to counter the moderate political line of an established Allahabad daily, the *Leader*. It failed to impress and, falling foul of the then restrictive Press laws, was compelled to close down within two years. The *National Herald* continues.

Nehru's interest in journalism has never been as close or consistent as Gandhi's, who was proud to describe himself as a journalist. Gandhi was in fact a superlative journalist who could write as persuasively in English as in his mother tongue, Gujarati. Nehru's newspaper writings have been forceful, and though necessarily dealing with ephemeral themes, they had during the struggle for independence strong evocative appeal, directed as they were equally to heart and head.

The letters to his daughter, Indira, later published as *Glimpses of World History*, are a lively revelation of the range of Nehru's wide, almost encyclopaedic knowledge of and interest in history. Despite the fact that they were written from various prisons, the letters reflect the writer's objectivity and refusal to be depressed. In the last published letter Jawaharlal tries to communicate something of this attitude and spirit to his daughter.

Our age is . . . an age of disillusion, of doubt and uncertainty and questioning. We can no longer accept many of the ancient beliefs and customs; we have no more faith in them, in Asia or in Europe or America. So we search for new ways. . . . Sometimes the injustice, the unhappiness, the brutality of the world oppress us and darken our minds, and we see no way out. . . . And yet if we take such a dismal view we have not learnt aright the lesson of life or of history. For history teaches us of growth and progress and of the possibility of an infinite advance for man.

The search for new ways must go on. In Gandhi's lifetime Nehru had been accused of scaring Gandhiites by his socialism and shocking socialists by his Gandhism. Neither intellectually nor morally did he feel at home in either camp, for in his reckoning the right road lay between. India must adopt a distinctive way of life suited to her own conditions which accepted neither the doctrinaire theories of Marxism or socialism on the one hand nor Gandhi's belief in wealth as a trusteeship on the other.

But the path towards which the Mahatma pointed was the only path possible in the circumstances of pre-independent India, and must be followed. Even after independence Nehru accepted, albeit reluctantly, Vallabhbhai Patel's suggestion for a five-year truce or moratorium between labour and capital, in which period both would be put on their best behaviour. Had Patel been ten years younger he might have salvaged the situation for private enterprise on which he had drawn heavily for party funds in the years before independence. Patel was old, and plainly he was dying. Like one of the stricken lions of his own Gir forest in Saurashtra, he could roar feebly in protest but do little else.

The onslaught against private enterprise was mounted openly at the Avadi conference in January, 1955, shortly after Nehru's return from Red China. But even before this, the offensive had been launched against the landlord and the big industrialist. Jawaharlal had been critical of the Mahatma's economic outlook long before independence. In his autobiography, he asks with more than a hint of impatience and petulance:

With all his [Gandhi's] keen intellect and passion for bettering the down-trodden and oppressed, why does he support a system, and a system which is obviously decaying, which creates this misery and waste? He seeks a way out, it is true, but is not that way to the past barred and bolted? And meanwhile he blesses all the relics of the old order which stand as obstacles in the way of advance—the feudal States, the big *zamindaris* and *taluqdaris*, the present capitalist system. Is it reasonable to believe in the theory of trusteeship—to give unchecked power and wealth to an individual and to expect him to use it entirely for the public good? Are the best of us so perfect as to be trusted in this way?

From this explosive mood of expostulation many were led to infer that Nehru was merely engaged in a rhetorical exercise. Even Gandhi when his attention was drawn to these outbursts was wont to smile indulgently. Patel's reaction was a droop of his heavy eyelids and a slow wintry smile of scorn. After all, as the controller of the Congress party's purse strings, he knew where the funds came from.

But Nehru knew better. He could wait and bide his time. The strong calculating streak in his character which even his closest associates appear never to have suspected led him to temporise and talk of subordinating his long-term aims to "larger considerations" and the "long view." So the legend grew of Nehru as the Hamlet of Indian politics, noble but vacillating.

In reality, no man was in more deadly earnest. Nehru knew that all he had to do was to temporise and compromise. As far as Gandhi was concerned, he satisfied himself intellectually by observing that the Mahatma's methods were advancing India more quickly than any other way towards her political goal. He appreciated and admitted that Patel's realism tempered his own idealism, that the older man's nationalism was a curb on perhaps his too exuberant internationalism, and that Patel never let his impulses run away with his ideas. But it is doubtful if either the Mahatma or the Sardar in their lifetime ever visualised that with their passing Nehru would press boldly forward with his own ideas.

In effect, what Gandhi and Patel urged was that if they opened a quarrel between the present and the past they would find that they had lost the future. Nehru never completely accepted this thesis. In his mind, as he had impliedly indicated at the first Asian conference of November, 1946, unless they drew a line between the present and the past, while remembering the historic continuity which linked the two, the future would be merely a projection of past and present evils and mortgaged to both.

He had startled many and upset a few when at the height of the Congress dispute with the Muslim League he had remarked with a show of wilfulness: "Mr. Jinnah complains that I am out to create new situations. I *am* out to create new situations."

For the greater part of his political life Nehru has attempted to do so. Gandhi had taught him that only good means led to good ends, a lesson that has burned itself in his memory. So Nehru's mind, travelling back, characteristically satisfies his conscience by equating Gandhi's call to lift the weight from the backs of the indigent, the oppressed and the downtrodden with his own politico-economic philosophy of mulcting the rich in order to help the poor. Hence his justification of the offensive against private enterprise.

In Gandhi's lifetime Jawaharlal had chafed at the idea that he was not able intellectually to reconcile Gandhism with socialism. Now, by a simple equation, he has enabled himself and his Government to do so, identifying his objective of an equalitarian society with Gandhi's ideal of a just State, and meanwhile limiting his methods or means to persuasion or legislative compulsion but never technically to expropriation without compensation.

It is interesting in this connection, and not without irony, to recall Nehru's comment in his autobiography on Gandhi's methods of persuasion which to him often seemed dangerously like compulsion:

Since then [his South African days], he has had a fixed basis for all his ideas, and his mind is hardly an open mind. He listens with the greatest patience and attention to people who make new suggestions to him, but behind all his courteous interest one has the impression that one is addressing a closed door. He is so firmly anchored to some ideas that everything else seems unimportant. To insist on other and secondary matters would be a distraction and a distortion of the larger scheme.

Every word of this criticism might faithfully be applied to Nehru today in his attitude to free enterprise.

Yet as Vinoba Bhave, the leader of the Bhoodan movement, has said of Jawaharlal, "After Gandhi's his is the one name that stands for India—is India." In the contradictions of his nature, his simplicity and charm, the wilfulness of his spirit, his brooding aloofness, the pride, the temper, the tantrums, the faith and doubts, in his seeming arrogance but innate humility, his lack of religiosity but high moral fervour, and in his determination coupled with a curious diffidence Jawaharlal does represent the new and modern India of our day. Like Krishna who lured the *gopis*[2] with his flute, Nehru lures India's masses with the magic of his name.

"His weaknesses," writes a friend, "are on the surface and make him the more likable." There is in his ebullience of spirit and speech a schoolboy charm which contrasts strangely with his ascetic and reflective mien. Like Krishna, Nehru also loves to indulge in playful pranks, these for the most part expressing themselves in exhibitions of temper and tantrums which over the years India's people have grown accustomed to and have learned to expect and accept, even to delight in.

"I am a great believer in being aggressive," Nehru once remarked

[2] Milkmaids.

in pre-independence days. "If the Government knows it can't frighten you into keeping still, it has to think carefully before putting you in prison, and count the consequences."

It is part of his offensive-defensive strategy.

Long years ago India took the measure of this man and learned to love him. The basis of his patriotism is pride, and India instinctively responds to that urge. But there also persists in Nehru's nature a strong streak of sentiment and humility.

At a meeting of the Congress Working Committee many years ago the atmosphere was stormy and tempers ran high, not least that of Jawaharlal, who resigned from the General-Secretaryship in protest. Yet at the end of the meeting, walking over to one of his opponents, he said wistfully, "I wish we would not break each other's hearts so easily and so constantly."

That phrase might appropriately be whispered on the international stage today.

Tagore once likened Nehru to the *rituraj*, to the spirit of spring which is the spirit of eternal youth. And always Nehru sees India, particularly the India which Gandhi founded and which he himself is helping to build, in the majestic vision of Tagore's *Gitanjali*:

Where the mind is without fear and the head is held high;
Where knowledge is free;
Where the world has not been broken up into fragments by narrow
    domestic walls;
Where words come out from the depth of truth;
Where tireless striving stretches its arms towards perfection;
Where the clear stream of reason has not lost its way into the dreary
    desert sand of dead habit;
Where the mind is led forward by thee into ever widening thought and
    action—
Into that heaven of freedom, my Father, let my country awake.

APPENDIX

This Congress is of opinion that to enable the masses to appreciate what swaraj, as conceived by the Congress, will mean to them, it is desirable to state the position of the Congress in a manner easily understood by them. In order to end the exploitation of the masses, political freedom must include real economic freedom of the starving millions. The Congress, therefore, declares that any constitution which may be agreed to on its behalf should provide or enable the swaraj government to provide for the following:

(1) Fundamental rights of the people, including: (i) Freedom of association and combination; (ii) Freedom of speech and of the press; (iii) Freedom of conscience and free profession and practice of religion, subject to public order and morality; (iv) Protection of the culture, language, and scripts of the minorities; (v) Equal rights and obligations of all citizens, without any bar on account of sex; (vi) No disability to attach to any citizen by reason of his or her religion, caste or creed or sex in regard to public employment, office of power or honour, and in the exercise of any trade or calling; (vii) Equal rights to all citizens in regard to public roads, wells, schools and other places of public resort; (viii) Right to keep and bear arms in accordance with regulations and reservations made in that behalf; (ix) No person shall be deprived of his liberty, nor shall his dwelling or property be entered, sequestered or confiscated, save in accordance with law.

(2) Religious neutrality on the part of the state; (3) Adult suffrage; (4) Free primary education; (5) A living wage for industrial workers, limited hours of labour, healthy conditions of work, protection against the economic consequences of old age, sickness and unemployment; (6) Labour to be freed from serfdom or the conditions bordering on serfdom; (7) Protection of women workers, and adequate provisions for leave during maternity period; (8) Prohibition against employment of children of school-going age in the factories; (9) Right of labour to form unions to protect their interests with suitable machinery for settlement of disputes by arbitration; (10) Substantial reduction in agricultural rent or

revenues paid by the peasantry, and in case of uneconomic holdings exemption from rent for such period as may be necessary, relief being given to small zamindars wherever necessary by reason of such reduction; (11) Imposition of a progressive tax on agricultural incomes above a fixed minimum; (12) A graduated inheritance tax; (13) Military expenditure to be reduced by at least one half of the present scale; (14) Expenditure and salaries in civil department to be largely reduced. And no servant of the state, other than specially employed experts and the like, to be paid above a certain fixed figure which should not ordinarily exceed Rs.500 per month; (15) Protection of indigenous cloth by exclusion of all foreign cloth and foreign yarn from the country; (16) Prohibition of intoxicating drinks and drugs; (17) No duty on salt manufactured in India; (18) Control over exchange and currency policy so as to help Indian industries and bring relief to the masses; (19) Control by the state of key industries and ownership of mineral resources; (20) Control of usury.

It shall be open to the A.-I.C.C. to revise, amend or add to the foregoing so far as such revision, amendment or addition is not inconsistent with the policy and principles thereof.

BIBLIOGRAPHY

By Jawaharlal Nehru

Autobiography (London, John Lane, The Bodley Head, Ltd., 1936; New York, John Day, 1941, under the title *Toward Freedom*).
The Discovery of India (Calcutta, Signet Press, 1946; New York, John Day, 1946).
Eighteen Months in India (Kitabistan, 1938).
Glimpses of World History (London, Lindsay Drummond, Ltd., 1939; New York, John Day, 1942).
India and the World (London, George Allen & Unwin, Ltd., 1936).
Mahatma Gandhi (Signet Press, 1949).
Soviet Russia (Chetana, Bombay, 1929).
Towards a Socialist Order (Indian National Congress, 1955).
The Unity of India (London, Lindsay Drummond, Ltd., 1941; New York, John Day, 1942).

Speeches and Biographical Sources

Independence and After, a collection of more important speeches from September, 1946, to May, 1949 (Government of India, 1949; New York, John Day, 1950).
Jawaharlal Nehru's Speeches 1949–53 (Government of India, 1954).
Speeches in America (New Delhi National Bookstall, 1950).
Visit to America (New York, John Day Company, Inc., 1950).
Prime Minister Jawaharlal Nehru in China (Embassy of the People's Republic of China, New Delhi, 1955).
Speeches of Bulganin and Khrushchev in India (Tass in India, 1956).
Jawaharlal Nehru Press Conferences 1952 (Information Service of India, 1955).
Nehru Abhinandan Granth (a volume presented to the Prime Minister on his sixtieth birthday, November 14, 1949).
Nehru Your Neighbour, edited by P. D. Tandon (Signet Press, 1946).
Talks with Nehru, by Norman Cousins (New York, John Day Company, Inc., 1951).
So I Became a Minister, by Vijayalakshmi Pandit (Kitabistan, 1939).
With No Regrets, by Krishna Hutheesing (Padma Publications, Bombay, 1944).

495

Prison and Chocolate Cake, by Nayantara Sahgal (New York, Alfred A. Knopf, Inc., 1954).

GANDHIANA

The Story of My Experiments with Truth, by M. K. Gandhi (Navajivan Press, 2nd ed., 1940).
Mahatma, by D. G. Tendulkar and Vithalbhai K. Jhaveri (8 vols., 1953–1954).
The Life of Mahatma Gandhi, by Louis Fischer (New York, Harper & Brothers, 1950; London, Jonathan Cape, Ltd., 1951).
Lead, Kindly Light, by Vincent Sheean (New York, Random House, 1949).

REFERENCE WORKS

Indian Annual Register (Calcutta), a record of events in India (from January, 1937, to June, 1953).
History of the Indian National Congress, by Pattabhi Sitaramayya (Congress Working Committee, 2 vols., 1935, 1947).
India in World Affairs, by K. Karunakaran (London, Oxford University Press, 1952).
Apart from these, reference was made to various Government communiqués, hand-outs, articles, speeches and official reports.

ON PAKISTAN

Jinnah, by Hector Bolitho (London, John Murray, 1954).
India Divided, by Rajendra Prasad (Hind Kitabs, 1946).
Pakistan, by Rajendra Prasad (Allied Publishers, Bombay, 1940).
Pakistan, by B. R. Ambedkar (Thackers, Bombay, 1945).
Islam Today, edited by A. J. Arberry and Rom Landau (London, Faber and Faber, Ltd., 1943).

INDIAN PRINCES AND STATES

White Paper on Indian States (Government of India, 1948).
Indian States and the Government of India, by K. M. Panikkar (London, Martin Hopkinson, Ltd., 1932).
Treaty Rights of Indian States, by C. P. Ramaswamy Aiyar (Indian Council of World Affairs, 1945).
The Making of the Indian Princes, by Edward J. Thompson (New York, Oxford University Press, 1943).

THE MOUNTBATTENS

Mission with Mountbatten, by Alan Campbell-Johnson (London, Robert Hale, Ltd., 1951).

Time Only to Look Forward, speeches of Lord Mountbatten as Viceroy and Governor-General of India (London, N. Keye, 1949).

Lady Louis: Life of the Countess Mountbatten of Burma, by Dennis Holman (London, Odhams Press, Ltd., 1952).

CONSTITUTIONAL PROBLEMS

Rise and Fulfilment of British Rule in India, by Edward J. Thompson and G. T. Garrett (London, Macmillan, 1934).

The Constitutional Problem in India, by Reginald Coupland (London, Oxford University Press, 1944).

The Cripps Mission, by Reginald Coupland (London, Oxford University Press, 1942).

An Indian Diary, by Edwin S. Montagu (London, Heinemann, Ltd., 1930).

Our Constitution (Government of India, 1950).

Our Government (Government of India, 1950).

KASHMIR, HYDERABAD, ETC.

Danger in Kashmir, by Josef Korbel (Princeton University Press, 1954).

Defending Kashmir (Government of India, 1949).

Kashmir—A Survey, by M. A. Gurmani, Minister for Kashmir Affairs (Government of Pakistan, 1952).

World Opinion on Kashmir and Indian Reactions to It (Pakistani Mission to the U.N., 1951).

Crisis in Kashmir Explained, by Bakshi Ghulam Mohammad (Lalla Rookh Publications, Srinagar, 1953).

Kashmir in the Security Council (Lalla Rookh, Srinagar, 1953).

The Kashmir Story (Government of India, 1949).

Hyderabad in Retrospect, by a former official of Hyderabad (*Times of India*, 1949).

MISCELLANEOUS

The Indian Struggle, by Subhas Bose, 2 vols. (Calcutta, Thacker, Spink & Co., 1948).

Sardar Vallabhbhai Patel, by Narhari D. Parikh, Vol. I (Navajivan Press, 1953).

The Hindu View of Life, by S. Radhakrishnan (London, George Allen & Unwin, Ltd., 1927).

Hinduism and the Modern World, by K. M. Panikkar (Kitabistan, 1938).

The Sikhs, by J. C. Archer (Princeton University Press, 1946).

Halfway to Freedom, by Margaret Bourke-White (New York, Simon & Schuster, 1949).

Ambassador's Report, by Chester Bowles (New York, Harper & Brothers, 1954).

The New Dimensions of Peace, by Chester Bowles (New York, Harper & Brothers, 1955).

Inside Asia, by John Gunther (New York, Harper & Brothers, 1939; London, Hamish Hamilton, Ltd., 1942).

OFFICIAL REPORTS

First Five-Year Plan (Government of India, December, 1952).

Second Five-Year Plan: A Draft Outline (Government of India, 1956).

Draft Note on Second Five-Year Plan, by Federation of Indian Chambers of Commerce and Industry, 1955.

Second Five-Year Plan: The Framework (Government of India, 1955).

Education in the Plan (Government of India, 1954).

Housing in India (Government of India, 1954).

Building for Tomorrow, First Year of Community Projects (Government of India, 1954).

Road to Welfare State (Government of India, 1954).

Community Development Programme in India (paper prepared by India at the Asian-African Conference at Bandung, 1955).

Evaluation Report on Second Year's Working of Community Projects, 2 vols. (Planning Commission, 1955).

Millions on the Move: The Aftermath of Partition (Government of India, 1948).

Bhakra Dam and Power Plant (Public Works Department, Punjab-India, 1955).

Kosi and Public Co-operation (Government of India, 1955).

Planning, Power and Irrigation (Government of India, 1954).

Statement on the Progress of Work on the Centrally Financed Multi-Purpose Projects up to August 31, 1955 (Ministry of Irrigation and Power, 1955).

The First Year (Government of India, 1948).

Three Years of Progress (Government of India, 1954).

After Partition (Government of India, 1948).

In addition the author has consulted numerous pamphlets, magazines, newspaper articles and reports, Security Council proceedings, U.N. bulletins, and other official hand-outs, both from the Government of India and from the Government of Pakistan.

INDEX

499